To Cynthia and Whitney, for the joy you continue to bring into my life each day.
SHG

To my family, friends, and students, for your continuing support and encouragement.
PMF

To my very special people: Jody, Chris, and Carlos.
JFM

To my family, for your unwavering support of my efforts.
PSL

About the Authors

STEPHEN H. GOODMAN

Stephen H. Goodman is an associate professor of management information systems at the University of Central Florida. He received his Ph.D in business administration from Pennsylvania State University, where he specialized in operations management and operations research. Prior to his doctoral study he received a B.S. in aeronautical engineering and an M.B.A., also from Penn State. During his academic career, he has taught, researched, and published primarily in production planning and control. He has also served as a coauthor of a textbook in the field of production/operations management. Currently he has a major teaching and research focus in quality management. He is an active member of the Decision Sciences Institute (DSI) and the American Production and Inventory Control Society (APICS), having held offices in each, has engaged in journal review activities, and has conducted professional training classes. He has achieved the distinction of Certified Fellow in Production and Inventory Management (CFPIM) from APICS.

PATRICIA M. FANDT

Patricia M. Fandt is professor emeritus at the Milgard School of Business, University of Washington, Tacoma, a faculty associate in educational leadership at the University of North Carolina at Charlotte, and a director with The Geneva Foundation. Dr. Fandt earned her doctorate in management and organizational behavior from Texas A&M University in 1986.

Throughout her academic career, Dr. Fandt has published numerous peer-reviewed articles and books on leadership performance, accountability, team dynamics, and organization change. Currently, her research extends from her recently published book *The 2nd Language of Leadership* and involves the integration of the personality/leadership behavior framework with the impact of change.

Her undergraduate and graduate teaching is primarily focused on team development, leadership, and organization change, and she has been recognized with awards for teaching and curriculum development excellence.

Dr. Fandt's industry experience includes a career in marketing as a sales representative with Procter & Gamble, an account manager with Kendall Surgical Corporation, and a regional sales manager in the surgical division of 3M Corporation. She was a flight attendant with Delta Airlines and worked for the Red Cross in Southeast Asia as a dietitian.

In the consulting arena, Dr. Fandt has worked with a broad range of companies in health care, service, and technology industries. She consults with several universities on curriculum development and accreditation review.

JOSEPH F. MICHLITSCH

Joseph F. Michlitsch teaches strategic management in the School of Business at Southern Illinois University Edwardsville (SIUE) and is chair of the Management and Marketing Department. He holds a Ph.D. in management from the University of Minnesota, an M.B.A. from the University of South Dakota, and a bachelor of science degree in economics from South Dakota State University. He is licensed to present the Stephen Covey 7 Habits of Highly Effective People workshops at SIUE.

Dr. Michlitsch publishes in the areas of strategy development, strategy implementation, managerial decision making, and the teaching of management. Outlets for his work include *Strategy & Leadership, Industrial Management, Business Insights, Supervisory Management, Journal of Education for Business, Research in Higher Education, Labor Law Journal, Public Personnel Management, Journal of*

Management

Challenges for Tomorrow's Leaders

Stephen H. Goodman
University of Central Florida

Patricia M. Fandt
University of Washington, Tacoma

Joseph F. Michlitsch
Southern Illinois University Edwardsville

Pamela S. Lewis
Queens University of Charlotte

THOMSON
SOUTH-WESTERN

Australia · Brazil · Canada · Mexico · Singapore · Spain · United Kingdom · United States

Management: Challenges for Tomorrow's Leaders

Stephen H. Goodman, Patricia M. Fandt, Joseph F. Michlitsch, Pamela S. Lewis

VP/Editorial Director:
Jack W. Calhoun

Director of Development/Sr. Publisher:
Melissa S. Acunã

Executive Editor:
John Szilagyi

Developmental Editor:
Monica Ohlinger
Ohlinger Publishing Services

Sr. Marketing Manager:
Kimberly Kanakes

Production Project Manager:
Robert Dreas

Sr. Marketing Communications Manager:
Jim Overly

Manager of Technology, Editorial:
Vicky True

Technology Project Editor:
Kristen Meere

Web Coordinator:
Karen Schaffer

Manufacturing Coordinator:
Doug Wilke

Production House:
Pre-Press Company Incorporated

Printer:
China Translation & Printing Services, Ltd.

Art Director:
Linda Helcher

Internal Designer:
Grannan Graphic Design, LTD.

Cover Designer:
Grannan Graphic Design, LTD.

Cover Images:
© Getty Images

Photography Manager:
John Hill

Photo Researcher:
Susan Van Etten

Printed in China
1 2 3 4 5 08 07 06

International Student Edition:
ISBN 0-324-36084-3

Library of Congress Control Number:
2005935616

For more information about our products, contact us at:

Thomson Learning Academic
Resource Center
1-800-423-0563

Thomson Higher Education
5191 Natorp Boulevard
Mason, OH 45040
USA

Technical Writing and Communication, and *Perceptual and Motor Skills*. He also consults in strategy development and the many parts of strategy implementation (organization development, individual development, team building, and communication).

Previously, he taught at several colleges in South Dakota and at the University of Minnesota while completing his Ph.D. degree. He worked with the Planning Department at Monsanto Chemical Company, now Solutia, during one sabbatical leave from SIUE, and during a second leave assisted the director of management consulting at Grace & Company in writing the second edition of a strategy book for practitioners.

PAMELA S. LEWIS

Pamela S. Lewis is president of Queens University of Charlotte in Charlotte, N.C. Prior to becoming president, Dr. Lewis served as the dean of the McColl School of Business at Queens and as dean of the LeBow College of Business at Drexel University in Philadelphia. Throughout her career, Dr. Lewis has distinguished herself through her commitment to providing innovative and high-quality education. Her particular focus has been on increasing community involvement and forging industry and academic partnerships that enhance the relevance and applicability of academic programs. Dr. Lewis, who holds a Ph.D. in strategic planning and international business from the University of Tennessee, has written numerous articles in the areas of strategic planning, international strategy, and entrepreneurship/new venture strategy. Dr. Lewis also has been active in executive education and consulting, serving as a strategic planning consultant for numerous organizations across a wide variety of industries. Dr. Lewis serves on the Board of Directors for three public companies—Sonoco Products Company, C&D Technologies, and Charming Shoppes—as well as on the board of numerous not-for-profits such as Presbyterian Hospital, Charlotte Chamber of Commerce, Communities in Schools, Charlotte Museum of History, and YMCA of Greater Charlotte.

Brief Contents

Contents

Preface

This new international edition presents us with an opportunity to reflect on significant events that have occurred within the past few years, and to assess their impact on the matter at hand—the study of management. As the 21st century approached we saw a frenzy of activity as the business community prepared itself for the dreaded Y2K problem. Although this glitch in computer date coding resulted in dire predictions of computer system malfunctions, it barely caused a blip on the radar screen when we rang in the new millennium. The economy continued to soar. We saw the rapid ascent and subsequently equally rapid fall of many dot-com organizations. We have seen changes in political administrations and public policy. Early in the new millennium we find ourselves facing an economy that is not riding the crest of the wave that it once surfed. Businesses have had to tighten belts, and business leaders are finding it necessary to turn their full attention to meeting the challenges of a highly dynamic and rapidly changing business environment. U.S. involvement in wars in Iraq and Afghanistan has shaken the confidence of many. We have been introduced to political terrorism on our own home front. The pernicious events of September 11, 2001, have altered the face of business and to some extent, have altered our way of life. Boarding a commercial airplane is no longer the simple task it once was. Meanwhile, many of the major air carriers struggle to remain solvent in the wake of costly security measures.

Mother Nature has also played a role in emphasizing the importance of studying management. Our nation has suffered several natural disasters that have dramatically affected the availability and movement of resources. Within a six-week span in 2004 hurricanes Charley, Frances, Ivan, and Jeanne wreaked havoc in Florida. As bad as they seemed at the time, they pale in comparison to what blew in from the Gulf of Mexico in 2005. In August of that year Hurricane Katrina inflicted catastrophic damage to the Louisiana, Mississippi, and Alabama Gulf Coast. Antebellum mansions that had stood proudly for one and a half centuries disappeared in the blink of an eye. New Orleans, which had the distinction of being a major U.S. port city, a center for petrochemical production, and a cultural and tourism icon, lay submerged beneath a pool of toxic water. Such a cataclysmic event was destined to have an economic impact for years to come. Countless businesses would struggle to get back on their feet. Major reconstruction, renovation, and preservation efforts would severely tax material supplies in the construction industry. Damage to U.S. oil refining capacity in Louisiana would push fuel prices to dizzying heights. Less than one month after Katrina, that problem was compounded by hurricane Rita's blow to Texas and Louisiana refineries. Those same airlines that were reeling under the pressures of heightened security were now struggling with the rising cost of jet fuel and mounting financial losses.

Looking beyond the physical destruction and other consequences of Hurricane Katrina, we see signs pointing to the importance of studying management. People around the world were horrified as they helplessly watched the tragic events unfold on their television screens. U.S. citizens could be seen huddled in squalid conditions within evacuation shelters. Others could be seen clinging to rooftops waiting to be rescued. All had to endure days in sweltering heat with little food or water. Meanwhile, leadership at federal, state, and local levels was ineffective in getting relief to those who were suffering. Effective decision making and decisive leadership might have prevented much of the loss of life that resulted.

As students of management, and future business and civic leaders, you must prepare to face challenges like these, for the business, social, and political environment is destined to remain on this volatile course. As the times continue to change, so too do the roles of leaders. Change is coming from many directions: the global marketplace has redefined the competitive structure of many industries; the increasing predominance of entrepreneurial and service-based organizations has altered the structure of our economy; quality management has radically changed the way many organizations do business; and extremist militant groups are doing all in their power to disrupt the world's free-market economy. Organizations are being restructured and redesigned to be lean, flexible, and adaptable to change; leaders in all areas and at all levels of the organization are expected to be proactive, team-oriented, and focused on results; and diversity in the workforce has become the rule rather than the exception. Succeeding as a leader in the organization of today and tomorrow requires a special set of management skills and competencies.

Management: Challenges for Tomorrow's Leaders should pique your excitement about this discipline. As you progress through the chapters you will be exposed to the new challenges and contemporary issues that the leaders of today and tomorrow will continually face.

Global competition; organizational restructuring; entrepreneurial, service-based, and quality initiatives; and an emphasis on gender, ethnic, and racial diversity in the workforce are just a few of the issues that you and other contemporary managers will confront. Our overriding objective in developing this book was to capture the excitement and challenges that business leaders will face in the environment of the 21st century.

In a few short years much has happened in the business environment that needed to be captured in this new edition. As authors, we also have had to adapt to change. While significant changes have been made in each chapter, the theoretical content of the chapters remains true to earlier editions and the pedagogical objective has not wavered. *Management: Challenges for Tomorrow's Leaders* provides comprehensive coverage of traditional and emerging management theory, and has a special focus on honing the leadership skills that will be necessary for survival in the dynamic, global environment of business.

The application orientation of the book has also remained strong. A number of features provide you with an opportunity to implement the material you learn and to understand a wide variety of real-world management situations. In short, the book is designed to help you develop an understanding of the field of management and to develop the competencies and skills that will enable you to succeed in the business environment of the future.

Changes in this Edition

- In the prior editions of this book, each chapter opened with an incident that details a real-life organizational problem or situation that is related to the content of the chapter. This pedagogy was very well received, and continues in this international edition. However, each chapter opening, now called "Facing the Challenge," has been changed to provide fresh illustrations of situations or problems, and how they were dealt with within the realm of the content and theory of the chapter. The challenge is referred to often as the chapter unfolds. At the close of the chapter, "Meeting the Challenge" describes how the problem was solved or the situation was addressed.
- The boxed material (highlighted examples) in each chapter has been replaced with updated or new illustrations and applications of contemporary management practice. These highlighted examples fall into the categories of Leaders in Action, At the Forefront, Now Apply It, and of course the Facing the Challenge and Meeting the Challenge so prominent in each chapter.
- Every chapter has been updated to reflect many of the changes that have occurred in the business world during the past few years. Along with the major features noted above, many new illustrative examples have been woven into the fabric of each of the chapters.

In all, more than 50 new company situations and scenarios have been developed to accompany the theoretical content of the chapters, as well as numerous additional company examples interspersed through the text.

Text Highlights

This book includes a number of features designed to prepare students to be leaders in this new millennium. These features focus on: (1) meeting the challenges inherent in a dynamic, rapidly changing business environment, (2) developing the competencies and skills that leaders will need in the future, (3) bridging the gap between management theory and practice, and (4) responding to the contemporary management trends that will affect both organizations and managers in the 21st century.

- *Challenges for Tomorrow's Leaders.* The underlying, integrating theme that forms the foundation of this book is meeting the leadership challenge as we begin the new millennium. As tomorrow's leaders, you will be challenged continually to respond to opportunities and threats that arise in the dynamic, global environment of business. You will need to be creative in the way you think about and respond to these challenges. As competitive pressures continue to escalate and consumers around the globe demand increasing levels of quality, you will find it necessary to strive for excellence in all facets of your organizations. Our focus in this book is to prepare you to meet these challenges as they affect the activities in which you will engage and the roles you will play.
- *Competencies and Skills.* Beyond our theme of meeting the challenge, we have developed this book with an emphasis on the competencies and skills needed by contemporary leaders. As students of management, you must be prepared to translate theory into practice as you move into the workplace. To do so, you will need to develop fully your skills in such important areas as teamwork, critical thinking, problem solving, communication, and adapting to change.
- *Theory and Practice.* This book bridges the gap between management theory and practice by using an interdisciplinary, applied approach to the material in

the text. Because leaders come from all areas of an organization (for example, production departments, finance and accounting departments, sales and marketing departments), it is important to understand how the concepts of management are applied in the various functional areas of organizations of all sizes. Further, an interdisciplinary approach to the study of management is essential given the blurring of the lines separating the traditional functions of business (for example, management, marketing, and finance) and the increasing predominance of cross-functional work teams within contemporary organizations.

- *Contemporary Management Trends.* Finally, we have identified and highlighted several contemporary management trends that present challenges for organizations and leaders today. They include global management, entrepreneurship, service management, quality, team-based management, ethics, and cultural diversity. Rather than adding a separate chapter on each of these trends, we introduce them very early in the text and then integrate the topics into each and every chapter of the book.

ORGANIZATION

Part 1 of the text addresses the basic concepts of management, the roles of the manager, and the changing nature of both the contemporary organization and the contemporary manager. The contemporary management trends discussed above are introduced, and a foundation is laid for examining how these trends affect management theory and practice. In addition, the history of management thought is reviewed, and the topics of social responsibility and ethics are addressed in light of their increasing importance in modern organizations.

Part 2 explores the managerial function of planning. This section examines the basic principles of the planning process, as well as planning from a strategic perspective. Strategy is examined as a tool for responding to challenges in today's highly competitive, global business environment and for achieving quality in every aspect of an organization's operations. Further, decision making is addressed as a key managerial responsibility, and a number of tools and techniques for decision making are presented.

Part 3 of the text focuses on the organizing function of management. More specifically, this section addresses the fundamental principles of organizing, as well as the models of organizational design that are appropriate for contemporary, team-oriented organizations. Issues of organizational culture, change, and human resource management are also addressed in this section. Particular emphasis is placed upon organizing to improve flexibility, facilitate change, utilize team management, and respond to the challenges of a diverse and heterogeneous work environment.

Part 4 explores the managerial function of leadership. This section focuses on factors that influence the behavior of people. Separate chapters examine individual and group behavior, what motivates members of the workforce, the nature of leadership, and communicating with others. Special attention is given to developing a leadership style that empowers the members of diverse organizations to excel in everything they do and to work as a team to achieve the goals and objectives of the organization.

Part 5 examines the management function of control. The foundational principles of control are addressed, and specific attention is given to productivity, quality control, and information systems control. Control is presented as a principal tool for achieving quality in the products, services, and processes of the organization, as well as a tool for developing a competitive advantage based on enhanced productivity, increased efficiency, and superior quality.

APPLICATION ORIENTED APPROACH

Consistent with our application-oriented approach to the presentation of contemporary management trends, we have included the following elements, which are designed to help you become a more effective manager:

- *Chapter Overview.* Every chapter opens with a summary that describes the general content of the chapter. This opening summary highlights the primary topics and concepts to be covered in the chapter and explains why the information is important to the manager of the future.
- *Learning Objectives.* Each chapter contains a well-defined set of learning objectives. These objectives focus on the specific topics covered in the chapter and provide a checklist of important points discussed in the chapter. Each learning objective is keyed to the appropriate section of the chapter text, the chapter summary, and the chapter review questions.
- *Facing the Challenge/Meeting the Challenge.* An opening Facing the Challenge in each chapter details a real-life organizational problem or situation that is related to the content of the chapter. This incident is referred to often as the chapter unfolds. At the close of the chapter, a Meeting the Challenge describes how the problem was solved or the situation was addressed using the management concepts discussed in the chapter. This allows the student to see how the concepts and theories presented in each chapter

are applied to business situations in actual companies.

- *Chapter Summary*. Each chapter closes with a summary of the major points presented in the chapter. This overview of the chapter contents provides students with an overall perspective on the topics covered. Each chapter's summary is tied directly to that chapter's learning objectives.
- *Review/Discussion Questions*. A set of review and discussion questions is provided at the end of each chapter. The review questions relate directly to the content of the chapter and are keyed to the learning objectives. The discussion questions are application-oriented in that they require students to respond to real-world situations or issues using the knowledge gained from the chapter.
- *Now Apply It*. In each chapter, Now Apply It provides an opportunity for students to practice the management principles they have studied. For example, students are given the opportunity to use self-assessment instruments to describe their own personal management or leadership styles, and organizational assessment skills to evaluate organizations.
- *Key Terms*. Key terms are highlighted throughout the chapter and are defined in the margins. A comprehensive glossary is provided at the back of the text.
- *Highlighted Examples*. Throughout the book, organizations that provide examples of contemporary management practices are highlighted. These examples are designed to profile real companies that are confronting management challenges and responding in proactive and innovative ways. Each of the chapters contains the following highlighted examples:

  Leaders in Action. Business leaders who have achieved excellence through their management practices and leadership skills are featured in Leaders in Action.

  At the Forefront. Companies that have achieved excellence through their management practices are featured in At the Forefront. Of particular interest are those organizations that have adopted a quality orientation in everything they do.

SUPPLEMENT PACKAGE

A professor's job is demanding. Because of this, we expect professors to demand a lot in return from the publisher and the authors of *Management*. Both the textbook and the accompanying ancillary materials (available for download at http://aise.swlearning.com) have been developed to help instructors excel when performing their vital teaching function. We also include a number of supplements to aid students in their study of the material.

Instructor's Manual
(available at http://aise.swlearning.com)
The instructor's manual for *Management* was prepared by David A. Foote, and provides important information for each chapter. Each chapter of the manual includes the following information:

- Learning Objectives.
- Chapter Overviews.
- Pedagogy Grids to highlight the main points covered in the feature boxes.
- Lecture Notes with narratives under each major point to flesh out the discussion and show alternative examples and issues to bring forward.
- Detailed Responses to the review questions and discussion questions.
- Cases with suggested answers for those instructors who wish to supplement the text material.

Test Bank
(available at http://aise.swlearning.com)
Special attention was given to the preparation of the test bank because it is one of the most important ancillary materials. Linda Putchinski, University of Central Florida, has updated this international edition of the test bank. The test bank contains over 3,500 multiple choice, true/false, matching, case, and essay questions.

PowerPoint ™ Presentation Slides
(available at http://aise.swlearning.com)
Developed by Charlie T. Cook, Jr., University of West Alabama, in close coordination with the text authors, over 600 slides are available to supplement course content, providing a comprehensive review of each chapter in the book.

Acknowledgments

A book such as this does not come to fruition solely by the hands of the authors. Many individuals have had significant involvement with this project, and their contributions must not go unrecognized. Our reviewers made insightful comments and valuable suggestions on the preliminary drafts of this book. Although criticism is sometimes a bitter pill to swallow, we can now look back and agree that the reviewer comments led to modifications that greatly strengthened the final product. We would like to express our gratitude to each of the following reviewers:

International Edition Reviewers:
- Barbara Barrett, St. Louis Community College
- Bruce Barringer, University of Central Florida
- Rochelle R. Brunson, Alvin Community College
- Maxine Christensen, Aims Community College
- Gerald Ellis, DeVry University
- Gregory Gomez III, Southern Illinois University Edwardsville
- Mary Kiker, Auburn University, Montgomery
- Tish Matuszek, Troy University
- Linda Beats Putchinski, University of Central Florida
- Joan Reicosky, University of Minnesota, Morris
- James Saya, College of Santa Fe
- Gail Thomas, New Hampshire Community Technical College/Laconia

Previous Edition Reviewers:
- Maha W. Alul, Maryville University
- Bruce Barringer, University of Central Florida
- Jerry Biberman, University of Scranton
- Donna Cooke, Florida Atlantic University
- Max E. Douglas, Indiana State University
- Lorena B. Edwards, Belmont University
- Kathleen Jones, University of North Dakota
- Thomas R. Mahaffey, Siena College
- John Mastriani, El Paso Community College
- Susan S. Nash, University of Oklahoma
- Charles Stubbart, Southern Illinois University
- Cynthia L. Sutton, Metropolitan State College of Denver
- Andrew Ward, Emory University

In addition to these manuscript reviewers, other colleagues have contributed greatly by developing several of the high-quality, comprehensive supplements that support this book. These individuals, and their contributions for which we are so grateful, include:

Instructor's Manual	David A. Foote, Middle Tennessee State University
Study Guide	Tish Matuszek, Sorrell College of Business at Troy University
Test Bank	Linda Putchinski, University of Central Florida
PowerPoint Slides	Charlie T. Cook, Jr., University of West Alabama

Our executive editor, John Szilagyi, and other individuals at South-Western made valuable contributions to this project. They include Monica Ohlinger, our developmental editor, who played a critical role in linking the huge network of contributors to this project. We also acknowledge the stamina of Bob Dreas, our production project manager, who not only tolerated our continual changes to the manuscript as it moved through production, but actually encouraged us to change whatever was necessary to make this product the very best possible. Our thanks also go to Kim Kanakes, senior marketing manager, for coordinating the outstanding sales and marketing efforts awarded this text.

Finally, we'd like to thank our families for their support throughout this project. Their tolerance of our absence from many family activities, their understanding of the time commitment a project like this requires, and their continual encouragement to push on enabled us to endure the long nights and lost weekends that made it possible for us to complete this book. For that support and commitment, we will always be grateful.

Stephen H. Goodman
Patricia M. Fandt
Joseph F. Michlitsch
Pamela S. Lewis

part 1

Meeting the Challenges of the 21st Century

Chapter

1

Management and Managers

© ASSOCIATED PRESS/AP

CHAPTER OVERVIEW

Each year, *BusinessWeek* publishes "The Best and Worst Managers of the Year".[1] In discussing the accomplishments of the "best" managers, words such as *vision, goals, strategy, customer-driven, innovation, strong diverse leadership,* and *increasing profitability* are common.

Here are some managers to whom these words apply. Ann Mulcahy took over at Xerox in 2001 and brought the company back to profitability. She says, "it's getting your people focused on the goal that is still the job of leadership."[2] At PepsiCo, Steven Reinemund is pulling ahead of Coca-Cola[3] by introducing many products each year that are purchased by customers throughout the world and by developing managers through mentoring and teaching. Carlos Ghosn brought Nissan Motor Co. from near bankruptcy in 1999 to one of the most profitable car companies in the world.[4] Meg Whitman, CEO of eBay Inc., is not only on *BusinessWeek's* list, but is also featured in *Fortune* as the "most powerful woman in business."[5]

What do these managers do to be successful? These managers do "everything" that a manager is supposed to do. That is, they successfully engage in the management functions of planning, organizing, leading, and controlling.

This chapter introduces you to overall management. Management is defined and the basic managerial functions are explained. Then things that managers do to carry out the basic functions of planning, organizing, leading, and controlling are discussed. These are the roles that managers play, the scope of their jobs, the levels of management, and the skills that managers need. Next, major changes in the 21st century are discussed. The chapter concludes with an overall framework that will be useful to coordinate learning about management and why it is important to study management.

LEARNING OBJECTIVES

When you have finished studying this chapter, you should be able to

1. Define what management is.
2. Identify and explain the basic managerial functions.
3. Understand the roles that managers play.
4. Discuss the scope of responsibilities of functional and general managers.
5. Describe the three levels of managers in terms of the skills that they need and the activities in which they are involved.
6. Identify major changes in the 21st century and explain how they will affect management of organizations.
7. Explain the interactions between all the major functions that managers perform and the interactions between planning, organizing, leading, and controlling.
8. Explain why it is important to study management.

Facing The Challenge

Can Anyone Save Nissan Motor Co., Ltd.?

Throughout the 1990s, Nissan Motor Co., Ltd. was getting deeper and deeper into trouble. Honda pushed the company out of second-place market share in the Japanese market, and its market share was small in other countries. Worse, costs were too high, and profit was gone. Nissan had losses in 6 of the last 7 years, from 1993–1999. The company had very high debt. There were too many brands that were not differentiated from each other or from the competitors. Nissan had to discount the price of its vehicles heavily in order to sell them. This resulted in excess capacity and further losses because it could not sell enough vehicles.

At the same time, because the overall competition was very strong, car companies around the world were merging and acquiring others because a company had to be very large in order to sell enough cars to make a profit. It appeared that Nissan could not survive, so the company tried to get large carmakers such as Ford and DaimlerChrysler for partners or to buy Nissan. This was not successful.

Finally, in March 1999, Renault purchased controlling interest in Nissan. The problem was that Renault was not in much better condition than was Nissan. The future for Nissan looked very bleak.

Louis Schweizer, CEO of Renault, assigned Carlos Ghosn, then an executive vice president at Renault, to take over Nissan. Although born in Brazil, Ghosn is a Lebanese citizen because his father was from Lebanon. His mother was French. Ghosn's education began in Lebanon and continued with degrees from the two most prestigious schools in France, Ecole Polytechnique and Ecole des Mines de Paris.

Then 30 years old, Ghosn worked for Michelin Tire Co. and went to Brazil to turn around the business there. He later became manager of U.S. operations and in 1996 joined Renault where he acquired the nickname of "le cost killer" for his efforts to improve Renault's situation.

In 1999 Ghosn headed to Japan to take over Nissan. Very quickly, he established a plan to revive Nissan. Is it possible to save a company that is in so much trouble?

Sources: M. Yoshino and M. Egawa, *Nissan Motor Co., Ltd., 2002* (Boston: Harvard Business School Publishing, 2002); "Nissan Aims for More Market Share with First New U.S. Plant in 20 Years," *St. Louis Post-Dispatch,* 28 May 2003, C1–C3; B. Bremner, G. Edmondson, C. Dawson, D. Welch, and K. Kerwin, "Nissan's Boss Carlos Ghosn Saved Japan's No. 2 Carmaker: Now He's Taking on the World," *BusinessWeek,* 4 October 2004, 50–58; G. Edmondson, "Smoothest Combo on the Road," *BusinessWeek,* 4 October 2004, 58–60; B. Bremner, "The Gaijin Who Saved Nissan," *BusinessWeek,* 17 January 2005, 18.

Introduction

Why did so many of the dot-com companies, or e-business companies, go out of existence very quickly only a year or two after they were founded during the years 1999 and 2000? It seemed that using the Internet and information technology was the way to go. Many of those starting the dot-com companies believed that brick-and-mortar businesses, as traditional businesses were called, would be extinct in a very short time.

Rather than many of the traditional businesses going out of existence, many of the dot-com companies went out of existence. A basic reason why this happened is because many of the dot-com managers forgot that a business still has to deliver something of value to customers, actually has to deliver it when the customers want it, and has to do this in a way that will result in profits, at least in the long run. Amazon.com is an example of a company that has hung on and is now becoming successful. It has been profitable only for a short part of its life, however. Amazon and the other companies that have survived and those that have been started and have become successful recently have figured out how to do it. They are employing basic management and business principles and practices.[7]

The same issues apply to traditional businesses and other types of organizations. Certainly, not all traditional businesses and organizations are successful either. However, as with the dot-com companies, the more successful ones also employ basic business and management principles well.[8]

That is why this book is about basic management. It is intended to help you learn about management and to help understand how changes that are likely to occur will affect management in the 21st century.

The purpose of this chapter is to introduce you to the field of management. It will set the stage for understanding the foundations of management that are discussed in the rest of the chapters.

Leaders in Action

The Avon Lady

Andrea Jung joined Avon Products in 1994 as president of the Product Marketing Group. She was promoted to president of Global Marketing in 1996, executive vice president and president of Global Marketing and New Business in 1997, and chief executive officer in 1999. The title of chair of the board was added in addition to CEO in 2001. When she became CEO in 1999, she was the first woman to hold that position in the 115-year history of the company.

She also took over a company that was in very serious trouble. Profits were sinking, products were not inspiring, competitors were eroding Avon's sales, and the notion of selling cosmetics door to door with "Avon ladies" seemed out of date.

Jung demonstrated that she is a good leader by engaging every major principle of good overall management with successful results. She started by defining the vision of Avon as the company for women. This includes focus on customers and what they need as well as the many, mostly women, who sell Avon products. Then Jung overhauled almost everything at Avon, from manufacturing, to packaging, to advertising, to selling. The updated selling included rejuvenating the sales representatives' jobs by adding rewards for representatives who recruited more representatives and by making them partners in Internet sales, which could have replaced the door-to-door representatives.

In addition to employing the basic management principles very well, Jung has embraced the Internet as a powerful tool to do business. She has also taken the company global by introducing Avon products in many countries, including Japan and most recently China. Diversity is also important to Jung. With 86% of its managers being women, Avon has the largest percentage of women managers of any other Fortune 500 company. These are all good reasons why *Fortune* magazine ranks Andrea Jung as the third most powerful woman in business.

Sources: G. Brewer, "How Avon's CEO Implements Diversity," *Sales and Marketing Management* 149 (no. 1) (January 1997): 1; N. Byrnes, "Avon: The New Calling," *BusinessWeek,* 18 September 2000, 136; K. Brooker, "It Took a Lady to Save Avon," *Fortune,* 15 October 2001, 158; J. Tarquinio, "Aging Gracefully at Avon," *Kiplinger's Personal Finance,* September 2004, 49; "50 Most Powerful Women," *Fortune,* 18 October 2004, 181–198.

What Is Management?

1 Management has been defined in many ways. Mary Parker Follett, an early management scholar, offered what has come to be known as the classic definition when she described management as "the art of getting things done through people."[9] Although this definition captures the human dimension of management, a more comprehensive definition is needed.

Management is defined as the process of administering and coordinating resources effectively, efficiently, and in an effort to achieve the goals of the organization.[10] Of course, management includes establishing appropriate overall organizational goals. The degree to which the goals are achieved is defined as **effectiveness. Efficiency** is achieved by using the fewest inputs (such as people and money) to generate a given output. In other words, effectiveness means "doing the right things" to achieve the appropriate goal, and efficiency means "doing things right."[11] The end result of effective and efficient management will be organizational success.

Management occurs within an organizational context. But what is an organization? An **organization** is a group of individuals who work together toward common goals. Organizations can be for profit, such as the business organizations with which we are all familiar (for example, Starbucks, Wal-Mart, and Dell), or not for profit, such as churches, fraternities, and public universities. Organizations also include the group that you might put together for a trip or for an intramural softball team. No matter what kind of organization it is, all organizations are made up of people. The efforts of these people must be coordinated if the organization is to accomplish its goals. Let's examine the management process in which managers establish overall goals and then achieve them effectively and efficiently. That is, let's study the managerial process.

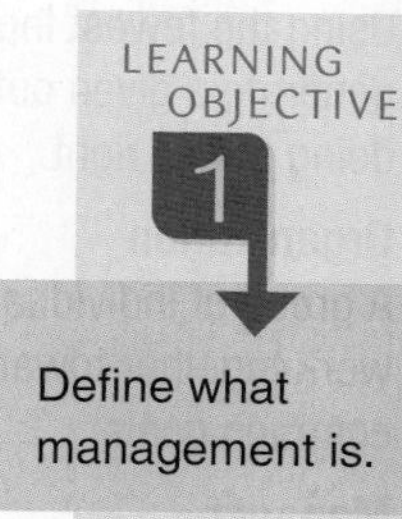

Define what management is.

KEY TERMS

Management
The process of administering and coordinating resources effectively and efficiently in an effort to achieve the goals of the organization.

Effectiveness
The degree to which goals are achieved; doing the right things.

What Managers Do

Four overall functions tend to include essentially everything that **managers** do in the management process. They are planning, organizing, leading, and controlling (Figure 1.1). Although the details of what each manager does varies considerably from manager to manager, from organization to organization, and from time to time, these basic functions have been useful over time to help understand the broad functions that all managers carry out.[12]

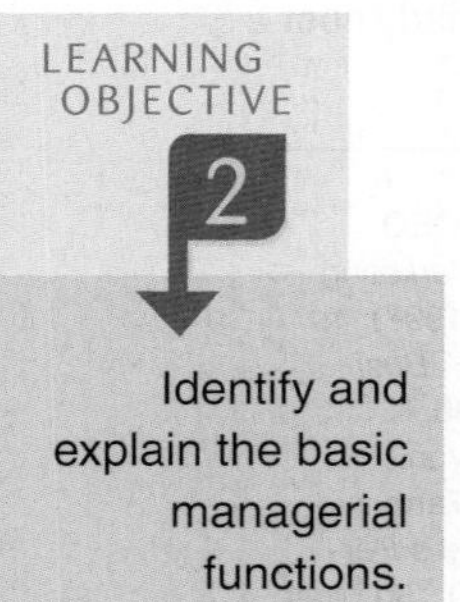

LEARNING OBJECTIVE 2

Identify and explain the basic managerial functions.

PLANNING

Planning includes setting goals and defining the actions necessary to achieve the goals, in light of the situation. That is, the situation must be analyzed and understood and the appropriate goal(s) and actions must be determined in order to take advantage of opportunities and/or to solve problems. While top-level managers establish overall goals and strategy, managers throughout the organization must develop goals, strategy, and operational plans for their work groups that contribute to the success of the organization as a whole. In addition, they must develop a plan for administering and coordinating the resources for which they are responsible so that the goals of their work groups can be achieved.

KEY TERMS

Efficiency
Using the fewest inputs to generate a given output; doing things right.

Organization
A group of individuals who work together toward common goals.

Manager
An organizational member who is responsible for planning, organizing, leading, and controlling the activities of the organization so that its goals are achieved.

Planning
Setting goals and defining the actions necessary to achieve those goals.

Organizing
The process of determining the tasks to be done, who will do them, and how those tasks will be managed and coordinated.

ORGANIZING

Organizing involves determining the tasks to be done, who will do them, and how those tasks will be managed and coordinated. Managers must organize the members of their work groups and organization so that information, resources, and tasks flow logically and efficiently through the organization. Organizing also includes defining and assigning authority and responsibility for decisions to enable tasks to be carried out effectively. Issues of organizational culture and human resource management are also related to this function. Overall, the organization must be structured in a way that will lead to achievement of its mission and organizational goals and allow it to be responsive to changes in the organization's environment.

LEADING

Managers must also be capable of **leading** the members of their work groups toward the accomplishment of the organization's goals. To be effective leaders, managers must understand the dynamics of individual and group behavior, be able to motivate their employees, and be effective communicators. In today's business environment, effective leaders must also have vision. They must be capable of understanding and predicting what will happen in the future, and they must be capable of sharing that vision and guiding, empowering, and influencing their employees to make the vision a reality. When this is accomplished, the results are very positive. A WorkUSA 2002 survey report found a significant effect in financial results that came from how companies managed their people.[13]

CONTROLLING

Managers must monitor the performance of the organization as well as their progress in implementing strategic and operational plans. **Controlling** includes establishing and understanding what is required to achieve goals, measuring what actually happened or is being done, identifying deviations between planned and actual results, and taking corrective action if there is a deviation. Such actions may involve pursuing the original plan more aggressively or adjusting the plan to the existing situation. Control is an important function in the managerial process because it provides a method for ensuring that the organization is moving toward the achievement of its goals.

Roles of Managers

3 In performing the four overall functions, most of what managers do can be categorized into basic roles. **Role** refers to the behavior that is expected in a

Figure 1.1 The Process of Management

particular situation. For example, think about the behavior that is expected in your role as a daughter or son, as a friend, as an employee, or as a supervisor. Knowing the basic roles that managers play will help us to better understand what managers do.

The work of Henry Mintzberg is widely used to explain the roles that managers typically perform. Mintzberg conducted a project in which he studied the actual behaviors of managers. He found that there were ten roles grouped into three categories: interpersonal, informational, and decisional[14] (Figure 1.2). Considerable evidence over time supports Mintzberg's findings.[15]

INTERPERSONAL ROLES

Interpersonal roles involve interactions and relationships with organizational members and other constituents. The three interpersonal roles played by the manager are figurehead, leader, and liaison.

As the heads of organizational units, managers must perform certain duties that are primarily ceremonial in nature. For example, managers may have to appear at community functions, attend social events, or host luncheons for important customers. In doing so, managers fulfill their role as figureheads.

Because managers are responsible for the success or failure of their organizational units or the organizational overall, they must play the role of leader. In this capacity, managers work with and through their employees to ensure that the organization's goals are met.

Finally, managers must serve as liaisons. That is, they coordinate the activities between individuals and work groups within the organization and develop favorable relationships with outside constituents. Being politically sensitive to important organizational issues helps them develop relationships and networks both within and beyond their organizations.

INFORMATIONAL ROLES

LEARNING OBJECTIVE

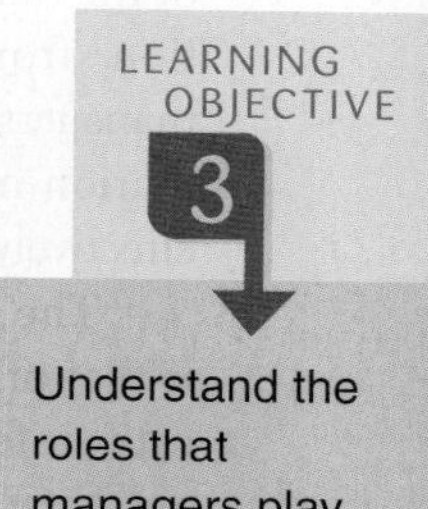

Understand the roles that managers play.

In their **informational roles**, managers are responsible for ensuring that the people with whom they work have sufficient information to do their jobs effectively. By the very nature of managerial responsibilities, managers become the communication centers of their units and are a communication source for other work groups within the organization. People throughout the organization depend on the management structure and the managers themselves to disseminate information or provide access to the information that they need to do their jobs. Informational roles include monitor, disseminator, and spokesperson.

As monitors, managers continually scan the internal and external environments of their organizations for useful information. Managers seek out information from their subordinates and liaison contacts and may receive unsolicited information from their networks of personal contacts. From this information, managers identify potential opportunities and threats for their work groups and organizations.

In their role as disseminators, managers share and distribute much of the information

KEY TERMS

Leading
Motivating and directing the members of the organization so that they contribute to the achievement of the goals of the organization.

Controlling
Monitoring the performance of the organization, identifying deviations between planned and actual results, and taking corrective action when necessary.

Role
The behavior that is expected in a particular situation.

Interpersonal role
The role of a manager that involves relationships with organizational members and other constituents.

Figure 1.2 Mintzberg's Managerial Roles

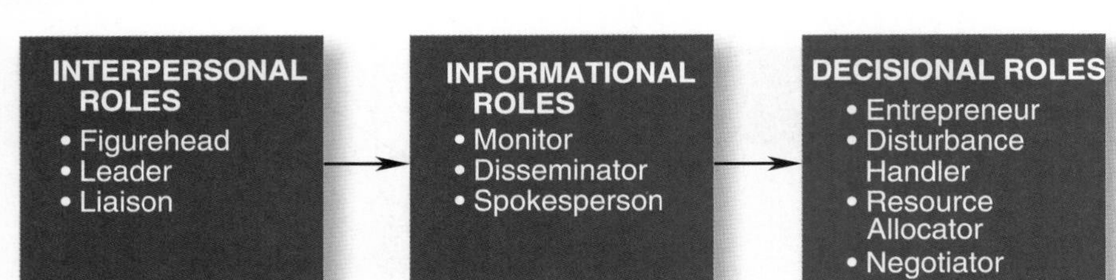

Reprinted by permission of Harvard Business Review. From "The Manager's Job: Folklore and Fact," Henry Mintzberg, *Harvard Business Review*, March–April 1990, 49–61.

they receive as information monitors. As disseminators, managers pass on important information to appropriate members of their work groups. Depending on the nature of the information, managers may also withhold information from work group members. Most important, managers must ensure that their employees have the information necessary to perform their duties efficiently and effectively.

The final informational role played by managers is that of spokesperson. Managers must often communicate information to individuals outside their units and their organizations. For example, directors and shareholders must be advised about the financial performance and strategic direction of the organization; interest groups must be assured that the organization is fulfilling its social obligations; and government officials must be satisfied that the organization is abiding by the law.

DECISIONAL ROLES

Finally, managers play the role of decision maker. In their **decisional roles**, managers process information and reach conclusions. Information in and of itself is nearly meaningless if it is not used to make organizational decisions. Managers make those decisions. They commit their work groups to courses of action and allocate resources so that the groups' plans can be implemented. Decisional roles include entrepreneur, disturbance handler, resource allocator, and negotiator.

KEY TERMS

Informational role
The manager's responsibility for gathering and disseminating information to the stakeholders of the organization.

Decisional role
The role in which a manager processes information and reaches conclusions.

Recall that in the monitor role managers scan the internal and external environments of the organization for changes that may present opportunities. As an entrepreneur, the manager initiates projects that capitalize on opportunities that have been identified. This may involve developing new products, services, or processes.

Regardless of how well an organization is managed, things do not always run smoothly. Therefore, managers will have to handle disturbances. They must cope with conflict and resolve problems as they arise. This may involve dealing with an irate customer, negotiating with an uncooperative supplier, or intervening in a dispute between employees.

As a resource allocator, the manager determines which projects will receive organizational resources. Although we tend to think primarily in terms of financial or equipment resources, other types of important resources are allocated to projects as well. Consider, for example, the manager's time. When managers choose to spend their time on a particular project, they are allocating a resource. Information is also an important resource. By providing access to certain information, managers can influence the success of a project.

Managers also must be negotiators in certain situations. Studies of managerial work at all levels have found that managers spend a good portion of their time negotiating. Managers may negotiate with employees, suppliers, customers, or other work groups. Regardless of the work group, the manager is responsible for all negotiations necessary to ensure that the group is making progress toward achieving the goals of the organization.

Managerial Scope, Levels, and Skills

4 We have looked at the various functions that managers perform and roles that managers play within the organization. To this point, however, we have not distinguished among types of managers. Managers differ with

regard to both the scope of their responsibilities and their level within the vertical structure of the organization. All managers need the same basic skills, but the importance of a certain skill may be higher with some types of managers than others.

SCOPE OF RESPONSIBILITY

The nature of the manager's job will depend on the scope of his or her responsibilities. Some managers have functional responsibilities, whereas others have general management responsibilities.

Functional managers are responsible for work groups that are segmented according to function. For example, a manager of an accounting department is a functional manager. So are the managers of a production department, a research and development department, and a marketing department. Work groups segmented by function tend to be relatively homogeneous. Members of the group often have similar backgrounds and training and perform similar tasks. Functional managers often have backgrounds similar to those of the people they manage. Their technical skills are usually quite strong because they are typically promoted from within the ranks of their work groups. The greatest challenge for these managers lies in developing an understanding of the relationship between their work groups and the other work units within the organization. Equally important, functional managers must convey information back to their work groups and ensure that the members of their units understand their roles within the organization as a whole.

General managers are responsible for ensuring that several functions or parts of the organization work together effectively. In doing so, they must coordinate and integrate the work of diverse parts of the organization. For example, the manager of a supermarket is responsible for managing the overall supermarket by coordinating all the departments within the store. The produce manager, grocery manager, bakery manager, and floral manager all report to the general manager. Because general managers manage diverse departments, their technical skills may not be as strong as the skills of the people they manage. The manager of the supermarket, for example, may not know the difference between a tenderloin or flank steak or have little idea how croissants are made. However, general managers must be able to coordinate various parts of the organization in an effective way.

LEVELS OF MANAGEMENT AND RELATIVE IMPORTANCE OF SKILLS

In general, there are three levels of managers: first-line managers, middle managers, and top-level managers. Figure 1.3 illustrates these managerial levels, as well as the *operational employees,* or the individuals who are not in the managerial ranks but who actually deliver the product or service of the organization. The pyramid shape of the figure reflects the number of managers at each level. Most organizations have more first-line managers than middle managers and more middle managers than top-level managers. (This will be discussed more in the organizing chapters.)

Managers at all organizational levels engage in planning, organizing, leading, and controlling. Carrying out these functions requires a set of overall skills. However, managers at different levels in the organization tend to be more or less involved in certain types of activities, so the degree to which they are immersed in the basic functions varies. For example, a study of over 1000 managers examined the extent to which managers at each level engaged in certain activities, elements of planning, organizing, leading, and controlling, such as managing individual performance, instructing subordinates, planning and allocating resources, coordinating interdependent groups, managing group performance, monitoring the business environment, and representing one's staff. The results of the study suggest that managers at different levels of the organizational hierarchy are involved in these activities to varying degrees.[16] Consequently, the degree to which managers at different levels employ certain skills also varies. This is shown in Figure 1.4 , summarized in Table 1.1 and discussed next.

LEARNING OBJECTIVE 4

Discuss the scope of responsibilities of functional and general managers.

LEARNING OBJECTIVE

Describe the three levels of managers in terms of the skills that they need and the activities in which they are involved.

First-Line Managers: One-to-One with Subordinates

First-line managers supervise the individuals who are directly responsible for producing the organization's product or delivering its service. They carry titles such as production supervisor, line manager, section chief, or account manager. First-line managers are often promoted from the ranks, based on their ability to deliver the product or service of the organization as well as their ability to manage others who do the same.

KEY TERMS

Functional manager
A manager who is responsible for managing a work unit that is grouped based on the function served.

General manager
A manager who is responsible for managing several different departments that are responsible for different tasks.

First-line manager
The manager who supervises the operational employees.

Figure 1.3 Managerial Levels

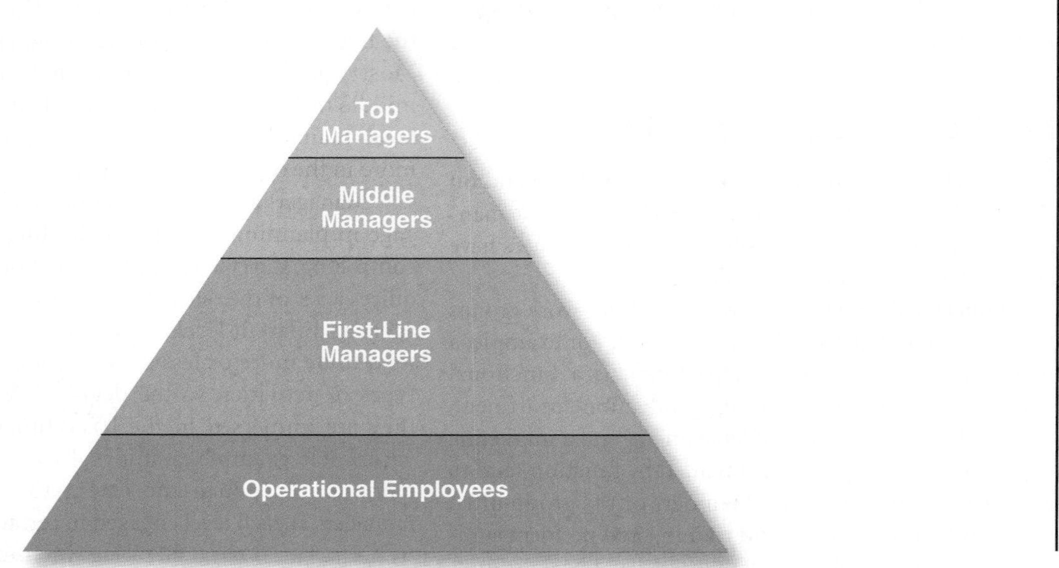

The primary objective of first-line managers is to ensure that the products or services of their organization are delivered to customers on a day-to-day basis.

Technical skills tend to be most important for first-line managers. These skills refer to the knowledge and use of the tools, techniques, and procedures that are specific to their particular field.

Because first-line managers are also involved in two of the basic activities listed earlier—managing individual performance and instructing subordinates—they also use **human skills,** the ability to work effectively with others. Managing individual performance involves motivating and disciplining subordinates, monitoring performance, providing feedback, and improving communications. Instructing subordinates includes training, coaching, and instructing employees on how to do their jobs.

First-line managers are also involved in tasks that require **conceptual skills,** the ability to analyze complex situations. This may involve planning, scheduling, and related tasks. However, the first-line manager normally does not get involved in conceptual issues to the degree that a higher-level manager might.

Middle Managers: Linking Groups

Middle managers supervise first-line managers or staff departments. They carry titles such as department head, product manager, or marketing manager. Middle managers may come from the ranks of first-line managers in a particular department or from other areas of the organization. These managers are typically selected because they have a strong understanding of the overall strategy of the organization and a commitment to ensuring that

KEY TERMS

Technical skill
The ability to utilize tools, techniques, and procedures that are specific to a particular field.

Human skill
The ability to work effectively with others.

Conceptual skill
The ability to analyze complex situations.

Middle manager
A manager who supervises the first-line managers or staff departments.

Table 1.1 Managerial Level, Main Skill, and Typical Activities

Top Management	Conceptual	Monitoring the organization environment. Set strategic direction
Middle Management	Human	Planning and allocating resources. Coordinating interdependent groups. Managing group performance.
First-line	Technical	Use appropriate tools, techniques, procedures. Instructing, guiding subordinates. Managing individual performance.

Figure 1.4 Skills Needed at Different Levels of Management

FIRST-LINE MANAGEMENT	MIDDLE MANAGEMENT	TOP MANAGEMENT
Conceptual	Conceptual	Conceptual
Human	Human	Human
Technical	Technical	Technical

it is implemented well. Essentially, middle managers perform as linkages between the top managers and related overall strategy and the first-line managers. A primary objective of most middle managers is to allocate resources effectively and manage the first-line managers who supervise the work group so that the overall goals of the organization can be achieved.[17]

Middle managers tend to be most involved in three basic activities—planning and allocating resources, coordinating interdependent groups, and managing group performance. The importance of these three activities rises sharply as one moves from first-line to middle management, but interestingly, as we will see later, it declines slightly for the top-level management group.

Human skills are most important for middle managers because these managers must coordinate the efforts of members of one's work group as well as coordinate with other work groups within the organization. Within the work group, middle managers must manage group dynamics, encourage cooperation, and resolve conflicts. When interacting with outside work groups, middle managers serve as liaisons, communicating the needs and issues of their teams to other members of the organization and conveying information from other work groups back to their units. Of course, the other tasks of middle managers also require technical and conceptual skills but perhaps not as much as human skills.[18]

© MICHAELNEWMAN/PHOTO EDIT

Managers must be able to organize the members of their work groups and lead them toward the accomplishment of the organization's goal.

Top-Level Managers: An Eye on the Outside

Top-level managers provide the strategic direction for the organization. They carry titles such as chief executive officer (CEO), president, chief operations officer, chief financial officer (CFO), chief information officer, and executive vice president.

Occasionally, top-level managers work their way up the organizational hierarchy from the first-line management level. However, it is also fairly common for organizations to hire top-level managers from other organizations.

Regardless of their background, top-level managers should be selected because they have a vision for the organization and the leadership skills necessary to guide the organization toward reaching that vision. Top-level managers must set the strategic direction of the organization in light of organizational resources, assets, and skills and the opportunities and threats that were found in monitoring the external environment.

Top-level managers need to have strong conceptual

KEY TERMS

Top-level manager
The manager who provides the strategic direction for the organization.

skills if they are to effectively accomplish these things. Conceptual skills enable managers to process a tremendous amount of information about both the external and the internal environment of the organization and to determine the implications of that information. Conceptual skills also enable top-level managers to look at their organization as a whole and understand how separate work groups and departments relate to and affect each other. Finally, strong conceptual skills enable top-level managers to develop a distinctive personality or culture for their organizations. Some examples of very effective top-level managers include Herb Kelleher, cofounder and chair of the board at Southwest Airlines; Meg Whitman, CEO of eBay; Howard Schultz,[19] founder of Starbucks; Andrea Jung, CEO of Avon Products; Carlos Ghosn, CEO of both Nissan and its parent, Renault, at the same time;[20] Jack Welch, former CEO of General Electric;[21] and Andy Grove, cofounder of Intel. In fact, Grove was voted the "most influential business leader of the past quarter-century"[22] by the prestigious Wharton Business School in 2004.

LEARNING OBJECTIVE 6

Identify major changes in the 21st century and explain how they will affect management of organizations.

As is true of managers at other organizational levels, top-level managers also need human and technical skills. Top-level managers definitely must work effectively with people, inside and outside the organization, and have technical skills so that they can understand the financial ramifications and other effects of the technical parts of the organization. However, most of the tasks of top-level managers tend to fall in the conceptual area, requiring an ability to think and to analyze causes, effects, and consequences.

Managing in the 21st Century

6 The 21st century is still very young, but it has already seen some amazing things. When it began, the economy in the United States was booming and dot-com companies appeared ready to take over from the so-called brick-and-mortar companies. It was said that there was a "new economy" and that everything was different. The old ways of running a business did not apply anymore. In a very short period of time, the economy cooled and many of the dot-com companies became dot-bombs and imploded.[23] This was made even worse by the 9/11 (2001) terrorist attacks. Yes, there were many changes in the economy and in society, there will continue to be changes, and the rate of change continues to increase. However, the same basic business, economic, and managerial principles still apply. An organization still has to provide products or services to its customers that are valued by those customers. Then the customers will pay a price that will allow the organization to be prosperous, so long as it keeps its costs in line.

Let's now discuss important factors that have changed considerably, some in a very short time and some that continue to change. They all have important consequences for managing an organization. These factors are the Internet and information technology, increasing globalization, increasing diversity, intellectual capital, and increased emphasis on ethics.

THE INTERNET AND INFORMATION TECHNOLOGY

Jeff Bezos, the founder and CEO of Amazon.com, shocked the business world on January 22, 2002, when he announced that his company had made its first profit ever for the third quarter of the previous year.[24] Why was this a shock? Up to that time, most dot-com companies experienced large financial losses and were not close to earning a profit. After the first profitable quarter, Amazon took a loss the next quarter and several after that. However, Amazon.com was profitable during 2003, and its profitability is continuing.[25] Finally, dot-com companies were beginning to be financially successful. E-business was working. During 2002, roughly one fourth of e-business companies were profitable.[26] In addition to Amazon.com, this included Expedia, Priceline, and WebMD. How did they do it? "It [Amazon.com] earned a profit by getting the basics right: tangible operational efficiencies, heads-down cost cutting, and savvy partnership deals with the likes of Toys R Us Inc. and Target Corp."[27] E-businesses are using basic managerial and business principles and are profitable.[28]

Traditional, brick-and-mortar businesses also added the use of the Internet, not to replace how they did business but to compliment their existing businesses. Now one can buy products from Wal-Mart, Barnes & Noble, Sears, REI, and the local auto dealership at the stores and on the Internet.[29]

Of course, the Internet and information technology has changed some of the aspects of how business is conducted. Organizations can have almost instant feedback about results with sophisticated information systems. They can also give needed information to people throughout the organization so that they can perform better. Very tight links can be established between suppliers and organiza-

© ZAVE SMITH/CORBIS

Because technology continues to advance and become more widespread, effective managers should have strong technological skills.

tions that can exchange information to coordinate their operations.

Customers can get more information about products and services on the Internet. They can "comparison shop" to see which businesses have the products they want and at what price. One effect of this is the physical arrangement and location of retail stores are changing because informed customers now do not spend time "shopping" inside of the store.[30]

Blogs, which are essentially an individual's online personal journal, also contain information about products, services, and organizations. Being personal, some of the information is favorable, some unfavorable, and much of it based on personal tastes and opinions. Organizations are now starting blogs, including the blog set up by Robert Lutz (vice chairman of General Motors), to use for advertising and otherwise sending out positive information.[31]

All these things increase the bargaining power of customers. The Internet also makes the market for many products and services global. Now a business in most any country can compete with anyone else as long as the product can be shipped easily to customers. Of course, with information-based products and services (for example, concert tickets and airline tickets), competitors can come from anywhere in the world.[32]

INCREASING GLOBALIZATION

The Internet makes possible the access to geographic markets that were previously out of reach of many companies. It makes many markets, especially those for many services and those where the product is information, truly global. An important example of this is the high-tech call-centers that many U.S. companies have moved to other countries, especially India.[33]

In addition to the influence of the Internet in continued **globalization**, there continues to be more companies moving various parts of their operations to a larger number of countries. For example, many companies have located research labs in China. General Electric has 27 labs there, MicroSoft Corp. has 200 researchers there, and companies such as DaimlerChrysler, Cisco, Intel, and IBM are moving labs to China.[34]

Globalization also continues on another front: the combinations and partnerships between businesses from various countries. TCL Corp. from Huizhou, China, merged with Thomson from France to create the largest television maker in the world. One of the popular television brands that the company makes is RCA, a brand that got its start in the United States with the RCA Co. Shanghai Automotive Industry Corp. purchased 48.9% of Ssangyong, a truck maker in Korea. Perhaps the most interesting and complex combination of all is the acquisition of controlling interest of the personal computer operations of IBM by Lenovo Group Ltd. from China.[35] That deal will allow IBM to gain access to the Chinese market for many of its products and services and allow the Chinese company to move into the United States. The headquarters of Lenovo will be relocated from Beijing to Armonk, New York, which is close to IBM's headquarters. IBM managers will manage the new Lenovo headquarters. IBM also has an 18.9% ownership in Lenovo.[36]

The pace and pervasiveness of globalization will continue. Managers at all levels of organizations will need to understand the effects of operating in a global environment.[37]

INCREASING DIVERSITY

Closely connected to the globalization of business has been the globalization of the

KEY TERMS

Globalization
Various companies moving to multiple countries and doing business in multiple countries.

labor market. Just as goods and services flow relatively freely across national boundaries, so do human resources. The result has been increased diversity of the population base in the United States as well as other countries and increased diversity in the workplace.[38] In the broad sense, diversity is defined as differences or variety. That applies to all types of differences. However, as the word is normally used, **diversity** refers to the heterogeneity of the population and workforce, mostly in terms of gender and race.

Diversity presents new challenges for businesses and managers. As we will see in subsequent chapters, organizational success requires a strong organizational culture and group cohesiveness. Achieving this may be more difficult when the workplace includes people with different backgrounds, from different nations, or with different cultural frames of reference. Men, women, Caucasians, Hispanics, African Americans, and others with diverse racial, national, and ethnic backgrounds often have very different perceptions about the same situations. As a consequence, it may be more difficult for diverse groups to reach a consensus on common goals and on the methods for achieving those goals.[39]

Many organizations today have established training programs to help employees develop an appreciation for diversity and to foster cooperation among culturally diverse groups. Most of these programs focus on valuing, even celebrating, diversity and the breadth of thought and experience that results from diverse work groups. Some organizations have implemented such programs because they feel it is "politically correct" to do so. Many other organizations, however, have implemented aggressive diversity-training programs because they believe that a diverse workforce provides a significant competitive advantage. For example, companies such as Allstate Insurance, Qwest, Avon, Wal-Mart, and General Electric view diversity as a key strategic tool for ensuring success in the highly competitive markets.[40]

The globalization of business will undoubtedly continue to escalate. Therefore, issues of diversity will continue to influence the thinking and behaviors of managers.

KEY TERMS

Diversity
The heterogeneity of the workforce, mostly in terms of gender and race.

Intellectual capital
The total of an organization's knowledge, experience, relationships, processes, discoveries, innovations, market presence, and community influence.

Structural capital
The accumulated knowledge of the organization represented by its patents, trademarks and copyrights, proprietary databases, and systems.

Customer capital
The value of established relationships with customers and suppliers.

Human capital
The cumulative skills and knowledge of the organization.

© MARK RICHARDS/PHOTOEDIT

Diversity of gender and race in the workforce presents a challenge in reaching a consensus on common goals and the methods for achieving these goals.

INTELLECTUAL CAPITAL

For most of the 20th century, the critical factors of production were considered to be land, labor, and raw materials. The job of managers was to use these production factors to create products that were more valuable than the sum of their parts. In the 21st century, intellectual capital is becoming a critical resource. More and more products will become intellectual, or knowledge-based (for example, investment services and advice, registering for classes at a school, computer software), and may be better referred to as services. Services such as travel and entertainment are becoming more important, and they rely heavily on knowledge. Even the traditional products will make more use of knowledge in design, production, and marketing of them. According to Gary Hamel, a well-known consultant, we are now an "economy of heads" rather than an "economy of hands."[41]

What is intellectual capital? In general, **intellectual capital** refers to the total of an organization's knowledge—what its people know, experiences, relationships, processes, discoveries, innovations, market presence, and community influence.[42] Thomas Stewart, the author of *Intellectual Capital: The Wealth of New Organizations*,[43] provides a classification for knowledge assets. The three major categories of intellectual capital are

- **Structural capital**: the accumulated knowledge and know-how of the organization represented by its patents, trademarks and copyrights, proprietary databases, and systems.
- **Customer capital**: the value of established relationships with customers and suppliers.
- **Human capital**: the cumulative skills and knowledge of the organization.

At the Forefront

Managing in the 21st Century

Five factors are identified in this chapter as having special importance in the 21st century. Many organizations are engaged in all of these areas, and here are some notable examples:

- **Internet and Information technology** e-Bay and Amazon.com are prime examples of using the Internet and information technology because they are "Internet companies." Everything they do is on the Internet. Many traditional businesses also conduct part of their business with the help of the Internet (for example, Wal-Mart and Starbucks). Most organizations have a website.
- **Increasing globalization** Essentially all automobile companies operate on a global scale, from selling vehicles in many countries, to having ownership and partnership across the world: DaimlerChrysler, a German and U.S. company; Renault-Nissan, in France and Japan; Ford, who owns Volvo, Land Rover, and Jaguar, in European countries. Avon Products markets its products in many countries (see "Leaders in Action").
- **Increasing diversity** Of Avon's managers, 86% are women; PepsiCo stresses diversity in its management ranks so that managers can understand markets in different countries; many companies, including Wal-Mart, General Electric, Denny's Restaurants, and Allstate Insurance, have diversity-training programs.
- **Intellectual capital** All companies need to manage their knowledge to keep up in very competitive, fast-moving markets. Some companies deal almost exclusively in knowledge, such as Expedia, Travelocity, and brokerage companies. Others rely heavily on knowledge to deliver products and services, such as Amazon.com and e-Bay.
- **Ethics** Ethical behavior of managers and others in organizations has always been important. Because a notable and large number of unethical behavior has occurred in recent years, there is special attention on ethical behavior. Jeffrey Immelt is leading General Electric in becoming more aware so that it won't sell products to people that might cause physical damage in the long run. Salie Krawcheck, now chief financial officer at CitiBank, cleaned up practices of brokers that were considered unethical in the brokerage business as chief executive officer of Smith Barney, part of CitiBank. Edward Breen took over as CEO at Tyco after Dennis Kozlowski was fired and was tried by the courts for larceny because of the large sums of company money that he allegedly used for his own purposes.

Sources: K. Brooker, "It Took a Lady to Save Avon," *Fortune,* 15 October 2001, 158; J. Tarquinio, "Aging Gracefully at Avon," *Kiplinger's Personal Finance,* September 2004, 49; "eBay's Secret," *Fortune,* 18 October 2004, 161–178; "50 Most Powerful Women: Who's Up? Who's Down?" *Fortune,* 18 October 2004, 181–198; H. Hof, "The Wizard of Web Retailing," *BusinessWeek,* 20 December 2004, 18; "The Best & Worst Managers of the Year," *BusinessWeek,* 10 January 2005, 55–68.

Stewart and others contend that contemporary organizations must develop, measure, and manage these intellectual assets if they are to be successful.

The management of this overall knowledge, or intellectual capital, is a critical strategic resource for contemporary organizations. Managers must attract the right people and manage them in a way that turns their brainpower into profitable products and services. Some examples of companies that are doing this are Amazon.com, Dell, General Electric, Wal-Mart, and Southwest Airlines.

ETHICS

Ethical behavior of managers continues to fill the news. There are headlines in magazines and newspapers such as "They Fought the Law: A Parade of Alleged Corporate Wrongdoers Faced Their Accusers,"[44] "Former Charter Executive Pleads Guilty,"[45] and "Businesses are Pushing Against Requirements of Sarbanes-Oxley Act."[46] The Sarbanes–Oxley Act is a relatively new law that is one of the more obvious remnants related to the questionable business practices that led to legal problems and charges of unethical behavior of an unusually large number of top-level managers recently. The law requires businesses to use certain accounting rules that would prohibit the many financial abuses by managers that came to light in recent years. Surprisingly, some managers are resisting the requirements of the Sarbanes–Oxley Act, as the headline above suggests. That may be one reason why stories continue to fill the media about managers, especially the more notorious high-level managers, who engaged in behavior that most consider unethical and for which the managers are being tried, or have been tried, in court. For

KEY TERMS

Ethical behavior
Behavior that is considered by most to be acceptable.

Figure 1.5 An Overall Framework of Management

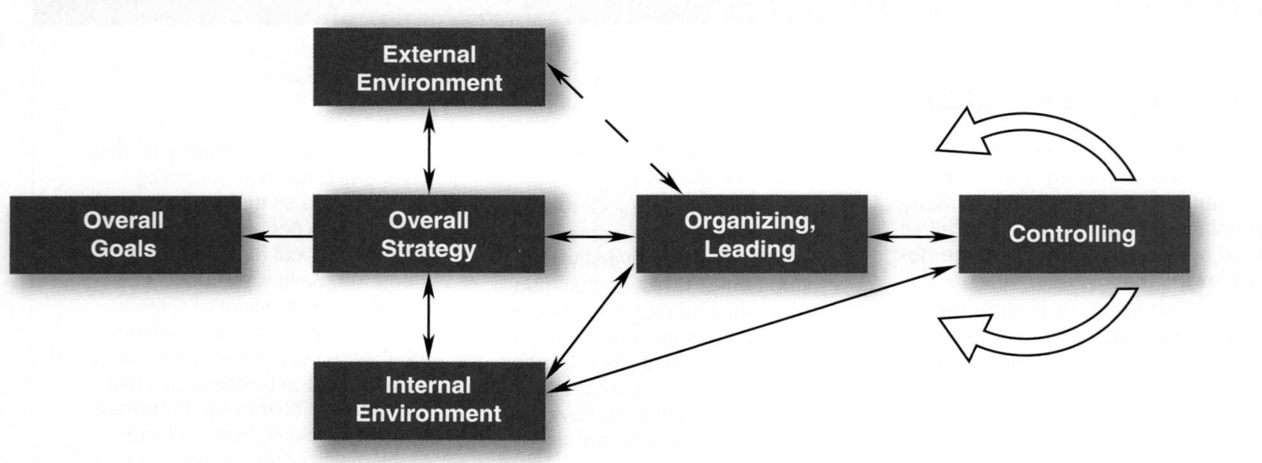

example, Martha Stewart finished her time in jail. Facing court cases are Bernard Ebbers, fired CEO of WorldCom—now MCI; Richard Scrushy, fired CEO of HealthSouth; Kenneth Lay and Jeffrey Skilling, both from the now-extinct company Enron; and others.[47] Former Tyco CEO, Dennis Kozlowski, and former CFO, Mark Swartz, were even charged with larceny for their lavish and alleged personal use of the company's cash.[48] The *Academy of Management Executive,* a publication for both practitioners and academics, published an issue devoted entirely to "Ethical Behavior in Management."[49]

Ethics is important in managing organizations. We discuss this topic in Chapter 3, along with social responsibility.

An Overall Framework

An overall framework of management is useful to coordinate what we have discussed so far and to set the context not only for the rest of this book but also for how this course fits in your overall study of business and organizations (Figure 1.5).

As we discussed earlier, the purpose of an organization is to achieve its overall goals. To do that effectively and efficiently, planning must be done to first establish the overall goals and then to set the strategy to achieve the goals. The planning includes understanding the markets and industry (**external environment**) and the **competencies,** weaknesses, and operations inside the organization. (The arrows suggest interactions between these factors; the broken line suggests an indirect relationship.) Understanding these things is necessary to establish appropriate goals and strategy. (This is discussed later in more depth in the strategy and planning chapters.)

Understanding the competencies, weaknesses, and operations inside of the organization or inside the department for managers other than the chief executive officer, is what organizing and leading are all about. A manager needs to understand the state of organizational design; authority and responsibility; reporting relationships, communication, human behavior, and leadership in the organization; how they interact with each other; and how they all must support the overall strategy. Consequently, other chapters in this book discuss these topics.

The other courses that you are studying also are part of the analysis of the external and internal environments of organizations. For example, here is where a manager uses knowledge of such things as economics, political science, government, and sociology to judge the nature of the overall organizational environment. Other courses and disciplines, such as finance, marketing, production, and computer information systems/information technology, provide knowledge that is needed to assess the competencies, weaknesses, and operations inside the organization. A manager uses knowl-

KEY TERMS

External environment
The setting in which an organization operates; the markets and industry.

Competencies
The things that an organization can do well; the skills and abilities.

edge from all these other areas in carrying out the basic functions of management: planning, organizing, leading, and controlling.

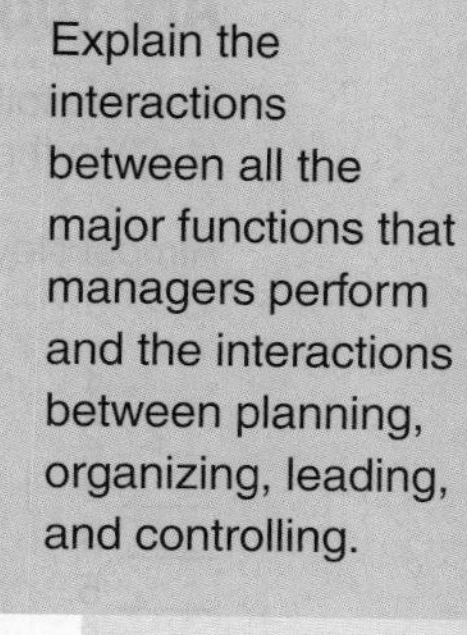
LEARNING OBJECTIVE 7

Explain the interactions between all the major functions that managers perform and the interactions between planning, organizing, leading, and controlling.

7 Because the purpose of an organization is to achieve an overall goal or goals, everything that is done in the organization must be evaluated and guided so that it is all directed to achieving the overall goal. This is the overall definition of control. While some procedures need to be established to ensure an overall control system (discussed in Chapter 15 on control), many of its components are parts of the other operations in the organization. For example, job descriptions, authority and responsibility, influence of the manager as leader, communications, and motivation all guide, monitor, and reward what is accomplished.

Finally, analysis that goes into understanding all parts of the organization and its environment and overall control require feedback in order to understand consequences of what has been done so far. If the consequences are positive, then the managers in an organization can continue to do what they are doing. The feedback will also help them understand why things worked well. If the consequences are negative, that needs to be known so that corrective action can be taken. The arrows in Figure 1.5, including the larger arrows pointing back, indicate the necessity of feedback.

Overall, this framework will help you understand how all the other courses that you take relate to the functions of management. Also, the framework indicates how the functions of management all interact with each other, and together they lead to effective and efficient achievement of an organization's overall goals.

Why Study Management?

LEARNING OBJECTIVE 8

Explain why it is important to study management.

8 The ideas discussed in this chapter and those that will be discussed in the remaining chapters are useful ideas for managers. But what if you are not a manager or are not thinking about being one? Let's discuss the reasons why it is important for everyone to study management.

For those of you who are managers or want to be managers, it is reasonable to say that it is important to learn about management. The basic functions that managers perform, the roles that managers play, and the skills that managers use are **universal.** They apply to the management of all organizations, from Starbucks to Dell Computer Co., from the New England Patriots football team to a NASCAR race, from your local church to state government, from your university to the student group of which you are the president or other officer. The details and the types and levels of roles and skills used across these organizations vary, but the basics apply. The basics are contained in planning, organizing, leading, and controlling.

It is relatively easy to see how the above applies to top-level managers. However, what if you are or want to be a middle manager of a first-line manager, and that is the level at which you want to stay? The same question applies to all top-level managers as they move through these levels on their way to the top. Certainly, details of what a marketing manager or an accounting manager does vary, but again, the same basics apply. A first-line production manager at a factory also uses planning, organizing, leading, and controlling, just as do the night manager at the convenience store and the organizer of a softball league.

Okay, what if you do not plan on being a manager? First, chances are very high, almost 100%, that even in your first job, no matter what that is, you will be required to do some planning. You probably will also be required—or at the least, find it very useful—to engage in organizing and perhaps controlling. Although you may think it quite unlikely, you probably very soon will be supervising one or more people, calling for leading skills. Even if you do not consider official jobs, everyone is a member of some type of informal organization, such as a sorority, fraternity, softball league, and so on. These organizations also need to be managed and will benefit from applying management principles.

The conclusion is that management is universal. The basic functions—planning, organizing, leading, and controlling—are required in every organization. Of course, the details of the roles that managers play, the skills that managers need, and the specifics tools that managers use vary across types of organizations, levels of managers, types of managers, and specific situations. However, the basic functions are the same, so it is useful to study management.

KEY TERMS

Universal
Something that applies in all situations. The basic management principles apply in all situations.

Now Apply It

Are You Ready to Lead in the 21st Century?

Use the following scale to rate the frequency with which you perform the behaviors described below. Place the number (1–7) in the blank preceding the statement.

Almost Never	Irregularly	Occasionally	Sometimes	Usually	Frequently	Almost Always
1	2	3	4	5	6	7

_____ 1. I thrive in uncertain situations where the outcome is unknown.
_____ 2. I provide guidance to others.
_____ 3. I am willing to make mistakes when learning a new process.
_____ 4. I recognize the contributions and performance of others.
_____ 5. I see change as an opportunity, not a threat.
_____ 6. I challenge others to consistently do a better job.
_____ 7. I seek new ways to do things better and faster.
_____ 8. I motivate others to reach their highest potential.

Transfer your scores to the columns below. Circle your highest score.

Column A	Column B	Column C	Column D
Question 1 ____	Question 2 ____	Question 3 ____	Question 4 ____
Question 5 ____	Question 6 ____	Question 7 ____	Question 8 ____
Total ____	Total ____	Total ____	Total ____

If your highest score was for column A, you demonstrate Adapting leadership skills. You recognize that change is a natural part of growth and are comfortable in dealing with ambiguity. If your highest score was for column B, you demonstrate Coaching leadership skills. You see the importance of motivating people around you and are willing to help others when necessary. If your highest score was column C, you recognize the role of Learning in being an effective leader. You consistently look for new ways to work more effectively and realize that making mistakes is a part of the learning process. If your highest score was for column D, you demonstrate Empowering leadership skills. You know the importance of developing others and encourage the people around you to reach their potential. Of course, you may show a mixed pattern of leadership skill sets. In any case, examine your answers to these questions. They may reveal information about your management and leadership orientation. Once you have studied all of the chapters in this book, complete this exercise again to see if your responses have changed.

Implications for Leaders

All organizations need to be managed. The purpose of all organizations is to achieve their overall goals. Management is needed first of all to set the overall goals of the organization. These goals are established by employing the theories, concepts, principles, and tools that are part of planning. Then "everything else" must be coordinated with the overall goals so that they can be achieved. This includes organizing, leading, and controlling.

Anyone who wants to be a manager, who is, or will be a manager would be well served to learn about management. Those who implement the principles of management well will lead successful organizations.

Meeting The Challenge

Carlos Ghosn, Star of Nissan and the Auto Industry

By 2003 Carlos Ghosn enjoyed the status of a celebrity. He is swamped by people seeking his autograph when he tours Nissan manufacturing plants. He is adored in Japan for saving Nissan and is featured in manga comic books. He is the star at auto shows in Paris, New York, and Beijing, where he gets along fine, speaking five different languages. Some people in Lebanon suggested that he run for the presidency of that country because he is a Lebanese citizen.

Immediately upon arriving at Nissan in 1999, Ghosn established the revival plan. This included setting up cross-functional teams that studied essentially everything about Nissan and its markets. Nothing was "sacred." The markets were studied. Vehicles were redesigned, including a goal of 28 new vehicles by 2004. Goals also included cutting costs in purchasing and manufacturing. The sales organization was redesigned to focus on getting cars that people wanted to market.

The goals and actions that Ghosn led also included some very sensitive issues. In a country where *keiretsu* (interrelationships between companies, including cross-ownerships, much like the interlocking directorates in the United States) is very important and group reward is common, Ghosn broke up Nissan's *keiretsu* to free cash and to get rid of poor suppliers and implemented a reward system based at least partly on individual performance. And people were definitely held accountable for performance.

Nissan made a profit by 2001, achieving its overall goals a year early! By 2004 Nissan was one of the most profitable car companies in the world and had retaken the number-two spot in market share in Japan back from Honda. In 2005 Ghosn became the CEO of Renault, while continuing as CEO of Nissan.

Carlos Ghosn clearly applied the basic functions of management and added many of the details. In addition, he succeeded as a manager and leader by using his deep knowledge and appreciation for the different cultures of the countries in which he lived and worked to introduce changes in Japan that were unusual.

Sources: M. Yoshino and M. Egawa, *Nissan Motor Co., Ltd., 2002* (Boston: Harvard Business School Publishing, 2002); "Nissan Aims for More Market Share with First New U.S. Plant in 20 Years," *St. Louis Post-Dispatch,* 28 May 2003, C1–C3; B. Bremner, G. Edmondson, C. Dawson, D. Welch, and K. Kerwin, "Nissan's Boss Carlos Ghosn Saved Japan's No. 2 Carmaker: Now He's Taking on the World," *BusinessWeek,* 4 October 2004, 50–58; G. Edmondson, "Smoothest Combo on the Road," *BusinessWeek,* 4 October 2004, 58–60; B. Bremner, "The Gaijin Who Saved Nissan," *BusinessWeek,* 17 January 2005, 18.

SUMMARY

1. The simple definition of management is "the art of getting things done through people." A more detailed definition is that management is the process of coordinating resources in an effort to effectively and efficiently achieve the goals of the organization.

2. The process of management involves four primary functions: planning, organizing, leading, and controlling. Planning involves setting goals and defining actions that are necessary to achieve the goals, in light of the situation. Organizing includes determining the tasks to be done, who will do them, and how those tasks will be managed and coordinated to achieve the organization's goals. Leading means that managers must guide and motivate employees in ways that will lead to effective and efficient achievement of the organization's goals. Controlling requires establishing what is required to achieve the goals and to guide operations so that the goals are achieved.

3. According to Henry Mintzberg, managers play three primary roles: interpersonal roles, informational roles, and decisional roles. In their interpersonal roles, managers act as figureheads, leaders, and liaisons. In their informational roles, managers serve as monitors, disseminators, and spokespeople. Managers in their decisional roles function as entrepreneurs, disturbance handlers, resource allocators, and negotiators.

4. Managers' scope of responsibility varies depending on whether they are functional or general managers. Functional managers are responsible for work groups that are segmented according to function. General managers oversee several different departments that are responsible for different tasks.

5. Most large organizations have three levels of managers: first-line, middle, and top-level managers. These managers differ in terms of both the skills that they require and the way they spend their time.
6. First-line managers supervise individuals who are directly responsible for producing the organization's product or service. Although all managers use technical, human, and conceptual skills, first-line managers tend to employ more technical skills relative to human and conceptual skills. Middle managers supervise first-line managers and tend to use human skills more than the other two. Top-level managers provide strategic direction for the organization. In doing so, they tend to use conceptual skills more than other skills.
7. Important changes in the 21st century that will affect how managers do their job are increasing use of the Internet and information technology, increasing globalization, increasing diversity of the workforce, increasing use of intellectual capital, and a renewed emphasis on ethical behavior of managers.
8. All managers perform the same basic functions in managing organizations: planning, organizing, leading, and controlling. Most people in organizations will perform some managerial functions during their lifetimes.

REVIEW QUESTIONS

1. (LEARNING OBJECTIVE 1) Define *management.*
2. (LEARNING OBJECTIVE 2) Define the concept of management within an organizational context. Describe the major functions of the management process and why they are important.
3. (LEARNING OBJECTIVE 3) Describe the roles of the manager as outlined by Mintzberg.
4. (LEARNING OBJECTIVE 4) Describe the responsibilities of the functional manager. Describe the responsibilities of the general manager.
5. (LEARNING OBJECTIVE 5) Distinguish among the three levels of managers in terms of the skills that they need and the activities in which they are involved.
6. (LEARNING OBJECTIVE 6) What are the major changes in the 21st century, and how will they affect management?
7. (LEARNING OBJECTIVE 7) Explain the meaning of the overall framework presented in the chapter. Explain how the basic management functions interact.
8. (LEARNING OBJECTIVE 8) Explain why it is important to study management.

DISCUSSION QUESTIONS

Improving Critical Thinking

1. How is the increasing diversity of the United States influencing the student body at your university? Is the university administration taking proactive steps to ensure diversity on your campus? Does it maintain programs to ensure that diversity is celebrated rather than simply tolerated? With a small group, discuss how diversity in a team must be managed to have the diversity result in better team performance rather than cause difficulties with team performance.
2. Discuss the overall framework for management that is presented in the chapter with one or more other students. Why does "everything" that an organization does have to be focused on the overall goals of the organization?

Enhancing Communication Skills

3. Write a short paper in which you explain how and why the Internet will affect how businesses operate.
4. Identify a company that you believe has a strong global presence and one that you believe does not. Compare and contrast these organizations. Present your assessment to several classmates orally.

Building Teamwork

5. Organize a small group of students in which each student comes from a different country. Discuss each student's view about the importance of teamwork. Is each student's view influenced by the country from which he or she came?

6. With a small group of classmates, discuss the importance of leading in overall management. Should you appoint a leader of this discussion group before you begin? What happens if you do not? Does one emerge?

Chapter

2

Evolution of Management Thought

© SUSAN VAN ETTEN

CHAPTER OVERVIEW

The concept of management and the basic management functions of planning, organizing, leading, and controlling are not new phenomena. Throughout recorded history, activities have been conducted that most certainly would have required careful attention to these management functions. The Great Wall of China, the Pyramids of Egypt, and many other wonders of the ancient world would not have been possible without management of the activities required to complete them. Endeavors such as these certainly would have required planning, organizing, leading, and controlling. Not only was management important in the past, but it also continues to be important in the present as governments construct massive public works projects, private enterprise engages in the delivery of large-scale projects, and business leaders engage in commerce and industry around the globe. Management will continue to be important as long as humans survive on earth.

Despite management's lengthy tenure, formal theories on management began to emerge only during the past 100 years or so. In this chapter, we examine the historical evolution of management theories and philosophies and the factors that helped influence their development. This historical tour explores the five major schools of management thought that have emerged over the years. Our trip through time will reveal that the degree of support for and use of these different perspectives have shifted as times, conditions, and situations have changed. Despite this shifting support and use, components of each of these schools of thought still exist in current management thinking. Furthermore, they are likely to continue influencing management thought in the future. If we understand the managerial philosophies of the past and present, we will be better equipped to be successful leaders in the future.

LEARNING OBJECTIVES

When you have finished studying this chapter, you should be able to

1. Describe the major influences on the development of management thought.
2. Identify the five major perspectives of management thought that have evolved over the years.
3. Describe the different subfields that exist in the classical perspective of management and discuss the central focus of each.
4. Describe the theories of the major contributors to the behavioral perspective of management.
5. Describe the characteristics of the quantitative perspective of management.
6. Describe the systems perspective building blocks and their interactions.
7. Discuss the nature of the contingency perspective of management.
8. Discuss the future issues that will affect the further development of management thought.

Facing The Challenge

"Sony Shock": Crisis at the Electronics Giant

Mention Sony and many people will immediately think "electronics giant." After all, these are the folks who invented a litany of devices whose names are immediately recognizable to most of us. Sony was established in 1946 as a maker of telecom and measuring equipment, but it was to be Sony's electronics innovations that began a few decades later that would make the company a household name. Beginning with the Triniton color television in 1968, Sony continued its pioneer developments with such consumer electronics items as the Betamax video cassette player, the Walkman personal headphone stereo player, the world's first compact disc player, the portable Discman CD player, the Digital8 Handycam 8-mm video camcorder, Mavica digital cameras, the first DVD player, WEGA televisions, the Memory Stick flash media player, and several generations of the PlayStation video game console. With over 1000 Sony products, the collection is much too lengthy to list in its entirety. For decades Sony had the reputation of a world leader and a world beater in this industry. When Sony's electronics were coupled with its more recent acquisitions of CBS records, Columbia Studios, and assorted other media ventures, Sony became a formidable conglomerate. With more than 151,000 employees worldwide (27,000 in the United States), the corporation generated worldwide sales in the neighborhood of $67 billion (more than $18 billion of that in the United States) for the fiscal year that ended in March 2005. Despite those impressive numbers, all was not rosy at Sony in recent years.

Between June 2000, when Nobuyuki Idei assumed the role of chairman and CEO of Sony, and early 2005, Sony's stock suffered a 60% slide. A big portion of that slide occurred during a 2-day period in April 2003 after a company announcement of a $1 billion quarterly loss. This period when the bottom fell out of its earnings and its shares began to plunge has been referred to in the industry as the "Sony Shock." Under Idei's watch, Sony was outmaneuvered by rivals Sharp Corporation and Matsushita Electric Industrial Company (maker of the Panasonic brand) in flat-panel televisions and lost its lead in the portable music business to Apple Computer and its popular iPod player. Even Samsung, a once inferior South Korean rival, has embarrassed Sony by leaping ahead in flat-panel televisions. Despite Sony's pioneer work with digital photography, Canon and Nikon have regained their edge as digital photography has matured. Even in the area of gaming devices, where Sony still thrives, the next generation of its PlayStation will face a much stiffer challenge from rival Microsoft's next-generation Xbox. In early 2005, Sony's core electronics division was in danger of falling into the red for a second straight year amid tough price competition and a lack of hit products. A fragmenting brand and diverse competition are not the only problems holding back Sony's electronics business. Its increasingly poor performance can be attributed in part to its failed efforts to combine consumer electronics and media content inside one firm. In early 2005, Sony's big challenges were to start making electronic devices more profitably and to solve the dilemma of how to get its gadgets and media content working together in a fashion that would make consumers willing to pay a premium price for them.[1]

Introduction

By early 2005, leadership at Sony finally recognized that the management style and practices that had worked well in the past were no longer capable of maintaining the company as a leader in the consumer electronics industry. Despite some cost-cutting moves in the prior 2 years, Sony's electronics division seemed to be heading toward its second straight year of red ink. The company was faced with challenges that dictated a major change was necessary. As we saw in Chapter 1, changes are occurring that are causing business leaders to revise their managerial styles and become more creative in their thinking. But change is nothing new—all that is new are the types of change and the speed of change. Management thinking has evolved throughout the centuries to deal with the ever-changing environment. Today, management thinking continues to evolve to meet the challenges raised by rapid and dramatic societal changes. These factors will undoubtedly continue to influence future management developments. Before examining the historical developments in management thinking, let's first identify those factors that have influenced the evolution of modern management thought.

Environmental Factors Influencing Management Thought

LEARNING OBJECTIVE 1

Describe the major influences on the development of management thought.

1 Through the years, many environmental factors have caused management theorists and management practitioners to alter their views on what constitutes a good approach to management. These environmental factors can be conveniently categorized as economic, social, political, technological, and global influences. Let's examine each of these influences and the effects that they have had on the evolution of management thought in turn.

ECONOMIC INFLUENCES

Economic influences relate to the availability, production, and distribution of resources within a society. In "At the Forefront," we can see the economic impact of declining markets and declining prices on one segment of the agriculture industry. We also see how that segment was able to rebound by introducing a product that seemed to fit a niche market. With the advent of industrialization, the goal of most manufacturing organizations was to find the most profitable way to provide products for newly emerging markets. They needed a variety of resources to achieve this objective. Some resources were material, and some were human, but in each case, they tended to become scarcer over time.

When there was a seemingly endless expanse of virgin forests, loggers didn't think twice about clear-cutting a mountainside. Coal reserves were once stripped away with no thought of depletion. Burning off surplus natural gas was once a common practice. But as resources became scarcer, it became increasingly important that they be managed effectively. Time and circumstances

At the Forefront

The Golden Goose Is a Potato

Rural Florida potato farmers have taken a beating in recent years. They were once counted on to provide a fresh product for the East Coast during the off season for potato farmers in Idaho and Washington. However, those states have developed potatoes that can be stored for 6 months or more, severely cutting into the market for Florida potatoes. The trend toward lower-carbohydrate consumption has further cut into demand. In one Florida potato region, the number of potato farmers has dropped from more than 300 to only 38 in the last 25 years. Potato acreage has shrunk from about 32,000 to about 19,000 in the last 10 years alone. With many farmers selling potatoes at prices below the cost of production and much of the farmland being sold to developers, the future of this industry looked bleak.

In stepped a savior in the form of potato specialist Chad Hutchinson from the University of Florida's Institute of Food and Agricultural Sciences. He introduced a handful of growers to a new potato with some attractive characteristics that had been crossbred in Holland. This Dutch spud has fewer calories and fewer carbohydrates than its U.S. cousin. Furthermore, it requires less fertilizer to grow and has a more uniform and attractive shape. Its golden color was to be an omen. In 2004 six growers seized control of their destinies and formed the SunFresh of Florida Marketing Cooperative, focusing all their efforts on this new potato, which they dubbed the SunLite potato.

The numbers are impressive on this boutique tuber. When compared to a typical russet potato, the SunLite has one-third fewer carbohydrates, 25% fewer calories, and perhaps most important to the farmers, sells for almost three times the price of the russet. In the eyes of the farmers, each of these golden-hued beauties truly was a nugget of gold coming out of the ground. The growers unabashedly proclaim that theirs is a potato that is healthier, tastier, easier on the eyes, and easier on the environment. What a quadruple threat! In Hutchinson's own words, "It turned out this variety has the whole package. The lower carbs and lower calories will encourage people to try it, but we think they'll keep buying it because it truly is a gourmet potato with a lot of flavor and a great appearance." SunLites began appearing in grocery stores in early 2005, and the early results are very encouraging.

Sources: W. Smith, "Farmers See 'Lite' Spud as a Salvation," *Orlando Sentinel,* 28 January 2005, A1ff.; SunFresh of Florida Marketing Cooperative, Inc., http://www.sunfreshof-florida.com, 16 July 2005; Ellen Boukari, "Low Carb, High Hopes," http://www.rurdev.usda.gov/rbs/pub/mar05/lowcarb.htm, 16 July 2005.

dictate that supplies will not always be available when needed. Through gradual depletion over time, resources can simply run out.

Disruptions of supplies can also occur because of temporary but immediate circumstances. Drought in Brazil in early 2005 caused coffee prices to soar.[2] The 2003 war in Iraq and the subsequent turmoil in the Mideast have had a pronounced impact on crude oil supplies, causing a steady upward spiral in the price of gasoline. Four major hurricanes in the span of 6 weeks during the summer of 2004 had a sudden and dramatic impact on the management of resources as the storms crisscrossed the state of Florida. These storms led to some of the largest evacuations in U.S. history, causing manufacturers and distributors of construction materials to quickly rethink their manufacturing and distribution strategies so that they could act in a socially responsible manner. The leaders of businesses that engaged in the retail sale of these commodities also found it necessary to manage their resources differently. For example, Home Depot and Lowes closely monitored the tracks of the storms and moved such items as emergency generators, plywood, and building materials around the state in conjunction with each storm's projected path.[3] Then, in the wake of these hurricanes, a scarcity of materials used in lighted advertising signs slowed the repair of many businesses' only means to mark their locations.[4] As bad as these storms seemed at the time, they pale in comparison to the consequences of Hurricane Katrina in 2005. With a huge portion of the Gulf coast wiped out and large sections of New Orleans destined to be rebuilt, the impact on building materials and the petrochemical supplies produced in that area will be felt for years to come.[5] In short, scarcity makes it necessary for resources to be allocated among competing users.

© STEPHANIE MAZE/CORBIS

This Hispanic store front is a reminder that the ethnic, racial, and gender composition of today's workforces and communities is becomingly increasingly diverse.

SOCIAL INFLUENCES

Social influences relate to the aspects of a culture that influence interpersonal relationships. The needs, values, and standards of behavior among people help form the social contract of the culture. The social contract embodies unwritten rules and perceptions that govern interpersonal relationships, as well as the relationships between people and organizations. Business leaders need to be familiar with these perceptions if they are to act effectively. The ethnic, racial, and gender composition of today's workforce is becoming increasingly diverse. Recognizing and satisfying the varying needs and values of this diverse workforce and society as a whole present a challenge to business leaders. In "Leaders in Action," we can see how the president of a large supermarket chain responded to the changing ethnic composition in some areas served by his stores. Total conversion to Hispanic-format supermarkets was to be his response.

Throughout modern business history, management thinking and practice have been shaped in part by work stoppages, labor insurrections, and strikes by mineworkers, autoworkers, teamsters, and many others. Most of these incidents were precipitated not just by demands for more pay but by safety concerns, welfare issues, and other social considerations. Just recently, General Motors Corporation was pressured into expanding existing job-security protections to effectively give many of its United Auto Workers employees lifetime protection against losing their jobs to subcontracting or efficiency gains.[6]

Although some of these examples of social influence have a negative flavor, this need not always be the case. In recent years, the social contract of our culture has been changing. Workers have become more vocal in their desire to be treated as more than just muscle to do the job. They are insisting on using their mental abilities as well as their physical skills. As we will see throughout this book, these changes have led to some of the contemporary approaches that empower workers, giving them decision-making authority and responsibility for their activities. This approach has had a positive impact on organizations that have tried it.[7] Empowered workers often exhibit pride of ownership for their work and a dedication to quality and excellence in all that they do. From a somewhat amusing perspective, changing individual behavior has had an impact on producers of two breakfast staples. Individual obsession with low-

Leaders in Action

Publix's New Flavor

If you ran a successful supermarket chain and you were confronted by a rapidly growing Hispanic population with a skyrocketing buying power, what would you do? Here's what William Crenshaw, president of Publix Supermarkets, did. He began converting stores into completely Hispanic-format supermarkets. Publix Supermarkets is a Lakeland, Florida, based chain of 853 supermarkets. Publix is the largest supermarket chain in Florida and the ninth largest chain in the United States. Until recently, Publix operated exclusively in Florida, and although the company has begun branching out into neighboring states, the bulk of its stores (626) are located in the Sunshine State. Crenshaw's decision to begin converting stores was precipitated by demographic studies revealing that Hispanic buying power grew 160% to $542 billion in the last decade of the 20th century, and it was likely to top $650 billion in 2005. In central Florida alone, Hispanics were spending close to $7 billion annually, and that figure was projected to continue rising. These same studies revealed that Hispanics tend to shop more frequently and spend more money than non-Hispanic households.

The store conversions involved more than simply beefing up the Hispanic offerings. Stores were shut down while construction crews altered the look and layout of the new prototype supermarkets. Bilingual employees were hired, hard-to-find imports were obtained, and Spanish music was piped through the stores' loudspeakers. Catering to the growing Hispanic market is not new for Publix. The company recently launched its own house brand of Hispanic foods. Such private-label foods offer savings of 10–30% over national or imported brands. But, this new strategy of total conversion of stores to Hispanic format represents a much larger step than the introduction of house brands. "We want to be proactive in anticipating trends," said Crenshaw. To avoid alienating non-Hispanic customers, Publix Sabor (translation; Publix flavor) conversions will only occur where there are other conventional Publix markets nearby. The performance of the prototype Publix Sabor stores will be closely monitored. If the results are favorable, as most insiders predict they will be, the concept will be expanded to additional communities with high Hispanic concentrations.

Sources: S. H. Meitner, "Publix's New Flavor," *Orlando Sentinel,* 4 March 2005, C1ff.; "Publix to Launch Hispanic Food Line," *Orlando Sentinel,* 5 January 2005, C1ff.

carbohydrate diets has severely impacted sales of both orange juice and Krispy Kreme Doughnuts, causing financial difficulties for companies who process and manufacture those products.[8]

POLITICAL INFLUENCES

Political influences relate to the impact of political institutions on individuals and organizations. At a basic level are the various civil and criminal laws that influence individual and organizational behavior. In addition, the political system has bestowed various rights upon individuals and organizations that also impact behavior. Among these rights are the right to life and liberty, contract rights, and property rights. Finally, government regulations are yet another source of political influence. The laws, rules, and regulations that form the political influences on management in many instances have been the outgrowth of economic and social influences. Environmental regulations have often been precipitated by reckless disregard for the preservation of our natural resources. Child labor laws and OSHA (Occupational Safety and Health Administration) regulations trace their origin to social outcries over exploitative and dangerous working conditions.

Political forces have influenced management thinking in a variety of ways. For example, over the years increasing concern for individual rights has forced management to adapt to a shorter workweek for employees, provide a safe work environment, and make increasing contributions to employees' welfare. Such political influences can extend across international boundaries in today's global economy. Nike, Inc. found it necessary to increase wages for its workers in Indonesia in the face of that government's plan to raise the minimum wage.[9] Pressures from the court of public opinion have also prompted Nike and other companies such as Kmart and Wal-Mart to eliminate child-labor practices in foreign countries producing their merchandise. Regulations against monopolies have caused some businesses to restructure and some industries to reorganize. Increased environmental regulation has caused changes in many organizations. Deregulation of banking and trucking has had a dramatic influence on organizations in these industries. Increased bans on smoking in public places and the resulting reduced demand for smoking products has prompted many tobacco farmers to alter their choice of crops.[10] In short, evolving laws, rules, and regulations have tended to transform the way many organizations conduct business, necessitating changes in their management philosophies and styles over the years.

TECHNOLOGICAL INFLUENCES

Technological influences relate to advances and refinements in any of the devices used in conjunction with conducting business. As was noted in Chapter 1, advances in transportation, communication, and information technology have made it possible to conduct business on a global basis. Business leaders in the global economy must be alert to all opportunities for improvement. They must stay abreast of the new technology so that they can make intelligent, informed decisions. The stakes are high because these decisions affect both the human and the technical aspects of operations. Whether or not an organization adopts the new technology may determine whether it retains its competitive edge.[11]

As we will see in more detail in Chapter 17, electronic commerce (e-commerce) and its associated product sales via the Internet are becoming increasingly critical to the competitiveness of many organizations. As the 20th century wound to a close, Compaq, then the world's largest personal-computer manufacturer, replaced its CEO and CFO because they failed to adapt quickly enough to this new technology. Compaq's profits were starting to be squeezed as upstart competitor Dell Computer Corporation dramatically outperformed Compaq by embracing e-commerce more quickly than Compaq.[12]

Business leaders are seeing constant innovations in communications and information-exchange capabilities, including voice mail, electronic mail, fax transmission of documents, electronic data interchange, and the growth of the Internet. Cellular (cell) telephones and portable computers provide two familiar examples of dramatic technological advances that have occurred in the past few years. Early cell phones were not very portable and required separate battery packs carried over the shoulder in briefcase-sized satchels. Now a host of manufacturers offer battery-powered units that can fit into a shirt pocket or be concealed in the palm of one's hand. For instance, consider the latest from Motorola, the Moto Razr V3, a razor-thin cell phone that incorporates Bluetooth wireless technology and boasts a huge color screen and many other features in its ultrathin design. These will no doubt shrink even more as technological innovations continue. Notebook-style computers that weigh a few pounds now allow managers to exchange information with their company computers while flying virtually anywhere in the world. Using these same devices, information can be quickly retrieved from almost any source in the world by means of the Internet. Factories of the future will incorporate such technologies as computer-aided design (CAD), computer-aided manufacturing (CAM), computer-integrated manufacturing (CIM), computerized numerically controlled machines (CNCM), automated storage and retrieval systems (AS/RS), and flexible manufacturing systems (FMS). Innovations such as these are transforming workers' job responsibilities and, consequently, the way in which they should be managed.[13]

GLOBAL INFLUENCES

Global influences relate to the pressures to improve quality, productivity, and costs as organizations attempt to compete in the worldwide marketplace. The international, or global, dimension of an organization's environment has had the most profound impact on management thinking in recent years. In the world of business, national boundaries are quickly disappearing. Global competition has begun to affect all businesses. For example, U.S. automakers can no longer claim this country as their exclusive domain. Foreign competitors continually penetrate the U.S. market with high-quality, low-priced cars. To survive, U.S. automakers have found it necessary to compete on the same quality and price dimensions as their foreign competitors and to seek foreign markets of their own.[14]

As time progresses, even the lines between domestic and foreign automobiles continue to become more blurred. U.S. automobiles continue to incorporate more and more imported components, while "foreign" automobiles are increasingly being manufactured in the United States with U.S.-made parts and U.S. labor. For example, Marysville, Ohio, boasts a Honda manufacturing plant, and Georgetown, Kentucky, claims a Toyota manufacturing plant.

Similar situations in electronics and other industries could be cited. In all cases, increasing global competition has caused organizations to focus on using all the skills and capabilities of their workers in an effort to improve quality, productivity, and costs. Although the Sony Corporation described in "Facing the Challenge" is a Japanese corporation, it has manufacturing operations spread around the world. We saw that such increased competition was eroding Sony's profitability, posing a major challenge to the health of this organization. Increased globalization, coupled with the immediate access organizations have to one another through the Internet, has led to many global partnerships. Small companies that are seemingly isolated in small-town America can easily become suppliers to foreign companies and vice versa. Contemporary and future perspectives on management have been and will continue to be influenced most heavily by the global dimension of the environment.[15]

Schools of Management Thought

LEARNING OBJECTIVE 2

Identify the five major perspectives of management thought that have evolved over the years.

2 Beginning in the late 19th century and continuing through the 20th century, managers and scholars developed theoretical frameworks to describe what they believed to be good management practice. Their efforts have led to five different perspectives on management: the classical perspective, the behavioral perspective, the quantitative perspective, the systems perspective, and the contingency perspective. Each perspective is based on different assumptions about organizational objectives and human behavior. To help place these perspectives in their proper chronological sequence, Figure 2.1 displays them along a historical time line.

You might wonder why it is important to study the historical development of management thought. We've probably all heard it before in our secondary education: Studying history allows us to learn about mistakes made in the past so that they can be avoided in the future. Furthermore, it allows us to learn of past successes so that they can be repeated in the appropriate future situations. This certainly applies to the study of management history.

As Figure 2.1 shows, all these perspectives continue to influence the thinking of business leaders although opinions differ as to how influential each is. Consequently, it is important that future leaders become familiar with the basic concepts of each school of thought. The following sections examine these major perspectives on management thought in more detail.

CLASSICAL PERSPECTIVE

The oldest of the "formal" viewpoints of management emerged during the late-19th and early-20th centuries and has come to be known as the classical perspective. The classical perspective had its roots in the management experiences that were occurring in the rapidly expanding manufacturing organizations that typified U.S. and European industrialization. Early contributions came from management practitioners and theorists in several corners of the world.

Figure 2.1 Chronological Development of Management Perspectives

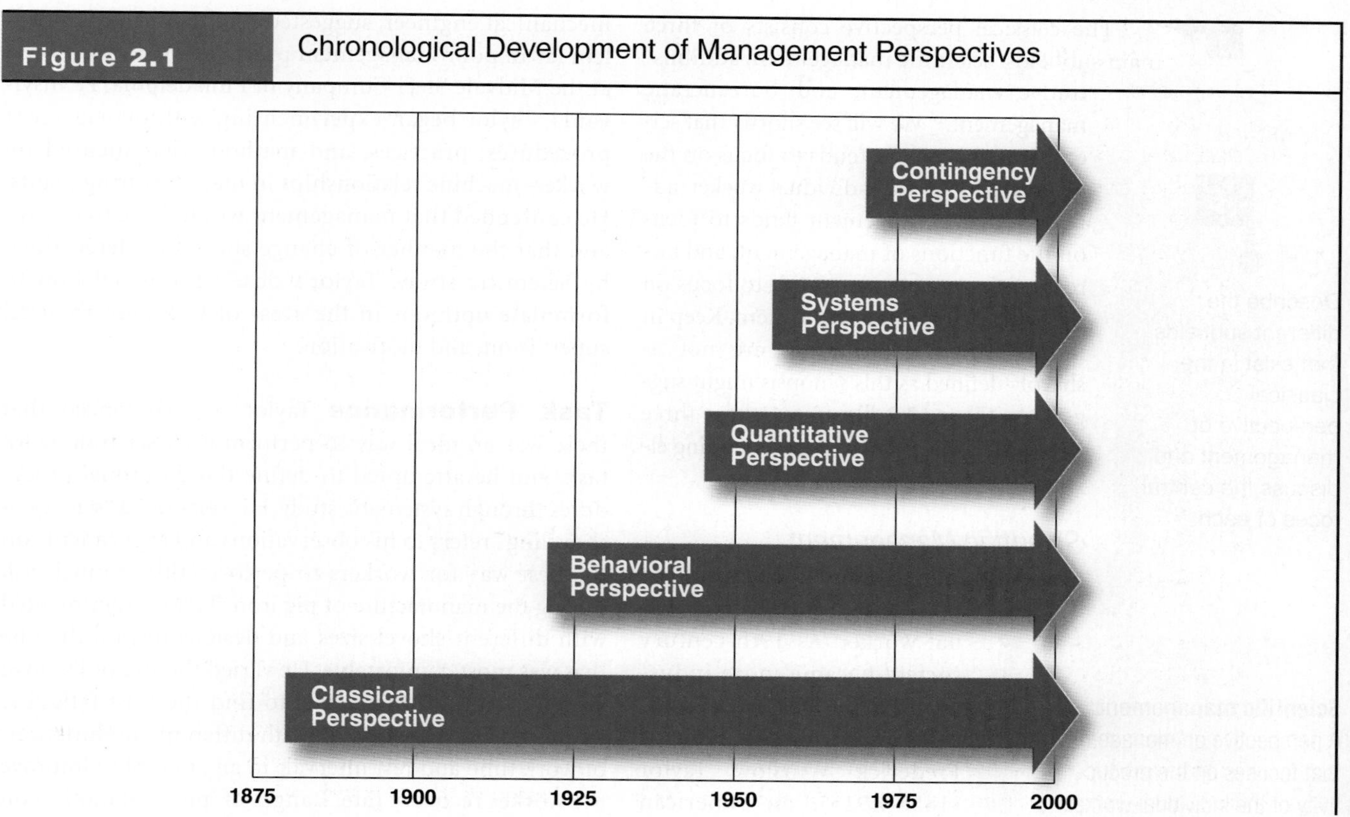

Figure 2.2 Subfields of the Classical Perspective on Management

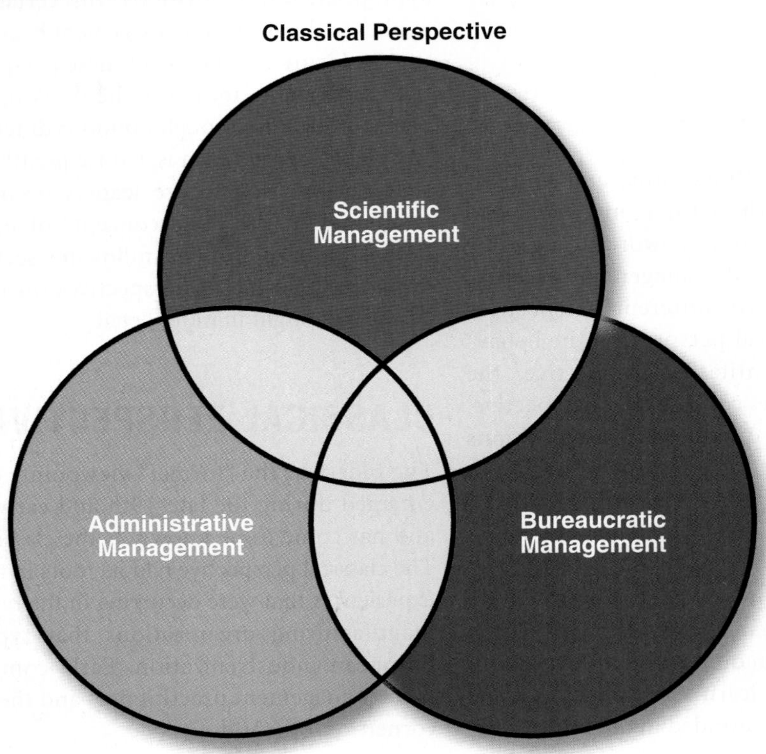

LEARNING OBJECTIVE 3

Describe the different subfields that exist in the classical perspective of management and discuss the central focus of each.

3 The classical perspective consists of three main subfields: scientific management, administrative management, and bureaucratic management.[16] We will see shortly that scientific management tends to focus on the productivity of the individual worker, administrative management tends to focus on the functions of management, and bureaucratic management tends to focus on the overall organizational system. Keep in mind, though, that things are not as sharply defined as this synopsis might suggest. As Figure 2.2 illustrates, these three subfields also contain some overlapping elements and components.

Scientific Management

Scientific management focuses on the productivity of the individual worker. As 19th-century society became more industrialized, businesses had difficulty improving productivity. Frederick Winslow Taylor (1856–1915), an American mechanical engineer, suggested that the primary problem lay in poor management practices. While employed at the Midvale Steel Company in Philadelphia, Pennsylvania, Taylor began experimenting with management procedures, practices, and methods that focused on worker–machine relationships in manufacturing plants. He contended that management would have to change and that the manner of change should be determined by scientific study. Taylor's observations led him to formulate opinions in the areas of task performance, supervision, and motivation.[17]

KEY TERMS

Scientific management
A perspective on management that focuses on the productivity of the individual worker.

Task Performance Taylor was convinced that there was an ideal way to perform each separate work task, and he attempted to define those optimal procedures through systematic study. His celebrated "science of shoveling" refers to his observations and experiments on the best way for workers to perform this manual task during the manufacture of pig iron. Taylor experimented with different shovel sizes and designs to find the one that was most comfortable. He varied the size of the load scooped up onto the shovel to find the least fatiguing amount. He experimented with different combinations of work time and rest intervals in an attempt to improve the worker recovery rate. Ranges of physical motion on the part of the workers were also examined. Based upon Taylor's suggestions, Midvale was able to reduce the number of shovel handlers needed from 600 to 140, while more than tripling the average daily worker output.[18]

These types of observations and measurements are examples of time-and-motion studies. Time-and-motion studies identify and measure a worker's physical movements while the worker performs a task and then analyze the results to determine the best way of performing that task. In the attempt to find the best way of performing each task, scientific management incorporates several basic expectations of management, which include the following:

- *Development of work standards.* Standard methods should be developed for performing each job within the organization.
- *Selection of workers.* Workers with the appropriate abilities should be selected for each job.
- *Training of workers.* Workers should be trained in the standard methods.
- *Support of workers.* Workers should be supported by having their work planned for them.

While Taylor is most remembered for his contributions in the area of task performance, his scientific management contributions went well beyond determining the one best way of performing a task. He also maintained strong convictions about supervision and motivation.[19]

Supervision In the area of supervision, Taylor felt that a single supervisor could not be an expert at all tasks. This was because most supervisors were promoted to their positions after demonstrating high levels of skill in performing a particular function within the organization. Consequently, each first-level supervisor should be responsible only for workers who perform a common function familiar to the supervisor, such as machine operator, material handler, or inspector. Each supervisor's area of expertise would become an area of authority. In Taylor's era these supervisors were referred to as foremen, so Taylor called this concept functional foremanship. Several foremen would be assigned to each work area, with each having a separate responsibility for such duties as planning, production scheduling, time-and-motion studies, material handling, and so forth.

Motivation In the area of motivation, Taylor felt that money was the way to motivate workers to their fullest capabilities. He advocated a piecework system in which workers' pay was tied to their output. Workers who met a standard level of production were paid at a standard wage rate. Workers whose production exceeded the standard were paid at a higher rate for all of their production output. Taylor felt that such financial incentives would induce workers to produce more so that they might earn more money. He also felt that management should use financial incentives judiciously. If the increased employee earnings were not accompanied by higher profits generated by the productivity increases, then the incentives should not be used. While Taylor's views on the power of money as a motivator may have been well suited to the conditions that prevailed in the early part of the 20th century, ample evidence suggests that, with a few exceptions, now it is not usually the most important motivator of workers. In some instances today, it can be something as simple as allowing casual dress that is a prime motivator of workers.[20]

Although Frederick Taylor is generally acknowledged to be the father of scientific management, the husband-and-wife team of Frank and Lillian Gilbreth also made substantial pioneering contributions to the field.[21] Frank Gilbreth specialized in time-and-motion studies to determine the most efficient way to perform tasks.[22] He identified 17 work elements (such as lifting, grasping, and positioning) and called them therbligs (roughly the reverse spelling of his last name).[23] In one of his more notable studies, Gilbreth used the new medium of motion pictures to examine the work of bricklayers. He was able to change that task's structure in a way that reduced the number of motions from 18 to 5, resulting in a productivity increase of more than 200%. Contemporary industrial engineers still use Frank Gilbreth's methods to design jobs for the greatest efficiency.

Lillian Gilbreth concentrated her efforts on the human aspects of industrial engineering. She was a strong proponent of better working conditions as a means of improving efficiency and productivity. She favored standard days with scheduled lunch breaks and rest periods for workers. She also strived for the removal of unsafe working conditions and the abolition of child labor. The Gilbreths' time-and-motion experiments attracted quite a bit of notoriety. In fact, their application of time-and-motion studies and efficiency practices to their personal lives and the raising of their 12 children was eventually chronicled in the long-running Broadway play and subsequent motion picture *Cheaper by the Dozen*. By the way, many readers are probably familiar with the 2003 and 2005 Steve Martin movies of the same name. It should be noted that these recent motion pictures bear almost no resemblance to the story line of the original classic. About the only thing the three have in common are families consisting of 12 children!

Although Taylor and the Gilbreths dominated the scientific management subfield of the classical perspective with their focus on the productivity of the individual worker, their views were not embraced by all classical

Table 2.1 Fayol's General Principles of Management

1. *Division of work.* By dividing the work into smaller elements and assigning specific elements to specific workers, the work can be performed more efficiently and more productively.
2. *Authority and responsibility.* Authority is necessary to carry out managerial responsibilities. Managers have the authority to give orders so that work will be accomplished.
3. *Discipline.* To ensure the smooth operation of the business, it is essential that members of the organization respect the rules that govern it.
4. *Unity of command.* To avoid conflicting instructions and confusion, each employee should receive orders from only one superior.
5. *Unity of direction.* Similar activities within an organization should be coordinated under and directed by only one manager.
6. *Subordination of individual interest to the common good.* The goals of the overall organization should take precedence over the interests of individual employees.
7. *Remuneration of personnel.* Financial compensation for work done should be fair both to the employees and to the organization.
8. *Centralization.* Power and authority should be concentrated at upper levels of the organization with managers maintaining final responsibility. However, managers should give their subordinates enough authority to perform their jobs properly.
9. *Scalar chain.* A single, uninterrupted chain of authority should extend from the top level to the lowest position in the organization.
10. *Order.* Materials should be in the right place at the right time, and workers should be assigned to the jobs best suited to them.
11. *Equity.* Managers should display friendliness and fairness toward their subordinates.
12. *Stability of personnel tenure.* High rates of employee turnover are inefficient and should be avoided.
13. *Initiative.* Subordinates should be given the freedom to take initiative in carrying out their work.
14. *Esprit de corps.* Team spirit and harmony should be promoted among workers to create a sense of organizational unity.

Source: Based on Henri Fayol, *General and Industrial Management*, trans. Constana Storrs (London: Pittman & Sons, 1949).

thinkers. Others focused on the functions of management or the overall organizational structure, as seen in the next two sections.

Administrative Management

Administrative management focuses on managers and the functions they perform. This approach to management is most closely identified with Henri Fayol (1841–1925), a French mining engineer whose major views emerged in the early 20th century.[24] Fayol made his mark when he revitalized a floundering mining company and turned it into a financial success. He later attributed his success as a manager to the methods he employed rather than to his personal attributes. Fayol was the first to recognize that successful managers had to understand the basic managerial functions. He identified these functions as planning, organizing, commanding (leading), coordinating, and controlling. He also contended that successful managers needed to apply certain principles of management to these functions. Fayol developed a set of 14 general principles of management, which are listed in Table 2.1.[25]

KEY TERMS

Administrative management A perspective on management that focuses on managers and the functions they perform.

Many of Fayol's principles are quite compatible with the views of scientific management. For example, the objective of Fayol's principle on the division of work is to produce more and better work with the same amount of effort. Taylor was attempting the same thing with his shoveling experiments. Fayol's order principle, stating that everything and everyone should be in their proper place, is consistent with the orderly objective of time-and-motion studies.

Some of Fayol's classical theories and principles may not seem compatible with contemporary management as described in Chapter 1. For example, his principle of centralization of power and authority at upper levels of the organization is contrary to the contemporary management view of allowing frontline workers more autonomy and authority for making and carrying out decisions. Furthermore, contemporary managers rarely demand that the goals of the overall organization take precedence over the interests of individual employees. Contemporary management thinking views employees as a valuable resource whose interests must be considered. Therefore, considerable importance is placed on satisfying the wants, needs, and desires of individual workers.

Despite the apparent incompatibility between some of Fayol's principles and the philosophies of contemporary management, several of his principles continue to be embraced by today's managers. His managerial functions of planning, organizing, leading, and controlling are routinely used in modern organizations. In fact, these functions form the framework for the organization of the material in this textbook. In addition, Fayol's principles on subordinate initiative, harmony, and team spirit are particularly applicable to the modern trend toward encouraging creativity and teamwork in the workplace.

Whereas scientific management focuses on the productivity of the individual worker and administrative management focuses on the functions of the manager, bureaucratic management, the final subfield of classical management, shifts its focus to the overall organizational system.[26]

Bureaucratic Management

Bureaucratic management focuses on the overall organizational system and is based upon firm rules, policies, and procedures; a fixed hierarchy; and a clear division of labor. Max Weber (1864–1920), a German sociologist and historian, is most closely associated with bureaucratic management.[27] Weber had observed that many 19th-century European organizations were managed on a very personal basis. Employees often displayed more loyalty to individuals than to the mission of the organization. As a consequence, resources were often used to satisfy individual desires rather than the organization's goals.

To counter this dysfunctional consequence, Weber envisioned a system of management that would be based upon impersonal and rational behavior.[28] Management of this sort is called a bureaucracy, and it has the following characteristics:

- *Division of labor.* All duties are divided into simpler, more specialized tasks so that the organization can use personnel and resources more efficiently.
- *Hierarchy of authority.* The organization has a pyramid-shaped hierarchical structure that ranks job positions according to the amount of power and authority each possesses. Power and authority increase at each higher level, and each lower-level position is under the direct control of one higher-level position, as in Figure 2.3.
- *Rules and procedures.* A comprehensive set of rules and procedures that provides the guidelines for performing all organizational duties is clearly stated. Employees must strictly adhere to these formal rules.
- *Impersonality.* Personal favoritism is avoided in the operation of the organization. The specified duties of an employee dictate behavior. The rules and procedures are applied to all employees impersonally and uniformly.
- *Employee selection and promotion.* All employees are selected on the basis of technical competence and are promoted based upon their job-related performance.[29]

Weber felt that an organization exhibiting these characteristics would be more efficient and adaptable to change, for such a system would be able to maintain continuity. Regardless of the individual personalities who might enter or leave the system over the years, the formal rules, structure, and written records would allow the organization to continue to operate as it had in the past.

Weber believed there were three different types of authority: traditional, charismatic, and rational–legal.[30] **Traditional authority** is based upon custom or tradition. **Charismatic authority** occurs when subordinates voluntarily comply with a leader because of his or her special personal qualities or abilities. **Rational–legal authority** is based on a set of impersonal rules and regulations that apply to all employees. Superiors are obeyed because of the positions they hold within the organization. Table 2.2 briefly describes these three types of authority and provides examples of each.

The term *bureaucracy* has taken on a negative connotation today. In many cases, negative opinions about a bureaucracy are fully justified,

© TIM PANNELL/CORBIS

Bureaucratic management involves a division of labor, a hierarchy of authority, rules and procedures, impersonality, and employee selection and promotion.

KEY TERMS

Bureaucratic management A perspective on management that focuses on the overall organizational system.

Traditional authority Subordinates comply with a leader because of custom or tradition.

Charismatic authority Subordinates voluntarily comply with a leader because of his or her special personal qualities or abilities.

Rational–legal authority Subordinates comply with a leader because of a set of impersonal rules and regulations that apply to all employees.

Figure 2.3 Bureaucratic Hierarchical Power Structure

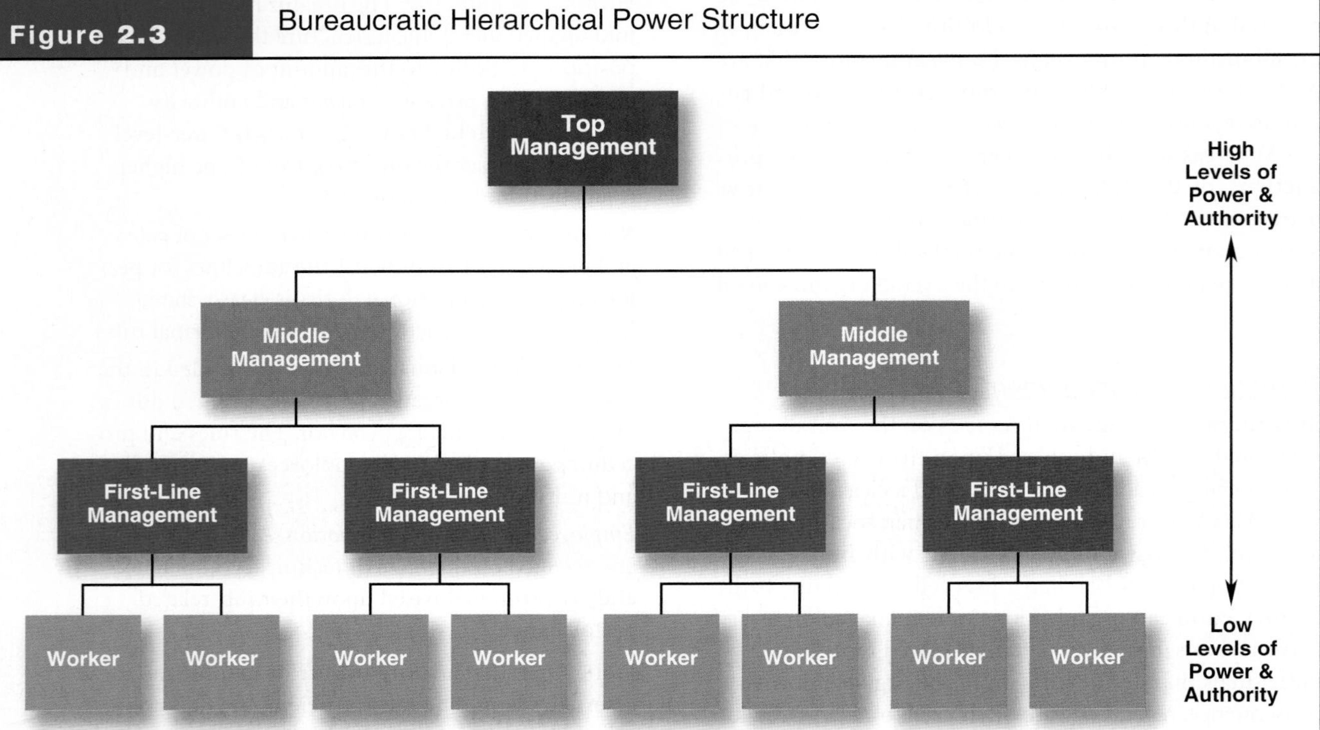

especially when its rules and regulations are imposed in an inflexible and unyielding manner. Who among us has not been frustrated by an encounter with the bureaucratic "red tape" of some government agency or university office? At a recent Compaq shareholders meeting, frustration over not getting anyone in the company to listen to them was summed up by one angry shareholder who fumed, "Try getting a human being on the phone at Compaq." These complaints prompted Compaq's chairman to admit that the company had become too "bureaucratic."[31] An inflexible and unyielding imposition of the rules and regulations is in direct conflict with the changing face of contemporary organizations as described in Chapter 1. There we noted that future leaders must typically display a greater reliance on work teams that are empowered to use their creativity, self-motivation, and initiative to make decisions and solve problems as they work toward achieving the organization's goals.

Table 2.2 Weber's Three Types of Authority

Type	Description	Examples
Traditional	Subordinate obedience based on custom or tradition	Native American tribal chiefs, royalty (kings, queens, etc.)
Charismatic	Subordinate obedience based on special personal qualities associated with certain social reformers, political leaders, religious leaders, or organizational leaders	Martin Luther King, Jr., Cesar Chavez, Mahatma Gandhi, Billy Graham, Bill Gates (Microsoft), Mary Kay Ash (Mary Kay Cosmetics), Dave Thomas (Wendy's)
Rational–legal	Subordinate obedience based on the position held by superiors within the organization	Police officers, organizational executives, managers, and supervisors

Even though the trend is toward less bureaucracy, we should not be too quick to bury its basic tenets. Despite its associated rules and red tape, it can still provide some effective control devices in organizations where many routine tasks must be performed. Low-level employees should be able to accomplish such work by simply following the rules. Unfortunately, the rules and red tape of bureaucracy can sometimes be carried to an unhealthy extreme. When General Motors wanted to construct a truck assembly plant in Egypt, the proposal had to pass through many ministries and required a multitude of signatures to gain approval. As a result of this sea of red tape, more than 3 years elapsed before final approval was granted.[32]

The classical thinkers of the late-19th and early-20th centuries made many valuable contributions to the theory and practice of management. However, their theories did not always achieve desirable results in the situations that were developing in the early-20th century. Changes were occurring in the workplace that gave rise to new perspectives on management. As a result, the behavioral perspective of management, which represents a significant departure from classical thinking, emerged.

BEHAVIORAL PERSPECTIVE

4 During the first few decades of the 20th century, the industrialized nations of the world were experiencing many social and cultural changes. Standards of living were rising, working conditions were improving, and the length of the average workweek was declining. Although these improvements temporarily stopped during the Great Depression and World War II, they did continue during the remainder of the century. One of the most profound changes was the newfound ability of workers to influence managerial decisions through the formation of powerful labor unions. Amid these changes, managers were increasingly finding that workers did not always exhibit behaviors that were consistent with what classical theorists had called rational behavior. Furthermore, effective managers were not always being true to the principles laid down by these traditionalists. Managers were being presented with more and more evidence that human behavior has a significant impact on the actions of workers. Observations and evidence such as this gave rise to the behavioral perspective of management, which recognizes the importance of human behavior patterns in shaping managerial style. The next sections describe the observations and research findings of several of the major contributors to this behavioral perspective.

Mary Parker Follett

In the first decades of the 20th century, Mary Parker Follett, an early management scholar, made several significant contributions to the behavioral perspective of management. Follett's contributions were based on her observations of managers as they performed their jobs. She concluded that a key to effective management was coordination. It was Follett's contention that managers needed to coordinate and harmonize group efforts rather than force and coerce people. She developed the following four principles of coordination to promote effective work groups:[33]

1. Coordination requires that people be in direct contact with one another.
2. Coordination is essential during the initial stages of any endeavor.
3. Coordination must address all factors and phases of any endeavor.
4. Coordination is a continuous, ongoing process.

Follett believed that management is a continuous, dynamic process in which new situations and problems are likely to arise as the process is applied to solve a problem. She felt that the best decisions would be made by people who were closest to the decision situation. Consequently, she thought that it was inappropriate for managers to insist that workers perform a task only in a specifically prescribed way. She argued that subordinates should be involved in the decision-making process whenever they are likely to be affected by the decision. Follett's beliefs that workers must be involved in solving problems and that management is a dynamic process rather than a static principle are certainly in contrast to the earlier views of Taylor, Fayol, and Weber, but they are more consistent with contemporary management philosophy.

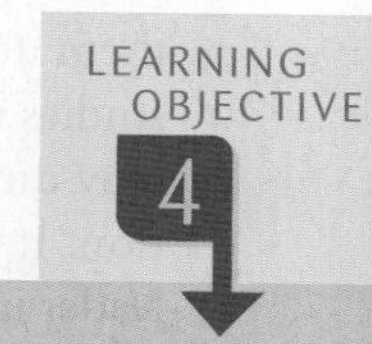

Describe the theories of the major contributors to the behavioral perspective of management.

Follett also made early contributions in the area of conflict management. She felt that managers could help resolve interdepartmental conflict by communicating with one another and with the affected workers. She recognized that conflict could actually be a positive force in an organization, for, if managed properly, it could serve as an integrating factor that stimulates production efforts.[34]

Elton Mayo

Beginning in 1924, studies of several situational factors were being performed at the Western Electric Company's plant in Hawthorne, Illinois. One of these experiments was designed to demonstrate that increased levels of lighting could improve productivity.[35] Test groups and control groups were formed. The test group was subjected to a variety of lighting conditions, while the control group operated under constant lighting conditions. The results demonstrated that when illumination levels were increased, the productivity of the test group improved, as was expected. The experimenters were surprised, however, to find a similar increase in productivity when the test group's level of illumination was dramatically decreased. Equally puzzling was the fact that the control group's productivity also increased, even though its lighting conditions remained constant.

Elton Mayo, a Harvard professor and management consultant, was brought in to investigate these puzzling results. After reviewing the results of these and other newly designed experiments, Mayo and his colleagues explained the results by what has come to be known as the **Hawthorne effect.** Productivity increases were being caused not by a physical event but by a human behavior phenomenon. Workers in both groups perceived that special attention was being paid to them, causing them to develop a group pride, which in turn motivated them to improve their performance. The Hawthorne studies revealed that factors not specified by management may directly influence productivity and worker satisfaction. It was found, for example, that an informal group leader in a task group may have more power among group members than the formal supervisor. Although the Hawthorne studies were conducted between 1924 and 1933, they did not have much impact until the 1950s because of world events (the Great Depression and World War II).[36]

It has been said that the Hawthorne studies "represent the transition from scientific management to the early human relations movement" and that they "brought to the forefront the concept of the organization as a social system, encompassing individuals, informal groups, and intergroup relationships, as well as formal structure."[37] In short, the Hawthorne studies added the human element to management thinking, an element that had been missing in the classical approaches to managerial thought.

KEY TERMS

Hawthorne effect
The phenomenon whereby individual or group performance is influenced by human behavior factors.

Theory X
Advocates that a manager perceives that subordinates have an inherent dislike of work and will avoid it if possible.

Theory Y
Advocates that a manager perceives that subordinates enjoy work and will gain satisfaction from their jobs.

Douglas McGregor

Douglas McGregor, whose background and training were in psychology, had a variety of experiences as a manager, consultant, and college president. McGregor was not totally satisfied with the assumptions about human behavior that were to be found in the classical perspective and the early contributions to the behavioral perspective. His experiences and background helped McGregor formulate his Theory X and Theory Y, which pose two contrasting sets of assumptions with which managers might view their subordinates. Table 2.3 provides a summary of the assumptions inherent in these contrasting views.[38]

McGregor proposed that **Theory X** managers perceive that their subordinates have an inherent dislike of work and that they will avoid it if at all possible. This theory further suggests that subordinates need to be coerced, directed, or threatened to get them to work toward the achievement of organizational goals. Finally, Theory X assumes that subordinates have little ambition, wish to avoid responsibility, and prefer to be directed. Managers who subscribe to this theory are likely to exercise an authoritarian style, telling people what to do and how to do it.

In contrast, **Theory Y** managers perceive that their subordinates enjoy work and that they will gain satisfaction from performing their jobs. Furthermore, this theory assumes that subordinates are self-motivated and self-directed toward achieving the organization's goals. Commitment to the organization's goals is a direct result of the personal satisfaction that they feel from a job well done. Finally, Theory Y assumes that subordinates will seek responsibility, display ambition, and use their imagination, creativity, and ingenuity when working toward the fulfillment of organizational goals. Managers who subscribe to Theory Y are likely to exercise a participatory style, consulting with subordinates, soliciting their opinions, and encouraging them to take part in decision making.[39] In Chapter 1, we looked at the ways management and managers are changing. The greater reliance on employees as decision makers, problem solvers, and team players is a strong endorsement for McGregor's Theory Y assumptions. This chapter's "Now Apply It" provides a self-assessment exercise that allows you to assess your own tendency toward Theory X or Theory Y assumptions. This exercise can be used to apply the theory to yourself and others with whom you work to assess your management styles.[40]

Chester Barnard

Chester Barnard studied economics at Harvard, and although he never completed the requirements for his degree, he had a very successful management career. He started in the statistical department of AT&T, and by

Table 2.3 Comparison of Theory X and Theory Y Assumptions

Factor	Theory X Assumptions	Theory Y Assumptions
Employee attitude toward work	Employees dislike work and will avoid it if at all possible.	Employees enjoy work and will actively seek it.
Management view of direction	Employees must be directed, coerced, controlled, or threatened to get them to put forth adequate effort.	Employees are self-motivated and self-directed toward achieving organizational goals.
Employee view of direction	Employees wish to avoid responsibility; they prefer to be directed and told what to do and how to do it.	Employees seek responsibility; they wish to use their creativity, imagination, and ingenuity in performing their jobs.
Management style	Authoritarian style of management	Participatory style of management

Now Apply It

Theory X and Theory Y

Complete the following questionnaire. Indicate your agreement or disagreement with each of the statements by placing the appropriate number next to the statement. This is not a test, and there are no right or wrong answers. Use the following scale: Strongly Agree: 5; Agree: 4; Undecided: 3; Disagree: 2; Strongly Disagree: 1

_____ 1. Most people prefer to be directed and want to avoid responsibility.

_____ 2. Most people can learn leadership skills regardless of their particular inborn traits and abilities.

_____ 3. The best way to encourage high performance is by using rewards and punishment.

_____ 4. A leader will lose influence over subordinates if he or she allows them to make decisions without direction and strict rules.

_____ 5. A good leader gives detailed and complete instructions to subordinates, rather than depending on their initiative to work out the details.

_____ 6. Because groups do not set high goals, individual goal setting offers advantages over group goal setting.

_____ 7. A leader should give subordinates only the information necessary for them to do their immediate tasks.

_____ 8. People are bright, but under most organizational conditions, their potentials are underutilized.

_____ 9. Most people dislike work and, when possible, avoid it.

_____ 10. Leaders have to control, direct, and threaten employees to get them to work toward organizational goals.

_____ 11. Most people will exercise self-direction and self-control if they are committed to the objectives.

_____ 12. People do not naturally dislike work; it is a natural part of their lives.

_____ 13. Most people are internally motivated to reach objectives to which they are committed.

_____ 14. People are capable of innovation in solving organizational problems.

_____ 15. Most people place security above all other work factors and will display little ambition.

Scoring key: Reverse score items 2, 11, 12, 13 (1 = 5, 2 = 4, 3 = 3, 4 = 2, 5 = 1). Sum all 15 items. A score of more than 55 indicates a tendency to manage others according to the principles in Theory X. A score of less than 35 indicates a tendency to manage others according to the principles in Theory Y. Scores between 35 and 55 indicate flexibility in the management of others.

1927 he had become the president of New Jersey Bell. Barnard made two major contributions to management thought: One dealt with the functions of executives, and the other was his theory of authority. He felt that executives serve two primary functions. First, executives must establish and maintain a communications system among employees. Barnard regarded organizations as social systems that require employee cooperation and continuous communication to remain effective. Second, executives are responsible for clearly formulating the purposes and objectives of the organization and for motivating employees to direct all their efforts toward attaining these objectives.

Barnard's other major contribution was his theory on authority. According to Barnard, authority flows from the ability of subordinates to accept or reject an order. His acceptance theory of authority suggests that employees will accept a superior's orders if they comprehend what is required, feel that the orders are consistent with organizational goals, and perceive a positive, personal benefit.[41] Many management scholars consider Barnard the father of the behavioral approach to management. In fact, many believe that his work laid the foundation for several contemporary approaches to management.

LEARNING OBJECTIVE 5

Describe the characteristics of the quantitative perspective of management.

As the mid-20th century was approached on the time line shown in Figure 2.1, new problem-solving and decision-making tools were developed, giving rise to a quantitative perspective on management. As you will see, the quantitative school provided managers with sophisticated new analytical tools and problem-solving techniques.

QUANTITATIVE PERSPECTIVE

5 The quantitative perspective had its roots in the scientific management approaches and is characterized by its use of mathematics, statistics, and other quantitative techniques for management decision making and problem solving. The most significant developments in this school of thought occurred during World War II when military strategists had to contend with many monumentally complex problems, such as determining convoy routes, predicting enemy locations, planning invasion strategies, and providing troop logistical support.[42] Such massive and complicated problems required more sophisticated decision-making tools than were available at that time. To remedy this situation, the British and the Americans assembled groups of mathematicians, physicists, and other scientists to develop techniques to solve these military problems. Because the problems often involved the movement of large amounts of materials and the efficient use of large numbers of people, the techniques that they devised could be readily transferred from the military arena to the business arena.

The use of mathematical models and quantitative techniques to solve managerial problems is often referred to as *operations research*. This term comes from the names applied to the groups of scientists during World War II (operational research teams in Great Britain and operations research teams in the United States).[43] This approach is also referred to as *management science* in some circles. Regardless of the name, the quantitative perspective has four basic characteristics:

1. *Decision-making focus.* The primary focus of the quantitative approach is on problems or situations that require some direct action, or decision, on the part of management.
2. *Measurable criteria.* The decision-making process requires that the decision maker select some alternative course of action. To make a rational selection, the alternatives must be compared on the basis of some measurable criterion, or objective, such as profit, cost, return on investment, or output rate, to name a few.
3. *Quantitative model.* To assess the likely impact of each alternative on the stated criteria, a quantitative model of the decision situation must be formulated. Quantitative models make use of mathematical symbols, equations, and formulas to represent properties and relationships of the decision situation.
4. *Computers.* Although many quantitative models can be solved manually, such a process is often time-consuming and costly. Consequently, computers are quite useful in the problem-solving process (and often necessary for extremely complex quantitative formulations).[44]

In the past few decades, giant strides in microchip capability have enabled computer sophistication to advance tremendously. Computer hardware that fits in the palm of one's hand can outperform hardware that filled rooms a few decades ago. It has been said that today's average consumers have more computing power in their wristwatches than existed in the entire world before 1961. Similarly, a host of quantitative decision-making tools evolved in this century, including such tools as linear programming, network models, queuing (waiting line)

Figure 2.4 Basic Structure of Systems

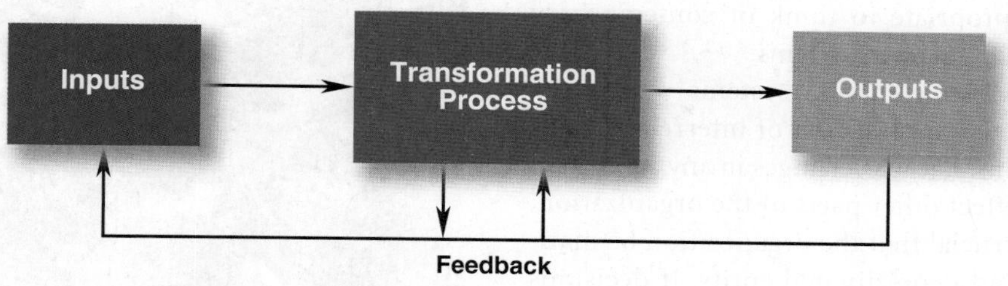

models, game theory, inventory models, and statistical decision theory.

SYSTEMS PERSPECTIVE

6 An approach to problem solving that is closely aligned with the quantitative perspective is **systems analysis.** Because many of the wartime problems reflected exceedingly complex systems, the operations research teams often found it necessary to analyze them by breaking them into their constituent elements. Since any system is merely a collection of interrelated parts, identifying each of these parts and the nature of their interrelationships should simplify the model-building process. Systems can be viewed as a combination of three building blocks: inputs, outputs, and transformation processes. These blocks are connected by material and information flows.[45] Figure 2.4 illustrates the interaction of these blocks and flows.

Although a more thorough discussion of inputs, outputs, and transformation processes can be found in Chapters 15 and 16, the basic components of the systems model can be briefly introduced here. **Inputs** can vary greatly depending upon the nature of the system. Such diverse items as materials, workers, capital, land, equipment, customers, and information are potential inputs. **Outputs** typically consist of some physical commodity or some intangible service or information that is desired by the customers or users of the system. The **transformation process** is the mechanism by which inputs are converted to outputs. We usually think in terms of a physical transformation process in which material inputs are reconfigured into some desired output. This scenario would be typical of a manufacturing system. Several other types of transformation processes are found in nonmanufacturing types of systems, however.[46] For example, in a transportation or distribution system such as Delta Air Lines or United Parcel Service, the transformation process merely alters the location of the inputs, not their form. In storage systems such as a U-Haul storage facility or a Bank of America safety deposit box, the inputs change in the time dimension, but not in form or location. **Feedback** represents information about the status and performance of the system.

Systems are often further distinguished by whether they interact with the external environment. **Open systems** must interact with the external environment to survive. The interactions can be reflected in the exchange of material, energy, information, and so forth. **Closed systems** do not interact with the environment. In both the classical and early behavioral perspectives, systems were often thought of as closed. In fact, the quantitative perspective often uses a closed-system assumption to simplify problem structures. Nevertheless, the difficulty of totally eliminating environmental interactions makes it hard to defend the concepts of open and closed systems in the absolute. Perhaps more appropriately, we might view systems as relatively open or relatively closed.[47] Thus, we might think of the production department of an organization as a relatively closed system. It can manufacture products in a continuous fashion while maintaining little interaction with the external environment. Meanwhile, the marketing department would be more appropriately viewed as an open system because it must constantly interact with external

LEARNING OBJECTIVE 6

Describe the systems perspective building blocks and their interactions.

KEY TERMS

Systems analysis
An approach to problem solving that attacks complex systems by breaking them down into their constituent elements.

Input
A diverse item such as material, worker, capital, land, equipment, customer, and information used in creating products and services.

Output
The physical commodity, or intangible service or information, that is desired by the customers or users of the system.

customers to assess their wishes and desires. Long-run organizational survival requires that all organizations have some interaction with the external environment; therefore, it is appropriate to think of contemporary business organizations as open systems.

LEARNING OBJECTIVE 7

Discuss the nature of the contingency perspective of management.

Most complex systems are often viewed as a collection of interrelated subsystems. Because changes in any subsystem can affect other parts of the organization, it is crucial that the organization be managed as a coordinated entity. If decisions are made independently at the subsystem level, the organization as a whole will often achieve less-than-optimal performance. But when all organizational subsystems work together, the organization can accomplish more than when the subsystems are working alone. This property, in which the whole is greater than the sum of its parts, is referred to as **synergy.**

Another important property of systems is **entropy,** which refers to their tendency to decay over time. As is the case with living systems, organizations must continuously monitor their environments and adjust to economic, social, political, technological, and global changes. Survival and prosperity often require that new inputs be sought. A system that does not continually receive inputs from its environment will eventually die.

© ASSOCIATED PRESS/AP

A manufacturing system represents the transformation process in which inputs are converted to outputs.

KEY TERMS

Transformation process
The mechanism by which inputs are converted to outputs.

Feedback
Information about the status and performance of a given effort or system.

Open system
A system that must interact with the external environment to survive.

Closed system
A system that does not interact with the environment.

Synergy
A phenomenon whereby an organization can accomplish more when its subsystems work together than it can accomplish when they work independently.

Entropy
The tendency for systems to decay over time.

Contingency perspective
Perspective on management proposing that the best managerial approach is contingent on key variables in a given organizational situation.

CONTINGENCY PERSPECTIVE

7 In the 1960s, managers were becoming increasingly aware that the effectiveness of different management styles varied according to the situation. With this awareness came the emergence of the **contingency perspective,** which proposes that there is no one best approach to management. This perspective recognizes that any of the four previously discussed management perspectives might be used alone or in combination for different situations.[48] In the contingency perspective, managers are faced with the task of determining which managerial approach is likely to be most effective in a given situation. This requires managers to first identify the key contingencies, or variables, in the given organizational situation. For example, the approach used to manage a group of teenagers working in a fast-food restaurant would be quite different from the approach used to manage a medical research team trying to discover a cure for AIDS.

The young fast-food worker might best be managed in a classical, authoritative style. Bureaucratic rules and regulations might be put in place to guide all worker actions and behaviors. Scientific management principles would probably be used to define the best way to perform each work task. Variation from the prescribed method would not and probably should not be tolerated in this situation. This is not the time or place to experiment with different ways to fry the burgers or mix the shakes!

It is doubtful that the medical research team would succeed under this approach to management. The team is faced with a very complex, unstructured endeavor that will require the team members to bring together all of their unique problem-solving skills. Such a situation requires that the team be given the autonomy to try out different solutions, pursue different avenues, and take risks that would simply be out of the question for the teenaged burger flippers.

Table 2.4 Production Technology Examples

Production Technology	Examples
Small-batch technology	Custom-fabrication machine shop, manufacturer of neon advertising signs, print shop specializing in personal business cards, trophy-engraving shop
Mass-production technology	Manufacturer of automobiles, manufacturer of refrigerators, manufacturer of hair dryers, manufacturer of pencils
Continuous-process technology	Oil refinery, flour mill, soft-drink bottler, chemical processor

Because the contingency perspective proposes that managerial style is situation specific, it has not yet developed to the point where it can dictate the preferred way to manage in all situations. A particularly important factor to consider in the contingency approach is the type of technology being used by the organization. In pioneering contingency studies conducted in the 1960s, Joan Woodward discovered that a particular managerial style was affected by the organization's technology. Woodward identified and described three different types of technology:

1. *Small-batch technology*. Organizations of this type exhibit job-shop characteristics in which workers produce custom-made products in relatively small quantities.
2. *Mass-production technology*. Organizations of this type exhibit assembly-line characteristics in which standardized parts and components are used to produce large volumes of standardized products.
3. *Continuous-process technology*. Organizations of this type have a process in which the product flows continuously through the various stages of conversion.

The level of human interaction varies with each of these technology types. Small-batch technology tends to have the most human involvement (that is, it is the most labor intensive) due to the customized outputs. Mass-production technology tends to have less human involvement due to the automated and robotic equipment that typifies assembly-line operations. Continuous-process technology has the lowest level of human involvement as the product flows through the stages of conversion. Consider, for example, how little hands-on human involvement is needed in an ExxonMobil oil refinery as crude oil flows through the various processing stages on its way to becoming gasoline. Examples of each of these production technologies appear in Table 2.4, and all three are discussed more thoroughly in Chapter 16.[49]

Some of Woodward's findings showed that bureaucratic management methods were most effective in organizations using mass-production technology. Conversely, organizations using small-batch and continuous-process technologies had little need for the formalized rules and communication systems of the bureaucratic style.[50] Continued studies of this type will fill in all the gaps and eventually provide more definitive guidelines as to which managerial style is desirable for a particular situation.

Other important factors to consider in defining the contingencies for each situation include environment, organizational size, and organizational culture.[51] For example, large organizations may find it necessary to use more structured and rigid rules, regulations, and policies to control organizational activities. On the other hand, smaller organizations may find that they can rely less on the formal structure and allow workers the autonomy to make decisions for the situations and problems that they encounter. In this example, the larger organization would undoubtedly tend toward a more bureaucratic management style, while the smaller organization would display a more behavioral orientation. As Figure 2.5 shows, parts of all of the management perspectives that we have examined might be combined to form a contingency approach.

Information Technology and Management Style

In recent years, we have all been witness to the tremendous advances that have occurred in the systems and devices that can process, disseminate, and transfer information. Each of our lives has been affected by cell phones, micro-

Figure 2.5 Blending Components into a Contingency Perspective

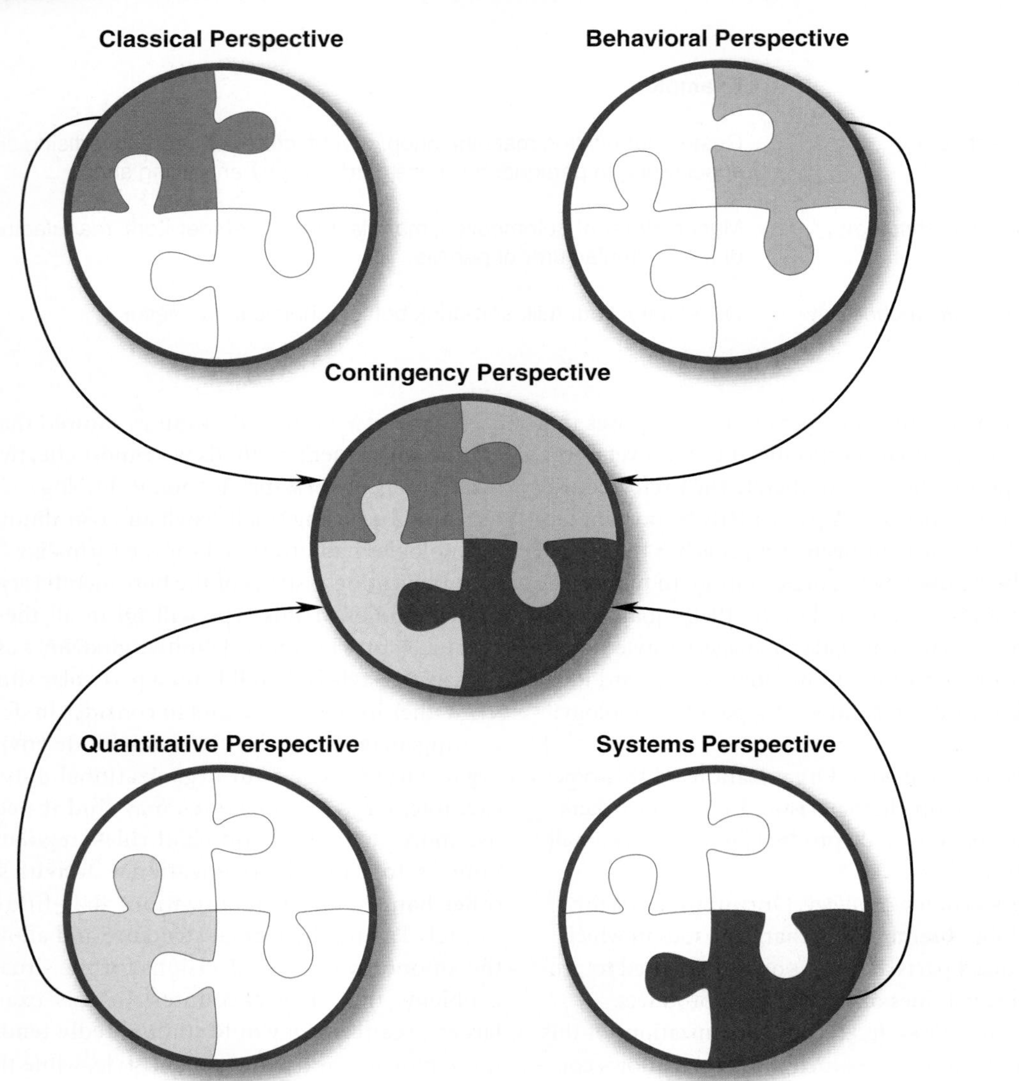

computers, fax machines, specialty software packages, and access to information on the Internet. These same devices and systems can have a profound effect on the choice of a management style. In many instances, they can facilitate the adoption of a particular style.

The most obvious areas in which technological advances in information processing facilitate the use of a particular style are the quantitative and systems perspectives. The geometric increase in microchip processing capability makes it easier to develop ultrasophisticated quantitative models of complex management systems. Rapid processing and feedback of information in these system models allow the organization to be managed as a coordinated entity. Perhaps less obvious is the impact that information-processing technology has on the subfields of the classical perspective on management. For example, classical theories might suggest how many workers should report to a single superior (span of control) and how many hierarchical levels of authority are needed in a particular organization. But these can be altered when each employee has at his or her disposal devices that relay critical decision-making information. In addition, the centralization principle of Fayol may not be desirable in these new situations. When low-level workers are empowered to make decisions and have the needed information readily available, it is not necessary for all decisions to be made at upper levels of management.

But technological advances can be a two-edged sword. In addition to facilitating the adoption of a particular management style, they may, at times, force a change. This was the situation at United Parcel Service (UPS) in recent years. The additional workload and stress to drivers brought on by a new, computerized package-tracing system forced UPS to ease up on its traditional bureaucratic management style.[52]

Future Issues: Diversity, Globalization, and Quality

LEARNING OBJECTIVE 8

Discuss the future issues that will affect the further development of management thought.

8 As you might expect, the theories and ideas that have emerged thus far do not represent the end of the road in the evolution of management thought. The economic, social, political, technological, and global forces that influence management thinking continue to change. A major trend in recent years has been heightened concern for diversity within the workplace. The workforce has become increasingly more varied, and the number of minority-owned businesses has continued to increase. Census Bureau data indicate that the recent growth rate of Hispanic-owned businesses in the United States is triple that of general business growth. In the words of one Commerce Department official, "Entrepreneurship is the flame that heats the American melting pot; it is the vehicle through which racial and ethnic minorities can enter the American mainstream, and it is visibly their most productive method for doing so."[53] The ranks of management need to exhibit a level of diversity that is similar to these levels of workforce and entrepreneurial diversity. Diversity within an organization can have an added side benefit. When government contracts stipulate that minority suppliers must be used, businesses displaying cultural, ethnic, and gender diversity stand a better chance of winning government business.

In recent years, Japanese management styles have received considerable scrutiny due to the tremendous successes achieved by Japanese industries. Most readers are surely aware of the degree to which the Japanese have taken control of the global automobile and electronics markets. This success has been achieved in part because of a managerial philosophy that is committed to quality and a just-in-time operating philosophy (a concept that is treated in more detail in Chapter 16).[54] This is a concept that has been adopted by virtually all of the world's other automobile manufacturers. Its benefits are not limited to automakers, however. Many other industries have successfully adopted its principles.

The successes of the Japanese management style are not due entirely to the technical operating system, however. Many aspects of the Japanese management style follow the prescriptions for successful management in the 21st century that were discussed in Chapter 1. A focus on quality is certainly central to the Japanese style. It is somewhat ironic that the Japanese emphasis on quality was a result of the teachings of the noted American quality philosophers W. Edwards Deming and Joseph Juran. Another noted American, Armand Feigenbaum, originated the concept of total quality control, which was quickly adopted by the Japanese. Many American firms have now embraced the concept of quality and have been successful enough to win the coveted Malcolm Baldrige National Quality Award. Some of the more recognizable recent winners of this award include AT&T, Cadillac, Corning, Eastman Kodak, Federal Express, GTE, IBM, Motorola, Ritz-Carlton Hotels, Texas Instruments, Westinghouse, and Xerox.[55]

It would be difficult to dispute that the Japanese maintain a global focus. Although not as apparent to observers from abroad, their management style also incorporates the concept of workers as decision makers, problem solvers, and team players. These were all identified in Chapter 1 as keys to operating successfully in the 21st century. It should also be noted that the Japanese management style embraces aspects from several of the historically evolving management perspectives discussed in this chapter. The Japanese philosophy includes a strong behavioral component because it recognizes the importance of workers as decision makers and problem solvers. There is also a hint of bureaucratic management in the Japanese philosophy with its tradition of lifelong career commitment to employees. But even that is in a state of evolution. The mounting pressure to streamline in the increasingly competitive global business environment is causing many Japanese organizations to abandon the lifetime employment concept.[56] In this chapter's closing "Meeting the Challenge," you will learn of Sony's decisions to terminate many employees in an effort to regain profitability.

The Japanese management style spawned the development of **Theory Z** by William Ouchi, a contemporary management scholar.[57] Theory Z is a management approach that advocates trusting employees and making them feel like an integral part of the organization. According to the theory, once a trusting relationship is established with workers, production will increase.

Many question whether the Japanese management style has developed and evolved to the point where it can be considered a major school of

KEY TERMS

Theory Z
Advocates that a manager places trust in the employees and makes them feel like an integral part of the organization.

Meeting The Challenge

Sony Makes an Historic Leap

When the announcement hit the newswires on March 7, 2005, it was like a bombshell blast in the electronics industry. The Sony Corporation proposed the creation of a new management structure and a new management team to lead the company. Most notable among the changes was the replacement of Chairman and CEO Nobuyuki Idei with Sir Howard Stringer, the first non-Japanese person to assume the helm of the company. Stringer, a native of Wales with dual British and U.S. citizenship, doesn't even speak the Japanese language! A few years earlier he had become the first non-Japanese member of the board, placed there in 2003 when the "Sony Shock" of missed profits drove down its share price. Stringer is a former TV journalist, having joined Sony from CBS. He turned around Sony Pictures and then took over control of first the music side of Sony in the United States, then entertainment globally. Where Stringer had recently ruled (in music and pictures), there had been a remarkable turnaround at Sony. Between the beginning of 2002 and early 2005, Sony Pictures Entertainment films generated more than $8 billion in worldwide ticket sales through a steady series of hits. During that span of time, Sony produced 26 films that were number 1 at the box office. The next closest studio had only 15. Under Stringer's watch, Sony Music was successful in cutting costs and becoming profitable.

Upon assuming his new leadership role, Stringer articulated two main goals: (1) to simplify Sony's management so that it can start making electronic devices more profitably and (2) to solve the long-running puzzle of how to make Sony's gadgets and content work together compellingly enough that consumers will pay a premium price for them. "I have said before that without content, most gadgets are just junk," said Stringer. To facilitate the accomplishment of the first goal, cost-cutting measures would have to be implemented. Some of those cost-cutting measures would be tactics that were foreign to the Japanese management style. Employees would have to be terminated, possibly by as many as 10,000 in Japan alone. Additional options included the abolishment of seniority-based salary systems and the implementation of a U.S.-style incentive pay program based on performance.

Industry analysts observed that Stringer's second goal could only be accomplished if he knocked down the walls of each division's fiefdom and achieved better integration between Sony's entertainment services and its consumer electronic devices. This is precisely what Stringer himself envisioned when he commented that "together we look forward to joining our twin pillars of engineering and technology with our commanding presence in entertainment and content creation to deliver the most advanced devices and forms of entertainment to the consumer." Will Stringer's management style and changes reverse Sony's fortunes? Only time will tell. However, if his proven track record of success is any indicator, chances are good that Sony will once again rise to a preeminent position in the consumer electronics industry.[58]

management thought. Perhaps the bigger question is whether we should be calling this style "Japanese management" or something else. Much of what we call the Japanese management philosophy originated in the Japanese automobile industry. However, these manufacturers readily admit that most of their technical innovations and ideas were borrowed from the methods used by U.S. automobile manufacturers in the heyday of Henry Ford. The Japanese simply refined these technical practices and principles, as they did the behavioral and classical components that form the total package. With this awareness, perhaps a name other than "Japanese management" would be more appropriate. Whatever the name, we must still ask whether this management style has evolved to the point where it can be considered a major school of management thought. Probably not yet, for it still must stand the test of time. Nevertheless, in time this philosophy or another might be more thoroughly developed and added to the list of major management schools of thought. Any new philosophy that emerges will undoubtedly contain bits and pieces from prior theories, but these will most assuredly be combined with new elements that have evolved in response to political, economic, social, technological, and global influences. Each era presents new problems and challenges, and new management styles arise to deal with them.

Implications for Leaders

Over the years, management theorists have developed several views on the best way to manage an organization. Each of these views is based on differing assumptions about organizational objectives and human behavior. To demonstrate quality in the management of an organization, it is important that leaders use the appropriate management approach. Therefore, tomorrow's leaders must be

- Thoroughly schooled in the different management perspectives that have evolved over the years.
- Able to understand the various economic, political, social, technological, and global influences that have affected management thinking over the years and will continue to shape future evolutionary changes in management thought.
- Capable of identifying and understanding such key variables as environment, production technology, organization culture, organization size, and international culture as they relate to the organization.
- Prepared to select elements from the various management perspectives that are appropriate for the situation.
- Adaptable to change because future conditions and developments can quickly render the chosen approaches obsolete.

In this chapter, we toured the major historical developments in the evolution of management thought. We saw the emergence of five major perspectives on management and many subfields within those major classifications. This march through time has revealed that certain aspects of every one of these evolutionary views are still appropriate for use in both today's and tomorrow's organizations. The successful leaders of tomorrow will be the ones who can blend together the appropriate components from the wide body of management theory.

SUMMARY

1. As agricultural societies were transformed into industrial societies as a result of the Industrial Revolution, managerial thinking was shaped by a variety of economic, political, social, technological, and global influences. Such influences continue to affect the way in which leaders function.

2. In the past century, five major perspectives of management thought have evolved: the classical, behavioral, quantitative, systems, and contingency perspectives. The classical perspective developed in the later part of the 19th century and the first part of the 20th century. The behavioral perspective began to evolve in the first third of the 20th century. Development of the quantitative perspective began in earnest during World War II. The systems perspective began to evolve in the 1950s, and the contingency perspective is the most recent, having begun in the 1960s.

3. The classical perspective includes scientific management, administrative management, and bureaucratic management subfields, each of which has a different focus. Scientific management focuses on the improvement of individual worker productivity. Time-and-motion studies observe and measure a worker's physical movements in order to determine the best way of performing a task. The expectation in scientific management is that managers will develop standard methods for performing each job, select workers with the appropriate abilities for each job, train workers in standard methods, and support workers by planning their work. Scientific management proponents believe that financial incentives are the major motivating factor that will induce workers to produce more. Administrative management focuses on the managerial process and the functions of the manager. Fayol identified planning, organizing, leading, coordinating, and controlling as the basic managerial functions. Bureaucratic management has as its primary focus the overall structure of the organization. This subfield emphasizes the division of labor into specialized tasks, a hierarchy of authority in which power and authority increase at higher levels of the organization, a comprehensive set of rules and procedures for performing all organizational duties, a climate of impersonality in which personal favoritism is to be avoided, and an employee selection and promotion process that is based on technical competence and performance.

4. The behavioral perspective of management had several major contributors. Mary Parker Follett emphasized the importance of coordination and harmony in group efforts. Elton Mayo recognized that the human element could play a significant role in determining worker behavior and output. Douglas McGregor proposed Theory X and Theory Y to explain employee attitudes and behavior. Chester Barnard examined the

functions of executives. He contended that executives are responsible both for establishing and maintaining a communications system among employees and for clearly formulating the purposes and objectives of the organization and motivating employees toward attaining those objectives. Barnard also contributed an acceptance theory on authority, which was a new way of describing how subordinates accept or reject orders from their superiors.

5. The major impetus for the emergence of the quantitative perspective of management was World War II and the many monumentally complex problems associated with the war effort. The quantitative perspective has a decision-making focus in which an alternative course of action must be selected as a solution to some problem. It requires the establishment of some measurable criteria so that alternatives can be compared prior to selection. Quantitative models are used to assess the impact of each alternative on the stated criteria, and computers are often helpful in the problem-solving process.

6. The systems perspective takes a set of inputs and subjects them to some transformation process, thereby generating some type of output. Inputs, transformation processes, and outputs can be quite varied, but the basic structure remains the same. Throughout this process, feedback loops constantly filter information about the status and performance of the system.

7. The contingency perspective of management suggests that there is no one best approach to management. It is a situational approach because the proper managerial style depends on the key variables, or contingencies, within the given situation.

8. In the future, cultural, racial, and gender diversity will have a huge influence on management thinking. In addition, quality and globalization will have an enormous impact on how businesses and industries are managed.

REVIEW QUESTIONS

1. (LEARNING OBJECTIVE 1) Describe the major factors that have influenced the evolution of management thought.
2. (LEARNING OBJECTIVE 2) Identify the five major perspectives of management thought.
3. (LEARNING OBJECTIVE 3) Describe the central focus of the scientific management, administrative management, and bureaucratic management subfields of the classical perspective on management.
4. (LEARNING OBJECTIVE 4) Describe the major behavioral perspective contributions of Follett, Mayo, McGregor, and Barnard.
5. (LEARNING OBJECTIVE 5) Discuss the four basic characteristics of the quantitative perspective of management.
6. (LEARNING OBJECTIVE 6) Describe the various building blocks of a systems perspective and indicate how they interconnect and interact.
7. (LEARNING OBJECTIVE 7) What is the main contention of the contingency perspective of management?
8. (LEARNING OBJECTIVE 8) What future issues are likely to affect further development of management thought?

DISCUSSION QUESTIONS

Improving Critical Thinking

1. Reexamine Weber's characteristics of a bureaucracy and Taylor's opinions in the areas of task performance, supervision, and motivation. Discuss aspects of their views that are similar in nature.
2. Some suggest that Japanese management is just the same old stuff in a new package, whereas others suggest that this style is a new and different departure. Provide arguments in support of both of these views.

Enhancing Communication Skills

3. In your own life experiences, you probably have had some occasion to use aspects of the scientific management approach. Try to recall some physical task that you analyzed to determine the best or most efficient way to perform it. To enhance your oral communication skills, prepare a short (10–15 minute) presentation for the class in which you describe that task and the results of your analysis.

4. Based on your personal observations of well-known authority figures, identify at least two authority figures in each of Weber's authority types (traditional, charismatic, and rational–legal). To enhance your written communication skills, write a short essay describing these authority figures and why you classified each of them as you did.

Building Teamwork

5. Have you ever been influenced by the Hawthorne effect? Try to recall some incident in which your performance was affected because you knew you were being watched. To refine your teamwork skills, meet with a small group of students who have been given this same assignment. Compare and discuss your experiences and then reach a consensus on the group's two most interesting experiences with the Hawthorne effect. The group members whose experiences were judged the most interesting will act as spokespersons to describe these experiences to the rest of the class.

6. Try to recall an encounter that you have had with a bureaucratic organization. Think about both the positive and negative aspects of that experience. To refine your teamwork skills, meet with a small group of students who have been given this same assignment. Compare and discuss your experiences and then reach a consensus on which two experiences represented the most rigid and unwavering bureaucratic response from the organizations. The group members whose experiences were judged to have the most rigid bureaucratic response will act as spokespersons to describe these experiences to the rest of the class.

Chapter

3

Social Responsibility and Ethics

CHAPTER OVERVIEW

As discussed in Chapter 1, ethical behavior of top-level managers, or more likely unethical behavior, continues to get attention. Almost every day brings reports about the latest company that restated its earnings because of questionable accounting practices or about the progress of court cases against former high-level managers.[1]

Obvious relationships exist between ethical behavior and social responsibility. For example, some consider it unethical and socially irresponsible for a company to outsource operations and jobs from the United States to another country.

The views and beliefs that managers have about social responsibility and ethics are very likely to influence the decisions they make in managing organizations. Managers must know what their views and beliefs are. That is why we discuss social responsibility and ethics before discussing the functions that managers perform.

Presenting social responsibility before ethics seems logical in that social responsibility is a broader issue, many times resulting from the ethical perspectives and values of the people in organizations.

To set the framework, we begin with a discussion of the stakeholder view of the firm. With that foundation, we explore the concept of social responsibility, examine four perspectives of social responsibility, and consider strategies for approaching social issues. In addition, recommendations for developing a socially responsive position are offered.

With regard to ethics, we consider values and the role that they play in shaping one's ethical behavior. Approaches for addressing ethical dilemmas are discussed as well. Our examination of ethics concludes with a discussion of ways to encourage and support ethical behavior in an organizational environment. Implications for tomorrow's managers are also discussed.

LEARNING OBJECTIVES

When you have finished studying this chapter, you should be able to

1. Discuss the stakeholder view of the firm and the impact of the globalization of business on social responsibility and ethics.
2. Describe the concept of corporate social responsibility and the primary premises on which it is based.
3. Distinguish between the four perspectives of corporate social responsibility.
4. Identify and evaluate approaches for responding to social issues.
5. Explain what values are, how they form the basis of an individual's ethical behavior, and how they may vary in a global business environment.
6. Describe how advances in information technology have created new ethical challenges.
7. Identify and discuss the differences in the utility, human rights, and justice approaches to ethical dilemmas.
8. Explain the methods used by organizations to encourage ethical organizational behavior.
9. Describe the different approaches used in ethics-training programs.
10. Discuss what is meant by whistle-blowing in monitoring ethical behavior.

Facing The Challenge

General Electric: Social Responsibility and Ethics

For essentially all of its life, General Electric Corporation (GE) has been well known and continues to be one of the most admired companies in the world. Its previous CEO, Jack Welch, is still considered to be one of the best managers ever, if not *the* best. *Fortune* magazine named him "manager of the century" in 1999.

There was good reason for the popularity and prominence of GE and Jack Welch. Welch was a strong believer in the things that lead to profitability and high returns for stockholders. In the 20 years that he was CEO, he led the company from a market value of $14 billion to $400 billion. The company continues to have the highest market value of any company in the world.

How then can one explain why GE was ranked 72nd in social responsibility in a survey conducted of investors, high-level managers, activists, and regulators in the United States and Europe? But is that a problem? GE is still very successful financially.

GE has been involved in some practices that are considered questionable; the most notable case is the dumping of PCBs, a very toxic substance to people and animals, into the Hudson River over many years. Perhaps more troublesome is the company's slow pace in cleaning it up. GE's conducting business with the country of Iran is considered questionable by some also.

Jack Welch was known for being a very successful manager and being extremely successful in increasing the financial value of GE. He was not necessarily known for making GE a leader in corporate social responsibility. The current CEO, Jeffrey Immelt, is trying to change that. Is that a good move?

Sources: D. Corbett, "Excellence in Canada: Healthy Organizations Achieve Results by Acting Responsibly," *Journal of Business Ethics* 55, no. 2 (December 2004): 125; "Money and Morals at GE," *Fortune,* 15 November 2004, 176–182; J. Veiga, "Bringing Ethics into the Mainstream: An Introduction to the Special Topic," *Academy of Management Executive* 18, no. 2 (May 2004): 37–38.

Introduction

LEARNING OBJECTIVE

Discuss the stakeholder view of the firm and the impact of the globalization of business on social responsibility and ethics.

If you are asked to list a company that is known for socially responsible and ethical behavior, General Electric probably would not be the name that came to mind first. (See "Facing the Challenge" box.) In recent years, the company has been in the news because of a few things, especially the slow cleanup of PCBs that it dumped into the Hudson River in the past. However, under the leadership of its CEO, Jeffrey Immelt, General Electric is engaging in many actions that can easily be labeled as good corporate social responsibility and very ethical. Not everyone will agree about the overall level of corporate social responsibility and ethical behavior in which General Electric is engaging, but the company is an example of one that is making a very serious effort to combine being profitable with being socially responsible and ethical.

As we examine social responsibility and ethics, you will see examples that illustrate the benefits of responsible and ethical behavior as well as others that illustrate the negative consequences of irresponsible or unethical behavior. First, however, we must answer a very important question: To whom is business responsible? (Although the ideas discussed apply to all types of organizations, it is easier to discuss the issues by focusing on businesses.) Is it the stockholders of the company? The customers? The employees? Answering this question requires an understanding of the stakeholder view of the firm.

KEY TERMS

Stakeholders
All those who are affected by or can affect the activities of the organization.

Organizational Stakeholders in a Global Environment

1 Central to the issues of social responsibility and ethics is the concept of stakeholders. **Stakeholders** are all those who are affected by or can affect the activities of the organization. Although it has long been accepted that a business must be responsible to its stockholders,

contemporary social responsibility theory maintains that a business has obligations to all of its stakeholders. This perspective broadens the scope of the business's obligations beyond a relatively narrow group of shareholders to a much broader set of constituents that includes such groups as government, consumers, owners, employees, and communities throughout the globe. [2]

Figure 3.1 illustrates the various groups that can be stakeholders in a given organization. The primary stakeholders are those that have a formal, official, or contractual relationship with the organization. They include owners (stockholders), employees, customers, and suppliers. Peripheral to this group are the secondary stakeholders. This includes other societal groups that are affected by the activities of the organization, and in turn, can have an impact on the organization. Consider, for example, which might represent primary and secondary stakeholders for your college or university. As a student, are you a primary or secondary stakeholder? What about the employers in your community? Are they primary or secondary stakeholders? What about Wal-Mart's stakeholders? Which stakeholders were affected by General Electric's actions?

As organizations become involved in the international business arena, they often find that their stakeholder base becomes wider and more diverse. Organizations that must cope with stakeholders from across the globe face special challenges that require a heightened sensitivity to and awareness of economic, political, and social differences among groups. For example, international businesses must be responsive to customers with very different needs, owners with varied expectations, and employees with distinct and perhaps dissimilar motivations.[3] Dealing effectively with such groups requires a focus on understanding the global nature of stakeholders and developing strategies that recognize and respond to such differences. As an example of the challenges that come from managing within an international environment, consider the controversy over purchasing products from economically depressed nations. Many people believe that big U.S. corporations take advantage of poorer nations and exploit their labor by purchasing goods at an unreasonably low price.

With the stakeholder view of the organization in mind, let's move on to examine the concepts of social responsibility and ethics. Certainly, these two topics are

Figure 3.1 The Stakeholder View of the Firm

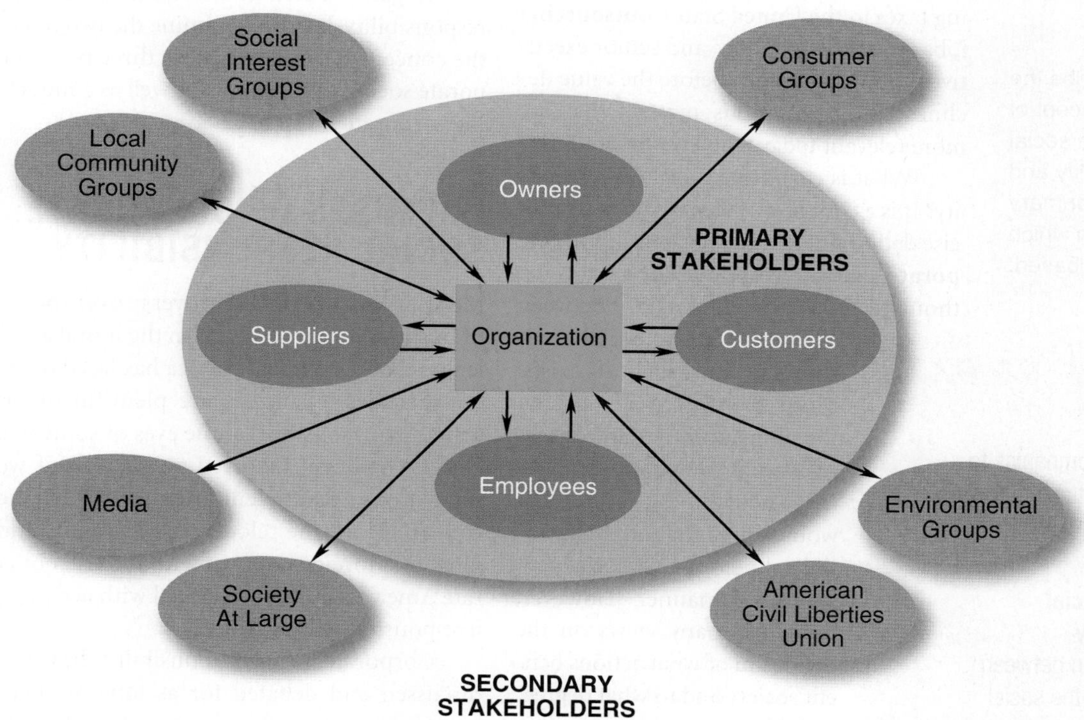

Source: From *Business & Society, Ethics and Stakeholder Management,* 3rd edition, by Carroll. © 1996. Reprinted with permission of South-Western, a division of Thomson Learning: http://www.thomsonrights.com. Fax 800-730-2215.

integrally related, as discussed above. We begin with the broader topic of corporate social responsibility that is an organizational issue relating to the obligation of business to society. Then we discuss the topic of ethics, an issue more relevant at an individual level. Both are important topics that have significant implications for the long-term success of any organization.

© ASSOCIATED PRESS/AP

As Wal-Mart develops stores in Asia, it must be sensitive to customers and employees who perhaps have different needs and different expectations.

Social Responsibility

2 The nature and extent of the obligations that business has to society have been debated for decades. Perspectives on the issue of corporate social responsibility have varied dramatically over the years, and even today, achieving consensus on the subject is difficult.[4]

In the wake of the collapse of Enron and the actions of many other companies, questions surrounding corporate social responsibility are being asked more intently than ever before. Issues such as hiding debt from investors, losing the retirement pensions of loyal employees, artificially inflating revenue amounts, moving a company's headquarters to another country to avoid paying taxes in the United States, **outsourcing** jobs to another country, and senior executives selling their stock before the value declines are very serious matters that are more relevant today than ever before.

LEARNING OBJECTIVE

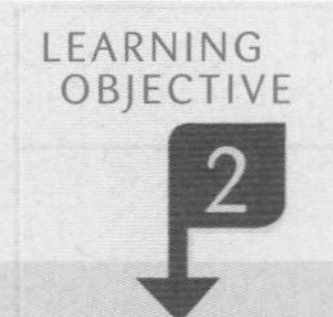

Describe the concept of corporate social responsibility and the primary premises on which it is based.

What is corporate social responsibility? It is a complex concept that resists precise definition. In a very general sense, **corporate social responsibility** can be thought of as the interaction between business and the social environment in which it exists. More specifically, it refers to the obligation that an organization has to operate in a way that benefits society. Most would agree that all organizations should act in a socially responsible manner. However, there are many views on the definition of what actions benefit society and to what degree.

The debate over corporate social responsibility focuses on the nature of socially responsible behavior. Does being socially responsible mean that the corporation's actions must not harm society, or does it mean that the corporation's actions should benefit society? How does one distinguish between nonharm and benefit? These issues are at the heart of the controversy over corporate social responsibility.

To gain a better understanding of corporate social responsibility, let's first examine the two basic premises of the concept. Then, we explore three perspectives of corporate social responsibility as well as a model for evaluating corporate social behavior.

KEY TERMS

Outsourcing
Using other companies to provide operations that were previously done inside the company.

Corporate social responsibility
The interaction between business and the social environment in which it exists. More specifically, the obligation that an organization has to society.

PREMISES OF CORPORATE SOCIAL RESPONSIBILITY

Many argue that the controversy over the responsibility of business is inevitable, given the moral and ethical challenges that corporate America has faced over the last several decades. Examples are plentiful of organizations acting "irresponsibly" in the eyes of some segment of society. Whether it involved a violation of worker-safety regulations, insufficient attention to product safety for consumers, or the relocation of a plant (and numerous jobs) to a foreign country with lower labor costs, corporate America has been besieged with accusations of social irresponsibility in recent years.

Corporate social responsibility has no doubt been discussed and debated for as long as there have been businesses, but one main piece of work that helps frame the discussions today was established by H. R. Bowen in the early 1950s. He proposed that businesses and managers have an obligation to "pursue those policies, to make those

Table 3.1 Four Perspectives of Social Responsibility

Type of Responsibility	Societal Expectation	Explanations
Economic	Required by society	Be profitable. Make sound strategic decisions. Provide adequate and attractive returns on investment.
Legal	Required by society	Obey all laws and regulations. Fulfill all contractual obligations. Honor warranties and guarantees.
Ethical	Expected by society	Avoid questionable practices. Respond to spirit as well as letter of law. Assume law is floor of behavior and operate above minimum required. Do what is right, fair, and just.
Philanthropic	Desired/expected by society	Be a good corporate citizen. Give back. Improve quality of life overall.

Source: From *Business and Society: Ethics and Stakeholder Management,* 6th ed. by Carroll/Buchholtz. © 2006. Reprinted with permission of South-Western, a division of Thomson Learning: http://www.thomsonrights.com. Fax 800-730-2215.

decisions, or to follow those lines of action that are desirable in terms of the objectives and values of our society."[5]

Bowen's assertions rest on two fundamental premises, social contract and moral agent, which can be summarized as follows:

- **Social contract.** Business exists at the pleasure of society, and as a result, it must comply with the guidelines established by society. An implied set of rights and obligations is inherent in social policy and assumed by business. This set of rights and obligations can be thought of as a social contract between business and society.
- **Moral agent.** Business must act in a way that is perceived as moral. In other words, business has an obligation to act honorably and to reflect and enforce values that are consistent with those of society. Furthermore, business can be held accountable as a moral agency.

These two premises have provided the foundation for the concept of social responsibility, but they have also served as targets for critics of the concept. In fact, there are several perspectives on social responsibility that differ mainly in their view of these two premises. Let's examine these perspectives in greater detail.

PERSPECTIVES OF SOCIAL RESPONSIBILITY

3 Four primary perspectives of corporate social responsibility have emerged over the years: economic responsibility, legal responsibility, ethical responsibility, and philanthropic responsibility.[6] The ethical responsibility perspective has been added to the other three only in recent times, reflecting the increased awareness of the effects of ethics. Table 3.1 outlines the bases of these perspectives. Each perspective views Bowen's two premises somewhat differently and, consequently, offers a different view of the concept of corporate social responsibility.[7]

LEARNING OBJECTIVE

Distinguish between the four perspectives of corporate social responsibility.

Economic Responsibility

Although many hold the **economic responsibility** perspective, one of its most outspoken proponents is Milton Friedman. Friedman maintains that the only social responsibility of business is to maximize profits within the "rules of the game." In his opinion, the only constituents to whom business is responsible are the stockholders, and it is the firm's responsibility to maximize the wealth of this constituent group. This is the only social contract to which business should be committed. If socially responsible behavior on the part of the corporation serves to reduce the financial return to the stockholders, the managers of the business have undermined the market mechanism for allocating resources and have violated the social contract of business as it should be in a free-market society.

KEY TERMS

Social contract
An implied set of rights and obligations that are inherent in social policy and assumed by business.

Moral agent
A business's obligation to act honorably and to reflect and enforce values that are consistent with those of society.

Economic responsibility
The perspective that says the social responsibility of an organization is to make profits and provide attractive returns on investment.

Proponents of the economic responsibility perspective also argue that corporations cannot be moral agents. Only individuals can serve as moral agents. When individuals choose to direct their own assets or resources toward the public good, that behavior is appropriate and to the benefit of society. However, when they begin to direct corporate resources toward that end, they have violated their commitment to the owners (that is, the stockholders) of those assets or resources.

Critics of the economic responsibility perspective argue that many of today's business organizations are not merely economic institutions and to view them as such is both unrealistic and naïve. Many large corporations wield significant political power and have tremendous influence on a wide variety of public policies and regulations across the globe. Examples of the enormous power and influence that some business have include General Electric (see "Meeting the Challenge" box), Airbus, Boeing, Procter and Gamble, Wal-Mart, and others. It is even suggested that Wal-Mart's influence is so strong that it affects wage levels, pricing, and many aspects of business in not only retail but also the entire economy and the world. Some of these effects are considered to be very positive, such as lower prices for consumers, jobs for many employees, and assisting many communities with various types of support. Others are considered very negative: driving some wages below the poverty level, squeezing profits out of suppliers, and lowering the profitability of entire industries.[8] Clearly, Wal-Mart and other companies have influence beyond just the economic.

Moreover, the activities of many corporations are essential to realizing important social goals such as equal opportunity, environmental protection, and increased global competitiveness in critical industries. Viewing the modern corporation as simply an economic institution is myopic and ignores the reality of the worldwide evolution of business.[9]

Legal Responsibility

Focusing almost exclusively on the social contract premise, proponents of **legal responsibility** argue that business should act in ways that are consistent with public policy. Rather than viewing public policy as simply the laws and regulations with which business must comply, supporters of this philosophy define public policy as "the broad pattern of social direction reflected in public opinion, emerging issues, formal legal requirements, and enforcement or implementation practices."[10] In other words, public policy refers to the overall perceptions and expectations of the public with regard to the interaction between business and society.

Some critics of the legal responsibility position argue that it tends to be applied too narrowly. If public responsibility means adhering to existing public policy, which is traditionally considered to be the laws and regulations of the legal system, then this perspective differs little from the economic perspective. Like the economic perspective, this view would imply only that business should comply with the "rules of the game." If, however, a broader view of public policy is assumed, the legal responsibility perspective begins to suggest some of the things in the ethical responsibility perspective.

KEY TERMS

Legal responsibility
The perspective that the social responsibility of an organization is to obey laws and public policy.

Ethical responsibility
The perspective that an organization should respond to the spirit as well as the letter of the law.

Ethical Responsibility

The perspective of **ethical responsibility** says that a business should engage in behavior and actions that not only meet the minimum requirements of law and public policy (the letter of the law) but also fulfill the "spirit of the law." Laws are normally considered to be the minimum or maximum that is expected or required by society. Ethical responsibility suggests that businesses tune into society and respond to or sometimes encourage major movements in society. Frequently, these major movements will lead to laws and official policy later.[11]

One example of decisions and behavior that are based on the perspective of ethical responsibility is related to pollution and gas mileage of vehicles. There are laws that require minimum estimated mileage for new cars. Some auto manufacturers have resisted and will continue to resist these minimum requirements. However, other automakers focus on not only producing cars that attain mileages much higher than the minimum required but also on engines that use alternative sources of energy and/or a hybrid engine. Honda and Toyota are the leaders in this area, but Ford also has a vehicle with a hybrid engine.[12]

Related to the example of going beyond the minimum requirements concerning things associated with pollution and use of fossil fuels is British Petroleum (BP). That company is running a series of advertisements that is highlighting the problem of pollution and alternative energies as one possible solution. Most people think that it is unusual for a fossil-fuels company (oil and gas) to be suggesting the development of fuels and energy sources that could reduce the use of fossil fuels. While working on alternative fuels and sources of energy because it is ethically responsible to do so may be an admirable thing, this also is related to BP's vision and strategy for the future. (See the chapters that discuss overall strategy and planning.)[13]

Certainly, the idea that a business might be engaged in certain actions for both a socially responsible and a profit motif concerns some people. They argue that if a

Table 3.2 Examples of Corporate Social Responsibility

Company	Actions
B.J. Communications, Inc. (public relations firm)	Encourages its employees to get involved in community; provides free services to nonprofit organizations.
Coca-Cola Co.	Uses recycled content in packaging, programs to reduce waste and increase efficiency.
De Beers	Contributes to efforts to fight HIV/AIDS.
Ford, Honda, Lexus, Toyota	Produce at least one vehicle that runs on a fuel-efficient, lower-polluting hybrid engine.
General Electric	Contributes money to Ghana and other countries for hospitals, water-treatment facilities, etc.
Jones Studio, Inc.	Designs environmentally friendly buildings.
Nissan	Donates money to the American Red Cross and matches employee contributions.
One World Health (nonprofit pharmaceutical company)	Markets drugs to developing countries.
People's Bank	Provides shelter and services to homeless people.
Shell Oil Co.	Uses many minority- and women-owned suppliers.
Starbucks	Works with coffee bean growers to encourage environmentally friendly practices.
Target Stores	Donates approximately $2 million per week to support medical research, literacy, and education.

Sources: "Corporate Volunteerism Awards Small Company: B.J. Communications," *Business Journal* (Phoenix, AZ), 9 May 2003, 29; E. Schrage, "Supply and the Brand," *Harvard Business Review* (June 2004): 20; J. Hempel, "Nonprofit Drugs for the Poor," *BusinessWeek,* 9 May 2005, 16; J. Snider, R. P. Hill, and D. Martin, "Corporate Social Responsibility in the 21st Century: A View from the World's Most Successful Firms," *Journal of Business Ethics* 48, no. 2 (December 2003): 175–188; L. Armstrong, "Are You Ready for a Hybrid?" *BusinessWeek,* 25 April 2005, 118–126; "People's Bank," *Fairfield County Business Journal,* 14 October 2002, 24; R. Bates, "De Beers Honored for AIDS Work," *Jewelers Circular Keystone,* August 2004, 42; Target Stores advertisement, *St. Louis Post-Dispatch,* 15 May 2005, A7; "Valley Forward Selects Honorees for Environmental Excellence," *Business Journal* (Phoenix, AZ), 15 September 2000, 8.

company does something that is profitable, then it does not really "qualify" as a socially responsible action.[14]

Philanthropic Responsibility

The fourth perspective of social responsibility is that of **philanthropic responsibility.** Proponents of this perspective argue that corporate social responsibility should not be simply an obligation on the part of business to meet the minimum expectations of society. Rather, modern corporations should proactively seek to act in ways that improve the welfare of society. Philanthropic responsibility implies a proactive and tangible effort to contribute to the well-being of society.

The philanthropic responsibility perspective also recognizes the moral agency aspect of corporate social responsibility. While proponents of this perspective agree with the economic responsibility proponents that morality is an individual rather than an organizational obligation, they maintain that the organization is responsible for creating and maintaining an environment in which moral behavior on the part of individual organizational members is encouraged and supported.

Many have endorsed the philanthropic perspective, arguing that profitability and social responsibility are not antagonistic concepts but rather are interdependent. In fact, some argue that there are several trends that are converging to shape a new social imperative in the 21st century. These trends include a deepening consumer conscience, an increase in socially conscious investing, more use of ecologically friendly "green" practices and products, and the growing impact of global media[15] (Table 3.2). Despite the increasing acceptance of or at

KEY TERMS

Philanthropic responsibility The perspective that organizations should be good corporate citizens; organizations should seek to improve the welfare of society.

least attention to the philanthropic perspective, however, this philosophy sparks some interesting and legitimate questions. One of the most pervasive has been the question of how much philanthropic responsibility is enough. At what point do the efforts of the organization come at the expense of profitability?

Evaluating the social behavior of organizations can be quite difficult given the diversity of perspectives regarding social responsibility. The following section describes one framework for evaluating the extent to which organizations demonstrate socially responsible behavior.

THE FOUR FACES OF SOCIAL RESPONSIBILITY

In a very general sense, an organization's social behavior can be categorized according to two dimensions: legality and responsibility. As illustrated in Figure 3.2, four combinations of legal and responsible behaviors are possible (1) legal/responsible, (2) legal/irresponsible, (3) illegal/responsible, and (4) illegal/irresponsible.[16]

Although one would hope that all organizations would operate in a legal and responsible manner, the evidence suggests otherwise. In fact, there are far too many examples of firms that have behaved in an illegal or irresponsible way. Why would a company choose to behave illegally or irresponsibly? Let's consider a situation where that might happen.

Suppose a manufacturing company has been notified of a new pollution regulation that will affect one of its plants. The cost of complying with the regulation is \$1.2 million, but the fine for failing to comply is \$125,000. Assume that the likelihood of being caught in noncompliance is 10%, and even if the organization is caught, there will be little publicity. Although noncompliance would be both illegal and irresponsible, a cost–benefit analysis might suggest that the organization not comply with the regulation. Is this an appropriate decision? Ideally, everyone would say that this is not an appropriate decision. It is irresponsible and illegal. Yet some companies facing such a situation might make that choice. When the penalty associated with breaking the law is less costly than complying with the law, an organization may make an inappropriate decision.

Look at the same idea applied to a personal action. Assuming that the speed limit on the highway was established on a very rational basis, then to drive above the speed limit is irresponsible behavior. Of course, it is illegal, by definition of "speed limit." Why might you engage in this illegal/irresponsible action?

Consider the other two quadrants in the model. Can you think of examples of organizations that have acted legally but irresponsibly? Illegally but responsibly? Under

Figure 3.2 The Four Faces of Social Responsibility

Legal/Responsible	Legal/Irresponsible
Illegal/Responsible	Illegal/Irresponsible

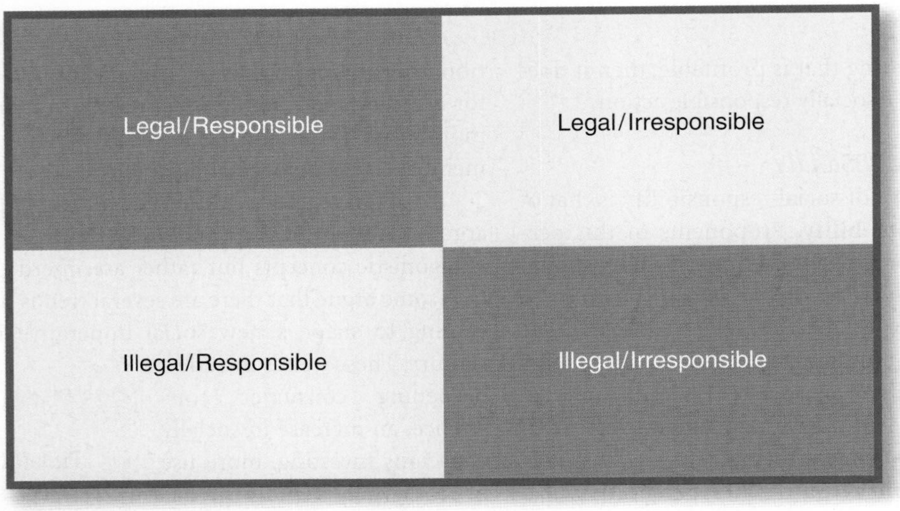

Source: Printed from *Business Horizons,* D. R. Dalton and R. A. Cosier, "The Four Faces of Social Responsibility." May/June 19–27, 1982 with permission from Elsevier.

what conditions might an organization choose to act in such ways? Consider the incidents profiled in Table 3.2. Do all of these incidents fall in the legal/responsible quadrant? Also consider these incidents from the four perspectives of social responsibility. Do some of the incidents fall into more than one perspective? Is it acceptable if an incident fits both the philanthropic and economic responsibility categories?

Organizations typically will behave in ways that are consistent with their overall strategy for responding to social issues. Social responsibility strategies may range from doing nothing to making an attempt to benefit society in tangible ways. The following section identifies four different strategies for social responsibility and examines reasons why an organization might choose a particular strategy.

Table 3.3 Approaches to Corporate Social Responsibility

Approach	Posture or Strategy	Performance
Reaction	Fight all the way.	Do less than required.
Defense	Do only what is required.	Do the least that is required.
Accommodation	Be progressive.	Do all that is required.
Proaction	Lead the industry.	Do more than required.

Source: Academy of Management Review, by Klimeski, Richard J. Copyright 1995 by Academy of Management. Reproduced with permission of Academy of Management in the format Textbook via Copyright Clearance Center.

SOCIAL RESPONSIBILITY APPROACHES

4 As we know, organizations take very different approaches to corporate social responsibility. Some organizations do little more than operate to ensure profitability for their stockholders, while others maintain aggressive and proactive social responsibility agendas. Table 3.3 illustrates a continuum of social responsibility strategies that range from being reactive to proactive. Four distinct approaches are identified along this continuum: reaction, defense, accommodation, and proaction.[17]

Reaction

An organization that assumes a **reaction** stance simply denies responsibility for its actions. There are two classic cases of that, both still controversial today, even after more than 50 years have passed. One is the case of asbestos; the other is tobacco.

Approximately 50 years ago, a company then known as Johns Manville, a large producer of asbestos, discovered evidence to suggest that asbestos inhalation causes a debilitating and often fatal lung disease. Rather than looking for ways to provide safer working conditions for company employees, the firm chose to conceal the evidence.

Why? That's hard to say, but evidence suggests that the company was more concerned about profitability than about the health and safety of its employees. Presumably, top executives at Manville thought it would be less costly to pay workers' compensation claims than to develop safer working conditions.

Manville's irresponsibility did not go without notice, however. Eventually, as a result of litigation, the company was forced to pay a $2.6 billion settlement, which forced a reorganization that left the company on very shaky ground. Stockholders lost 97.5% of

LEARNING OBJECTIVE 4

Identify and evaluate approaches for responding to social issues.

KEY TERMS

Reaction
An approach to corporate social responsibility that includes an organization denying responsibility for its actions.

The Enron Corporation has become a well-known touchstone for violating many dimensions of social and ethical responsibility.

their ownership of the company as a result of this and the resulting company, called Manville Corporation, has to make annual contributions to a trust fund set up for future claims.[18] To this day, people who believe they may have an ailment caused by exposure to asbestos continue to sue producers and sellers of products containing asbestos. This has gone far beyond just employees working with asbestos who claim damages. The situation now includes customers of products that contain asbestos.[19]

Tobacco was handled in a similar manner. Even though some cigarette producers had evidence over 50 years ago that nicotine in tobacco was addictive, they hid the evidence. As summarized in a claim by the U.S. Justice Department, "cigarette makers fraudulently denied the health risks and addictiveness of smoking, marketed to teens and falsely touted the benefits of light cigarettes."[20] Even after the landmark settlement between tobacco producers and most states in which tobacco companies agreed to pay billions of dollars over many years, there continues to be court cases related to smokers' health being damaged and to disagreements about the requirement of tobacco companies paying up to $10 billion over 25 years for smoking-cessation programs.[21]

Defense

Organizations that pursue a **defense** approach respond to social challenges only when it is necessary to defend their current position. They tend to admit responsibility but fight it.

Actually, most tobacco companies probably have moved from reaction to defense. Most have now admitted that nicotine is addictive, and some are cooperating with the requirements of the settlement mentioned above, including producing advertisements that suggest stopping smoking.[22] However, the actions tend to be the least that is required by the settlement.

Accommodation

Organizations using an **accommodation** approach to corporate social responsibility readily adapt their behaviors to comply with public policy and regulation where necessary and, more important, attempt to be responsive to public expectations.

Consider, for example, financial services companies that are required by regulation to disclose certain information. Although virtually every financial services company meets the minimum requirements of disclosure regulation, some companies maintain a more proactive code for voluntary, on-demand disclosure of appropriate information.[23]

Proaction

Organizations that assume a **proaction** approach to corporate social responsibility subscribe to the notion of philanthropic responsibility. They do not operate solely in terms of profit; nor do they consider compliance with public policy to be sufficient. These organizations proactively seek to improve the welfare of society. Here are a few examples. Since its beginning, McDonald's has helped sick children and their families through the Ronald McDonald Houses; Mary Kay Cosmetics focuses on women's health issues such as breast cancer; Target Stores supports medical research, literacy, education, and the arts through support of live-theater students; Ford, Honda, and Toyota all produce at least one vehicle with a hybrid engine, and other automakers are working on hybrid engines and/or fuel cells—both of which will increase gas mileage and produce fewer pollutants.[24] These are only a few examples of businesses that are attempting to better conditions overall. (See Table 3.2 for more examples.)

Which approach is the best? Should all organizations assume a proaction approach with respect to corporate social responsibility? Not necessarily.

Social Responsibility in the 21st Century

Evidence suggests a growing emphasis on social responsibility in the future. The issues surrounding asbestos, tobacco, global warming, outsourcing of jobs, the collapse of Enron and questionable actions of top-level managers in many other companies, and similar issues will only intensify the emphasis on social responsibility as employees, customers, and investors demand accountability from the actions of corporate leaders. Organizations that wish to attract socially conscious consumers know they must be socially conscious themselves if they are to meet the needs of those consumers.

Similarly, organizations that have invested in their communities and have demonstrated more socially responsible behaviors often find it easier to attract high-quality workers. All of this is summed up in *Fortune* mag-

KEY TERMS

Defense
An approach to corporate social responsibility that an organization takes only when it is necessary to defend its current position.

Accommodation
An approach to corporate social responsibility that adapts to public policy in doing more than the minimum required.

Proaction
An approach to corporate social responsibility that includes behaviors that improve society.

azine's "America's Most Admired Companies" because one of the eight categories used to select the companies is "Social Responsibility." Further, the rankings of the most admired companies are done by over 12,000 senior managers and other business and financial leaders. In addition, *Fortune*'s ranking of "The 100 Best Companies to Work For" and *BusinessWeek*'s selection of "The Best and Worst Managers of the Year" include management of people and overall evaluations that include various types and levels of corporate social responsibility.[25]

Social responsibility is important throughout the world. In England, there is the "Queen's Awards for Enterprise." This award not only shows the prevalence of social responsibility but also suggests the future in that the awards now include a category for "Sustainable Development" because "business as usual" is no longer acceptable or not sustainable. Sustainable development is defined as doing business in such a manner that new environmental, social, and economic demands are met.[26] In addition to "everything else," this does include making a profit. Similarly, the future of social responsibility, now commonly called corporate social responsibility, and conveniently referred to as CSR, tends to be seen by many as "business practices with a positive impact on People, Planet and Profit."[27] Notice the capital letters. We may be getting closer to what was suggested in 1984 in "The Ten Commandments of Corporate Social Responsibility,"[28] in Table 3.4.

Table 3.4 The Ten Commandments of Corporate Social Responsibility

- *I* Take corrective action before it is required. Compliance with self-imposed standards is almost always preferable to compliance with standards that are imposed by outside constituencies.
- *II* Work with affected constituents to resolve mutual problems.
- *III* Work to establish industry-wide standards and self-regulation.
- *IV* Publicly admit your mistakes. Few things are worse for a company's image than being caught trying to cover up socially irresponsible behavior.
- *V* Get involved in appropriate social programs.
- *VI* Help correct environmental problems.
- *VII* Monitor the changing social environment.
- *VIII* Establish and enforce a corporate code of conduct.
- *IX* Take needed public stands on social issues.
- *X* Strive to make profits on an ongoing basis. An organization cannot provide jobs and employ workers if it is not in a position to make consistent profits.

Source: L. Alexander and W. Mathews, "The Ten Commandments of Corporate Social Responsibility," *Business and Society Review*, 1984; 50, 62–66.

Now we turn our attention to ethics. A person's beliefs and values related to ethics influence the decisions and actions in which one engages in organizations and thereby influence the type and degree of corporate social responsibility.

Ethics

Ethics is everyone's business, from top-level managers to employees at the lowest levels of the organization. One of management's most important challenges is to conduct business ethically while achieving high levels of economic performance. Why ethical problems arise in business and what can be done about them are the issues that are addressed in this section.

UNDERSTANDING BUSINESS ETHICS

Would you "bend" the accounting rules to show higher revenue for your division when you are under strong pressure from your supervisor to increase sales? Should you pay a bribe to obtain a business contract in a foreign country? Is it acceptable to allow your company to dispose of hazardous waste in an unsafe fashion? Can you withhold information that might discourage a job candidate from joining your organization? Is it appropriate to engage in instant messaging with your friends while on company time? These are just a few examples of ethical and moral dilemmas that you probably will face at various times during your career in an organization.

Ethical behavior has always been important, but the many high-profile cases that occurred over the last several years keep concern about ethical behavior in the news. Damage is still being repaired from the more notorious cases of unethical behavior at Enron, WorldCom, Tyco, Arthur Andersen, and Adelphia Communications (see the "Leaders in Action" Box.). The managers and companies involved are still being discussed in attempts to learn more about ethical and unethical behavior and what tends to influence it.[29] Let's now explore more about ethics.

Ethics reflect established customs and morals and fundamental human relationships that may vary throughout the world. Often ethical issues are controversial because they

KEY TERMS

Ethics
Reflects established customs and morals.

Leaders in Action

Cleaning Up Adelphia Communications

Adelphia Communications Corporation was an important player in the cable television business, even as it prepared to exit bankruptcy protection. That exit included an agreement to sell itself to Time Warner Inc. and Comcast Corporation.

Imagine being the person who is in charge of cleaning up the huge mess left by the founder, John Rigas, and his son, Timothy. They were accused and convicted of stealing billions of dollars from the company by using fraudulent accounting practices and doing many things that were certainly unethical; many were illegal. The offenses were so serious that prosecutors in the case requested sentences of 215 years. Eighty-year-old John received a 15-year sentence; Timothy received a 20-year sentence.

Vanessa Wittman signed on to be chief financial officer of Adelphia several years ago. Her job was to prepare the company to emerge from bankruptcy protection. In doing so, she had to deal with the Securities and Exchange Commission (SEC), the Justice Department, and angry shareholders and creditors, all the while trying to understand all the fraudulent accounting that had taken place under the management of the Rigases.

By all accounts, she did an admirable job. She quickly arranged an operating budget that was the foundation for a line of credit of $1.5 billion. This was needed to keep the cable lines in good and upgraded condition to retain their value during constant fierce competition. Wittman negotiated a financial settlement of $725 million with the SEC and the Justice Department to settle claims of accounting fraud. During her 16-hour days, in addition to everything else, she supervised 100 accountants who sifted through 7 million entries to prepare new and accurate accounting statements.

Because the major parts of the company have been sold as a result of the exit from bankruptcy protection, what does someone like Vanessa Wittman do next? With her previous experience at Andersen Consulting, Morgan Stanley, Microsoft, and a few other companies, she certainly will be a valuable manager for many companies. Or, perhaps she may take on the assignment to "clean up the mess" at another company in bankruptcy or other trouble. In recent years, major breaches in ethical behavior have created companies in that condition.

Sources: D. Searcey and L. Yuan, "Adelphia's John Rigas Gets 15 Years," *Wall Street Journal*, 21 June 2005, A3. P. Grant and S. Young, "Federal Prosecutors Request 215-Year Sentences for Rigases," *Wall Street Journal*, 13 June 2005, C4; T. Lowry, "The CFO behind Adelphia's Rescue," *BusinessWeek*, 11 April 2005, 68–69.

raise emotional questions of right and wrong behaviors. For our purposes, we define **ethical behavior** as behavior that is morally accepted as "good" and "right" as opposed to "bad" or "wrong" in a particular setting. Right behavior is considered ethical behavior, and wrong behavior is considered unethical. Corporate executives are concerned with business ethics because they want their companies to be perceived as "good" and "right" in their interactions with stakeholders. In many cases, the goal is to avoid illegal or unethical corporate behavior leading to adverse governmental or societal reactions such as warnings, recalls, injunctions, monetary or criminal penalties, adverse public opinion, or loss of contracts.[30]

In the business world, however, the difference between right and wrong behavior is not always clear—particularly when organizations are operating in an international, multicultural environment.[31] Although many unethical behaviors are illegal in the United States, some may be within the limits of the law in other countries. The three international ethical issues that have been subject to the greatest scrutiny by the media, government, and other social agencies are corruption (for example, bribery and improper payments), inadequate labor conditions, and environmental responsibility.[32] For many years, international social activists have been calling for U.S. corporations to develop global codes of ethics that would be applied in all international markets. Recent surveys suggest that U.S. companies have moved boldly in that direction, developing global ethical principles to guide their overseas organizations.[33]

KEY TERMS

Ethical behavior
Behavior that is morally accepted as good or right as opposed to bad or wrong.

Foundations of Ethics

Although ethical behavior in business does reflect social and cultural factors, it is also highly personal and is shaped by an individual's own values and experiences. In your daily life, you face situations in which you can make ethical or unethical decisions. You make your choices based on what you have learned from parents, family, teachers, peers, friends, and so forth. From what you have learned, you developed a set of values that influence your ethical decisions.

5 **Values** are the relatively permanent and deeply held preferences of individuals or groups; they are the basis on which attitudes and personal choices are formed. Values are among the most stable and enduring characteristics of individuals. Much of what we are is a product of the basic values that we have developed throughout our lives. An organization, too, has a value system, usually referred to as its organizational culture. (We discuss organizational culture in more detail in Chapter 10.)

To better understand the role of values as the foundation for ethical behavior, let's look at a basic values framework. Rokeach developed a values framework and identified two general types of values: instrumental values and terminal values.[34] **Instrumental values,** also called means-oriented values, prescribe desirable standards of conduct or methods for attaining an end. Examples of instrumental values include ambition, courage, honesty, and imagination. **Terminal values**, also called ends-oriented values, prescribe desirable ends or goals for the individual and reflect what a person is ultimately striving to achieve. Terminal values are either personal (such as peace of mind) or social (such as world peace). Examples of terminal values are a comfortable life, family security, self-respect, and a sense of accomplishment.

Although values are an individual characteristic, there are some similarities between members of groups. For example, business school students and professors tend to rate ambition, capability, responsibility, and freedom higher than do people in general. They tend to place less importance than the general public on concern for others, helpfulness, aesthetics, cultural values, and overcoming social injustice.[35] In most cases, the ethical standards and social responsibility of an organization or business reflect the personal values and ideals of the organization's founders or dominant managers.[36] Over the years, those values and ideals become institutionalized and become integral to the organization's culture. For example, Herb Kelleher's personal values and ethics formed the basis of the culture of Southwest Airlines.[37] Bill Gates set the foundation for the culture at Microsoft. At Wal-Mart, the influence of its founder, Sam Walton, continues to strongly influence the company years after Sam Walton passed away.[38] In each case, these individuals were the source of their organizations' experiences, values, and principles. They were the behavioral role models for the organizations' ethical behavior and commitment to social responsibility.

An organization's culture and the practices of its senior managers can influence the ethical behavior of not only its employees but also other individuals and entities associated with the organization. Therefore, the challenge facing an organization is how to successfully develop, sustain, review, and adapt its ethical standards and its commitment to socially responsible behavior.[39]

LEARNING OBJECTIVE

Explain what values are, how they form the basis of an individual's ethical behavior, and how they may vary in a global business environment.

Business Ethics

Business ethics is not a special set of ethical rules that differ from ethics in general. **Business ethics** is the application of the general ethical rules to business behavior. If a society deems dishonesty to be unethical, then anyone in business who is dishonest with employees, customers, creditors, stockholders, or competition is acting unethically.

Businesses pay attention to ethics because the public expects a business to exhibit reasonable levels of ethical performance and social responsibility. Many ethical rules operate to protect society against various types of harm, and business is expected to observe these ethical principles. High ethical standards also protect the individuals who work in an organization. Employees resent invasions of privacy, being ordered to do something against their personal convictions, or working under hazardous conditions. Normally, businesses that treat their employees with dignity and integrity gain rewards in the form of improved productivity. People feel good about working for an ethical company because they know they are protected along with the general public. In contrast, most employees do not feel good about working for companies that demonstrate unethical behaviors.

LEARNING OBJECTIVE

Describe how advances in information technology have created new ethical challenges.

6 Recent improvements in information technology have raised new issues with regard to business ethics. From an employee perspective, concerns about information privacy have escalated in recent years, as business organizations and government agencies have gained greater access to private information about individuals.[40] From an organizational perspective, unethical acts by employees are increasing as a result of access to information technology in the workplace. In fact, according to a recent study conducted by International Communication Research, nearly half of

KEY TERMS

Values
Relatively permanent and deeply held preferences upon which individuals form attitudes and personal choices.

Instrumental value
A standard of conduct or method for attaining an end.

Terminal value
A goal an individual will ultimately strive to achieve.

Business ethics
The application of general ethics to business behavior.

American workers engaged in unethical behavior as a result of technology. Such behaviors include accessing personal files, sabotaging data, and using the computer for personal reasons.[41] Another area of concern raised by sophisticated information technology relates to businesses providing customer information to other organizations. Such concerns have led some companies to publicly express their promise to protect their customers' privacy.[42]

Pressures to Perform

In the past few years, the negative and questionable ethical practices of many public figures and corporations have attracted considerable media attention. Many such incidents have been mentioned in Chapter 1 and earlier in this chapter. Because of pressure to keep the price of the stock up or to keep revenues rising, managers have "bent" various accounting rules or simply broke them to please stockholders. Another reason why managers may have done these things is because they could gain very large bonuses by increasing revenues or the price of the stock.

LEARNING OBJECTIVE 7

Identify and discuss the differences in the utility, human rights, and justice approaches to ethical dilemmas.

Unethical behavior is often blamed on the emphasis on materialism as well as on economic and competitive pressures to perform. In today's environment of intense competition, some have even questioned whether ethics is a liability that limits an organization's ability to succeed. Yet, most would agree that good ethics makes good business sense. In fact, long-term costs to unethical behavior can have very negative consequences for any organization.[43]

The pressures to perform are nowhere more evident than in the sports industry. Coaches often feel pressure from demanding fans and/or owners—so much so that they are tempted to "bend the rules" to ensure a winning season. But according to Penn State University head football coach Joe Paterno, that's just not necessary. Despite a few less than stellar records in recent years for Coach Paterno's teams, he is still widely known for having winning teams and for maintaining a highly principled football program. He is up front with all players about his personal commitment to do the right thing in each and every circumstance. For many years, Coach Paterno's "investments" in a solid ethical environment in his football program have earned his teams tremendous respect from fans and others.

Managers must continually choose between maximizing the economic performance of the organization (as indicated by revenues, costs, profits, and so forth) and improving its social performance (as indicated by obligations to customers, employees, suppliers, and others). Many ethical trade-offs are conflicts between these two desirable ends—economic versus social performance. Making decisions in such situations is not merely a matter of choosing between right and wrong or between good and bad. Most of the alternatives are not so clear-cut. Individuals who effectively manage these ethical trade-offs have a clear sense of their own values and the values of their organization. They have developed their own internal set of universal, comprehensive, and consistent principles upon which to base their decisions.

KEY TERMS

Ethical dilemma
A situation in which a person must decide whether or not to do something that, although benefiting oneself or the organization, may be considered unethical and perhaps illegal.

Utility approach
A situation in which decisions are based on an evaluation of the overall amount of good that will result.

MANAGERIAL GUIDELINES FOR ETHICAL DILEMMAS

7 An **ethical dilemma** is a situation in which a person must decide whether to do something that, although beneficial to oneself or the organization or both, may be considered unethical. Ethical dilemmas are common in the workplace. In fact, research suggests that managers encounter such dilemmas in their working relationships with supervisors, subordinates, customers, competitors, suppliers, and regulators. Common issues underlying the dilemmas include honesty in communications and contracts, gifts and entertainment, kickbacks, pricing practices, and employee terminations.

Organizations need a set of guidelines for thinking about ethical dilemmas. These guidelines can help managers and employees identify the nature of the ethical problem and decide which course of action is the most likely to produce the most ethical results. The following three approaches—utility, human rights, and justice—provide managerial guidelines for handling ethical dilemmas.

Utility Approach

The **utility approach** emphasizes the overall amount of good that can be produced by an action or a decision. It judges actions, plans, and policies by their consequences. The primary objective of this approach is to provide the greatest good for the greatest number of people. It is often referred to as a cost–benefit analysis because it compares the costs and benefits of a decision, a policy, or an action. These costs and benefits can be economic (expressed in dollars), social (the effect on society at large),

Child labor in countries outside the United States presents a serious human rights dilemma. The degree to which human rights are protected and promoted is an important ethical benchmark for judging the behavior of individuals and organizations.

or human (usually a psychological or emotional impact). This type of results-oriented ethical reasoning tries to determine whether the overall outcome produces more good than harm—in other words, more utility, or usefulness, than negative results. The utility approach supports the ethical issues of profit maximization, self-interest, rewards based on abilities and achievements, sacrifice and hard work, and competition.[44]

The main drawback to the utility approach is the difficulty of accurately measuring both costs and benefits. For example, some things, such as goods produced, sales, payrolls, and profits, can be measured in monetary terms. Other items, such as employee morale, psychological satisfactions, and the worth of human life, do not easily lend themselves to monetary measurement. Another limitation of the utility approach is that those in the majority may override the rights of those in the minority.

Despite these limitations, cost–benefit analysis is widely used in business. If benefits (earnings) exceed costs, the organization makes a profit and is considered to be an economic success. Because this method uses economic and financial outcomes, managers sometimes rely on it to decide important ethical questions without being fully aware of its limitations or the availability of other approaches that may improve the ethical quality of decisions. One of these alternative approaches is the impact of the decisions on human rights.

Human Rights Approach

The **human rights approach** is a second method for handling ethical dilemmas. This approach to ethics holds that human beings have certain moral entitlements that should be respected in all decisions. These entitlements guarantee an individual's most fundamental personal rights (life, freedom, health, privacy, and property, for example). These have been spelled out in such documents as the U.S. Bill of Rights and the United Nations Declaration of Human Rights.[45] A right means that a person or group is entitled to something or is entitled to be treated in a certain way. The most basic human rights are those claims or entitlements that enable a person to survive, make free choices, and realize his or her potential as a human being. Denying those rights to other persons and groups or failing to protect their rights is considered to be unethical. Respecting others, even those with whom we disagree or whom we dislike, is the essence of human rights, provided that others do the same for us.

The human rights approach to ethical dilemmas holds that individuals are to be treated as valuable ends in themselves simply because they are human beings. Using others for your own purposes is unethical if, at the same time, you deny them their rights to their own goals and purposes. For example, an organization that denies female employees an opportunity to bid for all jobs for which they are qualified is depriving them of some of their rights.

The main limitation on using the human rights approach as a basis for ethical decisions is the difficulty of balancing conflicting rights. For example, using a polygraph test to evaluate an employee's honesty to protect the organization's financial responsibilities may be at odds with the employee's right to privacy. Rights also clash when U.S. multinational corporations move production to a foreign nation, causing job losses at home while creating new jobs abroad. In such cases, whose job rights should be protected?

The degree to which human rights are protected and promoted is an important ethical benchmark for judging the behavior of individuals and organizations. Most people would agree that the denial of a person's fundamental rights to life, freedom, privacy, growth, and human dignity is generally unethical. Thus, the protection of such rights becomes a common denominator for making ethical decisions.[46]

Justice Approach

A third method of ethical decision-making concerns justice.

KEY TERMS

Human rights approach
A situation in which decisions are made in light of the moral entitlements of human beings.

Now Apply It

Ethics in the Workplace

Ethics in the workplace is a critical issue that affects all employees. The following three scenarios highlight specific potential ethical issues. As you read these scenarios, consider how you might react.

Scenario 1 John is a production manager at a toy-manufacturing plant. In his role, he selects vendors for a number of the materials used in the production process. You know that John usually picks suppliers with whom he has a good relationship, even when they are not the lowest bidder. Most recently, you have noticed that a very large purchase was made from a vendor that regularly hosts John at the local pro-basketball games. You know another vendor has a significantly lower price, and you wonder whether John's decisions are biased. When you ask him about it, he explains that having a good relationship with your supplier ensures good-quality service, which is more important than price.

Scenario 2 Janice travels frequently for her company, and, because she is a bit disorganized, maintaining accurate expense records has never been her strength. She tends to tuck receipts in her suit pockets, briefcase, bag, or even books she may be carrying. Many of the receipts (especially those from taxi drivers) are blank because Janice has failed to note the amount of her expenditure at the time she made it. Janice turns in her receipts sporadically, guessing at the expenditures she has made. You, as her office mate, note the sloppy fashion in which Janice reports her expenses and bring it to her attention. Janice responds by saying that she is sure that it all balances out in the end.

Scenario 3 Robert is the equivalent of a "class clown" in the office. He is always telling jokes, playing silly pranks, and otherwise entertaining the office staff. While most of Robert's antics are harmless, he occasionally tells ethnic jokes that could be offensive to others. When you mention this to Robert, he tells you to "lighten up." No one else in the office seems to be offended.

Under the **justice approach,** decisions are based on an equitable, fair, and impartial distribution of benefits (rewards) and costs among individuals and groups. Justice is essentially a condition characterized by an equitable distribution of the benefits and burdens of working together, according to some accepted rule. For society as a whole, social justice means that a society's income and wealth are distributed among the people in fair proportions.[47]

A common question is, Is it fair or just? For example, employees want to know whether pay scales are fair; consumers are interested in fair prices when they shop. When new tax laws are proposed, there is much debate about their fairness: Where will the burden fall, and will all taxpayers pay their fair share? Using the justice approach, the organization considers who pays the costs and who gets the benefits. If the shares seem fair, then the action is probably just.

Determining what is just and what is unjust can be a complex issue, especially if the stakes are high. Because distributive rules usually grant privileges to some groups based on tradition and custom, sharp inequalities between groups can generate social tensions and clamorous demands for a change to a fairer system.

KEY TERMS

Justice approach
A situation in which decisions are based on an equitable, fair, and impartial distribution of benefits and costs among individuals and groups.

As with the utilitarian approach, a major limitation of the justice approach is the difficulty of measuring benefits and costs precisely. Another limitation is that many of society's benefits and burdens are intangible, emotional, and psychological. People unfairly deprived of life's opportunities may not willingly accept their condition. Few people, even those who are relatively well off, are ever entirely satisfied with their share of society's wealth. For these reasons, the use of the justice approach can be tricky. Although everyone is intensely interested in being treated fairly, many are skeptical that justice will ever be fully realized. Despite these drawbacks, the justice approach to ethical dilemmas can still be applied in many business situations.

FOSTERING IMPROVED BUSINESS ETHICS

More and more organizations are recognizing that their culture and values are affecting how people at all levels behave and how they make decisions. The predominant belief is that a manager's leadership will influence behaviors of people in the organization, either positive or negative. Managers must become the ethics leaders in their organizations.[48]

To foster improved business ethics in an organization, action must be directed at five levels: the international, societal, association, organizational, and individual levels. The most fundamental effort is directed at the individual.

Agreements among nations help foster ethical behavior at the international level. Laws established by international governing bodies such as the World Trade Organization and the United Nations help shape ethical behavior across nations. Nongovernmental organizations (NGOs) also play an important role in promoting ethical behavior on a global basis. NGOs are nonprofit, voluntary citizens' groups that are organized on a local, national, or international level to address international issues. You can learn more about NGOs and their activities by visiting http://www.ngo.org.

Societal ethics are fostered to the extent that laws and regulations discourage unethical behavior, and systems exist for recognizing and rewarding behaviors that epitomize strong ethical values. For example, the Foreign Corrupt Practices Act governs the actions of U.S. firms engaged in international business activities. Award programs, such as the Business Ethics Award given annually by the Center for Business Ethics at Bentley College, help reinforce the value of ethical behavior within our society.

At the association level, groups can join together and establish codes of ethics for their industry or profession and provide mechanisms for monitoring and disciplining members who violate the code. For example, the Society of Professional Journalists, an organization of 13,500 people involved in journalism, has developed a code of ethics that provides guidance for journalists across the world. Not only has the association established such a code, but it also invites online debate about proposed changes to the code. This debate has evolved to include discussions of both real and hypothetical ethical issues in the journalism profession.

At the organizational level, improving business ethics requires leaders who can model the expected ethical behavior, set realistic goals for workers, and encourage ethical behavior by providing an organizational environment that rewards such behavior and punishes violators. Leadership is perhaps the most important ingredient in developing an ethical organizational culture.

At the individual level, the challenge for organizations is to develop employees' awareness of business ethics (Table 3.5) as well as to help them confront complex ethical issues. Employees find it helpful when their organization publicly announces what it believes in and expects in terms of employee behavior.[49]

In the next section, we examine two of the most common ways in which organizations foster ethical behavior: (1) creating codes of conduct and (2) developing ethics-training programs. In general, such activities must reflect relevant employee concerns and must be tailored to specific needs and value statements.

Table 3.5 Developing Employee Awareness of Ethics

1. Enable the ethical component of a decision to be recognized.
2. Legitimize the consideration of ethics as part of decision making.
3. Avoid variability in decision making caused by lack of awareness of rules or norms.
4. Avoid ambivalence in decision making caused by an organizational reward system that psychologically pulls a person in opposite directions.
5. Avoid ambivalence in decision making caused by confusion as to who is responsible for misdeeds, particularly when the employee has received an order from a superior.
6. Provide decision-making frameworks for analyzing ethical choices and helping employees to apply such frameworks.

Source: Academy of Management: The Thinking Manager's Source by S.J. Harrington. Copyright 1991 by Academy of Management. Reproduced with permission of Academy of Management in the Textbook via Copyright Clearance Center.

LEARNING OBJECTIVE 8

Explain the methods used by organizations to encourage ethical organizational behavior.

Codes of Ethics

8 A **code of ethics** describes the general value system, ethical principles, and specific ethical rules that a company tries to apply. It can be an effective way to encourage ethical business behavior and raise an organization's standards of ethical performance. Such a document may be called a code of ethics, code of conduct, credo, declaration of business principles, statement of core values, or something similar.

In response to the ethical problems that have been arising in the United States, many companies and professional societies are now publishing codes of conduct. In fact, about 90% of Fortune 500 firms and almost half of all other firms have ethics codes.[50]

Typically, a code of ethics covers a wide range of issues and potential problem areas that an organization and its members may encounter. It is a set of carefully articulated statements of ethical principles rooted in the organization's goals, objectives, organizational history, and traditions. A code contains explicit statements and precepts intended to guide both the organization and its employees in their professional

KEY TERMS

Code of ethics
The general value system, principles, and specific rules that a company follows.

At the Forefront

Guides to Organization Behavior

Below are statements from the websites of two companies. Do you think that these statements are good guides to behavior that would be profitable, socially responsible, and ethical, all at the same time?

Bristol Technology
(http://www.bristol.com/careers/)

"Bristol's Core Values

- Earn profits and respect.
- Show respect for fellow Bristolites.
- Create a superior work environment.
- Spend company money wisely.
- Think BIG, be aggressive, and win!"

"We look to hire 'the best.' The attributes we think are most important are:

- Intelligence
- A Sense of Urgency
- Integrity"

Southwest Airlines (http://www.southwest.com/about_swa/mission.html)

"The Mission of Southwest Airlines

The mission of Southwest Airlines is dedication to the highest quality of Customer Service delivered with a sense of warmth, friendliness, individual pride, and Company Spirit."

"To Our Employees

We are committed to provide Employees a stable work environment with equal opportunity for learning and personal growth. Creativity and innovation are encouraged for improving the effectiveness of Southwest Airlines. Above all, Employees will be provided the same concern, respect, and caring attitude within the organization that they are expected to share externally with every Southwest Customer."

behavior. A code helps employees know what is expected when they face uncertain ethical situations. It becomes the basis for establishing continuity and uniformity in managerial action and can be a unifying force that holds the organization together so that its employees can act in a cohesive and socially responsible manner. (See the "At the Forefront" box.)

An organization's code of ethics can serve several purposes. First, it creates employee awareness that ethical issues need to be considered in making business decisions. Second, it demonstrates that the organization is fully committed to stating its standards and incorporating them into daily activities. Third, a code can contribute to transforming an "us–them" relationship between the organization and its employees into an "us–us" relationship.[51] A code's impact on employee behavior is weakened if the code's purpose is primarily to make the company look good or if it is intended to give the company's top executives a legal defense when illegal or unethical acts are committed by lower-ranking employees.

A code of ethics can resemble a set of regulations ("Our employees will not . . ."), aspirations ("Our employees should . . ."), or factual statements ("Our organization is committed to . . ."), but all effective codes appear to share at least three characteristics:

1. They generally govern activities that cannot be supervised closely enough to ensure compliance.
2. They ask more of employees than would otherwise be expected.
3. They can serve the long-term interest of the organization.

In today's global business environment, a growing number of organizations are establishing global ethics codes. Companies such as Shell, Sara Lee Corporation, and General Electric have led the way in developing comprehensive codes of ethics that are disseminated on a worldwide basis. Table 3.6 outlines the major issues addressed by a majority of global codes of ethics.

Table 3.6 Subjects Addressed by a Majority of Global Codes of Ethics

- Bribery/improper payments
- Conflict of interest
- Security of proprietary information
- Receiving gifts
- Discrimination/equal opportunity
- Giving gifts
- Environment
- Sexual harassment
- Antitrust
- Workplace safety
- Political activities
- Community relations
- Confidentiality of personal information
- Human rights
- Employee privacy
- Whistle-blowing
- Substance abuse
- Nepotism
- Child labor

Source: R. Berenbeim, "Global Corporate Ethics Practices," *Conference Board Research Report,* 121243-99-RR, 1999.

Merck & Company has been particularly aggressive with regard to developing a comprehensive and relevant code of ethics. The company has long subscribed to a belief that core values and an adherence to the highest standards of ethical behavior are key to global success, and Merck is committed to ensuring that the company culture reflects this philosophy. How did the company achieve this? First, the company conducted an organizational analysis that involved participation of over 10,000 employees in 21 countries. Based on the feedback from the interviews and surveys of these employees, an ethics code was drafted. The final document, which was translated into 22 languages, was tested with focus groups in each major geographic region of the company. Ultimately, the company's code was distributed to employees across the globe, who simultaneously participated in ethics training. Key to Merck's success was ensuring that the code was embraced by the leadership of the company. By selecting leaders throughout the organization and across the globe who subscribe to and support fully its core values and code of ethics, Merck has created an organizational culture that is based on ethical standards.[52] After the many questionable practices by various managers at Citigroup related to helping companies such as Enron and WorldCom hide questionable and illegal practices, Chuck Prince, CEO, is attempting a similar approach to improve ethical behavior at Citigroup.[53]

Ethics statements and social responsibility policies are not sufficient by themselves to cause people to behave in a socially responsible manner. A 20-page policy statement by General Dynamics failed to prevent a widespread lapse in ethical conduct involving government contracts. The real challenge for top-level management is to create an environment that sustains, promotes, and develops ethical behavior and a commitment to social responsibility. The effort must begin at the highest levels of the organization. Unless top-level management, beginning with the CEO, provides leadership, commitment, and role modeling, no organization can hope to attain high ethical standards or consistently behave in a socially responsible manner. Top-level management must also ensure that the organization's expectations of ethical behavior and social responsibility are clearly conveyed to its employees and to all parties involved with the organization—that is, the stakeholders. This requires extensive communication among all parties and the establishment of systems within the organization to reinforce ethical behavior.[54]

Ethics Training Programs

9 Many organizations and associations provide ethics training for employees. In fact, a recent Conference Board report suggests that 78% of companies that have an ethics code reinforce it with ethics training.[55] The combination of a widely distributed code of ethics and comprehensive ethics training for all employees can greatly enhance the ethical environment within an organization.

LEARNING OBJECTIVE 9

Describe the different approaches used in ethics-training programs.

The reasons for ethics training vary widely from organization to organization. Some of the most prominent reasons include avoiding adverse publicity, potential lawsuits, illegal behavior, and monetary and criminal penalties. Many organizations also use ethics training to gain a strategic advantage, increase employee awareness of ethics in business decision making, and help employees become more attentive to ethical issues to which they may be exposed.[56]

Ethics-training programs have been shown to help employees avoid rationalizations often used to legitimize unethical behavior. Among the rationalizations often advanced to justify organizational misconduct are believing that (1) the activity is not really illegal or immoral, (2) it is in the individual's or the corporation's best interest, (3) it will never be found out, or (4) the company will condone it because it helps the company.

Ethics-training programs can help managers clarify their ethical framework and practice self-discipline when making decisions in difficult circumstances. Hershey Foods, General Electric, and Abbott Laboratories are among the prominent companies with training programs for managers, supervisors, and anyone else likely to encounter an ethical question at work.[57]

The content and approach of ethics-training programs may differ depending on the organization's goals. Case studies, often specific to the business functions of the organization's audience, are the most widely used approach. Other popular approaches include presenting rules or guidelines for deciding ethical issues (such as the Golden Rule or the utilitarian approach), developing a checklist to aid managers in making ethical decisions, or using cognitive approaches that attempt to develop higher levels of ethical understanding such as the one shown in Table 3.7.[58]

LEARNING OBJECTIVE

Discuss what is meant by whistle-blowing in monitoring ethical behavior.

Whistle-Blowing

10 One method of evaluating the ethical conviction of the organization is to observe its approach to professional dissent or, as it is more commonly called, whistle-blowing. **Whistle-blowing** occurs when an insider reports alleged organizational misconduct to the public. A whistle-blower is someone who exposes organi-

KEY TERMS

Whistle-blowing
Reporting alleged organizational misconduct or wrongdoing to the public.

Table 3.7 A Manager's Guide for Developing a Strong Ethics Policy

1. Develop a written policy on ethics and communicate it regularly to your employees.
2. Make sure that all employees understand the policies and procedures in place for determining ethical behavior.
3. Establish fair and consistent rules for disciplining violators.
4. Develop and continually monitor audit systems to prevent and detect violations of the law or corporate policy.
5. Create a safe environment where employees can report suspected violations anonymously without fear of retribution.
6. Allow those accused of violating ethics policies the opportunity to explain or defend their behavior.

zational wrongdoing in order to preserve ethical standards and protect against wasteful, harmful, or illegal acts.

Whistle-blowing has become a staple on the front pages of newspapers and magazines and an all-too-frequent segment on *60 Minutes*.[59] An employee—or, more often, a former employee—of a big corporation or government agency goes public with charges that the organization has been playing dirty. The next step is a lawsuit that sets out the details of the misconduct and charges that the whistle-blower was at best ignored and at worst harassed, demoted, or fired.

Doubtless, some whistle-blower suits are brought by employees with an ax to grind or who see an opportunity for large monetary gain. For example, under the False Claims Act, whistle-blowers can receive up to 25% of any money recovered by the government from a business that has gained it illegally in transactions with the government. A classic case that illustrates the magnitude of potential payoffs for whistle-blowers was that of Christopher M. Urda. Urda was awarded $7.5 million in July 1992 for providing evidence that his - employer, then a unit of Singer Corporation, cheated the Pentagon out of $77 million in the 1980s.[60]

Generally, employees are not free to speak out publicly against their employers because there is an expectation that organizational problems are handled internally. Organizations face countless ethical issues and internal conflicts in their daily operations. Choices must be made where there are differing opinions and beliefs. Mistakes are made and waste does occur, but usually corrective action is taken.

Although whistle-blowing typically exposes unethical practices, how it is done and how it is handled may also be ethically questionable. The costs of whistle-blowing are high for both the company and the whistle-blower. The company's reputation is damaged whether it wins or loses, which can create considerable internal conflict. The company spends much time and money defending itself and may damage general employee morale by seeming to be unsympathetic to legitimate concerns expressed by employees. The whistle-blower also suffers. Many times, whistle-blowers are subject to retaliatory action by disgruntled employers, and they often are blackballed for not being team players. Even if the whistle-blower wins, the costs can be high: legal expenses, mental anguish, ostracism by former coworkers, or a damaged career.

To avoid the costs for both the company and the employee but to encourage reports of serious wrongdoing, many companies have become more receptive to employee complaints. Some organizations have established regular procedures for professional dissent, such as hotlines that employees can use to report dangerous or questionable company practices or the use of ombudspersons who can act as neutral judges and negotiators when supervisors and employees disagree over a policy or practice. These things are being done because most observers of wrongdoing do not report it.[61] Confidential questionnaires are another device to encourage potential whistle-blowers to report their concerns before they become a big issue. In these ways, progressive companies attempt to lessen the tensions between the company and its employees and maintain the confidence and trust between them.

Anonymous reporting of financial wrongdoing is actually a requirement of the Sarbanes–Oxley legislation.[62] It does appear to be working well because the number of complaints of wrongdoing to the Department of Labor are those protected by Sarbanes–Oxley.[63]

Table 3.8 shows a model whistle-blower policy developed by the Conference Board.[64] The policy can work if managers emphasize that ethics is more than an ideal statement. Employees must have confidence in the company's ethics system and believe that exposing internal wrongdoing is part of their job. Whistle-blowers who raise real issues should be rewarded.[65] Whatever technique is used, it should permit individuals to expose unethical practices or lapses in socially responsible behavior without disrupting the organization.

There are several well-known cases of whistle-blowers in recent years. One is Sherron Watkins, then a vice president at Enron, who wrote a letter to the chairman, Ken Lay, in which she said, "I am incredibly nervous that we will implode in a wave of accounting scandals."[66] Of course, that is exactly what happened. A second noteworthy whistle-blower is Cynthia Cooper, an internal auditor at WorldCom. She found $3.8 billion of "accounting irregularities" in WorldCom's books and reported it to the Board of Directors. One month later, that company filed for bankruptcy protection.[67] Finally, Coleen Rowley made a public statement that high-ranking managers of the FBI did not pay attention to clear evidence that could have predicted the 9/11 terrorist attacks. *Time* magazine named these three people "Persons of the Year" for 2002.[68]

Does Socially Responsible and Ethical Behavior Pay?

There has been research over the years on this question. Several studies report a positive statistical correlation between socially responsible and/or ethical behaviors and financial performance of companies. A few studies suggest the opposite. We must keep in mind, however, that statistical correlation by itself does not show cause and effect. It may be that socially responsible and ethical behaviors do lead to financial success, or it may be that financial success leads to the behaviors. Overall, the interactions between specific behaviors and financial performance are too complex to find a direct cause and effect.[69]

Even if there is not a direct link between socially responsible and ethical behavior and financial performance, there are many incidents of the high cost of negative behavior. A few examples: the multibillion dollars that tobacco companies must pay to states;[70] the \$2 billion fine that Citigroup paid for its actions related to Enron;[71] the total failures of Enron itself and the accounting firm, Arthur Andersen, for its role in the Enron case; the high costs related to a large number of court cases; the costs of keeping various former managers in prison; and the very large decreases in market values of many companies, such as the 80% decline in the value of Krispy Kreme.[72] These costs probably do have an overall negative effect on the economy. If in no other way, these costs eventually show up in prices and various taxes.[73]

Implications for Leaders

We have explored two important concepts in this chapter: social responsibility and ethics. Achieving social responsibility and business ethics at an organizational level is a challenge that tomorrow's managers will face.

Table 3.8 A Model Whistle-Blower Policy

- Publicize a reporting policy that encourages reporting of valid complaints of wrongdoing.
- Establish a reporting procedure that allows anonymous complaints (required by Sarbanes–Oxley, at least for financial wrongdoing) or complaints to someone outside of the chain of command.
- Investigate the situation immediately.
- Go public. Publicize the outcomes of investigations. This shows employees and other stakeholders that complaints are taken seriously.

Sources: N. Swartz, "Whistleblower Complaints Growing," *Information Management Journal* 38, no. 3 (May/June 2005): 8; T. Mohr and D. Slovin, "Making Tough Calls Easy," *Security Management* 49, no. 3 (March 2005): 51–56; L. Driscoll, "A Better Way to Handle Whistle-Blowers: Let Them Speak," *BusinessWeek,* 27 July 1992, 36.

Tomorrow's leaders must be highly cognizant of the importance of strong character for leadership effectiveness. Character can be best demonstrated by acting ethically and fully considering the impact of decisions on the community at large. Toward that end, keep the following tips in mind as a leader:

- Explore ways in which the organization can be more socially responsive.
- Recognize the effect of the organization's actions on its stakeholders.
- Make sure that a code of ethics is put in place and followed.
- Ensure that whistle-blowing and ethical concerns procedures are established for internal problem solving.
- Involve employees in the identification of ethical issues to help them gain understanding and resolve issues.
- Determine the link between departments and issues affecting the company and make them known to employees in the departments.
- Integrate ethical decision making into the performance appraisal process.
- Publicize, in employee communications and elsewhere, executive priorities and efforts related to ethical issues.

By following these guidelines, managers will be taking a major step toward achieving a high level of social responsibility in the organization and increasing employee awareness of ethical issues. Managers of the future will be expected to address important social issues proactively and to maintain a high standard of ethical behavior.

Meeting The Challenge

Social Responsibility, Ethics, and Profits at GE

In the fall of 2004, Jeffrey Immelt, CEO of General Electric (GE), presented a list of the four things that he believed it would take to keep GE successful; virtue, execution, growth, and great people. Virtue was listed first. The other three seem quite reasonable. It would be very unusual for any business to even list virtue as necessary for overall success, let alone list it first. Then Immelt said that GE being a good citizen is imperative to business.

General Electric is now involved in a wide variety of actions that generally fall into the categories of corporate social responsibility and ethical behavior. The company is helping the country of Ghana with hospitals, water systems, and teaching health workers management skills. It invests in exploring wind power as a source of energy. GE is auditing its supply chain to try to not do business with companies that operate sweatshops. The company grants domestic-partner benefits. It is careful not to sell products to countries that might use them for questionable purposes, such as ultrasound machines to select the sex of a baby that could lead to abortions. GE refuses to conduct business in Myanmar because of that country's violations of human rights.

What is Immelt's plan? He believes that it is imperative to "be a good neighbor." More and more managers and academics believe now that there is a link between socially responsible and ethical behavior and long-term sustainable business success. Think about how GE's contributions in Ghana and other African countries might lead to future markets for GE's products and services; how the company's treatment of employees with regard to domestic benefits and no sweatshops might help attract great people. It appears that the things that Immelt and GE are doing have at least a reasonable chance of leading to profitability in the long run. In fact, that is what Immelt is counting on.

Now what about doing business in Iran? GE does not conduct business directly with that country. Its wholly owned subsidiaries in France and Italy do. This is totally legal. However, some still question this practice. Immelt believes that by working with countries such as Iran, reform in that country can be achieved better and sooner than by ignoring the country.

GE is still a very successful and well-known company. Immelt continues to manage the company for profit, as did Jack Welch. Immelt believes that being socially responsible and ethical are linked to profitability in the long run.

Sources: D. Corbett, "Excellence in Canada: Healthy Organizations Achieve Results by Acting Responsibly," *Journal of Business Ethics* 55, no. 2 (December 2004): 125; "Money and Morals at GE," *Fortune*, 15 November 2004, 176–182; J. Veiga, "Bringing Ethics into the Mainstream: An Introduction to the Special Topic," *Academy of Management Executive* 18, no. 2 (May 2004): 37–38.

SUMMARY

1. The concepts of social responsibility and ethics require an understanding of the stakeholder view of the organization. Whereas the traditional view of socially responsible behavior considers only the stockholders, contemporary theory recognizes a much broader group of constituents—stakeholders. Stakeholders include any individual or group that is affected by or can affect the organization.

As the business environment becomes more and more global, the stakeholders of many organizations have become more diverse. As a company's operations become more international, managers will be required to understand and respond to a broader group of stakeholders.

2. Corporate social responsibility has been the subject of much controversy and debate over the last several decades. Although the concept defies precise definition, in a very general sense, social responsibility refers to the interaction between business and the social environment in which it exists. The concept of social responsibility rests on two premises: social contract and moral agent.

3. Four perspectives of corporate social responsibility have significant support from both practitioners and academics. The economic responsibility perspective suggests that the only social responsibility of business is to maximize profits within the "rules of the game." The economic responsibility perspective argues that business has an obligation to act in a way that is consistent with society's overall expectations of business. The ethical responsibility perspective suggests that business not only follow the letter of the law but also the spirit of the law. Supporters of the philanthropic responsibility perspective suggest that businesses act proactively to improve the welfare of society.

4. There are four approaches for responding to social issues. (a) reaction, (b) defense, (c) accommodation, and (d) proaction. A reaction approach results in fighting the requirements. Defense includes doing only what is required. Accommodation suggests a progressive approach—do more than is required. Proaction suggests that a business be a leader in the industry in order to better society.

5. Values are the relatively permanent and deeply held desires of individuals or groups. They form the foundation of an individual's ethical behavior. Instrumental, or means-oriented, values describe desirable standards of conduct or methods for attaining an end. Terminal, or ends-oriented, values describe desirable ends or goals for the individual and reflect what a person is ultimately striving to achieve. People from different international and cultural environments may hold very different values and thus have different perspectives on ethical issues.

6. As information technology has become more sophisticated, new ethical issues have emerged. Issues regarding privacy of individual information and the personal use of computers in the workplace are just two of the technology-related ethical concerns in today's business environment. Additional ethical issues may arise as technology improvements continue.

7. Three primary approaches can be taken in dealing with ethical dilemmas. The utility approach emphasizes the overall amount of good that can be produced by an action or a decision. The human rights approach holds that decisions should be consistent with fundamental rights and privileges such as those of life, freedom, health, privacy, and property. Under the justice approach, decisions are based on an equitable, fair, and impartial distribution of benefits (rewards) and costs among individuals and groups.

8. Organizations often develop codes of ethics along with training programs to encourage and reinforce ethical business behavior. A code of ethics describes the organization's general value system, its ethical principles, and the specific ethical rules that it tries to apply.

9. Several approaches can be used in ethics training programs. These approaches include case studies, the presentation of rules or guidelines for deciding ethical issues, and cognitive approaches that attempt to develop higher levels of ethical understanding.

10. A whistle-blower is someone who exposes organizational wrongdoing in order to preserve ethical standards and protect against wasteful, harmful, or illegal acts. Organizations should develop and maintain policies and procedures that encourage reports of wrongdoing yet discourage employees from making frivolous or unjustified allegations against others.

REVIEW QUESTIONS

1. (LEARNING OBJECTIVE 1) Describe the stakeholder view of the organization. How does the stakeholder view differ from the stockholder view, and what are the implications of these differences for the concept of corporate social responsibility?
2. (LEARNING OBJECTIVE 1) How has the globalization of the business environment impacted issues of social responsibility and ethics?
3. (LEARNING OBJECTIVE 2) Define the concept of corporate social responsibility. What are the two premises advanced by Bowen in his original definition of social responsibility?
4. (LEARNING OBJECTIVE 3) Compare and contrast the four perspectives of corporate social responsibility.
5. (LEARNING OBJECTIVE 4) Evaluate the four different approaches for dealing with social responsibility. Describe how these approaches differ, and give an example of a company that has pursued each approach.
6. (LEARNING OBJECTIVE 5) What are values? Why are they the basis of an individual's ethical behavior? How might values vary across multinational, multicultural environments?

7. (LEARNING OBJECTIVE 6) Describe how advances in information technology have created new ethical challenges.
8. (LEARNING OBJECTIVE 7) Describe the utility, human rights, and justice approaches to ethical dilemmas and explain how they differ.
9. (LEARNING OBJECTIVE 8) What is a code of ethics? Describe several goals an organization can have for developing a code of ethics.
10. (LEARNING OBJECTIVE 9) What are the common approaches used in ethics training programs?
11. (LEARNING OBJECTIVE 10) Explain what is meant by whistle-blowing. What are the benefits that come from whistle-blowing? What are some of the problems it might cause?

DISCUSSION QUESTIONS

Improving Critical Thinking

1. Consider the implications of self-regulation versus government-imposed regulation. Why is it preferable for an industry to be self-regulated?
2. Describe an ethical dilemma that you have experienced at work or as part of a business or social organization. What was your response? If you faced a similar dilemma now, would your response differ?

Enhancing Communication Skills

3. Select an organization with which you are familiar or that you are interested in researching. Evaluate the social responsibility approach of that company with regard to the following social issues: (a) environmental protection, (b) worker health and safety, and (c) product safety. Has this company been in a reaction, defense, accommodation, or proaction mode with regard to these social issues? Make an oral presentation of your findings to the class.
4. Using current business periodicals or newspapers, find an example of an organization that has faced an ethical problem. How did it solve the problem? Did the organization have a code of ethics? Write a summary of your findings as a way to demonstrate your understanding of the issue and practice your written communication skills.
5. Examine the policy your college or university has for handling academic dishonesty. How is dishonesty defined? How appropriate is the policy? Would you suggest any changes? Write up your suggestions and discuss them with a small group or your class.

Building Teamwork

6. As part of a small group, consider the following argument: If one looks far enough into the future, the interests of all stakeholders converge. That is, all stakeholders ultimately benefit from a strong economy, well-paid employees, and a healthy and clean environment. Thus, organizations should not find a conflict between their primary stakeholders (stockholders) and their secondary stakeholders (the community at large). Is this statement true? Why or why not? Provide an example of an organizational situation that supports your position.
7. In small groups or as directed by your instructor, select a company that is considering relocating its major manufacturing plant from a domestic site to a country with lower labor costs. What are the social considerations that are most relevant for this company? Evaluate how this decision would be viewed by proponents of each of the four perspectives of social responsibility (economic responsibility, legal responsibility, ethical responsibility, and philanthropic responsibility).
8. As part of a small group, develop a code of ethics for an organization to which one or more of you belong, such as a fraternity, a sorority, a business association, or your college. What are the key issues that need to be addressed? Share your code with the class and the organization.

part 2

Planning Challenges in the 21st Century

Chapter

4

Strategic Management and Planning in a Global Environment

© SUSAN VAN ETTEN

CHAPTER OVERVIEW

In Chapter 1, we learned that management is about administering and coordinating resources in a way that results in effectiveness and efficiency, achieving the organization's goals in an efficient manner. In Chapter 2, we learned valuable lessons from experiences of managers through time. Then in Chapter 3, we explored social responsibility and ethics, important foundations that will influence managers as they manage—as they plan, organize, lead, and control in a way that will accomplish the organization's goals.

Now we have learned about the basics on which we can build our understanding of management. This chapter first recalls the overall framework of management that was presented in Chapter 1 and presents it in a way that focuses on overall planning, or strategic planning, which refers to the process of making plans and decisions that are focused on long-run performance. (Review Figure 1.5.) It discusses strategic analysis, which includes analyzing the external and internal environments of organizations along with establishing the overall purpose, or mission, of an organization. Then developing strategy for the organization is discussed. Essentially, this refers to a skill or knowledge that helps an organization accomplish something better than its competitors and, thus, gives the organization a competitive advantage over its competitors. Implementation of the overall strategy and evaluation and control of it are briefly discussed as a way to introduce the rest of the book.

Strategies can be categorized as either grand or generic strategies, and they should be implemented in light of the organization's mission, vision and goals as well as its strengths, weaknesses, opportunities, and threats. The most common ways to evaluate strategies are portfolio assessment models and decision matrices. The topics in the remaining chapters explain the many things that make up implementation of the overall strategy and evaluation and control so that the overall strategy can be achieved successfully.

LEARNING OBJECTIVES

When you have finished studying this chapter, you should be able to

1. Define strategic management and describe its purpose.
2. Explain the four stages of the strategic management process.
3. Identify and explain the components of strategic analysis, as well as explain the value of conducting this analysis.
4. Explain how an organization can develop a competitive advantage.
5. Explain the purpose of strategy formulation and describe the two levels of strategic alternatives.
6. Explain the role of strategy implementation.
7. Explain the importance of evaluation and control of strategy and its implementation.
8. Discuss the importance of strategic planning.

Facing The Challenge

Changes at Hewlett-Packard

Hewlett-Packard (HP) had a long history of being a very successful company over many years, first in the area of mainframe computers and later in PCs, printers, consulting—especially managing information technology (IT) services for companies—and related products and services. In 1999 HP hired a new CEO, Carly Fiorina, who came from a successful career at several previous companies; the latest was Lucent Technologies. Her challenge was to revitalize the company. She wanted HP to be the leading technology company in the world.

HP's success was acceptable, but it was facing increasing challenges. There was a proliferation of products resulting in many brands that were not known and not profitable. Major business customers such as Ford and Boeing were not pleased that they had to interact with many different HP sales teams, rather than deal with one team that could handle all their needs. Dell was now the dominant producer of PCs and was coming into the printer market, two of HP's major product areas.

Fiorina made some quick changes in cutting the small and nonprofitable brands. She reorganized parts of the company into broader units, for example, by combining printers and PCs. She reorganized sales so that major business customers could interact with one sales force. Then, she completed the merger between HP and Compaq, intended to strengthen HP overall. However, many investors and some members of the HP Board of Directors had serious reservations. She made predictions to financial analysts that were positive. The predictions turned out to be too positive.

An article written by Stewart Alsop in *Fortune* in early 2002 suggested what might be the real problem or at least the outcome of the problems at HP. In the article, Alsop explained the many difficulties he had with purchasing a PC for his son, including the product not being in stock at the retailer, high-pressure salespeople, difficulty with repair, and major bureaucracy in purchasing the PC and later repair. Perhaps if HP had so much trouble with the actual sale of a product, there were serious problems.

These problems included conflicts between HP's culture and Fiorina's intended changes, a negative reaction from managers when she dismissed top-level managers whom she said were not performing profitably, and changes in the competitive environment that resulted in HP not being dominant in any product area except for printers. And Dell was attacking there.

In early 2005, Fiorina was dismissed. After several months, HP hired a new CEO, Mark Hurd. In discussing his selection as CEO, business publications were suggesting that perhaps Fiorina's strategy for HP was too broad. Will Hurd have better success?

Sources: C. Loomis, "Shy Carly's Big Bet Is Failing," *Fortune,* 7 February 2005, 50–64; B. Elgin, "Carly's Challenge," *BusinessWeek,* 13 December 2004, 98–108; G. Anders, "The Carly Chronicles," *Fast Company* (February 2003): 66–73; P. Tam, "The Economy: H-P's First Results Including Compaq Stir Doubts," *Wall Street Journal,* 27 August 2002, A2; S. Alsop, "If You Can't Get This Right," *Fortune,* 7 January 2002, 36.

Introduction

LEARNING OBJECTIVE 1

Define strategic management and describe its purpose.

An organization needs a mission, a focus that guides its operations, and a plan to accomplish the mission. The mission and plan, together known as overall strategy, then must be implemented to achieve success. Perhaps Hewlett-Packard (HP) ("Facing the Challenge") did have a good mission: to be the leading technology company in the world. Perhaps its difficulties were in problems with the plans for achieving that mission, or perhaps the problem was that the plan was not implemented. Then again, perhaps the mission was too broad and did not give enough guidance that would focus day-to-day operations so that they could target something meaningful.

After you read this chapter, look at what HP is attempting to do currently. (See the "Meeting the Challenge" box.) Do its mission and plans fit the competitive situation better now than they did in the situation described in the "Facing the Challenge" box?

Strategic Management and Strategic Planning

1 The terms *strategic management* and *strategic planning* are sometimes used interchangeably. However, there is an important difference. **Strategic management** refers to overall, long-run management.

Figure 4.1 The Strategic Management Process

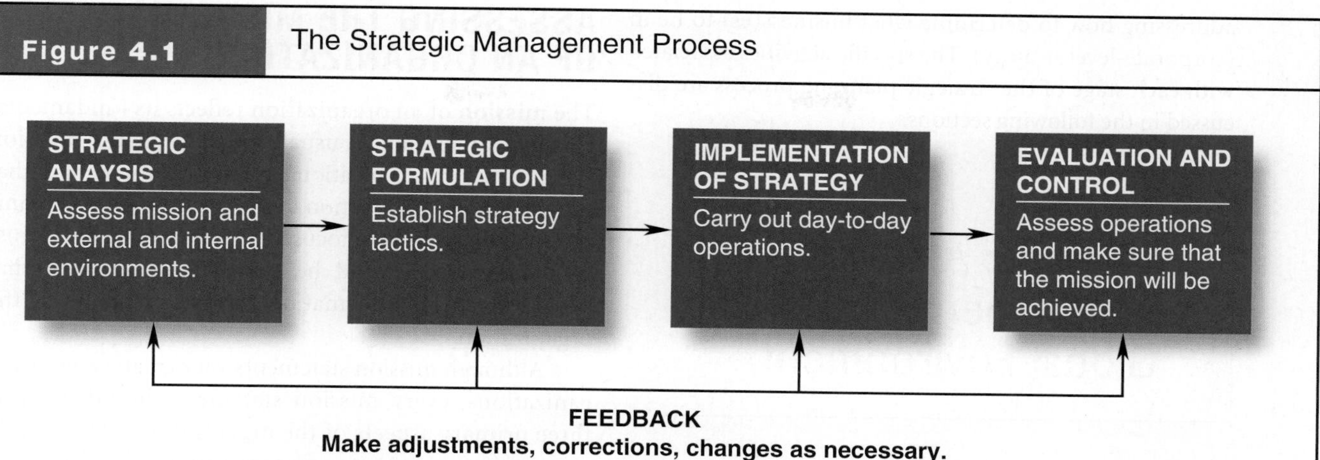

That includes planning, organizing, leading, and controlling effectively and efficiently over the long run—that is, successful management overall. Strategic planning deals with the planning function of management. Figure 4.1 illustrates these ideas. It also presents strategic management and its parts, planning, and other functions as processes. That is, one part of management leads to and interacts with another, and all parts may need adjusting and changing depending on the outcomes.

2 We now turn our attention to **strategic planning,** which refers to the process of making plans and decisions that are focused on long-run performance. The resulting comprehensive plan that provides overall direction for the organization is known as a **strategic plan.** Although the level of sophistication and formality of the strategic planning process will differ among organizations, the process itself is similar across all organizations.[1]

As Figure 4.1 indicates, the strategic management process is carried out in four stages. Although strategic planning deals directly with the first two stages, planning is also related to the other stages. Furthermore, the feedback lines in the model suggest that the strategic planning process is interactive and self-renewing, continually evolving as changes in the environment or in the organization create a need for revised strategic plans.

The **strategic analysis** phase of the strategic planning process addresses the question, What is the current position of the organization? Accordingly, the mission and external and internal environmental conditions faced by the organization are evaluated during this phase of the process. The information gathered during the strategic analysis serves as a foundation for the formulation of the organization's strategic plan.

Strategy formulation deals with establishing strategy and tactics necessary to achieve the mission of the organization. This includes both short-run and long-run strategies and tactics. Strategies are developed with the intention of bridging the gap between the current and desired position of the organization.

The **strategy implementation** phase of the process involves doing the things necessary to ensure that the strategy of the organization is achieved effectively and efficiently. Implementation includes the day-to-day operations and involves all other managerial functions being exercised.

LEARNING OBJECTIVE 2

Explain the four stages of the strategic management process.

The final stage of the strategic planning process is **evaluation and control.** This phase is designed to monitor the organization's progress toward implementing its plans and achieving its goals. Strategic control mechanisms identify deviations between actual and planned results so that managers can make the adjustments necessary to ensure that organizational goals can be achieved in the long term.[2]

The strategic planning process is the focus of the remainder of this chapter. Although the strategic planning process can and should be applied at both the corporate and business levels (see Chapter 5), this chapter focuses on developing strategies at the business level. In other words, this chapter highlights the process of strategic planning as it relates to determining how to operate a specific business (business-level strategy), rather than

KEY TERMS

Strategic management
Overall, long-run management.

Strategic planning
The process of making plans and decisions that are focused on long-run performance.

Strategic plan
A comprehensive plan that provides overall direction for the organization.

Strategic analysis
An assessment of the external and internal environments of an organization.

Strategy formulation
Establishing strategy and tactics necessary to achieve the mission of the organization.

addressing how to determine what business(es) to be in (corporate-level strategy). The specific activities associated with each stage of the strategic planning process are discussed in the following sections.

Strategic Analysis: Assessment in a Global Environment

3 The purpose of a strategic analysis is to assess the current condition of the organization and the environment in which it operates.[3] Until you understand where an organization is in its development and the factors that it faces in the markets in which it operates, it is impossible to determine where it could and should be. Strategic analysis requires three primary activities: (1) assessing the mission of the organization, (2) conducting an external environmental analysis, and (3) conducting an internal environmental analysis.[4] Figure 4.2 illustrates these three components of a strategic analysis.

LEARNING OBJECTIVE 3

Identify and explain the components of strategic analysis, as well as explain the value of conducting this analysis.

As you will learn in the following section, an organization's mission expresses its fundamental purpose for existence by describing its target markets, what the target markets want in terms of products and services, sometimes expressed as the customers' wants that are satisfied, and basically how these wants will be satisfied. An assessment of an organization's external and internal environments involves the identification of its primary strengths, weaknesses, opportunities, and threats. Such an assessment is often referred to as a SWOT analysis—S (strengths), W (weaknesses), O (opportunities), and T (threats). By understanding the mission of the organization, as well as its current SWOTs, managers are prepared to identify and assess the strategic alternatives that are appropriate for the organization. Let's examine the components of a strategic analysis more closely.

KEY TERMS

Strategy implementation
Doing the things necessary to ensure that the strategy of the organization is achieved effectively and efficiently.

Evaluation and control
The methods by which the performance of the organization is monitored.

Mission
The reasons for which the organization exists.

ASSESSING THE MISSION OF AN ORGANIZATION

The **mission** of an organization reflects its fundamental reasons for existence, usually expressed in a mission statement.[5] An organizational mission is a statement that provides strategic direction to the members of an organization and keeps them focused on common goals. A mission statement should be a "living" document that provides critical information for the members of the organization.[6]

Although mission statements vary greatly among organizations, every mission statement should describe three primary aspects of the organization: (1) its target markets (who), (2) its primary products and services (what), and (3) an outline of the overall strategy for delivering these products and services to satisfy the customers in the target markets (how), thereby ensuring long-term success. This information serves as the foundation on which strategies are built. For example, if the mission of your university is to meet the educational needs of individuals in your state by offering innovative programs in the arts, science, business, engineering, and health care, the strategy of the university should be developed to fulfill that mission.

Although some management experts have questioned the real value of mission statements,[7] most believe missions to be of critical importance in setting the strategic direction of an organization and for providing

© SUSAN VAN ETTEN

A SWOT analysis discussion helps managers to identify the strategic alternatives that are appropriate for an organization's internal and external environments.

Figure 4.2 The Components of Strategic Analysis

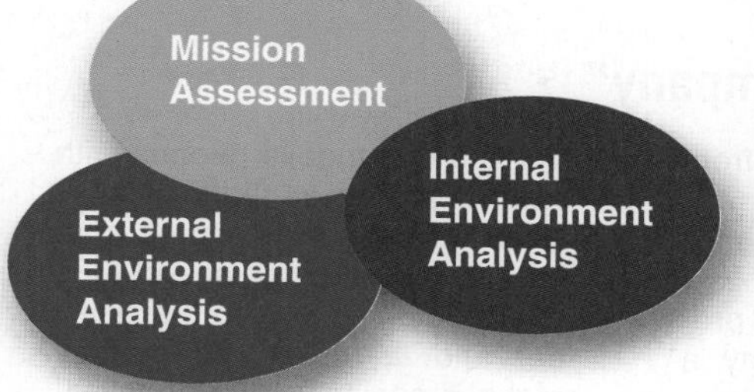

a foundation for the development of business strategy.[8] In fact, one study indicated that mission-driven companies outperformed their rivals by an average of 30% in key financial measures.[9] The results of a Gallup poll strongly support the value of mission statements. Of the people surveyed in that poll, 60% said that when they understood the mission of their company it made their job feel important, which caused them to be engaged in their work. Although no direct measure was included in the poll, people engaged in their jobs probably leads to higher productivity and profitability.[10] Of course, the key to all of this is that people must understand the mission and how their jobs fit and help achieve the mission.

The achievement of some of the most successful companies can be attributed to the commitment of their managers to providing a compelling mission for their organizations. Examples of managers who have done this exceptionally well include Sam Walton (Wal-Mart), Bill Gates (Microsoft), Herb Kelleher (Southwest Airlines), Jeff Bezos (Amazon.com), and Steve Jobs (Apple Computer Company and Pixar), who shaped their views of a particular market environment into a mission that could be understood and acted on by all members of their organizations. Their commitment to developing and communicating the mission of the organization contributed greatly to the success of their companies.[11]

The main reasons why there are different views concerning the value of mission statements are that they are difficult to construct and, even if stated well, they might not be communicated to nor understood by people in the organization. Organizations state missions differently. However, in addition to the mission, many include "philosophy," "values," "principles" and/or vision. (See Table 4.1.) What do you think of the mission statement that Newport News Shipbuilding wrote in 1886 and etched in bronze? "We shall build good ships here—at a profit if we can—at a loss if we must—but always good ships."[12] The company still uses this mission statement today. "At the Forefront" shows examples of missions that may need to change.

Now Apply It

Setting Mission and Strategic Goals

Review Experiential Exercise 4.1, "Developing a Conceptual Image Document." This is similar to an external and internal analysis in preparation for a personal plan. You may also wish to read *The 7 Habits of Highly Effective People* by Stephen Covey, especially the chapter that deals with establishing a personal mission statement.

Now, write your personal mission statement. Remember that it should be focused on what you want to be, who you want to be, or what you want to achieve in the long run.

After you have written your personal mission statement, write down several strategic goals, major, long-term goals that you will need to achieve to reach your mission.

At the Forefront

The Future "Phone Company"

- Do you get phone service from an Internet provider?
- Does your house have a "landline"?
- Is your television service provided by a satellite company, a cable company, or your telephone company?
- Do you take pictures with or watch television on your mobile phone? Do you post to your blog from your mobile phone?
- Does caller ID information for home phone calls display on your television screen?
- Can you access the Internet from your television equipment?
- Will your phone company provide electricity and natural gas soon?
- Is your refrigerator connected to your phone service or the Internet? Can it order milk and other things when you are running low?

Defining mission as who customers are, what customers want, and how to provide it seems to be very practical. To identify and understand these things is difficult enough when the industry in which a company operates is relatively simple and stable. Many industries have become more complex over time, probably none more so than the phone service industry—or what once was the phone service industry.

Consider the following:

- Sprint Nextel has mobile phones that wirelessly connect to broadband Internet service, offers GPS navigation, and has walkie-talkie capability. Of course, Sprint Nextel wants to be the sole provider for your home or business, so it may also provide a landline and, perhaps, television service.
- Verizon has mobile phones with color screens that display weather and sports scores from the Internet. Its high-speed DSL offers quick access to the Internet and its color screen may make it possible to offer television service. In the meantime, access to the Internet with large data bases made it easier for Verizon to sell its phone directory business. This business was sold because it is in a commodity type industry where it is difficult to differentiate the product.
- Time Warner offers some customers a package that includes Internet, phone, and television service. In some markets, caller ID can be shown on television screens.
- Comcast offers a complete package—cable television, Internet access, and phone service, both landline and mobile.
- SBC purchased AT&T and will be known as AT&T which provides both landline and mobile phones with high-speed Internet service.
- Motorola is producing mobile phones that can connect to your Internet and cable TV service. Some phones can keep you in touch with television service away from home.
- Google may offer phone service over its Internet network.
- Cablevision Systems Corp. is working to offer phone and Internet service along with cable television.
- Apple has an iPod that shows videos, most downloaded from the Internet along with music, and also serves as a phone. Might Apple enter into providing phone service as it did with distributing music?
- Dell is making and selling televisions. With the merging of television, Internet, and phone service, will Dell enter the phone service business?
- Intel is making components for digital televisions along with components for computers and Internet-related services. Would it make sense for Intel to enter the phone and/or television service business?

While all this is happening, wireless mobile phone service providers are ranked below health-maintenance and cable TV providers in customer satisfaction. The service is just not reliable and there are far too many "dropped calls" and static. In addition, there are serious questions about whether one electronic device can hold all the technology that would be required to deliver phone, television, and Internet service. This is now true of mobile phones, but is also true of computers and televisions that are expected to deliver all services while at the same time, be light-weight and small.

Source: J. Granelli, "Cell phone operators try to reduce the static," *St. Louis Post-Dispatch,* December 7, 2005, B4; D. Searcey, J. Drucker, and S. Ali, "As telecom shifts, providers seek new connections," *Wall Street Journal,* December 6, 2005, A1, A8; D. Searcey and D. Berman, "Verizon to shed phone-book unit," *Wall Street Journal,* December 5, 2005, A3; "It's time to reinvent the yes-man," *Fortune,* November 28, 2005, 1; C. Rhoads, "Handset sales help Motorola return to profit," *Wall Street Journal,* July 20, 2005, A1.

Table 4.1 Ford Motor Company's Mission Statement

Ford Motor Company

Our Vision

"To become the world's leading consumer company for automotive products and services."

Our Mission

"We are a global family with a proud heritage passionately committed to providing personal mobility for people around the world.

We anticipate consumer need and deliver outstanding products and services that improve people's lives."

Our Values

"Our business is driven by our consumer focus, creativity, resourcefulness, and entrepreneurial spirit.

We are an inspired, diverse team. We respect and value everyone's contribution. The health and safety of our people are paramount.

We are a leader in environmental responsibility. Our integrity is never compromised and we make a positive contribution to society.

We constantly strive to improve in everything we do. Guided by these values, we provide superior returns to our shareholders."

Source: Ford Motor Credit http://www.ford.com/en/company/about/overview.htm, June 30, 2005.

By providing **strategic direction,** the mission suggests guidance not only for current operations but also the future. This guidance for the future is called a **vision.** Vision can be considered from two perspectives. One is the **vision statement** that is intended to guide the organization into the future, what the organization wants to become or where it wants to be.

The other way to look at vision is from the perspective of a skill. One frequently hears the statement that a manager must have vision. What does that mean? It means that a manager can predict problems and opportunities that are likely in the future. How can this be accomplished? How can this skill be acquired, or can it be acquired? If a manager learns to carefully analyze the external and internal environments of an organization (discussed below), that manager can probably predict what is more or less likely to happen. This skill is important for all managers to develop and is even critical for top-level managers. With a supportive organizational culture, discussed in a later chapter, most or all people in an organization can learn to predict what might happen, at least to some degree.[13]

CONDUCTING AN EXTERNAL ENVIRONMENTAL ANALYSIS

Strategic analysis requires a thorough understanding of the external environment in which an organization operates. The purpose of an external analysis is to identify those aspects of the environment that represent either an opportunity or a threat to the organization. **Opportunities** are those environmental trends on which the organization can capitalize and improve its competitive position. External **threats** are conditions that jeopardize the organization's ability to prosper in the long term.

Figure 4.3 illustrates the primary dimensions of a global external environment. The external environment is divided into two major components—the general environment and the task environment. The **general environment** includes environmental forces that are beyond the influence of the organization and over which it has no or little control. Forces in the **task environment** are within the organization's operating environment and may be influenced to some degree.

General Environment

An organization's general environment includes economic, sociocultural, technological, and political–legal factors. A strategic analysis must consider the global dimensions of all these factors as well as their domestic effects. Table 4.2 on page 97 lists examples of trends

KEY TERMS

Strategic direction
Direction of the organization toward success in the long run.

Vision
The ability to predict opportunities and threats in the future.

Vision statement
A statement representing what the organization wants to become and where it wants to be in the future.

Opportunities
Environmental trends on which the organization can capitalize.

Threat
A condition in the environment that may cause trouble for the organization.

General environment
Those environmental forces outside of the organization over which the organization may have no control.

Figure 4.3 Dimensions of the Global External Environment

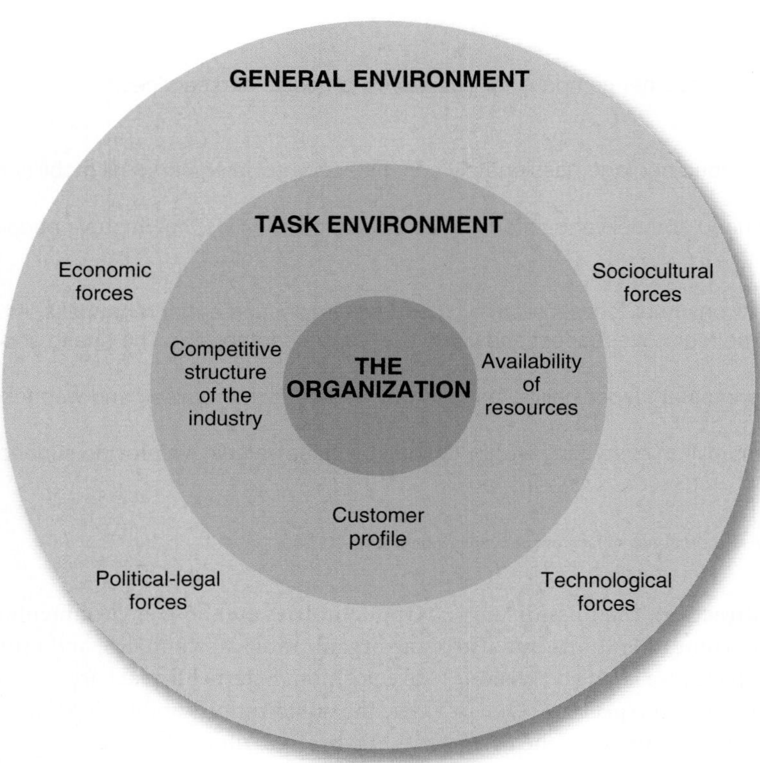

in each of these areas that might represent an opportunity and/or a threat that would influence an organization's strategic plan.[14]

Economic Environment The **economic environment** contains components of the general environment and is represented by the general state of both the domestic and the world economy. The health of the economy is reflected by variables such as total gross domestic product (GDP), growth in the GDP, interest rates, the inflation rate, the consumer price index, wage rates, and unemployment rates. Similar measures can be used to evaluate the world economy. World trade and foreign direct investment trends are also useful for such an analysis.

A favorable economic climate represents opportunities for growth for most businesses. For example, in times of economic prosperity, people typically spend more money on consumer goods. They tend to eat out more frequently, travel more often, and purchase more products and services. So hotels, restaurants, and retailers are just some of the organizations that would typically find growth opportunities when economic conditions are positive.

However, the demand for some products and services grows during times of economic decline. For example, mobile homes, bologna, and car-repair services are products and services that tend to be in greater demand during poor economic times. Other products and services are essentially recession proof and remain in relatively constant demand irrespective of the economic conditions. Consider Denstply, for example, the world's largest manufacturer of products used by dentists. Even during the economic downturn that began in the summer of 2000, Dentsply experienced steady sales and profitability. According to CEO John Miles, the demand for dentistry service remains relatively steady irrespective of economic conditions. This means that the demand for products from his company tends to be very stable, which has implications for his company's strategic plan.[15]

With increasing globalization, as discussed in Chapter 1, managers must pay attention to the economic environments in many countries. Economic conditions in other countries may affect demand for products and services as

KEY TERMS

Task environment
Those environmental forces that are within the firm's operating environment and over which the organization may have some degree of control.

Economic environment
The economic components of the general environment.

Table 4.2 Sample Issues in the General Environment

Economic	Sociocultural	Technological	Political–Legal
• Inflation rates • Unemployment rates • Wage rates • Exchange rates • Stock market fluctuations • Per capita income • GDP trends • Economic development	• Norms and values • Demographic trends • Age groups • Regional shifts in population • Household composition • Diversity • Ecological awareness • Life expectancy	• Spending on research and development • Internet availability • Availability of information technology • Production technology trends • Productivity improvements • Telecommunications infrastructure	• Tax laws • Environmental protection • International trade regulation • Antitrust regulation • Federal Reserve policy • Intellectual property and patent laws

well as many other aspects of operations. For example, wage and unemployment rates may give some companies an advantage or disadvantage in competition. A company might outsource some of its operations to another country that has cheaper wage rates, assuming that the appropriate skill levels are there. Outsourcing is a common occurrence, and it probably will increase.[16]

The economy can be a strong determinant of the demand for many goods and services, and it can affect many other components of the operations of an organization. Consequently, forecasts of economic activity will influence the strategic plans of most organizations.

Sociocultural Environment The **sociocultural environment** is represented by the attitudes, behavior patterns, and lifestyles of the individuals who ultimately purchase the products or services of the organization. Components of the sociocultural environment influence not only what products and services are wanted but also many things related to how these products and services are produced and sold. As the aspects of the sociocultural environment change, so must the strategy of organizations that are affected by such changes.

Although some sociocultural trends cross national boundaries (such as the popularity of jeans among young people), not all developments occur on a global basis. In fact, many aspects of the sociocultural environment are specific to certain groups of people in one country, to a certain country, or to groups of countries. Consequently, organizations that operate internationally often must cope with multiple heterogeneous sociocultural environments and therefore must develop strategies to deal with different environmental conditions.

There are many sociocultural components and trends. Some of the most important are the following:

- *Changes in age groups* In all developed countries, the fastest-growing age group is people over 50 years old. In the United States, these people make up the largest age group and are known as "baby boomers," and many of them are "woofies" (well-off old folks). Campbell Soup Company recognized that older consumers eat more soup than their younger counterparts and responded. CBS, once plagued by declining viewership ratings, refocused on its traditional market of older viewers and is enjoying high television network ratings. Yet other companies, Levi's, for example, find the aging baby-boomer market to represent a strategic threat. Since older people do not wear jeans as much as younger people, Levi's is trying to shed its image of serving the aging baby boomers and associate its products with the very different emerging youth market. However, the company is having trouble getting Generation Y (born after 1980) to prefer the Levi brand. Generation Y could be even larger than the baby-boomer group.[17]
- *Increase of niche markets* Many factors have combined to encourage customers to demand products and services matched closely to what they want. Dell Computer company can assemble a computer that fits the exact specifications of the customer. L'Oreal produces a range of cosmetics with many of its brands aimed at a

KEY TERMS

Sociocultural environment The attitudes, behavior patterns, and lifestyles of individuals who purchase products and services of organizations.

specific market.[18] Mobile phone services can offer packages of calling and related electronic services that meet specifications of customers. Advances in such things as customer knowledge and information and marketing have made these things possible along with advances in production and operations that allow mass customization.[19] Without mass customization (matching products and services to small markets in a way that still allows efficiency and operating on a large scale), organizations could not accomplish serving small niche markets profitably.

- *Household composition* It is estimated that before 2010 the most common household type in the United States will be single-person households. The composition of the household affects demand for many products and services.[20]
- *Increasing diversity* Between 1996 and 2050, it is predicted that the percent of the racial categories in the United States will change as follows: Caucasians, from 83% to 75%; Hispanics, from 10% to 25%; African Americans, from 13% to 15%; Asians, from 4% to 9%; and American Indians, possibly a slight increase. Hispanics can be of any race, so the total percentage adds to over 100%.[21] People in various ethnic groups are increasingly being identified as target markets.
- *Environmental awareness* Although it is difficult to track the effects of environmental awareness on purchases and the way companies operate, there probably is a gradual increase in its effects. Several years ago, McDonald's switched from Styrofoam containers to cardboard ones, under pressure from school-aged children. Many cities and communities offer some sort of recycling of at least some materials. There is some effect of "going green," using recycled products and/or those that can be regrown and do not pollute.[22] And, while some still dispute whether "global warming" is real, many people now believe that something has to be done to reduce the use of products and services that contribute to the pollution that causes global warming.

KEY TERMS

Technological environment
Changes in technology in the external environment.

B2B
An initialism representing business-to-business transactions.

B2C
An initialism representing business-to-consumer interactions.

Political–legal environment
The part of the external environment that includes political and legal issues that affect organizations.

Technological Environment Technological forces are the third component of the general environment. The **technological environment** includes changes in technology that affect the way organizations operate or the products and services they provide.

Clearly, the most significant technological advances of the recent past have been related to information technology. Not only have new software applications, such as enterprise resource planning (ERP) systems, revolutionized many organizational processes, but the advent of the Internet has also changed the way organizations operate and consumers purchase goods and services. Business-to-business (**B2B**) e-commerce has enabled more efficient supply-chain management strategies for virtually all organizations, and business-to-consumer (**B2C**) e-commerce has radically changed the retail industry, from books to music to apparel. Even greater changes will be likely in the years to come.

The success of virtually all organizations today depends, at least in part, on their ability to identify and respond to technological changes. Both UPS and Fed Ex, for example, have made tremendous inroads in its industry by investing heavily in technology and utilizing the Internet as a sales channel. Both companies offer customers a wide array of services made possible by advanced information technology. The result is that UPS and Fed Ex together deliver the majority of products purchased on the Internet.[23]

Technology improvements have also affected the health care industry dramatically. Computer-based and Internet-based technologies make possible innovative new monitoring products that enable clinicians to better track daily patient measurements, store and retrieve historical data, and generate patient reports. No longer will health care professionals have to be at each patient's bedside because they will be able to monitor patients from remote sites.[24]

From a more creative perspective, consider how improvements in technology have affected the entertainment industry. A "digital convergence" of Hollywood and Silicon Valley has made possible the production of movies such as *Shrek, Shrek2, Finding Nemo,* and the *Incredibles* taking the movie industry to a new level of creativity and innovation.[25] The music industry has been heavily impacted as well. The availability of music in a digital format has created new challenges and opportunities for artists and music producers.[26] Clearly, technology is impacting all kinds of industries, organizations, products, and services.[27]

Political–Legal Environment The final component of an organization's general environment is its **political–legal environment.** The political–legal environment includes the regulatory parameters within which the organization must operate. Tax policy, trade regulations, minimum-wage legislation, and pollution standards are just a few kinds of political–legal issues that can affect the strategic plans of an organization. Below are a few examples.

How do you think McDonald's and other fast-food restaurants would be affected by increases in the minimum wage? How about retail apparel stores like Gap and American Eagle? Given an increase in the minimum wage, these companies would likely look for new ways to maximize the efficiency of their human resources. In addition, new pricing strategies might be necessary in light of increased labor costs.

A major legal effect of the corporate corruption, which first came to light with the Enron scandal and escalated quickly with the Arthur Andersen, Worldcom, Adelphia, and Tyco debacles, is the Sarbanes–Oxley Act of 2002 that became law in the United States. That law requires organizations to follow tighter accounting rules and Section 404 of that law requires CEOs of companies to state that the accounting is accurate. As a result, thousands of publicly traded companies had to adjust the way they conducted business to meet those regulations.[28]

In an effort to abate the economic decline that began in 2000, the Federal Reserve established fiscal policies, mostly reducing basic interest rates, meant to stimulate economic activity.[29] Of course, the Federal Reserve continues to monitor the economy and sets policies accordingly to keep the economy healthy. All these policy and regulatory changes had implications for the strategic plans of many organizations.

© SPENCER GRANT/PHOTOEDIT

An organization, such as a car dealership, must know its customers' demographic and psychographic characteristics.

Like the other parts of the general environment, the political–legal environment of an organization often varies dramatically from nation to nation. As a consequence, organizations that operate internationally must develop a strategy for dealing with multiple political–legal systems.

Task Environment

In addition to general environmental issues, organizations must be aware of trends in the task environment. Critical variables in the task environment include **customer profiles,** the **competitive structure** of the industry, and the availability of resources.

Customer Profiles Would there be a need for an organization that had no customers, the stakeholders who purchase the products and services of a company? Even though organizations have multiple stakeholders, without customers, there is no revenue and eventually no profits. Therefore, it is imperative to have an in-depth understanding of the characteristics, needs, and expectations of the organization's customers.

An organization's customer may be another company in the production chain, or it may be the individual consumer. When an organization's customers are mainly industrial or wholesale clients, it needs information about the types of organizations that are using its products and services, their specific needs and expectations, their financial health, and the extent to which they depend on the organization's products and services.[30]

When an organization's customers are individuals, their specific wants and expectations must be understood. Demographic and psychographic characteristics such as average age, income level, gender, and marital status can help. Psychographic characteristics related to the consumer's lifestyle and personality may also be critical determinants of buying behavior.

Historically, a number of prominent companies, including American Express, have learned the hard way that understanding customers is essential for success in fast-changing, highly competitive markets. At one time, American Express seemed to turn a deaf ear to consumers who wanted more innovative product features and retailers who wanted better rates. As a result, American Express lost market share to its two largest competitors, MasterCard and

KEY TERMS

Customer profile
A description of customers that will help managers understand what products and services that customers wish to purchase.

Competitive structure
The nature and type of competition between competitors in an industry.

Figure 4.4 Five Forces Model of Industry Analysis

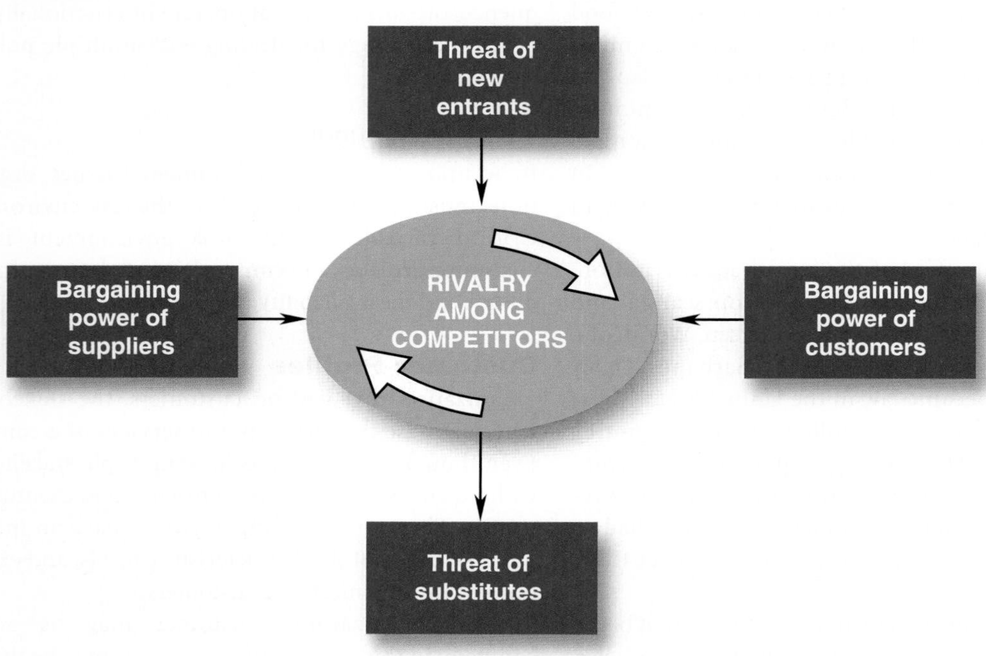

Source: Reprinted by permission of Harvard Business Review. From "How Competitive Forces Shape Strategy," by Michael E. Porter, March/April 1979: 137–145. Copyright © 1979 by the Harvard School Publishing Corporation; all rights reserved.

Visa.[31] Today, however, American Express is back with a variety of credit card options and an aggressive Internet strategy that could make it a powerful player in online banking and smart cards.[32]

Other companies—Amazon.com, for example—have always prioritized the customer. Jeff Bezos, founder and CEO of Amazon.com, describes his company as having a culture of "customer obsession." That customer obsession has earned Amazon.com its place as the Internet's most powerful merchant.[33] Even though Southwest Airlines says that its employees come first, the company clearly understands who its target customers are and what they want in terms of a traveling experience on an airline. Of course, Southwest then expects its employees to deliver that traveling experience to its customers.[34] (See "At the Forefront" in Chapter 3 for how Southwest incorporates this into its mission statement.)

As with all parts of management, the globalization of the marketplace has complicated the process of customer analysis. With customers spread across the globe, the relevant dimensions for analysis are more difficult to identify, evaluate, and predict. Therefore, managers in international organizations must take special care to ensure that they have a clear understanding of their customers in each national market served.

Competitive Structure of the Industry One of the best-known and widely used tools for assessing the competitiveness of an industry is Michael Porter's **five forces model** (Figure 4.4). The nature and degree of competition is influenced by interactions among the five main factors.

- *Bargaining power of customers* It is of course crucial for an organization to know who its customers are and what they want. However, an organization must also know how much bargaining power customers have because it will affect the final price and other conditions under which the customer will purchase the product or service. The bargaining power of customers has generally increased over time because customers have more information available to them,

KEY TERMS

Five forces model
A model developed by Michael Porter that uses five forces to assess the competitive structure of an industry.

especially with help of the Internet. For example, how much information can you get when you prepare to buy a new car?

- *Threat of substitute products or services* If another product or service can satisfy what customers want, then the level of competition in an industry increases because now an organization has to try harder or try other things to influence the customer to purchase its product or service rather than that of a competitor. When other products or services are seen as substitutes by customers, it is easy for customers to switch to the products or services of competitors; that is, switching costs are low. On the other hand, when a customer is loyal to one product or brand, others are not seen as substitutes. Generally, customers are willing to pay a higher price in those cases. For example, many people perceive Harley-Davidson Motorcycles to be superior to others and will pay a higher price.[35]
- *Bargaining power of suppliers* The concept here is the same as bargaining power of customers. Just as it is important to have loyal customers, it is also important, sometimes absolutely necessary, to have strong and positive working relationships with key suppliers. However, even in those cases, the bargaining power that suppliers have will influence the details of the working relationship.
- *Threat of new entrants* New organizations coming into the industry or businesses already in the industry that are now entering specific markets also tend to increase the degree of competition. An organization that has products, services, or efficiencies that are highly valued by customers normally will be able to stand up to increased competition.
- *Rivalry among competitors* The strategies of various competitors and the way various high-level managers compete influence the degree of rivalry in an industry. The more strengths that competitors have or the more aggressive they are in their tactics, the higher the competitiveness in an industry will be.

The five forces model can guide managers through an analysis of the important factors in an industry. That analysis will help them understand the overall nature and degree of competition.[36]

As the model suggests, in addition to knowing about customers and suppliers, companies need to understand a great deal about each other. Consider the degree of **competitive analysis** that takes place between Coca-Cola and Pepsi, Anheuser-Busch and Miller, or Nike and Reebok. These companies make it their business to know as much about their competitors as they know about themselves. In doing so, they are better able to anticipate what their competitors might do and how these actions might influence the marketplace.

Competitive analysis has become increasingly complex as more and more industries have become global. Some organizations simply overlook important international competitors because they are "hard to see."[37] Even if such competitors are easily identified, it is often difficult to obtain information about them because few international organizations are subject to the same disclosure regulations as U.S. organizations. Nevertheless, competitive analysis is an essential aspect of the strategic planning process, and managers must commit the time and energy necessary to gain a clear understanding of their competitors both domestically and globally.

Resource Availability Resource availability is the final component of the organization's task environment. The term **resource** can be applied to a broad range of inputs and may refer to raw materials, personnel or labor, and capital. To the extent that high-quality, low-cost resources are available to the organization, opportunities exist to create marketable products or services. When any resource is constrained, the organization faces a threat to its operations. Thus, strategic plans will be affected by the availability of the resources needed, both domestically and globally, to produce goods and services.

Consider, for example, the labor shortage experienced in the United States as it entered 2000. While the labor supply was inadequate in nearly every worker category, the scarce supply of professional and technical personnel was particularly problematic. Employers, desperate to attract qualified workers, turned to more creative methods of compensation in an effort to address the problem.[38] Nonmonetary forms of compensation, such as flexible work arrangements, were often more effective in attracting workers than enhanced salary packages. For organizations that had the flexibility to design creative compensation programs, the labor shortage might have actually provided an opportunity to "out-hire" their more traditional competitors.

Yet, how quickly times can change. With the recession of 2001–2002, labor shortages abated as corporation after corporation announced layoffs in response to weakening demand for their products and services. As staffs were reduced, those who remained in

KEY TERMS

Competitive analysis
Analysis conducted to understand the strengths and weaknesses of competitors.

Resource
An input that an organization can use to achieve its strategy.

their jobs were expected to do more and more to make up for the loss of their coworkers. In fact, the most recent recession was the first since World War II in which the productivity of the labor force rose rather than fell. According to a study by the Bureau of Labor Statistics, this rise in productivity was due in part to the fact that nearly 20% of the workforce reported spending more than 49 hours a week at work.[39]

An organization must also analyze and understand the situation related to all of its other resources. The availability, relative quality, cost, and other conditions of resources can have a significant impact on the strategic plans of virtually all organizations.

Once an organization understands who its customers are, what they want, the competitive structure of the industry, and the state of the resources available, it is ready to conduct an analysis of the internal environment to understand its strengths and weaknesses. Why conduct the external analysis first? Simply stated, changes in external environmental conditions can affect the value of any particular organizational strength. Consider some historical examples of this phenomenon: General Electric's capabilities in transistor technology were devalued with the introduction of semiconductors; American Airlines' strong relationship with the Civil Aeronautics Board became far less valuable when the airline industry was deregulated; and the advent and growth of the personal computer devalued IBM's capability in the mainframe computer business. Most recently, consider how advances in e-commerce have affected the competitive advantages of traditional bricks-and-mortar bookstores such as Borders and Barnes & Noble.[40] Although internal strengths are clearly an important source of competitive advantage, organizations must be sensitive to the ways in which changing external environmental and competitive conditions might affect the relative value of any particular strength.

Resource availability is the final component of the organization's task environment. When high-quality, low-cost resources are available, an organization can create marketable products or services.

CONDUCTING AN INTERNAL ANALYSIS

The purpose of an **internal analysis** is to identify assets, resources, skills, and processes that represent either strengths or weaknesses of the organization. Strengths are aspects of the organization's operations that represent distinctive competencies that can lead to competitive advantages, whereas weaknesses are areas that are in need of improvement.[41]

Essentially, to understand strengths and weaknesses, the entire organization must be examined. The most obvious areas to consider are marketing, operations, finance, and human resources (Table 4.3). It is crucial to understand whether the organization is even producing products and services that customers want. If it is, then the organization must produce them how and when the customers want them and do so in an efficient manner so that profits can be earned. It is also obvious that it takes employees with the right skills to do this.

Other areas that may not be as obvious but nevertheless important are the organization's structure, research and development, information systems and technology, purchasing, engineering, organizational culture, and overall control. All these areas can have very strong influences on the products and services and how they are delivered to customers.[42]

Notice that only some of the topics and areas to be analyzed of the internal components of an organization are discussed in this book. Topics that deal with organizational structure, culture, communication, leadership, motivation, control, and closely related issues are discussed later in this book. All other topics are included in other courses in your program. You will learn in those courses the important principles, theories, concepts, and tools that are part of those disciplines. The framework for strategic management and strategic planning presented in this chapter shows you how all other areas of an organization must fit together in arriving at an overall strategy and mission.

KEY TERMS

Internal analysis
Assessment of the strengths and weaknesses of an organization.

Table 4.3 Internal Factors for Analysis

Marketing	Operations	Finance	Human Resources	Other Factors
Product, service	Productivity	Profitability	Skills	Organization culture
Brand equity	Quality	Revenue	Selection	Overall control
Market research	Facilities	Asset utilization	Training and development	Information system
Sales force	Supply chain	Debt/leverage	Leadership	Information technology
Market share	Technology	Equity	Motivation	Organizational structure
Size of market	Purchasing	Per unit costs	Communication	
Distribution channels	Safety	Profit margins	Rewards	
Price	Ecological issues	Cash flow		
Promotion				

Strengths and weaknesses of an organization must be aligned with the competitive situation. That is, if the organization has a weakness in an area that is important, the weakness must be repaired. On the other hand, a strength that is not important in the competitive environment is not really a strength, at least not in this situation. Further, an organization might have a strength, but so do the competitors. Let's look at this deeper.

4 A strength is more valuable if it represents a distinctive competency that can lead to a competitive advantage. A **distinctive competency** is a unique skill or knowledge that an organization can use to accomplish something better than its competitors. Accomplishing something better than its competitors gives the organization an advantage over its competitors, a **competitive advantage.** A distinctive competency can be developed if the skill or knowledge has four characteristics: It adds value to the customer, it is rare, it is difficult to imitate, and it is organized.[43]

First, to develop into a distinctive competency, the customers of the product or service must see it as adding some value for them. For example, Wal-Mart's customers expect products to be on the shelf and to have a relatively low price. The company's information technology and inventory control system ensures that both of these are accomplished. Similarly, Southwest Airlines' operations get customers to where they want to go quickly and at a relatively low price.[44] Starbucks' coffee drinks and other drinks are perceived by Starbucks customers to very good and to be part of a "Starbucks experience." Consequently, customers readily pay relatively high prices for Starbucks products.[45]

Second, if a competency can be achieved by all competitors, no one has an advantage. Therefore, it must be rare. Patents for companies such as DuPont, Monsanto, and Pfizer can keep a competency rare, at least until the patent expires. Southwest Airlines' target markets and point-to-point flights were rare for a long time. Other airlines are attempting to copy Southwest now, but it still is not sure that they can.[46]

LEARNING OBJECTIVE 4

Explain how an organization can develop a competitive advantage.

Third, if a competency is difficult to imitate, then an organization can develop a competitive advantage. Southwest Airlines has a culture, in which its operations are embedded, that make it very difficult for other airlines to imitate. Other airlines could imitate using only one type of airplane or reduce some costs. However, it seems impossible to copy the organizational culture that keeps all parts of Southwest operating together very effectively and efficiently. On the other hand, Xerox assumed that no one could develop its expertise in

KEY TERMS

Distinctive competency
A unique organizational skill or knowledge that will help an organization accomplish something better than its competitors.

Competitive advantage
An advantage over competitors.

duplicating equipment. Companies such as Canon and Kodak clearly did, and Xerox lost its dominance.[47]

Finally, if competencies are well organized, they all work together to achieve overall results very effectively and probably efficiently. Again, look at Southwest Airlines. Essentially everything that Southwest does is well planned, tightly coordinated, and focused on its target market. Although some airlines may be catching up, Southwest has enjoyed a competitive advantage over a long period of time because its competencies add value, are rare, are difficult to imitate, and are well organized.

Another example of a company that also, in one way or another, meets all four tests is Wal-Mart. Clearly, what Wal-Mart does adds value in the eyes of customers. While the basics of some of its operations are not rare, Wal-Mart's size certainly is. The size gives it efficiencies that others cannot match. That makes it difficult to imitate. And, of course, Wal-Mart is well organized throughout. The competencies of these companies are distinctive; they are better than the competitors. Because of this, these companies have a competitive advantage.[48] Southwest Airlines and Wal-Mart accomplished this in some of the toughest industries.[49]

Strategy Formulation: Achieving a Competitive Advantage

5 Once the strategic analysis is completed and the position of the organization has been assessed, corporate and business strategy can be formulated. Strategy formulation includes (1) casting or reaffirming the organization's vision and mission, (2) setting strategic goals, (3) identifying strategic alternatives, and (4) evaluating and choosing the strategy that provides a competitive advantage and optimizes the performance of the organization in the long term.

LEARNING OBJECTIVE 5

Explain the purpose of strategy formulation and describe the two levels of strategic alternatives.

KEY TERMS

Strategic goal
The result that an organization seeks to achieve in the long term.

CASTING OR REAFFIRMING THE ORGANIZATION'S VISION AND MISSION

As we discussed earlier, central to any strategic plan are the vision and mission for the organization. Whereas a mission statement describes the products and services (what), target markets (who), and strategies (how) for an organization, a vision statement describes what the organization aspires to be in the long term. It is a description of the way in which the organization wants to be perceived by others at some future date. Based on the strategic analysis, an organization must either reaffirm its mission and vision, adjust it, or change it. Most organizations will conclude that it is appropriate to reaffirm the mission and vision. However, it may be necessary occasionally to change the mission. Intel did this in the mid-1980s when it found that Japanese producers had become very good at making memory chips that resulted in making that industry very unattractive for Intel. (See the "Leaders in Action" box.) Intel switched its focus to microprocessors.[50]

SETTING STRATEGIC GOALS

Once the vision and mission of the organization have been established, strategic goals can be determined. **Strategic goals** are statements of the results that an organization wishes to achieve in the long term. Such goals relate to the mission and vision of the organization and specify the level of performance that it desires to achieve.

Most organizations establish their goals to reflect their perception of success. In many organizations, managers look at profit as an indicator of success, and maximizing profit becomes their primary strategic goal. However, the late Peter Drucker, a prominent management theorist, warns against focusing solely on profit as a measure of success. He suggests that a preoccupation with profits alone can lead to short-term thinking and reactive management behavior. Rather, success should be operationalized more broadly and should include such things as market standing, innovation, productivity, physical and financial resources, profitability, managerial performance and development, worker performance and attitudes, and public responsibility.[51]

It is important to recognize that strategic success can vary greatly across organizations and between industries. Two organizations may measure and evaluate success in dramatically different ways. For example, a growth-oriented company may stress market-share gains, whereas an organization that operates in a mature, slow-growth industry may place its emphasis on maximizing bottom-line profitability.

Strategic goals by definition are focused on relatively broad accomplishments over the long run. Frequently, several more specific, shorter-term goals are necessary to achieve the overall goal. Similarly, goals need to be set at all levels of the organization—those at the lowest levels

Leaders in Action

Andrew Grove of Intel

Andrew Grove must have accomplished a great deal in order to be designated "the most influential business leader of the past quarter-century" in early 2004 by the Wharton School. Or course, that title fits nicely with the fact that many management experts see him as a great role model for future top-level managers.

Grove is a cofounder of Intel, the company that is the "Intel Inside" many personal computers (PCs) and now mobile phones and other digital electronic devices. Intel started out being a company that produced memory chips. It did very well in that industry until Japanese companies began to dominate the industry in the mid-1980s. That is when Grove decided that Intel should change its focus.

Grove literally fired himself from the company and reentered with the new Intel mission of being a microprocessor company. It was a large change of direction. With excellent adaptation to the changing competitive situation, Intel became very successful as a microprocessor company, with the exception of the defective Pentium chip in 1994. However, Grove and Intel handled that very serious crisis quite well. Although this hurt Intel's reputation with some users, the overall outcome probably strengthened the brand with most customers.

Then in 1997, Grove became the chairman of the board of Intel. From that time until his retirement from the board in early 2005, he established an outstanding record of selecting, developing, and managing a Board of Directors. This was especially important in light of the many questionable and illegal practices that sunk major businesses in the early 2000s. He separated the roles of the CEO and chair of the board, frequently held by one peson. He selected outside board members—members who were not also managers in the company. Grove has developed a board that truly guides, or governs, the company rather than is simply a "rubber stamp" on the one hand or a meddling board on the other. Intel's board is one of only 22 out of 2121 boards that have been rated a perfect 10 (on a 1 to 10 scale, 10 being highest), by Governance Metrics International, an organization that rates board performance.

Grove has excelled in every role that he played at Intel. Management experts say that he has the abilities and skills to understand very complex situations, to establish strategies, to set clear and high expectations, and then to guide and influence people to achieve. Grove believes that a CEO must manage to ensure that the company's success outlasts the tenure of the CEO. That is why he manages for the "quarter-century" or beyond—to manage the company so that it is successful in the long run.

Sources: "Jim Collins on Tough Calls," *Fortune,* 27 June 2005, 89–94; J. Garten, "Andy Grove Made the Elephant Dance," *BusinessWeek,* 11 April 2005, 26; "The Best Advice I Ever Got," *Fortune,* 21 March 2005, 104; B. Schlender, "Inside Andy Grove's Latest Crusade," *Fortune,* 23 August 2004, 68–78.

working together to achieve the ones at the next level, and so on up to the mission.

No matter at what level in the organization, goals must be **SMART.** That is, they need to be specific, measurable, achievable, results oriented and have a time line, or deadline. Having these characteristics increases the probability that they can be achieved.[52] Without these characteristics, goals essentially become meaningless.

- Specific: "To increase productivity per employee by 10% over last year" defines what is expected. "To do the best you can" does not. How do you know when you have done the best you can?
- Measurable: If a goal is not measurable, one will never know when it is achieved. Of course, some goals are difficult to measure. For example, "to increase customer satisfaction" might be difficult to measure. However, more specific goals, perhaps the number sold of a certain product or the total dollar amount of sales to a customer, could be defined that would give an indication of increased customer satisfaction.
- Achievable: There are varying beliefs concerning whether achievable (or realistic or attainable) should be a characteristic of a goal. Certainly, if people do not believe that they can achieve a goal, they might not even try. On the other hand, a goal that is set too low is not motivational either.

Recent research on this issue is based on the idea of goal commitment—the degree to which a person is committed to achieving the goal. A manager can use various motivational, communication, and leadership techniques to influence the degree to which employees can be committed to goals. First, the man-

KEY TERMS

SMART
The acronym standing for the characteristics that goals should possess; **s**pecific, **m**easurable, **a**chievable, **r**esults oriented, and **t**ime line.

ager can specify and clarify expectations. Then the manager can use encouragement recognition as well as other things that might assist and encourage the employees to achieve the goal. Under these circumstances, goals that might otherwise seem too high and unachievable can be seen as quite achievable. General Electric and Goldman Sachs use this approach and label some goals "**stretch goals,**" goals that are designed to be relatively high.[53] Some therefore suggest that the "A" in SMART should be "audacious," especially at the top of the organization.[54]

- **R**esults oriented: The goal should focus on a final outcome, not just on activity. For example, "to increase advertising expenditure to $3 million dollars during the next year" may not necessarily lead to success. Rather, it might just result in increased expenses. The increase in advertising expenditures must be linked to some measurable change in sales.
- **T**ime line: Without a deadline, one does not know when the goal is to be achieved. "To increase employee productivity by 10%" has no meaning if there is no time associated with it. "To increase employee productivity by 10% during the next 12-month period in order to reduce per unit cost by 2%" is better.

IDENTIFYING STRATEGIC ALTERNATIVES

The third stage of the strategy formulation process involves identifying strategic alternatives. These alternatives should be developed in light of the organization's mission and vision; its strengths, weaknesses, opportunities, and threats; and its strategic goals.

Strategy can be defined in a variety of ways. The following sections describe two ways to define strategic alternatives—grand strategies and generic strategies.

Grand Strategies

Many organizations define their strategic alternatives in terms of grand strategies. A **grand strategy** is a comprehensive, general approach for achieving the strategic goals of an organization.[55] Grand strategies fall into three broad categories: stability, growth, and retrenchment strategies.

KEY TERMS

Stretch goals
Goals that are intended to be high.

Grand strategy
A comprehensive, general approach for achieving the strategic goals of an organization.

Stability Strategy A stability strategy is intended to ensure continuity in the operations and performance of the organization. At the business level, stability strategies require very little if any change in the organization's product, service, or market focus. Organizations that pursue a stability strategy continue to offer the same products and services to the same target markets as in the past. They may, however, attempt to capture a larger share of their existing market through market penetration or improve bottom-line profits through greater operational efficiency.

Market penetration is the initial strategy of most start-up organizations. At the outset, organizations enter a specific geographic market with a particular set of products and services. Stability is the primary goal of organizations at this stage of development because they are focused on generating the sales and revenues to succeed in their businesses. Once the market they serve has been fully penetrated, the organization may move on to pursue the next category strategies—growth.

Growth Strategy A growth strategy is designed to increase the sales and profits of the organization. At the business level, growth strategies involve the development of new products for new or existing markets or the entry into new markets with existing products. The purpose of growth strategies is to increase the sales and profits of the organization in the long term and to position the organization as a market leader within its industry.

In many cases, growth strategies focus on being innovative, seeking out new opportunities, and taking risks. Such strategies are suitable for organizations that operate in dynamic, growing environments in which creativity, innovation, and organizational responsiveness are often more important than efficiency. Sony is an example of a company that pursues a growth strategy by offering a steady stream of new, innovative products. Some new product innovations even displace existing products, but they all contribute to the organization's long-term growth in sales and profits.

Over the last several decades, many organizations have pursued a growth strategy by entering the international marketplace. When an organization has fully penetrated the domestic marketplace, international markets provide an opportunity to grow sales further.

Retrenchment Strategy The purpose of a retrenchment strategy is to reverse negative sales and profitability trends. At the business level, retrenchment strategy focuses on streamlining the operations of the organization by reducing costs and assets. Such reductions may require plant closings, the sale of plants and equipment, spending cuts, or a reduction in the organization's workforce. Furthermore, new systems, processes, and procedures must be designed to support the new, leaner organization. If the retrenchment strategy is successful, stability or growth strategies may be considered in the long term.

Figure 4.5 Generic Strategies Matrix

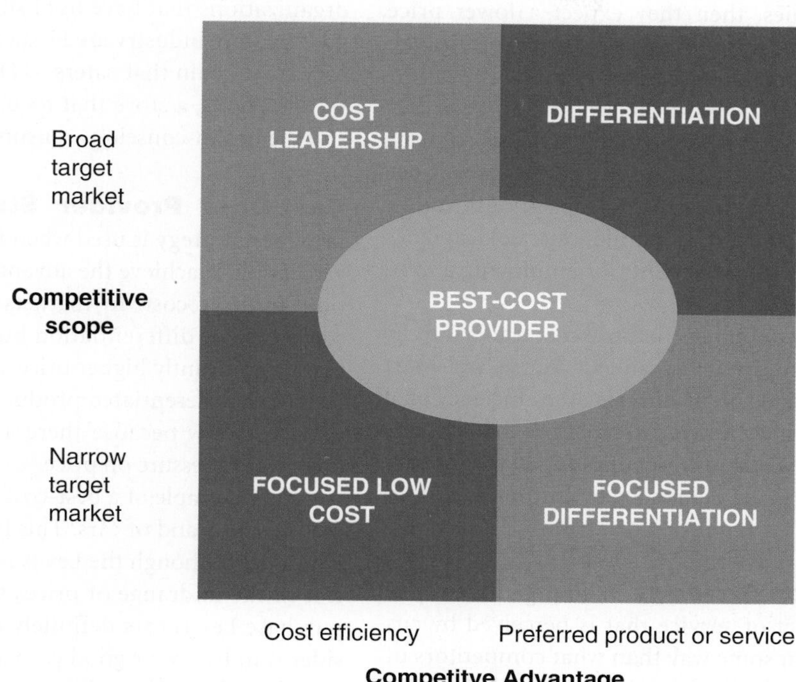

During the economic troubles of 2001–2002, made more difficult by the 9/11 terrorist attacks, many companies in the United States pursued retrenchment strategies, at least for the short run. For example, airlines grounded roughly 20% of their fleets and began the painful process of layoffs and restructuring.[56] Aerospace companies that served the airline industry also had to retrench their operations. Boeing laid off 30,000 workers, approximately one third of its workforce, and cut production by nearly half. Suppliers of tires, engines, and other parts of aircrafts, such as Goodrich and General Electric, also shaved thousands of jobs.

But it was not just the airlines and aircraft manufacturers who were hurt. The hotel business was negatively affected, as were car rental companies. In fact, ANC Rental, the parent company of Alamo Rent A Car and National Car Rental, was forced into bankruptcy following the September 11, 2001, tragedy. [57]

Generic Strategy

A **generic strategy** reflects the primary way in which an organization competes in its market. Michael Porter, a well-known Harvard professor, identified generic strategies that can be used to describe the strategy of most organizations. Porter originally identified three strategies; cost leadership, differentiation, and focus. Initially the focus strategy included focused low cost and focused differentiation, which are shown separately in Figure 4.5, but are usually thought of as separate strategies now. At the time, Porter suggested that a company had to choose either low cost or differentiation; to attempt both would cause a company to achieve neither and be "stuck in the middle."[58]

However, over time, many industries have changed, requiring a company to accomplish the benefits of both low cost and differentiation. Also, some companies have actually used a low-cost approach as a way to differentiate themselves from competitors—for example, Southwest Airlines and Edward Jones.[59] Therefore, a strategy usually called best-cost provider depicts a strategy that combines the advantages of both low cost and differentiation. [60]

Porter defines the generic strategies along two primary dimensions—competitive scope and competitive advantage provided by the strategy. Competitive scope refers to the target market chosen by the organization. The organization's focus in how it intends to serve its customers and manage its operations in order to outperform its competitors is called competitive advantage.

Cost Leadership Strategy The basic reason for why an organization would pursue

KEY TERMS

Generic strategy
The fundamental way in which an organization competes in the marketplace.

a **cost leadership strategy** is that a relatively low price is important to customers. That is, if customers do not see important differences between products or services from different companies, then they expect a lower price. When there is downward pressure on price, profit margins are squeezed, making it necessary for organizations to reduce the per unit cost of the product or service. To do so, the organization must be highly efficient so that it can achieve a low-cost position in the industry. Costs may be minimized by maximizing capacity utilization, achieving size advantages (economies of scale), capitalizing on technology improvements, or employing a more productive workforce.

Examples of companies that use cost leadership include Bic pens, Timex watches, and, of course, Wal-Mart. Each has concentrated on maximizing the efficiency of all its systems, achieving a lower-cost structure than its competitors. This allows these companies to sell for the relatively low prices that are demanded by customers and still be profitable.

Differentiation Strategy If an organization can produce a product or service that is perceived by customers as better in some way than what competitors offer, then that organization should pursue a **differentiation strategy.** When customers believe that a certain type or brand of product or service is better than another, the organization can charge a higher price based on the differentiated product or service feature. Distinctive characteristics may include exceptional customer service, quality, dependability, availability, innovation, or image.

Many organizations pursue a differentiation strategy. Examples of products that have succeeded through such a strategy include Cross pens, Movado watches, Starbucks coffee, and Jaguar automobiles.

Focus Strategy A **focus strategy** occurs when an organization targets a specific, narrow segment of the market and thereby avoids competing with other competitors that target a broader segment of the market. Companies that pursue a focus strategy may compete in their niche market with either a cost leadership (focused low cost) or a differentiation (focused differentiation) strategy. Therefore, the focus strategy appears in two boxes of the matrix shown in Figure 4.5.

Examples of products that have succeeded based on a focus strategy include BMW motorcycles, A&W root beer, and White Castle hamburgers. Prime examples of organizations that have used such a strategy within the grocery store industry are Fiesta Mart, a Texas-based grocery store chain that caters to Hispanic consumers, and Whole Foods, a store that focuses on organic products and the health-conscious consumer.

Best-Cost Provider Strategy The **best-cost provider strategy** is used when it is important for an organization to achieve the advantages of both differentiation and low cost. In markets where customers want some type of differentiation but also are not willing to pay a significantly higher price, a company must work to provide a differentiated product but also must keep per unit costs low because there a ceiling on price, if not downward pressure on price.

One example of a best-cost provider strategy is Toyota's Lexus brand of cars. This is especially true with the ES model. Although the Lexus is considered a luxury car, it is in the midrange of prices for cars. Customers who purchase Lexus cars definitely do so because they consider it to be a very good car with an image with which they identify. It is a differentiated product for them. However, there are many cars of very similar quality. Therefore, there is a ceiling on how high the price can go. Because the features that help differentiate a Lexus do cost more and there is a ceiling on price, profits can be squeezed. Lexus must work to both keep its cars differentiated plus keep per unit costs down or at least keep them from rising.[61]

EVALUATING AND CHOOSING STRATEGY

Designing strategy can be a challenging task. When determining an optimal strategy for the organization, managers can draw on a variety of tools and techniques to generate, evaluate, and choose among strategic alternatives. Among the most popular evaluation and decision-making techniques are portfolio assessment models and decision matrices.

Portfolio assessment models provide a mechanism for evaluating an organization's portfolio of businesses, products, or services. These models classify the organization's portfolio of holdings into categories based on certain important criteria such as growth rate or competitive position. Based on that classification, the organization's portfolio is assessed as to the appropriateness of the mix of business units, products, or services. The optimal strategy for each business unit, product, or service may

KEY TERMS

Cost leadership strategy
A strategy for competing on the basis of low per unit cost.

Differentiation strategy
A strategy for competing by offering products or services that are different from those of competitors.

Focus strategy
A strategy for competing by targeting a specific and narrow segment of the market.

Best-cost provider strategy
A strategy based on achieving the benefits of both low-cost and differentiation strategies.

vary according to its position in the portfolio. Popular portfolio assessment models include the Boston Consulting Group (BCG) growth-share matrix and the General Electric industry attractiveness–business strength matrix. Both of these portfolio assessment models will be discussed in Chapter 6.

Decision matrices help managers choose among strategic alternatives. A *decision matrix* provides a method for evaluating alternative strategies according to the criteria that the organization's managers consider most important such as contribution toward sales growth, market share growth, profitability, and the like. Managers rate strategic alternatives according to the established criteria and select the alternative that has the best overall rating. Chapter 6 also provides a detailed discussion of decision matrices that can be used to make strategic choices.

Once the strategy formulation stage of the strategic planning process is complete, it is time to begin implementing the strategy. Strategy implementation is a critical and complex component of the strategic management and strategic planning processes.

Strategy Implementation: Focusing on Results

6 The importance of strategy implementation should never be underestimated because the best-formulated strategy is virtually worthless if it cannot be implemented effectively. If an organization is to achieve the best results from its strategic planning efforts, it must ensure that its strategy is put into action. That many times is even more difficult than establishing the strategy. Why is that so? Often, managers simply underestimate and under-manage the strategy implementation process.[62] Organizations that achieve strategic success commit a tremendous amount of time, energy, and effort to making sure that the strategy is implemented effectively.[63] That, however, does not mean that the strategy needs to be long and drawn out. In fact, successful companies such as Barclays Bank, Cisco, 3M, and Southwest Airlines "keep it simple," making it specific with very direct and clear language that states what the company will and will not do.[64]

A direct, specific, clear strategy is a good foundation for people to understand what they are to do because implementation of strategy involves "everything" in the organization as the organization carries out its day-to-day operations. Everything that the people in an organization do should be directly or at least indirectly focused on achieving goals and, ultimately, the mission of the organization. Of course, the implementation of strategy must also be planned.

The planning part of implementation includes the necessity for establishing strategies at other levels of the organization and in all parts of the organization. For example, each major part of an organization should have its mission and overall goals, which must be aligned with the organization's overall mission and goals. There also needs to be guidelines in the form of other plans, policies, procedures, rules, and the like. Although all these things are important, the organization also needs a culture that supports everything that the organization intends to do and helps keep focus on the overall mission.[65] These are discussed in the next chapter.

As with internal analysis, the remaining chapters of this book and other courses in your program deal with other aspects of managing an organization. Assuming that the overall mission and strategy of an organization are proper, everything in an organization must be aligned with them to achieve success. The remaining chapters of this book discuss the important topics of the organizational structure, the right people and related human resource practices, the organizational culture, good communication, leadership, motivation, and the effective control that must be in place to guide everything to success.

Important principles, theories, concepts, and tools needed for other parts of implementation will be learned in other courses in your program. For example, knowledge of marketing, finance, production, information systems and information technology, economics, accounting, and other knowledge will be needed to successfully achieve the overall mission of an organization. As you study the other topics in this book and those in your other classes, think about where and how they fit into overall strategic management.

LEARNING OBJECTIVE 6

Explain the role of strategy implementation.

Evaluation and Control: Achieving Effectiveness and Efficiency

The last stage of the strategic planning process is evaluation and control. This involves evaluating progress toward the mission in order to understand what works and what does not and to guide operations of the organization so that the mission is achieved. Although this is conceptually logical, it is made very practical by the provisions of Sarbanes-Oxley Act, discussed earlier. Because Section 404 of that law requires CEOs to not only certify financial reports as accurate but also take responsibility for anything that is erroneous or misleading in the reports, managers must be sure that overall control is in place.[66]

As was discussed in the overall framework to studying management in Chapter 1, many aspects of evaluation and control are built into the functions that managers perform. Job descriptions, performance appraisals, communications with managers, the organizational culture, and the like all guide behavior of the people as they perform the operations of the organization. Other details of control are discussed in Chapter 15. There, we discuss evaluation and control from a strategic perspective (comprehensive and long run).

LEARNING OBJECTIVE 7

Explain the importance of evaluation and control of strategy and its implementation.

In general, control mechanisms can be either feedforward or feedback controls. Let's examine what each involves.

FEEDFORWARD CONTROLS

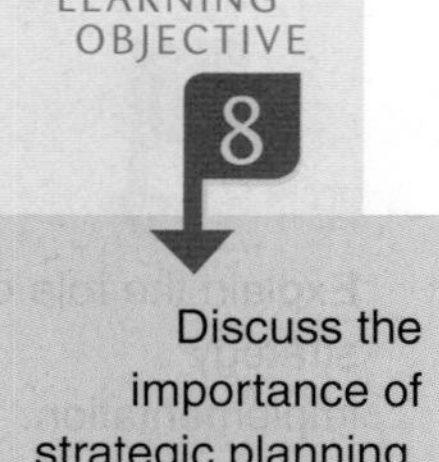

7 **Feedforward controls** are designed to predict changes in the external environment or the internal operations of the organization that may affect its ability to fulfill its mission and meet its strategic goals. Feedforward controls are designed to identify changes in any condition, internal or external, upon which the strategy of the organization was based.

LEARNING OBJECTIVE 8

Discuss the importance of strategic planning.

Consider, for example, a large construction company that plans to develop 500,000 acres of residential property over the next 3 years. By the end of the first year of the company's plan, the economy begins to deteriorate, and interest rates, inflation, and unemployment begin to rise. If feedforward controls are in place and are designed to detect changes in the economic conditions on which the construction company's plan is based, the company will know to adapt its strategy to the changing economic conditions.

KEY TERMS

Feedforward control
A control designed to predict changes in the external environment or the internal operations of the organization that may affect an organization's ability to fulfill its mission.

Feedback control
A control that compares the actual performance of the organization to its planned performance.

FEEDBACK CONTROLS

Feedback controls compare the actual performance of the organization to its planned performance. These controls usually target the goals established in the organization's strategic and operational plans. One of the primary benefits of feedback control is that it focuses the attention of managers on the results for which they are responsible in the organization's plan. This may discourage managers from spending too much time on situations and issues that are unrelated to the overall goals of the organization. Often, feedback controls evaluate financial results such as revenues, profitability, stock price, and budget variances. Other feedback controls monitor nonfinancial results such as customer relations, product and service quality, productivity, and employee turnover.

Organizations should maintain both feedforward and feedback controls. Relying on only one type of control could be a mistake because these controls focus on different issues that could affect the organization's plans. Just as organizations establish different goals and pursue different strategies, they should develop control systems to meet their specific strategic needs.

An organization's control system must be in alignment with its strategic initiatives.[67] For example, an organization pursuing a growth strategy is unlikely to develop the same control system as one that is pursuing a retrenchment strategy. The growth-oriented firm would monitor such variables as forecasts for demand, sales levels, sales growth, increases in market share, and brand awareness. In contrast, the organization pursuing retrenchment would monitor such variables as supply costs, productivity, sales per employee, sales-to-assets ratios, gross and net margins, and other indicators of efficiency and bottom-line profitability.

Information Technology and Strategic Planning

8 The increasing availability and sophistication of information technology have had a tremendous impact on the ability of organizations to develop effective strategic plans. Such technology has made both internal and external sources of information more readily available to managers who are responsible for strategic planning. For example, tracking the sales of individual products in specific regions and at various price levels is much simpler given the information technology available today.

Meeting The Challenge

Focus and Implementation at Hewlett-Packard

In less than 3 months after he became CEO of HP, Mark Hurd is gaining the reputation for focusing on execution—that is, making the strategy work. He has reversed the combination of the printer division with the PCs division and is rethinking the sales force organization, two major parts of the previous strategy. In addition, he is hiring new managers who have credentials as being "operations types." The overall strategy before was broader and attempted to gain synergies between HP's divisions. Hurd is choosing much more focus.

Not only is the printer division separate again, but it is also focusing on the most attractive segments of the printer market: discontinuing the printers that are not in attractive, profitable segments. Similarly, Hurd intends to reorganize the overall sales force so that smaller groups can focus on the specific products and markets, something that is in line with narrower product groups. Hurd is also looking at the entire organization to identify areas where costs can be cut.

Will this rethinking of HP's strategy changing from a focus on being the best technology company in the world to a focus on specific markets, products, and implementation be successful?

Sources: P. Burrows, "The Un-Carly Unveils His Game Plan," *BusinessWeek,* 27 June 2005, 36; P. Tam, "H-P's New Chief Separates PC Unit from Printer Arm," *Wall Street Journal,* 14 June 2005, A3, A6; P. Burrows, "Why HP Is Pruning the Printers," *BusinessWeek,* 9 May 2005, 38–39.

Similarly, information regarding such things as market-share fluctuations, profitability, and productivity measures is more readily available, and operational activities such as purchasing, inventory management, and human resource management are more easily monitored.

Competitive intelligence, a method by which companies track the strategies and actions of their competitors, has been enhanced greatly through the use of comprehensive databases and analytical tools. New approaches to meeting the needs of customers have emerged as companies use information technology to better understand their customers' profiles and track their preferences.[68] Clearly, a well-designed management information system can provide accurate, timely information to managers throughout the organization.[69]

Strategic planning is a critical organizational activity that will affect the long-term performance of most organizations. We conclude by exploring the implications of strategic planning for the manager and leader of tomorrow.

Implications for Leaders

Successful leaders must have excellent strategic thinking and planning skills. It is much easier to influence employees to follow your strategy when they have a clear understanding of the present and a vision for the future. As you engage in strategic planning, keep the following tips in mind:

- Understand the realities of the external environment in which you operate.
- Understand the importance of a thorough and accurate assessment of the current situation of the organization.
- A plan will be only as good as the analysis on which it is based.
- Strategic vision is critical for ensuring a common strategic direction for the organization.
- Make sure that the mission statement is a working document that provides direction for the members of the organization.
- Strategic goals serve as targets for achievement. Make sure that they are specific, measurable, results oriented, and have a established time for their achievement.
- Strategy should be designed to provide the organization with a distinctive competitive advantage in the long run.
- A strategic plan is meaningless if it is not implemented well.
- Provide for evaluation and control to be sure that operations are on track for accomplishment of the organization's mission.

In this chapter, you have learned about the process of strategic planning and how it fits into overall strategic management. This process provides a strong foundation for the development and implementation of effective strategy.

SUMMARY

1. Strategic planning is the process by which an organization makes decisions and plans actions that affect its long-term performance. The purpose of strategic planning is to move the organization from where it is to where it wants to be.
2. The strategic planning process consists of four primary stages: (a) strategic analysis, (b) strategy formulation, (c) strategy implementation, and (d) evaluation and control.
3. The purpose of strategic analysis is to assess the current condition of the organization. Strategic analysis requires three primary activities: (a) assessing the mission of the organization, (b) conducting an external environmental analysis to identify the opportunities and threats facing the organization, and (c) conducting an internal environmental analysis to identify the strengths and weaknesses of the organization.
4. Strategy formulation requires the development or reaffirmation of an organizational mission and vision, the determination of strategic goals, the identification of strategic alternatives, and the evaluation and selection of a strategy that distinguishes the organization from its competitors.
5. Strategy can be described as grand strategies or generic strategies. Grand strategies include stability, growth, and retrenchment. Generic strategies include cost leadership, differentiation, focused low cost, focused differentiation, add best-cost provider.
6. Strategy implementation is the action phase of the strategic planning process as it puts the strategy of the organization into effect.
7. Strategic evaluation and control involves monitoring the organization's progress toward implementing its plans and achieving its goals. Strategic control mechanisms identify deviations between actual and planned results so that managers can make the adjustments necessary to ensure that organizational goals can be achieved in the long term. In general, control mechanisms can be either feedforward or feedback controls.
8. Information technology can be used to improve the strategic planning efforts of most organizations. From data collection to support strategic analysis to the monitoring of performance indicators, management information systems provide managers with data that can enhance the effectiveness of the strategic planning process.

The rapidly changing business environment creates many challenges for managers who must plan strategically. Managers of the future must remember the basic principles of strategic planning as they attempt to ensure the competitiveness of their organizations through the development of effective strategy.

REVIEW QUESTIONS

1. (LEARNING OBJECTIVE 1) Define strategic management.
2. (LEARNING OBJECTIVE 2) Describe the process of strategic management. How are the four stages of the process interrelated?
3. (LEARNING OBJECTIVE 3) What is involved in conducting a strategic analysis? More specifically, how does one (a) develop or assess an organizational mission, (b) identify the opportunities and threats facing an organization, and (c) identify the strengths and weaknesses of an organization?
4. (LEARNING OBJECTIVE 4) Explain how an organization can establish a competitive advantage.
5. (LEARNING OBJECTIVE 5) What is the purpose of strategy formulation? What roles do vision and goals play in formulating strategy?
6. (LEARNING OBJECTIVE 5) Describe the three grand strategies and the generic strategies. Give examples of organizations that have pursued each of these strategic alternatives.
7. (LEARNING OBJECTIVE 6) What role does strategy implementation play in the strategic planning process? What aspects of a firm's organizational system need to be in alignment with its strategy?
8. (LEARNING OBJECTIVE 7) Describe the elements of strategic evaluation and control.
9. (LEARNING OBJECTIVE 8) How has information technology affected the strategic planning process in contemporary organizations?

DISCUSSION QUESTIONS

Improving Critical Thinking

1. If an organization has competencies but they are not distinctive, can it develop a competitive advantage? Explain why or why not.
2. How has the emergence of a global marketplace complicated the process of strategic analysis for organizations that pursue international strategies?

Enhancing Communication Skills

3. Consider an organization that you have worked for at some time or that you currently work for. Would you classify that organization as having a stability, growth, or retrenchment strategy? Do the organization's culture, leadership, and control systems match its strategy? To improve your oral communication skills, prepare a brief presentation for the class.
4. Under what conditions might an organization choose to shift from a cost leadership strategy to a differentiation strategy? Would this be a difficult adjustment for most organizations? To practice your written communication skills, write a one-page summary of your response.

Building Teamwork

5. Discuss the following with a group of four or five students. Describe the effect each of the following would have on an organization:
   a. Ineffective implementation of a good strategy
   b. Effective implementation of a poor strategy
   c. Ineffective implementation of a poor strategy
6. Form teams of four or five students. For each of the following strategies, identify an organization (beyond those cited in the text) that can be characterized as pursuing each strategy: (a) cost leadership, (b) differentiation, and (c) best-cost provider. Why did you choose these particular organizations? Be prepared to discuss your selections with the class.

Chapter

5

Planning in the Contemporary Organization

CHAPTER OVERVIEW

In Chapter 4, we discussed strategic planning, which deals with establishing comprehensive plans for the long run. We discussed strategic analysis, establishing mission and vision, formulating plans and strategic goals (strategy), implementing the plans, and evaluating and controlling to make sure that the mission and strategic goals are accomplished. It was also mentioned in Chapter 4 that planning and implementation required plans at all levels of the organization.

In this chapter, we discuss why planning is important and explain the difference between strategic planning and planning at other organizational levels, called operational planning. Planning is important because it ensures that the organization is both effective and efficient in its activities; it provides the members of an organization with guidance and direction in how to deliver products and services to its customers. Most organizations engage in both strategic and operational planning. Strategic planning has three levels: corporate, business, and functional. Operational planning deals with the process of determining the necessary day-to-day activities to achieve the long-term goals of the organization. We also discuss the types of operational plans. These include standing plans that deal with organizational issues or problems that recur frequently and single-use plans that address specific organizational situations that typically do not recur. Finally, we discuss common barriers to effective and efficient planning and how to overcome them. The barriers to effective planning include demand on the manager's time, ambiguous and uncertain operating environments, and resistance to change. Overcoming these barriers involves learning to apply managerial functions, such as organizing and leading, more effectively; involving employees in decision making; taking advantage of a diversity of views, and encouraging strategic thinking among employees.

LEARNING OBJECTIVES

When you have finished studying this chapter, you should be able to

1. Describe the managerial function of planning and explain why planning is critical for effective leadership.
2. Explain the benefits and costs of planning.
3. Discuss the potential advantages and disadvantages of top-down and bottom-up planning.
4. Define strategic planning and describe the three levels of strategic planning.
5. Define operational planning and distinguish between standing and single-use plans.
6. Describe individual planning systems such as management by objectives and the Balanced Scorecard.
7. Define contingency planning and identify the circumstances under which contingency planning would be appropriate.
8. Discuss how advances in information technology have affected operational planning.
9. Describe common barriers to effective planning and explain ways to reduce these barriers.

Facing The Challenge

Can Motorola Survive?

Motorola Inc. has a very long, proud, and successful past. It built some of the first radios for cars, walkie-talkies for use by the military in World War II, equipment used for communication between astronauts on the moon and NASA headquarters on earth, and was a leader in mobile phones. In fact, until 1998 Motorola had secured over 50% of the global market for mobile phones.

In 1998 Nokia surpassed Motorola's share of the global mobile phone market. Then Samsung pushed Motorola to third place for a time during 2004. Profits were shrinking. During the early 2000s, the company cut 60,000 jobs, 40% of the people it had in 2000. The reasons: Customers saw Motorola as "shoddy" quality, outdated products, and a boring styling; and the company had a late shifting from analog to digital technology.

The organizational culture did not stress keeping up with customer preferences and the nature of competition in the industry. The organizational structure worked to insulate one business unit from another rather than help them coordinate and communicate with each other. The reward system was based on financial incentives geared to the performance of each business unit separately, which added to the conflict rather than cooperation between parts of the company. Many employees saw the company as a huge bureaucracy with business units at war with each other.

CEO Christopher Galvin, grandson of the founder, Paul Galvin, tried to turn things around. He spun off a semiconductor business because it did not fit the focus of the company and cut costs to try to get back the profitability. However, in early 2004, he left the company. The Board of Directors then selected a new CEO, Edward Zander, formerly the second in command at Sun Microsystems, Inc. Zander's vision is to get Motorola back to the top of the communication industry.

Sources: C. Rhoads, "Motorola's Modernizer," *Wall Street Journal,* 23 June 2005, B1, B5; B. Stone, "Motorola's Good Call," *Newsweek,* 14 March 2005, 42–43; E. Corcoran, "Making Over Motorola," *Forbes* 174, no. 12 (December 2004): 103–108; R. Crockett, "Reinventing Motorola," *BusinessWeek,* 2 August 2004, 82–83; "Hello, Moto," *Economist* 370, no. 8357 (January 2004): 58.

Introduction

Edward Zander certainly has an interesting vision for Motorola (see the "Facing the Challenge" box). If achieved, it would get Motorola back to a position that it enjoyed for a long time in the past. But why did Motorola fall out of a leading position in its industry? As with most situations, "it's not just one thing."

Apparently, Motorola did not keep up to date with understanding customers and the changes in technology and competitors in the industry. It also set up plans, policies, rules, an organizational structure, reward system, and an organizational culture, all of which interfered with keeping up rather than helping to keep up. As you read this chapter, think of the types of plans that Zander needs to get Motorola back to a successful position. Then, think about what Motorola needs to do as you read the rest of the chapters, especially those dealing with organizational structure, motivation, and organizational culture.

Planning provides a foundation for all organizational activities. Through planning, managers coordinate organizational activities so that the goals of the organization can be achieved. Organizational success depends on the ability of managers to develop a plan that brings together, in a logical way, the diverse set of tasks that occur within the organization. In its simplest form, planning involves understanding the current situation of the organization, knowing what results the organization desires to achieve, devising the means to achieve those results, and guiding and controlling operations so that the results are achieved (Figure 5.1). Organizational leaders must understand the importance of planning and be prepared to provide guidance to other organizational members in devising and implementing plans.

Managerial Planning

Planning is an essential but potentially complex managerial function. To gain a better understanding of the planning function, we discuss a few key issues: What is planning, why should managers plan, and where should the planning process begin?

Figure 5.1 Planning as a Linking Mechanism

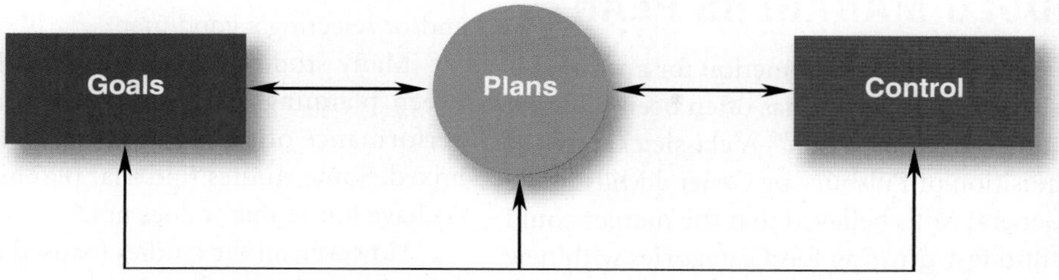

WHAT IS PLANNING?

LEARNING OBJECTIVE 1

Describe the managerial function of planning and explain why planning is critical for effective leadership.

1 We already discussed strategic planning in the previous chapter. Here, we focus on the **planning** that provides the details necessary to achieve the overall mission and strategic goals. This planning is the process of outlining the activities that are necessary to achieve the goals of the organization. Through planning, managers determine how organizational resources are to be allocated and how the activities of the organization will be assigned to individuals and work groups. The output of the planning process is the plan. A **plan** is a blueprint for action; it prescribes the activities necessary for the organization to realize its goals.[1]

The purpose of planning is simple—to ensure that the organization is both effective and efficient in its activities. In a broad sense, an organization must develop a plan that ensures that the appropriate products and services are offered to its customers. More specifically, planning gives guidance and direction to the members of the organization about their role in delivering those products and services.[2] As indicated in

At the Forefront

Is Failing to Plan Planning to Fail?

The success rate of new businesses is less than 5% over the first 24 to 30 months. It is even less than that for new products and services, from idea to a marketable product or service. The success rate of new businesses and new products and services will probably decrease because speed to the marketplace is becoming more important because of the effects of competition related to globalization and technology development. How can the success rate be increased, or can it?

A major study of 233 business start-ups found that planning actually helped new businesses to survive, at least past 30 months. That is significant because approximately 95% of them normally do not survive that long, as indicated above.

The study found that planning helped the business to "get off the ground," by guiding overall management, and also helped the new businesses with product development—a base of success. Specifically, planning helped new businesses make better decisions that included clearer understanding of what needed to be done. In addition to the typical components of plans, the study found that goals were a major factor that guided operations, providing measures and a timetable. Interestingly, planning helped do all of this in less time than it might take without planning because analysis was conducted well beforehand.

Sources: B. Matherne, "If You Fail to Plan, Do You Plan to Fail?" *Academy of Management Executive* 18, no. 4 (November 2004): 156; F. Delmar and S. Shane, "Does Business Planning Facilitate the Development of New Businesses?" *Strategic Management Journal* 24, no. 12 (2003): 1165–1185.

Figure 5.1, plans and the guidance, or control, in implementing them lead to accomplishment of goals.

WHY SHOULD MANAGERS PLAN?

Planning is a critical managerial function for any organization to be successful. In fact, it has often been said that "failing to plan is planning to fail."[3] A classic example of this is the acquisition of Pillsbury by General Mills in the recent past. General Mills believed that the merger could help it break into fast-growing food categories with new products to augment its tried and true, yet quite mature, cereal product lines (Cheerios, Wheaties, and Chex). But it took far longer and at a greater cost than expected, largely because of a failure to plan effectively. Integrating Pillsbury into the General Mills organization proved to be more challenging than expected, so much so that new product development efforts had to be delayed. Competitors, sensing the turmoil at General Mills, took advantage of the company's lack of focus, launching many new products that cut into General Mills' market share. By the time the merger was complete, General Mills' profits had declined significantly, the stock price had fallen, and the company had lost its market leadership position in the cereal business to Kellogg. With the integration of Pillsbury finished, General Mills finally started to achieve the benefits of acquiring the Pillsbury Company.[4]

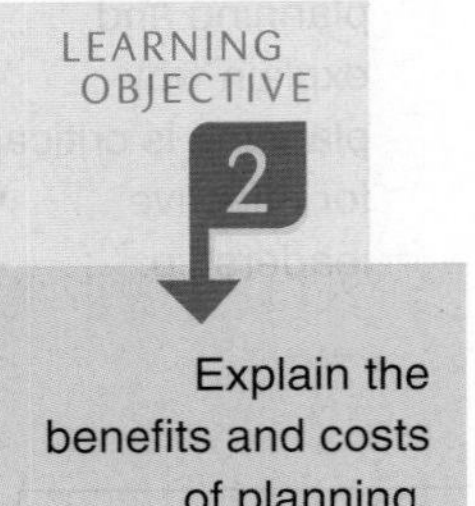

Explain the benefits and costs of planning.

Although there are benefits to planning, there certainly are costs also. Each will be discussed.

Benefits of Planning

2 Ideally, planning leads to superior performance for the organization. From a general perspective, the planning process offers four primary benefits: It provides (1) a "road map," (2) better coordination, (3) a focus on forward thinking, and (4) more effective control systems.

KEY TERMS

Planning
Setting goals and defining the actions necessary to achieve those goals.

Plan
A blueprint for action that prescribes the activities necessary for the organization to realize its goals.

A Road Map "If you don't know where you are going, any road will take you there"[5] (paraphrase of Cheshire Cat to Alice in the movie *Alice in Wonderland*). Of course, you do not know where you will end up. Organizations are created for a purpose, so that will not do. Organizations are set up to arrive at a certain place. That is reflected in their missions and strategic goals. Assuming that an organization has a good mission, it then needs a map that will help select the best or at least better roads that will guide the organization to the mission. Planning is constructing and/or selecting a good map.

Many studies have dealt with the relationship between planning and performance, especially financial performance of an organization. The results have been mixed. Some studies find that planning does "pay." Others have found that it does not.[6]

However, all the studies focused on whether or not a formal planning process was involved. It is quite possible that a formal planning process, involving formal meetings and processes and a formal plan, may not lead to better performance for several reasons. One reason is that even with a formal plan, if it is not followed or implemented, it will not lead to success. Another reason is that a formal process does not guarantee a good plan. Still another reason is that organizational members can undertake very effective planning without necessarily going through an elaborate process. It might be that the people in an organization have learned to think strategically, as was suggested in both Chapters 1 and 4.[7]

Herb Kelleher, cofounder and now chair of the board of Southwest Airlines, says that his company does not do planning. At the same time, he says that Southwest must always understand its industry, its customers, and its employees—every aspect of conducting successful operations, now and in the future. Also, essentially everything that the company does is clearly and directly linked to the overall strategic goals of Southwest. Southwest is the most financially successful airline in the United States, and its financial success is high compared to many companies overall. Here is an example of a company that does planning very well yet does not get bogged down in the formalities and details of planning that can decrease, or destroy, the benefits of planning. It has a clear mission and a very good road map to get there.[8]

The important issue with planning is not whether an organization does it formally or not. It is whether the organization has a clear mission and a road map that members of the organization understand. Complete the exercise in the "Now Apply It" box to help understand this.

Better Coordination Planning provides a much-needed foundation for the coordination of a broad range of organizational activities. Most organizations consist of multiple work groups, each of which is responsible for contributing to the accomplishment of the goals of the organization. A plan helps both to define the responsibilities of these work groups and to coordinate their activities. Without such a mechanism for coordination, directing the efforts of organizational

Now Apply It

Developing a Professional Development Plan

Developing a professional development plan helps you focus on your primary career objectives. The planning process includes three major activities: goal setting, developing a plan of action, and monitoring your progress. Start by identifying a professional goal. This goal can be either short term (such as making the dean's list) or long term (such as owning your own business). With that goal in mind, develop a list of three things that you can do to achieve it. Finally, develop a method to control your progress. How can you make sure that your plan is being implemented properly?

Goal: Establish a professional goal.

____

Plan: Delineate activities that will help you attain your professional goal.

1. ______________________________
2. ______________________________
3. ______________________________

Control: Identify ways to monitor the implementation of your plan.

1. ______________________________
2. ______________________________
3. ______________________________

members and groups toward common organizational goals would be difficult.

At a broader level, consider the coordination needed to establish global brand recognition for a particular product. Global brand recognition requires that the product's market position, advertising strategy, personality, look, and feel must be essentially the same from one country to another. Many companies, such as IBM, Visa, and Coca-Cola seek to achieve a consistent brand image across the dozens of international markets that they serve. These companies, like many other global organizations, use the planning process to help build consistency in their brands across international markets. Using the same planning template, terminology, and process helps managers coordinate their efforts to achieve the same brand attributes and identity throughout the global marketplace.[9]

Focus on Forward Thinking The planning function forces managers to think ahead and consider resource needs and potential opportunities or threats that the organization may face in the future. Although the identification of organizational problems and solutions is an important part of the planning process, its overriding focus should be on preparing the organization to perform more effectively and efficiently in the future than in the past.

Today's highly competitive and dynamic business environment demands that managers be forward thinking, but many companies find it challenging to anticipate the changes that will affect their businesses. Consider, for example, the music industry. It wasn't so long ago that the distribution channels for music were easy to understand and to control. But with the arrival of digital media for distributing music, the entire industry has changed dramatically. Stores that sold recorded music in the form of CDs, tape cassettes, and even some vinyl records now face tremendous challenges from all forms of downloads of music. Digital media made it possible for Wal-Mart, Starbucks, iTunes, and others to compete with stores that traditionally sold music. How will music, movies, and even books, be distributed in the future?

More Effective Control Systems An organization's plan provides a foundation for control of the processes and progress of the company. The implementation of the activities prescribed by the plan can be evaluated, and progress toward the achievement of performance objectives can be monitored. Controls provide mechanisms for ensuring that the organization is moving in the right direction and making progress toward achieving its goals.[10] For example, General Mills could have likely benefited from a well-developed control system to ensure that its efforts to integrate Pillsbury into its operations were proceeding as planned. Such a control system may have alerted management to some of the integration problems in time to make some adjustments to their plan.

Costs of Planning

Despite these benefits, planning also entails costs.[11] These costs can be significant and may discourage managers from planning.

Management Time Done properly, the planning process requires a substantial amount of managerial time and energy. Managers must work with their employees to evaluate existing resources, identify opportunities to improve the operations of the work group, and establish organizational goals. Some work groups may find that planning requires an assessment of external information related to the products, prices, and strategies of competing firms. The collection, analysis, and interpretation of such information can be time-consuming and costly.[12]

Interestingly, a study of planning in new businesses found that planning actually speeds up making decisions.[13] The reason is that planning helps people understand assumptions and consequences before things happen, and it also helps identify missing information. In addition to saving time directly, it may also allow managers to make decisions very quickly when the competitive environment requires it.

Organizations participating in the global business environment often find that planning is more complex and time-consuming than it is for the domestic market. International firms must analyze multiple economies, market forces, customer profiles, and other such variables. Yet taking the time to plan carefully may be the key to the success of an international initiative.

Delayed Decision Making Another potential cost of planning is that it may delay decision making. This is particularly true when planning processes require time-consuming acquisition of information and data.[14] Further, some managers argue that planning directs the focus toward evaluating rather than doing—that is, **paralysis by analysis.** This can delay the organization's response to changes in the industry, marketplace, or internal operations. The delay can be particularly detrimental when an organization's success depends on its ability to respond to change quickly.

KEY TERMS

Paralysis by analysis
While planning, spending so much time on analysis that nothing is accomplished.

Distribution channels for music have changed dramatically since the advent of digital media.

Nevertheless, taking the time to plan effectively may be more important to the success of the initiative than the loss of time it takes to do so. (See the preceding discussion about planning leading to speedier decisions.)[15]

In the business environment of the 21st century, speed in response time is critical for success in most industries. Nimble competitors will seize opportunities that are missed by those who are too slow at the planning process. According to Barbara Kux, once vice president of Switzerland's Nestlé S.A., global managers have to be able to analyze, plan, and execute quickly to stay on top in the international marketplace. As she explained, "The first trait of a global manager is to be nimble. Move fast, but don't hip-shoot. Do some analysis, but not too much analysis, and then act . . . it's better to be 70 percent right and move fast than to be perfect and wait."[16]

WHERE SHOULD PLANNING BEGIN?

Planning is carried out at various levels of the organization and for various departments, work groups, and individuals at each level. Although it must be initiated at the top level of the organization, information is needed from all levels. Eventually, people at all organizational levels need to understand their part in the plans, at a minimum. Beyond that, people at all levels

Table 5.1 Top-Down and Bottom-Up Planning

	Top-Down	Bottom-Up
Organizational level	CEO, Board of Directors	People/department closest to product, service, customer.
Role of organizational unit	As the plan moves down the hierarchy, units determine actions needed to support the plan.	Units develop goals and plans. As plans move up the hierarchy, they are evaluated and adjusted for accuracy and feasibility.
Specificity of plan	Begins broad, becomes more specific as it moves down the hierarchy.	Begins specific and probably fragmented; becomes cohesive and integrated as it moves up the hierarchy.
Potential advantages	Plans are driven by top-level managers who are most knowledgeable about all factors affecting the organization.	Those closest to customers, suppliers, and operating systems provide focus of plans.
Potential disadvantages	Top-level managers may be removed from the front line.	Lower-level managers may lack understanding of all factors affecting the organization.

might be included to varying degrees in the actual planning process.

3 Two overall perspectives on planning are presented, the top-down approach and the bottom-up approach, to help us think about the potential advantages and challenges of involving people at different levels in the organization. Table 5.1 illustrates the differences between these two perspectives. Of course, the planning process in most organizations probably lies somewhere between the two extremes, including advantages and challenges from each perspective.

The **top-down** perspective involves the CEO and/or Board of Directors who determine the general direction of the organization and establish a master plan to achieve its overall goals. The master plan establishes the parameters within which the organization's work groups develop their plans. Managers develop plans for their work groups based on what their units must accomplish to support the master plan.

The **bottom-up** perspective involves people at the lowest levels of the organizational hierarchy and/or those who are most directly involved in the delivery of the organization's products and services, and they establish their goals and plans. The managers and employees at the operational level begin the planning process by estimating sales potential, describing needed product and service modifications or new product and service developments, and identifying potential problems or opportunities in the supply of input resources. As these plans move up through the organization, they are developed further, refined, and evaluated for accurateness and feasibility. Finally, the Board of Directors and top-level executives bring together all the plans of the organization's work groups to develop a cohesive and well-integrated master plan that establishes the overall direction of the organization.[17]

Both the top-down and bottom-up approaches to planning have advantages and disadvantages. The primary advantage of top-down planning is that the top-level managers, who presumably are most knowledgeable about the organization as a whole, drive the development of the plan. Although one might argue that the people at other levels of the organization know more about how the organization actually operates, top-level management has a more comprehensive understanding of the wide variety of internal and external factors that affect the overall success of the organization.

Having those closest to the operating system, customers, and suppliers provide the focus for the planning process does have advantages. These individuals may have a better understanding of the

LEARNING OBJECTIVE 3

Discuss the potential advantages and disadvantages of top-down and bottom-up planning.

KEY TERMS

Top-down
Planning that starts at the top-level of the organization.

Bottom-up
Planning that starts at the lower levels in the organization.

competitive and operational challenges faced by the organization than the top-level executives, who are far removed from the front line.

Which approach is better? The answer to that question depends on the specific circumstances facing the organization. Perhaps most important, these planning perspectives, or approaches, are not mutually exclusive. Organizations must take advantage of the benefits of both approaches and minimize the disadvantages. Charming Shoppes, Inc., a speciality retailer of women's apparel, uses both approaches simultaneously. While the board of directors and the top-level management team are focused on growing the company through acquisition strategies, such as the recent acquisitions of Catherine's and Lane Bryant, the managers and employees of the functional areas of the business are developing plans for integrating the operations and systems of the merged companies.

LEARNING OBJECTIVE 4

Define strategic planning and describe the three levels of strategic planning.

Now that we have discussed important basic issues related to planning, let's examine the two primary types of planning that occur in most organizations: strategic and operational planning.

Strategic and Operational Planning

In general, most organizations engage in both strategic and operational planning. Although strategic and operational planning differ in a number of ways, they are also interrelated. Let's explore both of these important types of planning.

STRATEGIC PLANNING

As we discussed in Chapter 4, planning that is strategic in nature focuses on enhancing the competitive position and overall performance of the organization in the long term. It defines the markets in which the organization competes, what the customers in those markets want, and how the organization will deliver products and services to satisfy what customers want.[18] The purpose of strategic planning is to move the organization from where it is to where it wants to be and, in the process, to develop and maintain a competitive advantage within the industries in which it competes.[19]

Levels of Strategic Planning

4 Strategic planning occurs at three primary levels within the organization: the corporate, business, and functional levels.[20] Each level can be distinguished by the focus of the strategic planning process, the participants in the process, the specificity of the strategy, and the time horizon of the plan. Table 5.2 summarizes the key differences in these three levels of strategic planning; the discussion that follows elaborates on each.

Corporate Strategic Planning Strategic planning that occurs at the top level of the organization focuses on developing corporate strategy. **Corporate-level strategy** addresses the question, What business should we be in? It is relevant for organizations that operate in single or multiple lines of business. Corporate

Table 5.2 Levels of Strategic Planning

Level	Focus	Specificity	Participants	Time Horizon
Corporate strategy	To develop a mix of business units that meets the company's long-term growth and profitability goals.	Broad	Board of directors Top-level executives	5–10 years
Business strategy	To develop and maintain a distinctive competitive advantage that will ensure long-term profitability.	More specific than the corporate strategy	Top-level executives Managers within the business unit	1–5 years
Functional strategy	To develop action plans that ensure that corporate and business strategies are implemented.	Very specific	Middle-level managers Lower-level managers	1–2 years

strategic planning involves assessing the organization's portfolio of businesses to determine whether an appropriate mix exists.[21] The objective is to develop a mix of business units that meets the long-term goals of the organization.

Diversification is often at the core of corporate strategy.[22] **Diversification** occurs when an organization chooses to add a new business unit to its portfolio of businesses. A company may pursue a strategy of diversification if it wishes to reduce its dependence on its existing business units or to capitalize on its core competencies by expanding into another business. Diversification can be **unrelated** (entering markets or industries that are different from the ones in which it operates) or **related** (adding a business or product that is related to the mission or core competencies).

While PepsiCo's portfolio of products and companies was not totally unrelated, it decided to sharpen its overall focus in the late 1990s. Consequently, PepsiCo spun off Kentucky Fried Chicken, Taco Bell, and Pizza Hut into a separate, independent company and its soft-drink bottling company into another. PepsiCo acquired Cracker Jack, Tropicana, Gatorade, and Quaker granola bars (Gatorade and granola bars came with its acquisition of Quaker Oats Company) to joins its Lay's snacks, Aquafina, Lipton, Doritos, and Mountain Dew and Pepsi beverages to fit a corporate strategy with a tighter focus on convenience foods and beverages. This is related diversification that benefits from a clear focus and sharing of PepsiCo's competencies in marketing convenience foods.[23]

Because corporate strategy defines the very nature of the organization, it is formulated by the organization's top-level managers and usually must be approved by the Board of Directors. In developing their strategic plans, however, these individuals rely to a great extent on information provided by middle- and lower-level managers.

Corporate strategy is relatively broad and general in nature and may extend as far as 5 to 10 years into the future. While many would argue that it is impossible to formulate strategy 10 years into the future in today's rapidly changing business environment,[24] it is important for corporate leaders to have a strategy for the long-term future of the organization—even if that strategy has to be adapted and adjusted in light of environmental and competitive changes that occur over the years.

Business Strategic Planning Business-level **strategy** defines how each business unit in the organization's corporate portfolio will operate in its market arena. Strategy formulated at this level addresses the question, How do we compete in our existing line(s) of business?

Carrying the PepsiCo example further, the portfolio of products might be divided into division, or departments, of soft drinks, snack foods, sports drinks, and Quaker Oats. While coordinating with corporate managers and other division managers, the top-level managers in the soft-drinks division would focus on the overall management of soft-drink products. The managers of the other divisions would focus on their divisions.

Assume that an organization held a group of unrelated products or companies—say, for example, an airline, a hotel chain, and a rental car company. In that case, business-level strategy would mean that the manager of each business would focus on all aspects of the one business, the manager of the airline company on the airline business, and so on.

Business strategy should be formulated by the individuals who are most familiar with the operations of the business unit. Consequently, the Board of Directors and corporate executives are typically not involved with strategy formulation at the business level. Instead, this responsibility lies with the top-level executives and managers within the specific business units, and usually the CEO of the business unit is responsible for the outcomes of the business unit.[25] In this situation, the business unit is referred to as a **strategic business unit (SBU)**. For example, PepsiCo has a manager who is responsible for the Tropicana and Gatorade group and another for Frito Lay Snacks.[26]

Functional Strategic Planning Functional strategic planning leads to the development of functional strategy. **Functional-level strategy** specifies the production, research

KEY TERMS

Corporate-level strategy
Decisions and actions at the top level of the organization that define the portfolio of business units that an organization maintains.

Diversification
Adding new products, services, or businesses to an organization.

Unrelated diversification
Adding products, services, or businesses that are different from the ones an organization currently has.

Related diversification
Adding products, services, or businesses that have some relationship to the ones an organization currently has or share a core competency.

Business-level strategy
Focused plans that define how each business unit in an organization's corporate portfolio will operate in its market arena.

Strategic business unit (SBU)
A part of an organization that is responsible for its outcomes.

Functional-level strategy
Strategy at the department level that specifies such things as the production, research and development, financial, human resource management, and/or marketing activities necessary to implement the organization's corporate and business strategies.

Table 5.3 Examples of Functional Strategies

Human Resource Strategies	Finance Strategies
• Recruit for management positions.	• Secure debt financing.
• Design commission structure.	• Evaluate capital structure.
• Develop training program.	• Initiate and manage budget process.
• Design benefit package.	• Review and revise credit policies.
Marketing Strategies	**Production Strategies**
• Develop market research study.	• Evaluate robotics system.
• Identify additional distribution channels.	• Redesign quality control processes.
• Create promotional program.	• Locate alternative sources of supply.
• Evaluate pricing structure.	• Develop inventory management system.

and development, financial, human resource management, and marketing activities necessary to implement the organization's corporate and business strategies.[27] Table 5.3 lists some of the areas in which functional planning occurs and gives examples of functional strategies in each area.

LEARNING OBJECTIVE

Define operational planning and distinguish between standing and single-use plans.

Strategy formulation at the functional level addresses the question: What needs to be done functionally to implement our business and corporate strategies? Whereas an organization's business and corporate strategies address what should be done, functional strategy focuses on how things will get done.

Inside the Frito Lay part of PepsiCo, the production department will have to prepare to manufacture the products, and the marketing department must develop appropriate pricing, promotion, and advertising plans. Each activity represents functional strategy.

Functional strategic planning is carried out by middle- and lower-level managers, who develop functional strategies to ensure that their units are supporting the corporate and business strategies of the organization. Strategic planning at the functional level is more specific than corporate and business strategic planning, and functional strategies typically span a shorter time frame, usually 1 or 2 years at most.

KEY TERMS

Operational planning
The process of determining the day-to-day activities that are necessary to achieve the long-term goals of the organization.

Operational plan
An outline of the tactical activities necessary to support and implement the strategic plans of the organization.

Standing plan
A plan that deals with organizational issues and problems that recur frequently.

OPERATIONAL PLANNING

5 **Operational planning** focuses on determining the day-to-day activities that are necessary to achieve the long-term goals of the organization. **Operational plans** outline the tactical activities that must occur to support the ongoing operations of the organization. They are more specific than strategic plans, address shorter-term issues, and are formulated by the middle- and lower-level managers who are responsible for the work groups in the organization.

In general, plans can be categorized as standing or single-use plans, depending on whether they address recurring issues or are specific to a given set of circumstances. Most organizations maintain both standing and single-use plans because both are applicable to a broad range of organizational situations. Although standing and single-use plans are usually developed for work groups within the organization, operational planning can also occur for individual organizational members.

Standing Plans

Standing plans are designed to deal with organizational issues or problems that recur frequently. By using standing plans, management avoids the need to "reinvent the wheel" every time a particular situation arises.[28] In addition, such plans ensure that recurring situations are handled consistently over time. This may be particularly important for an organization with a highly diverse workforce. Individuals from different cultural and social backgrounds may react to certain situations differently. Standing plans ensure that such situations will be handled in prescribed ways.

Standing plans can, however, limit employees' flexibility and can make it more difficult to respond to the customer, if customers require different things over time

© DAVID YOUNG-WOLFF/PHOTO EDIT

Universities maintain policies about admittance to academic programs, grade appeals, and course waivers that guide each decision maker in evaluating specific circumstances in individual student cases.

or from customer to customer. Therefore, standing plans work best in situations that are stable and there is little change.

Standing plans include policies, procedures, and rules. Each provides guidance in a different way.

Policies **Policies** are guidelines that govern how certain organizational situations will be addressed. They provide guidance to managers who must make decisions about circumstances that occur frequently within the organization. For example, human resource management departments maintain policies concerning sick leave, vacation leave, and benefit options. Production departments establish policies for procurement and inventory management. A university's administration maintains policies about admittance to certain academic programs, grade appeals, and permissible course waivers or substitutions. These policies provide a framework for decision making that guides the decision maker in evaluating the specific circumstances surrounding each individual case. Therefore, policies do not state specifically what the decision will be. Rather, they state the boundaries of the decision and/or what must be considered in the decision. In doing these things, policies do guide decisions so that they will be similar in situations that are similar. You will see how policies are necessary to delegate authority when we discuss that in Chapter 7.

Procedures **Procedures** are more specific and action oriented than policies and are designed to give explicit instructions on how to complete a recurring task. Most companies maintain some sort of procedures manual to provide guidance for certain recurring activities. Many use a standard operating procedures (**SOPs**) manual to outline the basic operating methods of the organization. For example, human resource management departments develop procedures for filing benefit claims, documenting the reasons for sick leave, and requesting vacation time. Production departments establish procedures for identifying and evaluating suppliers and ordering supplies, operating the inventory management system, and identifying and implementing specific quality-control criteria. Universities maintain specific procedures for applying for admittance to certain programs, appealing grades, and requesting course waivers and/or substitutions.

Rules **Rules** are the strictest type of standing plan found in organizations.[29] Rules are not intended to serve as guidelines for making organizational decisions; instead, they provide detailed and specific regulations for action.[30]

For example, a human resource management department may have rules governing the number of sick days an employee may take with pay, the months in which vacation time can be scheduled, and the length of time an organizational member must be employed before qualifying for benefits. The production department may have rules governing the percentage of supplies that can be purchased from a single supplier, the method in which inventory must be accounted for, and the way in which products of substandard quality are handled.

KEY TERMS

Policy
A guideline for decision making within the organization.

Procedure
An instruction on how to complete recurring tasks.

SOP
Standard operating procedure.

Rule
A detailed and specific regulation for action.

A university may have rules to govern the minimum grade point average necessary for admission to a given academic program and the specific courses that may be substituted for one another.

Experiential Exercise 5.1 provides an opportunity for you to evaluate and adapt standing plans for an organization with which you are familiar. Based on this exercise, you should see the potential value of establishing standing plans to cope with recurring organizational situations.

Single-Use Plans

Single-use plans are developed to address a specific organizational situation. Such plans are typically used only once because the specific situation to which they apply does not recur. Consider, for example, the plan of SAP Americas, a leading provider of enterprise resource planning (ERP) and e-commerce solutions, to build a new corporate headquarters. A sophisticated plan was necessary to finance, construct, and move into the new building. This was a single-use plan because SAP would not need to build such a building or relocate its employees again for a very long time.

LEARNING OBJECTIVE 6

Describe individual planning systems such as management by objectives and the Balanced Scorecard.

The most common types of single-use plans are programs, projects, and budgets. Each offers a different degree of comprehensiveness and detail. Programs are the most comprehensive plans; projects have a narrower scope and, in fact, are often undertaken as a part of a program; and budgets are developed to support programs or projects.

KEY TERMS

Single-use plan
A plan that addresses specific organizational situations that typically do not recur.

Program
A single-use plan that governs a comprehensive set of activities designed to accomplish a particular set of goals.

Project
Directs the efforts of individuals or work groups toward the achievements of a specific goal.

Budget
A plan that specifies how financial resources should be allocated

Programs **Programs** are single-use plans that govern a relatively comprehensive set of activities designed to accomplish a particular set of goals. Such plans outline the major steps and specific actions necessary to implement the activities prescribed by the program. The timing and sequencing of the efforts of individuals and units are also articulated in the plan.

Many organizations today have implemented diversity programs. Such programs are designed to recruit and hire a more diverse workforce as well as to educate employees on issues related to diverse work environments. For example, Allstate Corporation took proactive steps to recruit minority candidates and to provide diversity training for managers and employees at all levels of the organization. This program was developed to meet Allstate's goal of having a productive and diverse workforce that reflects the organization's customer base.[31]

Projects **Projects** direct the efforts of individuals or work groups toward the achievement of specific, well-defined goals. Projects are typically less comprehensive and narrower in focus than programs and usually have predetermined target dates for completion. Many projects are designed to collect and analyze information for decision-making purposes or to support more comprehensive planning efforts, such as programs.

For example, the marketing department at Allstate might be asked to undertake a project to heighten awareness of Allstate among minority populations. This project would have a narrower scope than the overall diversity program, but it would be undertaken to support Allstate's overall efforts to create a more diverse employee base. Similarly, the food services group might take on a project to create a diversity week, featuring different cultural foods, entertainment, and artwork in the company lounge. Again, the project would be of narrower scope than the diversity program as a whole, but it would contribute to the overall diversity goals of the company.

Budgets **Budgets** often are undertaken as a part of other planning efforts because they specify the financial resource requirements associated with other plans such as programs and projects. In addition, budgets serve as a mechanism for controlling the financial aspects of implementing the plan.[32]

Allstate would undoubtedly establish a budget to support the implementation of the overall diversity program and to ensure that it is carried out in an effective and efficient manner. In fact, the size of that budget might provide some insight as to the importance of the project to the organization.

Although all the types of standing and single-use plans discussed here can be used for specialized planning purposes, they are often interrelated. For example, projects are often subcomponents of more comprehensive programs or are undertaken in an effort to develop or implement policies, procedures, and rules. In fact, most organizations engage in all of these forms of planning over time.

Individual Plans

Increasingly, organizations are looking for ways to translate broader organizational plans to the level

Figure 5.2 Management by Objectives: The Cycle

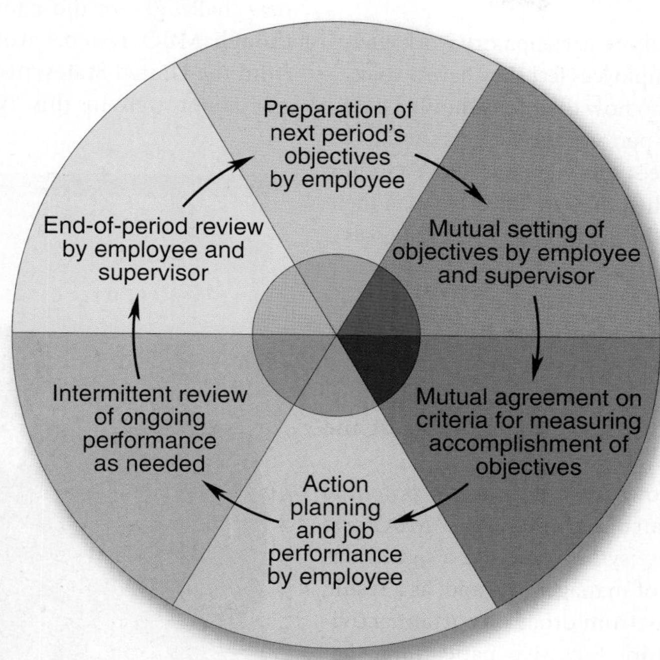

Source: K. Davis and J. Newstrom, *Human Behavior at Work: Organizational Behavior* (New York: McGraw-Hill, 1989), 209. Reproduced with permission of the McGraw-Hill Companies.

of individual employees. Two approaches for doing so are management by objectives and the Balanced Scorecard.

Management by Objectives A special planning technique, **management by objectives (MBO)**, provides a method for developing personalized plans that guide the activities of individual members of the organization (the words *objectives* and *goals* are used interchangeably). The MBO approach to planning helps managers balance conflicting demands by focusing the attention of the manager and the employee on the tasks to be completed and the performance to be achieved at an individual level.[33]

Figure 5.2 outlines the primary steps in an MBO program. As the figure illustrates, MBO programs are circular and self-renewing in nature. The process begins when employees, in conjunction with their managers, establish a set of goals that serve as the foundation for the development of their work plans. Once a set of mutually agreeable goals has been determined, criteria for assessing work performance are identified. Next, employees formulate and implement the action plans necessary to achieve their goals and review their progress with their managers on an intermittent basis. At the end of the MBO period, the performance of the employees is compared to the goals established at the beginning of the period. Performance rewards should be based on the extent to which the goals have been achieved. Once the MBO cycle is complete, employees begin formulating goals to drive the next MBO-planning period.

As originally conceived, MBO programs provide three primary benefits:

1. MBO programs provide a foundation for a more integrated and system-oriented approach to planning. Establishing goals and action plans for individual employees forces managers to examine how the activities of each individual in the work group contribute to the achievement of the overall goals of the group. As an MBO system works its way up the hierarchy of the organization, it provides a mechanism for ensuring systemwide coordination of work efforts.
2. The MBO approach to planning requires communication between employees and their managers because they

KEY TERMS

Management by objectives (MBO)
A method for developing individualized plans that guide the activities of individual members of an organization.

must agree on the performance goals outlined in the plan. This increased communication often serves to build stronger relationships between managers and their employees.

3. MBO systems lead to more participatory work environments in which employees feel they have a voice and can have input into how their jobs should be designed and what their performance targets should be. Furthermore, employees gain a greater understanding of the organization when they are forced to plan their activities in line with the organization's overall goals.

In addition to these general benefits, MBO systems offer the more specific advantages listed in Table 5.4.[34] These benefits include such things as higher individual performance levels, prioritized goals, and greater opportunities for career development for both managers and employees.[35]

At the same time, however, a number of potential disadvantages are associated with the use of MBO systems (see Table 5.4). These systems require a significant commitment on the part of management and, as a result, may divert attention away from other important activities. Many systems require excessive paperwork that complicates the administrative processes within the organization. Furthermore, some argue that MBO programs focus attention on short-run goals rather than on issues that are relevant to the long-term success of the organization. Finally, goals may be difficult to establish and put into operation in some cases. As a consequence, MBO systems may not be suitable for all job designs.[36]

The increasing diversity of the workforce has created new challenges for those involved in MBO programs. Although MBO systems work well for many employees from the United States, people from other cultures may not adapt well to this type of planning. The MBO

While MBO systems work well for many employees from the United States, people from other cultures may not adapt well to this type of planning. Managers must be sensitive to the diversity of their work teams.

Table 5.4 Potential Advantages and Disadvantages of MBO

Potential Advantages	Potential Disadvantages
Can result in better achievement of goals.	Requires time and commitment of top-level managers.
Forces managers to establish priorities and measurable goals or standards of performance.	May require excessive paperwork.
Encourages participation of employees and managers in establishing goals.	May create tendency to focus on short-term goals.
Facilitates control.	Can be difficult to establish and put into operation.
Lets individuals know what is expected.	Goals of individuals may not be coordinated with higher-level goals.
Can help improve communication.	
Increases motivation and commitment of employees.	

Source: Gordon/Mondy/Sharplin/Premeaux, Management and Organizational Behavior, 1st Edition, © 1990, pp. 129, 131. Adapted by permission of Pearson Education, Inc. Upper Saddle River, NJ.

Table 5.5 Measuring Performance with the Balanced Scorecard

Key Principles	Measurement Criteria	Implications for Leaders
Align organization to the strategy.	Customers	Understand the "big picture."
Translate the strategy to operational terms.	Internal processes	BSC measures performance at all levels.
View strategy as a continual process.	Innovation	Execute strategy into action.
Make strategy everyone's job.	Growth	Empower frontline employees.

Source: Manage by J. Steele. © 2001 by National Management Association Foundation, Inc. Reproduced with permission of National Management Association Foundation Inc. in the Textbook via Copyright Clearance Center.

concept is predicated on an employee's desire to be reasonably independent and willingness to work toward predetermined goals—both of which are relatively common characteristics of workers in the United States. In many other cultures, however, such attitudes toward work are not common. MBO programs may be far less effective when used with individuals from such cultures. Consequently, managers must be sensitive to the diversity of their work teams and may need to modify the MBO concept to suit different individuals.

In general, MBO systems can be an effective tool. Although they can be cumbersome if implemented throughout every unit of an organization, these programs can be beneficial to overall management when used selectively. MBO includes all aspects of management from planning as well as guiding employees in terms of communication, leadership, and motivation, and it helps with control. Siemens Company is an example of a firm that has embraced the MBO approach to planning. Corporate executives credit this system for the high level of commitment of Monsanto employees to the overall plans and strategy of the firm.[37]

Balanced Scorecard More recently, organizations have developed systemwide performance measurement processes that align individual goals with the strategic goals of the organization. One widely popular process, the **Balanced Scorecard** (BSC), has been used in a variety of organizations across both the private and public sectors.[38]

The BSC process allows an organization to translate its strategy into operational actions at every level. Thus, employees can ensure that their individual action plans and goals are consistent with the overall strategic direction of the organization. Many organizations, including AT&T, UPS, CIGNA, and the Department of Defense, have successfully developed and implemented BSCs to help measure progress toward their strategic objectives. Table 5.5 provides an overview of the BSC system.

Contingency Planning for Changing Environments

7 **Contingency planning** is a popular approach in today's rapidly changing business environment.[39] Virtually all organizations face strategic and operating conditions that are subject to change and could therefore benefit from a contingency approach to planning. This approach is especially useful when an organization's effectiveness is highly dependent on a set of business conditions that are particularly volatile.[40]

Contingency planning requires flexibility. There are at least two variations on how this can be achieved. Both variations rest on sound strategic analysis, as discussed in Chapter 4. One variation is the development of two or more plans (the idea of "**plan B**"), each of which is based on a different set of strategic or operating conditions that could occur. Which plan is implemented is determined by the specific circumstances that come to pass.[41] For example, an organization may plan to begin production at a new plant facility in June 2007, but managers should develop a contingency plan that ensures

LEARNING OBJECTIVE

Define contingency planning and identify the circumstances under which contingency planning would be appropriate.

KEY TERMS

Balanced Scorecard
A planning system that aligns the goals of individual employees with the strategic goals of the organization.

Contingency planning
Development of two or more plans each based on different conditions.

Plan B
Referring to a second contingency plan.

Leaders in Action

Ann Mulcahy: Turnaround at Xerox

Ann Mulcahy is on *BusinessWeek*'s 2005 list of "The Best Managers." The reasons why include not only her turnaround of the troubled company, but also her use of sound management to develop and manage a successful company.

When she became CEO of the company in 2001, Xerox was in serious trouble. Competitors such as Canon and Hewlett-Packard had taken much of the copier market away (Dell would join the group later). The company had high debt and was close to bankruptcy, it was being investigated by the Securities and Exchange Commission for accounting practices, and the previous CEO left after failing to change the sales force into a successful unit.

Mulcahy began by getting a better understanding of the competition and customers. Then she streamlined the company to better fit the situation, cutting costs wherever possible, including reducing the number of employees. Her plans also involved selecting a new chief financial officer, managing cash flow better to stay financially solvent, encouraged faster decision making, and implemented a Six Sigma Program to improve efficiency. The company has met financial expectations of investors during the past several years and has new products coming to market.

Whether turning a company around or managing any company well, Mulcahy says the most important job of a manager is the same. That job is to get everyone in the company focused on the goal.

Sources: "The Best Advice I Ever Got," *Fortune,* 21 March 2005, 104; "The Best Managers," *BusinessWeek,* 10 January 2005, 62; A. Harrington and P. Bartosiewicz, "50 Most Powerful Women: Who's Up? Who's Down?" *Fortune,* 18 October 2004, 183.

uninterrupted production in the event that the plant opening is delayed for some reason. The plan probably should include making a decision at some specified time if demand does not grow enough to need the new plant.

As another example, consider the airline industry. Herb Kelleher, chairman of the board of Southwest Airlines, says that it is virtually impossible to employ traditional long-range planning in the airline industry. Things change too much and too quickly—schedules, routes, competitors, and fares change continually. Therefore, contingency planning is particularly important in that industry. Nevertheless, it is important to note that effective contingency planning requires that potential changes in strategic and operating conditions are somewhat predictable. Do you think that Southwest had a contingency plan to deal with the chaos that hit the airline industry in the wake of 9/11/2001? Should the company have had such a plan?

LEARNING OBJECTIVE 8

Discuss how advances in information technology have affected operational planning.

A second variation of contingency planning rests on the skill and ability of people in the organization to think strategically and flexibly. That means that the people must be informed continually and understand the important trends, causes, effects, and interactions of the conditions in both the external and internal environments of the organization. This skill and ability is called having "prepared minds"[42] by some. If people in the organization are prepared, they can think strategically, as was suggested while discussing vision in Chapter 4 (long term and comprehensively), and can make decisions to keep aligned with what is happening in the industry. Of course, this does not rule out having plan B; rather, it probably includes having a second plan, at least in the heads of the people, if not written down.

Royal Dutch/Shell, an early pioneer in the area of contingency planning, has developed a sophisticated system of scenario planning to support the creation of its contingency plans.[43] The company creates a set of scenarios that reflect potential changes in the world that would affect its operations. Contingency plans can be developed based on the conditions in each scenario. If you would like to read more about Royal Dutch/Shell's scenarios, visit the web site at http://www.shell.com/scenarios.

The Impact of Information Technology on Planning

8 As we have learned, operational plans include standing plans such as policies, procedures, and

rules. Advances in information technology in recent years have supported the more efficient development of such plans as well as more effective implementation. Consider, for example, how a university might use information systems to communicate policies, streamline procedures, and monitor compliance with rules. Policies related to such things as admission to certain programs, grade appeals, permissible course waivers, and substitutions can be communicated to students via the Internet or a campus local area network. This enables students to have online, real-time access to important information rather than having to wait for the next year's catalog to be distributed. Class registration procedures have also been improved through the use of information technology. At many universities, students can register via the Internet. This is a dramatic improvement over the long registration lines of days gone by. Monitoring compliance with rules such as minimum grade point average, prerequisite completion, and course substitution is also more efficient with the use of information technology. Database systems that maintain individual student records allow university administrators to readily identify students who are in violation of university rules.

Facilitating the Planning Process

Although most managers admit that they need to plan, many would also admit that they do much less planning than they should. This situation is a result of a number of barriers to planning.

BARRIERS TO EFFECTIVE PLANNING

Why do some managers fail to plan effectively? They do so for a number of reasons, all of which may be overcome by developing an organizational culture that encourages and supports the planning process. However, this requires a clear understanding of the main reasons why managers fail to plan effectively.

Demands on the Manager's Time

Some managers may simply be too busy "putting out fires" to take the time to plan properly. Managers often feel as though they face a continuous stream of problems from the time they arrive at work until they leave. Although this constant troubleshooting may seem to leave few opportunities for planning, the hectic nature of the manager's day in itself suggests that planning is very much needed. Through better planning, such as policies, rules, and the like, managers can develop operational systems that are more effective and less problematic and demanding of their time.

Ambiguous and Uncertain Operating Environments

Environmental complexity and volatility are other commonly cited reasons for not planning. Managers who are uncomfortable with ambiguity may find it difficult and frustrating to plan under conditions of uncertainty. Yet, while it may be difficult to develop plans under such circumstances, effective managers make an effort to do so. Organizations that operate in rapidly changing and complex environments often find that planning provides a mechanism for coping with such conditions.

Resistance to Change

Finally, managers may hesitate to plan because they are resistant to change. Organizational members may associate planning with a need to change the way they do their jobs. Their hesitancy to change may discourage them from initiating the planning process.[44] Given the current focus on quality and continuous improvement, resistance to change can have very detrimental results for the organization in the long term.

OVERCOMING THE BARRIERS TO PLANNING

9 As discussed previously, achieving success through planning requires the participation of a broad range of organizational members. Consequently, organizations must develop and maintain a culture that encourages planning and rewards those who plan effectively. Here are important things that can help.

LEARNING OBJECTIVE 9

Describe common barriers to effective planning and explain ways to reduce these barriers.

Learn to Apply the Managerial Functions Better

Better planning can be achieved by not only learning how to plan more effectively and efficiently but also by applying better the other managerial functions that are discussed in this book: organizing, leading, communicating, motivating, and developing/teaching employees. A few specific examples are the following:

- Learn to identify what is really important as opposed to what is urgent but not important.[45] Much time could be saved by not paying attention to urgent but not important things.
- Use well-thought out goals, policies, procedures, and rules.
- Delegate authority well.
- Communicate expectations clearly.
- Teach employees to be more self-guiding.

Involve Employees in Decision Making

Seek information from employees and keep them informed about expectations. Input from all levels of the organization is essential to the success of the organization's planning. Managers should solicit the opinions and views of their employees when formulating plans, and they should encourage individual members of the organization to communicate about the planning efforts of the unit and the organization. Discouraging employees from sharing information that might be important to the planning process will result in less effective organizational plans.[46]

Take Advantage of a Diversity of Views

Diverse views and perspectives lead to a broader assessment and evaluation of organizational problems and opportunities. In fact, this can be one of the primary benefits of maintaining a diverse workforce.[47] Organizations that encourage a wide range of different ideas and views and have learned to manage diverse groups are more likely to produce plans that are comprehensive and fully developed. It is imperative to learn to manage diverse work groups well.

Encourage Strategic Thinking

Developing an organizational culture that encourages strategic and results-oriented thinking will lead to more effective planning.[48] Thinking is a skill and, as is the case with most skills, can be developed through training and practice.[49] Employees should be provided with the training necessary to develop strategic thinking skills and given the opportunity to practice those skills in their work environment. Furthermore, individuals should be rewarded for thinking strategically when developing their plans.[50]

Implications for Leaders

Tomorrow's manager will face many challenges in developing effective strategic and operational plans. Planning has become increasingly difficult as the pace of change in the business environment has accelerated. Although change makes the planning process more difficult, it also makes planning more critical. Managers of the future must be forward thinking and focused on achieving the goals of their work groups and their organizations through effective planning. Managers need effective planning skills, which are among the key competencies that ensure an organization's success.

The ultimate objective of the planning process is the development of good plans. Plans are good if they can be implemented successfully and result in the accomplishment of the goals for which they were designed. Managers are more likely to develop good plans when they

- Recognize and communicate the importance of planning in achieving organizational success.
- Understand the difference between and the relationships among strategic and operational planning initiatives.
- Involve those responsible for implementing the plan to understand their role. If appropriate, involve them in the planning process itself.
- Use contingency planning as a means of maintaining flexibility in rapidly changing business environments.
- Utilize technology to enhance the effectiveness and efficiency of the planning process.
- Remove the barriers to planning at the work group and individual levels.
- Reward those who think strategically and follow through with operational planning.

In this chapter, we have examined the managerial function of planning. Our focus, at both the strategic and operational levels, has been on achieving organizational success through planning.

Meeting The Challenge

Ed Zander Has a Plan for Motorola

The year 2004 was one of the most profitable ever for Motorola. Continuing with the changes that were started by former CEO Christopher Galvin, Edward (Ed) Zander worked on updating Motorola's out-of-date image. This included a modern "batwings" logo combined with effective advertising and the new RAZR mobile phone that became very popular immediately after it was introduced in late 2004. However, without other changes, the new phone, advertising, and logo would not have accomplished much.

To realize his vision of bringing Motorola back to the top of the communication industry, Zander's strategic goal is to transform the company into a unified technology company. To realize this ambitious vision and strategic goal, Zander is working out long-term and short-term plans. The new RAZR phone is part of the short-term plans, more specifically, the execution of existing plans. Execution includes Zander's insistence that Motorola puts the customers first again, making products that they want. Of course, that is based on keeping up with understanding the markets and industry.

Execution also includes tearing down the stifling bureaucracy that resulted in people and departments fighting with each other rather than cooperating when it was necessary to produce and sell products that customers wanted. The company is being reorganized around customers and markets, including a simplified sales force to better serve the customers. Also, new polices and rules now encourage cooperation between people and departments where it is needed to understand and serve the markets. A new bonus plan is based on cooperation, customer satisfaction, and product quality.

The short-term plan is working well. The true test is whether Zander can establish a long-term strategy and plan to rebuild the company. That will certainly include new products and services and probably more changes to the company, including some parts of the organizational culture and getting costs down relative to the revenue generated.

Sources: C. Rhoads, "Handset Sales Help Motorola Return to Profit," *Wall Street Journal,* 20 July 2005, A1; C. Rhoads, "Motorola's Modernizer," *Wall Street Journal,* 23 June 2005, B1, B5; B. Stone, "Motorola's Good Call," *Newsweek,* 14 March 2005, 42–43; E. Corcoran, "Making Over Motorola," *Forbes* 174, no. 12 (December 2004): 103–108; R. Crockett, "Reinventing Motorola," *BusinessWeek,* 2 August 2004, 82–83; W. Schaff, "Restructuring Pays Off for Motorola," *Information Week,* 26 July 2004, 72; "Hello, Moto," *Economist* 370, no. 8357 (January 2004): 58.

SUMMARY

1. Planning is an important managerial function through which managers outline the activities necessary to achieve the goals of the organization. The purpose of planning is to ensure organizational effectiveness and efficiency in both the short term and the long term.
2. When done well, planning is essential. When not done well, it can interfere with success and can be costly.
3. Most organizations today plan from an integrative perspective, incorporating aspects of a top-down approach and a bottom-up approach.
4. There are three levels of strategic planning—corporate, business, and functional—and they vary with respect to focus, specificity, time horizon, and the participants in the planning process.
5. Operational planning determines the day-to-day activities that are necessary to achieve the long-term goals of the organization. Standing plans, which include policies, procedures, and rules, are developed to address issues that recur frequently in the organization. Single-use plans address a specific issue or problem that the organization experiences only once.
6. Individual planning systems guide the behaviors and actions of individual organizational members. Management by objectives (MBO) and the Balanced Scorecard (BSC) focus the attention of the manager and the employee on the tasks to be completed and the performance to be achieved at an individual level.

7. Contingency planning involves the development of a set of plans that are designed for the varied strategic or operating conditions the organization might face. Contingency planning is most appropriate for organizations operating in environments that are subject to frequent or significant change.

8. Advances in information technology have improved both the effectiveness and efficiency of the planning function.

9. Common barriers to planning are demands on the manager's time, ambiguous and uncertain environmental conditions, and resistance to change. Overcoming the barriers to planning requires the development of an organizational culture that supports and encourages planning.

REVIEW QUESTIONS

1. (LEARNING OBJECTIVE 1) Describe the managerial function of planning, explaining what it is and why managers should plan.
2. (LEARNING OBJECTIVE 2) Explain the benefits and costs related to planning.
3. (LEARNING OBJECTIVE 3) What are the advantages and disadvantages associated with top-down and bottom-up planning?
4. (LEARNING OBJECTIVE 4) Define strategic planning. What are the three levels at which strategy is formulated, and how do they differ in terms of (a) focus, (b) participants, (c) specificity, and (d) time horizon?
5. (LEARNING OBJECTIVE 5) What is operational planning, and how does it differ from strategic planning?
6. (LEARNING OBJECTIVE 5) Describe standing and single-use plans and identify the various types of plans that fall into these two categories.
7. (LEARNING OBJECTIVE 6) Describe the two types of individualized planning systems outlined in the chapters. What are some advantages and disadvantages of these types of planning?
8. (LEARNING OBJECTIVE 7) What is contingency planning? Under what circumstances would it be most appropriate to use a contingency approach to planning?
9. (LEARNING OBJECTIVE 8) How have advances in information technology affected operational planning?
10. (LEARNING OBJECTIVE 9) What are the common barriers to planning? What might a manager do to reduce the barriers to planning?

DISCUSSION QUESTIONS

Improving Critical Thinking

1. Evaluate the benefits of MBO as an employer and as an employee. Would you want to participate in an MBO program? Why or why not?

2. Planning can begin at the top of the organization and flow downward or start at the bottom of the organization and move upward. As an employee of an organization, would you prefer a top-down or bottom-up approach to planning? What would you consider to be the advantages and disadvantages of each from an employee's perspective? From an employer's perspective?

Enhancing Communication Skills

3. Consider an organization with which you have been affiliated as an employee or a member, such as a business, church, sorority, and the like. Describe the planning system of this organization. Was it effective? If not, why? What might the managers of the organization have done to ensure better planning? To improve your oral communication skills, present your analysis of this situation to the class.

4. How might the planning process for a new business venture differ from the process in an established business? How would it differ for small versus large

businesses? To practice your written communication skills, prepare a one-page written summary of your response.

Building Teamwork

5. We know that planning occurs at the strategic and operational levels. Is it more important to plan at one level than at the other? Why or why not? Discuss this question in teams of four to five students and develop a position that you can present to the class.

6. Identify and evaluate some of the standing plans at your university or college that directly affect you as a student. From your perspective, do the policies, procedures, or rules that you identified help or hinder the students? Why do you think the administration at your school believes that it is necessary to have well-defined standing plans? What would happen if none of the plans that you identified existed? Form teams of four to five students, answer the preceding questions and present your responses to the class.

Chapter

6

Managerial Decision Making

© JEFF GREENBERG/PHOTOEDIT

CHAPTER OVERVIEW

Consider all the decisions necessary to carry out any major effort—from launching a space satellite to marketing and producing a new line of automobiles. The leaders responsible for these decisions rely on good decision-making skills. A manager's responsibility as a decision maker is very important. Although all managers are called upon to make decisions, the kinds of decisions that are required will vary with their level of authority and type of assignment. Poor decisions can be disastrous to a department and an organization. Good decisions facilitate the smooth flow of work and enable the organization to achieve its goals.

This chapter introduces concepts and models that focus on the demands of managerial decision making. Managers and leaders may not always make the right decision, but they can use their knowledge of appropriate decision-making processes to increase the odds of success. Skill in decision making is a distinguishing characteristic of most successful managers. We explore how leaders in organizations make decisions by discussing the seven steps in the decision-making process and examining two commonly used models of decision behavior. Because leaders are frequently involved with groups and teams, we focus on the participative model of group decision making by looking at techniques that leaders can use to improve this process. We conclude by examining several strategic decision-making tools.

LEARNING OBJECTIVES

When you have finished studying this chapter, you should be able to

1. Describe the nature of the decision-making process and explain each of its seven steps.
2. Describe the rational–economic model of decision making.
3. Discuss the behavioral decision model and its related concepts of bounded rationality, intuition, satisficing, and escalation of commitment.
4. Describe the participative approach to decision making.
5. Discuss the advantages and disadvantages of participative decision making.
6. List the various techniques used to improve participative decision making.
7. Discuss the basic classifications for managerial decisions.
8. Describe the nature of strategic decision making as well as the strategic decision-making matrix approach for strategy selection.
9. Identify the differences between the growth-share matrix and the industry attractiveness/business strength matrix approaches for evaluating business portfolios.

Facing The Challenge

Goodbye Cypress Gardens

When the topic of central Florida amusement parks and attractions comes up, most people immediately think of the assortment of Disney parks (Magic Kingdom, EPCOT, MGM Studios, and Animal Kingdom), Universal Studios (and its sister Universal Islands of Adventure), and Sea World. But, these are mere infants next to the granddaddy of them all—Cypress Gardens. On January 2, 1936, Dick Pope opened the gates on his showplace for 8000 varieties of flowers and plants from over 90 countries around the world. Guests could take a leisurely stroll through the grounds and drink in the beauty. Within a few years of opening, the park added electric boats to cruise the canals and provide guests with an even more sedate way to soak up the ambience. The strolling Southern Belles outfitted in antebellum dresses first appeared near the entrance gate in the winter of 1940 to distract guests from the sight of some freeze-damaged vegetation. They proved to be so popular they remained as a permanent fixture throughout the park. In 1943 when some visiting World War II servicemen expected to see a show, the Pope children were enlisted to perform a waterskiing exhibition on adjacent Lake Florence. This was to be the birth of the famous Cypress Gardens water-ski show. Who among us hasn't seen the vintage photos of the multi-level pyramid of skiers with the American flag fluttering at the apex? Celebrities and Hollywood movie producers discovered Cypress Gardens in the decades of the 1940s through the 1960s. Several movies were filmed in the park's lush tropical waterways. Additional attractions and displays, like an ice-skating show and elaborate model train setups, were added over the years.

Cypress Gardens was a theme park in that it had themed areas. But, perhaps its distinguishing characteristic was not what it was, but rather what it wasn't. Cypress Gardens was not a ride park. There were no roller coasters or other thrill-based attractions that were to become the trademark of the newer parks that began to dot the central Florida landscape in the 1970s. That fact may have led to the park's downfall. At the beginning of the new millennium, 89% of the park's guests were senior citizens. In the words of the Winter Haven Area Chamber of Commerce executive director, "There was no reason for a child over 8 to go there." The park just didn't have much to offer young families. Competition from the newer parks was quite intense. The post 9/11 tourism downturn didn't help matters either. On peak days, park attendance would barely reach 3000 guests, which pales in comparison to the tens of thousands visiting the surrounding parks each day. When debt mounted to $6 million, the owners decided to throw in the towel. With only 3 days notice, Florida's first commercial tourist theme park closed its gates on April 13, 2003, after almost seven decades of operation. While developers licked their lips over this prime piece of real estate, a grassroots organization called Friends of Cypress Gardens quickly sprang up. With members in 117 Florida cities, all 50 states, and 15 countries, the group lobbied hard for a savior. In stepped Kent Buescher, owner of a Valdosta, Georgia, amusement park. He was intent upon resurrecting this Florida tourist icon.[1]

Introduction

LEARNING OBJECTIVE 1

Describe the nature of the decision-making process and explain each of its seven steps.

Any person or organization faced with a decision has a rather straightforward task at hand. The decision maker must select a course of action (the decision) from a set of potential alternatives. Some decisions are critical and can have a major impact on personal and organizational lives. Other decisions are more routine but still require that we select an appropriate course of action. In "Facing the Challenge," Kent Buescher was destined to face many decisions and challenges as he sought to restore Cypress Gardens to its past glory. This chapter introduces concepts and models that focus on the demands of managerial decision making. Before examining specific tools and techniques for decision making, we review the conditions under which a decision situation might arise. Then we present a structured, multistep process for making quality decisions.

Sources of Organizational and Entrepreneurial Decisions

1 **Decision making** is the process through which managers and leaders identify and resolve problems and capitalize on opportunities. Good decision

making is important at all levels in the organization. It begins with recognition or awareness of problems and opportunities and concludes with an assessment of the results of actions taken to solve those problems. A **problem** occurs when some aspect of organizational performance is less than desirable. This definition is purposely broad so that it covers any aspect of organizational performance, such as overall bottom–line profits, market share, output productivity, quality of output, or worker satisfaction and harmony, to name just a few of the countless possibilities. When such unsatisfactory results have occurred, the successful manager will both recognize the problem and find a solution for it.[2]

Numerous examples can be cited where organizations and individuals have made a decision in response to some problem. In 2005 the Ford Motor Company recalled nearly 800,000 pickup trucks and sport utility vehicles because the cruise control switch could short circuit and cause a fire under the hood.[3] In the same year, the Florida Turnpike Enterprise made the decision to install protective barriers along sections of Florida's turnpike where out-of-control motorists have either crashed into oncoming traffic or plunged into ponds and canals.[4] Again in 2005, many restaurants made the decision to relocate the carbon dioxide source for their carbonated beverages to the exterior of the restaurant in the wake of two McDonald's workers being asphyxiated from carbon dioxide stored in a confined, interior space.[5] In the wake of mad cow disease scares, the menus in European Hard Rock Cafes had to be altered to focus less on beef.[6] In a similar vein, in the wake of the 2004 Southeast Asia tsunami, top hotels in several Asian capitals removed many fish items from their menus to ease diners' concerns that fish might be feasting on human corpses.[7] In the case of Cypress Gardens, the problems facing the previous owners were lack of attendance and mounting losses. The decision made in response to those problems was sudden and drastic. The park abruptly ceased operation, and the assets were put up for sale.

Managers do not always make decisions in response to problem situations. Often decisions are made because an opportunity arises. An **opportunity** is any situation that has the potential to provide additional beneficial outcomes. When an opportunity presents itself, success will be achieved by those who recognize the potential benefits and then embark upon a course of action to achieve them. For example, consider PepsiCo's decision to add a freshness date on its beverage containers.[8] This decision was precipitated by a perceived opportunity to capture additional market share by offering something that Pepsi's competitors were not offering. Not to be outdone, Coca-Cola soon followed with freshness dates on its own products. Eventually, this service was to become standard practice in the beverage industry. The next salvo in the cola wars was the introduction of flavors, and soon lemon- , cherry- , vanilla- , and, most recently, lime-flavored colas were lining up for shelf space.[9] Low calorie has also been a battleground, with catchy names like Pepsi One and Coke Zero.[10]

Much like the freshness-dating situation in soft drinks, the battery industry provides an example of companies following the lead of their competitors to cash in on an opportunity. Duracell first introduced the concept of a battery tester contained in its packaging. However, the Energizer Bunny topped that by introducing batteries with the test mechanism designed as an integral part of the battery. One needed only to squeeze the buttons on the battery and its LCD display would indicate the strength of its charge. Duracell soon followed suit with a version of that innovation. The list of company decisions precipitated by opportunity can go on and on. Apple Computer's digital music player, the iPod, has prompted many companies to enter the iPod aftermarket, with an assortment of gadgets, accessories, and add-ons for this popular MP3 player.[11] The post-9/11 era presented many opportunities that companies seized on. When the U.S. Postal Service had an episode of anthrax-tainted letters, the Bayer Corporation more than tripled its production of the anthrax antibiotic Cipro.[12] In early 2002, heavyweights Boeing, Northrup Grumman, TRW, Raytheon, and eventual winner Lockheed Martin all began preparing bids, seeking to win a federal airport security contract for a system to screen passengers and baggage in the post-9/11 era.[13] In the "At the Forefront" box, we can see how several south Florida entrepreneurs seized upon an opportunity in this strife-torn world with their focus on converting stock automobiles into armored cars.[14]

It is hard to top the serendipitous opportunity that presented itself to Chris Mike, director of Marketing and Advertising for Nike Golf, during the 2005 Masters Golf Tournament. The "Leaders in Action" box describes how Mike seized a golden opportunity when a Tiger Woods chip shot miraculously found the bottom of the cup on the 16th hole at the Augusta National Golf Course on the final day of the tournament.[15] Recognizing the importance of finding new opportunities, the 3M Corporation spends nearly twice the industry average on research and development. In fact, researchers spend about 15% of their time brainstorming and working on projects of their own choosing. This initiative is in support of the company's objective to maintain an innovative spirit, and its goal to generate 30% of annual revenue from products

KEY TERMS

Decision making
The process through which managers identify and resolve problems and capitalize on opportunities.

Problem
A situation in which some aspect of organizational performance is less than desirable.

Opportunity
A situation that has the potential to provide additional beneficial outcomes.

At the Forefront

Danger Drives Demand for Armored-Car Makers

Personal security and safety has become a major concern in many areas of our strife-ridden world. In war-torn regions of the Middle East and Latin America, kidnappings and assaults on occupants of motor vehicles are increasing at an alarming rate. No one is immune from this extreme form of road rage. Politicians, government employees, military personnel, business leaders, celebrities, and common citizens have all been targets of such violence. Urban terror of this type has presented a golden opportunity for Juan Mundo, who with his father Jorge, owns CSI Armoring in Miami–Dade County. This company is in the business of retrofitting stock vehicles to make them almost invincible to violent attacks. The 20-year-old company traditionally depended on private businessmen throughout south Florida as its client base. Now the Mundos cater almost exclusively to contractors who export the vehicles to Iraq and to customers in Latin America. Demand is so great that the Mundos are searching for a larger warehouse to store the truckloads of sport utility vehicles that are brought in each week for bulletproofing.

At the CSI Armoring plant, more than 50 workers gut brand-new Chevy Trail Blazers in preparation for their future "war-zone" homes. Sheets of Kevlar are inserted in doors, floors, and body panels to bulletproof the auto bodies. Sheets of bulletproof glass that can block bullets from an AK-47 assault rifle are also installed. Most conversions include flat-proof tires and safes in the rear compartment. Occasionally, vehicles are outfitted with canisters that spray Mace. Additional accessories that can be added include a device that creates a smoke curtain, an armored grill to protect the radiator, and electrified door handles. What was once a James Bond fantasy has become a new-millennium reality. Although his vehicle conversions cost upwards of $130,000, Mundo rationalizes that "you can't really put a price on safety. We're living in real troubled times."

Other south Florida entrepreneurs who have cashed in on this opportunity include Martin Cardenal, who co-owns Square One Armoring Service of Miami. Square One is among the few vendors in the United States that has secured vehicle-armoring contracts with the U.S. government. Cardenal's company was recently awarded a $2.2 million government contract to equip vehicles shipped to the Middle East and ships an average of 200 vehicles a year for various government agencies. On an even larger scale, Labock Technologies in suburban Miami secured $60 million in orders in 2004. The company specializes in products for the military in Iraq and corporate security in Latin America. Although some would argue that these companies are profiting from war and chaos, it cannot be denied that they are making sound business decisions in response to an opportunity that has presented itself. According to one company official from Labock Technologies, "[We] provide a vital service that saves lives. We have pictures and proof that the grim situation out there could be worse without these services."

Sources: I Rodriguez, "Danger Drives Up Demand: South Florida Armored Car Suppliers Grow to Meet Increased Need for Security," *South Florida Sun-Sentinel,* 13 March 2005, 1B; I. Rodriguez, "Danger Drives Demand for Armored-Car Makers," *Orlando Sentinel,* 26 March 2005, C1ff.

that are less than 4 years old.[16] When Kent Buescher looked at the vacant property that was once Cypress Gardens, he viewed it as a marvelous opportunity to resurrect the once-proud tourist Mecca and turn it back into a profitable business venture.

Steps in the Decision-Making Process

An effective decision-making process generally includes the seven steps shown in Figure 6.1. Although the figure shows the steps proceeding in a logical, sequential order, managerial decision making often unfolds in a quite disorderly and complex manner. Keep in mind that managers are influenced at each step in the decision-making process by their individual personalities, attitudes, and behaviors (as we will discuss in Chapter 13), ethics and values (as discussed in Chapter 3), and culture, as we discuss later in this chapter. Before we begin to examine these steps in greater detail, think about how you make decisions. How skilled a decision maker are you? Take a few minutes to complete the decision-making process questionnaire (DMPQ) in the "Now Apply It" box. The DMPQ evaluates your current level of decision-making ability.[17] As we progress through this chapter, you will learn more about sharpening these skills, which are an important part of most managerial experiences. Now let's

Figure 6.1 Seven Steps in the Decision-Making Process

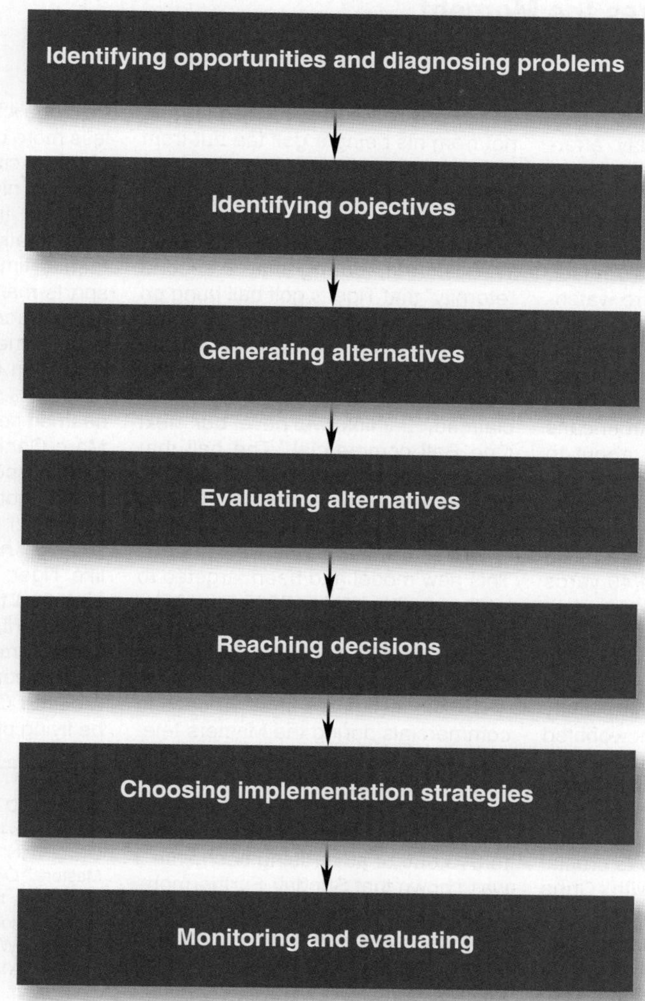

examine in more detail each of the seven steps in the managerial decision-making process.

IDENTIFYING OPPORTUNITIES AND DIAGNOSING PROBLEMS

Decision makers must know where action is required. Consequently, the first step in the decision-making process is the clear identification of opportunities or the diagnosis of problems that require a decision. Managers regularly review data related to their areas of responsibility, including both outside information and reports and information from within the organization. Discrepancies between actual and desired conditions alert a manager to a potential opportunity or problem. Identifying opportunities and problems is not always easy, considering human behavior in organizations. Sometimes, the origins of a problem may be deeply rooted in an individual's past experience, the complex structure of the organization, or some combination of individual and organizational factors. Therefore, a manager must pay particular attention to ensure that problems and opportunities are assessed as accurately as possible. Other times the problem may be so obvious that it is easily recognized, even by the casual observer.

An assessment of opportunities and problems will be only as accurate as the information on which it is based. Therefore, managers put a premium on obtaining accurate, reliable information. Poor-quality or inaccurate information can waste time and lead a manager to overlook the underlying causes of a situation.[18] This basic principle

Leaders in Action

Nike Executive Seizes the Moment

April 10, 2005, was a little different from most Sunday afternoon TV sports-viewing days. On this day, the final round of the Masters Golf Tournament was being played, so both avid and casual golf fans were likely to be tuned in. In fact, even many nongolf fans were watching the annual drama unfold. Chris Mike was comfortably positioned in front of his television in the basement of his Portland, Oregon, home, doing what 20 million plus other Americans were doing. They were all about to witness one of the most replayed moments in televised golf history. Tiger Woods was clinging to a one-stroke lead when his tee shot at the par-3 16th hole sailed long. From 40 yards off the green, Woods played a delicate chip that rolled up the slope, across a ridge, and then made what appeared to be a 90-degree turn to the right, trickling toward the vicinity of the hole. The ball then wobbled back to the left and stopped at the edge, hanging there for 2 full seconds before finally toppling into the cup. Woods had somehow conjured up a miracle birdie, a feat that was crucial to his achieving a tie with Chris DiMarco, and eventual victory in a playoff. At the sight of this "miracle," Chris Mike jumped from his chair and screamed so loudly that his two young children left the room shaking their heads.

Much of Mike's jubilation sprang not from his being a golf fan but from his being a golf executive. You see, Mike is the director of marketing and advertising for Nike Golf, whose products are endorsed and used by Tiger Woods. And, during that 2-second "eternity" that Tiger's golf ball hung on the lip of the cup, the Nike "swoosh" logo was plainly visible for all the world to see. Mike quickly got on his phone, called a colleague, and proclaimed, "I think we have our next One Ball commercial." The ball that Woods used was a model called One Platinum, a new model that Woods began using in January after switching over from another Nike model. This new model had been targeted to hit the market in May 2005, and Mike was determined to seize this marketing opportunity and cash in on this stroke of good fortune.

Mike estimated that 30-second commercials during the Masters telecast could cost as much as $250,000 apiece. The Nike logo was showcased on Woods' ball for 2 full seconds. A glimpse of the Nike swoosh amounted to $16,666 of advertising each time it was shown that Sunday. Furthermore, every TV station that replayed the moment during its sports coverage prominently featured the Nike logo. By the 60th replay on highlight shows and sportscasts that evening, Nike had received the equivalent of $1 million in free publicity. There would be countless more of these replays in the wake of this exciting and dramatic event. By Monday night, Mike offered that "the value of that shot far exceeds any mathematical evaluation of purchased media time." Many experts in the sports-marketing industry concluded that Woods's $20 million annual endorsement fee from Nike will rate as a bargain by the end of the summer. Nike's 9% share of the golf ball market seemed certain to rise. In the words of Marc Ganis, executive in a Chicago-based sports-marketing firm, "Nike could not have written a better script; (1) you had brand awareness, (2) you'll have people who want to be like Tiger, and (3) people will recognize that they have to have that ball because it's pretty cool." Mike's advertising campaign was under way, and he was certain that a lot of those $54-a-dozen One Platinum golf balls will be flying off the shelves.

Sources: D. Haugh, "Product Placement: Nike Execs Hope to Get Plenty of Mileage Out of Tiger Woods' Amazing Shot at the Masters," *Orlando Sentinel,* 13 April 2005, A1ff.; "Nike to Launch Ad Campaign on Woods' Shot," Forbes.com, 13 April 2005; T. Spousta, "Woods' Chip Lodged in Masters Lore," USAToday.com, 12 April 2005.

is well understood by U.S. business leaders, who spend millions of dollars each year on market research to identify trends in consumer preferences and buying decisions. For example, it was Mattel's monitoring the trends and shifting tastes of young girls that prompted the company to update its aging Barbie doll. The company reacted by introducing an array of new Barbies, including a soft-body version with glow-in-the-dark hair and pajamas—the perfect combination for little girls to bring to bed. Mattel's plan called for establishing Barbie as a ubiquitous "lifestyle brand," with a product for a girl's every fashion need.[19] Despite all efforts to thoroughly monitor the relevant information, crucial information is sometimes overlooked. In a classic blunder several years ago, the Coca-Cola Company developed the infamous "New Coke" after exhaustive taste tests were conducted. However, the company failed to assess one crucial factor: brand loyalty. The unveiling of the New Coke was one of the most spectacular marketing flops of all time.[20]

Even when high-quality information is collected, it may be misinterpreted. Sometimes, misinterpretations accumulate over time as information is consistently misunderstood or problematic events are unrecognized.[21] Many major disasters or accidents turn out to have had long incubation periods in which warning signs were misunderstood or overlooked. Consider the following revelations

© BOB DAEMMERICH/PHOTOEDIT

Managers are influenced at each step in the decision-making process by their individual personalities, attitudes, and behaviors as well as their ethics, values, and cultures.

regarding some news-headline-grabbing events. Months before ValuJet Flight 592 crashed into the Florida Everglades, killing all 110 people on board, the Federal Aviation Administration (FAA) had the safety data it later used to ground the airline. Unfortunately, this information was stored in warehouses out of sight of the FAA's key decision makers. In Saudi Arabia, U.S. authorities wanted to widen the security zone that surrounded the complex that housed U.S. troops, but the Saudis denied the request. It wasn't until 4 days after a terrorist bomb killed 19 Americans that Defense Secretary William Perry learned about the denial.[22] And none of us is likely to soon forget how the unrecognized hazards of insulating foam on external fuel tanks led to the space shuttle *Columbia* disaster, in which all crew members perished.[23]

To complicate matters further, even when managers have accurate information, it can be subject to different interpretations. Consider for the moment the Cypress Gardens situation described in the opening "Facing the Challenge." Previous owners perceived profitability problems, resulting in the decision to close the park. The potential new owner, Kent Buescher, was looking at the same piece of real estate and the same tourist pool of potential park visitors when he perceived the situation as a golden opportunity to have a profitable business venture. Even though managers will improve their chances of making good decisions by insisting on high-quality information and interpreting it carefully, there are no guarantees that solutions will always be clear cut.

IDENTIFYING OBJECTIVES

Objectives reflect the results the organization wants to attain. Both the quantity and quality of the desired results should be specified because these aspects of the objectives will ultimately guide the decision maker in selecting the appropriate course of action.

As you will recall from Chapters 4 and 5, objectives are often referred to as targets, standards, and ends. They may be measured along a variety of dimensions. For example, profit or cost objectives are measured in monetary units, productivity objectives may be measured in units of output per labor hour, and quality objectives may be measured in defects per million units produced.

Objectives can be expressed for long spans of time (years or decades) or for short spans of time (hours, days, or months). Long-range objectives usually direct much of the strategic decision making of the organization, whereas short-range objectives usually guide operational decision making. Regardless of the time frame, the objectives guide the ensuing decision-making process.

GENERATING ALTERNATIVES

Once an opportunity has been identified or a problem diagnosed correctly, a manager develops various ways to solve the problem and achieve objectives. This step involves the generation of **alternatives,** which are strategies that might be implemented in the decision-making situation. Creativity and imagination are often required in this step. In generating alternatives, the manager must keep in mind the goals and objectives that he or she is trying to achieve. Ideally, several different alternatives will emerge. In this way, the manager increases the likelihood that many good alternative courses of action will be considered and evaluated. In the never-ending burger wars, Burger King routinely considers many alternative additions to its menu to combat rival McDonald's menu changes. In an effort to provide more

KEY TERMS

Objective
The desired result to be attained when making decisions.

Alternative
A strategy that might be implemented in a decision-making situation.

Now Apply It

Assessing Your Decision-Making Skills

This decision-making process questionnaire (DMPQ) evaluates your current decision-making skills. These behaviors are part of most managerial experiences, but you will find that the questions are applicable to your own experience even if you are not yet a manager. If you do not have experience in a management-level position, consider a group you have worked with either in the classroom or in an organization such as a fraternity, sorority, club, church, or service group. Use the following scale to rate the frequency with which you perform the behaviors described in each statement. Place the appropriate number (1–7) in the blank preceding the statement.

Rarely:	Irregularly:	Occasionally:	Usually:	Frequently:	Almost Always:	Consistently/Always:
1	2	3	4	5	6	7

____ 1. I review data about the performance of my work and/or my group's work.
____ 2. I seek outside information, such as articles in business magazines and newspapers, to help me evaluate my performance.
____ 3. When examining data, I allow for sufficient time to identify problems.
____ 4. Based on the data, I identify problem areas needing action.
____ 5. To generate alternative solutions, I review problems from different perspectives.
____ 6. I list many possible ways of reaching a solution for an identified problem.
____ 7. I research methods that have been used to solve similar problems.
____ 8. When generating alternative courses of action, I seek the opinions of others.
____ 9. I explicitly state the criteria I will use for judging alternative courses of action.
____ 10. I list both positive and negative aspects of alternative decisions.
____ 11. I consider how possible decisions could affect others.
____ 12. I estimate the probabilities of the possible outcomes of each alternative.
____ 13. I study information about problems that require my decisions.
____ 14. I determine if I need additional data in light of my objectives and the urgency of the situation.
____ 15. To reach a decision, I rely on my judgment and experience as well as on the available data.
____ 16. I support my choices with facts.
____ 17. Before finally accepting a decision, I evaluate possible ways to implement it.
____ 18. I choose the simplest and least costly methods of putting my decisions into effect.
____ 19. I select resources and establish time frames as part of my implementation strategy.
____ 20. I choose implementation strategies that help achieve my objectives.

Enter your score for each category in the following table and sum the five category scores to obtain your total score. Enter that total score in the space indicated. Scores can range from a low of 4 to a high of 28 in each skill category. Total scores can range from a low of 20 to a high of 140. The higher the score in a particular category, the more refined your skill in that aspect of the decision-making process.

Skill Area	Statements	Score
Diagnosing the problem	1, 2, 3, 4	____
Generating alternatives	5, 6, 7, 8	____
Evaluating alternatives	9, 10, 11, 12	____
Reaching decisions	13, 14, 15, 16	____
Choosing implementation strategies	17, 18, 19, 20	____
Total score		____

Source: P. Fandt, *Management Skills: Practice and Experiences* (St. Paul: West, 1994).

choices, Burger King has evaluated such additions as a veggie burger, eggwich, Chicken Whopper, King Supreme, onion rings with zesty sauce, and an old-fashioned, ice cream–based milk shake.[24] Many nutritionists cringed when the company recently decided to offer its Enormous Omelet Sandwich—a two-egg, sausage, cheese, and bacon concoction stuffed between two halves of a bun.[25] As decadent as this 730-calorie, 47–fat gram sandwich may sound, it barely holds a candle to Hardee's new Monster Thickburger. This sandwich includes a slab of Angus beef with four strips of bacon, three slices of cheese, and mayonnaise on a buttered, sesame-seed bun, and weighs in at 1420 calories and 107 grams of fat.[26] These decisions certainly buck the trend toward lower-calorie fare at fast-food restaurants.

Managers may rely on their training, personal experience, education, and knowledge of the situation to generate alternatives. With prior experience in the amusement park industry, Buescher had a clear idea of several alternatives that might help turn around the fortunes of Cypress Gardens. Collectively, these decision choices would all focus on the concept of making the park more attractive to both families and individuals of all ages. Viewing the problem from varying perspectives is often helpful in generating good alternatives. This is usually best accomplished when input is solicited from other people such as peers, employees, supervisors, and groups within the organization. For example, consumer product companies such as Procter & Gamble often use customer focus groups to supply information that can be used in this stage of decision making.

The alternatives can be standard and obvious as well as innovative and unique. Standard solutions often include options that the organization has used in the past. Innovative alternatives may be developed using such approaches as brainstorming, nominal group technique, and the Delphi technique. These methodologies, which encourage consideration of multiple alternatives, are discussed in more detail later in the chapter as techniques for enhancing the quality of participative decision making.

EVALUATING ALTERNATIVES

The fourth step in the decision-making process involves determining the value or adequacy of the alternatives generated. Which solution is the best? Fundamental to this step is the ability to assess the value or relative advantages and disadvantages of each alternative under consideration. Predetermined decision criteria, such as the quality desired, anticipated costs, benefits, uncertainties, and risks of each alternative, may be used in the evaluation process. The result should be a ranking of the alternatives. For example, the manager might ask, "Will this alternative help achieve our objectives? What is the anticipated cost of this alternative? What are the uncertainties and risks associated with this alternative?" Later in this chapter, we examine some of the tools used by managers to evaluate strategic alternatives.

REACHING DECISIONS

Decision making is commonly associated with making a final choice. Reaching the decision is really only one step in the process, however. Although choosing an alternative would seem to be a straightforward proposition (that is, simply consider all the alternatives and select the one that best solves the problem), in reality, the choice is rarely clear-cut. Because the best decisions are often based on careful judgments, making a good decision involves carefully examining all the facts, determining whether sufficient information is available, and finally selecting the best alternative.[27]

In a classic example of cautious restraint, when Lou Gerstner took over as CEO of IBM Corporation, Wall Street expected him to take quick and bold action because IBM was losing its strong hold in the computer industry. When he took no action that Wall Street could see in his first year, he came under fire for being indecisive. But Gerstner was doing his homework, reviewing every IBM planning document that had been written since the late 1970s. Eventually, Gerstner decided to remove many ingrained operating procedures as he began reshaping IBM's organizational culture. Six billion dollars in expenses were cut, and stock prices doubled as IBM had its first profitable year since 1990.[28]

CHOOSING IMPLEMENTATION STRATEGIES

When decisions involve taking action or making changes, choosing ways to put these actions or changes into effect becomes an essential managerial task. The step that is the bridge between reaching a decision and evaluating the results is the implementation phase of the decision-making process. The keys to effective implementation are (1) sensitivity to those who will be affected by the decision and (2) proper planning and consideration of the resources necessary to carry out the decision. As will be seen in the closing "Meeting the Challenge," Buescher had a detailed plan for the implementation of his Cypress Gardens restoration decisions. New rides and attractions were secured, delivered, and installed with a schedule that had a "soft" opening planned within a year and a half of the park closing. This was quite an aggressive schedule, given the need to restore overgrown garden areas, install new attractions and venues, and repair the damage caused by the three major 2004 hurricanes that hit the park.

Those who will be affected by the decision must understand the choice and why it was made; that is, the decision must be accepted and supported by the people who are responsible for its implementation. These needs can be met by involving employees in the early stages of the decision process so that they will be motivated and committed to its successful implementation. This is advice that a top-level MCI executive would have been wise to heed a few years ago when he decided to relocate MCI's 4000-employee systems division from Washington, D.C., to Colorado Springs. This decision was made with the thought that the spectacular setting in this new location would inspire workers. Instead, numerous executives and engineers, as well as hundreds of the division's minority population, refused to relocate or left MCI shortly after relocating. These workers had been accustomed to living in larger, ethnically diverse urban areas and found Colorado Springs to be too isolated and politically conservative, with little diversity and fewer cultural activities.[29]

According to recent research, senior executives frequently complain that middle and operating managers fail to take actions necessary to implement decisions. Implementation problems often occur as a result of poor understanding and lack of commitment to decisions on the part of middle management.[30] Poor understanding and lack of commitment tend to be less prevalent at upper levels of management. This is certainly evident in the case of a recent major automobile recall by the Saturn Motor Company. Executives at Saturn operated swiftly and decisively when it was learned that there was a small chance of engine fires due to an alternator wiring problem. Although only 34 fires had been reported, company officials initiated a media blitz of information detailing the recall of over 380,000 automobiles to make the necessary repairs.[31]

The planning process is a key to effective implementation. Without proper planning, the decision may not be accepted by others in the organization, cost overruns may occur, needed resources may not be available, and the objectives may not be accomplished on schedule. To plan properly for implementation, managers need to perform the following activities:

- List the resources and activities required to implement each activity or task.
- Estimate the time needed for each activity or task.

Planning is key to effective implementation. Factors involved in the planning process include: listing resources and activities required to implement the task; estimating necessary time for each task; drawing up a chronological schedule of necessary activities; assigning responsibility for activities; and determining how the situation will look when the plan is fully operational.

- Draw up a chronological schedule of the activities and tasks that must be carried out to make the decision fully operational.
- Assign responsibility for each activity or task to specific individuals.
- Determine how things will look when the decision is fully operational.

Figure 6.2 displays a summary overview of the critical aspects of successful decision implementation.

MONITORING AND EVALUATING FEEDBACK

No decision-making process is complete until the impact of the decision has been evaluated. Managers must observe the impact of the decision as objectively as possible and take further corrective action if it becomes necessary. Quantifiable objectives can be established even before the solution to the problem is put into effect. For example, when 3M began a 5-year program dubbed "Challenge '95" to increase quality control and reduce manufacturing costs by 35%, the company constantly monitored its efforts to determine whether it was making progress toward those goals.

Monitoring the decision is useful whether the feedback is positive or negative. Positive feedback indicates that the decision is working and that it should be continued and perhaps applied elsewhere in the organization. Negative feedback indicates either that the implementation requires more time, resources, effort, or planning than originally thought or that the decision was a poor one and needs to be reexamined.

Figure 6.2 Keys to Effective Implementation of Decisions

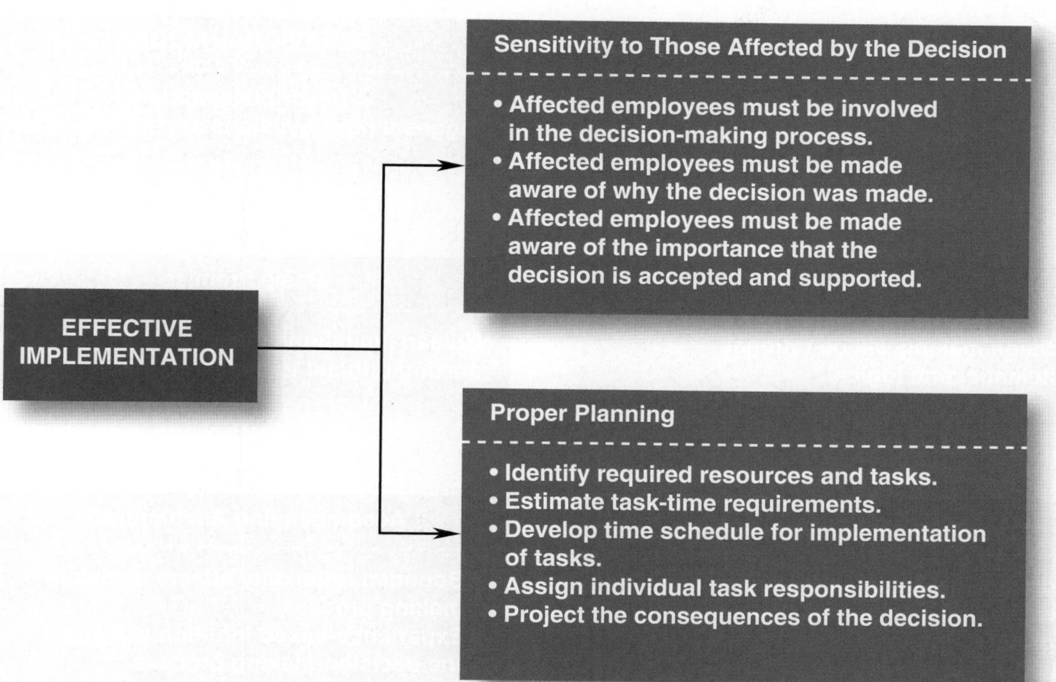

The importance of assessing the success or failure of a decision cannot be overstated. Evaluation of past decisions as well as other information should drive future decision making as part of an ongoing decision-making feedback loop.

Thus far, we have explored how managers in organizations make decisions by examining the seven steps in the decision-making process. The process starts when the organization recognizes a problem or becomes aware that an opportunity exists. It concludes with an assessment of the results of its decision actions. As we have stressed, the ability to make effective decisions is a distinguishing characteristic of most successful managers.[32] However, there are philosophical differences in how one approaches the decision-making process. In that context, we now examine two commonly used models of decision making.

Models of Decision-Making

Many models of the decision-making process can be found in the management literature. Although these models vary in scope, assumptions, and applicability, they are similar in that each focuses on the complexity of decision-making processes. In this section, we examine two contrasting decision-making models: the rational–economic model and the behavioral model. Our goal is to demonstrate the variations in how decision making is perceived and interpreted.[33] Figure 6.3 displays a summary comparison of many of the key aspects of each of these models. The discussions that follow elaborate on the points in this figure.

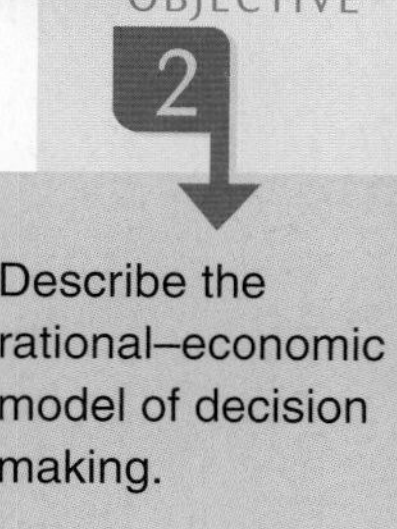

Describe the rational–economic model of decision making.

RATIONAL–ECONOMIC DECISION MODEL

2 The **rational–economic decision model** is prescriptive rather than descriptive; that is, it focuses on how decisions should be made, not on how they actually are made. The model makes the following important assumptions about the decision maker and the decision-making process:

- The decision maker is assumed to have "perfect"

KEY TERMS

Rational–economic decision model
A model that focuses on how decisions should be made.

Figure 6.3 Two Contrasting Decision Models

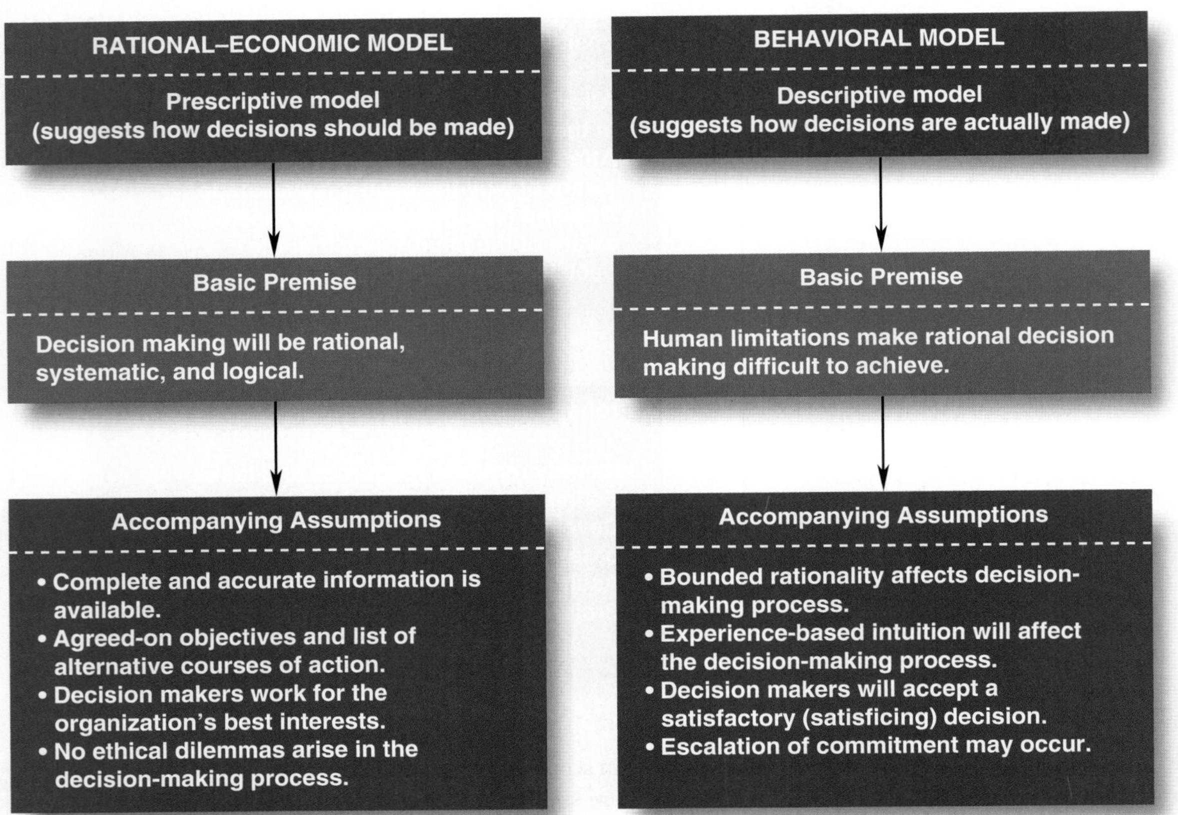

(that is, completely accurate) information and to have all the information that is relevant to the decision situation.

- The model assumes that the decision maker operates to accomplish objectives that are known and agreed on and has an extensive list of alternatives from which to choose.
- The model assumes that the decision maker will be rational, systematic, and logical in assessing each alternative and its associated probabilities.
- The model assumes that the decision maker will work in the best interests of the organization.
- The model assumes that ethical dilemmas do not arise in the decision-making process.

As these assumptions suggest, the rational–economic decision model does not address the influences that affect the decision environment or describe how managers actually make decisions; instead, it provides guidelines to help the organization or group reach an ideal outcome. As a consequence, in practice, the model may not always be a realistic depiction of managerial behavior. For example, the model portrays decision making as a straightforward process. In reality, there are several reasons why making a decision is not likely to be that simple. First, people rarely have access to complete and perfect information. Second, even if information about all possible alternatives were available, individuals are limited in their ability to comprehend and process vast amounts of information. Third, decision makers seldom have adequate knowledge about the future consequences of alternatives. Fourth, in most decision-making situations, personal factors (such as fatigue, emotions, attitudes, motives, or behaviors) are likely to intervene to prevent a manager from always acting in a completely rational manner. Finally, an individual's culture and ethical values may influence the decision process.

From a global perspective, it is especially important to be sensitive to how culture influences decision making. Individuals from different backgrounds and cultures have different experiences, values, and behaviors, which in turn influence the way they process information and make decisions. It is particularly important for managers

to recognize and appreciate this as modern organizations become increasingly global in their operations. We will discover in Chapter 16 the full extent to which organizations, large and small, are forming global alliances through e-commerce and Internet linkages. For example, Japanese managers follow a unique consensual decision-making process in which subordinates are involved in considering the future direction of their companies. Individuals and groups who have ideas for improvement or change discuss them extensively with a large number of peers and managers. During this lengthy information communication process, some agreements are hammered out. At this point, a formal document is drafted and circulated for the signature or personalized stamp of every manager who is considered relevant to the decision. Only after all the relevant managers have put their seals on the proposal is the idea or suggestion implemented.[34]

Managerial decision making is also influenced by the individual's ethics and values. As we discussed in Chapter 3, managers have power by virtue of their positions to make decisions that affect people's lives and well-being; consequently, the potential for ethical dilemmas is always present.[35] In an **ethical dilemma,** managers must decide whether or not to do something that will benefit themselves or the organization but may be considered unethical and perhaps illegal.

Ethical dilemmas are going to occur more and more frequently in the future as a result of the dramatic changes the business environment is undergoing. For example, managers may have to answer questions such as the following: What do companies owe employees who are let go after 30 years of service? Is it right to cancel a contract with a loyal distributor when a cheaper supplier becomes available? Is it proper to develop condominiums on land that is an unofficial wildlife refuge?

The following questions may help you when you face a situation that has ethical implications:[36]

- Have you accurately assessed the problem?
- Do you have all the necessary information?
- Where are your loyalties?
- Have you generated a list of possible alternatives and considered how each will affect the other parties involved?
- Have you tested each alternative by asking whether it is legal, fair, and just to all parties involved?
- Would your decision change if you were to disclose it to your family, your boss, or society as a whole?
- Does your decision have any symbolic potential? Could it be misunderstood?

Managers should encourage ethical decision making throughout the organization by providing subordinates with clear guidelines for making decisions and establishing rules for enforcing the guidelines. Both the guidelines and the rules should be communicated to subordinates on a regular basis.

BEHAVIORAL DECISION MODEL

LEARNING OBJECTIVE 3

Discuss the behavioral decision model and its related concepts of bounded rationality, intuition, satisficing, and escalation of commitment.

3 Unlike the rational–economic model, the **behavioral decision model** acknowledges human limitations that make rational decisions difficult to achieve. The behavioral decision model is descriptive and provides a framework for understanding the process that managers actually use when selecting from among alternatives.

The behavioral decision model suggests that a person's cognitive ability to process information is limited. In other words, a human being can handle only so much information before overload occurs. Even if complete information were available to decision makers, these cognitive limitations would impede them from making completely rational decisions.

Applying this assumption to managerial decision making, the model suggests that managers usually attempt to behave rationally within their limited perception of a situation. But most organizational situations are so complex that managers are forced to view problems within sharply restricted bounds. They frequently try to compensate for their limited ability to cope with the information demands of complex problems by developing simple models. Thus, managers' behaviors can be considered rational, but only in terms of their simplified view of the problem.

The behavioral decision model introduces several concepts that are important to understanding how we make decisions. These concepts include bounded rationality, intuition, satisficing, and escalation of commitment.

Bounded Rationality

The notion of **bounded rationality** recognizes that people cannot know everything; they are limited by such organizational constraints as time, information, resources, and their own mental capacities.[37]

KEY TERMS

Ethical dilemma
A situation in which a person must decide whether or not to do something that, although benefiting oneself or the organization, may be considered unethical and perhaps illegal.

Behavioral decision model
A descriptive framework for understanding that a person's cognitive ability to process information is limited.

Bounded rationality
Recognizes that people are limited by such organizational constraints as time, information, resources, and their own mental capacities.

Bounded rationality is a useful concept because it explains why different individuals with exactly the same information may make different decisions.

Bounded rationality affects several key aspects of the decision-making process. First, decision makers do not search out all possible alternatives and then select the best. Rather, they identify and evaluate alternatives only until an acceptable solution is found. Having found a satisfactory alternative, the decision maker stops searching for additional solutions. Other and potentially better alternatives may exist, but they will not be identified or considered because the first workable solution has been accepted. Therefore, only a fraction of the available alternatives may be considered due to the decision maker's information-processing limitations.

Intuition

Intuition has been described as everything from an unconscious analysis based on past experience to a paranormal ability called a "sixth sense."[38] Several theories have attempted to explain intuition, but none has been proved. We do know that intuition is based on the individual's years of practice and experience. For example, a decision maker who detects similarities between the current situation and one encountered previously will select or modify actions that proved effective in that situation in the past.[39] Managers use intuition to obtain a quick understanding of a situation and to identify solutions without going through extensive analysis. With four decades of experience in the theme park industry, Robert G. Gault, Jr., president and chief operating officer of Universal Orlando, relies heavily on intuition as he interacts with workers and surveys guests' opinions while walking around Universal Studios' two Orlando theme parks.[40] Buescher also relied on intuition a good bit as he made the various decisions to transform Cypress Gardens into a more family-friendly attraction. With his years of experience at the Valdosta, Georgia, amusement park, Buescher had a pretty keen sense of what it would take to turn this situation around. Some experts on corporate decision making feel that it would be a good thing if there was more behavior like this. They feel that many U.S. corporations place too much emphasis on decision analysis and suggest that managers should trust their feelings and experience more often.[41]

KEY TERMS

Intuition
An unconscious analysis based on past experience.

Satisficing
The search for and acceptance of something that is satisfactory rather than perfect or optimal.

Escalation of commitment
The tendency to increase commitment to a previously selected course of action beyond the level that would be expected if the manager followed an effective decision-making process.

Satisficing

Satisficing means searching for and accepting something that is satisfactory rather than insisting on the perfect or optimal. Satisficers do not try to find optimal solutions to problems but search until they find an acceptable or satisfactory solution and then adopt it. In short, managers tend to satisfice rather than optimize in considering and selecting alternatives. Some satisficing behavior is unavoidable because managers do not have access to all possible contingencies in making decisions. When Hewlett-Packard decided it was going to enter the home personal-computer business, it established a goal of simply becoming one of the top three competitors in this market. This could be viewed as a satisficing decision because Hewlett-Packard management had identified a level of performance that would be satisfactory but certainly not perfect.[42]

Escalation of Commitment

When managers face evidence that an initial decision is not working, they frequently react by committing more resources, even when feedback indicates the action is wrong.[43] This **escalation of commitment** phenomenon is the tendency to commit more to a previously selected course of action than would be expected if the manager followed an effective decision-making process.[44] One reason for escalation of commitment is that individuals feel responsible for negative consequences and try to justify their previous decisions. Managers may also stay with a course of action simply because they believe consistency is a desirable behavior. In addition, managers may worry that if they change course, others may regard the original decision as a mistake or a failure. For example, when Denver's new state-of-the-art international airport opened in 1995, it was supposed to have an equally state-of-the-art, computer-controlled luggage-handling system, complete with laser scanners reading barcodes on luggage tags, thousands of telecars carrying luggage around 21 miles of track, and photocells tracking the moving telecars. What Denver International got was a system that misdirected luggage, periodically jammed, and all too often crushed the luggage of irate passengers. Although many carriers soon abandoned the system in favor of the more conventional luggage-handling methods, United Airlines, Denver's largest carrier and long-time proponent of the system, remained committed to the system and continued to invest heavily to get it operable. Finally, after 10 years of futility and millions of wasted dollars, United threw in the towel and shut down the system in 2005.[45]

FOSTERING QUALITY IN THE DECISION-MAKING PROCESS

How can managers tell whether they have made the best possible decision? One way is to wait until the results are in, but that can take a long time. In the meantime, managers can focus on the decision-making process. Although nothing can guarantee a perfect decision, using vigilance can make a good decision more likely. **Vigilance** means being concerned for and attentive to the correct decision-making procedures. Vigilant decision makers use the following procedures:[46]

- Survey the full range of objectives to be fulfilled and identify the values and qualities implicated by the choices.
- Thoroughly canvass a wide range of alternative courses of action. This is the idea-gathering process, which should be separate from idea evaluation.
- Carefully weigh whatever they know about the costs and risks of both the negative and positive consequences that could flow from each alternative.
- Intensively search for new high-quality information relevant to further evaluation of the alternatives.
- Assimilate and take into account any new advice or information to which they are exposed, even when the information or advice does not support the course of action initially preferred.
- Reexamine all the possible consequences of all known alternatives before making a final choice, including those originally regarded as unacceptable.
- Make detailed provisions for implementing or executing the chosen course of action and give special attention to contingency plans that might be required if various known risks materialize.

Vigilance will not guarantee perfect decisions every time, but this approach can help managers be confident that they have followed procedures that will yield the best possible decision under the circumstances. Spending more time at this stage can save time later in the decision process.

Group Considerations in Decision Making

So far in this chapter, we have been examining how managers make decisions individually. In practice, managers often work with their employees and peers in the company and may need to solicit input from them. Decision making is frequently entrusted to a group—a board, standing committee, ad hoc committee, or task force—and as such, is referred to as participative decision making. Participative decision making is becoming more common as organizations push decision making to lower organizational levels in conjunction with their increased focus on improving customer service through quality management.[47] Accordingly, this section examines some of the issues related to using groups to make decisions.

PARTICIPATIVE DECISION MAKING

4 Participative decision making is not a single technique that can be applied to all situations. As we will see, managers can use a variety of techniques to involve the members of the organization in decision making. The appropriate level of subordinate participation in decision making depends on the manager, the employees, the organization, and the nature of the decision itself.

LEARNING OBJECTIVE 4

Describe the participative approach to decision making.

Participative Models

Vroom and Yetton laid the groundwork for participative decision making with their pioneer work in the development of a model to help managers determine when group decision making is appropriate.[48] According to this participative model, the effectiveness of a group decision is governed by both its quality and its acceptance (the degree to which group members are committed to the decision they have made). This model has seen a few updates over the years by Vroom and Jago to reflect the decision-making environment of managers more adequately.[49] The most recent version of this model employs five possible levels of subordinate participation in decision making, yielding the five decision styles described in Table 6.1. We see here that the five styles can be arranged along a continuum. The decision methods become progressively more participative as one moves from a highly autocratic style in which the leader makes the decision alone, to a highly participative style in which the leader permits the group to make the decision.[50]

According to Vroom and Jago, the degree of subordinate participation depends on

KEY TERMS

Vigilance
The concern for and attention to the process of making a decision that occurs when the decision maker considers seven critical procedures.

Table 6.1 Vroom–Jago Decision-Making Styles

Decide style	Leader makes the decision alone and announces or sells it to the group. Leader uses his/her own expertise and may collect information from the group to help solve the problem.
Consult individually style	Leader presents the problem to group members individually, gets their ideas and suggestions individually, and then makes the decision.
Consult group style	Leader presents the problem to group members in a meeting, gets their suggestions, and then makes the decision.
Facilitate style	Leader presents the problem to the group in a meeting and acts as a facilitator by defining the problem to be solved and the constraints within which the decision must be made. Leader seeks concurrence from group members on a decision.
Delegate Style	Leader permits the group to make the decision within prescribed limits. Group undertakes the identification and diagnosis of the problem and the development of alternative solutions and makes the decision on the selection of alternative(s).

Source: Adapted and reprinted from Leadership and Decision-Making, by Victor H. Vroom and Philip W. Yetton, by permission of the University of Pittsburgh Press © 1973 by University of Pittsburgh Press.

seven situational contingencies. They provide the following list of diagnostic questions to help managers select the appropriate level of participation.

1. *Decision significance* How significant is this decision for the project or the organization?
2. *Importance of commitment* How important is subordinate commitment for enacting the decision?
3. *Leader expertise* What is the level of the leader's expertise in relation to the problem?
4. *Likelihood of commitment* Would subordinates have high or low commitment if the leader were to make the decision alone?
5. *Team support* What is the level of subordinate support for the team's or organization's goals associated with this decision?
6. *Team expertise* What is the level of knowledge and expertise on the part of team members in relation to the problem at hand?
7. *Team competence* How skilled and committed to working together as a team are the subordinates?

Figure 6.4 shows how these questions can be used in a matrix format to arrive at the appropriate decision style. The leader enters the left side of the matrix at Problem Statement and examines the seven situational contingency questions in sequence from left to right. Each question calls for a response of either high (H) or low (L), and each response to a question moves the user one column to the right to answer the next situational contingency question. Following these sequential questions eventually leads the user to a choice of a decision-making participation style in the last column.

To illustrate the use of this model, assume that the leader entered the matrix at the left with a problem statement and answered H to the *decision significance* question. Suppose the response to the second question, *importance of commitment,* was also H. The leader would then proceed to the *leader expertise* question. Let's assume that the response here was also H. The leader then proceeds to the *likelihood of commitment* question. We'll assume that the response to this question was L. Let's also assume that a response of L was given to the next question, *goal alignment.* If you have been following the responses on the matrix, you will now encounter dashes the rest of the way to the right. This means that the subsequent questions do not need to be addressed. We proceed directly to the decision-making style in the last column, in this case the Consult group style.

Regardless of what type of participative decision-making model is used, generally speaking, a participative decision style is desirable when subordinates have useful information and share the organization's goals, when subordinates' commitment to the decision is essential, when timeliness is not crucial, and when conflict is unlikely. At the same time, group decision making is more complex than decision making by individuals, but good communication and conflict-management skills can overcome this difficulty.[51]

It is important to note that inappropriate use of either group or individual decision making can be costly. Ineffective use of groups wastes organizational resources because

Figure 6.4 Vroom and Jago Decision Model

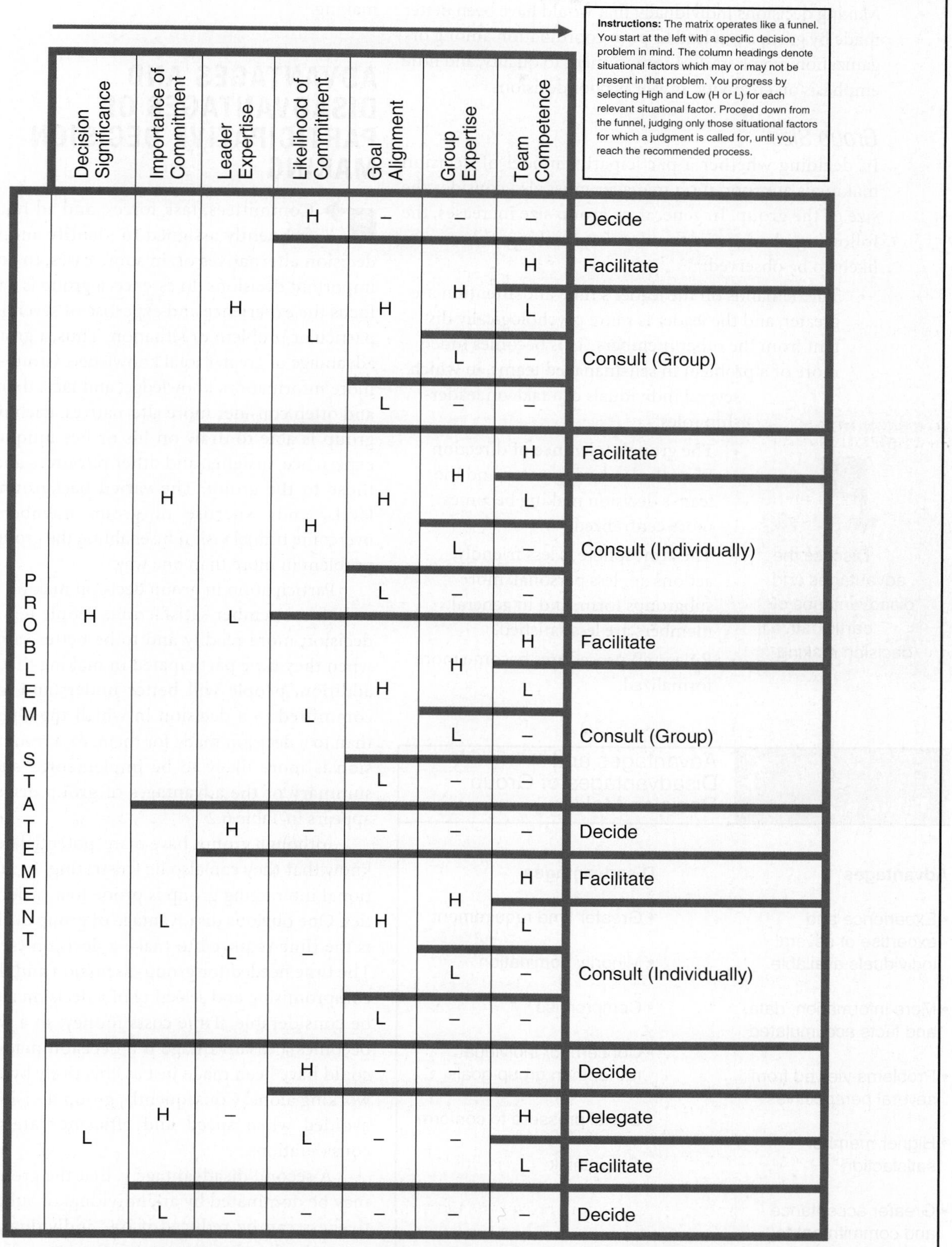

Instructions: The matrix operates like a funnel. You start at the left with a specific decision problem in mind. The column headings denote situational factors which may or may not be present in that problem. You progress by selecting High and Low (H or L) for each relevant situational factor. Proceed down from the funnel, judging only those situational factors for which a judgment is called for, until you reach the recommended process.

PROBLEM STATEMENT

Decision Significance	Importance of Commitment	Leader Expertise	Likelihood of Commitment	Goal Alignment	Group Expertise	Team Competence	
H	H	H	H	–	–	–	Decide
H	H	H	L	H	H	H	Facilitate
H	H	H	L	H	H	L	Consult (Group)
H	H	H	L	H	L	–	Consult (Group)
H	H	H	L	L	–	–	Consult (Group)
H	H	L	H	H	H	H	Facilitate
H	H	L	H	H	H	L	Consult (Individually)
H	H	L	H	H	L	–	Consult (Individually)
H	H	L	H	L	–	–	Consult (Individually)
H	H	L	L	H	H	H	Facilitate
H	H	L	L	H	H	L	Consult (Group)
H	H	L	L	H	L	–	Consult (Group)
H	H	L	L	L	–	–	Consult (Group)
H	L	H	–	–	–	–	Decide
H	L	L	–	H	H	H	Facilitate
H	L	L	–	H	H	L	Consult (Individually)
H	L	L	–	H	L	–	Consult (Individually)
H	L	L	–	L	–	–	Consult (Individually)
L	H	–	H	–	–	–	Decide
L	H	–	L	–	–	H	Delegate
L	H	–	L	–	–	L	Facilitate
L	L	–	–	–	–	–	Decide

Source: Adapted and reprinted from Leadership and Decision-Making, by Victor H. Vroom and Philip W. Yetton, by permission of the University of Pittsburgh Press © 1973 by University of Pittsburgh Press.

the participants' time could have been spent on other tasks; it can also lead to boredom and reduce motivation when participants feel that their time has been wasted. Making decisions individually that would have been better made by groups can lead to poor coordination among organization members, less commitment to quality, and little emphasis on creativity, as well as poor decisions.[52]

Group Size

In deciding whether a participative model of decision making is appropriate, a manager must also consider the size of the group. In general, as group size increases, the following changes in the decision-making process are likely to be observed:[53]

- The demands on the leader's time and attention are greater, and the leader is more psychologically distant from the other members. This becomes much more of a problem in self-managed teams, in which several individuals can take on leadership roles.
- The group's tolerance of direction from the leader is greater, and the team's decision making becomes more centralized.
- The atmosphere is less friendly, actions are less personal, more subgroups form, and in general, members are less satisfied.
- Rules and procedures become more formalized.

LEARNING OBJECTIVE 5

Discuss the advantages and disadvantages of participative decision making.

Table 6.2 Advantages and Disadvantages of Group Decision Making

Advantages	Disadvantages
• Experience and expertise of several individuals available	• Greater time requirement
• More information, data, and facts accumulated	• Minority domination
• Problems viewed from several perspectives	• Compromise
• Higher member satisfaction	• Concern for individual rather than group goals
• Greater acceptance and commitment to decisions	• Social pressure to conform
	• Groupthink

Participative decision making offers potential advantages, but it is not without its disadvantages. Let's now briefly examine these aspects of participative decision making.

ADVANTAGES AND DISADVANTAGES OF PARTICIPATIVE DECISION MAKING

5 Committees, task forces, and ad hoc groups are frequently assigned to identify and recommend decision alternatives or, in some cases, to actually make important decisions. In essence, a group is a tool that can focus the experience and expertise of several people on a particular problem or situation. Thus, a group offers the advantage of greater total knowledge. Groups accumulate more information, knowledge, and facts than individuals and often consider more alternatives. Each person in the group is able to draw on his or her unique education, experience, insights, and other resources and contribute those to the group. The varied backgrounds, training levels, and expertise of group members also help overcome tunnel vision by enabling the group to view the problem in more than one way.

Participation in group decision making usually leads to higher member satisfaction. People tend to accept a decision more readily and to be better satisfied with it when they have participated in making that decision. In addition, people will better understand and be more committed to a decision in which they have had a say than to a decision made for them. As a result, such a decision is more likely to be implemented successfully. A summary of the advantages of group decision making appears in Table 6.2.

Although groups have many potential benefits, we all know that they can also be frustrating. In fact, the traditional interacting group is prone to a variety of difficulties. One obvious disadvantage of group decision making is the time required to make a decision (see Table 6.2). The time needed for group discussion and the associated compromising and selecting of a decision alternative can be considerable. Time costs money, so a waste of time becomes a disadvantage if a decision made by a group could have been made just as effectively by an individual working alone. Consequently, group decisions should be avoided when speed and efficiency are the primary considerations.

A second disadvantage is that the group discussion may be dominated by an individual or subgroup. Effectiveness can be reduced if one individual, such as the group leader, dominates the discussion by talking too much or being closed to other points of view. Some group leaders try to control the group and provide the major input. Such dominance can stifle other group members' willingness to participate and could cause decision alternatives to be ignored or overlooked. All group members need to be encouraged and permitted to contribute.

Another disadvantage of group decision making is that members may be less concerned with the group's goals than with their own personal goals. They may become so sidetracked in trying to win an argument that they forget about group performance. On the other hand, a group may try too hard to compromise and consequently may not make optimal decisions. Sometimes this stems from the desire to maintain friendships and avoid disagreements. Often groups exert tremendous social pressure on individuals to conform to established or expected patterns of behavior. When they are dealing with important and controversial issues, interacting groups may be prone to a phenomenon called groupthink.[54]

Groupthink is an agreement-at-any-cost mentality that results in ineffective group decision making. It occurs when groups are highly cohesive, have highly directive leaders, are insulated so that they have no clear ways to get objective information, and—because they lack outside information—have little hope that a better solution might be found than the one proposed by the leader or other influential group members.[55] These conditions foster the illusion that the group is invulnerable, right, and more moral than outsiders. They also encourage the development of self-appointed "mind guards" who bring pressure on dissenters. In such situations, decisions—often important decisions—are made without consideration of alternative frames or alternative options. It is difficult to imagine conditions more conducive to poor decision making and wrong decisions.

Research indicates that groupthink may also result when group members have preconceived ideas about how a problem should be solved.[56] Under these conditions, the team may not examine a full range of decision alternatives, or it may discount or avoid information that threatens its preconceived choice.

Irving Janis, who coined the term *groupthink*, focused his research on high-level governmental policy groups faced with difficult problems in complex and dynamic environments. The groupthink phenomenon has been used to explain numerous group decisions that have resulted in serious fiascoes. Classic examples of such decisions include the Bay of Pigs invasion, the Watergate cover-up, and NASA's decision to launch the ill-fated, space shuttle *Challenger*.[57] Of course, group decision making is common in all types of organizations, so it is possible that groupthink exists in private-sector organizations as well as in those in the public sector. Table 6.3 summarizes the characteristics of groupthink and the types of defective decision making that will likely result.

Table 6.3 Characteristics of Groupthink and the Types of Defective Decisions That May Result

Characteristics of Groupthink	Types of Defective Decisions
• Illusion of invulnerability	• Incomplete survey of alternatives
• Collective rationalization	• Incomplete survey of goals
• Belief in the morality of group decisions	• Failure to examine risks of preferred decisions
• Self-censorship	• Poor information search
• Illusion of unanimity in decision making	• Failure to reappraise alternatives
• Pressure on members who express arguments	• Failure to develop contingency plans

Groupthink is common in tightly knit groups that believe in what they are doing, such as citizen groups who censor book acquisitions for the local library, environmental groups who will save us from ourselves at any price, business leaders who presume that they control other people's economic destinies, or government functionaries who think they know better than the voters what is in the national interest. None of the decisions made by these groups is necessarily wrong, but that is not the point. Rather, it is the single-mindedness of the decision process, the narrow framing, and limited deliberation that are of concern.[58]

TECHNIQUES FOR ENHANCING THE QUALITY OF PARTICIPATIVE DECISION MAKING

LEARNING OBJECTIVE 6

List the various techniques used to improve participative decision making.

6 Managers can use several structured techniques to foster quality in group decision making.[59] Here, we briefly explore brainstorming, the nominal group technique, the Delphi technique, devil's advocacy approach, and dialectical inquiry.

KEY TERMS

Groupthink
An agreement-at-any-cost mentality that results in ineffective group decision making.

Brainstorming

Brainstorming is a technique that encourages group members to generate as many novel ideas as possible on a given topic without evaluating them. As a group process, brainstorming can enhance creativity by overcoming pressures for conformity that can retard the development of creative decision making. Brainstorming primarily focuses on generating ideas rather than on choosing an alternative. The members of the group, usually 5 to 12 people, are encouraged to generate ideas during a specific time period while withholding criticism and focusing on nonevaluative presentation.[60] In this way, individuals who may be concerned about being ridiculed or criticized feel more free to offer truly novel ideas.

The following rules should guide the brainstorming process:[61]

- Freewheeling is encouraged. Group members are free to offer any suggestions to the facilitator, who lists ideas as people speak.
- Group members will not criticize ideas as they are being generated. Consider any and all ideas. No idea can be rejected initially.
- Quantity is encouraged. Write down all the ideas.
- The wilder the ideas are, the better.
- Piggyback on or combine previously stated ideas.
- No ideas are evaluated until after all alternatives are generated.

© TAXI/GETTY IMAGES

Managers can use several techniques, such as brainstorming, to foster quality in group decision making.

KEY TERMS

Brainstorming
A technique used to enhance creativity that encourages group members to generate as many novel ideas as possible on a given topic without evaluating them.

Nominal group technique (NGT)
A structured process designed to stimulate creative group decision making where agreement is lacking or where the members have incomplete knowledge concerning the nature of the problem.

Delphi technique
An approach that uses experts to make predictions and forecasts about future events without meeting face to face.

Brainstorming enhances creativity and reduces the tendency of groups to satisfice in considering alternatives. One advocate of brainstorming is Bill Gates, CEO of Microsoft. He often joins programmers in the brainstorming sessions that give birth to new products. According to Gates, it is very important to him and to those who work with him at Microsoft to encourage creative group decision making.[62]

Nominal Group Technique

The **nominal group technique (NGT)** is a structured process designed to stimulate creative group decision making in which agreement is lacking or the members have incomplete knowledge of the nature of the problem.[63] It is a means of enhancing creativity and decision making that integrates both individual work and group interaction with certain basic guidelines. NGT was developed to foster individual as well as group creativity and to further overcome the tendency of group members to criticize ideas when they are offered.

NGT is used in situations in which group members must pool their judgments to solve the problem and determine a satisfactory course of action. First, individual members independently list their ideas on the specific problem. Next, each member presents his or her ideas one at a time, without discussion. As with brainstorming, members are asked to generate ideas without direct comment, but the idea-generation phase of NGT is more confined than it is with brainstorming because group members present ideas in a round-robin manner rather than through freewheeling. Members' ideas are recorded so that everyone can see them. After all members' ideas are presented, the group discusses the ideas to clarify and evaluate them. Finally, members vote on the ideas independently, using a rank-ordering, or rating, procedure. The final outcome is determined by the pooled individual votes and is thus mathematically derived.

NGT may be most effective when decisions are complex or when the group is experiencing blockages or problems, such as a few dominating members. NGT is generally effective in generating large numbers of creative alternatives while maintaining group satisfaction.[64]

Delphi Technique

The **Delphi technique** was originally developed by Rand Corporation to enable groups to consult experts and use their predictions and forecasts about future events.[65] Using survey instruments or questionnaires, a group leader solicits and collects written expert opinions on a topic. The leader collates and summarizes the information before distributing it to the participants. This process continues until the experts' predictions are systematically refined through feedback and a consensus emerges.

Like NGT, the Delphi technique can be used to define problems and to consider and select alternatives. The Delphi technique is also best used under special circumstances. The primary difference between NGT and the Delphi technique is that with the Delphi technique participants do not meet face to face.

A significant advantage of the Delphi technique is that it completely avoids group-interaction effects. Even NGT is not completely immune to the social facilitating pressure that results from having an important person in the same room. With Delphi, participant experts can be thousands of miles apart.

Devil's Advocacy Approach

The last two techniques to enhance group decision making, devil's advocacy approach and dialectical inquiry, were developed to deal with complex, strategic decisions. Both techniques encourage intense, heated debate among group members. One study found that disagreement in structured settings like meetings can lead to better decision making.[66] Disagreement is particularly useful for organizations operating in uncertain environments.

The **devil's advocacy approach** appoints an individual or subgroup to critique a proposed course of action. One or more individuals are assigned the role of devil's advocate to make sure that the negative aspects of any attractive decision alternatives are considered.[67] The usefulness of the devil's advocacy technique was demonstrated several years ago by Irving Janis in his discussion of famous fiascoes attributed to groupthink. Janis recommends that everyone in the group assume the role of devil's advocate and question the assumptions underlying the popular choice. An individual or subgroup can be formally designated as the devil's advocate to present critiques of the proposed decision. Because groups often exhibit a desire to agree, using this technique avoids the problem of having this tendency interfere with the decision-making process. Potential pitfalls are identified and considered before the decision is final.

Dialectical Inquiry

With **dialectical inquiry,** a decision situation is approached from two opposite points, and advocates of the conflicting views conduct a debate, presenting arguments in support of their positions. Each decision possibility is developed, and assumptions are identified. The technique forces the group to confront the implications of their assumptions in the decision process.[68] The Bausch and Lomb Company successfully uses this technique by establishing "tiger teams" composed of scientists from different disciplines. Team members are encouraged to bring up divergent ideas and offer different points of view. Xerox uses round-table discussions composed of various functional experts to encourage divergent and innovative decision making.

Now that we have examined the decision making process from both an individual and a group perspective, let's turn our attention to a mechanism for classifying decision situations.

LEARNING OBJECTIVE 7

Discuss the basic classifications for managerial decisions.

Classifying Decision Situations

7 On a very basic level, Herbert Simon, a management scholar and prolific researcher in the area of decision making, proposed that decisions can be classified as either programmed or nonprogrammed.[69] When the decision situation is one that has occurred in the past and the response is routine, the decision is referred to as a **programmed decision.** Identifying alternative courses of action in such situations is usually routine because the alternatives are quite familiar to the decision maker. As an example of a programmed decision, consider the customer assistance operator for the Mills-Pride Company, a manufacturer of kits of unassembled furniture and cabinetry. If a customer discovers that a component or hardware item is missing from her kit, she can call an 800 number for assistance. The operator routinely obtains the missing part number from the customer and then authorizes immediate UPS shipping of that part.

When a decision is made in response to a situation that is unique, unstructured, or poorly defined, it is called a

KEY TERMS

Devil's advocacy approach
An approach in which an individual or subgroup is appointed to critique a proposed course of action and identify problems to consider before the decision is final.

Dialectical inquiry
A method that approaches a decision from two opposite points and structures a debate between conflicting views.

Programmed decision
A decision made in response to a situation that is routine or recurring.

nonprogrammed decision. These decisions often require considerable creativity, cleverness, and innovation to elicit a list of reasonable alternative courses of action. When an investment group took control of the Schwinn Bicycle Company and tried to reverse the slide that Schwinn had been in for years, many nonprogrammed decisions were made as they restructured the company, shifted to a customer focus, and developed some hot new models. These decisions helped Schwinn roll back to its former prominence in the industry.[70]

Whether programmed or nonprogrammed, organizational decisions can be further described as either long-range strategic decisions or short-range operational decisions. As the names suggest, long-range strategic decisions are those that are made infrequently and commit resources for long time spans into the future. On the other hand, short-range operational decisions are those that are made on a recurring basis and deal with the day-to-day or week-to-week operation of the organization.

The changing nature of today's business environment presents an interesting dilemma for decision makers. On one hand, the rapidly changing, global business environment creates a need for more nonprogrammed decisions than ever before. With quality and continuous improvement as major strategic initiatives, organizations are constantly being challenged to find creative and innovative solutions to unique new problems and opportunities. On the other hand, the changing composition of the workforce suggests that more programmed decisions might be beneficial. Today's workforce continues to become more diverse in racial, ethnic, and gender composition. Workers with diverse backgrounds and cultural values often have different perceptions of appropriate organizational goals and objectives and therefore respond differently to the same decision situation. In such circumstances, the more programmed the decision responses can be, the more likely that workers will make consistent, high-quality decisions.

LEARNING OBJECTIVE

Describe the nature of strategic decision making as well as the strategic decision-making matrix approach for strategy selection.

KEY TERMS

Nonprogrammed decision
A decision made in response to a situation that is unique, unstructured, or poorly defined.

Strategic decision-making matrix
A two-dimensional grid used to select the best strategic alternative in light of multiple organizational objectives.

Regardless of the type of decision situation, managers have at their disposal certain tools and techniques to achieve excellence in the decision-making process. Let's look at a few of the more popular tools used in making long-range strategic decisions within an organization.

Strategic Decision-Making Tools

8 Strategic decision making occurs at the highest levels in organizations. As we saw in Chapter 5, this type of decision making involves the selection of a strategy that will define the long-term direction of the firm. Two important areas for strategic decision making are in strategy selection and evaluation of portfolios.

STRATEGY SELECTION: THE STRATEGIC DECISION-MAKING MATRIX

Many times, organizations find that there is not one clear-cut, obvious strategy that should be pursued. Instead, several potentially attractive alternatives may exist. The task for management is to select the strategy that will best facilitate the achievement of the multiple objectives of the organization. A tool that can be helpful in such cases is the **strategic decision-making matrix.**[71]

When management faces several strategic alternatives and multiple objectives, it is helpful to organize these factors into a two-dimensional decision-making matrix.[72] To illustrate, let's consider the case of an organization that has established a goal of strong growth and has implemented that goal by specifying three objectives: increased profit, increased market share, and increased production output. Suppose management has determined that three alternative growth strategies are reasonable options for the organization—product development, horizontal integration, and a joint venture. To form the strategic decision-making matrix, the alternative strategies are listed along the side of the matrix, and the objectives are listed along the top, as in Table 6.4.[73]

Because the objectives of the organization won't always be equally important, different weights can be assigned to them. Management usually assigns the weights based on its subjective assessment of the importance of each objective. The weights are shown directly below the objectives in Table 6.4. In this example, increased profit is the most important objective; therefore, it has received the highest weight. Note that the sum of the weights must equal 1.0.

Table 6.4 Strategic Decision-Making Matrix

	Objectives			
	Increased Profit	**Increased Market Share**	**Increased Production Output**	**Total Weighted Score**
Alternative Strategies/Weight	0.5	0.3	0.2	
Product development	2	2	3	0.5(2) + 0.3(2) + 0.2(3) = 2.2
Horizontal integration	4	2	2	0.5(4) + 0.3(2) + 0.2(2) = 3.0
Joint venture	5	3	3	0.5(5) + 0.3(3) + 0.2(3) = 4.0

To use the matrix, management must first rate each alternative strategy on its potential to contribute to the achievement of each objective. A 1-to-5 rating scale is used, with 1 indicating little or no potential for achieving an objective and 5 indicating maximum potential. Once an alternative strategy has been rated for each objective, the strategy's total weighted score can be computed by multiplying its rating for each objective by the corresponding weight of the objective and then summing across all objectives, as shown in the last column in Table 6.4. The decision maker can then select the strategy with the highest weighted score. In this example, the joint venture strategy is the most desirable alternative because it will allow the organization to achieve the best combination of profitability, market share, and production output.

EVALUATION OF PORTFOLIOS

Whenever an organization becomes involved in several businesses and industries or with several products and services, it becomes necessary to make decisions about the role each business line will play in the organization and the manner in which resources will be allocated among the business lines. Although this discussion of the portfolio approach focuses on the evaluation of multiple business lines, these approaches can also be used at the product or service level. This is done by replacing business lines on the matrix with products or services. The most popular technique for assessing the balance of the mix of business lines in an organization is portfolio matrix analysis. A **business portfolio matrix** is a two-dimensional grid that compares the strategic positions of each of the organization's businesses.

A portfolio matrix can be constructed using any reasonable pair of indicators of a firm's strategic position. As we will see, usually one dimension of the matrix relates to the attractiveness of the industry environment and the other to the strength of a business within its industry.[74] The two most frequently used portfolio matrices are the growth-share matrix and the industry attractiveness/ business strength matrix.

LEARNING OBJECTIVE 9

Identify the differences between the growth-share matrix and the industry attractiveness/ business strength matrix approaches for evaluating business portfolios.

The Growth-Share Matrix

9 The earliest business portfolio approach to be widely used for corporate strategy formulation is the growth-share matrix. This technique was developed by the Boston Consulting Group (BCG), a leading management consulting firm. Figure 6.5 illustrates a BCG matrix.[75]

The **BCG matrix** is constructed using market-growth rate and relative market share as the indicators of the firm's strategic position. Each indicator is divided into two levels (high and low) so that the matrix contains four cells. The rows of the matrix show the market-growth rate, and the columns show the relative market share. Market-growth rate is the percentage at which the market in which the business operates is growing annually. In the BCG matrix, 10% is generally considered the dividing line between a low rate and a high rate of market growth. Relative market share is computed by dividing the firm's market share by the market share of its largest competitor.

KEY TERMS

Business portfolio matrix
A two-dimensional grid that compares the strategic positions of each of the organization's businesses.

BCG matrix
A business portfolio matrix that uses market growth rate and relative market share as the indicators of the firm's strategic position.

Figure 6.5 The BCG Growth-Share Matrix

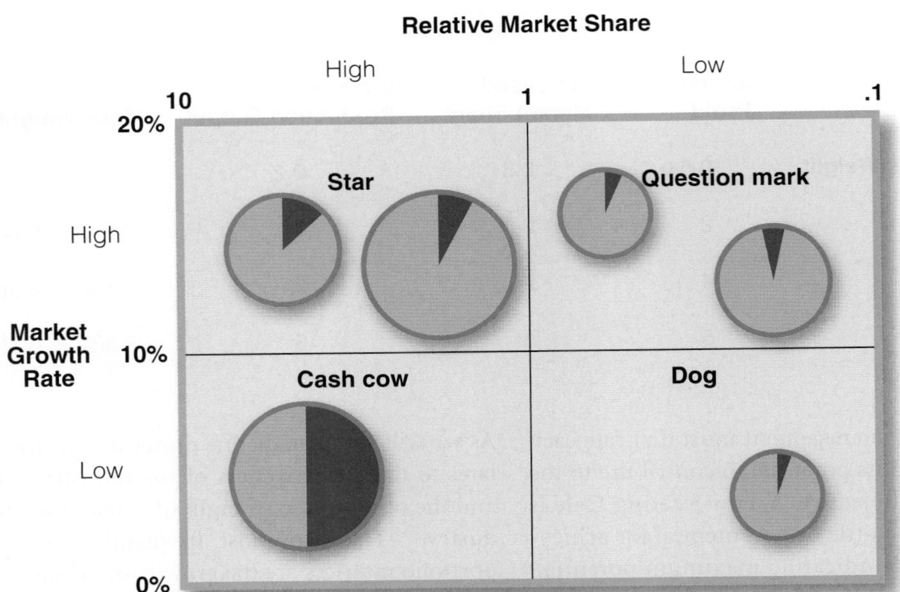

For example, a relative market share of 0.4 means that the sales volume of the business is only 40% of the largest competitor's sales volume. In the BCG matrix, a relative market share of 1.0 is usually set as the dividing line between high- and low-relative market shares.

To use the BCG matrix, each of the organization's businesses is plotted in the matrix according to its market-growth rate and relative market share. Figure 6.5 illustrates a BCG matrix for an organization with six businesses. Each circle represents a business unit. The size of a circle reflects the proportion of corporate revenue generated by that business, and the pie slice indicates the proportion of corporate profits generated by that business.[76] Note that each cell in the BCG matrix has a descriptive label; these labels reflect the roles that the businesses in the cells play in the overall strategy of the firm.

Stars Businesses that fall into the high market-growth/high market-share cell are referred to as **stars.** These businesses offer attractive profit and growth opportunities. However, they also require a great deal of money to keep up with the market's rate of growth. Consequently, in the short term they are often cash-using rather than cash-generating units, but usually this situation reverses in time. BCG analysis advocates retaining stars in the corporate portfolio.

Cash Cows Businesses that fall into the low market-growth/high market-share cell are referred to as **cash cows.** These businesses generate substantial cash surpluses over what they need for reinvestment and growth. Cash cows are generally yesterday's stars whose industries have matured. Although not attractive from a growth standpoint, they are quite valuable because the cash surpluses they generate can be used to pay bills, cover dividends, provide funds for investment, or support struggling businesses, such as the question marks described in a following section. BCG analysis also views cash cows favorably and advocates keeping them in the corporate portfolio.

Dogs Businesses that fall into the low market-growth/low market-share cell are known as **dogs.** These businesses typically generate low profits, and in some cases they may even lose money. They also frequently consume more management time than they are worth. Unless there is some compelling reason to hold onto a dog, such as an expected turnaround in market-growth rate, BCG analysis suggests that such businesses be removed from the portfolio.

KEY TERMS

Star
A business that falls into the high market-growth/high market-share cell of a BCG matrix.

Cash cow
A business that falls into the low market-growth/high market-share cell of a BCG matrix.

Dog
A business that falls into the low market-growth/low market-share cell of a BCG matrix.

Question Marks Businesses that fall into the high market-growth/low market-share cell are referred to as **question marks.** The rapid market growth makes these businesses look attractive from an industry standpoint. Unfortunately, their low market share makes their profit potential uncertain. Question mark businesses are often called *cash hogs* because they require large infusions of resources to keep up with the rapid growth and product development of the market. BCG analysis suggests that the organization must consider very carefully whether continued funding for a question mark is worthwhile. Management must consider the question mark's potential to gain market share and move into the star category.

The BCG business portfolio matrix makes valuable contributions in the area of strategic decision making. This method of analysis can be used in both for-profit and not-for-profit organizations and in manufacturing and service organizations. It enables a corporation to highlight the flow of cash resources among the units in its portfolio, and it provides a sound rationalization for resource allocation, investment, expansion, and contraction decisions. It also enables management to assess the balance among the units within its portfolio. A balanced portfolio should contain units in several cells. The status of individual business units can shift over time. For example, question marks can move into the star category, and stars will eventually evolve into cash cows. For these reasons, it is important to have question marks "waiting in the wings" to replace stars and stars waiting to replace any cash cows that might slip into the dog category.

Darden Restaurants (parent company to Red Lobster and Olive Garden restaurants) is a classic example of a service organization that tries to balance its portfolio to ensure its long-term success. In addition to the seafood and Italian segments of casual dining, Darden has ventured into the Caribbean and barbeque segments with its Bahama Breeze restaurants and Smokey Bones BBQ Sports Bars. In early 2005, Darden began testing still another concept restaurant with its unveiling of a few Seasons 52 restaurants. This concept offers a casually sophisticated grill and wine bar, which features a low-calorie, seasonally changing menu. Each restaurant chain is in a different stage of development and occupies a different position on the BCG matrix. With 679 restaurants in mid-2005, Red Lobster is a mature chain in a mature segment of the restaurant industry. Although Red Lobster still has opportunities for expansion, its growth rate has subsided since the early 1980s when units were popping up everywhere. When Olive Garden was started in 1982, the intention was to build this chain into a leader in its segment by penetrating the domestic market. Olive Garden, with its 556 restaurants, has already achieved this leadership position and is moving beyond the middle-growth stage, and it will continue to enjoy significant growth for several years to come. Expansion plans for Olive Garden will increase its footprint to over 700 restaurants in the next several years.[77] Placing these restaurant chains on a BCG matrix, we find that Red Lobster is a cash cow and Olive Garden is a star that is rapidly approaching the cash cow category.

In the early 1990s, Darden moved into the Chinese segment with its China Coast restaurants. As the China Coast venture was beginning its growth, it fell into the question mark category. With only 51 restaurants and a short track record, its future was uncertain. The questions about China Coast were certainly answered when Darden abruptly closed all China Coast restaurants in August 1995. Darden replaced China Coast in its portfolio with the Bahama Breeze restaurants. This segment has been setting and resetting records for Darden at each of its restaurants since opening. With 32 restaurants thus far, it is quickly moving from the question mark category toward the star category. Smokey Bones BBQ Sports Bar has seen a growth rate that has exceeded Bahama Breeze. Although once a question mark, Smokey Bones, with its 101 restaurants, is quickly gravitating to star status.[78] Darden's newest concept restaurant, Seasons 52, currently falls into the question mark category with only 3 prototype outlets being tested thus far.[79] The BCG matrix will continue to be an important tool for Darden as long as it continues to experiment with new dining concepts.

The BCG business portfolio matrix approach is not without its shortcomings. Some critics have argued that the four-cell classification scheme is overly simplistic. Others contend that accurately measuring market share and growth rate can be difficult. Furthermore, when the analysis is based on just these two factors, other important variables may be overlooked.[80] In an attempt to overcome some of the limitations of the BCG approach, more refined models have been proposed. One of the early refinements of the BCG approach is the General Electric model, which attempts to overcome some of the BCG shortcomings.

The Industry Attractiveness/Business Strength Matrix

General Electric (GE) developed a nine-cell business portfolio matrix that overcomes some of the limitations of the BCG matrix. The **GE matrix** uses several factors (listed in Table 6.5) to assess industry attractiveness and business strength.[81] The GE approach

KEY TERMS

Question mark
A business that falls into the high market-growth/low market-share cell of a BCG matrix.

GE matrix
A business portfolio matrix that uses industry attractiveness and business strength as the indicators of the firm's strategic position.

Table 6.5 Factors Contributing to Industry Attractiveness and Business Strength

Industry Attractiveness	Business Strength
Market Forces	
Size (dollars, units, or both)	Your share (in equivalent terms)
Size of key segments	Your share of key segments
Growth rate per year:	Your annual growth rate:
Total	Total
Segments	Segments
Diversity of market	Diversity of your participation
Sensitivity to price, service, features, and external factors	Your influence on the market
Cyclicality	Lags or leads in your sales
Seasonality	
Bargaining power of upstream suppliers	Bargaining power of your suppliers
Bargaining power of downstream suppliers	Bargaining power of your customers
Competition	
Types of competitors	Where you fit, how you compare in terms of products, marketing capability, service, production strength, financial strength, and management
Degree of concentration	
Changes in type and mix	
Entries and exits	Segments you have entered or left
Changes in share	Your relative share change
Substitution by new technology	Your vulnerability to new technology
Degrees and types of integration	Your own level of integration
Financial and Economic Factors	
Contribution margins	Your margins
Leveraging factors, such as economies of scale and experience	Your scale and experience
Barriers to entry or exit (both financial and nonfinancial)	Barriers to your entry or exit (both financial and nonfinancial)
Capacity utilization	Your capacity utilization
Technological Factors	
Maturity and volatility	Your ability to cope with change
Complexity	Depths of your skills
Differentiation	Types of your technological skills
Patents and copyrights	Your patent protection
Manufacturing process technology required	Your manufacturing technology
Sociopolitical Factors in Your Environment	
Social attitudes and trends	Your company's responsiveness and flexibility
Laws and government agency regulations	Your company's ability to cope
Influence with pressure groups and government representatives	Your company's aggressiveness
Human factors, such as unionization and community acceptance	Your company's relationships

Source: Abell, Derek; Hammond, John S.; Strategic Market Planning: Problems and Analytical Approaches, 1st Edition, © 1979, p. 214. Reprinted by permission of Pearson Education Inc., Upper Saddle River, NJ.

also allows for three levels of industry attractiveness and business strength, resulting in its nine-cell structure.

To use the GE matrix, each of the organization's businesses is rated as to industry attractiveness and business strength. To measure the attractiveness of an industry, the decision maker first selects from Table 6.5 those factors that are likely to contribute to the attractiveness of the industry in question. Each factor is assigned a weight based on its perceived importance. These weights must sum to 1.0. The industry is then assigned a rating for each of these factors using some uniform scale (for example, a 1-to-5 rating scale). Finally, a weighted score is obtained by multiplying weights by factor scores and then adding to obtain a total weighted value. To arrive at a measure of business strength, each business is rated using the same procedure as for industry attractiveness. Table 6.6 illustrates these calculations for a hypothetical business in a corporation's portfolio.

The total weighted scores for industry attractiveness and business strength are used to locate the business on the nine-cell matrix. Figure 6.6 illustrates a GE business portfolio matrix that contains eight businesses, with each circle reflecting one business.[82] The area of a circle is proportional to the size of the entire industry, and the pie slice within the circle represents the business's share of that market.

The GE matrix provides the decision maker with rationalization for resource allocation, investment, expansion, and contraction decisions within different cells, in much the same way as the BCG matrix. Businesses that fall into the three green cells at the upper left of the GE matrix are given top investment priority. These are the combinations of industry attractiveness and business strength that are most favorable. The strategic prescription for businesses located in these three cells is to invest and grow. Businesses positioned in the three gold

Table 6.6 Illustration of Industry Attractiveness and Business Strength Computations

Industry Attractiveness	**Weight**	**Rating (1–5)**	**Value**
Overall market size	0.20	4.00	0.80
Annual market growth rate	0.20	5.00	1.00
Historical profit margin	0.15	4.00	0.60
Competitive intensity	0.15	2.00	0.30
Technological requirements	0.15	3.00	0.45
Inflationary vulnerability	0.05	3.00	0.15
Energy requirements	0.05	2.00	0.10
Environmental impact	0.05	1.00	0.05
Social/political/legal	Must be acceptable		
	1.00		3.45
Business Strength	**Weight**	**Rating (1–5)**	**Value**
Market share	0.10	4.00	0.40
Share growth	0.15	4.00	0.60
Product quality	0.10	4.00	0.40
Brand reputation	0.10	5.00	0.50
Distribution network	0.05	4.00	0.20
Promotional effectiveness	0.05	5.00	0.25
Productive capacity	0.05	3.00	0.15
Productive efficiency	0.05	2.00	0.10
Unit costs	0.15	3.00	0.45
Material supplies	0.05	5.00	0.25
R&D performance	0.10	4.00	0.40
Managerial personnel	0.05	4.00	0.20
	1.00		3.90

Source: Hosmer, Larue T., Strategic Management: Text&Cases on Business Policy, 1st Edition, © 1982. Reprinted by permission of Pearson Education, Inc., Upper Saddle River, NJ.

Figure 6.6 The GE Industry Attractiveness/Business Strength Matrix

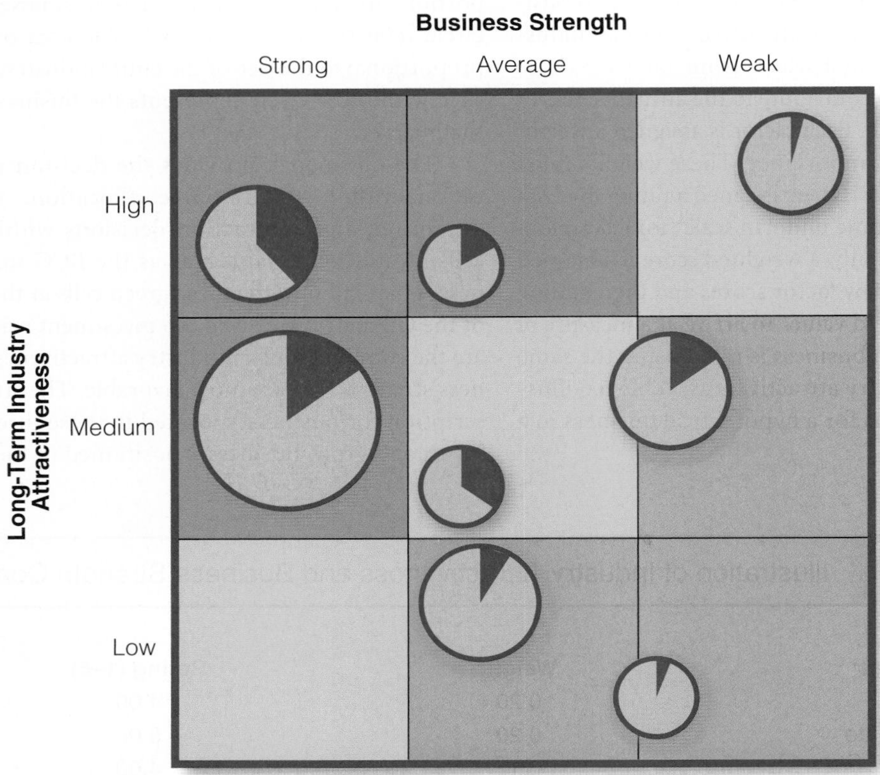

cells are next in priority. These businesses deserve selective reinvestment to maintain and protect their industry positions. Finally, businesses positioned in the three orange cells at the lower right of the matrix are serious candidates for divestiture due to their low overall strength.[83]

Although similar to the BCG approach, the GE matrix offers several improvements. For one thing, it allows for intermediate rankings between high and low and between weak and strong, yielding nine rather than four cells. A second improvement is that it incorporates a much wider variety of strategically relevant variables. Whereas the BCG matrix considers only two factors (industry growth rate and relative market share), the GE matrix takes many factors into consideration (see again Table 6.5) to determine industry attractiveness and business strength. Finally, and perhaps most important, the GE approach emphasizes allocating corporate resources to businesses with the greatest chance of achieving competitive advantage and superior performance.[84]

Despite these improvements, the GE matrix does have its critics. Like the BCG matrix, it prescribes only a general strategic posture and provides no real guidance on the specifics of the business strategy. Another criticism of the GE approach (and the BCG approach, for that matter) is that they are static. They portray businesses as they are at one point in time and do not take into account that businesses evolve over time. Consequently, these approaches do not detect businesses that are about to become winners because their industries are entering the takeoff stage or businesses that are about to become losers as their industries enter the decline stage.[85] This was certainly the case as Darden was expanding the China Coast restaurant chain. The BCG matrix was not capable of helping management foresee this chain's sudden demise.

Ethical and Social Implications in Decision Making

The treatment of decision making presented thus far may leave the impression that all managers need to do is plug in the numbers to generate the best choice of an alternative. However, managers must also be careful to consider more than just the numbers. Often they will have to look beyond the numbers and consider the ethical and social implications of their decisions. Many examples can be cited for decisions that went beyond bottom-line profitability and included a component of ethical behavior and social responsibility. At considerable expense the Walt Disney Company has been refurbishing many of its resort swimming pools into "zero-entry" pools. Also called "zero-grade" or "zero-barrier" pools, these pools lack a traditional elevated ledge, instead offering a gradual "shorelike" entrance and exit. Handicapped bathers can simply roll into the pool in special water-resistant wheelchairs.[86] Burger King made the decision to double the number of welfare recipients hired.[87] In response to tragic incidents of children dying after becoming trapped in car trunks, General Motors announced its decision to equip its family cars with an infrared-sensing device that automatically unlocks the trunk if anyone is trapped inside.[88] Partly due to the rising number of fatal handgun incidents (and partly due to corresponding liability issues), the Colt Manufacturing Company has decided to remove itself from the consumer handgun business.[89] In an effort to help the homeless break out of the endless cycle of poverty, the Orlando/Orange County Expressway Authority made hiring the homeless a condition for contractors bidding on a highway project.[90] And how about Bob Thompson? When he sold his road-building firm, one of the conditions of the sale was that his employees would not lose their jobs. Then, as a reward for their loyalty and hard work, he decided to split $128 million from the sale among his 550 flabbergasted workers. More than 80 of them became instant millionaires![91]

Information Technology and Decision-Making Tools

Early in this chapter, we were introduced to a seven-step decision-making process and focused on how timely and accurate information is extremely beneficial in the first step (problem identification) and the last step (monitoring and evaluating). The tools and techniques introduced in this chapter are quantitative models that enable us to assess the promise of various alternative courses of action. Consequently, these tools and techniques have their biggest impact on the midsection of the decision-making process in which alternatives are evaluated and decisions reached. When we use quantitative models of this type, the old axiom rings true: garbage in, garbage out. Regardless of how sophisticated these analytical tools are, their output (decision recommendations) will be worthless if the information being processed is suspect. Once again, the huge advances in information-gathering, -processing, and -dissemination technology serve to make this aspect of the decision-making process more reliable. The confidence that we can place in our decisions will only increase as the technological advances in information handling continue.

Implications for Leaders

Decision making has always been one of the primary activities of business leaders. As the global business economy continues to expand and change dramatically, the level of managerial decision making can only be expected to increase in the future. If leaders are to make high-quality decisions, they will have to become thoroughly familiar with the structure of decision making while equipping themselves with the tools and techniques that can aid in the decision-making process. To be effective decision makers, tomorrow's leaders should

- Be able to recognize quickly problems and opportunities that call for a decision.
- Be able to recognize the different time frames and scopes of strategic decisions versus operational decisions.
- Be equipped with all the tools and techniques that can aid in making strategic decisions.
- Be familiar with the framework for operational decision making as well as the structural components for displaying operational decisions.
- Be able to recognize the different decision-making environments in which their operational decisions will be made.
- Have an awareness and understanding of the various quantitative tools that can aid in making operational decisions.

This chapter has presented a structured methodology that can aid in making both strategic and operational decisions. Various analytical tools, techniques, and decision-making aids are available, suggesting that we need only "plug in the numbers" to select the best alternative. However, we saw several times in our discussions that decision making cannot always go entirely by the numbers. Many times, experience, good judgment, and even intuition are valuable commodities when making decisions about future courses of action, especially because we can never be entirely certain about what the future holds in store.

Meeting The Challenge

Hello Cypress Gardens Adventure Park

The historic grounds that encompassed Cypress Gardens were spared from the developers' bulldozers when Kent Buescher, owner of a Valdosta, Georgia, amusement park, stepped in and offered to purchase this Florida landmark. The deal was closed in February 2004. Buescher's experiences in the amusement park industry convinced him that these grounds had potential, but something had to be done to make the attraction more family friendly. Buescher's solution involved keeping a lot of the old but introducing much more that was new. The famed botanical gardens, topiaries, water-ski show, and Southern Belles would remain as park fixtures. These were to be complimented with a wide array of rides, new attractions and shows, shopping areas, and dining facilities. Buescher pledged to invest $36 million in the first 18 months of restoration. He had an aggressive schedule that called for reopening the park by late 2004, a daunting task given that the gardens had suffered almost a year of neglect and the new attractions would require a major construction effort.

Unanticipated events occurred that might have challenged the resolve of even the strongest of entrepreneurs. Six months after restoration had begun, the park found itself in the crosshairs of three major hurricanes in 6 weeks. After the first and most devastating hurricane, Buescher commented that "we had spent so much time restoring and rejuvenating the park that it was heartbreaking to see six months of hard work disappear over night." These catastrophes would set back the opening by several months and raise the price of the first wave of investments to $50 million. But Buescher was undeterred, and work proceeded at a fever pitch. By late November 2004, the park was able to have the first of several "preview days" to work out the "bugs" prior to its December 9, 2004, grand reopening as Cypress Gardens Adventure Park. Workers toiled around the clock at a frenzied pace making some major "final touches" with things like paving, painting, construction, and landscaping. When the park finally had its official opening, park visitors were thrilled with what they found. When you go through the following scorecard, you will understand why the park was renamed Cypress Gardens *Adventure Park:*

- 38 rides: 11 are coasters/thrill rides, 16 are family rides, 2 are water rides, and 9 are children's rides
- 9 shows, including comedy, song and dance, magic, ice skating, waterskiing, and more more than 50 all-star concerts and special events yearly
- A bustling village where shopping takes an entertaining old-fashioned twist and dining options range from quick bites and confections to elegant dining
- A water park containing slides and attractions for everyone from tiny tots to bold thrill seekers, a 20,000–square foot wave pool, a 1000-foot meandering river pool, and a full range of dining facilities
- A teen-oriented arcade, complete with interactive games and a disc jockey

Early indications are that this has been a successful transformation. In the first few months of operation, annual pass sales were brisk, and daily attendance was averaging four to five times what the park averaged prior to Buescher's transformation decisions. These early successes prompted park officials to raise their first-year attendance projections to more than 1.2 million guests. Many longtime Cypress Park visitors have been effusive in their praise of the transformation, but perhaps the highest compliment was paid by Dick Pope, Jr., son of the original founder and one of the original water-skiers. In his words, "It's just beautiful. It's going in the right direction."

SUMMARY

1. Decision making is the process through which managers and leaders identify and resolve problems or capitalize on opportunities. The decision-making process includes seven steps: (a) identifying and diagnosing the problem, (b) identifying objectives, (c) generating alternatives, (d) evaluating alternatives, (e) reaching decisions, (f) choosing implementation strategies, and (g) monitoring and evaluating.
2. The rational–economic decision model assumes that the decision maker has completely accurate information and an extensive list of alternatives from which to choose. It also assumes that he or she will be rational and systematic in assessing each alternative and will work in the best interests of the organization.

3. The behavioral decision model acknowledges human limitations to decision making and addresses the issues of bounded rationality, intuition, satisficing, and escalation of commitment. Bounded rationality recognizes that people cannot know everything and are limited by such organizational constraints as time, information, resources, and their own mental capacities. Intuition has been described as everything from an unconscious analysis based on past experience to a paranormal ability called a "sixth sense." Satisficing means searching for and accepting something that is satisfactory rather than optimal. Escalation of commitment is the tendency to commit more resources to a previously selected course of action than would be expected if the manager followed an effective decision-making process.

4. The increased involvement of groups and teams in management actions requires that leaders understand group considerations in decision making. The participative model of group decision making provides guidelines for the appropriate level of subordinate participation in decision making.

5. A leader must consider both the advantages and disadvantages of participative decision making. The advantages include greater experience and expertise, more information, higher satisfaction, and greater acceptance of and commitment to the decisions. The disadvantages are that group decisions take more time, one member or subgroup may dominate, individual goals may supplant group goals, social pressure to conform may be brought to bear on members, and groupthink may develop.

6. Leaders can use several structured techniques to aid in participative decision making. These include brainstorming, the nominal group technique, the Delphi technique, devil's advocacy approach, and dialectical inquiry.

7. On a basic level, decisions can be classified as either programmed or nonprogrammed. Programmed decisions are routine responses to decision situations that may have occurred in the past or with which the decision maker is familiar. Nonprogrammed decisions are responses to situations that are unique, unstructured, or poorly defined.

8. Strategic decision making occurs from a broad perspective and is performed at the highest levels within organizations. It involves the selection of a corporate-level strategy and the choice of competitive strategies to be pursued by the various business units of the organization. Strategic decision making is most often nonroutine by nature. Selection of a business strategy can be facilitated by means of the strategic decision-making matrix approach. This tool allows the decision maker to evaluate a variety of potential strategies in conjunction with several objectives. Objectives are ranked by their importance, and strategies are rated by their likelihood of achieving those objectives. This method ultimately allows for the ranking of alternative strategies.

9. Two popular matrix approaches for evaluating a business portfolio are the BCG growth-share matrix and the GE industry attractiveness/business strength matrix. Although both have two dimensions, they measure different factors and include a different number of levels for each factor. The two factors in the BCG matrix are market-growth rate and relative market share. With two levels for each factor, a four-cell matrix results. The GE matrix uses industry attractiveness and business strength as its factors. Three levels for each factor are defined, resulting in a nine-cell matrix. In both approaches, an organization's business units are placed in the appropriate cell; then prescriptions for strategic decision making are made relative to the cell occupied by the business unit.

REVIEW QUESTIONS

1. (LEARNING OBJECTIVE 1) Describe the nature of the decision-making process and list each of its seven steps.
2. (LEARNING OBJECTIVE 2) Describe the rational–economic model for decision making.
3. (LEARNING OBJECTIVE 3) Describe the behavioral model for decision making and indicate how it differs from the rational–economic model.
4. (LEARNING OBJECTIVE 4) Describe the participative decision-making approach.
5. (LEARNING OBJECTIVE 5) Describe the advantages and disadvantages of participative decision making when compared to individual decision making.
6. (LEARNING OBJECTIVE 6) Discuss the concepts of brainstorming, nominal group technique, Delphi technique, devil's advocacy approach, and dialectical inquiry as devices that can enhance quality in participative decision making.

7. (LEARNING OBJECTIVE 7) Identify and describe the two basic classifications for managerial decisions.
8. (LEARNING OBJECTIVE 8) Describe the strategic decision-making matrix technique for selecting from among strategy alternatives.
9. (LEARNING OBJECTIVE 9) Describe the structure, purpose, and approach of the four-cell BCG matrix and the nine-cell GE matrix.

DISCUSSION QUESTIONS

Improving Critical Thinking

1. Recall a situation in which you made a decision for which the outcome was satisfactory but not optimal. Describe the reasons you accepted this satisficing decision rather than pushing on to make an optimal decision.
2. Discuss the pros and cons associated with the two business portfolio matrix techniques described in this chapter. Which, if either, do you find more appealing? Why?

Enhancing Communication Skills

3. What types of ethical dilemmas do you think future managers will face? How can you prepare yourself to handle ethical dilemmas? To develop your written communication skills, find some recent examples in business publications and/or the news media and write a short paper on this subject.
4. Consider an important decision that you recently made, such as choosing a major or buying a car. How much vigilance did you exercise to ensure making a quality decision? To practice your oral communication skills, be prepared to present your decision process to the class or a small group as directed by your instructor.

Building Teamwork

5. Interview one of your college professors. Ask the professor to describe a decision that was made regarding one of the policies on the course syllabus and to explain the process that led to that decision. Analyze the professor's decision with regard to the two models of decision making described in the chapter. Form small groups and share the results of your interview with the team. Did the team members find any issues in common among all the professors interviewed?
6. Reflect on recent decisions made by groups with which you were involved in various college courses. Try to recall an experience that showed signs of groupthink. Be prepared to report this experience to the class and describe what might have been done to prevent this phenomenon.

part 3

Organizing Challenges in the 21st Century

Chapter 7
Organizing for Effectiveness and Efficiency

Chapter 8
Organizational Design

Chapter 9
Strategic Human Resource Management

Chapter 10
Organizational Culture and Change

Chapter

7

Organizing for Effectiveness and Efficiency

CHAPTER OVERVIEW

The previous chapters discussed the establishment of vision and mission of an organization or reaffirming or adjusting the vision and mission, as is the most likely case in existing organizations. Then goals and operational plans were discussed, and we have learned about decision making and ethical and socially responsible behavior so that, as managers, we can make better decisions concerning all of these issues. In other words, we have learned about establishing an overall strategy for an organization. Now we learn about organizing the many tasks that need to be done to achieve the strategy and, consequently, the mission and vision.

This chapter begins by discussing the necessity to understand the tasks and jobs that need to be done to work toward the goals and overall strategy. It also discusses relationships that need to be established and tools that can be used to organize the jobs into an overall organizational structure that will help the organization operate effectively and efficiently. Constructing the overall organizational structure and design will be discussed in the next chapter.

The remaining chapters in this book discuss the other managerial functions that must be performed to plan, organize, and carry out the operations successfully. Take another look at Figures 1.1 and 1.5 to refresh your memory about how everything must be focused on achieving the mission and vision of an organization.

LEARNING OBJECTIVES

When you have finished studying this chapter, you should be able to

1. Explain why organizing is an important managerial function, describe the process of organizing, and outline the primary stages of the process.
2. Discuss the concept of job design and identify the core job dimensions that define a job.
3. Explain how and why the perspectives on job design have evolved.
4. Describe the job-design approaches that came from the classical management, behavioral management, and employee/work team–centered perspectives.
5. Understand both the vertical and horizontal associations that exist between individuals and work groups within the organization.
6. Define delegation and discuss why it is important for managers to delegate.
7. Explain why managers often fail to delegate and suggest methods for improving delegation skills.

Facing The Challenge

Procter and Gamble Stumbles

It is almost unimaginable that Procter and Gamble (P&G), the company that introduced Tide in 1946 and disposable diapers (Pampers) in 1961, as well as a vast variety of consumer products, would be in financial difficulty. By 2000 revenues were not increasing but costs were, driving down profit margins. In turn, the price of the stock fell 43% in a year.

It is not that P&G under CEO Dirk Jager was not trying. In fact, when Jager became CEO, he began immediately to try to change the organization's culture, which was very resistant to new ideas and change. Rather, the culture was rule bound, and everyone stayed in his or her own department and job. There was little cooperation and communication from person to person, job to job, and department to department. Jager used a very aggressive approach to try to get the people to change and to try to get new products developed because new products and/or new uses for existing products were necessary in the very slow-growing markets of household products.

Instead of changing to keep up with the industry, P&G stagnated. Although the company was in no danger of failing soon, the long term looked much less bright. Over the previous 15 years, only one product, the Swiffer dust mop, was financially successful. The company had to get more profitable.

After only 17 months as CEO, the Board of Directors replaced Jager. In the summer of 2000, the board selected A. G. Lafley, a 23-year P&G veteran to be its new CEO. Lafley's main job was not to necessarily change the company but to get profits back to reasonable levels.

Sources: S. Ellison, "P&G Chief's Turnaround Recipe: Find Out What Women Want," *Wall Street Journal* (Eastern Edition), 1 June 2005, A1; "It Was a No-Brainer," *Fortune,* 21 February 2005, 97–102; P. Sellers, "P&G: Teaching an Old Dog New Tricks," *Fortune,* 31 May 2004, 166–180; R. Berner, "P&G New and Improved," *BusinessWeek,* 7 July 2003, 52–60.

Introduction

LEARNING OBJECTIVE 1

Explain why organizing is an important managerial function, describe the process of organizing, and outline the primary stages of the process.

You may have heard the saying, "form follows function." In organizing terms, the form of the organizational structure should be designed so that it can help an organization achieve its function. Procter and Gamble's organizational structure did not seem to be appropriate for achieving profitability any more ("Facing the Challenge"). The organizational structure, with its rigid rules and tightly defined jobs and organizational units, interfered with rather than assisted designing, making, and marketing products that customers wanted. As you read this chapter, think about what Procter and Gamble could do to return to success.

What Is Organizing?

1 **Organizing** refers to the process of determining the tasks to be done, who will do them, and how those tasks will be managed and coordinated. It is an interactive and ongoing process that occurs throughout the life of the organization. As an organization develops and matures, so must its organizational system. Many times companies must adapt their organizational systems to cope with changes that occur in their competitive environment. As you read in "Facing the Challenge," CEO Dirk Jager of Procter and Gamble attempted this, but it was not done successfully.

The process of organizing can be divided into two primary stages (Figure 7.1). In the first stage, the foundation of the organizational system is developed. Work activities are determined and assigned to specific job positions, and working relationships between individuals and work

Figure 7.1 The Process of Organizing

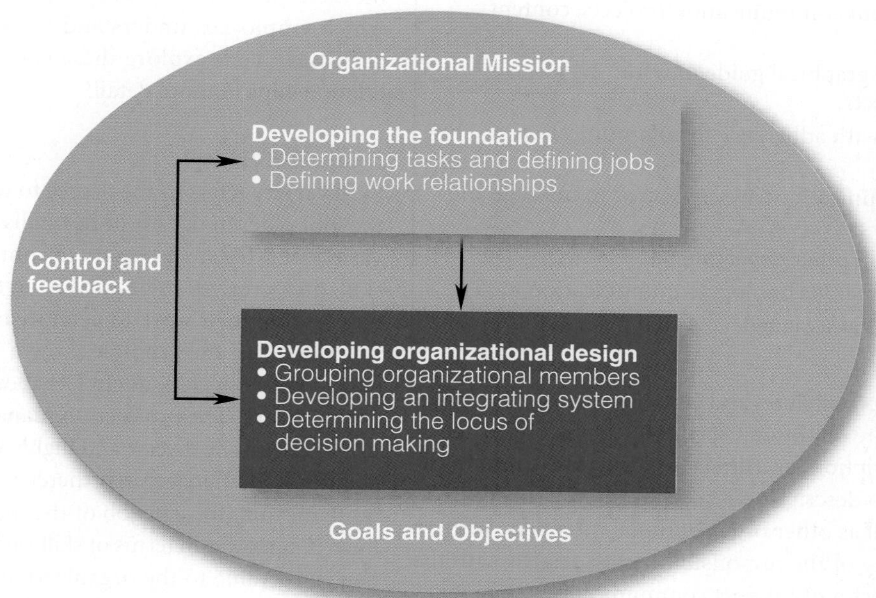

groups are defined. This chapter focuses specifically on these aspects of the organizing process. The second stage of the organizing process involves developing an organizational design that supports the strategic and operational plans of the organization. This requires grouping organizational members into work units, developing integrating mechanisms to coordinate the efforts of diverse work groups, and determining the extent to which decision making in the organization is centralized or decentralized. These aspects of organizing will be addressed in Chapter 8.

Job Design

2 As we noted, the first stage of the organizing process involves outlining the tasks and activities to be completed and assigning them to individuals and groups within the organization. Before managers can design specific jobs, they need to identify the work that must be done to achieve the organization's strategic and operational goals.

Consider, for example, an organization that manufactures and distributes small appliances. To fulfill its mission and achieve its goals, the organization must complete a number of tasks and activities. Raw materials must be acquired and inventoried; people must be hired, trained, and compensated; the plant must be managed and maintained; and the product must be delivered to customers. These are just a few of the activities that must occur.

Once the tasks and activities that must be completed have been identified, jobs must be designed and assigned to employees within the organization. **Job design** refers to the set of tasks and activities that are grouped together to constitute a particular job position. The importance of effective job design should not be underestimated because the overall productivity of the organization will be affected by the way jobs are structured. Managers commonly blame an employee's poor performance on his or her lackluster efforts, but in many cases the real problem is poor job design.

The design of a job can be assessed, to a degree, by reviewing the associated **job description.** A job description

LEARNING OBJECTIVE 2

Discuss the concept of job design and identify the core job dimensions that define a job.

KEY TERMS

Organizing
The process of determining the tasks to be done, who will do them, and how those tasks will be managed and coordinated.

Job design
The set of tasks and activities that are grouped together to define a particular job.

Table 7.1	Job Description of a Director of Internet Communications

- Develop and implement communication projects, content through completion.
- Develop editorial and graphical guidelines for communication projects.
- Monitor compliance with adherence to communication guidelines.
- Ensure that all communications are consistent in message and tone.
- Direct technical staff in other departments.
- Monitor developments in technology/communication media.
- Perform related duties as assigned.

details the responsibilities and tasks associated with a given position[1] (more on this in Chapter 9). Table 7.1 provides a position description for a director of Internet communications. This job description is intended to provide the jobholder, as well as other organizational members, with an understanding of the responsibilities associated with the job of the director of Internet communications.

Although job descriptions are commonly used to describe how jobs are designed, some relevant job characteristics may not be evident from a job description. Before we go on to discuss the various job perspectives that have evolved over the years, it is important to examine the fundamental characteristics that can be used to describe most jobs.

KEY TERMS

Job description
Details of the responsibilities and tasks associated with a given position.

Skill variety
The degree to which a job challenges the jobholder to use various skills and abilities.

Task identity
The degree to which a job includes the completion of an identifiable piece of work.

Task significance
The degree to which a job contributes to the overall efforts of the organization.

Autonomy
The degree to which a job includes freedom, independence, and decision-making authority.

CORE JOB DIMENSIONS

A set of core job dimensions can be used to characterize any job: (1) skill variety, (2) task identity, (3) task significance, (4) autonomy, and (5) feedback.[2] Each of these core job dimensions can significantly affect the performance and satisfaction of the individual who occupies the job. As Table 7.2 illustrates, these dimensions affect the degree to which employees find their work meaningful, feel responsibility for the outcomes of their job, and understand the results of their work activities. More specifically, skill variety, task identity, and task significance can affect the degree to which employees find their work meaningful; autonomy can affect the extent to which employees feel responsible for the outcomes of their jobs; and feedback can affect the degree to which employees understand the results of their work activities.[3] Let's explore these core job dimensions and relationships in more detail.

Skill Variety

Skill variety refers to the degree to which a job challenges the jobholder to use his or her skills and abilities. When a variety of skills are necessary to complete a task and those skills are perceived to be of value to the organization, employees find their work to be more meaningful.

Consider, for example, how a production manager and a mailroom clerk might feel about the meaningfulness of their work. The production manager's job requires the use of a relatively diverse and highly valued set of skills and abilities. That manager may therefore perceive the job to be quite meaningful. The job of the mailroom clerk, in contrast, is narrower in terms of skill variety and usually of less perceived value to the organization than the production manager's job. As a result, the mailroom clerk may feel that the job is less meaningful.

Task Identity

Task identity refers to the degree to which the job requires the completion of an identifiable piece of work—a tangible outcome that can be attributed to the employee's efforts. For example, individuals who design computers will likely find their jobs to have higher task identity and to be more meaningful than employees who simply slide a chip into place on the circuit board of the computer and thus have low task identity.

Task Significance

Task significance relates to the degree to which the job contributes to the overall efforts of the organization or to the world at large. Where task significance is high, the work probably will be perceived as more meaningful. For example, civil engineers who design an entire highway system will likely find their jobs to be more meaningful than assembly-line workers who are responsible for producing a component that goes into other products. This is particularly true when the employees don't know what the end product is, what it does, or who uses it.

Autonomy

Autonomy reflects the degree to which jobholders have freedom, independence, and decision-making authority in their jobs. When employees are highly autonomous in their work roles, their success depends on their own capabilities and their desire to complete the task. Therefore, they tend to feel greater responsibility for the success or failure of their efforts and, in general, greater job satisfaction.[4] When there is low autonomy, employees tend to feel less accountable for the outcomes of their work.

Consider, for example, organizational trainers who teach a seminar that prepares participants to pass a national certification exam. These trainers may have little latitude in selecting the material to be covered in the course and often must employ a course design that is prescribed by the testing agency. They have little autonomy in conducting their jobs. In contrast, consider trainers who teach a management development seminar that is intended to help participants learn more about their own management style. These trainers are free to determine both the material to be covered and the methods by which it should be delivered. They are likely to feel more personal responsibility for their work than the trainers who deliver a prepackaged training seminar.

Recently, The Limited used highly creative approaches to learning to revitalize the company's training function. Training programs took a game-show approach wherein employees played *Let's Make a Deal* to learn more about The Limited's products, participated in a session inspired by *Jeopardy!* to demonstrate their knowledge of critical financial metrics, and competed with one another in *Lingo Bingo,* which helps them develop a mastery of retail buzzwords. Members of the training group designed a successful program, largely because they were given the autonomy to be creative and they felt responsible for their work.[5]

Table 7.2 The Core Dimensions of a Job

Core Job Dimension		Effect of Dimension
• Skill variety • Task identity • Task significance	→	Meaningfulness of the work
• Autonomy	→	Responsibility for outcomes of the work
• Feedback	→	Knowledge of results of the work activities

Source: California Management Review Volume/Edition 5th by Hackman, Oldhan, Janson C. Pardy. Copyright 1975 by California Management Review. Reproduced with permission of California Management Review in the format Textbook via Copyright Clearance Center.

© SUSAN VAN ETTEN

When employees have less autonomy, as might be indicated by the obligation to record the times they arrive and leave work, they tend to feel less accountable for the outcomes of their work.

Feedback

Feedback refers to the extent to which jobholders have information about the results of their efforts. When feedback is frequent and constructive, employees develop a better understanding of the relationship between their efforts and the outcomes of their work. When feedback is insufficient, employees have little understanding of the value of their efforts.[6]

Some organizations even provide customer feedback to their employees. Such feedback encourages employees to be more customer oriented in their work. Solectron, the world's largest contract equipment manufacturer, attributes much of its success to its system of providing comprehensive customer satisfaction feedback to its employees on a weekly basis.[7]

Because the core dimensions of job design affect the extent to which jobholders find their work meaningful, feel responsibility for their efforts, and understand the relationship between their activities and the results of those activities, they have a significant effect on the commitment and attitudes of the jobholders.[8] Motivation, quality of work performance, job satisfaction, absenteeism, and turnover will all be a function of the core job dimensions to some degree. Consequently, managers should consider the effect of various job designs on each core dimension as they assign tasks and work activities to individuals within the organization.

KEY TERMS

Feedback
Information about the results of efforts in a job.

Now Apply It

Job Design

Focus on the job that you currently hold or one that you have held recently. Analyze the design of that job.

Part A: Using the scales below, rate the job that you are assessing in terms of its skill variety, task identity, task significance, autonomy, and feedback. If your responses fall toward the left side of the scales, what is your feeling about the job? If your responses tend to fall toward the right side, what are your feelings about the job? Find someone who has rated his or her job on the end of the scales opposite of yours. Compare your feelings about your respective jobs.

Part B: Based on your responses to Part A, how might you redesign your job to improve each of the five core job dimensions? Would your suggested changes help make you more effective and more efficient in your job?

High									Low

Skill variety

High									Low

Task identity

High									Low

Task significance

High									Low

Autonomy

High									Low

Feedback

The increasing diversity of the workforce has made the assessment of job design more complicated. Individuals from diverse cultural backgrounds may view certain job characteristics differently. For example, whereas many people from the United States may perceive a job with low autonomy negatively, people from other cultures may perceive low autonomy favorably. In any case, managers must be aware of how an individual employee might view a job.[9]

LEARNING OBJECTIVE 3

Explain how and why the perspectives on job design have evolved.

How does your job stack up with regard to these job characteristics? The "Now Apply It" box provides an opportunity for you to assess a past or present position that you have held in an organization (such as a business, church, social club, or student organization) in terms of skill variety, task identity, task significance, autonomy, and feedback. At this point, you are prepared to complete the assessment aspect (Part A) of the exercise. After reading the next section, you'll be prepared to suggest ways in which the job could be redesigned to improve it (Part B).

THE EVOLUTION OF JOB-DESIGN PERSPECTIVES

3 As management theory has evolved, so have many of the perspectives of job design. As we discussed in Chapter 2, classical management theory and scientific

management theory supported the concepts of division of labor and specialization. These early theories of management gave rise to perspectives of job design in which jobs were highly structured. The movement toward the human relations school of thought introduced other job-design variables, most of which dealt with human behavior.[10] As a result, more behavioral approaches to job design gained acceptance. Today, we consider issues of job design in the organizations of the 21st century. Clearly, in industrial economies, machinery, metal, and muscle define how work is done. But in postindustrial societies, the raw material is information, and the production worker is the knowledge worker. Thus, in many ways, contemporary management thought has focused on a different type of work. Let's examine how each of these approaches has affected the concept of job-design, as well as the core job dimensions.

Table 7.3 Potential Advantages and Disadvantages of Job Specialization

Potential Advantages	Potential Disadvantages
Task or job is easier to learn.	Task or job may be dull to some.
Can perform very well—high quality.	Productivity may decrease if employee sees job as dull and has negative reaction.
Greater efficiency—can do job faster.	Productivity may decrease if employee has negative perspective that contributes to absence.
Can select employee based on specific qualifications.	

Perspectives from Classical Management

4 Recall from Chapter 2 that classical management theorists emphasized the benefits of division of work and specialization. Productivity and efficiency were the driving forces for job design. Repetition, skill simplification, and time-and-motion efficiency were the primary focus of job-design efforts. The result was highly specialized jobs that were routine, repetitive, and highly efficient.

In a classic book, *Wealth of Nations,*[11] Adam Smith explained how specialization can lead to high quality and efficiency. At the time, one pin-maker performing all the tasks necessary to make a pin could make only ten pins per day. The total productivity of ten pin-makers making pins in this fashion would be 100 pins per day. But if the ten pin-makers organized the activities of the group so that one pin-maker drew the wire, another straightened it, a third cut it, and a fourth sharpened it to a point, while others were performing the operations necessary to complete the head of the pin and prepare the final product, the group could produce 48,000 pins per day—an average of 4800 pins per pin-maker per day. Obviously, the productivity of the group improved dramatically when jobs were redesigned to be highly specialized.

The benefits of specialization are easy to identify (Table 7.3). Specialized tasks can lead to high quality and efficiency because work activities are broken down into routine, repetitive actions. Furthermore, such actions can be mastered readily by individual workers and require less training than more complex tasks. Additionally, when tasks are highly specialized, workers may be selected based on specific characteristics that make them uniquely qualified to perform the task effectively and efficiently.

Specialization may also have disadvantages. Often, the skill variety, task identity, and task significance associated with such tasks are low. Jobholders typically have less autonomy and may receive little feedback or feedback that is inconsequential. To the extent that these conditions exist, some jobholders may find little challenge in their work and may lose interest in their jobs.

LEARNING OBJECTIVE

Describe the job-design approaches that came from the classical management, behavioral management, and employee/work team–centered perspectives.

It is easy to see that the assembly-line manufacturing design is founded on the concept of highly routine and specialized tasks. Consider, for example, the traditional automobile manufacturing plant. As the chassis of the car flows through the assembly line, workers perform a series of highly specialized tasks that contribute in some way to the production of the final product. While any given worker may do little more than attach a specific component or insert and tighten several screws, the result of the combined efforts of all the participants in the assembly process is a complete and fully functioning vehicle. Today, robotics technology has replaced many specialized jobs, particularly in the manufacturing environment.

Now consider how the idea of specialization permeates almost all organizations. Almost everyone's major, specialization, or concentration, including advanced degrees in education, is based on specialization, at least to some degree. The marketing major focuses on marketing, the accounting major on accounting, and so on. Within each major or discipline there is further specialization; in accounting, one may specialize in tax or auditing. Within an organization, one's job may focus on accounts receivable, accounts payable, tax, or auditing. In human resources, one's job may focus on payroll, benefits, recruiting, or training. This specialization tends to be true for not only lower-level employees but also most managers. Specialization helps us focus on a particular job or task in order to improve our skills and perform better and more efficiently. Of course, specialization may lead to the disadvantages mentioned in Table 7.3.

Perspectives from Behavioral Management Approaches

The theorists who were part of the human relations and other behavioral movements in management believed that highly specialized jobs could be redesigned in ways that would improve both productivity and employee satisfaction. Their emphasis moved from division of labor and specialization toward job designs that had greater breadth, depth, and challenge. From that came job enlargement, job enrichment, and job rotation.

Job Enlargement To understand job-enlargement programs, one must understand the concept of job scope. **Job scope** refers to the number of different activities that a specific job requires and the frequency with which each activity is performed. Jobs that involve many different activities have broader scope than jobs that are limited to a few activities. Jobs with broad scope typically rate more favorably in terms of skill variety, task identity, and task significance than do jobs with a narrower scope.

Consider, for example, how the job scope of an office manager and a data-entry clerk might differ. The office manager's job will involve a relatively broad set of tasks and thus will have relatively wide scope. In any given day, the office manager may prepare a letter, complete and sign time cards, make travel arrangements, schedule appointments, order supplies, and interview, hire, or fire office staff. The data-entry clerk's job, in contrast, is much narrower in that it involves only entering data into a database file.

Job enlargement broadens the scope of a specific job. The intent of job enlargement is to increase the horizontal tasks and responsibilities associated with a given job and provide greater challenge for the employee. For example, a data-entry clerk's job could be enlarged by assigning additional job responsibilities such as answering the phones, processing payroll forms, and providing copying services. The data-entry clerk would be responsible for a greater variety of tasks.

KEY TERMS

Job scope
The number of different activities required in a job and the frequency with which each activity is performed.

Job enlargement
Adding more of similar tasks to a job.

Job depth
Adding tasks to a job that require a wider range of skills, usually including autonomy.

Job enlargement has typically been considered as a means of making jobs more interesting that hopefully leads to better productivity. However, sometimes *reducing* job scope has a positive impact on productivity and job satisfaction. Consider, for example, the situation at United Parcel Service (UPS). UPS was experiencing high turnover among its drivers. Management was very concerned about this issue because the drivers are critical employees for the company. Not only did it take several months to train every new driver on a particular route, but also, over time, these drivers tended to develop strong relationships with the customers on their route. So, when UPS lost a driver, it incurred significant training costs and put customer satisfaction at risk. As the company explored the cause of the driver turnover, it discovered that it was the front end of the work—loading the packages on to the truck—that was causing the turnover. Management restructured the job to provide loaders for the drivers, reducing their job scope. This action improved job satisfaction greatly and reduced turnover among drivers. The relatively simple change in the job design had big benefits for UPS and its customers.[12]

Job Enrichment Central to the concept of job enrichment is the notion of **job depth,** which refers to the degree of control that individuals have over the jobs they perform. Job depth is high when the planning, doing, and controlling aspects of the job are the responsibility of the jobholder. When one or more of these aspects is the responsibility of some other organizational member, job depth is lower. Jobs that have high job depth typically rate more favorably on the core job dimensions of skill variety, task identity, and autonomy than jobs with low job depth. Just as specialization has led to jobs with a narrow job scope, highly specialized jobs often lack depth. In such cases, the planning, doing, and controlling aspects of a job may be separate.

For example, consider a computer services center within an organization and how the tasks might be divided to provide high or low job depth. Assume that this computer services center has three employees. If all three employees are responsible for receiving work orders, clarifying instructions with the originator of the work, setting priorities for scheduling the work orders they receive, providing the technical services required by the work order, and confirming the acceptability of the work with the originator, their jobs are of significant depth as they plan, do, and control their work. In contrast, if the tasks of the computer services center were divided among the three employees such that one person received work orders, clarified instructions, and scheduled the work, while another performed the services required, and yet another followed up with the originator of the work to ensure that the services were performed satisfactorily, the tasks performed would be more highly specialized, and the three members of the group would have lower job depth.

By vertically loading the job, closing the gap between planning, doing, and controlling, **job enrichment** gives the jobholder greater discretion in setting schedules and planning work activities, determining appropriate methods for completing the task, and monitoring the quality of the output from the work process.[13] For many, job enrichment can be an effective means of motivating employees and improving job satisfaction.[14]

Job Rotation **Job rotation** involves shifting individuals from one position to another to gain a more well-rounded experience. Employees rotate through a number of job positions that are at approximately the same level and have similar skill requirements. Job rotation is a type of **cross-training** in that employees learn to complete several tasks, or jobs, not just one.

Although job rotation has proven particularly beneficial in manufacturing settings,[15] it can also be used effectively in service organizations. For example, an individual who works in a bank might rotate between being a teller, a customer-service representative, a loan processor, a proof operator, and a safe deposit box attendant. At a higher organizational level, a financial manager who works for a multinational firm might rotate among positions at various foreign subsidiaries to gain international business experience.

Job rotation offers several advantages. Organizations that use job rotation typically have more flexibility in developing work schedules, making work assignments, and filling vacancies within the company quickly. In addition, some employees are more challenged and less bored with their jobs and usually have a better understanding of the organization as a whole. At the level of the individual employee, job rotation has been found to have a positive effect on both promotion rates and salary growth.[16] In fact, in many companies, job rotation is considered essential for grooming managers for executive-level positions because it provides the breadth of experience necessary for top-level management roles.[17]

A new form of job rotation emerged in response to the downsizing activities of the 1990s. As organizations reduced their workforces, their employees had far fewer internal career opportunities available. With fewer promotions available, some companies tried to motivate employees by shifting them sideways instead of up. American Greetings, for example, found lateral moves to be very effective in rejuvenating employees who had become bored in their present positions. Nabisco Foods, Corning, Inc., and Eastman Kodak are other companies that have looked to lateral job moves as a method of motivating employees whose career progression has been stymied by the restructuring efforts of the organization. Sony and Canon even attribute much of the success at product innovation to the job rotation of their engineers.[18] Ultimately, employees often find that lateral career moves enhance their long-term job satisfaction and career advancement.[19]

Job enlargement, job enrichment, and job rotation are methods of redesigning specialized jobs. Such efforts often have a positive effect on overcoming the disadvantages that might be associated with highly specialized jobs.

Employee-Centered and Team-Centered Perspectives

In recent years, both management theorists and practitioners have been rethinking the traditional approaches to job design.[20] Efforts to develop more innovative and effective approaches to job design have been inspired by increasing competitive pressures in many industries. From airlines to banks to manufacturing companies, organizations have had to rethink job design to ensure high product and service quality at the lowest possible cost.

Approaches that incorporate elements of participatory decision making that include employees more directly have been used to supplement the job-design methods discussed above. The most popular are employee-centered work redesign and self-managed teams.

Employee-Centered Work Redesign **Employee-centered work redesign** is an innovative approach to job design that presents a practical solution to one of the most significant challenges of job design—bridging the gap between the individual and the organization. This method of job design links the mission of the organization with the needs of the individual by allowing employees to design their work roles to benefit the organization as well as themselves. The unique aspect of this job-design approach is that employees are accountable for justifying how their job will support the mission of the organization as well as improving their productivity and job satisfaction.[21]

KEY TERMS

Job enrichment
Adding tasks to a job that require a wider range of skills.

Job rotation
Assigning individuals to a variety of job positions, usually positions at a similar level.

Cross-training
Teaching a variety of skills to a jobholder, usually skills that can be used in other, similar jobs.

Employee-centered work redesign
An approach whereby employees design their work roles to benefit the organization and satisfy their individual goals.

A number of benefits are associated with employee-centered work redesign. Because jobs are designed by the jobholder, this approach tends to favorably affect the core job dimensions that are most relevant to the individual employee. Studies suggest that tangible improvements in both productivity and job satisfaction result from employee-centered work redesign efforts. Furthermore, this approach fosters an organizational climate that supports cooperative efforts between individuals and work groups. Finally, employee-centered work redesign can be consistent with the quality improvement efforts of many companies. If employees of an organization are in a position to know where quality improvements can be achieved, their jobs can be designed so that quality problems can be identified and resolved more quickly.[22]

Today, many companies are looking to work-redesign programs to address a critical work problem that can result in significant losses in productivity—stress.[23] Based on a survey by International Survey Research in Chicago, about 40% of U.S. workers say workloads are excessive, and about the same percentage indicate that they are bothered by too much pressure on the job. A few companies, such as Bank of America, used innovative ways to redesign jobs to reduce stress and provide a better work/life balance. Bank of America's efforts began with 1100 employees at two customer-service call centers. The employees were asked to report on those aspects of their work that were frustrating and an impediment to balancing work and family life. A large number of suggestions poured in through focus groups and an 800-number hotline. When all was finished, 60% of the employees at the two call centers had offered suggestions on how to change their work. Bank of America moved quickly to implement many of the changes. Not only were the employees delighted, but the customers benefited as well. The proportion of customers reporting satisfaction with the service they received rose from 80 to 85% at one call center and from 79 to 82% at the other. Bank of America's experience in this case clearly demonstrates that employees and customers can both benefit from employee-centered work redesign, which ultimately benefits the business as a whole.[24]

Self-Managed Teams

All the approaches to job design discussed so far have focused on designing the jobs of individual organizational members. The **self-managed team (SMT)** approach to job design shifts the focus from the individual to a work group. Instead of managers dictating a set of narrowly defined tasks to each employee, responsibility for a substantial portion of the organization's activities is assigned to a team of individuals who must determine the best way to fulfill those responsibilities. Today, SMTs exist in organizations of all sizes and types and in and across departments within those organizations.[25] When SMTs exist across departments and include representatives from the different functional areas of the organization (for example, engineering, marketing, finance), they are considered cross-functional teams.[26]

The distinguishing feature of the SMT approach to job design is that the group is largely independent. The team must justify its choice of work methods only in terms of strong productivity and contribution to the overall effort of the organization. As with employee-centered work redesign programs, jobs that are designed by SMTs tend to reflect the core job dimensions that are most relevant to the individual employees of the work group.

Although research has suggested that SMTs can achieve higher productivity and deliver better-quality products and services with lower relative costs,[27] a number of situational factors appear to influence the effectiveness of such groups. These factors include the personalities of the group members as well as the nature of the job responsibilities.[28]

The SMT approach has been credited with improving overall organizational effectiveness in ways such as avoiding redundant efforts, increasing cooperation between organizational members, spawning new ideas, generating solutions to problems, maintaining motivation, improving product quality, and increasing profits.[29] Examples include the classic teamwork success at NUMMI (New United Motors Manufacturing, Inc.), the joint venture between General Motors and Toyota, and the more recent examples of success at 3M and BP.[30] Other companies have used the SMT approach to develop new products and processes. For example, companies as diverse as Chrysler, Medtronic, IBM, and Eli Lilly have used SMTs to create new processes so that they could develop new and better products.[31]

As businesses have become more international in nature, the need to develop global work teams has increased. Yet, many challenges exist in developing highly effective work teams that cross national borders. Cultural and communication differences among team members, as well as the barriers that arise from time-and-distance differences, all complicate the development of effective global teams. Nevertheless, some organizations, such as Digital Equipment, and 3Com, have developed innovative ways to make global teams work effectively.[32] In recent years, improvements in technology have enabled many global teams to overcome the barriers of time and distance. In fact, through the use of

KEY TERMS

Self-managed team (SMT)
A group of employees who design their jobs and work responsibilities to achieve the self-determined goals and objectives of the team.

© THE IMAGE BANK/GETTY IMAGES

Cultural and communication differences among team members, as well as the barriers that arise from time-and-distance differences, complicate the development of effective global teams.

advanced information technology, so-called virtual teams have emerged.[33] These teams can work together from all over the world as long as they share a common purpose and a means of communicating. The existence of virtual teams will likely change the way many people work in the years to come.

Now that we have concluded our discussion of job design, take a moment to go back to Part B of "Now Apply It." How might you redesign the position you evaluated to improve productivity, job satisfaction, quality?

Thus far, we have explored how managers determine the work to be done and assign that work to individual employees or work groups. Equally important, however, is the process of defining the working relationships, both vertical and horizontal, that exist within the organization. The next section examines how working relationships can be established to ensure that the organization fulfills its mission and achieves its goals.

Organizational Relationships

Now let's discuss how to arrange the jobs and tasks in a coordinated way so that they can work together to achieve the organization's mission. The plan, or guide, for this arrangement is called an **organizational structure,** or **organizational chart.** It is usually pictured as the arrangement of parts (jobs, departments, divisions) of the organization showing the relationships among the parts as they are focused on the organization's mission, as represented by the top-level manager, or chief executive officer (CEO). (See Figure 7.2 for examples of organizational structure.) Designing the overall structure will be discussed in the next chapter. However, first we need to discuss important concepts and tools that are needed to establish the relationships between the parts of the organization as the overall structure is designed.

5 The working relationships that exist within an organization will affect how its activities are accomplished and coordinated. Consequently, it is essential to understand both the vertical and horizontal associations that exist between individuals and work groups within the organization. Organizational relationships are defined by (1) chain of command, (2) span of control, (3) line and staff responsibilities, and (4) authority and responsibility.

LEARNING OBJECTIVE 5

Understand both the vertical and horizontal associations that exist between individuals and work groups within the organization.

CHAIN OF COMMAND

The vertical relationships that exist within an organization are defined by its chain of command. The **chain of command** delineates the line of authority and responsibility that flows throughout the organization and identifies the supervisor and subordinate relationships (who reports to whom) that govern decision making. This is also called the hierarchy of authority. Ideally, each employee should report to and be accountable to only one supervisor. This is called **unity of command.**

As you recall from Chapter 2, the concept of a well-defined chain of command was originally advanced by the classical management theorists. In its purest form, the concept is consistent with the bureaucratic organizational system. Although contemporary managers still embrace the idea of a chain of command, the flexibility of the organization to respond to change quickly and proactively may be severely limited when decision making is rigidly tied to the official hierarchy. For

KEY TERMS

Organizational structure
The plan representing the relationships between jobs and departments in an organization.

Organizational chart
The chart, or "picture" of the organizational structure.

Chain of command
The line of authority and responsibility that flows throughout the organization.

Unity of command
An employee in the organization is accountable to one and only one supervisor.

Figure 7.2 Alternative Ways to Structure an Organization

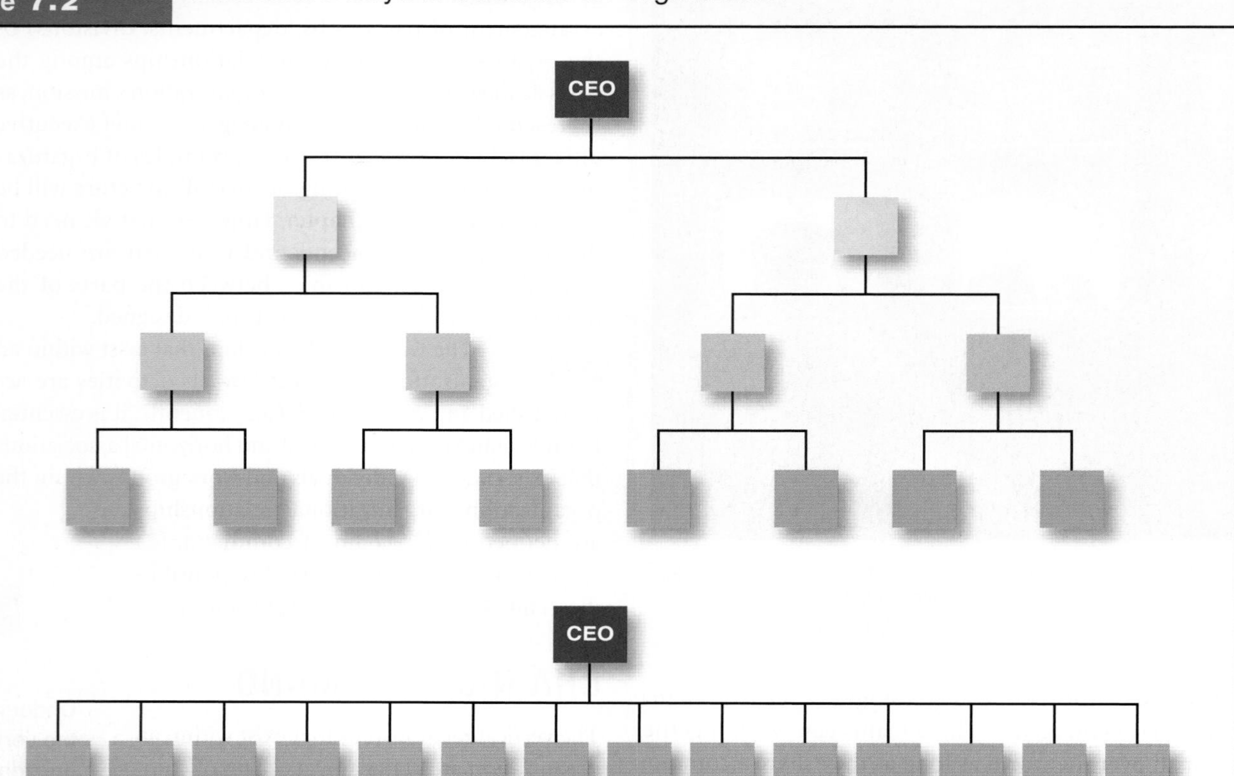

Source:: Adapted from *The Structuring of Organizations* by Mintzberg, © 1991. Reprinted by permission of Prentice-Hall, Inc., Upper Saddle River, NJ.

that reason, organizations may need to find ways to be flexible in their chain of command and yet find ways to hold people and departments accountable for results.

SPAN OF CONTROL

A second important aspect of working relationships is **span of control,** also known as span of management, which refers to the number of employees who report to a single manager.[34] At one time it was thought that there was a universally appropriate span of control (for example, six employees should report to each manager), but managers now recognize that span of control will vary in accordance with a number of variables.[35] Organizational characteristics such as task complexity, the volatility of the competitive environment, and the capabilities of both the employees and the manager will influence the appropriate span of control.

As an example of how certain conditions might affect span of control, consider the job characteristic of task complexity. Normally, when tasks are very complex, span of control should be relatively narrow. This allows the manager to spend more time with each subordinate to help him or her deal with the complexity of the job. In contrast, where jobs are highly standardized and routine (low complexity), a manager will not need to spend as much time supporting individual subordinates, and the span of control may be larger.[36]

Span of control is a critical organizational variable for a number of reasons. It defines the layers of management that exist within the company. An organization that maintains a relatively narrow span of control will have more hierarchical levels (tall) than an organization with the same number of employees but a wider span of control (flat) (Figure 7.2). Is it better to have narrower or broader spans and more or fewer levels in the hierarchy? That depends on the situation.[37]

Managers who have fewer subordinates to supervise might be less likely to be overcommitted and overburdened. Free from the burden of excessive numbers of subordinates, such managers may have more time to analyze situations, make effective decisions, and execute the actions associated with their decisions. Consequently, they may be more effective than managers with more subordinates reporting to them.[38]

KEY TERMS

Span of control
The number of employees reporting to a particular manager.

At the Forefront

No Organizational Chart at Semco, Inc.

How would you like to work for Semco, Inc.? There is no organizational chart. People decide when they will come to work, on what products to work, which meetings to attend—if any—and which manager they want to work with. There is no permanent CEO. Rather, the position is rotated among about six senior managers every 6 months. Everyone has access to the financial statements, and union leaders hold workshops to help people understand them. There are hammocks in the offices for naps.

Your reaction to this situation probably falls into one of four categories. One is that you are convinced that this situation would result in total chaos. Another is that you would like to work in this company because it sounds like a lot of fun. A third response might be that "there has to be something more going on here." A fourth reaction might be that it is obvious to you what the "something more" is.

In the early 1980s, Ricardo Semler took over the family business from his father. The business made industrial machinery in Sao Paulo, Brazil, but was not doing particularly well. Semler fired most of the managers and implemented the strategies mentioned above. Since Semler took over, the company's revenues have grown over 900%.

When Semler changed the business from one with traditional organizational characteristics, many of the people were fired, or they left on their own because they did not like the turmoil that they saw in the "new" company. The only people who remained were passionate about the new kind of company. When new people are hired, they go through unlimited numbers of interviews conducted sometimes by over a dozen people at one time. New hires must fit "the Semco way."

All employees sign a contract for a specific level of output or productivity, and they are held accountable for it. If they do not meet their contract, they are fired or they leave voluntarily.

What do you think is included in "the Semco way"?

Sources: S. Shinn, "The Maverick CEO," *BizEd* (January/February 2004): 16–21; G. Colvin, "The Anti-Control Freak," *Fortune,* 26 November 2001, 60.

Managers with wider spans of control have greater demands in terms of direct supervision. They may feel hassled, frustrated, and incapable of coping effectively with the nonsupervisory demands of their job.[39] Yet wide spans of control suggest a need for greater self-direction and initiative on the part of individual employees and may result in more effective employee development.[40]

Clearly, advantages and disadvantages are associated with both tall and flat structures. Therefore, organizations must choose a span of control that supports their particular strategic and operational goals.[41]

LINE AND STAFF RESPONSIBILITIES

Line and staff positions or departments exist within virtually all organizations, but the individuals who occupy these positions play very different roles. **Line departments** are directly involved in delivering the product or service of the organization. They have formal authority for decisions affecting the core production efforts of the organization. **Staff departments,** in contrast, are not part of the product or service delivery–system chain of command but rather provide support to line departments. Line personnel or work groups may call upon staff personnel to provide expert advice or perform specific support services. Staff personnel do not have authority or responsibility for decisions that relate to the core delivery system of the organization.

Distinctions between line and staff have sometimes caused conflicts. Some think that staff departments are not as important as line or that they are just cost, or "overhead"; that is, they do not contribute to profits. However, the differences in the way employees contribute is far less important than the commonality inherent in working to achieve the same organizational goals. Fortunately, the distinction between line and staff has become less important.

In addition, line and staff personnel now frequently coexist within work teams that collectively pursue a specific set of tasks. A company called AES has done everything it can to eliminate the staff function at the corporate level by moving

KEY TERMS

Line department
An organizational unit that is directly involved in delivering the products and services of the organization.

Staff department
An organizational unit that is not directly involved in delivering the products and services of the organization but provides support for line personnel.

all staff personnel onto the teams around which the organization is structured. The finance, marketing, and environmental compliance departments have all been eliminated and their staff personnel reassigned to teams that are responsible for delivering core products and services. AES believes this system enables all team members to understand all aspects of the business.[42]

LEARNING OBJECTIVE

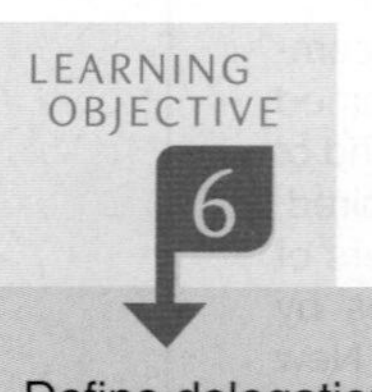

Define delegation and discuss why it is important for managers to delegate.

AUTHORITY AND RESPONSIBILITY

Various people in organizations need to make decisions about what is to be done, who is to do it, when it is to be done, and the like. The formal right inherent in an organizational position to make decisions—instruct or ask subordinates to do certain things and expect that they will—is called **authority.** When it is based on a position in the organization, it is called **formal authority.**[43] When an ability to influence people is based on personal attributes, such as knowledge or charisma, it is called **informal authority.** (See *position power* and *personal power* in the leadership chapter.)

With authority comes **responsibility** to use the authority properly. Responsibility is the obligation to perform the duties that were assigned with the authority. Although the words *responsibility* and **accountability** are used by some as two different things, they are essentially the same. To be accountable to a supervisor means that a subordinate is responsible to the supervisor for results of decisions made and actions taken by the subordinate.[44]

6 Managers at all levels in organizations probably cannot make all the decisions that need to be made in the parts of the organizations that they supervise. Therefore, they must delegate some of the authority to subordinates. **Delegation** refers to the process of transferring the authority for a specific task or set of tasks to another member of the organization and empowering that individual to accomplish the task effectively. Normally, authority is delegated by a manager to one or more of his or her subordinates.

KEY TERMS

Authority
The formal right inherent in an organizational position to make decisions.

Formal authority
Authority inherent in an organizational position.

Informal authority
Ability to influence others that is based on personal characteristics or skills.

Responsibility
The obligation to perform the duties assigned.

Accountability
Responsibility to the supervisor for results of decisions made and actions taken with delegated authority.

Delegation
The process of transferring the authority for a specific activity or task to another member of the organization and empowering that individual to accomplish the task effectively.

The Process of Delegation

Delegating authority well is an important, often complex task.[45] It is much more than just turning authority over to someone else. The person to whom authority is delegated must be capable and willing to use it well. The person with the authority is accountable to his or her supervisor. However, the manager who delegated the authority is still accountable for the results of his or her department, and now it includes the decisions of subordinates to whom authority was delegated.[46]

Delegating authority well includes important steps. They are (1) decide which goals or tasks to delegate, (2) make assignments, (3) grant authority, (4) hold responsible/accountable, and (5) monitor. All are essential to the success of the delegation process (Table 7.4).

Decide Which Goals or Tasks to Delegate

Deciding which goals or tasks to delegate can be complex. A manager might assign goals or tasks for many reasons including

- Goals or tasks for which a subordinate has a special skill or interest.
- A very capable subordinate.
- Goals or tasks for which the manager might not have expertise and/or interest.

Some might suggest that a manager should delegate tasks that he or she does not like. However, this is probably not a good guide to delegation. Joseph Liemandt of Trilogy Development Group believes that a manager should not keep tasks just because he or she likes them or delegate tasks just because he or she does not like them.[47]

In any case, delegation of authority will be more successful if the subordinate to whom goals or tasks are assigned understands the mission of the department and, ideally, the mission of the organization and is capable of making good decisions. Of course, the manager can teach and train the subordinate in these areas.

Make Assignments The manager must be clear in what is being transferred to the subordinate.[48] The subordinate must understand the mission, goals, and tasks for which he or she will now be responsible. If there are limits to what is an acceptable outcome or an acceptable decision, the manager must establish those limits. This can be done with the use of policies, which were discussed in Chapter 4. The manager and subordinate must agree on the results that are expected and what monitoring or feedback might be helpful to make the outcomes successful. Finally, the manager must give the subordinate information that is useful for the subordinate to make good decisions.

Grant Authority Managers must give their employees the authority to accomplish their work successfully.[49] The subordinate must have the formal right to make decisions and to commit resources. Without sufficient authority, it is unlikely that employees will complete delegated tasks successfully. As we mentioned in Chapter 4, a policy is a tool that can be used to set the limits or guidelines for what authority is to be delegated. This is what Jeffrey Immelt, CEO of General Electric, calls "manage by setting boundaries with freedom in the middle."[50]

Granting authority in a "public" way can help make the authority more clear and more "authentic." For example, putting it in writing offers a chance to clear up misunderstandings, and it is a more formal way to state the authority. Another form of making it public means that the manager should inform other people or departments affected by a person's authority so they know that the authority is legitimate.

Consider a simple example: A restaurant manager has to leave early one evening and says to one of the waiters, "Make sure that all the employees complete their closing duties." Assuming that the statement is made only to the waiter and not to the other employees and that the waiter has not previously been designated as a head waiter, the manager has put the waiter in a difficult position. The other employees are unlikely to feel compelled to cooperate with the waiter because they do not know that the waiter is now to have this authority.

Finally, managers must not interfere. Yes, managers should monitor and give feedback, as agreed in step 2. Beyond that, if a manager interferes, either the results will not be good and/or the subordinate will not learn to use authority well or will not be interested in doing so.

In today's age of greater access to information, employees may feel frustrated by the fact that they know about a problem but do not have the authority to address it. Consider, for example, the warehouse worker who can see that an order will be late but has no authority to expedite it. Or the airline reservationists who know that many seats are available on certain flights but cannot book a standby passenger on those flights because they do not have the authority to override the policy requiring standby passengers to register at the gate. In both cases, the employees have the knowledge to do their jobs better and create greater customer satisfaction, but they do not have the authority to act on that knowledge. As information becomes increasingly available to frontline workers, organizations must consider how to provide the authority for those workers to act appropriately in light of that information.[51]

Table 7.4 Delegating Authority

1. Decide which goals/tasks to delegate.
   - Teach the department or organization mission.
   - Find a capable person.
   - Teach/train the person.

2. Make assignments.
   - Agree on mission, goals, tasks.
   - Establish limits (policy).
   - Agree on results.
   - Establish monitors and feedback.
   - Give information.

3. Grant authority to act.
   - Transfer right to decide.
   - Transfer right to commit resources.
   - Make it public.
   - Do not interfere.

4. Hold responsible/accountable.
   - Check progress.
   - Treat problems and challenges as teaching/learning opportunities.

5. Monitor.
   - Teach.
   - Reward.
   - Communicate.
   - Give information.
   - Give resources.
   - Remove roadblocks.

Hold Responsible/Accountable Managers must hold their employees accountable for completing the tasks for which they assume responsibility and are given the necessary authority. When there is accountability for performance, employees understand that they must justify their decisions and actions with regard to the tasks for which they have assumed responsibility.

It is important for managers to be sure that subordinates are doing the "right things." These are the things that help achieve goals and, ultimately, the mission of the organization. Enterprise Rent-A-Car used a reward system that paid people a bonus based on the amount of profits that they help generate. To increase their bonus, some branch managers started focusing on short-term profits, which sometimes interfered with long-term profits. Consequently, Enterprise now bases bonuses on customer satisfaction plus profits in order to hold people accountable for long-term profits.[52]

Delegating decision-making authority without the associated accountability will compromise the overall benefits of the delegation process. Christopher Galvin, former CEO of Motorola, said, "Sometimes delegation does work and sometimes it does not." While he believes strongly in the power of delegation, he also knows that when it does not work, managers must learn to delegate better.[53]

If you are the manager, how do you hold some responsible? If the person made a decision that resulted in a positive outcome, reward that. That might be a simple acknowledgment or some other appropriate reward. However, look for signs that the person is aware of why and how the decision led to good results. If that is not the case, then the person has not necessarily made a good decision.

Now, what if the person made a decision that resulted in negative outcomes or created other problems? Turn this into a teaching/learning opportunity. If you are the manager, refer to the goals and assignments that were established in steps 1 and 2. Then help the subordinate learn how and why the results were not positive. If done well, the subordinate will learn how to make better decisions and use authority well. CEO Steven Reinemund of PepsiCo holds senior managers accountable for teaching their subordinates to delegate well. In turn, the next level of manager must mentor and teach their subordinates.[54]

Monitor Just as the overall management process and each managerial function must have feedback mechanisms built in to evaluate and control operations (see the discussion related to the overall framework shown in Figure 1.5), so too must the delegation process. The monitors and feedback mechanisms that were established in step 2 mean that not only the subordinate will be watching for how decisions are progressing but also the supervisor. The feedback probably will include things that the supervisor and subordinate will watch together, including meetings and discussions, as seem appropriate. Both the supervisor and subordinate should view and ensure that feedback and monitoring are constructive. Of course, if the subordinate cannot, or will not learn to correct mistakes and problems, then the authority must be taken back and/or the subordinate replaced.

Delegation of authority and decision making to employees also involves accountability of performance to managers.

The Benefits of Delegation

Delegation offers a number of advantages. When done properly, delegation can lead to a more involved and committed workforce, sometimes referred to as an empowered workforce.[55] Empowerment can lead to heightened productivity and quality, reduced costs, more innovation, improved customer service, and greater commitment from employees.[56] The end result can be a more effective organization.[57]

Delegating decisions and activities to individuals lower in the organizational hierarchy can lead to better decision making. Those who are closest to the actual problem to be solved or the customer to be served may be in the best position to make the most effective decisions. In addition, response time may be improved because information and decisions need not be passed up and down the hierarchy. This is particularly critical in organizations where delays in decision making can make the difference between success and failure.

Delegation is also beneficial from an employee development perspective.[58] By delegating tasks and decision-making responsibility to their employees, managers provide an opportunity for the development of analytical and problem-solving skills. The employees are forced to accept responsibility, exercise judgment, and be accountable for their actions. The development of such skills will benefit the organization in the long term.[59]

Leaders in Action

Was Tyco International Too Flexible?

Tyco International (Tyco) was one of the companies that was almost destroyed by a notorious CEO who was at the forefront of using unethical and illegal practices that artificially inflated profitability while enriching himself and some of the other top managers. Dennis Kozlowski is well known for paying himself a very high salary, living in a an expensive apartment in New York City that was paid for by the company, and purchasing lavish furnishing for the apartment with company money. Kozlowski faced legal problems because of use of illegal accounting practices and because he was charged with simply looting company funds.

Under Kozlowski, top-level managers earned large bonuses that were based almost entirely on revenues. Problems related to this included managers who would simply buy other companies to get the revenues and/or not watch costs in generating the high revenues. There was no concern about whether the companies fit together in any way that could take advantage of core competencies. Division managers were totally free to manage their companies. With emphasis on revenues without any on costs, profitability suffered. If the illegal activities had not shaken Tyco, the profitability problems were ready to cause trouble.

It was up to Edward Breen, newly hired CEO in mid-2002, to clean up the mess and try to restore Tyco to a grand company. He replaced the entire Board of Directors, fired 290 of the top 300 managers, and began to streamline and coordinate many parts of the company in order to cut costs that were way too high. We focus on restoring efficiency by cutting costs here.

All divisions of Tyco purchased almost all of what they needed on an individual basis; nothing was coordinated to be managed by headquarters. Phone services, office supplies, raw materials, and even computers (PCs) were purchased by various people and units throughout the organization. There was no attempt to take advantage of buying in quantity.

Breen formalized the purchasing operation and centralized it at headquarters. A few examples of the results: Purchasing PCs at headquarters reduced the cost of computers alone by $11 million a year. Reducing the number of packaging suppliers used by Tyco from 300 to 25 saved $40 million per year.

These examples show the results of Mr. Breen establishing policies, procedures, and rules that restricted the jobs of many Tyco managers. The result is better coordination of costs that resulted in supplies and services that were at least as good as before but now at a much lower cost. Now Breen is working on applying the same analysis to see where benefits can be achieved by combining and coordinating other parts of the organization. Managers probably had too much flexibility previously, or at least it was not managed well.

Sources: "Best Managers: Edward Breen," *BusinessWeek,* 10 January 2005, 63; S. Tully, "Mr. Cleanup," *Fortune,* 15 November 2004, 151–163

Finally, through proper delegation, managers magnify their accomplishments. By delegating tasks that their employees have the ability to complete, managers can use their time to accomplish more complicated, difficult, or important tasks. This can lead to a more creative and productive work group as a whole.[60]

Many organizations have benefited from empowering employees through proper delegation. Starbucks, Xerox, the American Society for Quality Control, and FedEx are a few examples of organizations that have claimed significant success from employee empowerment.[61]

7 Managers should be cautioned, however, about the potentially negative perceptions that ineffective delegation can create. Delegation must never be used to avoid work responsibilities that should legitimately be assumed by the manager. Delegation is not a way to "pass the buck" but rather a method for enhancing the overall productivity of the work group. If employees perceive the delegation as a way to reduce the manager's responsibilities and increase their own, their respect for the manager will deteriorate. This may be particularly problematic in diverse work groups in which perceptions of delegation may vary. In such situations, it may be appropriate for managers to explain to their employees how delegation benefits the entire work group.

LEARNING OBJECTIVE 7

Explain why managers often fail to delegate and suggest methods for improving delegation skills.

Effective delegation is a vital skill for successful managers. Yet it is a skill that many managers lack. Why? There are a number of reasons why managers fail to delegate.[62]

Reasons for Failing to Delegate

Delegation requires planning—and planning takes time. How often have you heard someone say, "By the time I get done explaining this task to someone, I could have done it myself"? This is a common excuse for maintaining authority for tasks rather than delegating them.[63] In some cases, such a decision may make sense. However, when tasks are recurring and would warrant the time to train someone who could assume authority and responsibility for the work, such a decision would not be appropriate. "Experiential Exercise 7.1" at the end of this chapter provides a tool for managers to use in determining whether a task is appropriate for delegation.

Another reason for failure to delegate is that managers may simply lack confidence in the abilities of their subordinates. Such a situation fosters the attitude "If you want it done well, do it yourself." This problem is particularly difficult to overcome when the manager feels pressure for high-level performance in a relatively short time frame. The manager simply refuses to delegate, preferring to retain authority for tasks to ensure that they are completed properly.

As a further complication, managers experience dual accountability. Managers are accountable for their own actions and the actions of their subordinates. If a subordinate fails to perform a certain task or performs it poorly, it is the manager who is ultimately responsible for the subordinate's failure. Therefore, when the stakes are high, managers may prefer to perform certain tasks themselves.[64]

Finally, managers may refrain from delegating because they are insecure about their value to the organization. Such managers may refuse to share the information necessary to complete a given task or set of tasks because they fear they will be considered expendable.

Learning to Delegate Effectively

Despite the perceived disadvantages of delegation, the reality is that managers can improve the performance of their work groups and their organizations by delegating well to their employees. So how do managers learn to delegate effectively? They apply the basic principles of delegation.

Principle 1: Match the Employee to the Task Managers should carefully consider the employees to whom they delegate. The individual selected should possess the skills and capabilities needed to complete the task and, when possible, should stand to benefit from the experience. Furthermore, managers should delegate duties that challenge employees somewhat but which they can complete successfully. There is no substitute for success when it comes to getting an employee to assume responsibility for more challenging assignments in the future.

Implicit in this principle is an acceptance of an incremental learning philosophy. This philosophy suggests that as employees prove their ability to perform effectively in a given job, they should be given tasks that are more complex and challenging. In addition to employee development benefits, such a strategy will be beneficial for the overall performance of the work group.[65]

Principle 2: Be Organized and Communicate Clearly Most cases of failed delegation can be attributed to either poor organization or poor communication. When managers or employees do not clearly understand what is expected, the delegation process is sure to fail. Both the manager and the employee must have a clear understanding of what needs to be done, what deadlines exist, and what special skills will be required.[66] Delegation is a consultative process whereby managers and employees gain a clear understanding of the scope of their responsibilities and how their efforts relate to the overall efforts of the group or organization.[67]

Furthermore, managers must be capable of communicating their instructions effectively if their subordinates are to perform up to their expectations.[68]

Principle 3: Transfer Authority and Accountability with the Task The delegation process is doomed to failure if the individual to whom the task is delegated is not given the authority to succeed at accomplishing the task and is not held accountable for the results. The manager must expect employees to carry the ball and let them do so.[69] This means providing employees with the necessary resources and power to succeed, giving them timely feedback on their progress, and holding them fully accountable for the results of their efforts.

Principle 4: Choose the Level of Delegation Carefully Delegation does not mean that the manager can walk away from the task or the person to whom the task is delegated. The manager may maintain some control of both the process and the results of the delegated activities. Depending on the confidence that the manager has in the subordinate and the importance of the task, the manager can choose to delegate at several levels (Figure 7.3).[70]

Many good managers find it difficult to delegate. Yet few managers have been successful in the long term without learning to delegate effectively.[71] As a future manager, you must develop effective delegation skills.

Figure 7.3 Degree of Delegation

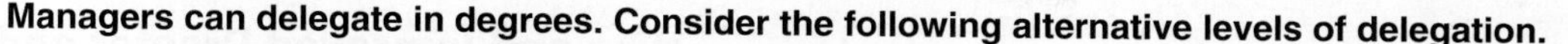

Managers can delegate in degrees. Consider the following alternative levels of delegation.

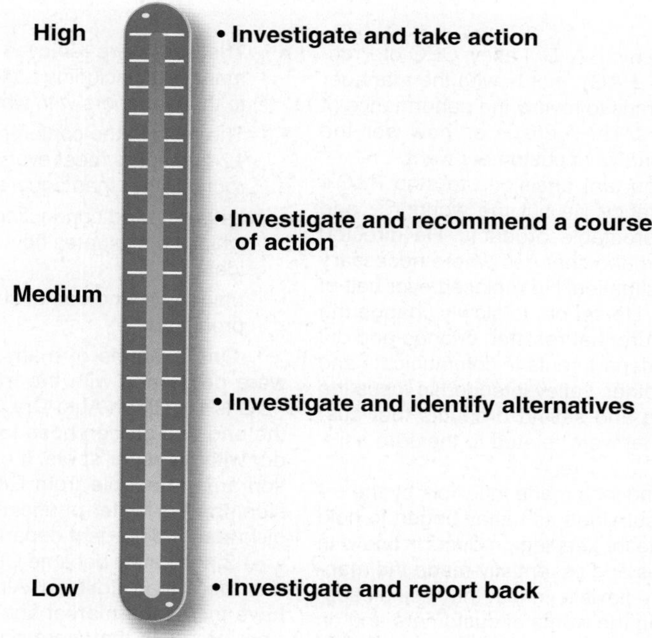

Source: Adapted from M. E. Haynes, "Delegation: There's More to It Than Letting Someone Else Do It!" 9–15. Reprinted, by permission of publisher, from *Supervisory Management*, January 1980. © 1980, American Management Association, New York. All rights reserved.

Implications for Leaders

In this chapter, we have learned how jobs are designed and organizational relationships are determined. Effective managers must demonstrate competence by designing jobs and working relationships in such a way that achieves the goals of the organization. As a future manager, you should keep the following organizing tips in mind:

- Identify the tasks and activities that must be completed for the goals of the organization to be achieved.
- Design jobs so that jobholders will find their jobs interesting and challenging.
- Understand the potential advantages and disadvantages of specialization, job enlargement, job enrichment, and job rotation.
- Understand the importance of chain of command and span of control.
- All successful managers delegate authority. Learn how to delegate well and hold people accountable.

This chapter focused on the first stage of the organizing process. The next chapter addresses the concept of organizational design, building the entire organization structure. The design of an organization defines the way that organizational members are configured or grouped together; the types of mechanisms used to integrate and coordinate the flow of information, resources, or tasks between organizational members; and the degree of centralization or decentralization of decision making within the organization. An understanding of these organizing concepts, along with those discussed in this chapter, are essential for understanding the managerial function of organizing.

Meeting The Challenge

New and Improved Procter and Gamble

Every Sunday evening, A. G. Lafley, CEO of Procter and Gamble (P&G), meets with the manager of human resources to review the performance of the top 200 managers. The focus is on how well the managers are delivering what customers want.

Lafley made important decisions to stop P&G's slide. To regain efficiency, he cut the workforce and eliminated some unprofitable products. He directed that pricing be studied and changed where necessary to fit the competitive situation. He replaced over half of the 30 top managers. He set out to slowly change the parts of the P&G culture that resisted change and did not allow people and departments to communicate and cooperate with each other. Lafley intended to focus the managers on making and selling products that customers wanted and that were related to the core competencies of P&G.

The tight rules and jobs made inflexible by the organizational culture subsided as Lafley began to hold managers accountable for keeping products in line with consumer preferences and essentially made the managers' jobs much more flexible so that they could cooperate to be focused on the wants of customers and on taking advantage of the company's core competencies. The main changes that made jobs more flexible, enhanced cooperation, and held managers accountable are the following:

- A quarterly meeting of the top-level people from the 15 biggest brands was initiated so that ideas can be shared across products and divisions.
- Internal trade shows were started so that managers could learn from each other across the corporation.
- The five division managers were moved from the corporate headquarters' 11th floor to the floors on which their managers were located.
- The walls were removed between the senior managers, including Lafley's whose desk is next to the managers with whom he interacts most.
- The table in the conference room where the top 12 managers meet every Monday morning is now round rather than square.
- Lafley started conducting "innovation reviews" in which he evaluates how well managers share ideas.
- Managers who do not share ideas are not promoted.

One example of many successful products that were developed with the much more flexible jobs in P&G is Mr. Clean Auto Dry, a product that attaches to the end of a garden hose to wash a car and help it to dry without water spots. It came about after cooperation among people from R&D in the home-care division, the Pur water-purification unit, and the Cascade dishwasher detergent department.

Since Lafley became CEO, the stock price of P&G has more than doubled. Almost all the major brands have increased market share. Core volume, revenue from products that were part of P&G's existing business, is up about 12% per year. Although work is still to be done, as there always is, the more flexible organization structure, culture, and jobs helped P&G get back to understanding what its customers want and help the company to deliver in a way that takes advantage of core competencies and results in profits.

Sources: S. Ellison, "P&G Chief's Turnaround Recipe: Find Out What Women Want," *Wall Street Journal* (Eastern Edition), 1 June 2005, A1; "It Was a No-Brainer," *Fortune,* 21 February 2005, 97–102; P. Sellers, "P&G: Teaching an Old Dog New Tricks," *Fortune,* 31 May 2004, 166–180; R. Berner, "P&G New and Improved," *BusinessWeek,* 7 July 2003, 52–60.

SUMMARY

1. For an organization to fulfill its mission and achieve its goals, the employees of the organization must complete many tasks and activities. These varied tasks and activities must be organized and coordinated to ensure the effectiveness and efficiency of the organization. First, the work that needs to be done must be clarified and assigned to specific jobholders. Then the work relationships necessary to support the organization's product and service delivery system must be established. After that, work groups must be assigned, the integrating system to coordinate the work of those groups must be established, and the locus of decision making in the organization must be decided.

2. Job design refers to the way tasks and activities are grouped to constitute a particular job. Core job dimensions that can be used to describe a job include (a) skill variety, (b) task identity, (c) task significance, (d) autonomy, and (e) feedback. The first three dimensions determine the meaningfulness of jobs;

the fourth dimension, autonomy, determines the degree to which individuals feel responsible for their work; and feedback relates to the extent to which jobholders understand the outcomes of their jobs.

3. Classical management theory and scientific management support the concepts of division of labor and specialization. These early theories of management gave rise to designing jobs that are highly structured. The human relations and behavioral approaches to management suggest designing jobs that include job enlargement, job enrichment, job rotation, and job design that might include participation from employees.

4. Classical management perspectives of job design focus on efficiency. Specialization and division of labor are key features. Behavioral approaches to job design focus on the human aspect of work and seek to enhance the motivation, satisfaction, and productivity by using job enlargement, job enrichment, and job rotation. Other approaches include jobs that are designed by employees, including self-managed teams.

5. Organizational work relationships are defined by the organization structure. Components of the organization structure are (a) chain of command, (b) span of control, (c) line versus staff responsibilities, and (d) authority and responsibility. Chain of command defines the vertical relationships that exist within the organization. Span of control refers to the number of subordinates who report to any supervisor. Line departments are those that have direct responsibility for the delivery of the organization's product or service, whereas staff personnel provide an advisory or support function to the line personnel. All managers need authority to make decisions and must be held accountable for the decisions.

6. Delegation of authority involves the assignment of deciding which goals and tasks to delegate, making the assignments, granting of the authority necessary to complete the task, holding people accountable for authority, and monitoring the entire process. Successful managers must be able to delegate effectively because delegation makes better decisions possible, provides development opportunities for employees, and magnifies the accomplishments of the manager.

7. Managers often fail to delegate because of a failure to plan, a lack of confidence in their subordinates, hesitancy to assume dual accountability for their own actions and the actions of those to whom they delegate, or insecurity about their own value to the organization. Effective delegation requires matching the employee to the task, clearly communicating task responsibilities, giving authority to and requiring accountability from the person to whom the task is delegated, and choosing the appropriate level of delegation.

REVIEW QUESTIONS

1. (LEARNING OBJECTIVE 1) Why is organizing an important managerial function? Describe the process of organizing. What does each stage in the process entail?
2. (LEARNING OBJECTIVE 2) Define job design. What are the core job dimensions that define a specific job?
3. (LEARNING OBJECTIVE 3) How and why have job-design perspectives evolved over the last century?
4. (LEARNING OBJECTIVE 4) Explain the potential advantages and disadvantages of specialization, job enlargement, job enrichment, job rotation, employee-centered design, and self-managed teams.
5. (LEARNING OBJECTIVE 5) Discuss the following concepts: (a) chain of command, (b) span of control, (c) line versus staff departments, and (d) authority and responsibility.
6. (LEARNING OBJECTIVE 6) What is delegation and why is it important to delegate?
7. (LEARNING OBJECTIVE 7) Why might managers find it difficult to delegate? How might they improve their delegation skills?

DISCUSSION QUESTIONS

Improving Critical Thinking

1. Consider an organization that you have either worked for or have been affiliated with in some way. How might you redesign the jobs that must be done in that organization to achieve (a) increased effectiveness—better products and services; (b) increased efficiency; and (c) improved employee satisfaction? Are these objectives mutually exclusive? Could you design the jobs so that all of these objectives could be achieved?
2. The concept of self-managed teams has gained popularity in recent years. Consider moving toward that type of job design in a job you have held or hold currently. What would be the advantages and disadvantages of this approach?

Enhancing Communication Skills

3. Certain advantages and disadvantages are associated with having a fairly strict chain of command. What are they? Can you identify certain business conditions and/or organizations in which a more strict chain of command would be appropriate? What conditions and/or organizations would benefit from the use of a more flexible chain of command? Present your conclusions to the class orally.
4. Consider the job design of the following grocery store positions: (a) cashier, (b) produce manager, and (c) general manager. How would these jobs differ with regard to the core job dimensions discussed in this chapter? How would these jobs rate in terms of meaningfulness, the responsibility the jobholder feels for outcomes, and the jobholder's understanding of the results of work activities? To practice writing, develop a written summary of your response.

Building Teamwork

5. The competitive pressures of today's business climate (such as stronger global competition, advancing technology, greater demands from consumers) have forced many organizations to reconsider how they might operate more effectively and more efficiently. Form a team with four or five fellow students. As a group, identify and research at least three organizations that have responded to such pressures by reassessing and adjusting their organizational system. Have their efforts been effective?
6. Your boss is a terrible delegator. She rarely delegates tasks, preferring to retain the authority for the efforts of your entire work unit rather than take a risk by assigning the task to a member of the group. Even when she does delegate a meaningful task, she rarely gives the authority necessary to complete the task successfully. Form a team of four to five fellow students and discuss ways to encourage your boss to delegate more.

Chapter

8

Organizational Design

CHAPTER OVERVIEW

Developing an organizational design that supports the strategic and operational goals of an organization can be a challenging managerial task. This is particularly true today as many organizations struggle to find that delicate balance between organizational responsiveness and operational efficiency. Achieving success depends, to a large degree, on the ability of managers to develop an effective organizational design and one that has the right degree of flexibility for the situation.

We discussed the basic components of organization design in the previous chapter. Here, we discuss "putting all of this together" into an overall organization design that will be effective and efficient. That is, we discuss arranging the jobs and tasks into departments or divisions in an appropriate overall organizational structure, coordinating the departments or divisions so that they work together appropriately, and deciding at what level in the organization major decisions should be made.

LEARNING OBJECTIVES

When you have finished studying this chapter, you should be able to

1. Explain why organizational design is important for organizational success.
2. Identify the three major components of organizational design.
3. Discuss the four types of organizational structure and the strategic conditions under which each might be appropriate.
4. Describe the factors that affect an organization's need for coordination and explain how integrating mechanisms can be used to coordinate organizational activities.
5. Explain the concept of locus of decision making and when centralized or decentralized decision making might be appropriate.

Facing The Challenge

IBM: Big Blue Has the Blues

Basically since its beginning, IBM was nearly synonymous with computing in organizations. Its blue mainframe computers, combined with the software that they used, set the standard in the industry, earning IBM the nickname "Big Blue." The computers and software were so entrenched in businesses that when IBM decided to enter the personal-computer (PC) market, it instantly helped set the standard for PCs also, preventing Apple Computer Company and others from capturing large shares of the PC market.

All of that was before Gateway, Dell, and Intel. Gateway and Dell built very efficient businesses that served primarily as assemblers of components, including important processing chips from Intel, to make PCs with the latest features that customers wanted. Dell continued to do this so well that it pushed aside Gateway and others, including Hewlett-Packard (HP) and Compaq, which became part of HP. At the same time, PC makers continued to supply sophisticated servers that, combined with powerful PCs, took over many of the functions that mainframes perform.

By the early 2000s, IBM's revenues and profits were showing the effects of the changes in the computing industry and the competition from PCs. The demand for mainframe computers was decreasing and profits from PCs were gone.

Sources: S. Hamm, "Two Pillars of IBM's Growth Look Shaky," *BusinessWeek* 1 August 2005, 35–36; C. Forelle, "IBM's Earnings Hint at Recovery," *Wall Street Journal,* 19 July 2005, A3, A10; S. Hamm, "Beyond Blue," *BusinessWeek,* 18 April 2005, 68–76; P. Hemp, "Leading Change When Business Is Good," *Harvard Business Review* (December 2004): 60–71; D. Kirkpatrick, "Sam Palmisano," *Fortune,* 9 August 2004, 96; D. Kirkpatrick, "Inside Sam's $100 Billion Growth Machine," *Fortune,* 14 June 2004, 80–90; D. Kirkpatrick and S. Palmisano, "IBM Has a Vision Too," *Fortune,* 25 November 2002, 158–162.

Introduction

Sam Palmisano faced serious challenges when he became CEO of IBM in 2002. The industry consisting of mainframe computers and, later, personal computers had changed dramatically. Mr. Palmisano decided that it was time to change the overall strategy of the company, and to support that change in strategy, a new organization design was necessary. Both of these major changes are complex and risky. However, once there was a change in strategy, the old organization structure would not work anymore.

LEARNING OBJECTIVE 1

Explain why organizational design is important for organizational success.

1 Organizational design is an important aspect of management. The way in which an organization is designed will determine how effectively and efficiently its activities are carried out. Palmisano made bold changes for IBM. Hopefully, its new strategy is in line with the external environment, and its organizational design changes will help achieve the new strategy.

Organizational Design

Organizational design is a plan for arranging and coordinating the activities of an organization for the purpose of fulfilling its mission and achieving its goals. More specifically, design defines (1) the configuration of organizational members, (2) the types of mechanisms used to integrate and coordinate the flow of information, resources, and tasks between organizational members, and (3) the locus of decision making—the level of the organizational hierarchy at which most decision making occurs. The ultimate success of an organization depends, at least in part, on the ability of its managers to develop an organizational design that supports its strategic and operational goals.

Design provides a mechanism for coping with the complexity that results from managing multiple tasks, functions, products, markets, or technologies. Although organizational design issues are important to all organizations, the more complex an organization's operations, the more sophisticated its design must be. For example, a small organization that produces a single product

At the Forefront

Meg Whitman: Running Tomorrow's Company

Some say that Meg Whitman, CEO of eBay, is running the type of company that will be more common in the future, a company with minimum actual employees and maximum profitability. In 2005 eBay had over 125 million registered users. They do all of the selecting of products, pricing, buying, selling, and shipping. None of them is an employee. Over 430,000 people earn most or all of their income selling products on eBay. If eBay employeed these 430,000, it would be the second largest employer on Fortune's 500 list. Only Wal-Mart would have more employees. However, none of these people is an employee of eBay. Yet eBay has grown faster in its first 8 years, measured by revenues, than any other company and has been very profitable. How do you manage 125 million people who are not employees?

Whitman does it very well. She talks to buyers and sellers at eBay's annual conference. She listens in on calls with buyers and sellers. She has established strong credibility not only with eBay users but also with employees and investors. When she says that she is going to do something, she does it.

Whitman has been very successful in managing a profitable, global company consisting mostly of people and other businesses, most of whom are not employees. She has done it so well that *Fortune* consistently selects her to be on its "The 50 Most Powerful Women in Business" list, being number 1 on the list in 2004. Similarly, she repeatedly appears on *BusinessWeek*'s "The Best Managers" list.

Sources: "eBay: Back on Track," *BusinessWeek*, 1 August 2005, 40; "The Best Managers: Repeat Performers," *BusinessWeek*, 10 January 2005, 68; P. Sellers, "50 Most Powerful Women: eBay's Secret," *Fortune*, 18 October 2004, 160–178.

with a small workforce will likely find it easier to organize and coordinate its organizational members than will a multinational organization with multiple product lines, operating facilities spread across the globe, and a highly diverse workforce. Furthermore, growth-oriented organizations will find that effective design is a key to managing the complexity that results from developing new products, entering new geographic markets, or pursuing new customer groups. In sum, all organizations—small, large, and growing—must maintain an organizational design that is appropriate for the level of complexity they face.

No universal design is appropriate for all organizations. Organizational design must be consistent with a fairly broad range of variables that are largely a function of the organization's strategy, size, level of development, product diversity, geographic coverage, customer base, and information-processing needs.[1] Consequently, just as strategy varies among organizations, so will organizational design.

The 1990s and early 2000s have been characterized by a need for corporate redesign as organizations struggled to find an alignment between their strategy and structure. The highly volatile and competitive business environment forced many companies to reconsider their strategic focus and, consequently, the way in which their organizations were designed.[2] This has also been true for nonprofit organizations.[3] Pressures for efficiency led some companies into reengineering efforts. Yet efficiency alone was not enough. Simultaneously, competitive pressures to have the highest-quality products and services forced companies to look at designs that fostered employee creativity and commitment.[4] Still other competitive pressures made it necessary for some organizations to change their entire focus. Companies such as Motorola, General Electric, Proctor and Gamble, and Semco have responded to these challenges effectively, reformulating their strategies in light of the competitive challenges they face and redesigning their organizations to support those strategies. IBM ("Meeting the Challenge") is a good example of an organization that changed its organizational structure to be in line with its change in focus.[5]

KEY TERMS

Organizational design
The way in which the activities of an organization are arranged and coordinated so that its mission can be achieved.

Components of Organizational Design

As noted earlier and illustrated in Figure 8.1, an organization's overall design is defined by three primary components: (1) organizational structure, (2) integrating mechanisms, and (3) locus of decision making. As a system, these components enable the members of the organization to fulfill their mission and work toward the achievement of their goals. Each component will vary with the overall strategy of the organization.

LEARNING OBJECTIVE 2

Identify the three major components of organizational design.

ORGANIZATIONAL STRUCTURE

As discussed in Chapter 7, **organizational structure** refers to the primary reporting relationships that exist within an organization. The chain of command and hierarchy of responsibility, authority, and accountability are established through organizational structure. These relationships are often illustrated in an organizational chart.

LEARNING OBJECTIVE 3

Discuss the four types of organizational structure and the strategic conditions under which each might be appropriate.

The structuring process involves creating departments by grouping tasks on the basis of some common characteristic such as function, product, or geographic market. If, for example, work units are created by grouping all production tasks together, all marketing tasks together, and all finance tasks together, then the units are organized by function. In contrast, if work units are formed by grouping together all tasks related to serving a specific region of the U.S. market (such as Northeast, Southeast, Central, or West), then the geographic market served is the basis for departmentalization.

KEY TERMS

Organizational structure
A phrase referring to the primary reporting relationships that exist within an organization.

Functional structure
A structure in which tasks and jobs are grouped according to the function they perform within the organization.

An organization's strategy has significant implications for its structure.[6] For example, an organization with significant product diversity will likely find a structure departmentalized by product to be most suitable for managing its broad range of products. If, in contrast, a firm has a relatively narrow product line but serves many geographic markets that are quite different from each other, it might find a geographically based structure to be most appropriate.

In general, four types of organizational structure are predominant in organizations today. Three of these—the functional, divisional, and matrix structures—are traditional organizational forms that have been used by U.S. corporations for decades. The fourth, the network structure, has emerged more recently as an approach to meeting the challenges of today's business environment. In the next several sections, we describe each structural alternative, suggest some strategic conditions for which each might be appropriate, and outline some of the major advantages and disadvantages associated with each structure.

Functional Structure: Specialization and Efficiency

The **functional structure** groups organizational members according to the particular function that they perform within the organization and the set of resources that they draw on to perform their tasks. It is based on discipline-specific specialization. Therefore, the departments have names such as Marketing, Production, Finance, Human Resources, and Information Technology (Figure 8.2). Because functional structures are based on specialization, they can help focus on a particular job or task in order to perform effectively and efficiently. Because of this, the functional structure is the most commonly used organizational form.

Table 8.1 outlines the major potential advantages and disadvantages associated with the functional structure. On the positive side, functional structures support task specialization and may help employees develop better job-related skills. In addition, work groups may be more cohesive because employees work with individuals with similar skills and interests and the group's leader has a common functional orientation with the group members. Finally, this structure supports tight, centralized control and tends to contribute to operational efficiency.

But this structure has potential disadvantages as well. Most of these disadvantages stem from the problems associated with coordinating diverse work groups. Work groups organized along functional lines can often be insulated from the activities of other departments and may not truly understand the priorities and initiatives of other work groups. Another potential disadvantage of the functional structure is that it leads to the development of specialized managers rather than generalists who may be more appropriate for top-level management positions.

Figure 8.1 Dimensions of Organizational Design

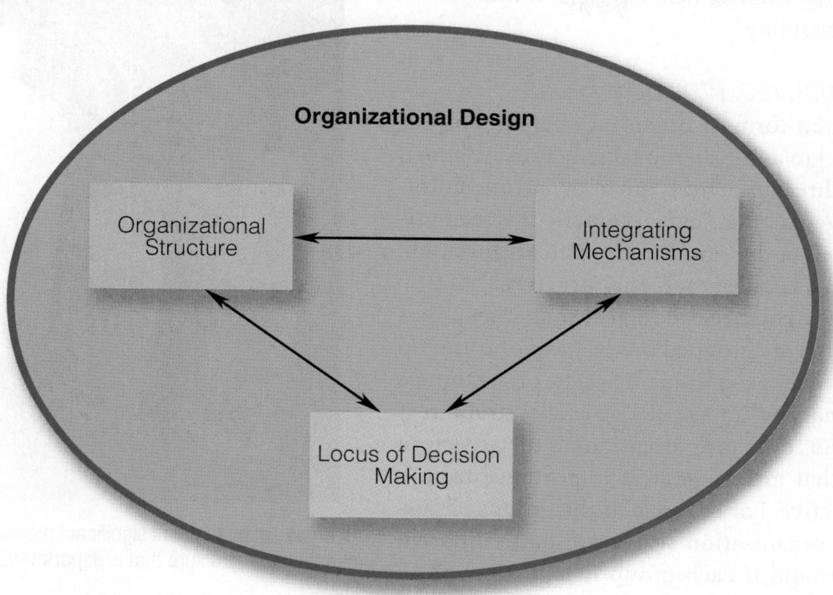

Figure 8.2 Functional Structure

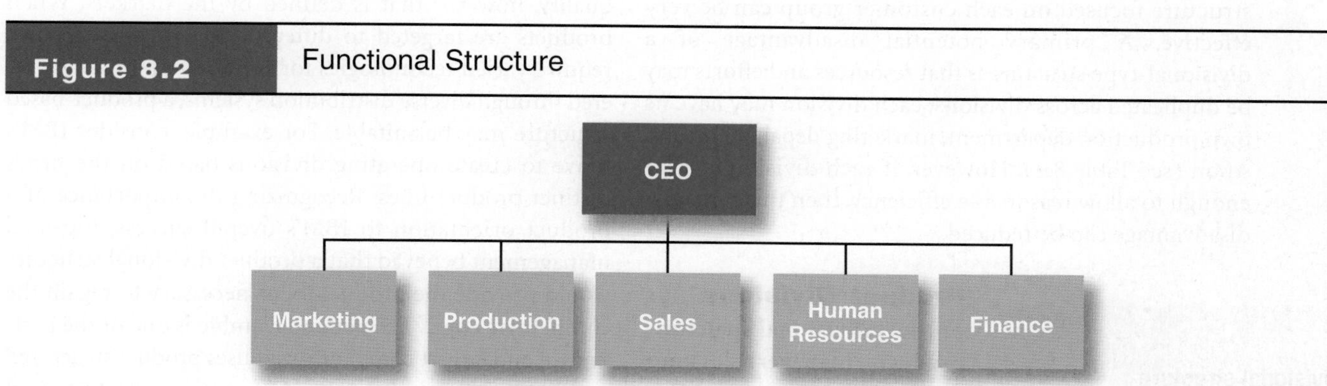

Table 8.1 Potential Advantages and Disadvantages of Organizational Structures

Types of Structure	Potential Advantages	Potential Disadvantages
Functional	Facilitates specialization. Cohesive work groups. Operational efficiency.	Focuses on departmental rather than organizational issues. Difficult to develop generalists needed for top-level management. Only top-level management held accountable for profitability.
Divisional	Focuses on specific product, geographic markets, or customers. Adapts to specific growth strategies.	Duplicates resources across divisions. Coordination among divisions difficult.
Matrix	Focuses on simultaneous goals. Develops managerial skills in several dimensions.	Complex and difficulties with implementation. "Two bosses." Difficult to plan and coordinate.
Network	Maximizes effectiveness of core unit. Can do more with fewer resources. Flexibility.	Fragmentation; difficult to control systems. Success depends on success in locating resources. Difficult to develop employee loyalty.

Finally, profit centers usually do not exist in a functionally structured organization. Therefore, only top-level corporate executives can be held clearly accountable for bottom-line profitability.

An organization that has significant product diversity will likely use a management structure that is departmentalized by product.

Divisional Structures: Providing Focus

A second common form of organizational structure is normally referred to as the divisional structure. Although it incorporates three different types of departmentalization—product, geographic, and customer—it is seen primarily at top levels or divisional levels in an organization. For convenience, it is called divisional structure.

A **divisional structure** is designed so that members of the organization are grouped on the basis of common products or services, geographic markets, or customers served. The primary advantage of a divisional structure is that it focuses the company's attention on the aspects of its operations that are of greatest importance from a strategic perspective. For example, if the groups of customers that an organization serves are quite different from each other and if each group is large enough to allow reasonable efficiency, then an organizational structure focused on each customer group can be very effective. A primary potential disadvantage of a divisional-type structure is that resources and efforts may be duplicated across divisions; each division may have its own production department, marketing department, and so on (see Table 8.1). However, if each division is large enough to allow reasonable efficiency, then this potential disadvantage can be reduced.

KEY TERMS

Divisional structure
A structure in which members of the organization are grouped on the basis of common products, geographic markets, or customers served.

Product divisional structure
A structure in which the activities of the organization are grouped according to specific products or product lines.

Geographic divisional structure
A structure in which the activities of the organization are grouped according to the geographic markets served.

Product Divisions In a **product divisional structure,** product managers assume responsibility for the production and distribution of a specific product or product line to all the geographic and customer markets served by the organization. These managers coordinate all functional tasks (finance, marketing, production, and so on) related to their product line. Product divisional structures can be based on services as well as products.

Product divisional structures are considered most appropriate for organizations with relatively diverse product lines that require specialized efforts to achieve high product quality, however that is defined by the markets. When products are targeted to different and distinct groups, require varied technologies for production, or are delivered through diverse distribution systems, a product-based structure may be suitable. For example, consider IBM's move to create operating divisions based on the firm's distinct product lines. Recognizing the importance of a product orientation to IBM's overall success, top-level management believed that a product divisional structure would provide the product focus necessary to regain the competitive edge.[7] Procter and Gamble is one of the best-known and largest companies that uses product structure.[8]

Look at Figure 8.3 to see Clariant's use of a product structure. Actually, this figure shows the use of a product structure for the main line divisions and a functional-based structure for the staff departments.

Many large organizations not only have diverse product lines but also operate several diverse and distinct businesses. In such cases, the product divisional structure actually takes the form of an SBU (strategic business unit) divisional structure in which each business unit is maintained as a separate and autonomous operating division. PepsiCo provides an excellent example of a company organized around its primary businesses—Pepsi Cola Company (soft drinks), Frito-Lay Company (snack foods), and others.[9]

Geographic Divisions The **geographic divisional structure** groups the activities of the organization along geographic lines. Each geographic division is responsible for distributing products or services within a specific

Figure 8.3 Product Divisional Structure: Clariant

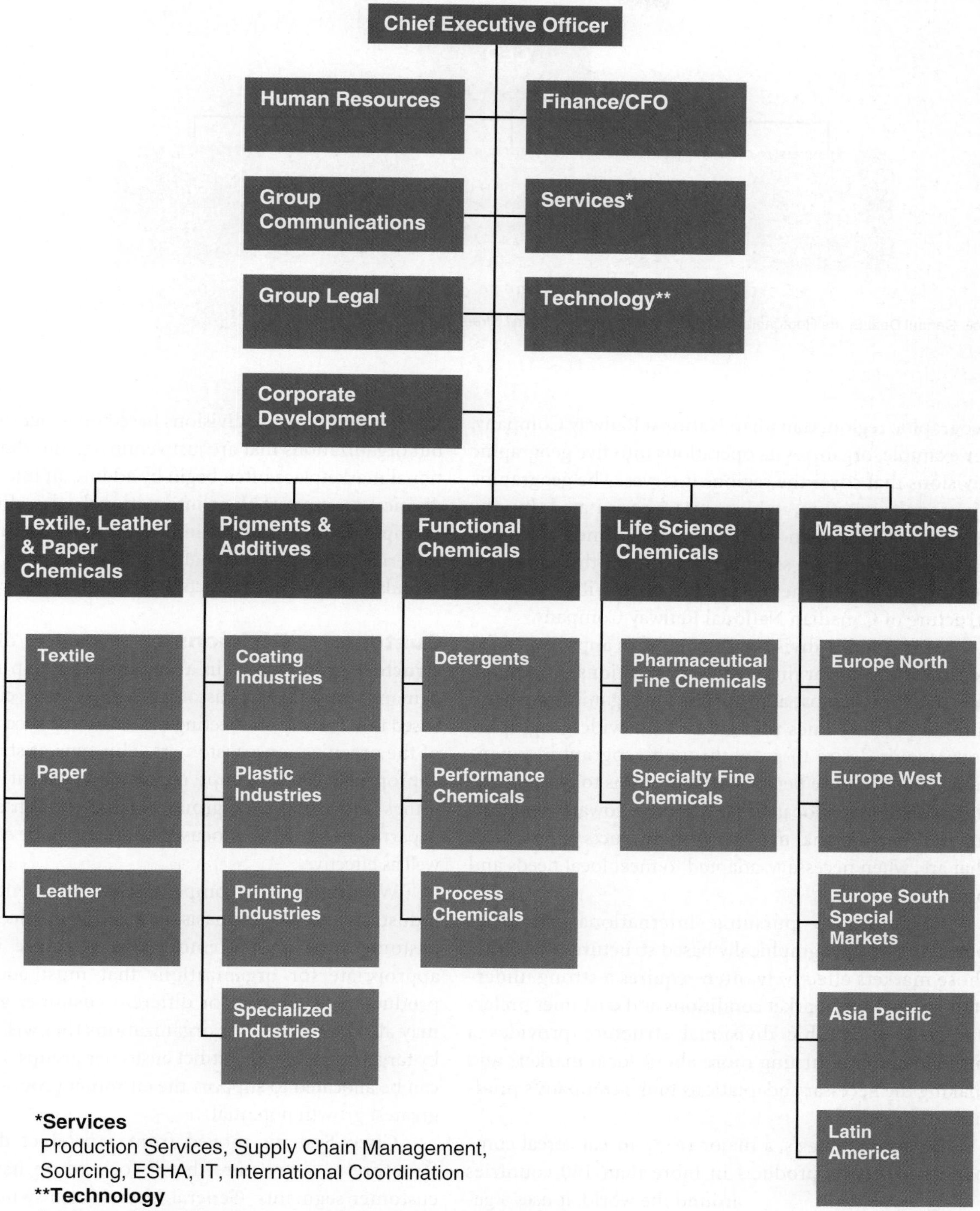

Chief Executive Officer

Human Resources

Finance/CFO

Group Communications

Services*

Group Legal

Technology**

Corporate Development

Textile, Leather & Paper Chemicals
- Textile
- Paper
- Leather

Pigments & Additives
- Coating Industries
- Plastic Industries
- Printing Industries
- Specialized Industries

Functional Chemicals
- Detergents
- Performance Chemicals
- Process Chemicals

Life Science Chemicals
- Pharmaceutical Fine Chemicals
- Specialty Fine Chemicals

Masterbatches
- Europe North
- Europe West
- Europe South Special Markets
- Asia Pacific
- Latin America

***Services**
Production Services, Supply Chain Management, Sourcing, ESHA, IT, International Coordination

****Technology**
Intellectual Property, Innovation & Knowledge Management, New Business Development

Source: http://www.clariant.com. August 19, 2005.

Figure 8.4 Geographic Divisional Structure: Canadian National Railway Company

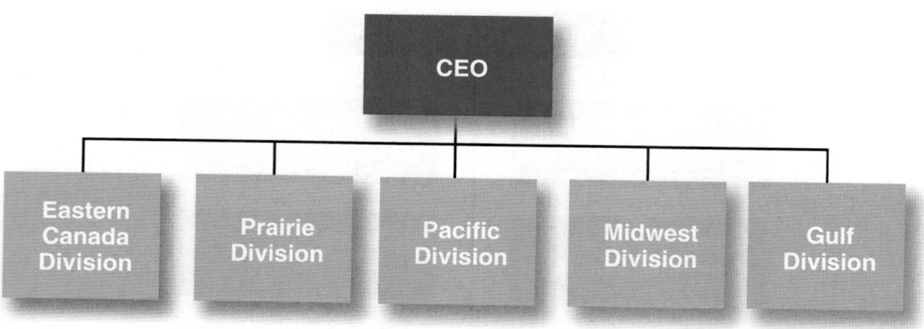

Source: "Illinois Central Deal Spurs Reorganization by Canadian National," *Wall Street Journal,* April 15, 1999, A4.

geographic region. Canadian National Railway Company, for example, organizes its operations into five geographic divisions that cover the regions it serves. The geographic divisional structure, which was precipitated by the merger of Canadian National with Illinois Central, focuses managers on serving the needs of the particular geographic market they serve.[10] Figure 8.4 illustrates the structure of Canadian National Railway Company.

A geographic divisional structure is appropriate for organizations of varying strategic conditions. In general, this structure is most appropriate for organizations with limited product lines that either have wide geographic coverage or desire to grow through geographic expansion. This structure permits organizations to concentrate their efforts and allocate their resources toward penetrating multiple regional markets with products and services that are, when necessary, adapted to meet local needs and preferences.[11]

Organizations pursuing international strategies often choose a geographically based structure.[12] Entering those markets effectively often requires a strong understanding of local market conditions and customer preferences. A geographic divisional structure provides a mechanism for learning more about local markets and making the necessary adaptations to the company's products and services.

Because Kellogg's, a major ready-to-eat cereal company, markets its products in more than 160 countries around the world, it uses a geographical structure with six main geographic regions—the United States, Europe, Latin America, Canada, Australia, and Asia.[13] Kellogg enjoys a strong international presence that justifies separate divisions based on geographic area, but organizations that are just venturing into the international marketplace often begin by adding an international division to support their international sales efforts. For example, Houghton Mifflin, a publisher of educational materials, added an international division in an effort to stimulate sales of its products overseas.[14]

KEY TERMS

Customer divisional structure
An organizational structure focused on customer groups.

Customer Divisions A **customer divisional structure** groups tasks in a way that will help meet the demands of different customer groups. Each customer-based unit focuses on meeting the needs of a specific group of the organization's customers. This type of structure is appropriate when groups of customers want different things and when each group is large enough so that a department or division focused on them can be efficient as well as effective.

With the intense competitive environment in most industries and the emphasis on meeting the needs of the customer first and foremost, this structure is highly appropriate for organizations that must adapt their products and services for different customer groups. It may also be suitable for organizations that wish to grow by targeting new and distinct customer groups. Resources can be allocated to support the customer groups with the greatest growth potential.

Cisco Systems moved from a product divisional structure to a structure that is focused on its primary customer segments. General Electric also switched to a structure in mid-2005 that is focused on what it calls industry groups.[15] Amazon.com added a division that is focused on helping other retailers to sell on the Internet.[16] Although Microsoft is organized into five semiautonomous product divisions, those divisions focus on very different customer segments.[17]

Figure 8.5 Matrix Structure

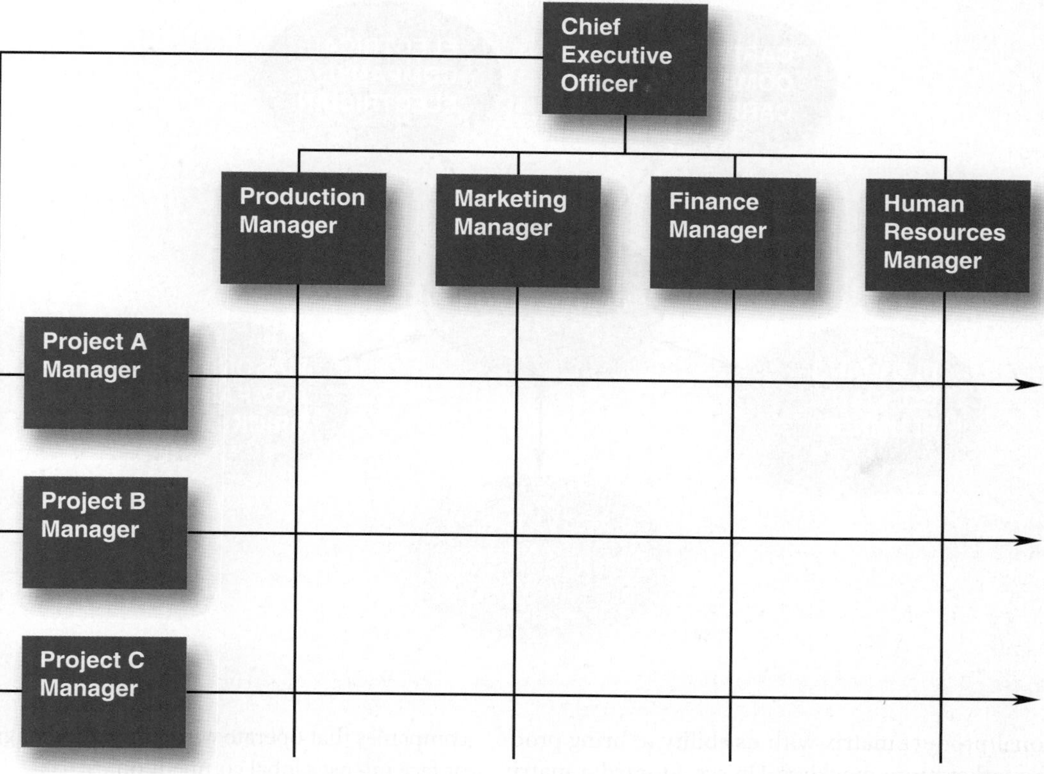

Matrix Structure: A Dual Focus

The organizational structures discussed so far have grouped activities along a specific, single dimension of the organization's operations (function, product, geographic region, or customer base). In some cases, there is a need to focus on two or more dimensions at the same time. For example, assume that a company has a functional structure but it also needs to be sure that each product or product group meets certain requirements. Similarly, an organization might have a product-based structure, but it also must tune into requirements of the different geographic markets. The **matrix structure** was developed to deal with these situations.[18] It defines work groups on the basis of two dimensions simultaneously (such as product/function, product/geographic region, and so on).

A matrix structure begins with a basic form of structure, usually functional, and then has a second type of structure superimposed upon it. A common form of matrix structure is a functional structure with a product, geographic, or customer structure laid over. The managers of the superimposed structure normally are called project managers, especially if the matrix structure is intended to be temporary. When the matrix is intended to be permanent, the project managers may be product managers or geographical managers (Figure 8.5).

The potential advantage of a matrix structure is to provide a way to focus on two important dimensions at the same time. It can also provide flexibility when the second focus is needed for only a short time. For example, if a project is to last for a certain time only, the organization does not have to build an organizational unit for the project. Instead, a project manager can be designated, and that manager can "borrow" or coordinate resources across the original organization in order to accomplish the project. When the project is finished, the resources can be used by their original organizational unit.

The matrix structure also has a number of disadvantages (see Table 8.1). Most notable is the complexity inherent in a dual chain of command. Managing within this structure requires extraordinary planning and coordination between work groups.[19]

A number of companies have found the matrix structure to be effective. For example, Texas Instruments credited a

KEY TERMS

Matrix structure
A technique that arranges work groups on two dimensions simultaneously.

Figure 8.6 Network Structure (Building Contractor)

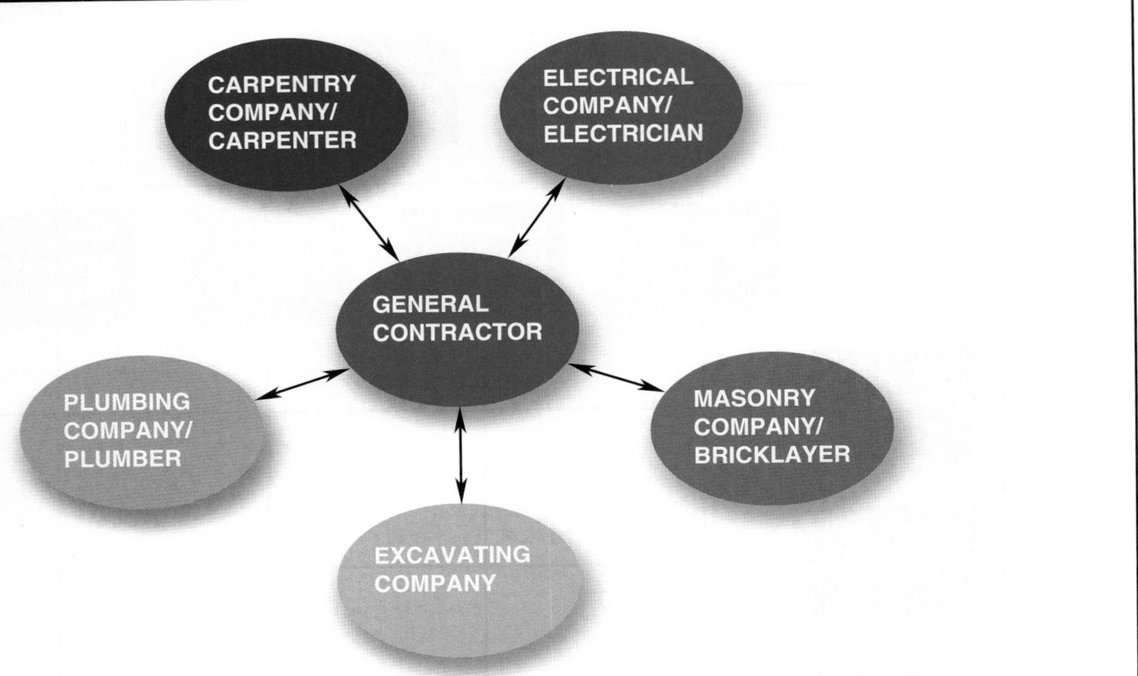

functional/product matrix with its ability to bring products to market more quickly.[20] Unisys adopted a matrix structure in an attempt to bring a stronger customer focus to the company. However, before Digital Equipment Company (DEC) was acquired by other companies, it reported a very different experience with the functional/product matrix structure. DEC found that the matrix structure led to "people spending endless hours in meetings trying to build consensus between the two factions in the matrix: the functional bosses and the team bosses."[21] The delays associated with the structure left DEC behind in the fast-paced technology race in the computer industry. DEC's experience provides an important reminder that although the matrix structure can be effective, the benefits of the design will come only with successful implementation.

Network Structures: Flexibility

For decades, organizations aspired to be large. Growth was considered to be synonymous with success, and the "bigger-is-better" syndrome governed the strategic decision making of most companies. But today, an alternative view has emerged. Organizations are finding that being lean and flexible is often preferable to being big. This may be particularly true for companies that operate within rapidly changing industries or face intense global competition.[22]

In response to these changes, a number of successful organizations have moved toward a form of organizational structure called the network structure. The **network structure** is built around alliances between organizations within the network. Each member of the network performs some portion of the activities necessary to deliver the products and services of the network as a whole.[23] At the core of each network is an organization that performs some key functions for the network and coordinates the activities of other network members. For example, the central organization may coordinate the production, marketing, financing, and distribution activities necessary to market a particular product without owning a single manufacturing plant, creating a single line of advertising copy, or even taking possession of the product. The central organization simply coordinates the activities of others so that the product reaches the ultimate consumer in an effective and efficient way.[24] Essentially, a network structure results in outsourcing various parts or operations of the organization. This is becoming increasingly popular, especially because many managers and other strategy experts suggest that a company should focus on its distinctive competencies (Chapter 4) and outsource the other things.[25] Figure 8.6 illustrates the network organizational structure in a very simple form.

KEY TERMS

Network structure
An organization that has a core coordinating with other organizations or organizational units.

Leaders in Action

Will Your Next TV Be a Dell?

When Michael Dell was 16, he bought a BMW with money earned from his paper route. He occasionally visited the courthouse to get names of new home buyers and newly married couples. Then he solicited them as customers for his paper route. By the mid-1980s, he understood that personal computers (PCs) were all made the same way, simply assembled from components that were readily available. So he started assembling PCs and declared that he was competing against IBM.

As the saying goes, the rest is history. Dell has built one of the most effective and efficient organization structures that ever existed. Even though Dell now produces servers, printers, and related products in addition to PCs, they all are produced in essentially the same way, assembled from readily available components. That is why Dell establishes alliances and partnerships with major component makers, such as Intel and Microsoft, and shippers such as FedEx and UPS.

Now Dell is planning to make televisions and is becoming a major competitor in the printer business, which was once dominated by Hewlett-Packard. And what about competing against IBM? IBM sold its PC division to a Chinese company, and Michael Dell is chairman of the "most admired company" in 2005.

Sources: A. Serwer, "The Education of Michael Dell," *Fortune,* 7 March 2005, 72–82; A. Park, "Thinking Out of the Box," *Newsweek,* 22 November 2004, 22; J. Baattelle and M. Dell, "Features/Titans of Tech," *Business 2.0* 5, no. 4 (May 2004): 99; G. McWilliams, "Dells' Founder to Step Down as CEO; President Rollins to Take That Post, while Mr. Dell Will Remain as Chairman," *Wall Street Journal,* 5 March 2004, A10; G. McWilliams and P. Tam, "Dell Price Cuts Put a Squeeze on Rival H-P," *Wall Street Journal,* 21 August 2003, B1; S. Pritchard, "Inside Dell's Lean Machine," *Works Management* 55, no. 12 (December 2002): 14–16.

Ikea, an international Scandinavian-style furniture company, is an example of a company that uses elements of a network structure. The company develops its own strategy and mission and controls all aspects of its operations. It controls design of the furniture, design of manufacturing techniques that result in quality furniture while keeping costs down, and all aspects of marketing. However, Ikea does not manufacture any of its furniture and does not actually perform some other operations. It outsources those operations.[26]

Similarly, Michael Dell, founder and CEO of Dell Computers, has created an innovative network structure that is considered by many to be the standard in not only the PC computer industry but also in many other industries. Dell does not make any of the parts of the PC. Rather, Dell has very strong alliances with suppliers of various components and with companies that deliver the PCs to the customers. Dell assembles the PCs and coordinates everything related to design, marketing, assembly-production, and the like.[27] (See the "Leaders in Action" box.)

On the other hand, IDEO is an organization to which other companies outsource. IDEO is a design company that helps Intel, Nestle, Lufthansa, Samsung, and others with design of products and related marketing tools.[28] As discussed in the "Meeting the Challenge" box, IBM is moving to become a company that also provides services for many others.

As globalization continues, companies that operate in many countries are using various forms of network structure. This allows the companies to work with partners in a local country.[29] The partner in that country, if chosen carefully, can help with adapting to the local conditions much more successfully and quickly.

Three primary types of network structures are found in organizations today—internal, stable, and dynamic networks.[30] These structures vary in the extent to which the central organization relies on outsourcing.

An **internal network** exists in organizations that choose to avoid outsourcing but wish to develop internal entrepreneurial ventures that are driven by market forces and thus are competitive with alternative sources of supply. These internal units operate independently and negotiate with the central unit like any outside vendor. Each unit functions as a profit center that specializes in a particular aspect of the organization's product delivery system.

The component business of General Motors (GM) is an

KEY TERMS

Internal network
A network structure that relies on internally developed units to provide services to a core organizational unit.

example of an internal network structure. GM's component business maintains independent divisions that specialize in the production of some aspect of the automotive system. These divisions are encouraged to conduct business on the open market, yet they cooperate with the central unit of GM's component business whenever appropriate. The net result is greater effectiveness for the corporation as a whole.[31]

Organizations that maintain a **stable network** rely to some degree on outsourcing to add flexibility to their product delivery system. The central organization contracts with outside vendors to provide certain products and services that are essential to its product delivery system. Although these vendors are independent of the central organization, they typically are highly committed to the core firm.

LEARNING OBJECTIVE 4

Describe the factors that affect an organization's need for coordination and explain how integrating mechanisms can be used to coordinate organizational activities.

BMW is an example of a company that has adopted a stable network structure. Somewhere between 55 and 75% of BMW's production comes from outsourcing. Although BMW does not own its vendor firms outright, it does maintain stable relationships with them and may even make a financial investment in these organizations where appropriate.[32] Dell has a longstanding alliance with Intel for processors.[33]

A **dynamic network** differs from internal and stable networks in that organizations with this structure make extensive use of outsourcing to support their operations. Partnerships with vendors are less frequent, and less emphasis is placed on finding organizations to service the central organization only. Typically, the central organization focuses on some core skill and contracts for most other functions. For example, Ikea focuses on its retailing strength, and although it coordinates everything else, it also outsources many of the other operations.[34] Reebok focuses on its design strengths and oursources the rest.[35]

KEY TERMS

Stable network
A network structure that continually uses a set of alliance partners.

Dynamic network
A network structure that makes extensive use of outsourcing through alliances with outside organizations.

Coordinating
Keeping organization units that interact with or influence each other in contact with each to share information and other things in a way that enhances accomplishment of tasks.

A number of potential advantages and disadvantages are associated with the network structure (see Table 8.1). The effectiveness and efficiency of the core unit can be maximized by the use of a network structure, particularly if the network is characterized by enduring, mutually beneficial business relationships.[36] The organization can do more with less because it is using others' resources. Flexibility is an inherent benefit of this organizational form because the core unit can change vendors quickly should product and/or component changes be necessary. Many international firms have found that the network structure provides them with the speed and flexibility necessary to compete effectively in highly competitive global markets. In fact, some multinationals have abandoned the matrix structure in favor of the more adaptable network form.[37]

The primary potential disadvantage of a network structure is that, because operations are fragmented, it may be difficult to develop a control system that effectively monitors all aspects of the product delivery system.[38] However, advanced information technology can be utilized to better monitor the activities of networked companies. In fact, specialized systems have been developed that address the unique needs of the network organization. Companies such as Dell, Benetton, and Nike are utilizing such systems to effectively coordinate the activities of their diverse networks. As business-to-business e-commerce solutions continue to evolve, more organizations may find the network structure feasible and appealing.[39]

We have examined the four basic types of structures that are commonly used in organizations. These structures define how the employees of the organization are grouped and specify reporting relationships within the organizational hierarchy. The "Now Apply It" box gives you an opportunity to assess the organizational structure of an organization with which you are familiar. Take some time to work through the exercise before moving on to learn about the second component of organizational design—integrating mechanisms.

MANAGING COMPLEXITY THROUGH INTEGRATION

4 Integrating the activities of an organization involves controlling and **coordinating** the flow of information, resources, and tasks among organizational members and work groups. Whereas structure serves to segregate organizational members into different work units, the goal of the integration component of organizational design is to coordinate the work of these distinct groups. An organization's many and diverse work groups are linked together through integrating mechanisms. As we will soon learn, integrating mechanisms include such things as management information systems, liaison personnel, and cross-functional work teams.

Now Apply It

Analyzing Organizational Structure

Identify a student organization in which you are involved. Draw an organizational chart showing how the organization is departmentalized. Now answer the following questions about its structure:

1. Is the structure consistent with the strategy of the organization?
2. Do the work units, or student officers, have titles that represent primary functions, services, or customers?
3. Would another organizational structure make more sense than the existing one? If so, why?
4. Where is the locus of decision making in this organization? Does it seem appropriate? Explain why or why not.

The complexity of an organization's operations will affect its need for integration. For example, a purely domestic firm with a narrow product line and a single manufacturing facility will find the integration of its work groups to be more manageable than will a multinational corporation with broad product lines and manufacturing facilities spread across the globe. Normally, the more complex an organization's operations, the more sophisticated its coordinating mechanisms must be.

In general, an organization's integration needs will vary with the level of interdependence that exists among work groups.[40] In organizations where work groups must closely coordinate their activities to achieve organizational goals, integration needs will be high. In contrast, where work groups exist relatively independently and without significant interaction, integration needs are low. Before we discuss specific integrating mechanisms that might be used to coordinate the activities of an organization, let's examine the various levels of interdependence that may exist in an organization and how that interdependence affects its integration needs.

Interdependence and Integration Needs

Central to the discussion of integration is the concept of interdependence. **Interdependence** refers to the degree to which work groups are interrelated and the extent to which they depend on one another to complete their work. The level of interdependence between work groups will affect the need for integrating mechanisms.[41] Figure 8.7 illustrates the three primary levels of work group interdependence, and the following discussion describes each in greater detail.

Pooled Interdependence Pooled **interdependence** occurs when organizational units have a common source of resources but have no interrelationship with one another as a particular task is performed. Consider, for example, a local bank with branch offices spread around the city. Although all branches must coordinate their efforts with the central office, they have limited interaction with one another. They have little need to cooperate and coordinate with one another to achieve their goals. Managers work independently to achieve the goals of their own work groups, which in turn contribute to the overall performance of the organization.

Sequential Interdependence **Sequential interdependence** exists when work groups must coordinate the flow of information, resources, or tasks from one unit to another. Sequential interdependence is associated with a typical manufacturing assembly line. The output of one unit becomes the input for another unit. Organizations with sequentially interdependent units have greater coordination needs than organizations with units that have pooled interdependence.

Reciprocal Interdependence **Reciprocal interdependence** represents the greatest level of interrelatedness between work groups, in that work is passed back and forth between work units. The final product requires the input of a number of different departments at varying times

KEY TERMS

Interdependence
The degree to which work groups are interrelated.

Pooled interdependence
When organizational units have a common resource but no interrelationship with one another.

Sequential interdependence
When organizational units must coordinate the flow of information, resources, and tasks from one unit to another.

Reciprocal interdependence
Occurs when information, resources, and tasks must be passed back and forth between work groups.

Figure 8.7 Levels of Work Group Interdependence

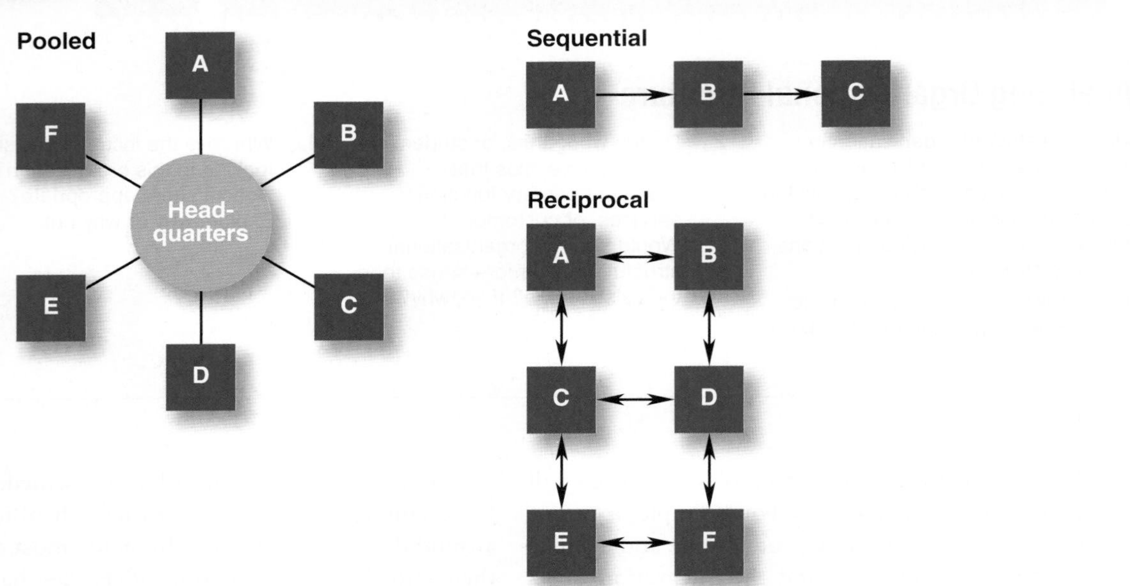

during the production process. Consider a university system in which students' registration materials must be shuffled from one administrative unit to another and back. These work groups are interrelated, and the effective functioning of the system requires a high level of integration among the groups.

The higher the level of interdependence of an organization's work groups, the greater its needs for coordination. The sophistication of an integrating system should be in alignment with its specific coordination needs. For example, an organization with pooled interdependence between its work groups may be able to function effectively with a few relatively simple integrating mechanisms. In contrast, an organization with reciprocal interdependence between work groups will require more sophisticated integrating mechanisms.

Integrating mechanisms are not without costs. As we will discuss, many of the tools for coordinating the activities of the organization have human or financial costs that are tangible and measurable. Therefore, organizations must carefully evaluate their coordination needs so that they can develop integrating mechanisms that are cost effective and in line with those needs.

KEY TERMS

Integrating mechanism
A method for managing the flow of information, resources, and tasks within the organization.

Integrating Mechanisms

At the foundation of an organization's ability to coordinate the activities of its subunits is its information-processing capacity. Effective coordination depends on the flow of information between the individual units of the organization so that work can be scheduled, resources shared and transferred, and conflicting objectives resolved. Toward this end, organizations develop integrating mechanisms that enhance their information-processing capacity and support their need for coordination. **Integrating mechanisms** are methods for managing the flow of information, resources, and tasks throughout the organization.

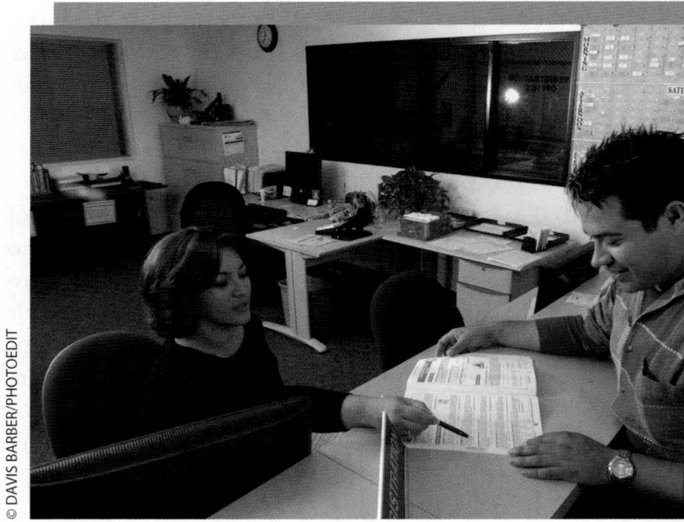

© DAVIS BARBER/PHOTOEDIT

A university student services office may control and coordinate the flow of student information for task purposes such as course registration, parking permits, and grading records.

Many different mechanisms can be used to process information and coordinate the activities of interdependent work units. Some of these mechanisms are characteristic of general management systems. Others are developed specifically to increase the coordination potential of the organization. Still others are designed to reduce the organization's need for coordination. Figure 8.8 illustrates the three major categories of integrating mechanisms, each of which is discussed next.[42]

General Management Systems Some coordination of work units may be achieved through the development of general management systems such as the managerial hierarchy, basic rules and procedures, and plans and goals. Such mechanisms form the foundation of an organization's integration system.

As we have discussed, an organization's managerial hierarchy is established by its organizational structure. Recall that organizational structure defines work groups on the basis of some type of familiarity (that is, function, product, geographic, market, or customer). By grouping organizational members in this fashion, coordination within the groups is enhanced. Consider the structures of Procter and Gamble and PepsiCo for example. These companies have designed their structures in such a way that separate business units focus on different products or serve different customer segments. Thus, they have grouped employees based on their need to coordinate with one another.[43]

Similarly, organizations develop plans, goals, policies, rules, and procedures that govern the behavior of their members. All of these serve as a means of integrating the operations of an organization. Plans that require implementation by multiple work groups provide a foundation for action by those units. A well-developed business plan details the activities of specific departments within an organization, thereby providing guidance about how those activities are to be coordinated. Similarly, certain behaviors are implied by specific achievement-based goals. The plans that result from such programs provide a foundation for integrating and coordinating the activities of diverse groups toward common quality-oriented goals.

Organizations that make extensive use of rules and procedures often are thought to be bureaucratic, highly formalized, and closely governed. In contrast, organizations that use fewer rules and procedures are considered to be more flexible, less formal, and participatory in nature. Yet too few rules can result in significant problems, particularly when coordination between organizational members is required.

Most universities make extensive use of rules and procedures to coordinate the activities of their colleges and departments. Student records must be processed according to specific guidelines; overrides into classes must be handled systematically; and parking tickets and overdue library books must be dealt with before the registration process can be completed. These rules and procedures are mechanisms ensuring that the activities of the various units of the university are well coordinated.

Increasing Coordination Potential Although general management systems can be very good coordination tools, they may not provide all the coordination that is needed. Information systems and lateral relationships are two of the most common mechanisms for increasing coordination potential both vertically and horizontally within the organization.

Figure 8.8 Integrating Mechanisms

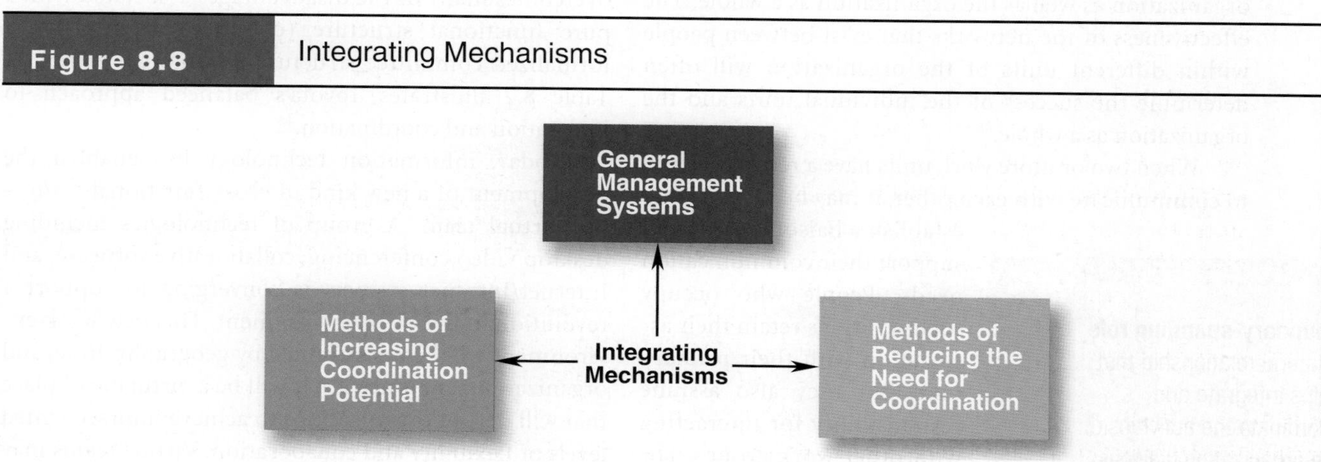

Source: Adapted by permission, J. R. Galbraith, "Organizational Design: An Information Processing View," *Interfaces* 4 (May 1974): 3. Copyright 1974, The Institute of Management Sciences and the Operations Research Society of America (currently INFORMS), 2 Charles Street, Suite 300, Providence, RI 02904 USA.

Information systems facilitate the flow of information up and down the traditional chain of command and across organizational units. The computerized transfer of important information and data provides a powerful tool for coordinating diverse departments or operating units. Additionally, information technology can provide control mechanisms ensuring that coordination problems are identified and resolved in a timely fashion. In fact, some have argued that information technology has advanced organizational coordination to the same magnitude that mass-production technologies advanced manufacturing in the Industrial Revolution.[44]

Many multinational corporations have developed sophisticated management information systems to support their global operations. With the advent of more sophisticated and affordable computer technology, decision-making data can be transmitted almost simultaneously from division to division around the globe. Computer and telecommunication networks provide the infrastructure for coordinating operations on a worldwide scale. E-mail, teleconferencing, and high-speed data systems are a few of the mechanisms used by multinational organizations. Wal-Mart is known for having one of the best, if not the best, information system in the world.[45]

The second important method for increasing coordination potential is to establish lateral relationships. Such relationships exist across horizontal work units and serve as mechanisms for exchanging decision making information. In general, lateral relationships can be thought of as **boundary-spanning roles.** The primary purpose of the boundary-spanning function is to develop an understanding of the activities of units outside the boundaries of one's own work group. Such knowledge helps employees and work groups understand how their actions and performance affect others within the organization as well as the organization as a whole. The effectiveness of the networks that exist between people within different units of the organization will often determine the success of the individual units and the organization as a whole.[46]

When two or more work units have a recurring need to communicate with each other, it may be beneficial to establish a liaison position to support their communication needs. People who occupy such positions retain their association with their primary unit, but they also assume responsibility for interacting with other work groups. For example, the marketing department of an organization might identify an individual to act as a formal liaison with the company's engineering department. Although this individual remains in his marketing role, he or she also serves as the primary contact point for the interaction between the marketing department and the engineering department.

KEY TERMS

Boundary-spanning role
A lateral relationship that helps integrate and coordinate the activities of the organization (liaisons, committees, task forces, integrating positions, and cross-functional work teams).

When the effective management of multiple interdependent units is critical to the success of the organization, it may be appropriate to establish a committee (a permanent group) or a task force (a temporary group) to facilitate communication between the groups. The committee or task force would be made up of representatives from each of the work groups involved. As was the case with the formal liaison position, the committee or task force assignment is only a part of each representative's job; the representatives' primary job responsibilities remain with the units they represent. Multinational corporations, for example, often use committees composed of corporate executives and representatives from both domestic and foreign subsidiaries. These committees assume responsibility for both assimilating and disseminating critical information needed by the operating units of the organizations.[47]

When an organization has very high integration needs, it may be appropriate to establish cross-functional work teams. Cross-functional work teams represent a more aggressive approach to integration in that members from various functional groups are permanently assigned to a team that is given responsibility for completing a particular set of tasks (see the discussions of self-managed teams in Chapter 7). Toyota, for example, uses a cross-functional team approach to support its vehicle development process. These teams enable the company to achieve cross-functional integration while still capturing functional expertise from the team members. The cross-functional team provides a balanced approach that overcomes many of the disadvantages associated with a pure functional structure (chimney extreme) or a formalized committee structure (committee extreme). Table 8.2 illustrates Toyota's balanced approach to integration and coordination.[48]

Today, information technology has enabled the development of a new kind of cross-functional team—the virtual team. A group of technologies including desktop video conferencing, collaborative software, and Internet/Intranet systems is converging to support a revolution in the work environment. This new work environment will be unrestrained by geography, time, and organizational boundaries; it will be a virtual workplace that will permit organizations to achieve unprecedented levels of flexibility and collaboration. Virtual teams may be geographically dispersed coworkers within the same organization, or they may exist across organizations as in a network organizational structure. What virtual teams

Table 8.2 How Toyota Avoids Extremes

Chimney Extreme	Toyota Balance	Committee Extreme
Mutual Adjustment		
Little face-to-face contact.	Succinct written reports for most communication.	Reliance on meetings to accomplish tasks.
Predominantly written communication.	Meetings for intensive problem solving.	Predominantly oral communication.
Direct Supervision		
Close supervision of engineers by managers.	Technically astute functional supervisors who mentor, train, and develop their engineers.	Little supervision of engineers.
Large barriers between functions.	Strong functions that are evaluated based on overall system performance.	Weak functional expertise.
Integrative Leadership		
No system design leader.	Project leader as system designer, with limitations on authority.	System design dispersed among team members.
Standard Skills		
No rotation of engineers.	Rotation on intervals that are longer than the typical product cycle, and only to positions that complement the engineers' expertise.	Rotation at rapid and broad intervals.
Standard Work Processes		
New development process with every vehicle.	Standard milestones—project leader decides timing, functions fill in details.	Lengthy, detailed, rigid development schedules.
Complex forms and bureaucratic procedures.	Standard forms and procedures that are simple, devised by the people who use them, and updated as needed.	Making up procedures on each project.
Design Standards		
Obsolete, rigid design standards.	Standards that are maintained by the people doing the work and that keep pace with current company capabilities.	No design standards.

Source: Reprinted by permission of *Harvard Business Review.* From "Another Look at How Toyota Integrates Product Development," by D. Sobek II, J. Liker, and A. Ward (July/August 1998).

have in common is that they are in separate physical locations, yet they are brought together by advanced telecommunications and information technologies to achieve a specific task.[49] Many organizations such as Microsoft, Intel, and Xerox are using virtual teams. British Petroleum (BP) has developed a virtual team network that has made it possible to flatten and decentralize its organizational design. By capitalizing on advances in information systems and digital communications, BP virtual team members can share knowledge and information with each other without concern for boundaries created by most organizational structures.[50]

Although integrating mechanisms designed to increase coordination potential can be quite costly, they may be warranted when strategic effectiveness requires close coordination and cooperation between organizational subunits. Most organizations today acknowledge that facilitating communication, integration, and coordination among work groups is critical to organizational success.[51]

Reducing the Need for Coordination The third method of integration is to reduce or eliminate the need for coordination between work groups. In essence, the organization creates "slack resources" that reduce the interdependence of the work groups and, as a result, the need for integrating mechanisms. For example, an organization might establish longer lead times for sequentially interdependent work to be completed or maintain larger inventories of work in progress. Both measures would reduce the need for tight coordination between units. Although this is an effective way to reduce the need for coordination, it is not necessarily the most efficient. Creating slack resources in this way is inconsistent with the need for improved productivity and efficiency. As a result, such a practice may lead to suboptimal organizational performance.

Another way that organizations can reduce the need for coordination is to create work units that have only pooled interdependence. By doing so, they minimize the need for integration. One benefit of cross-functional work teams is that work groups are relatively independent, thereby reducing the need for integration between diverse functional units. However, forming cross-functional teams simply to reduce integration needs may not be appropriate if it results in redundant resource utilization. In general, independent units should be formed only when there are other strategic reasons to do so.

LEARNING OBJECTIVE 5

Explain the concept of locus of decision making and when centralized or decentralized decision making might be appropriate.

Matching Integrating Mechanisms with Coordination Needs

It is important for an organization to develop an integration system that satisfies its coordination needs while minimizing the financial and managerial resources required to maintain the system. Without providing coordination that is necessary between work units in an organization, the organization might not be able to achieve its mission. On the other hand, coordination could be "overdone" to the point of interfering with the organization's operations, or it could simply cost more than the benefits it provides. Like everything else in the organization, this must be managed well.

KEY TERMS

Locus of decision making
The level of the organization at which decisions are made.

Centralized decision making
Authority is at the top of the organization.

Decentralized decision making
Authority is at the lower levels of the organization.

LOCUS OF DECISION MAKING

5 The third component of organizational design involves the locus of decision making within the organization. **Locus of decision making** refers to the level in the organization at which the authority resides for making major decisions. If the primary decision-making authority rests with corporate headquarters or the top levels of management of an operating facility, its organizational structure is said to be centralized. An organization that maintains its locus of decision making at lower levels, such as at the department or employee level, is decentralized.[52]

It is helpful to think of centralized and decentralized decision making as two ends of a continuum. The locus of decision making in most organizations is mixed, with decisions in some areas being relatively centralized and decisions in other areas being relatively decentralized.

Centralized and Decentralized Decision Making

Traditionally, **centralized decision making** has been associated with tight control at the top of the organization or organizational department. That is appropriate in some circumstances. However, if the top-level managers do not have all the appropriate information, it can hinder good decision making, and it can take a long time if the request for the decision has to go all the way up and down the chain of command. On the other hand, it is frequently argued that the people who are closest to the situation, usually referring to people at lower levels in the organization, could make better and faster decisions. The argument is that decision making should be **decentralized.** However, these people must have appropriate information and must be capable of making good decisions. Also, coordination between units may be hindered by decentralized decision making. Furthermore, the growing diversity of the workforce has increased the variability in decision-making styles.[53]

There are examples of organizations that have used both forms of decision making at different times in their history. Apple Computer, for example, has changed between a decentralized and centralized approach several times over the last three decades, depending on the organizational and competitive pressures at the time.[54] As discussed in the "Leaders In Action" box in Chapter 7, Edward Breen, the CEO brought to Tyco International in mid-2002, centralized purchasing from a very decentralized approach earlier and saved considerable amounts of money.[55]

John Brown, CEO of Stryker Corporation, believes that the locus of decision making should be flexible according to the circumstances. He has achieved remarkable success at Stryker, an orthopedic implant and medical equipment company, by both decentralizing decision making with some managers and retaining decision-making authority centrally when it comes to other managers. Brown drives decision making down to managers who are performing well and hitting targets. Those who are faltering, however, hear from Brown a lot more often.[56]

Although it is probably too simplistic, historically, the "popular" belief was that the decision to be centralized or decentralized involved a trade-off between control (characterized by centralized systems) and flexibility and responsiveness (characterized by decentralized systems). Today, however, we are learning how to manage ever-increasing complex situations, and advanced information technology can be used to resolve such trade-offs, allowing organizations to retain reasonable central control while decentralizing the decisions that are most critical to meeting the needs of customers[57] and providing instant information to improve the quality of centralized decisions.[58]

Many factors influence the degree of centralization or decentralization, but there are three main ones. They are the degree of stability in the external environment of the organization, the type of interdependence between work units, and the overall culture of the organization.

The Impact of Environmental Stability

The external environment for any organization can be characterized along a continuum ranging from stable to turbulent. In general, **stable environments** experience relatively little change, or the change is of low impact to the organization. This condition is associated with product life cycles being long and enduring, marketing strategies remaining relatively constant, and economic and political factors having little influence on the strategic or operational aspects of the firm. Competitive pressures are manageable, and changes in buyers' needs are minimal. Under these circumstances, most things are predictable. Although few industries would fit this description, some organizations do operate in relatively stable environments. For example, manufacturers of staple items such as detergents, cleaning supplies, and paper products enjoy relatively stable environmental conditions.[59]

Turbulent environments, in contrast, are characterized by rapid and significant change. An organization that faces turbulent environmental conditions must cope with shorter decision windows, changing buyer patterns, fragmented markets, greater risk of resource and product obsolescence, and a general lack of long-term control. Such conditions tend to be less predictable and intensify the pressure for organizations to respond effectively to change. For example, most computer-related companies (like Cisco, Unisys, Microsoft, and Dell) and other electronic product companies (such as Motorola and Samsung) face a relatively turbulent environment in which technological change creates competitive pressures for all industry players.[60] In addition, these industries tend to be crossing into each other. The key to success in such an environment lies in developing an organizational design that allows managers to identify and respond quickly to the opportunities and threats facing the organization.

In general, it is believed that organizations that operate in stable, predictable external environments find more centralization to be advantageous. This approach can be effective and efficient because things change slowly and they are predictable. In contrast, it is generally believed that organizations that operate in volatile and frequently changing environments need to be more decentralized because it allows the organization to respond to environmental change more proactively. However, for this to be successful, the people at various levels in the organization who make the decisions must be capable of doing so, must have the information, and must be coordinated well with the other parts of the organization that are impacted or must be involved in some way.[61] Refer to the discussion about delegating authority well in the previous chapter.

The Impact of Interdependence

As discussed earlier in this chapter, the type of interdependence between tasks or work units influences the type of coordination that is appropriate. When work groups are highly interdependent, such as with reciprocal interdependence, they either must be coordinated very well with some mechanism, or they could be coordinated with centralized decision making. A sequential interdependence can also be managed well with centralized decision making and authority because the work units must be kept in exact alignment with each other. On the other hand, pooled interdependence could be conducive to a decentralized approach as long as the work units are coordinated with an overall goal or mission.

The Impact of Organizational Culture

As discussed in Chapter 10, organizational culture refers to the dominant values or philosophy of an organization. In some organizations, the underlying philosophy, or belief, is that authority for decision making should be mostly kept toward the top. In others, the philosophy is to push it to the

KEY TERMS

Stable environment
An external environment that contains little change.

Turbulent environment
An external environment that includes rapid and significant change.

lowest possible level. With each philosophy and approach to centralization/decentralization, sometimes it works well; sometimes it does not. However, either approach could be made to work reasonably well as long as it is acknowledged that tasks are adapted to the approach, and people are selected for and trained/educated to work with that approach.

Certainly, people who work for Semco, Inc. ("At the Forefront" box in Chapter 7), where there is no formal organizational chart and people have great autonomy for making decisions, must be interested in and capable of making many important decisions. They must also deal with being held accountable for their decisions. On the other hand, an organization that is more centralized overall must be sure that appropriate decisions can be made in a timely manner.

Related to organizational culture that influences the relative degree of centralization is selecting and developing people who fit with the situation. When there is a higher degree of decentralization, capable people must be in place, either by proper selection and hiring or by training and development. Capable people must be combined with good delegation of authority, appropriate information, and rewards, all of which must support, coordinate, and control the decentralized decision making.

Multinational corporations have developed sophisticated management information systems to support global operations. Teleconferencing is a useful tool for a virtual, cross-functional team.

Implications for Leaders

Managers must be aware of the importance of organizational design to the long-term performance of the organization. The increasing availability and sophistication of technology will change the way organizations are designed and coordinated. The ever-increasing demands for quality will create additional pressures for achieving maximum efficiency and effectiveness in every aspect of an organization's operations. As more and more industries globalize, organizations will be faced with the challenge of coordinating their efforts across different nations and among diverse people. Effective leadership demands that one possess the competence to design organizations so that they are prepared to cope with and capitalize on a changing business environment. In preparing to meet such challenges, managers must

- Remember that organizational design provides an important mechanism for achieving the strategic and operational goals of the organization.
- Understand the makeup of the forms of organizational structure and under what conditions it would be appropriate to use each.
- Understand the potential advantages and disadvantages of the functional, division, matrix, and network structures.
- Look for ways to increase the integration potential of the organization or to reduce the need for integration.
- Understand the circumstances in which centralized or decentralized decision making would work well and how to use each approach.

Now we have learned how to design an overall organizational structure that will help us achieve the organization's overall strategy and mission. In the next chapter, we discuss finding and managing the right people to fit into the organization. Then, in the remaining chapters, we discuss the other basic components of overall management.

Meeting The Challenge

IBM: Changing Strategy and Structure

In mid-2005, Sam Palmisano, CEO of IBM, announced a major global reorganization of the company. This change was needed to support the change in overall mission and strategy. Although the company will definitely stay in the mainframe computer business, it will no longer be an IT (information technology) company. Rather, it now is a BPO (business process outsourcing) company. IBM wants other organizations to outsource major processes such as accounting, customer service, finance, research and development (R&D), supply chain management, inventory control, and human resource management to it. IBM wants to be the member of a network structure that provides services to the hub of the network structure.

IBM's focus now is mainly to provide services for other companies. Its new organizational structure is centered on grouping services into divisions with similar services or divisions targeted for specific industry customers. One division provides accounting services, another customer services and telemarketing, and so on. Another division is being developed to manage databases of patient information for health care organizations.

IBM will stay in the mainframe business. The hopes are that its new mainframe, named Danu, will reestablish it as the center of computing for large organizations. At the same time, IBM is doing R&D work for Honeywell International and Boeing; customer service for Nextel; human resources management for Proctor and Gamble; financial, customer support, telemarketing, and credit report work for Dun and Bradstreet; and others. The areas of supply-chain management, processing of insurance claims, and after-sales service are being developed. It seems to be working as a headline in the *Wall Street Journal* announced in mid-2005: "IBM's Earnings Hint at Recovery."

Sources: S. Hamm, "Two Pillars of IBM's Growth Look Shaky," *BusinessWeek,* 1 August 2005, 35–36; C. Forelle, "IBM's Earnings Hint at Recovery," *Wall Street Journal,* 19 July 2005, A3, A10; S. Hamm, "Beyond Blue," *BusinessWeek,* 18 April 2005, 68–76; P. Hemp, "Leading Change When Business Is Good," *Harvard Business Review* (December 2004): 60–71; D. Kirkpatrick, "Sam Palmisano," *Fortune,* 9 August 2004, 96; D. Kirkpatrick, "Inside Sam's $100 Billion Growth Machine," *Fortune,* 14 June 2004, 80–90; D. Kirkpatrick and S. Palmisano, "IBM Has a Vision Too," *Fortune,* 25 November 2002, 158–162.

SUMMARY

1. An organization's design serves as a mechanism for managing its tasks, functions, products, markets, and technologies effectively.
2. Organizational design determines the configuration of organizational members (structure); the flow of information, resources, and tasks throughout the organizational system (integration); and the centralization or decentralization of decision-making authority (locus of decision making).
3. Organizations structure their activities by grouping certain tasks and responsibilities into work units. The four primary forms of structure are functional, divisional, matrix, and network. Certain strategic conditions imply certain organizational structures. In general, an organization should employ a structure that is most conducive to achieving its mission.
4. An organization's need for coordination will be determined, to a large degree, by the level of interdependence among its subunits. Integrating mechanisms help coordinate the flow of information, resources, and tasks between work groups. Integrating mechanisms include general management systems (managerial hierarchy, rules and procedures, plans and goals), methods for increasing coordination potential (information systems and lateral relationships), and methods for reducing the need for coordination (creation of slack resources and independent work units).
5. Locus of decision making refers to the extent to which an organization centralizes or decentralizes decision-making authority.

REVIEW QUESTIONS

1. (LEARNING OBJECTIVE 1) What is organizational design? Why is it important for an organization to develop an effective design?
2. (LEARNING OBJECTIVE 2) What are the three primary components of organizational design?
3. (LEARNING OBJECTIVE 3) Identify and describe each of the four types of organizational structure discussed in the chapter.
4. (LEARNING OBJECTIVE 4) How does interdependence affect the need for coordination and integration? Outline the three major categories of integrating mechanisms.
5. (LEARNING OBJECTIVE 5) Explain the concept of locus of decision making. Under what circumstances would centralized decision making be appropriate? Under what circumstances would decentralized decision making be appropriate?

DISCUSSION QUESTIONS

Improving Critical Thinking

1. How might the organizational design of a research and development firm in the pharmaceutical industry differ from the organizational design of a consumer food products manufacturer?

2. Consider the organization you currently work for or one that you worked for in the past. Would you characterize that organization as having a centralized or decentralized locus of decision making? What are the advantages and disadvantages associated with the locus of decision making in that organization? If you had the power to change the locus of decision making, how would you change it, and why?

Enhancing Communication Skills

3. Suppose the dean of the College of Business hired you to coordinate the efforts of five different student organizations, each of which was affiliated with a different functional department within the college. What integrating mechanisms might you use to coordinate the activities of the groups? To practice your oral communication skills, make a brief presentation of your ideas to the class.

4. Identify a company that has a functional organization design at the top and one that has a product structure. Write an analytical report in which you explain why the structure is appropriate or not appropriate for each organization.

Building Teamwork

5. Think of a business that might be started on your campus to serve the needs of students. With a team of students, discuss how that business might be developed using a dynamic network system.

6. With a group of fellow students, identify an organization that could benefit from switching to being more of a network structure. Identify what the distinctive competency is or competencies are and which operations or functions could be outsourced. Develop a plan for managing the interactions between the center of the network structure and the other organizations that would support the center.

Chapter

9

Strategic Human Resource Management

CHAPTER OVERVIEW

"The one priority above all others in running a company today is to acquire as many of the best people as possible. And the biggest constraint on the success of the organization is the ability to get and to hang on to enough of the right people," so says Jim Collins, a highly respected management consultant and author.[1] If an organization does not have people with the knowledge, skills, abilities, and attitudes that are needed to achieve its overall strategy, it won't be successful. It won't be able to satisfy its customers. Coordinating and managing all the things that are necessary to find the right people and guide them toward achieving the overall strategy is called strategic human resource management (SHRM).

SHRM involves many other parts of overall management such as motivation, leadership, and communication, which are discussed in other chapters of this book. Although all managers need to understand the relatedness of these things to be successful managers, in this chapter we focus on the things that are normally managed or coordinated by managers who are specialists in human resource issues. We explore the major SHRM activities that help the organization attract, retain, and develop the quality and quantity of employees needed to meet organizational goals. The strategy of the organization both influences human resources and is influenced by human resources, as we discuss in this chapter.[2] Specifically, we examine the planning process involved in creating an effective internal organizational environment.

Specialists in the discipline of SHRM might coordinate and actually carry out many of the related details in forecasting, recruiting, selecting, and training, but every manager in an organization is directly or indirectly involved in all aspects of SHRM. Therefore, managers should be aware that their behavior and attitudes can and probably will influence many aspects of guiding people in their pursuit of the organization's overall strategy and goals.

LEARNING OBJECTIVES

When you have finished studying this chapter, you should be able to

1. Identify the components of the strategic human resource management planning process.
2. Define job analysis and explain its importance.
3. Summarize the different recruiting techniques used by organizations.
4. Clarify the major employee selection methods.
5. Discuss the different types of employee training.
6. Examine the role of performance appraisals in the organization.
7. Explain how compensation and benefits are used in organizations.
8. Describe the key factors of the legal environment in which human resource management functions.
9. Understand the importance of labor–management relations.

Facing The Challenge

JetBlue

In the short span of 6 years, JetBlue founder and CEO David Neeleman built a remarkably innovative company that has changed the rules of competition in its industry. JetBlue has gone from scratch to nearly $1 billion in annual revenue since 1999 and has forced its entrenched rivals to change tactics and strategies. It ranks among the industry's best operating margins, the highest percentage of seats filled, one of the top ratings for on-time arrivals, and makes a profit.

The real secret weapon of JetBlue is the employees, all of whom are called "crew members" (JetBlue lingo for employees), to emphasize the company-wide sense of teamwork. If you treat people well, the company's philosophy goes, they'll treat the customer well. "There is no 'they' in the organization. Instead, it's 'we' and 'us.'" The culture is based on "we succeed together or we fail together."

JetBlue's crew members aren't unionized. While insisting that they are not against unions, the leadership team makes it clear that they would prefer to avoid them. They believe if management and crew members trust one another and if people feel they're compensated fairly (in 2004 there was a 17% profit sharing), there's no need for a third party.

The work of JetBlue crew members transcends job titles. For example, all crew members help clean a plane when it lands. Employees traveling on their day off are expected to pitch in too, including the senior managers and the CEO. Like other practices at JetBlue, this involvement serves symbolic purposes as well as saving money.

JetBlue makes a very strong effort to find the right people and is highly selective. It looks for crew members who like people, not just certain people. In 2004 over 100,000 people applied for jobs, and JetBlue hired 1700.

The attention to employees is not to make them feel good or to keep them from unionizing. Ultimately, it's about building a system that consistently delivers a better experience to passengers, which is critical to JetBlue's survival. Despite evidence that the cost of a ticket is what matters most to airline passengers, JetBlue believes that it can compete on more than price. In some markets, its passengers are willing to pay fares that average $20 more than on competitors. The company believes that good service, delivered by passionate employees, will give JetBlue a lasting edge.

But as JetBlue grows, it relies more and more on employees who weren't there in the beginning, when the entire staff could fit in one room. That's why preserving the culture increasingly requires conscious effort, starting with orientation and emphasized in all training programs and strategic decisions.

On the first day of orientation, the CEO is the teacher. He explains the JetBlue brand, teaches how the company makes money, how each employee contributes to the bottom line, and how the numbers affect their profit sharing. He wants the group to know how important he considers them and their training.

Much about JetBlue is considered distinctive, from the enthusiasm of its employees to its relentless customer focus to its hip, slightly countercultural image. It depends on flexibility, speed, and a sense of intimacy with employees and customers alike.

Over the next 7 years, JetBlue expects to quadruple its workforce, growing from 6000 to 25,000 employees. Can it maintain the unique, passionate workforce as it evolves from a nimble startup into the bureaucracy that's required to manage a vastly more complex operation? This is the challenge JetBlue now faces.

Sources: J. Wyndbrandt, *Flying High: How JetBlue Founder and CEO David Neeleman Beats the Competition . . . Even in the World's Most Turbulent Industry* (New York: Wiley, 2004); B. Peterson, *Blue Streak* (San Francisco Portfolio, 2004); C. Salter, "And Now the Hard Part," *Fast Company* (May 2004): 66–73.

Introduction

To achieve the strategy of an organization, a certain set of actions, behaviors, and attitudes from the employees is necessary. To ensure the right behaviors and attitudes, an organization must have the "right" people who are guided by proper human resource policies and operations.[3] If this is done well, an organization will have people with the right skills and motivation to make the organization successful. The customers of the organization will be satisfied, and the organization will have a combination of people with the right skills and motivation and practices that would be impossible to imitate by another organization. The organization would have a sustainable competitive advantage.[4]

Figure 9.1 Strategic Human Resource Management Planning Process

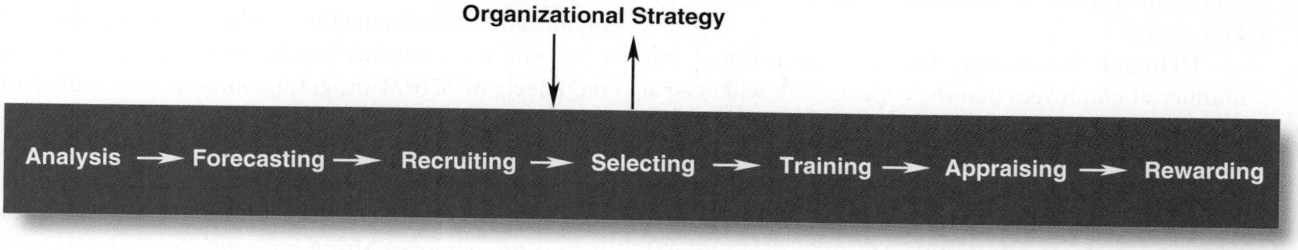

Strategic Human Resource Management

LEARNING OBJECTIVE 1

Identify the components of the strategic human resource management planning process.

1 Tying all of this together and focusing it on the overall strategy of an organization is called **strategic human resource management (SHRM).** This is all based on strategic planning and, as you recall from Chapter 1, the overall goals of the organization. Of course, main elements of these things are discussed in other chapters of this book. Here, we focus on the concepts and tools that are needed to guide the overall human resources planning process (Figure 9.1).

To begin with, we need to have some way to determine who the "right people" are, so we need to understand what knowledge, skills, and abilities are needed in each job through the process of job analysis.

ANALYSIS

LEARNING OBJECTIVE 2

Define job analysis and explain its importance.

2 **Job analysis** refers to studying a job in order to understand what knowledge, skills, abilities, and attitudes are needed as a foundation for the behaviors that would help the jobholder perform that job successfully.

To understand what behaviors are really required by the job, rather than what one might assume to be required, one must be very objective and careful when analyzing jobs. A salesperson's job in a retail store might require sincerely listening to customers and being able to interact with them well, especially if the company's strategy includes developing loyal long-term customers. A factory job might require skills needed to successfully engage in groups and group decision making, in addition to being able to operate certain equipment. A person's attitude and other personality characteristics may become a more important component of a job. The reason for this is that a person can be more successful if he or she fits into the culture of the organization, into the "way things are done." If a person really does not like working in groups or with very flexible work rules, then a culture that thrives on group work and flexible rules might not work well for the person. [5]

From the job analysis, a **job description** is established. The job description lists the tasks, behaviors, responsibilities, and other information that help explain the job. Related to this is the **job specification** that lists the specific knowledge, skills, abilities, and other employee characteristics that are needed to perform the job successfully.

Taken together, job descriptions and job specifications provide managers with a foundation for forecasting the supply of and demand for labor within the organization and for developing programs to meet the organization's human resource requirements. These activities are usually coordinated by or actually done by the human resource manager. Job descriptions and job specifications also help the organization comply with equal employment opportunity laws by ensuring that SHRM decisions are based on job-related information.

FORECASTING

An important aspect of SHRM planning is forecasting the demand for and supply of human resources for both short-term and long-term planning. Both types of forecasts require looking into the future. A significant demographic shift will

KEY TERMS

Strategic human resource management (SHRM)
Managing in such a way as to coordinate all human resource components and focus them on achieving organizational goals and overall strategy.

Job analysis
Studying a job to understand what knowledge, skills, abilities, and attitudes are required for successful performance.

occur in the coming years; the labor force will be older, with more minorities. By 2015 nearly one in five U.S. workers will be age 55 or older. The largest generation of American workers—76 million "baby boomers"—will soon retire.[6]

Demand forecasting involves determining the number of employees that the organization will need at some point in the future as well as the knowledge, skills, and abilities that these employees must possess. The organization's external and internal environments are the major determinants of the demand for human resources. For example, JetBlue is forecasting a growth from 6000 to 25,000 employees in the next few years.[7] Rapid technological change and the emergence of the global economy have created the necessity for profound change and the demand for a product or service, therefore requiring changes in a company's strategy and operations. As Hewlett-Packard moved into the digital entertainment market, an entirely new and different market for the company, it needed to identify the implications on the workforce. For example, the right designers, marketing people, and product specialists had to be identified, hired, and trained.[8]

LEARNING OBJECTIVE 3

Summarize the different recruiting techniques used by organizations.

Companies are increasing sales over the Internet. One reason for this is that the companies are developing the systems to do this. Another reason is that more and more customers are becoming comfortable with buying products over the Internet. Ultimately, this affects the need for employees with special skills.[9] In addition, demand is based on the organization's strategic goals and internal changes in the workforce, such as retirements, resignations, terminations, and leaves of absence.

Supply forecasting involves determining what human resources will be available both inside and outside the organization. Internal practices that affect promotions, transfers, training, and pay incentives are designed to meet demand with existing employees. To meet human resource demand, most organizations must rely to some extent on bringing in employees from the outside. Human resource professionals use labor-market analysis to forecast external labor supply. Together, internal and external supply forecasts allow the organization to estimate the number of people who will enter and leave various organizational jobs, as well as the effects of SHRM programs on employee skills and productivity.

After estimating the demand and supply of human resources, the human resource manager must reconcile the two forecasts. If a shortage is forecast, emphasis must be put on employee hiring, promotions, transfers, and training. If an excess is predicted, workforce reduction must be implemented. Although workforce reduction is a very serious issue, it tends to be one time or short term. Plus, if downsizing is done properly, it must include using the SHRM concepts and tools to identify those jobs that are no longer needed and the "right" people and jobs to remove from the organization. In the longer run, though, even those companies that downsize certainly have to continue to manage the remaining employees and probably have to add and replace people. Therefore, we turn our attention to recruitment.

KEY TERMS

Job description
Details of the responsibilities and tasks required by a job.

Job specification
A list of the knowledge, skills, abilities, and other employee characteristics needed to perform the job.

Demand forecasting
Determining the number of employees that the organization will need in the future as well as the knowledge, skills, and abilities these employees must possess.

Supply forecasting
Determining what human resources will be available both inside and outside the organization.

Recruitment
Finding and attracting qualified job candidates.

RECRUITING

3 **Recruitment** is the process of finding and attracting job candidates who are qualified to fill job vacancies. The qualifications are listed and explained in the job descriptions and job specifications, as we discussed earlier.

Recruitment can occur in a variety of settings, both inside and outside the organization. Both approaches have certain advantages and disadvantages. These are summarized in Table 9.1 and discussed in more detail below.

Internal recruitment involves identifying internal candidates and encouraging them to apply for and be willing to accept organizational jobs that are vacant. Methods of internal recruitment include job banks, employee referral systems, job postings, and advertisements in company newsletters. Every organization represents an internal labor market to some degree. Many employees, both entry level and upper level, aspire to move up the ranks through promotion. Promotion from within conveys a positive message that there are ways to move up within the organization. It becomes more feasible when companies invest in training and development activities. At higher levels, transfers can be an important development tool for acquiring additional job knowledge, as well as a means for upward mobility. Both promotion and transfer policies can create a favorable climate for attracting qualified employees and retaining valued ones.

Table 9.1 Internal versus External Recruitment

	Advantages	Disadvantages
Internal Recruitment	• Motivator for good performance • Causes succession of promotions • Better assessment of abilities • Increased commitment, morale • Lower cost for some jobs • Have to hire only at entry level	• Strong personnel development, training needed • Possible morale problems of those not promoted • Political infighting for promotions • Inbreeding
External Recruitment	• New ideas, insights • Possibly cheaper than training a professional • No group of political supporters in the organization already	• Selected person may not fit job or organization • Possible morale problems for internal candidates not promoted • Long adjustment time may be needed

UPS is one organization that maintains a policy to promote from within rather than recruiting from the outside. The company has a strong belief that employment longevity enables them to get experience across many different parts of the business. Such experiences and training delivers continuity. Most members of the company's executive team came up through the ranks, and they expect others to do the same.[10]

© MICHAEL NEWMAN/PHOTOEDIT

Recruitment is the process of finding and attracting job candidates who are qualified to fill job vacancies. Recruitment can occur both within and outside an organization.

External recruitment involves advertising for and soliciting applicants from outside the company. If internal sources do not produce an acceptable candidate or if it is decided that the best candidate would come from the outside, a wide variety of external sources are available.[11] These sources differ in terms of ease of use, cost, and the quality of applicants obtained.

External sources include walk-ins, public employment agencies, temporary-help agencies, labor unions, educational institutions, referrals from current and past employees, recruiting employees from competitors, newspaper and trade publications, and a growing use of the Internet. The source used will depend on the job skills required and the current availability of those skills in the labor market. For example, organizations frequently use external placement firms and private employment agencies to find applicants for upper-level managerial positions, but they look to educational institutions for candidates for entry-level managerial positions.

As technology develops, human resource managers are increasingly using computerized databases as well as the Internet. The Internet and employee referrals accounted for more than 61% of external hires in 2004 among companies surveyed by CareerXroads, a recruiting technology consultancy in Kendall Park, New Jersey. That figure has jumped in each of the past 3 years.[12]

The Container Store makes recruiting part of every employee's job, and all employees carry recruiting cards. Nearly a third of the company's employees come from referrals.[13] Employee referrals account for more than 40% at Cognizant Technology Solutions in Teaneck, New Jersey. These are primarily software engineers and MBA graduates with 6 to 8 years' work experience. Employees are rewarded with cash or reimbursement for external training.[14]

The search for high-tech workers has become increasingly difficult and controversial with the explosive growth of positions in technology. Many U.S. companies have developed a strategy of recruiting skilled workers from other countries, claiming that the labor pool of workers in the United States is not adequate. Opposing this strategy, many employee organizations claim that increasing the number of temporary visas issued to workers from other countries is a form of digital-age discrimination. They argue that the high-tech industries can pay lower salaries to temporary workers from other countries than they can to older and more experienced U.S. workers.[15]

A great company can't be built without great people, and that requires attention and commitment to the recruiting process.[16] According to a foremost authority on hiring, the best way to select people who will thrive in the company is to identify the personal characteristics of people who are already thriving and hire people just like them. To do this, it is necessary to understand star performers, identify their target behaviors and attitudes, and then use methods to find people with those attributes.[17]

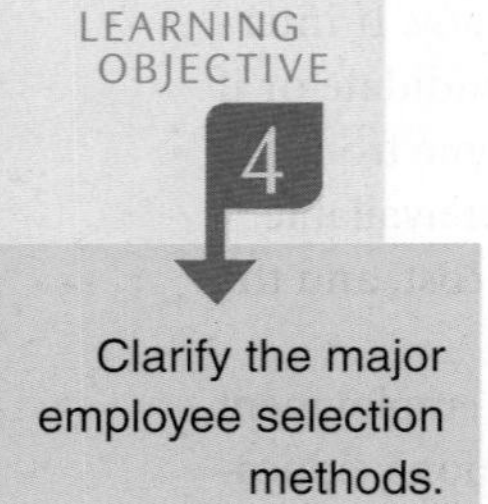

LEARNING OBJECTIVE 4

Clarify the major employee selection methods.

SELECTING

Selection is the process of evaluating and choosing the best-qualified candidate from the pool of applicants available for the position. It entails the exchange of accurate information between employers and job candidates to optimize the person–job match. Although organizations usually make these decisions, applicants also self-select into organizations that meet their requirements or choose to not join or to leave organizations that they think don't meet their needs.

At the heart of the selection process is the prediction of whether or not a particular applicant is capable of performing the job tasks associated with the position for which he or she is being considered. A wrong decision in either choosing a candidate who is not suited for the position or not choosing a candidate who would be very successful is costly. A "wrong candidate" is not productive and might have to be replaced. A "missed opportunity," not selecting a candidate who would have been very good, is a costly missed opportunity. Also, if a person is not selected for "nonvalid" reasons, illegal discrimination might be an issue. This could cause negative consequences in how the organization operates and could lead to a lawsuit.

To select the right person for a job, any method used to make an employment decision—for example, original selection, promotion, demotion, or selection for personal development—must demonstrate **validity.** That means the method must accurately measure or predict what it is intended to measure or predict. A strong relationship must exist between the selection method and some criterion. For example, if scores on a test are used to select a person for a job, then those scores must be associated with or predict performance on the job. An interview must be conducted in such a way that the person selected for the job as a result of the interview must be able to perform better than the person not selected. The same is true for all other employment or selection methods.

Now let's turn our attention to the more commonly used selection methods. Usually, some combination of the following methods is used. In any case, the methods must be used in such a way so that they are valid.

SELECTION METHODS

4 The **application form** and a **résumé** are usually the first sources of information about a potential employee. Both usually record the applicant's desired position and job-related qualifications and experience such as the applicant's educational background, previous job experience, and other information that may be useful in assessing the individual's ability to perform a job. Both the application form and résumé tend to serve as prescreening devices to help determine whether an applicant meets the minimum requirements of a position and allow preliminary comparisons with the credentials of other candidates.

Employers sometimes conduct background checks to evaluate the accuracy of information on the application form and résumé. Occasionally other things such as credit history and criminal record might be checked. Similarly, employers might contact references listed in a résumé, usually to check the accuracy of past employment or to ask for an appraisal of a candidate's past performance.

According to a Society for Human Resource Management survey, 69% of companies do some kind of a background check. This probably is wise because about 30% of applications contain misstatements of fact,

KEY TERMS

Selection
The process of evaluating and choosing the best-qualified candidate from the pool of applicants available for the position.

Validity
An employment tool must show that it predicts actual job performance.

Application form
A form used to gather information about a job applicant.

Résumé
Information prepared by a job applicant usually stating career goal, qualifications, and some related information.

usually claiming longer employment in previous jobs than was the case.

Background checks are costly especially in higher-level jobs. People who make employment decisions must therefore judge the extent of the background check. At the minimum, a manager would contact references listed on a résumé.

Tests

Any instrument, device, or information used to make an employment decision is considered an **employment test** by the EEOC's Uniform Guidelines on Employee Selection. An employment-testing measure is a means of assessing a job applicant's knowledge, skills, and abilities, for example, through written responses (such as a math test), simulated exercises, performance tests (such as a word-processing test), or verbal responses (such as a test of language skills). Regardless of what test is used, it should help select the best candidate for the position; that is, the test should predict the success of the candidate.[18] We discuss three categories of tests—written tests, performance tests, and personality (or personal characteristics) tests (Table 9.2). Although the personality test can be a written test, personality and personal characteristics can also be assessed through interviews and observations. We discuss the assessment of personality separately because it is being used with increased frequency and it may be controversial.

Table 9.2 Categories of Tests

Test Category	What It Measures	Example
Written	Knowledge	Driver's license exam
Performance	Ability, skills for a specific job	Assessment center, work sample
Personality	Characteristics, personality	Locus of control measure

Written tests usually are those that test knowledge, ability, skill, intelligence, or interest. They usually are called paper-and-pencil tests, although that title is outdated because many are now computerized. However, the tests still are designed to test one's knowledge about math, knowledge about a certain job or task, intelligence level, interest in certain types of careers, or other factors. If these tests are valid, the results of them predict job performance. A simple example of this type of test is the driver's license examination. It is presumed that the higher one's scores, the better driver that he or she is. Hopefully, the driver's exam is valid!

Performance tests require the job candidate to actually perform in the job usually some small part of the job or for a short time. Because performance tests are based directly on job analysis, they should accurately predict job performance. Performance tests consist of actual job behaviors. There are two common types of performance tests—work samples and assessment centers.

Work samples are more appropriate for jobs that might be more routine or more specific. For example, to see whether a person can install a computer, have the person actually perform the task. To judge whether a person might write creative and hopefully effective, advertisements, have the person prepare a portfolio (a collection or sample) of his or her work. If work samples are designed or selected well, then a person's performance in the work sample should accurately predict the person's performance on the job. In fact, work samples do show high validity scores, especially when compared to written aptitude, personality, or intelligence tests.[19]

Assessment centers are usually more appropriate to judge a candidate's predicted performance in a more complex job. For example, a candidate's readiness to be selected for a managerial position or to be promoted can be assessed by judging performance on a simulation of a group of tasks that a manager might actually do. The candidate typically is presented with a fairly large number and varying types of tasks to do. The tasks might include meetings to attend, speeches to make, decisions to make, among other tasks. This is sometimes called an "in-basket," referring to the tasks awaiting a manager.

The intent of the assessment center is to judge how a candidate would behave and perform in the selected tasks to predict performance as a manager. At the same time, the assessment center probably includes more tasks than can reasonably be done. This is usually included to see how the candidate selects which tasks to do and which to ignore.

In a typical assessment center, a team of managers, psychologists, and others trained in judging performance observe the candidate's performance and rate it. Assessment centers usually last several days, so they can be costly. However, assessment centers, like work samples, show good results in predicting performance in managerial jobs, so they may be worth it, especially for higher-level jobs.

KEY TERMS

Employment test
Any instrument or device used to assess the qualifications of a job applicant.

Work sample
A small part of an actual job completed by an applicant to predict performance on the job.

Assessment center
A type of simulation of a more complex or higher-level managerial job used to predict a job applicant's performance.

Personality tests are discussed here because increasing numbers and types of organizations are using some form of personality assessment to judge whether a person "fits," whether the organization hires the "right" people.[20] Studies indicate it is beneficial to hire people who already have characteristics and attitudes that are in line with the core values of the organization and with its culture. Teaching a person the details of a job is easier than teaching him or her to change deeply held attitudes or change personality characteristics.[21]

Personality tests include any method used to assess personal attributes or characteristics. It might be a written test that measures locus of control or self-esteem, an in-depth evaluation by a trained psychologist, or an assessment by an interviewer or a group of current employees.

Physical exams are required by many organizations. The physical exam is intended to ensure that a person is physically able to carry out certain job requirements. It also can be used to enroll employees in fringe benefits such as health, life, and disability insurance.

Drug tests are also used by some organizations, both for hiring and for continued employment. These tests tend to be very controversial. Occasionally, physical exams can be controversial also, depending upon how the information is used. The main thing to keep in mind with both physical exams and drug tests is that they must be important to the job.

Interviews

Interviews are relatively formal, in-depth conversations conducted for the purpose of assessing a candidate's knowledge, skills, and abilities, as well as providing information to the candidate about the organization and potential jobs. They are used for more than 90% of all people hired for industrial positions.

Interviews permit a two-way exchange of information. Most interview questions are straightforward inquiries about the candidate's experience or education. At Microsoft, however, prospective employees are asked questions that reveal the candidate's capabilities of (1) grasping new knowledge extremely quickly and generating acute questions on the spot, (2) possessing such familiarity with programming structures that a quick glance is sufficient for him or her to understand a long printout of code, and (3) having photographic recall of code that he or she has written. In other words, Microsoft is testing how the applicant thinks.

KEY TERMS

Personality test
Assessment of personality characteristics of a job applicant.

Interview
Relatively formal, in-depth conversations used to assess a candidate's readiness for a job, and to provide information to the candidate.

Related closely to the Microsoft example, many organizations use interviews to assess the job candidate's personal characteristics and attitudes to see whether the candidate will fit into the company culture. Carrying the interview a bit further, some organizations ask potential hires to make a presentation to current employees that solves an organizational challenge so that they can assess whether the candidate will function as part of a team.[22]

Interviews, overall, tend to have low validity. One reason for this is that although many people conduct interviews, many are not trained in how to do them well. Another reason is that interviews tend to be fairly informal, and no two are alike. This raises serious problems. In a typical interview, the interviewer draws a conclusion about the candidate within the first 2 minutes. The rest of the interview is spent looking for reasons to support the quick decision. Therefore, people who conduct interviews must take steps to increase their effectiveness. Typically, a structured interview format works best. This includes the interviewer asking the same questions, in the same order, and having the same type of information about each candidate in order to be more objective.

It is usually important for the interviewer to probe for more information and to follow up, based on what the candidate said, but this must be done carefully. If not done carefully, the interview could stray far from job-related issues. Also, the interviewer could easily be influenced by his or her biases, stereotypes, and previous information that the interviewer has about the candidate.

Interviewers can be effective by following these guidelines:

- Base the interview questions on a complete and current job analysis.
- Ask precise, specific questions that are job related.
- Avoid biases and making snap judgments, stereotyping, or looking for only negative or only positive information.
- Be careful about having a perception or stereotype of what the "good" candidate is.
- Be careful about making up your mind about the applicant in the first several minutes, as is usually the case.
- Avoid questions that can lead to discrimination (Table 9.3).
- Keep written records of the interview. Because there is questionable validity for interviews, they should never be the sole basis for selecting a candidate. Instead, they should be used along with other selection devices to provide additional information on candidates' strengths and weaknesses.

An interview can also include a realistic job preview. That is, the interviewer can explain to the job applicant what the job really requires rather than give just the positive points of a job or company and avoid the negative. For example, a candidate interviewing for a sales position might accompany a sales representative during a sales call in the field; a warehouse manager might observe warehouse operations; a training specialist might observe a training program and interact with participants. These experiences are important because they provide a sense of realism and greater accuracy of the job and the company than without a job preview.

Table 9.3 Interview Questions That Can Lead to Discrimination

Don't Ask	Ask This Instead
Are you married? Do you have children? Do you have child-care arrangements? What is your spouse's name?	Do you have any responsibilities that might conflict with job attendance or your availability for shift work?
What is your race?	No acceptable question.
What is your religion? Which church do you attend? What are your religious holidays?	Are you available for weekend work?
Are you male or female?	No acceptable question.
How old are you? What is your birth date?	If hired, can you prove that you are at least 18?
Have you ever been arrested?	Have you ever been convicted of a crime?
Are you a U.S. citizen? Where were you born?	Can you show proof that you are eligible to work in the United States?
Are you disabled? In your condition, do you think you can do the job?	Are you able to perform the essential functions of this job with or without reasonable accommodation?

TRAINING

Employees must know what to do in their jobs in order to perform well. Some or most of what they need to know may have been learned in some form of education or training before they got to the job. They might have a high school education, a college degree, a license, or experience in a similar job in the same or another organization. Or the job might require tasks that are quite new to them. In the latter case, training is obviously required. However, even with previous learning, a person will need to learn other duties as circumstances change in the industry. Also, new learning will probably be needed in order to move to a new job in the current organization or to move to a different organization. Some training will be necessary in almost every case.

Training is a planned effort to assist employees in learning job-related behaviors that will improve their performance. It is vital to the success of the organizations. This is evidenced by the fact that organizations spend $100 billion every year on formal training. The figure is much higher when all types of training are included. Rapidly changing technology requires that employees possess the knowledge, skills, and abilities needed to cope with new processes and production techniques.[23] Changes in management philosophy create a need for new approaches, skills, and knowledge.[24]

An organization's training needs can be identified through three types of needs assessment: organizational, task, and individual.[25] Organizational assessment determines where in the organization the training is needed; task assessment is what is to be trained; and individual assessment determines who needs to be trained based on actual versus desired skills.[26]

Types of Training

5 Once the training needs of the organization have been assessed, training must be designed and developed. The first step in the training process is to get new employees off to a good start. This is generally accomplished through orientation. **Orientation** is the formal process of familiarizing new employees with the organization, their job, and their work unit. Orientation procedures vary widely from organization to organization. Generally, their purpose is to enable new employees to fit in so that they become productive members of the organization. A newcomer may need several hours, several weeks, or several months of work with other employees to become completely familiar with the organization. In recent years, many organizations have realized that the socialization process begins

LEARNING OBJECTIVE 5

Discuss the different types of employee training.

in orientation and can make a significant difference to new employees. For example, at JetBlue, orientation is given a very high priority. Therefore, the senior leadership team and CEO participate in every new-hire orientation program.[27]

Technical training programs are designed to provide employees with specialized skills and knowledge in the methods, processes, and techniques associated with their jobs or trade. With advances in training technology, many organizations are using computer-assisted instruction and interactive video training. On-the-job training is conducted while employees perform job-related tasks. This type of training is the most direct approach and offers employers the quickest return in terms of improved performance.[28]

Management development programs are designed to improve the technical, interpersonal, and conceptual skills of supervisors, managers, and executives. On-the-job training for managers might include rotating through a variety of positions, regular coaching and mentoring by a supervisor, committee assignments to involve individuals in decision-making activities, and staff meetings to help managers become acquainted with the thinking of other managers and with activities outside their immediate area. Most of these on-the-job training methods are used to help managers broaden their organizational knowledge and experience. Some popular off-the-job training techniques include classroom training, simulations, roleplaying, and case discussion groups.

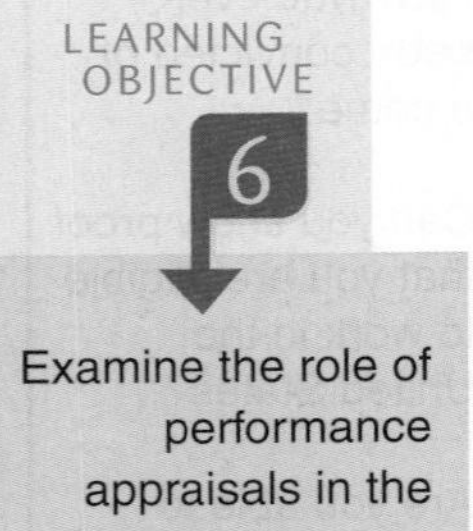

LEARNING OBJECTIVE 6

Examine the role of performance appraisals in the organization.

APPRAISING

6 Judging, or appraising, the performance of everyone in an organization is necessary so that the effort of everyone can be focused on achieving the mission of the organization. **Performance appraisal** is a systematic process of evaluating each employee's job-related achievements, strengths, and weaknesses, as well as determining ways to improve performance.[29]

Performance appraisals are valuable aids in making many SHRM decisions; they are essential for distinguishing between good and poor performers. Managers can use performance appraisal information in four ways:

1. *Motivation* Organizations try to motivate employees by rewarding them for good performance. This can be done by basing rewards, both financial (pay, bonuses) and nonfinancial (recognition, "pat on the back"), on good performance. Therefore, it is important to evaluate performance so that those rewards can be provided fairly and serve as a motivator for future performance. Merit pay plans, for example, are designed to compensate people according to their job performance.
2. *Personnel movement* Performance appraisal information helps managers develop an inventory of people appropriate for personnel movement. In other words, performance appraisals can be used to determine who should receive a promotion, transfer, or demotion, and who should be dismissed.
3. *Training* By identifying areas of poor performance, performance appraisals help the manager suggest training or other programs to improve certain skills or behaviors.
4. *Feedback for improvement and personal development* Performance appraisals provide a mechanism for

Organizations spend over $100 billion every year for formal training that assists employees in learning job-related behaviors that improve their performance.

KEY TERMS

Training
A planned effort to assist employees in learning job-related behaviors that will improve their performance.

Orientation
The process of familiarizing new employees with the organization, their job, and their work unit.

Performance appraisal
Any method used to assess a person's performance on the job.

giving employees feedback about their work performance. If employees are able to do their jobs better in the future, they need to know how well they have done them in the past so that they can adjust their work patterns as necessary for better performance or to get ready for a promotion.

Appraisal Methods

Effective performance appraisals usually consider various dimensions of a job. A variety of methods is available, but the most widely used approaches evaluate either behaviors or performance results.[30] Behavior-oriented approaches focus on assessing employee behavior based on the idea that certain behaviors will lead to successful performance on the job. Two commonly used methods are graphic rating scales and behavioral-anchored rating scales.

Graphic rating scales assess employees on a series of performance dimensions, such as initiative, tardiness, and accuracy of work, using a 5- or 7-point scale. For example, a typical rating scale ranges from 1 to 5, with 1 representing poor performance and 5 representing outstanding performance. The rater evaluates the employee on each performance dimension by checking the appropriate place on the scale.

Performance dimensions on a graphic rating scale tend to be fairly general and, as a result, the scales are relatively flexible and can be used to evaluate individuals in a number of different jobs. Because the graphic rating scale is general, considerable interpretation is needed to apply it to specific jobs. As a result, the scale sometimes produces inconsistent and inaccurate ratings of employees. In general, the more clearly and specifically the scales and performance dimensions are defined, the more effective is the evaluation.

To define various aspects of an employee's job more clearly, some organizations use behavioral-anchored rating scales (BARSs). BARSs are similar to graphic rating scales, but they use more detailed examples of job behaviors to represent different levels of performance. The BARS approach relies on job-analysis information to describe a range of desirable and undesirable behaviors for each performance dimension. Each of these behavioral descriptors is used as an anchor to distinguish between high, moderate, and low performance. Using BARS reduces subjective interpretation of performance because they are based on clearly stated job-related activities. They are costly to construct, however, and both subordinates and supervisors require training in their use.[31]

Results-oriented methods of performance appraisal are an alternative to the behavior-based ones. Results-based methods require the establishment of goals, targets, or results expected, and then a person's performance is judged against these.

Some organizations use **360-degree feedback** for performance appraisal. The approach includes feedback about performance from four sources: the supervisor, the subordinates, coworkers, and self-appraisal. Feedback from all these sources can give a more complete picture. However, this approach requires trust and communication skills. People need to understand how to give constructive feedback (see Chapter 11), and they must be comfortable with appraising their supervisor.[32]

Problems with Performance Appraisal

Although we would like to believe that every manager carefully assesses each employee's performance, most people who have given or received a performance appraisal are aware of the subjective nature of the process. This subjectivity can lead to the following common problems.[33]

Halo Effect The **halo effect** occurs when a manager rates an employee high or low on all items because of one characteristic. For example, a worker who has few absences might receive high ratings in all other areas of work, including quantity and quality of output. The manager may not really think about the employee's other characteristics separately. An employee may perform at the same level across all dimensions, but most people do some things better than others. Thus, the ratings should differ from one dimension to another.

Rater Patterns Managers may develop rating patterns. For example, some managers have a problem with central tendency. **Central tendency** occurs when the rater judges all employees as average, even though their performance varies.

Another common rater pattern is the leniency–severity error. A **leniency error** occurs when the rater evaluates some in a group higher than they should be or when the rater is unjustifiably easy in evaluating performance. In contrast, a **severity error** occurs when a rater tends to be unjustifiably harsh in evaluating employee performance.

KEY TERMS

360-degree feedback
Feedback from the supervisor, subordinates, coworkers, and self-appraisal.

Halo effect
Rating an employee high or low on all items because of one characteristic.

Central tendency
Judging all employees as average, even though their performance varies.

Leniency error
Evaluating someone in a group higher than the person should be rated or when the rater is unjustifiably easy in evaluating performance.

Severity error
Being unjustifiably harsh in evaluating employee performance.

A **contrast error** is the tendency to rate employees relative to each other rather than to performance standards. If almost everyone in a group is doing a mediocre job, then a person performing somewhat better may be rated as excellent because of the contrast effect. But, in a higher-performing group, the same person might have received only an average rating. Although it may be appropriate to compare people at times, performance appraisal ratings should evaluate performance against job requirements rather than against other employees.

If a manager bases an evaluation on the employee's most recent performance, it is considered a **recency error.** This is typically a problem when the evaluations are not frequent enough for the rater to recall performances over a long period of time. One way to help remedy this is to make weekly or biweekly notations on performance for all employees. When it is time for the performance review, information on the employee can be assembled with accurate documentation.

Eliminating the problems associated with performance appraisal is never simple. However, making raters aware of the potential problems through training programs is beneficial in overcoming the errors and the problems that result.[34]

© STONE/GETTY IMAGES

Incentive programs to provide good work/life balance might include an opportunity for employees to bring their dogs to work.

REWARDING

LEARNING OBJECTIVE 7

Explain how compensation and benefits are used in organizations.

Organizations must reward employees for doing a good job and for helping achieve the goals and mission of the organization. Frequently, when the word *reward* is used, we think of money. Certainly money is important, but there are very important nonmonetary rewards also.[35] Many of these nonmonetary rewards will be discussed in other chapters. For example, rewards like recognition, encouragement from the manager, coaching and mentoring from the manager, and supportive types of communication will be discussed in the chapters on motivation, leadership, and communication. Notice that many of these types of rewards are part of the manager being a good leader. Because these topics will be discussed elsewhere, we turn our attention to the direct and indirect aspects of compensation. The overriding goal is to design and implement equitable and effective reward systems.

KEY TERMS

Contrast error
The tendency to rate employees relative to each other rather than to performance standards.

Recency error
Evaluation on the employee's most recent performance rather than all of it.

Compensation
Direct and indirect payments to employees.

Compensation

7 **Compensation** consists of monetary payments and rewards that go to employees. This includes the direct financial payments such as wages, salaries, incentives, bonuses, and commissions. In addition, all indirect payments in the form of benefits such as insurance and vacation are forms of compensation.

Compensation rates are determined by an assessment of how valuable the job itself is to an organization, by economic forces in the labor market, by wages that competitors pay, by the level of education and specialized training needed, and in unionized firms, by negotiation.

To attract, retain, and motivate employees, organizations develop incentives programs. These incentives are designed to encourage employees to produce results beyond expected performance norms.[36] Traditionally, incentives were directly tied to performance such as profit-sharing plans and some form of stock options. More recently, many organizations are tailoring incentive programs to increase loyalty, decease turnover, and provide good work–life balance.[37] Read how David Brandon, CEO

Leaders in Action

PeopleFirst at Domino's

With turnover at 158%, Domino's CEO, David Brandon, realized the company was recruiting, hiring, and training 180,000 people a year. That was in 1999 when Brandon first took the leadership position. He vowed to make major changes and started by renaming the Human Resources department "PeopleFirst."

Brandon attacked turnover by focusing on store managers—hiring more selectively, coaching them on how to create better workplaces, providing access to financial data, and motivating them with the promise of stock options and promotions. To select better managers, Domino's implemented a new computer-testing process. Employees seeking a promotion to management are required to take a 30-minute online evaluation of their financial skills and management style. Candidates then receive training in specific performance areas. Technology systems were updated to provide managers with performance statistics and financial data tracking.

Brandon also introduced a program that grants stock options to about 15% of store managers, based on criteria such as sales growth and customer service. This is in addition to profit-linked bonuses that Domino's already had, which traditionally average about 30% of managers' compensation. Today, store managers' base salaries start at about $32,000. Brandon's strategy seems to be working. By 2005 the company's overall turnover had declined to 107%.

Sources: E. White, "To Keep Employees, Domino's Decides It's Not All about Pay," *Wall Street Journal,* 17 February 2005, A1; "CEO Interview: David Brandon—Domino's Pizza Inc.," *Wall Street Journal,* 11 April 2005, 1.

of Dominos, took an aggressive approach to turnover in the "Leaders in Action" box. Table 9.4 shows a sample of some creative incentive programs. Further discussion on the topics of incentives and motivation is in Chapter 14.

Benefits

Benefits are considered indirect compensation; that is, they are payments beyond wages or salaries that are given to employees as a reward for organizational membership. Benefits can be categorized into several types: required and voluntary security, retirement, time off, insurance and financial, and social and recreational. Examples of the benefits an organization can provide are listed in Table 9.5.[38]

Organizations commonly provide health, dental, disability, and life insurance coverage for employees and sometimes for their families. The costs of these plans may be paid entirely by the company or shared with the employee. Also, employees usually receive some pay for time that they don't work, such as vacations, sick days, and holidays. Retirement programs are also a common benefit.

Some organizations provide benefits such as counseling, wellness programs, credit unions, legal advice, tuition reimbursement for educational expenses, on-site child care, or emergency child-care arrangements. For example, M/C/C, an advertising agency in Dallas, Texas, built a Child Development Center that allows all employees to bring their children to work. The CEO contends that the center built loyalty, increased employee retention, and helped recruit new employees.[39]

A benefits package can represent a significant cost to an organization. However, it can be a key factor in attracting and retaining employees.

Most organizations attempt to develop a compensation system that carefully considers issues of equity or fairness. Compensation is often the prime reason that an individual works. However, compensation usually has several meanings to employees. It has economic meaning because it allows people to obtain the necessities and luxuries that they need and want; it is symbolic because it is a means of "keeping score" and a measure of achievement; and an increase in compensation indicates growth because it reflects how well employees' performance and capabilities have grown.

In practice, developing an equitable, or fair, compensation system is challenging, primarily because most organizations have very complex compensation systems. Equity theory, discussed in Chapter 14, is the basis for designing fair-pay plans. Compensation designers are concerned with three sources of fairness expectations: external fairness, internal fairness, and employee fairness.[40]

External fairness refers to expectations that the pay for a job in one organization is fair

KEY TERMS

Benefits
Indirect compensation given to employees as a reward for organizational membership.

External fairness
Pay in one organization is fair relative to the pay for the same job in other organizations.

Table 9.4 Creative Incentives Programs

SAS Institute Incorporated, Cary, North Carolina

- Provides performances of live music to keep its employees relaxed and healthy. Each day over lunchtime in the cafeteria of the company's headquarters, a pianist serenades employees with jazz standards, show tunes, and classical pieces. "The music doesn't cost a lot but adds a great deal to the company's culture," says Jeff Chambers, vice president of human resources.
- Operates several day-care centers and a summer camp for its employees' children at its 900-acre headquarters. Camp Awesome Adventure, for ages 9 to 14, features swimming, basketball, soccer, and nature hikes, among other activities.

Baystate Health System, Springfield, Massachusetts

- Sponsors 90-minute lunches, four times a year, during which employees with musical talent perform for their coworkers. The cost of that particular event is a few dollars per person for the food. Among the benefits is the opportunity for employees to network and get acquainted with peers, according to Anne-Marie Szmyt, director of work–life strategies.

Network Appliance Incorporated, Sunnyvale, California

- Installed a putting green and a beach volleyball court at headquarters for the company's employees to celebrate, relax, and exercise.

Orvis Company, Manchester, Vermont

- Offers employees free fishing classes and equipment that they can use during their breaks. The company, which specializes in fly fishing equipment, has a lake on its 377-acre property stocked with bass. "It helps align the associate with what we do and why we do it," says Mary Cheddie, vice president of human resources at Orvis.

MBNA Corporation, Wilmington, Delaware

- Provides newlyweds with limousine service on their wedding day, an extra week's vacation, and $500. Making employees "happier people" should also make them friendlier to customers, says spokesman Jim Donahue.

DDB Worldwide Communications Group

- Sponsors yoga classes in its conference rooms and on-site bicycles. In the firm's Paris office, it has a café serving wine and beer from the afternoon on, and the London office has a pub. In the U.S. office, beer is available to celebrate or to ease tensions during a hard project. Ken Kaess, DDB chief executive officer and president, considers these socializing opportunities a good way for employees to get to know each other. "Our whole business is based on people being able to work together."

Burton Snowboards, Burlington, Vermont

- Allows employees to bring their dogs to work, which a quarter of the company's 230 headquarters employees do everyday. "The humor and the morale boost that it brings far outweighs any lost productivity," according to Kathi Sporzynski, Burton's manager of benefits and compensation.

Source: Wall Street Journal Eastern Edition (Only Staff-produced materials may be used) by Jennifer Saranow. Copyright 2005 by Dow Jones & Co., Inc. Reproduced with permission of Dow Jones & Co., Inc. in the format Textbook via Copyright Clearance Center.

KEY TERMS

Internal fairness
Pay for the job within the organization is fair relative to the pay of higher- and lower-level jobs in the same organization.

Employee fairness
Expectations that individuals on a given job are paid fairly relative to coworkers on the same job.

relative to the pay for the same job in other organizations. Wage surveys are used to compare the organization's pay rates with other organizations in the industry to ensure that the pay remains competitive. **Internal fairness** refers to expectations that the pay for the job the individual is performing within the organization is fair relative to the pay of higher- and lower-level jobs in the same organization. Job-evaluation procedures use job specifications to determine the relative worth of jobs in the organization.

Employee fairness refers to expectations that individuals on a given job are paid fairly relative to coworkers on the same job. Differences in pay among coworkers are acceptable if the variations are based on differences in performance or seniority. Because compensation can be so complex, many organizations have compensation specialists in the human resource department who develop, administer, and oversee the compensation system. They ensure that the organization provides compensation that is both competitive and equitable.

Table 9.5 Examples of Benefits

Required Security	Voluntary Security	Retirement	Time-off	Insurance	Financial	Social and Recreational
Worker's compensation	Severance pay	Social Security	Vacation	Medical	Credit union	Recreational facilities
Unemployment compensation	Supplemental unemployment	Pension fund	Company-paid travel	Accident	House or car loans	Company publications
Old age, survivors', and disability insurance	Leave of absence	Early retirement	Holidays Sick pay	Group rates Disability	Legal services	Professional memberships
State disability insurance		Pre-retirement counseling	Military reserve pay	Life	Purchase discounts	Counseling
Medicare benefits		Disability retirement benefits	Social-service sabbatical	Auto	Stock plans	Sponsored events
					Financial counseling	Child care
					Moving expenses	Food services
					Tuition assistance	Wellness and health services
						Service awards

Disputes concerning fairness in pay have been one reason for legal issues surrounding human resource decisions. Certainly, pay disputes have not been the only reason, however. We now turn our attention to the legal environment of human resources.

Legal Environment of Strategic Human Resource Management

LEARNING OBJECTIVE 8

Describe the key factors of the legal environment in which human resource management functions.

8 One factor that has contributed to the increased importance of human resource managers is the number and complexity of legal issues faced by organizations. Federal and state laws that specify required, acceptable, and prohibited employment practices place many constraints on recruitment, selection, placement, training, and other human resource activities. For example, IBM sets recruitment and representation goals in accordance with federal guidelines and reviews them continually to make sure that they reflect workforce demographics. All companies with federal contracts are required to make this effort, but IBM extends the guidelines by setting diversity goals for its upper-level jobs and holding division and group managers accountable for reaching those goals.[41]

IMPORTANT LAWS

In an effort to reduce employment discrimination based on biases and stereotypes, Congress passed several laws

Table 9.6 Major Employment Laws

Law or Regulation	Year	Description
Fair Labor Standards Act	1938	Established minimum wage and 40-hour workweek; regulates child labor.
Social Security Act	1935	Established Social Security System.
Equal Pay Act	1963	Requires that men and women receive equal pay for equal work.
Title VII of Civil Rights Act	1964, amended 1972	Makes it illegal to discriminate on basis of race, color, religion, national origin, or gender.
Age Discrimination in Employment Act	1967, amended 1986	Prevents discrimination based on age for persons between 40 and 70.
Occupational Safety and Health Act	1970	Requires organizations to provide safe, nonhazardous working conditions.
Pregnancy Discrimination Act	1978	Broadens discrimination to include pregnancy, childbirth, and related conditions.
Americans with Disabilities Act	1990	Prohibits discrimination against persons with physical or mental disabilities or with chronic illness.
Civil Rights Act	1991	Amends and clarifies Title VII, Americans with Disabilities Act, and other EEO laws.
Family and Medical Leave Act	1993	Provides unpaid leave for care of family member, self, or child.

that directly address the problem of employee discrimination.[42] The Civil Rights Act of 1964, the Civil Rights Restoration Act of 1988, and the Civil Rights Act of 1991 are equal employment opportunity (EEO) laws that prohibit the consideration of race, color, religion, national origin, or gender in employment decision making. Other legislation, such as the Americans with Disabilities Act of 1990 and the Age Discrimination in Employment Act of 1967, prohibits employment decisions based on biases against qualified individuals with disabilities and the elderly. In general, the purpose of EEO legislation is to ensure that employment decisions are based on job-related criteria only. Toward that end, a substantial amount of legislation deals with various forms of employee protection. Table 9.6 summarizes the major federal laws and regulations that affect the management of human resources.

KEY TERMS

Bona fide occupational qualification
A qualification of a job that is legal to use even if it tends to rule out members of employee classes protected by Title VII.

There are exceptions to discrimination based on the protected areas listed previously. If a requirement of a job is very important in order to perform that job, then if a person in a protected class is not hired or promoted, it is not illegal discrimination. That is, if a **bona fide occupational qualification,** also known as business necessity, inadvertently discriminates, it is not illegal. For example, if a job requires certain physical strength, then it is not discriminatory to not hire someone if he or she does not have the strength, even if the strength level might be associated with gender or race or other biases. Managers have to be very careful here. The bona fide occupational qualification must be based on job analysis, not personal attitude, opinion, bias, or stereotype.

The most current piece of legislation to take effect is the Family and Medical Leave Act of 1993 (FMLA), which allows individuals to take up to 12 weeks of unpaid leave per year for the birth or adoption of a baby or the illness of a family member. Some companies have been slow to inform employees of their rights under this act because of the disruption that they perceive will happen in the workplace.

The Civil Rights Act of 1964 established the Equal Employment Opportunity Commission (EEOC). This organization is responsible for enforcing federal laws related to job discrimination. Although the EEOC can prosecute an organization that violates the law, it usually tries to persuade offending organizations to change their policies and pay damages to anyone who has encountered discrimination. To help organizations comply with federal employment regulations, the EEOC also publishes written guidelines that clarify the law and instruct organizations on their legal obligations and responsibilities. Current federal law prohibits discrimination on the basis of gender, age, physical or mental disability, military experience, religion, race, ethnic origin, color, or national origin. Check all of this out on the EEOC website, http://www.eeoc.gov.

Affirmative Action

Affirmative action refers to the legal requirement that federal contractors, some public employees, and private organizations under court order for short-term remedies must actively recruit, hire, and promote members of minority groups and other protected classes if such individuals are underrepresented in the organization. Individuals who fall within a group identified for protection under equal employment laws and regulations constitute a protected class. For example, if the qualified labor pool in a community is 20% African American and 12% Hispanic American, then 20% and 12% of the labor force of an organization operating in that community should be African American and Hispanic American, respectively, assuming that they are otherwise qualified.

Organizations often have patterns of employment in which protected groups are underrepresented relative to the number of group members who have appropriate credentials in the marketplace. To correct such imbalances, organizations may adopt affirmative action programs. An affirmative action program is a written, systematic plan that specifies goals and a timetable for hiring, training, promoting, and retaining groups protected by EEO laws and regulations. Although affirmative action is not synonymous with quotas, under federal regulations, all companies with federal contracts greater than $50,000 and with 50 employees or more are required to establish annual plans in the form of numerical goals or timetables for increasing employment of women and minorities.

In the past 10 years, there has been vocal opposition to affirmative action plans across the United States. California voters overwhelmingly supported the dismantling of the state's affirmative action programs. Similar actions have been passed in several other states. These initiatives banned race and gender preferences in public hiring, contracting, and education. Supporters said the goal was to create a color-blind society and eliminate gender preference in hiring. Opponents branded the initiatives as a negative attack on diversity and the needed affirmative action programs.[43]

Public institutions have created measures to manage the new mandates and have developed innovative programs to create opportunities for diverse populations while staying within the law. Many organizations have found that pursuing diversity for diversity's sake, rather than for the sake of good business, doesn't make sense.[44]

Workforce Diversity

Avon, Merrill Lynch, IBM, UPS, and Eastman Kodak are just a few of the organizations that have recognized the trend toward a more diverse workforce and have developed plans for managing that diversity effectively. Demographic changes in the workforce have forced organizations to introduce new SHRM programs, beginning with the recruiting and hiring of diverse individuals. The changing demographic profile of the available talent pool, such as the influx of women and minorities, is having a tremendous impact on the workplace. Women accounted for 60% of the total growth of the U.S. workforce between 1970 and 1985, and they made up a similar percentage of new entry-level employees between 1995 and 2004. Many of these women have children. In fact, the U.S. Census Bureau reports, in 2000, that 55% of mothers with infant children were in the workforce.[45] In addition, one third of the newcomers into the workforce between 1996 and 2000 were minority-group members.[46]

Diversity can be a competitive advantage if people in an organization are accepting of diverse perspectives and issues and are taught to work well together. For example, UPS has one of the most diverse workforces of any company. Minorities make up one third of the U.S. employee base and more than half of UPS's

KEY TERMS

Affirmative action
Emphasizing the recruiting, hiring, and promoting of members of minority groups and other protected classes if such individuals are underrepresented in the organization.

At the Forefront

Speaking Out on Diversity: Progress Energy

Progress Energy, a $9 billion diversified energy company headquartered in Raleigh, North Carolina, goes beyond talking about diversity. The company has an ambitious diversity program that started in 1999 with the establishment of the Corporate Diversity Council. The goal was to "harness . . . the diversity of our employees to not only improve operations, but to improve our workplace—because our differences will lead to success."

The council started with a company-wide survey to identify issues that needed to be addressed. All of its employees receive diversity training and participate in discussion groups in which they talk about diversity in all dimensions such as age, gender, race, sexual orientation, and disabilities. Participants talk about their experiences and help each other learn about and respect people's differences.

More recently, Progress Energy created a corporate diversity scorecard. This was a conscientious activity that will align diversity efforts with the company's strategic plan, leadership development, employee engagement, and retention.

The attention to diversity at Progress Energy's has been one of the issues that led to it being recognized for numerous awards.

Sources: See special advertising section, "Speaking Out On Diversity," *Business 2.0* (January 2005); http://www.progress-energy.com.

new hires. Minorities hold almost 30% of management positions. For 5 years, *Fortune* magazine has ranked UPS as one of the "50 Best Companies for Minorities." In addition, the UPS Community Internship Program deepens a manager's responsiveness to the needs of a diverse workforce.[47]

Diverse groups make better decisions, and for companies that operate globally, diversity means understanding minority marketing and customer relations in various ways that make big bottom-line differences. Progress Energy, our focus in the "At the Forefront" box, provides information about how it harnessed the diversity of its employees and its marketplace. But there are some challenges to managing a diverse work group. Considerable research shows that diversity in groups tends to reduce cohesion within the group, but innovation and performance tend to be good. The reduced cohesion could be a problem if adjustments are not made to deal with it.[48]

KEY TERMS

Sexual harassment
Actions that are sexually directed, are unwanted, and subject the worker to adverse employment conditions.

"Quid pro quo" harassment
Sexual harassment requiring sexual favors in exchange for positive job treatment.

Hostile environment harassment
Harassment produced by workplace conduct and/or setting that is considered to make an abusive working environment.

Sexual Harassment

A serious legal issue that organizations must be sensitive to is sexual harassment. **Sexual harassment** refers to actions that are sexually directed, are unwanted, and subject the worker to adverse employment conditions.[49] Part of the reason for the increase in complaints might just be that more people are aware of sexual harassment or that they can file a complaint. On the other hand, it might mean that there really is an increase in this type of harassment.

Sexual harassment or any type of harassment can disrupt performance in an organization and subjects some employees to unfair situations and treatment. These are serious enough reasons to be concerned about harassment and to learn how to get rid of it. In addition, it is illegal. The Supreme Court and the EEOC recognize two major forms of sexual harassment.[50]

The first is **"quid pro quo" harassment** in which sexual compliance is required for job-related benefits and opportunities such as pay and promotions. Harassment by supervisors and managers who expect sexual favors as a condition for a raise or promotion is inappropriate and unacceptable behavior in the work environment. The second form of sexual harassment has been termed **hostile environment harassment.** In this case, the victim does not suffer any tangible economic injury, but workplace conduct is sufficiently severe to create an abusive working environment. A pattern of lewd jokes and

Table 9.7 EEOC Guidelines for Preventing Sexual Harassment

- Establish a policy on sexual harassment and distribute a copy to all employees.
- Develop mechanisms for investigating complaints. The organization needs a system for complaints that ensures that they are satisfactorily investigated and acted upon.
- Develop mechanisms for handling accused people so that they are assured of a fair and thorough investigation that protects their individual rights.
- Communicate to all employees, especially to supervisors and managers, concerns and regulations regarding sexual harassment and the importance of creating and maintaining a work environment free of sexual harassment.
- Discipline offenders by using organizational sanctions up to and including firing the offenders.
- Train all employees, especially supervisors and managers, about what constitutes sexual harassment, and alert employees to the issues and behaviors involved.

comments in one instance and sexually oriented graffiti and posters in another have been viewed by the courts as sexual harassment.

Sexual harassment can occur between a manager and a subordinate, among coworkers, and among people outside the organization who have business contacts with employees. The vast majority of situations involve harassment of women by men although recent cases have involved harassment of men by women and harassment by someone of the same gender. More people are becoming increasingly aware of sexual harassment, and more research and writing is concerned with this issue.[51] Consequently, organizations are becoming more conscious of sexual harassment and are doing more to protect the rights of women and others who are victims. Training sessions, booklets, guidelines, and company policies regarding acceptable workplace behavior are some of the proactive methods for discouraging sexual harassment. Some actions suggested by the EEOC guidelines are listed in Table 9.7.

Certainly, the SHRM process is affected by the legal environment. Moreover, due to societal and political forces, the legal landscape of SHRM is constantly changing. Therefore, it is important for managers to keep abreast of which employment practices are permissible and which are prohibited. For example, many organizations have appearance and grooming rules and guidelines for employees, especially those who deal with the public. Although there have been cases of so-called appearance discrimination, businesses generally retain the right to require their employees to meet appearance standards. In contrast, there is growing pressure to prohibit employment decisions based on sexual preference.[52]

Labor–Management Relations

9 In many organizations, the strategic human resource process that we have been examining is affected by labor-management relations. The term **labor–management relations** refers to the formal process through which labor unions represent employees to negotiate terms and conditions of employment, including pay, hours of work, benefits, and other important aspects of the working environment.

LEARNING OBJECTIVE 9

Understand the importance of labor–management relations.

Given the turbulent history of labor–management relations, it should come as no surprise that the process of forming a union is closely regulated by the government. The National Labor Relations Board (NLRB) is the government agency that oversees this process in the private sector. It enforces the provisions of the Wagner Act of 1935 and the Taft–Hartley Act of 1947 (an amendment to the Wagner Act), two major laws governing labor–management relations. When recognized by the NLRB, unions have the legal right to negotiate with private employers over terms and conditions

KEY TERMS

Labor–management relations
The formal process through which labor unions represent employees in negotiating with management.

of employment and to help administer the resulting contract.

Unions have political power and use their lobbying efforts to support legislation that is in their own interests and the interests of all employees.[53] They can also provide workers with an opportunity to participate in determining the conditions under which they work. Studies have shown that workers who belong to a union perceive that they are treated with greater dignity and respect on the job than if they didn't belong to a union.

Management can pursue several different strategies in dealing with organized labor/unions. With a conflict orientation, management refuses to give in to labor and recognizes the union only because it is required to do so by law.[54] Managers can also use a more cooperative approach in which each party recognizes that the other party is necessary for attaining their respective goals. Recognition of shared interests has led to labor–management relationships characterized by mutual trust and friendly attitudes. Many organizations have established cooperative relations with unions in the hope that teamwork will boost productivity and quality and hold down costs.

Union membership has declined in the United States to less than 12% in the public sector and less than 8% in the private sector, continuing a gradual but steady slide since 1983.[55] There are several reasons for this decline. Effective SHRM practices in organizations have reduced the need for union protection. The very nature of high-tech industries also hampers organizing efforts. Many software designers and biotechnical engineers work for small start-up companies that unions find difficult and expensive to organize. Many young workers are taking jobs in the rapidly growing services sector, including banking, financial services, computer programming, and other types of services, that unions traditionally have not penetrated.

In some larger firms, workers are sometimes part of flexible teams that change tasks and work closely with management. This type of teamwork usually is associated with empowerment and leaves little role for unions to play. Other reasons for the decline in union membership include a decrease in union-organizing attempts, a decline in traditionally unionized industries, and a change in the economic well-being of organizations (making it more difficult for unions to pressure for better wages and benefits).

Some companies take a proactive approach to union organizing. Wal-Mart, for example, hired hundreds of staff members to support its in-store workers, managers, and human resources administrators. In addition, the company expanded the use of technology to improve communications between workers and managers and increased the frequency of its employee satisfaction surveys to keep tabs on potential issues and to gauge morale.[56]

As you read earlier in the chapter, JetBlue's staff isn't unionized. CEO Neeleman insists that he's not against unions and thinks that if employees feel they are compensated fairly and involved in the strategic direction of the company, there is no need for a third party.[57]

Implications for Leaders

In this chapter, you were introduced to the role of strategic human resource management in today's organizations. As a manager, you will be called on to make many decisions involving people. Therefore, it is important to remember the following points:

- Recognize that SHRM is a critical element of the strategic planning process and is essential for long-term organizational success.
- Keep in mind that job analysis is essential to understand what knowledge, skills, abilities, and attitudes each job requires.
- Carefully evaluate both internal and external sources for recruiting people.
- Base all SHRM decisions on job-related criteria and not on racial, gender, or other unjustified biases.
- To keep pace with rapid changes in technology, be sure to upgrade the knowledge and skill base of employees through training programs.
- Develop unbiased appraisal and reward systems that are effective and equitable.
- Be innovative in scheduling work, designing jobs, and rewarding employees so that you can respond effectively to the changing composition and needs of the workforce.

By managing human resources well, the organization will have the right people in the right jobs. The right people, guided and motivated to achieve the organization's goals and overall strategy, are the most important assets of the organization. The right people include managers who are successful leaders.

Meeting The Challenge

JetBlue

As JetBlue manages its growth, the company has standardized many things it does to avoid starting from scratch every time. For example, JetBlue has developed a checklist of what has to happen whenever it enters a new market. Everyone involved has access to the list on the corporate intranet. Each department sees what has been done, what remains to be done, deadlines, and problems.

These efforts also improve efficiency, which will be critical in the years ahead as JetBlue tries to offset rising costs for aging planes and more-senior employees. Low costs remain an obsession. JetBlue's reservation agents, for example, work from home rather than in an expensive call center.

To maintain the company culture while it grows rapidly, JetBlue has created an annual Speak-Up Survey of all crew members. They are asked how they feel, what it's like to work there, and what needs to be improved. The survey is considered an accountability tool that uncovers problems.

JetBlue tries to maintain the feel of a start-up by having senior officers practice "visible leadership." One of the reasons JetBlue has been so effective at building a dedicated staff is that visible leadership is a fundamental principle. To prevent management anonymity, each member of the leadership team is assigned one of the airline's destinations, a "Blue City." Once every 3 months, he or she visits that operation to meet with crew members and work alongside them. The visits help employees in the field form working ties to executives at headquarters. JetBlue wants to maintain the kind of culture where a customer service representative can pick up the phone and call a vice president at the company and get talk to him or her directly. In addition to flying JetBlue most weeks, they appear together at every first day of orientation for new hires.

Sources: J. Wyndbrandt, *Flying High: How JetBlue Founder and CEO David Neeleman Beats the Competition . . . Even in the World's Most Turbulent Industry* (New York: Wiley, 2004); B. Peterson, *Blue Streak* (San Francisco: Portfolio, 2004), C. Salter, "And Now the Hard Part," *Fast Company* (May 2004): 66–73.

SUMMARY

1. The components of strategic human resources management planning process include analysis, forecasting, recruiting, selecting, training, appraising, and rewarding. Job analysis is the primary process used for gathering current information about a job to understand what knowledge, skills, abilities, and attitudes are needed in order to perform well in the job. It involves assimilating all the information that is used to develop two important documents: the job description and job specifications.

2. Forecasting is determining the supply of and demand for human resources for both short-term and long-term planning. Two types of forecasting are used. Demand forecasting involves determining the number of employees the organization will need at some point in the future as well as the knowledge, skills, and abilities that these employees must possess. Supply forecasting involves determining what human resources will be available both inside and outside the organization.

3. Recruitment is the process of finding and attracting job candidates who are qualified to fill job vacancies. Both internal and external recruitment have certain advantages and disadvantages. Internal recruitment involves identifying potential internal candidates and encouraging them to apply for and be willing to accept organizational jobs that are vacant. External recruitment involves advertising for and soliciting applicants from outside the company.

4. Selection is the process of evaluating and choosing the best-qualified candidate from the pool of applicants recruited for the position. The major selection methods include application forms, employment testing, personal interviews, and sometimes, physical exams and drug tests.

5. Training is a planned effort to assist employees in learning job-related behaviors that will improve their performance. There is a variety of types of training. Orientation is the formal process of familiarizing new employees with the organization, their job, and their work unit. Technical training is designed to provide employees with specialized skills and knowledge in the methods, processes, and techniques associated with the job. On-the-job training is conducted while employees perform job-related tasks. Management development programs are designed to improve the technical, interpersonal, and conceptual skills of supervisors, managers, and executives.
6. Appraising performance is the process of evaluating each employee's job-related achievements, strengths, and weaknesses, as well as determining ways to improve performance.
7. Compensation consists of wages paid directly for time worked, incentives for better performance, and indirect benefits that employees receive as part of their employment relationship with the organization.
8. A key factor resulting in the increased importance of human resource managers is the number and complexity of legal issues faced by organizations. Federal and state laws that specify required, acceptable, and prohibited employment practices place many constraints on recruitment, selection, placement, training, and other human resource activities.
9. The increasing number of jobs in services and very flexible high-tech companies plus proactive SHRM practices may have caused declines in union membership.

REVIEW QUESTIONS

1. (LEARNING OBJECTIVE 1) Identify the components of the strategic human resource management planning process.
2. (LEARNING OBJECTIVE 2) Explain the importance of job analysis.
3. (LEARNING OBJECTIVE 3) Discuss the different recruiting techniques used by organizations.
4. (LEARNING OBJECTIVE 4) Clarify the major selection methods. What format is considered most appropriate?
5. (LEARNING OBJECTIVE 5) Discuss different types of training. How does an organization identify the need for training of its employees?
6. (LEARNING OBJECTIVE 6) Why are performance appraisals considered valuable in the organization?
7. (LEARNING OBJECTIVE 7) Explain the different ways the organization rewards employees. What are some of the common types of benefits used in organizations?
8. (LEARNING OBJECTIVE 8) Explain the key factors of the legal environment in which human resource management functions.
9. (LEARNING OBJECTIVE 9) Discuss some of the current trends in labor–management relations.

DISCUSSION QUESTIONS

Improving Critical Thinking

1. Explain why job analysis must be conducted first to be sure that the best-qualified people can be placed in a job.
2. Look for a current article in a newspaper or magazine that discusses a recent case of sexual harassment. Why is this a problem for managers?
3. Discuss why union membership is declining. Would you be interested in joining a union? Why or why not?

Enhancing Communication Skills

4. Obtain application forms from several different organizations. Include application forms from Internet sites. Analyze the forms and write a brief report that describes how the application forms differ and how they are similar. Point to any items that could be discriminatory. What are your impressions of the organizations based on the application form?

5. Examine the recruiting strategies of several organizations that you might be interested in joining. Create a chart to point out the types of employees that the companies hire and the variety of methods they use to recruit. Present your findings in a small group or to your class.

Building Teamwork

6. Develop a model of a college orientation program that provides all aspects of training that you think are important. Work in a small group as directed by your instructor. Present the group's model program to the class.

7. In a small group, create a detailed list of some of the best and worst questions asked of you in an interview. Are any questions common to several people? Work together to come up with some possible responses to the worst questions. Discuss how interviews can be improved.

Chapter

10

Organizational Culture and Change

© SUSAN VAN ETTEN

CHAPTER OVERVIEW

Change is an ever-present fact of life as companies respond to competitive pressures and capitalize on marketplace opportunities. The core of the matter involves the culture of the organization and the behavior of the people.[1]

When Louis Gerstner took over as CEO of IBM, he thought he could revive the company through a strategy of selling assets and cutting costs. He quickly found that those tools weren't nearly enough. He needed to transform the corporate culture. He focused on changing the behaviors of employees. IBM shifted from selling computer hardware to providing "services" and helping customers build and run their information-technology operations. Today, services have grown into IBM's core business and are the key to its success.[2]

Managers recognize that to build viable organizations, change must be viewed as an integral rather than a peripheral responsibility. After a decade of getting "leaner and meaner," organizations are also becoming "keener." Specifically, they are adopting new structures and practices to benefit from their competitive advantage. These organizations are developing their people and thereby the entire organization to keep up with the changes. If people in an organization can't change, that organization will die.

This chapter examines the issues associated with managing change, beginning with the organization's culture. We explore the components of organizational culture by examining organizational artifacts and then look at how culture affects the organization. Next, we turn our attention to the responsibility of bringing about change. We see that this can best be accomplished by analyzing the forces that drive change and those that resist it. Finally, we examine the processes and interventions that can be used to manage change and thereby develop the organization to be successful and meet its goals in the long run.

LEARNING OBJECTIVES

When you have finished studying this chapter, you should be able to

1. Discuss the foundations of organizational culture.
2. List and explain the two components of organizational culture.
3. Clarify the differences between the types of organizational artifacts.
4. Explain the impact of culture on the organization.
5. Explain how organizational culture can be changed.
6. Identify and discuss the targets of planned change.
7. Describe the framework for change.
8. List and explain the phases of planned change.

Facing The Challenge

Aveda: Culture in Balance

In an effort to stand off the ravages of time, most companies in the beauty industry turn to technology and chemistry for their instruments of war. However, Aveda turned the lifelong angst between age and beauty toward the first commandment of healing: Do no harm. The Aveda culture is evident in the commitment stated in the mission: "Our mission at Aveda is to care for the world we live in, from the products we make to the way we give back to society. At Aveda we strive to set an example for environmental leadership and responsibility, not just in the world of beauty, but around the world." To that effort, the company is committed to teaching employees and clients to release the habits that were so destructive to natural beauty.

Aveda is based on the principles of Ayurveda—the science of longevity. The commitment to longevity and nature is as evident in the organization's management style, stated in its beliefs (Table 10.1) as in its products. Employees are carefully recruited and then nurtured as much as trained in team and environmentally integrated business management. Holistic practices focus on retaining employees who would then teach customers to be loyal to the Aveda way. In addition, company policies dictate responsible environmental and safety practices and encourage the application of "pollution prevention, resource conservation, waste minimization, reuse and recycling practices."

When Estee Lauder acquired Aveda in 1997, it brought procedures and systems, written policies, and central purchasing that the company desperately needed to manage its growth. Lauder executives also brought a promise to Aveda employees that the holistic mission and culture would remain intact.

Sources: Aveda website (http://www.aveda.com); H. Rechelbacher, *Rejuvenation* (Rochester, VT: Healing Arts Press, 1987); H. Rechelbacher, *Aveda Rituals* (New York: Holt, 1999); GreenMoneyJournal.com 13, no. 53 (Winter 2004–2005).

Table 10.1 Aveda Beliefs

- We believe in treating ourselves, each other, and the planet with care and respect.
- We believe social responsibility is our responsibility.
- We believe ecological and profit goals are mutually achievable.
- We believe our authenticity and experience are our points of difference.
- We believe in inspiring and educating people to integrate wellness and beauty in their lives.
- We believe in the power of oneness: from our global image to a focused network.
- We believe learning never ends.
- We believe in encouraging innovation and empowered decision-making.
- We believe our actions, products, and services should always embody excellence.
- We believe personal and organizational balance is the key to sustainable success.
- We believe true leadership is delivered with passion and by example.

Source: http://www.aveda.com

Introduction

This chapter discusses organizational culture and change that are paramount to the organization reaching its goals. An organization's culture guides the behavior and actions of all employees inside the organization. Therefore, the culture needs to be aligned with the mission and the strategy. If not, the goals of the organization will not be achieved.

Change comes into play because it is pervasive in today's global and turbulent business environment. Organizations that survive accept change as a means of seeking new and better ways of doing business. In major changes, this might include changing the culture. In any case, change must be managed properly in order to train and teach people so that they can grow and develop to work successfully with the change.[3]

© ROYALTY FREE/CORBIS

Organizational cultures tell employees "what is to be done" and "how it is to be done."

Change comes in many forms. Transition involves a deliberate disturbance of the equilibrium and status quo and is a major event in the life of an organization and its employees. Most of the time, such events are drastic and intense, and the changes can be revolutionary and traumatic. Cultural change involves a disruptive break with the past and substantial changes in the way organizational members function.

Contemporary managers face extraordinary challenges.[4] As we have mentioned in previous chapters, today's dynamic, complex, and sometimes unpredictable environment demands that leaders and organizations take a proactive role in keeping up with and responding to change.

Change is a pervasive, persistent, and permanent condition. For many organizations, it is a huge threat and an opportunity for failure. Most change does not come in neatly defined segments; it seems constant and unrelenting. Often that makes change a bigger threat because there is no relief, no easy measure of success, and no sense of closure. Resisting change is natural, but in today's world, failing to change can be deadly. Businesses that do not change and develop disappear.

Foundations of Organizational Culture

1 Culture guides the behavior of and gives meaning to organizational members. Therefore, it has a direct and powerful influence on what the organization does and on what the people in the organization do. **Organizational culture** is the shared beliefs, values, and norms that bind people together and help them make sense of the systems within an organization. The beliefs, values, and norms tell people "what is to be done" and "how it is to be done." Cultures develop within organizations as their people interact and share ways of managing and coping.

Culture influences how people act in organizations—the ways employees relate to each other, to customers, to shareholders, and to business partners. It drives behaviors and unites employees around a shared set of values.[5] The strong culture of Aveda that we discussed in "Facing the Challenge" helped it rise to its success. The commitment to employees and long-held values of holistic practices and environmental responsibility are central to its culture.[6] That is why an increasing number of organizations today are creating a positive and supportive working environment and, as a result, a great place for customers to shop and do business.

Consider, for example, The Container Store, an organization that has consistently landed at the top of *Fortune* magazine's annual list of "100 Best Companies to Work For."[7] Founders Kip Tindell and Garrett Boone created a culture that recognizes employees as the company's greatest asset.[8] The founders' commitment to employees, their principled way of doing business, and the culture of this successful organization are described further in the "At the Forefront" box.

Cultures develop from a variety of factors. When a new organization is formed, the culture reflects the drive and imagination of the founding individual or group. Amazon.com founder and CEO Jeff Bezos prefers customers to visualize the virtual company on the Internet rather than at a physical location. Although customers never see the person whom they communicate with, a sense of personalization has been built from a culture of trust and comfort within Amazon.com.[9] The culture at Walt Disney Corporation was influenced by its creative founder, Walt Disney, who created entertainment that was focused on family values and traditional beliefs. Wal-Mart's culture remains distinctly Sam Walton.[10]

LEARNING OBJECTIVE 1

Discuss the foundations of organizational culture.

Cultures evolve and change in even the most stable periods. In times of trouble, they may change rapidly because, whatever else the culture may value, it prizes survival most of all. Economic crises, changes in

KEY TERMS

Organizational culture
The shared beliefs, values, and norms in an organization.

At the Forefront

The Container Store

In 1978 cofounders Kip Tindell (CEO and president) and Garrett Boone (chairman) opened the first The Container Store (TCS) devoted to offering an exceptional mix of storage and organizational products that would help people save time, space, and money. The privately held company has continued to expand strategically from coast to coast for 26 years, and retail sales have experienced healthy increases yearly.

TCS's goal never has been growth for growth's sake. Rather, it is to adhere to a fundamental set of business values, centered around deliberate merchandising, superior customer service, and constant employee input. The founders' commitment to its employees and their principled way of doing business have created a culture that has landed TCS at the top of *Fortune* magazine's annual list of "100 Best Companies to Work For". It was ranked as the third-best place in America to work in 2004, ranked second in 2003, and first in 2000 and 1999. Employees are recognized as the company's greatest asset and often described as motivated and enthusiastic. One of TCS's core business philosophies is that one great person equals three good people. It focuses on hiring only great people. Nearly a third of the company's employees come from referrals. Recruiting is part of everybody's job, and all employees carry recruiting cards. Staff members receive bonuses for every worker who is hired.

A major culture difference that TCS has over other retail companies is its philosophy and commitment to employee development. TCS matches employees' strengths with the needs and provides over 230 hours of training for new hires their first year.

TCS is known for its unique culture as well as a fun, high-energy work environment. It offers weekly yoga sessions free to employees, with 25% of the company's workforce attending. The company's official mascot is Gumby—a fitting symbol for the company's workers bending over backward to please customers and their coworkers. Other symbols of an employee-focused culture include monthly chair massages, stretching classes, and an online exercise and nutrition diary that is personalized for every worker.

Sources: L. Berry, *Discovering the Soul of Service: The Nine Drivers of Sustainable Business Success* (New York: Free Press, 1999); V. Powers, "Finding Workers Who fit," *Business 2.0* (November 2004): 74; L. Branham, "7 Hidden Reasons Employees Leave: How to Recognize the Subtle Signs and Act before It's Too Late," AMACOM, 2004; J. Gavin and R. Mason, "The Virtuous Organization: The Value of Happiness in the Workplace," *Organizational Dynamics,* 33 (December 2004): 379–392; TCS website: http://www.containerstore.com.

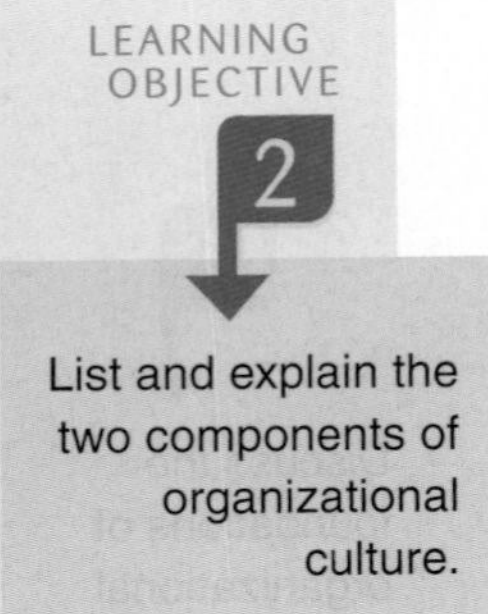

laws or regulations, social developments, global competition, demographic trends, explosive technological changes, and other events influence what an organization must do to survive, and its culture tends to evolve accordingly.[11]

Cultures also change when an organization discovers, invents, or develops solutions to problems it faces. Successful approaches to solving problems tend to become part of the culture and are used whenever the organization faces similar conditions. For example, as we mentioned earlier, the culture at IBM was refocused on the customer and that gave the workforce and the leadership team a renewed sense of purpose.[12]

Components of an Organization's Culture

2 Culture has two components. The first is substance, which consists of shared systems of beliefs, values, expectations, and norms; the second is form, which consists of the observable ways that members of a culture express ideas. These components are shown in Figure 10.1. They are illustrated as an iceberg because the surface elements—the artifacts—are based on much deeper-substance elements.[13] The visible

Figure 10.1 Components of Organizational Culture

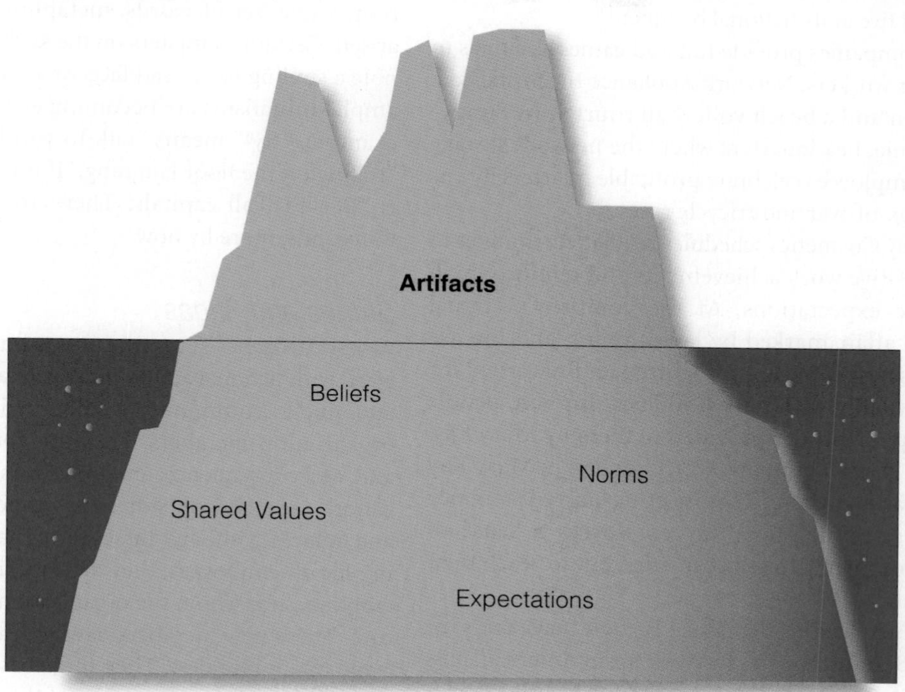

elements are the routines (practices) that constitute the organization's culture. These are sustained by the shared values, beliefs, expectations, and norms that are at the deepest level, or core, of the organization. Managers must recognize that it may not be possible to change the surface without changing what lies below.

EXAMINING CULTURE THROUGH ORGANIZATIONAL ARTIFACTS

3 The visible elements in Figure 10.1 consist of a number of artifacts. Artifacts are cultural routines, the rituals, and ceremonies that we see in public functions and events staged by the organization. Artifacts support and reinforce the organization's shared beliefs, value systems, expectations, and norms. Whether directed toward customers, employees, or both, events that tie into an organization's history are crucial to maintain its culture across small- or large-scale organizations.[14]

The artifacts level of cultural analysis is tricky because it is easy to obtain but hard to interpret. Although we can often describe the behavior patterns that are evident within organizations, it is hard to explain why these patterns exist.[15]

Rites, Rituals, and Ceremonies

Some of the most obvious displays of organizational culture are rites, rituals, and ceremonies. **Rites, rituals, and ceremonies** are a relatively dramatic, usually planned, set of recurring activities used at special times to influence the behavior and understanding of organizational members.[16] Evaluation and reward procedures, farewell parties, award banquets, and product promotions are examples. They are carried out through social interaction and usually occur for the benefit of an audience.

LEARNING OBJECTIVE 3

Clarify the differences between the types of organizational artifacts.

Through rituals and ceremonies, participants gain an understanding of and cement beliefs that are important to the organization's culture. Whether directed toward customers, employees, or both, events that tie into an organization's history are crucial to maintain its culture across small- or large-scale organizations. The "Be a Star" program at Compass Group North America—based in Charlotte, North Carolina—began in 1996 to promote the

KEY TERMS

Rites, rituals, and ceremonies
Relatively dramatic events that have special meaning for organizational members.

five core values: can-do attitude, diversity, teamwork, celebrating success, and quality. Every account sets five annual goals related to these values, and Compass honors units that attain all five at its national banquet.[17]

A few companies provide fun and games as rituals to support their workers. Network Appliance Inc. installed a putting green and a beach volleyball court at its Sunnyvale, California, headquarters where the network storage company's employees celebrate profitable quarters by engaging in tugs-of-war and tricycle races.[18]

Mary Kay Cosmetics schedules regular ceremonies to spotlight positive work achievements and reinforce high performance expectations. At the company's annual meeting, an affair marked by lavish pomp and intense drama, top salespeople are recognized and rewarded for high sales, usually with pink Cadillacs. Top salespeople praise the opportunities provided to them by Mary Kay, the heroine of the company. Until her death, Mary Kay herself was always there. This meeting-party is a major event that gives all Mary Kay employees a sense of purpose—not merely to sell cosmetics, but to reach their full potential.[19]

Most organizations that make *Fortune* magazine's list of the "100 Best Companies to Work for in America," plus thousands of others, also have a common theme of celebrating success through rites, rituals, and ceremonies.[20]

Language, Metaphors, and Symbols

Language, metaphors, and symbols are the ways that organizational members typically express themselves and communicate with each other. Language includes certain words, phrases, and speeches. Metaphors use familiar elements or objects to make behavior or other unfamiliar processes or actions comprehensible.[21] They include special terminology, abbreviations, jargon, slang, and gestures that can be unintelligible to outsiders but are used inside the organization to convey a sense of belonging or community. Symbols can be a picture, a shape, or a particular object.

For example, Levi Strauss management calls its open-door policy the "fifth freedom"; JetBlue's crew members (employees) respond positively to the company's belief that "if you treat people well, they'll treat the customer well"; the people who make the coffee at Starbucks are "baristas"; all the people at the Running Room are Team Members ; and Southwest Airlines' official "ticker" symbol, the official name that represents the company's stock in financial trades, is "LUV."

With the increasing use of electronic communication, a new set of words, metaphors, and symbols has arisen. Certain characters on the keyboard are used to denote a smiling face, a sad face, or a question mark, for example. Initialisms are becoming ever more popular. For example, "ttyl" means "talk to you later," and "rotfl" is "rolling on the floor laughing." If it is really funny, then it is "ROTFL," all capitals! There are hundreds, perhaps thousands, more by now.

Stories and Sagas

As narratives based on true events but frequently embellished with fictional additions, **stories and sagas** graphically and quickly communicate emotionally charged beliefs to organization members. They are apt to be entertaining and, as a consequence, are sometimes far fetched. Organizations are rich with stories of winners, losers, successes, and failures. Although these stories have important meaning for all employees, they are especially helpful for new employees for whom the organization is like a foreign culture. These new members have to learn how to fit in and avoid major blunders. Therefore, these organizational stories tell them the real mission of the organization, how it operates, what behavior is acceptable, and how individuals can fit into the organization.[22] For example, the founding of Southwest Airlines is celebrated in the following story:

> Early in 1967, Roland King consulted Herbert Kelleher, a corporate attorney in San Antonio, about legal matters pertaining to the dissolution of a small commuter airline owned by King. King was anxious to start another airline, and he believed that the major cities in Texas needed better air service. When he proposed his idea to Kelleher, the latter responded impulsively, "Roland, you're crazy. Let's do it." They went to dinner together and sketched out on a table napkin a simple triangle of a three-legged air route between Houston, San Antonio, and Dallas that became the original routes of Southwest Airlines. The napkin is now preserved in a wooden plaque hanging in Kelleher's office.[23]

Stories also serve as symbols of the organization's entrepreneurial orientation and promote values that unify employees from diverse organizational units. In many organizations, the members have a collection of stories that they tell repeatedly. Often one of the most important stories concerns the founding of the organization. Such stories may convey the lessons to be learned from the heroic efforts of an entrepreneur whose vision may still guide the organization.[24]

A story may become so embellished that it becomes a saga. Sagas are historical accounts describing the unique accomplishments of a group and its leaders or heroes. Many organizations, especially those with strong cultures,

KEY TERMS

Language, metaphors, and symbols
The way that organizational members typically express themselves and communicate with each other.

Stories and sagas
Narratives based on true events, frequently embellished.

Now Apply It

Culture Clash: Asking the Critical Questions

Whether you are searching for your first job or considering making a change in your career, consider how compatible you are with the company by examining the organization's culture. Culture clash is one of the biggest reasons that new hires fail.

The culture of a company can be a key factor determining whether you will succeed and be happy in your job. Although culture is intangible, there are several more important areas to consider than the job descriptions and compensation packages when weighing alternatives. The following are questions to ask that help you measure cultural fit during interviews:

1. Who are the company's star employees?
2. What are they like?
3. How long have they been with the company?

If stars run the best teams and foster a sense of team spirit, the company probably has a collegial culture. If they boast about individual accomplishments, the company may be very competitive.

4. How are yearly budgets developed?

This is often a clue to the way conflicts are resolved.

5. How are decisions made?
6. How does the leadership team communicate?
7. Do employees know the company mission and operating values?
8. Who are the founders, the company's early history, and its stories?

Firms, like people, often reflect their formative experiences, even many years later.

If you are particularly concerned about work–life balance, you might ask about a time when an employee's personal commitments conflicted with the immediate needs of the company and how the dilemma was resolved.

The information that you gain from asking questions can help you learn more about the corporate culture, but it won't guarantee that you will find all the information you need to make an informed decision. You can't fully understand the company culture until after you are hired.

Sources: E. White, "Savviest Job Hunters Research the Cultures of Potential Employers," *Wall Street Journal,* 29 March 2005 A5; K. Maher, "Career Journal: The Jungle," *Wall Street Journal,* 9 December 2003, D6; M. Siegel. "The Perils of Culture Conflict," *Fortune,* 9 November 1998, 257–258.

have a large number of sagas that tell about the exploits of the founder or other strong leaders. At Amazon.com, the premier e-commerce bookstore and retailer, sagas told by insiders feature the legendary creative accomplishments of the founder, Jeff Bezos, and the casual, friendly culture. One insider sums up Amazon.com as dynamic, hectic, casual, professional, and everything in-between all at once.

Are you searching for your first job or thinking about making a change in your career? The exercise in "Now Apply It" provides valuable information to help you understand how an organization's culture helps you succeed.

The Impact of Culture on the Organization

LEARNING OBJECTIVE 4

Explain the impact of culture on the organization.

4 In an organization with a strong culture, shared values and beliefs create a setting in which people are committed to one another and share an overriding sense of mission. This culture can be a source of competitive advantage.[25] Unique, shared values can provide a strong corporate identity, enhance collective commitment, create a stable social system, and reduce the need for formal and bureaucratic controls. A company named Trilogy (http://www.Trilogy.com) believes so strongly in the importance of culture that it puts all new employees through a 3-month boot camp, which is part of Trilogy University. The boot camp uses a method called action learning in which new employees work on real business problems under conditions with tight deadlines calling for intense teamwork. It serves as Trilogy's teaching, training, and orientation. While teaching the new employees about many parts of the company, it also teaches teamwork and the basic norms and culture. The intent of all of this is to prepare people to be ready for anything and to know the culture of Trilogy thoroughly.

Many other organizations, including General Electric, Cisco, Burger King, and General Motors, also have forms of boot camps or their own universities to teach many aspects of the organization, including culture. The basic issue is that culture must be aligned with the overall strategy and mission of the organization. If not, truly achieving the goals of the organization is much more difficult, perhaps impossible.

Companies with strong, formally articulated values that are focused on the needs of their constituencies have an important advantage over those without such values. For example, over its 155-year history, American Express has developed a strong sense of itself and what it stands for. The company's values have kept the company on course, regardless of challenges, and have helped American Express stand out in the marketplace. However, a strong culture can be a double-edged sword if it reinforces a singular view of the organization and its environment. If dramatic changes are needed, changing the organization may be very difficult unless the culture is also transformed. To avoid this potential difficulty, American Express has recently taken steps to renew its corporate values that has led to positive change and business growth.[26]

Many companies are striving to achieve high levels of performance coupled with high-quality customer service and satisfaction. To compete effectively, companies are increasingly hiring and retaining employees who fit the culture (see "At the Forefront"). Major investments in employee education and extensive training and development are important because they offer valuable benefits to both employer and worker. A common theme among *Fortune*'s 100 Best Companies to Work For is support for employee development and the encouragement of continuous learning.[27]

Read "Leaders in Action" and learn how the founder of Aveda, Horst Rechelbacher, created a holistic mission and strong culture that are still core to the company.

Two important issues are embedded in an organization's culture—ethics and diversity of employees. The culture strongly influences behavior of employees related to these issues as well as another very important factor—leadership behavior from the managers. How does it all fit together? Managers must use good leadership practices to be sure to introduce, develop, reward, and cement ethical practices and positive ways of working with diversity in the organization culture.[28] One of many examples of this is Carol Lavin Bernick, president of Alberto-Culver North America. She led a major culture change in her organization by implementing deliberate steps to focus on and to change the culture and make it part of everyday life in the organization. She further insists that the leader has to be passionate about it and must celebrate "what you'd like to see happen again."

Leaders in Action

Horst Rechelbacher, Founder of Aveda

Horst Rechelbacher founded Aveda in 1978 as a simple effort to bring healthy products into the hairdressing industry. Since that time, it has grown to be an exclusive line of more than 500 products, sold in approximately 10,000 professional salons and spas in more than 20 countries, with revenues expected to top $1 billion in the next few years.

Aveda was a labor of love, not only by Horst Rechelbacher but also by every employee. He came to the use of pure plant essence in all of his products quite naturally. Born just after World War II in impoverished Austria, Rechelbacher learned at the hand of his mother, an herbalist and naturalist. He devoted himself to the study of the relationship between the elements and essences of nature and their ability to balance if not counter the effects of aging.

Rechelbacher is proud of the financial success of the company, but money is not what drives him. Instead, he says that the company was part of himself, he was interested in feeling spiritually energized, and spiritual is how he behaves in the world. The underlying culture of the company is the belief that selfless service is a smart business decision.

Following the acquisition of Aveda by Estee Lauder in 1998, Rechelbacher became a more focused environmentalist, innovative business leader, author, speaker, and artist. For example, he started Intelligent Nutrients, a biodynamic and organic-based high-function food and nutraceutical corporation, and HMR Enterprises, which specializes in film, arts, and antiques.

Aveda has the experience of its parent company, Estee Lauder, to guide it and manage the more than 1100 employees. According to Aveda president Dominique Nils Conseil, the leadership values of Rechelbacher and Aveda's holistic mission and strong culture are still core to the company, and its founder continues to be the driving force behind the company.

Sources: H. Rechelbacker, *Aveda Rituals* (New York: Holt, 1999); GreenMoney Journal.com 13, no. 54 (Winter 2004–2005); D. Sack, "It's Easy Being Green," *Fast Company* (August 2004): 50–51; Aveda website: http://www.aveda.com.

Managers recognize that the world is changing at an unprecedented rate and everything is in constant flux, from the economy to markets. Just as cultures evolve, so do business organizations and their management styles. The workplace is beset by changes of all sorts from all sides. All the recent corporate strategies—pursuit of excellence, managing by walking around, reengineering, the learning organization, new organizational paradigms, and flattened hierarchies—are indicators of the evolutionary process. We now turn our attention to changing the culture of the organization.

Changing Organizational Culture

5 Changing an organization's culture can be very complicated. Management expert Peter Drucker suggested that managers can modify the visible forms of culture such as the organization's language, stories, rites, rituals, and sagas. They can change the lessons to be drawn from common stories and even encourage employees to see a different reality.[29] Because of their positions, top-level managers can interpret situations in new ways and adjust the meanings attached to important organizational events. Modifying the culture in these ways takes time and enormous energy, but the long-run benefits can be positive.

© JEFF GREENBERG/PHOTOEDIT

An organization's culture must be aligned with its overall strategy and mission. Employee training is important to ensure these connections.

Managers who strive for high-quality products and services understand that they must involve the keepers and holders of the culture, build on what all organizational members share, and teach new members how to behave. Sometimes managers attempt to revitalize an organization by dictating minor changes rather than building on shared beliefs and values. While things may change a bit on the surface, a deeper look often finds whole departments and key people resisting change. To be successful, change must be consistent with important values in the culture and emerge from participants within the organization.

The foundation of the Aveda Corporation's culture is a commitment stated in the mission statement: "To care for the world we live in, from the products we make to the way we give back to society. At Aveda we strive to set an example for environmental leadership and responsibility, not just in the world of beauty, but around the world."[30] When Estee Lauder acquired Aveda, it brought procedures and systems, written policies and central purchasing that the company desperately needed to manage its growth from 300 to 1100 employees, all the while keeping the holistic mission and culture intact. Aveda is an inspirational example of a culture that has staying power and continues to transform itself to meet demands and challenges over time.[31]

LEARNING OBJECTIVE 5

Explain how organizational culture can be changed.

The Leadership Challenge of Organizational Change

Change is essential to an organization's survival. Change leads to new ideas, technology, innovation, and improvement. Therefore, it is important that organizations recognize the need for change and learn to manage the process effectively. To be successful, the leadership team must be adept at taking their organization through major change by committing themselves to a better way, challenging existing norms, and taking risks.[32]

Organizational change is any alteration of activities in an organization. Alterations can involve the structure of the organization; the transfer of work tasks; the introduction of new products, systems, or technologies; or behavior among members.

KEY TERMS

Organizational change Any alteration of activities in an organization.

TARGETS FOR CHANGE

LEARNING OBJECTIVE 6

Identify and discuss the targets of planned change.

A variety of elements in an organization can be changed. Which elements are chosen is partly determined by the leaders' abilities to diagnose the organization's problems or opportunities accurately.[33] There are four primary targets for change: individual, group, organizational, and environmental.

At the individual level, organizations can target several areas. These changes fall under the general category of human resource changes; they include changing the number and skills of the human resource component as well as improving levels of employee motivation and performance. A manager may ask questions such as the following: Whom do we reward and how? On what basis will the reward be established—seniority, merit, innovation, bottom-line results, or other considerations?

Changes at the individual level may occur either as a result of new staffing strategies or because the company has embraced the strategic goal of recognizing and valuing diversity in the workforce. Individual targets are accomplished through employee training or development programs. For example, continuous training is an imperative at The Container Store, starting with a 240-hour training program for all new hires.[34]

Managers may consider changing the nature of the relationships between managers and subordinates or the relationships within work groups. This might include change or redirection of management leadership styles, group composition, or decision-making procedures. For example, when Intel Corporation opened its DuPont, Washington, plant, the assembly teams proposed a change in production scheduling. Team leaders and the plant manager suggested compressed, alternating shifts so that all workers rotated and the distribution of workdays would be more equitable.

LEARNING OBJECTIVE 7

Describe the framework for change.

At the organizational level, leaders can change (1) the basic goals and strategies of the organization, (2) the products, quality, or services offered, (3) the organizational structure, (4) the composition of work units, (5) organizational processes such as reward, communication, or information-processing systems, and (6) the culture. Consider whom the organization has to please. Is it customers, owners, shareholders, regulators, the media, or others? When? Nordstrom trains all employees to focus on service to the customer above all.[35]

An organization can also work to change sectors of its environment. As we discussed in earlier chapters, sectors in the external environment can be influenced and changed in a number of ways. For example, Weyerhaeuser modified its clear-cutting policy to meet community concerns before new forestry regulations were mandated.[36]

It is virtually impossible to change one aspect of an organization and not affect other aspects. Changes in products or services offered may require new technology, a new distribution system, new employee skills, or different relationships with consumers. Adopting new technology, such as using the Internet, has become an "e-wave," and it has changed the way organizations and customers learn about each other and communicate. It necessitates hiring different types of employees or revamping the corporate training system. Once again, the interconnection of systems and subsystems makes the job of management extremely complex and challenging.

KEY TERMS

Force-field analysis
A systematic process for examining pressures that support or resist a proposed change.

Leading Organizational Change

In recent years, a great deal of research and practical attention have focused on the necessity for change and the change process. If managers could design perfect organizations and if the scientific, market, and technical environments were stable and predictable, there would be no pressure for change. But such is not the case. We live in the midst of constant change.

Not only is change a constant of the modern business environment, but it is also becoming more complex, especially with continuing globalization. Organizations must manage change to be responsive to changing environments.[37] Managers must recognize that the forces of change are significant and pervasive. Learning to recognize and manage change is one of the most important skills that a manager can develop. Change is natural and managers must help their organizations work with it, not against it.

The following section examines the numerous issues involved with change. We examine the process as a sequence although in reality it may not always occur in that way.

A FRAMEWORK FOR CHANGE

One useful tool for understanding change is called **force-field analysis.** That approach is a systematic

Figure 10.2 Steps for Planned Change

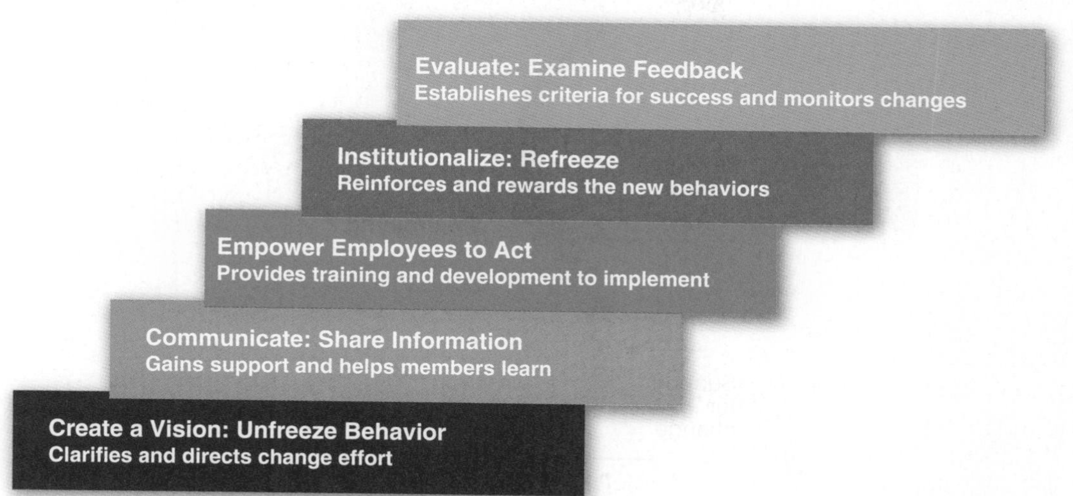

examination of the pressures that are likely to support or resist a proposed change. It is a framework proposed by organizational researcher Kurt Lewin, whose approach recognizes that merely introducing a change does not guarantee that the change will be successful. Force-field analysis includes the unfreezing process, how change occurs, and the refreezing process of new behaviors.[38] Within the framework for bringing about change, or transformation, in the organization are five phrases, as shown in Figure 10.2.

PHASES OF PLANNED CHANGE

8 The change process includes the following phases: (1) creating a vision, (2) communicating and sharing information, (3) empowering others to act on the vision, (4) institutionalizing the new approaches, and (5) evaluating.

Creating a Vision

Establishing a vision or goal is the first step in the process. The vision clarifies and directs the change effort and the strategies for achievement. In setting the vision, a number of critical issues must be considered.

The vision often triggers the beginning of the **unfreezing** process when an initial awareness of the need for change and the forces supporting and resisting change are recognized. Most people and organizations prefer stability and the perpetuation of the status quo. In such a state, forces for change, recognized as **driving forces,** are equally offset by forces that want to maintain the status quo, referred to as **restraining forces.** These forces are illustrated in Figure 10.3.

Driving forces for change are either internal or external. **External forces** are fundamentally beyond the control of management, but **internal forces** generally are within management's control. Changes in one or more of the key environmental sectors discussed in Chapter 4 might be the external forces that provide the impetus for change in an organization. The environment includes many economic, technological, political, and social forces that can trigger the change process. For example, in the economic domain, changes in the inflation rate, interest rates, and the money supply can affect the ability of an organization's managers to get needed resources. New laws and regulations, trade tariffs, and court decisions emanating from the political domain can affect the way an organization conducts its business.[39]

LEARNING OBJECTIVE 8

List and explain the phases of planned change.

KEY TERMS

Unfreezing
Developing an awareness of the need for change and the forces supporting and resisting change.

Driving forces
The forces that push for change.

Restraining forces
The forces to keep the status quo.

External forces
Forces that are fundamentally beyond the control of management.

Internal forces
Forces that are generally within the control of management.

Figure 10.3 Driving and Restraining Forces

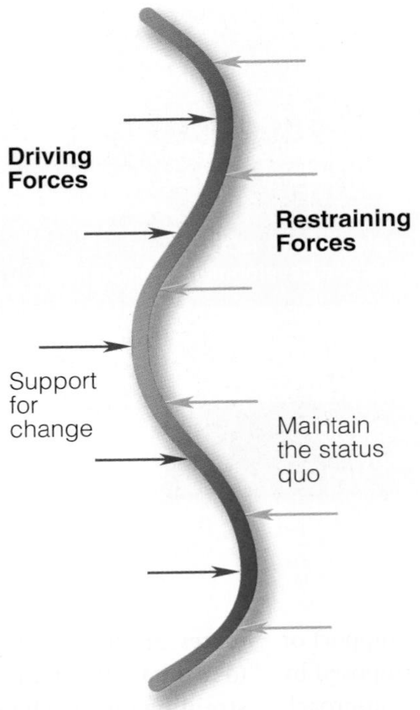

A vision can be initiated in response to internal forces at an organization. For example, in a Work USA Survey, workers who were contacted complained that workplace changes had an adverse impact on their workload and morale (44%); their relationship with the organization, such as satisfaction or commitment (37%); and the quality of the organization's products and services (23%).[40] Managers must recognize that external and internal driving forces can be highly interrelated. Because organizations operate as open systems, external and internal driving forces will always be connected. For example, employees' attitudes toward work may change because of a new organizational policy or as a result of new legislation. Additionally, employees must cope with changes in their personal lives as well as changes in the organization.

Regardless of the pressure these driving forces exert, the restraining forces are also important. People resist change for several reasons. First, they may genuinely believe that the change is not in their own best interests. They could be right, but often this belief is a result of fear of the unknown, habit, dependence, or the need for security. People may resist change because they lack the abilities or skills to cope with it. If proposed changes are going to require new skills, the organization must include skill training as part of the planned change effort.

Change can be threatening, and some individuals may assess the consequences of the change in a totally different way from those who are initiating the change. It may represent a loss and threaten vested interests such as power, responsibility, authority, control, or prestige.[41]

Finally, organizations have built-in resistance to change. Policies, rules, standard operating procedures, work methods, organizational charts, and job descriptions are examples of organizational infrastructures that serve to maintain the status quo. An organization's traditions, culture, and top-level management philosophy also resist change because they are developed over a long period of time and are not easily cast aside by organizational leaders. Changes that seem to violate the accepted culture will be more difficult to implement successfully than changes that seem to emerge naturally out of the culture.

Communicating and Sharing Information

The second phase in the change process is communication and information sharing. Communicating the new vision and the strategies that will be used is a valuable way to help organizational members learn to embrace change. New behaviors are learned from verbal, written, and nonverbal messages. Therefore, it is important for

The intent of the change process is to empower individuals to act on the institution's vision.

everyone to see and hear these messages.[42] For example, if the organization is establishing a work team environment, upper-level managers must act as role models for the new behavior.

The sharing of information and the messages sent to organizational members reduce resistance to change. Taking a proactive approach through open communication systems provides opportunities for a manager to listen to and gather feedback.

To gain the support of employees for the change efforts, management should consider their most commonly expressed concerns:[43]

1. *Information* Employees want the change described with answers to questions such as "What's going to happen? What does the change look like? What does it feel like?"
2. *Personal involvement* The change is already doomed if the questions "How will I fit in?" and "Will I survive the change?" can't be answered.
3. *Implementation* If answers to the first two sets of questions are provided, employees will be ready to ask: "How do I get started on the change?"
4. *Impact* Unless the first three concerns are resolved, employees won't want to hear about the possible benefits of the change. Expect questions such as "How will the change benefit us and the organization?" or "What will be different?"

Empowering Others to Act on the Vision

Often considered one of the most important steps in the change process is empowering others to act on the vision. This phase, the changing process, focuses on providing training and educational opportunities to help employees learn the new behaviors that they need to implement the vision. Many changes that occur in an organization, such as new equipment, policies, or products, are relatively easy to implement in isolation. However, major difficulties can arise when dealing with human reactions to such organizational changes or attempting to change human actions and relationships directly. For example, an organizational change that involves individual employees directly or indirectly can require changes in roles, technical skills, interpersonal skills, or values and attitudes.[44]

Groups must be encouraged to work as teams to solve problems and institutionalize ideas. Risk taking and nontraditional ideas, activities, and actions need to be encouraged and rewarded.

All these things are components of individual and organizational development. Individual development includes anything that helps an individual learn how to adapt to the change. It includes many forms of training from the organization, training or classes at educational institutions, mentoring from supervisors, and one's own learning from observation. Organizational development refers to teaching people to interact successfully with others in the organization. It includes group and team training, setting goals that coordinate with departmental and organizational goals, and anything else that helps people in the organization contribute in such a way that the organization overall is more successful. The intent of all of this is to improve and develop the people and thereby the entire organization.

Institutionalizing the New Approaches

The fourth phase is institutionalizing, or **refreezing,** the new approaches and behaviors. This step centers on reinforcing new behaviors, usually by positive results, feelings of accomplishment, or rewards from others.[45] Once management has implemented changes in organizational goals, products, processes, structures, or people,

KEY TERMS

Refreezing
The act of applying the new approaches and behaviors.

it cannot sit back and simply expect the change to be maintained over time. Laws of physics dictate that an object moved away from equilibrium will tend to return to the original equilibrium point unless new forces are present to prevent this. Lewin reminds managers that new goals, structures, and behaviors must be solidified, or institutionalized, if that change is to become the new status quo.

Behaviors that are positively reinforced tend to be repeated; therefore, new behaviors must be rewarded. In planning for change, attention must be paid to how the new behaviors will be reinforced and rewarded. Reward systems should be considered carefully and redesigned when necessary. If the rewards or reinforcements inherent in the change fall short of employee expectations, the change will likely fail.

In addition, the new way of doing things must be embedded in the culture or in the "new" culture, as the case may be. This includes rewards, as discussed previously. However, it also includes changing goals, policies, rules, performance appraisal, and perhaps mostly, the behavior of the manager. Here again, the leader has to establish the tone that sets or influences the culture.

Evaluating

The final phase in the change process is an important and often overlooked one—evaluation. Management needs to know whether the change has had the intended effects. Too many managers install changes, undertake training programs, and redesign structures with the mistaken belief that, simply because the change was made, it will be successful. In many cases, this assumption proves incorrect. This is particularly true when the change was unilateral or was made without those affected perceiving the need for change. Sabotage of changes imposed by management has been known to occur in such situations.[46]

Evaluation is also beneficial because it forces the manager making the change to establish the criteria for judging its success before the change is instituted. Doing so provides additional guidance when planning the tactics for making the change. It also forces the managers to give careful thought to how the results of the change will be measured.

Implications for Leaders

This chapter has focused on the need for managers to understand the culture of their organizations and the role that culture plays in managing change. Culture includes the basic values, beliefs, and norms of the organization. The values, beliefs, and norms essentially dictate what the people in the organization do, how they do it, and what the results are. Therefore, the culture must be aligned with the overall strategy, or mission, of the organization, or the mission will not be achieved.

Cultures change through evolution in light of changes in activities, in response to changing internal and external events, or through revolution as the organization deals with major challenges. Change is especially difficult in today's business environment of global competitiveness, diverse workforces, and technological innovations. It is part of the manager's job to help the organization and its members overcome resistance to change. Doing this requires an understanding of both the organization as it currently exists and its vision of what it wants to become. Research suggests a number of activities that will help managers achieve effective organizational culture and change:[47]

1. Solicit input from those who will be affected by organizational change. Involvement is essential to accepting the need for change.
2. Carefully formulate the message regarding the need for and nature of organizational change. The success of the change process will depend on effective communication.
3. Assess the organizational environment and be sure that the tone and the tempo of the change fit the organization. Timing is everything.
4. Serve as a role model, a leader, for the behaviors sought by the organizational change. Actions speak louder than words.

Meeting The Challenge

Aveda: A Culture in Balance

Aveda now employees over 1100 people. It has grown to be an exclusive line of more than 500 products, sold in approximately 10,000 professional salons and spas in more than 20 countries, with revenues expected to top $1 billion in the next few years. Expansion in the international marketplace is concentrated primarily in the United Kingdom and Japan.

Owners, employees, and customers remain loyal to Aveda in large part because Estee Lauder executives have wisely not meddled with the Aveda culture of socially responsible behavior. Aveda salons operate on the premise that businesses have not only the responsibility but also the opportunity to enhance the longevity of all living species.

Aveda president Dominique Nils Conseil has made a commitment to the biosphere in every business decision that he has made since he came on board to lead Aveda in 2000. His goal is to prove that exercising values and following the corporate culture can lead to leaner spending, better products, and ultimately a better product.

Aveda is an inspirational example of a culture that has staying power and continues to transform itself to meet demands and challenges over time. The mission of Aveda is still core to the company.

Sources: Aveda website (http://www.aveda.com); D. Atkin, *The Culting of Brands* (New York: Portfolio, 2004); D. Sack, "It's Easy Being Green," *Fast Company* (August, 2004): 50–51.; GreenMoneyJournal.com 13, no. 53 (Winter 2004–2005).

SUMMARY

1. Organizational culture is defined as shared beliefs, values, and norms that bind people together and help them make sense of the systems within an organization. People in organizations develop cultures as they interact and share ways of managing and coping. Culture influences how people act in organizations. The ways in which people perform, view their jobs, work with colleagues, and look at the future are largely determined by cultural norms, values, and beliefs and develop from a variety of factors. When a new organization is formed, the culture reflects the drive and imagination of the founding individual or group, and it evolves and changes over time.

2. Culture has two components. The first is substance, which consists of shared systems of beliefs, expectations, values, and norms; the second is form, which consists of observable ways that members of a culture express ideas.

3. Artifacts are cultural routines that form the substance of public functions and events staged by the organization. Rites, rituals, and ceremonies are the most obvious displays of organizational culture. They are a relatively dramatic, planned set of recurring activities used at special times to influence the behavior and understanding of organizational members. Language, metaphors, and symbols are ways that organizational members typically express themselves and communicate with each other. They include special terminology, abbreviations, jargon, slang, and gestures that are almost unintelligible to outsiders but are used inside the organization to convey a sense of belonging or community. Stories and sagas are narratives based on true events but distorted to incorporate fictional embellishment. They graphically and quickly communicate emotionally charged beliefs to newcomers and are likely to be entertaining and sometimes far fetched.

4. Changing an organization's culture can be very difficult. Leaders can modify the visible forms of culture such as the language, stories, rites, rituals, and sagas and the lessons to be drawn from common stories. They can interpret situations in new ways and adjust the meanings attached to important organizational events. Leaders must involve the keepers and holders of the culture, build on what all organizational members share, and teach new members how to behave.

5. The targets of change include the individual, group, organizational, and environmental. At the individual level, the targets fall under the general category of human resource changes and include changing the number and skills of the human resource component as well as improving levels of employee motivation and performance. At the group level, the targets are the relationships between managers and subordinates or the relationships within work groups. This might include change or redirection of management leadership styles, group composition, or decision-making procedures. At the organizational level, managers can change (a) the basic goals and strategies of the organization, (b) the products, quality, or services offered, (c) the organizational structure, (d) the composition of work units, (e) organizational processes such as reward, communication, or information-processing systems, and (f) the culture. An organization can also work to change sectors of its environment such as its customers, owners, shareholders, regulators, media, or legal institutions.

6. The culture of an organization can have a significant impact. Unique, shared values can provide a strong corporate identity, enhance collective commitment, create a stable social system, reduce the need for formal and bureaucratic controls, and create competitive advantage. A strong culture can be a double-edged sword if it reinforces a singular view of the organization and its environment. If dramatic changes are needed, changing the organization may be very difficult unless the culture is also transformed.

7. A tool for understanding change is called force-field analysis. This is a systematic examination of the pressures that are likely to support or resist a proposed change. Force-field analysis includes the unfreezing process, how change occurs, and the refreezing process of new behaviors.

8. The five phases for planned change include (a) creating a vision, or the unfreezing process, in which clarification and direction toward the change effort start and the strategies for achievement are created, (b) communicating and information sharing, which involve helping organizational members understand and learn to embrace change, (c) empowering others to act on the vision, which includes training and development to implement the vision, (d) institutionalizing or refreezing the new behaviors, which includes reinforcing and rewarding the new behaviors, and (e) evaluating, which establishes the criteria for success and monitors the changes.

REVIEW QUESTIONS

1. (LEARNING OBJECTIVE 1) How does an organization's culture evolve?
2. (LEARNING OBJECTIVE 2) What are the two basic components of organizational culture?
3. (LEARNING OBJECTIVE 3) Why are rites, rituals, and ceremonies important for organizational members?
4. (LEARNING OBJECTIVE 4) How can culture influence an organization's competitive advantage?
5. (LEARNING OBJECTIVE 5) Suggest ways managers can change organizational culture.
6. (LEARNING OBJECTIVE 6) Identify and describe the targets of planned change.
7. (LEARNING OBJECTIVE 7) What is a force-field analysis? How is it used to understand behavior during a change process?
8. (LEARNING OBJECTIVE 8) Describe the five phases of planned change and provide examples. What is the purpose in each step?

DISCUSSION QUESTIONS

Improving Critical Thinking

1. Because managers cannot actually see an organizational culture, what aspects of the organization might allow them to make some guesses about the nature of the culture?
2. What steps of planned change are managers most involved?
3. Provide some examples of situations in which resistance to change ended in a positive alternative.

Enhancing Communication Skills

4. Suggest ways in which a manager can maintain a culture. To practice your oral communication skills, prepare a presentation using some examples from the organization in which you work or one with which you are familiar.
5. Why do people resist change? Write a brief paper that gives some examples of this concept.

Building Teamwork

6. Describe the major differences between cultures in
   a. A high school and a college or university.
   b. Different college or university classes.
   c. Different campus organizations.
   d. A government (public) organization and a private organization.
7. In a small group, discuss each of these settings and report your findings to the class.
8. Working in a small group, think of a recent change that has taken place at your college or university. Analyze the driving and restraining forces. Write down the key issues that should be considered and report your findings to the class or instructor.

part 4

Leadership Challenges in the 21st Century

Chapter

11

Communicating Effectively within Diverse Organizations

CHAPTER OVERVIEW

Poor communication is a common problem in many workplaces. Leaders sometimes become so focused on meeting deadlines and demands that they fail to share vital information with employees, ignore input, or choose ineffective channels for conveying key messages. Experienced leaders know this can result in costly mistakes, low morale, and even turnover.[1]

Managers must understand the importance of building and sustaining human relationships through interpersonal communication.[2] Studies show that managers spend from 66 to 90% of their time communicating. If they do not understand the processes involved in good communication, their best-laid plans can fail. The need for effective communication is even greater as organizations become more global, employees become more diverse, technology becomes more complex, and change is more persistent.[3]

This chapter focuses on effective communication in organizations. Effective communication helps an organization increase profits by helping everyone understand the overall strategy and how to coordinate all the parts. We start by defining communication and the basic components of the process such as the social context, sender and message encoding, receiver and message decoding, the message, the channel, feedback, and noise. Next, we address interpersonal communication including oral, written, nonverbal, and technological communication. Then we turn to some of the barriers that prevent high-quality communication. Cultural factors, trust and credibility issues, information overload, perception, and language characteristics all have the potential to lead to misunderstandings. We explore ways in which managers handle organizational communication, including formal and spontaneous communication. Finally, we conclude by focusing on how managers can achieve communication competency by improving their feedback and listening skills.

LEARNING OBJECTIVES

When you have finished studying this chapter, you should be able to

1. Explain the role of communication in the organization and why it is so complex for managers to understand.
2. Define communication and explain how to achieve high-quality communication.
3. Describe the components of the communication process.
4. Identify the primary categories of interpersonal communication.
5. Discuss the role of technological communication and information use in the workplace.
6. Address the primary reasons why managers communicate.
7. Explain the barriers that interfere with effective communication.
8. Discuss the types of formal communication channels.
9. Describe the principles for effective feedback.
10. Specify the guidelines for becoming a good listener.

Facing The Challenge

TDIndustries

The commitment at TDIndustries (TDI) has more to do with creating a positive workplace than with financial or corporate-growth strategies. TDI's vision is communicated to employees starting on their first day with the organization. It is reinforced by all the company partners and customers.

TDI, located in Dallas, Texas, is an employee-owned construction company that works on new and existing commercial, industrial, and multifamily housing. The company provides mechanical and electrical construction and facility management services in areas such as heating, ventilation, air conditioning, plumbing, electrical, process and high-purity piping, automation systems, and refrigeration.

Beginning in 1998, TDI has ranked in the top seven of *Fortune* magazine's "The 100 Best Company's to Work For." It has consistently been evaluated by its employees as having a trusting and positive work environment, having open communication processes, and treating all members of the organization in a positive manner. Employees are called "partners," signifying their common goals and shared rights and responsibilities.

The company's practices communicate that the commitment to people is more than rhetoric. Partners are TDI stockholders. Education is a paramount concern for the company. Partners are encouraged to participate in the numerous in-house training and educational programs; partners who complete 32 hours of training on their own time receive an extra day off. Tuition and fees are covered for any work-related course. Monthly business meetings inform all partners about the company's financial condition and productivity.

The company follows an open-book management philosophy. For example, it trains employees how to read financial reports, resulting in money-saving collaborations. When the North Texas Service Group discovered that fuel and truck-repair costs were skyrocketing, the members changed their driving habits to control costs. Such collaboration emerges naturally from a supportive environment in which people feel cared for.

TDI conducts all of its business practices based on a deeply held philosophy of servant leadership, a philosophical idea originated by Robert Greenleaf. In 1971 TDI's founder, Jack Lowe, Sr., began to practice the philosophy and invited all employees to gather at his home to discuss its meaning. This monthly exchange became a ritual in which employees and leaders openly exchanged ideas.

A culture of trust is evident at TDI, and it has enabled the company to deal effectively with several major challenges. For example, when the company determined that there was a need for understanding and training about such sensitive areas as harassment, discipline, performance ratings, and the use of corporate resources, it looked within the organization to fill the need. Because partners participate actively in designing and conducting their own training, employee teams were formed and charged with creating effective training systems and process. With the trust and full support of management, the teams wrote, produced, and acted in all the training videos that are still used today. This was a highly effective means to communicate the company culture and values from employees to employees.

TDI has always maintained an open-door policy and encourages partners to visit members of the leadership team at any time to discuss concerns with them. CEO Jack Lowe, Jr., refers to the ease at which partners connect with the leadership team as "no-door" policy because everyone, including himself, work in offices that are the standard, open-cubicle space arrangement.

"We are committed to providing outstanding career opportunities by exceeding our customers' expectations through continuous aggressive improvements." This is TDI's vision. With more than 1400 employees, TDI faces the challenge to continue this vision.

Sources: http://www.greenleaf.org; http://www.tdindustries.com; R. Levering and M. Moskowitz, "How We Pick the Best 100," *Fortune,* 24 January 2005, 97; R. Levering and M. Moskowitz, "The 100 Best Companies to Work For," *Fortune,* 4 February 2002, 72–74; R. Levering and M. Moskowitz, "The 100 Best Companies to Work For," *Fortune,* 10 January 2000, 82–93; S. Branch, "The 100 Best Companies to Work For in America," 11 January 1999, 118–131; J. Gavin and R. Mason, "The Virtuous Organization: The Value of Happiness in the Workplace," *Organizational Dynamics* 33 (December 2004): 379–392. http://www.tdindustries.com.

Introduction

Excellence in communication can do more to advance an organization or a promising career than almost any other factor. Ask managers, lawyers, systems analysts, health care providers, CEOs, and businesspeople to name the most important aspect of their jobs. Is it the technical aspect, or is it interacting with people? Most will agree it is interacting and communicating with people.

Every day, you will face communication challenges such as getting and giving correct information, developing strong working relationships, attracting new customers, working in teams, solving disputes, building consensus, giving feedback, instructing others, and creating communication networks. All this requires communicating effectively and understanding the complexity of communication.

Communication Complexity

1 Communication is the process that managers use to interact with subordinates, peers, supervisors, customers, suppliers, owners, the general public, and others. It is not surprising then that the ability to communicate well is a critical skill in determining managerial success.[4] This ability involves a broad array of activities including reading, listening, managing and interpreting information, serving clients, writing, speech making, and using symbolic gestures.[5] All these communication activities become more complicated with the integration of technology, increased diversity, and more globalization.

Whether it is a face-to-face meeting or an overseas transmission, communication is a complex process that requires constant attention so that intended messages—that is, intended meanings, understandings, and feelings—are sent and received. Inadequate communication is the source of conflict and misunderstanding. It interferes with productivity and profitability.

© TAXI/GETTY IMAGES

Effective organizational communication is a complex process that requires constant attention so that intended messages are sent and received properly. Video conferencing may make this process even more challenging.

Communicating effectively is much more than just saying or writing the correct words. How we communicate is affected by frame of reference, emotional states, the situation, and preferred styles of communication. Consider, for example, a time when you experienced frustration because you just couldn't get through to someone. It felt as if you were speaking an unknown language or were on a different wavelength. Communication is essential to management because it encompasses all aspects of an organization and pervades organizational activity; it is the process by which things get done in organizations. Yet communication is a complicated and dynamic process with many factors influencing its effectiveness.[6]

LEARNING OBJECTIVE 1

Explain the role of communication in the organization and why it is so complex for managers to understand.

First, communication is a process in which the senders, messages, channels, and receivers do not remain constant or static. Second, communication is complex. Even a simple two-person interaction involves multiple variables—such as the individuals, the setting, the experiences each person has had, and the nature of the task—that impact the efficiency and effectiveness of the process. Third, communication is symbolic. We use a variety of arbitrary words and signs to convey meaning to those with whom we are communicating. Although there is some agreement about the meanings of most of our words and signs, meanings change over time.

The objective of communicating is to create some degree of accurate understanding among the participants. Clearly then, communication skills are essential for managerial success. This chapter explores the ways managers communicate, both formally and informally. Like the other aspects of the business environment that we have examined, communication is affected by the changing environment. In particular, technology, global issues, and diversity in the workforce pose challenges to the way managers communicate, and we look at these challenges in some detail. Throughout the chapter, emphasis is placed on ways managers use communication to support organizational goals.

Exploring and Achieving Effective Communication

A division head writes a memo and distributes it electronically. A flag flies at half-mast at the post office. An army officer praises the accomplishments of the unit. A pilot

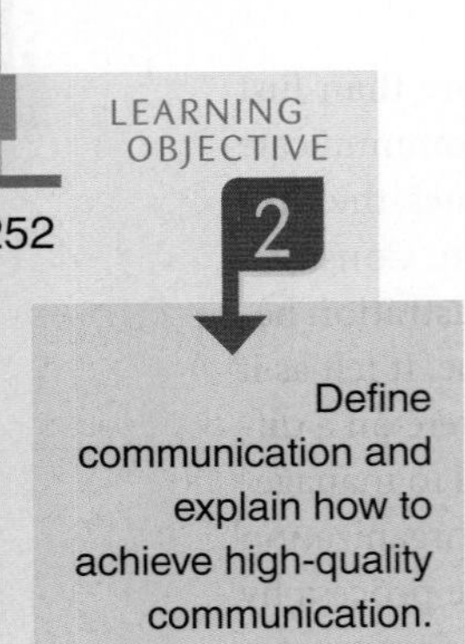

LEARNING OBJECTIVE 2

Define communication and explain how to achieve high-quality communication.

signals the ground crew that the flight is ready to depart. A professor writes a grade on a student's term paper. Employees in Seattle and Singapore attend a videoconference meeting. All these incidents involve some form of communication. But what exactly is meant by communication?

2 Communication is a complex and dynamic process, and like other management terms, it has no universally accepted definition. For our purposes, we will define **communication** as a process in which one person or group evokes an identical meaning in a second person or group. The meaning becomes shared by, or common, to both people or groups.[7] Indeed, the term *communication* stems from the Latin root word *communicare,* which means, "to make common." Defining communication is relatively simple, but achieving effective high-quality communication is complicated and difficult. Successful, high-quality communication results when the receiver of the message understands the exact meaning that the sender intended.

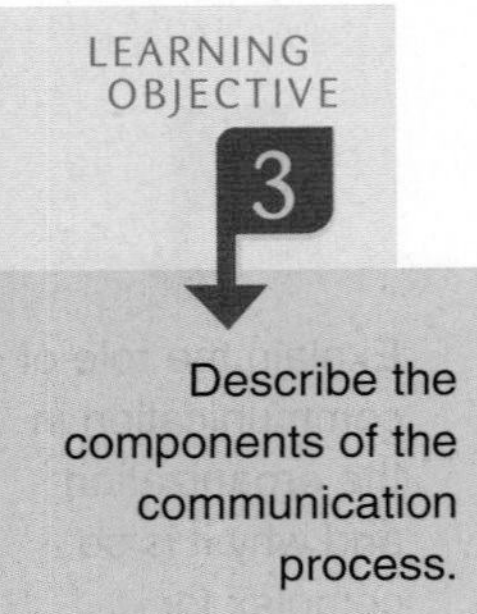

LEARNING OBJECTIVE 3

Describe the components of the communication process.

Components of the Communication Process

To improve the quality of communication, managers must understand how the process of communication works. The communication process begins when an individual or group has an idea or concept and wishes to make that information known to someone else. Let's explore the components of the basic communication model in more detail.

3 The primary components of the communication process are shown in Figure 11.1. They include the sender, the channel, the message, the receiver, feedback, and noise. Because the communication process does not occur in a vacuum, the social context in which the communication takes place is an influential variable that we include in the discussion.

KEY TERMS

Communication
A process in which one person or group evokes an identical or common meaning in another person or group.

Social context
The setting in which the communication takes place.

Sender
The person who initiates the communication process by encoding his or her meaning and sending the message through a channel.

CONTEXT: GLOBAL, DIVERSITY, AND TECHNOLOGY IMPACT

The **social context** is the setting in which the communication takes place. The setting has an impact on the other components of the communication process. For example, communication between a manager and a subordinate in the manager's office will be more formal and reserved than it would be if it occurred on the golf course. Fewer distractions may occur under these circumstances. However, the subordinate may be less inclined to give the manager candid feedback. The social context is an important consideration in light of the global nature of business and the diversity of employees' and customers' cultural backgrounds and the complexity of information technology. Conducting business in this arena presents many challenges to managers.

SENDER

The **sender** initiates the communication process by encoding his or her meaning and sending the message through a channel. The **encoding** process translates the sender's ideas into a systematic set of symbols or a language expressing the communicator's purpose. The function of encoding, then, is to provide a form in which ideas and purposes can be expressed as a message. Vocabulary, language, and knowledge play an important role in the sender's ability to encode. But our ability to encode ideas, thoughts, and feelings is far from perfect. A manager has to learn to encode meanings in a form that can be understood by a variety of recipients as well as other professionals in the same field. This of course is related to a basic rule for making a speech—analyze your audience. Knowing more about the receiver will help the sender select more effective language and symbols.[8]

MESSAGE

The result of encoding is the **message.** Messages are the tangible forms of coded symbols that are intended to give a particular meaning to the information or data. They are the thoughts and feelings that the communicator is attempting to elicit in the receiver. Words and symbols have no meaning in and of themselves. Their meaning is created by the sender and the receiver and, to a certain extent, by the situation or context. Sometimes messages are conveyed in ways that can be interpreted very differently.[9]

Figure 11.1 Basic Components in the Communication Process

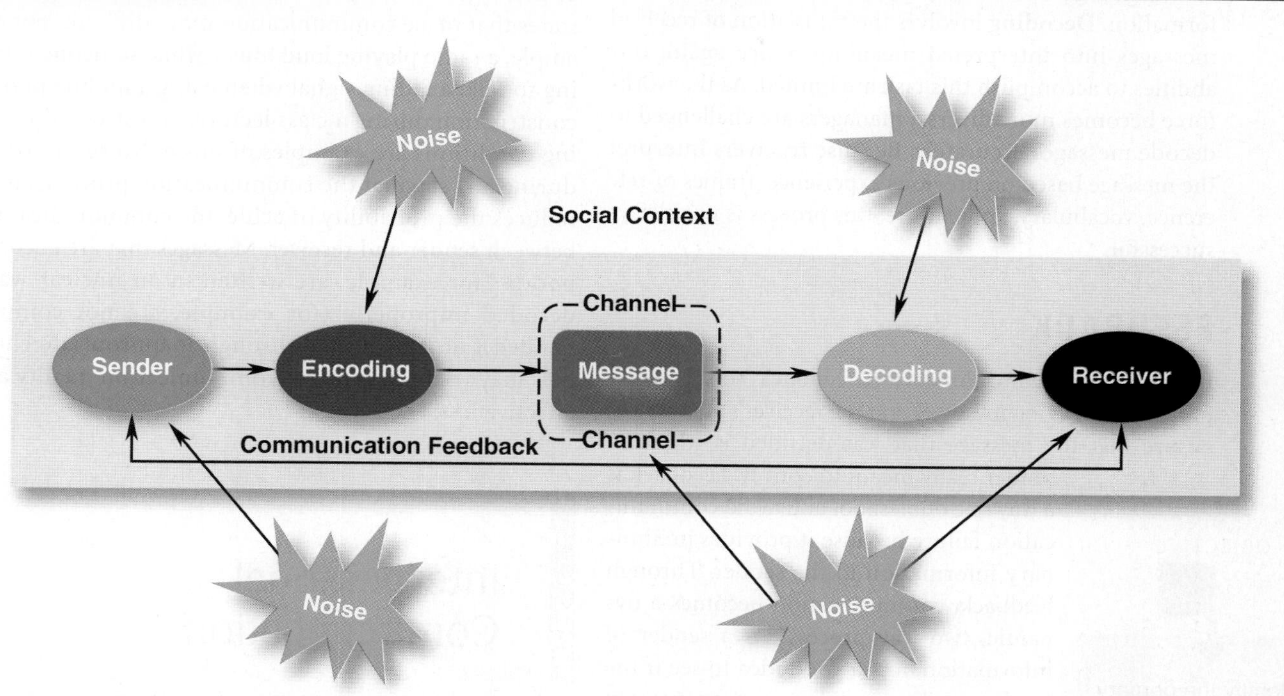

CHANNEL

Once the encoding is accomplished and a message emerges, another issue arises. How can this information be transmitted to the receiver? The answer depends in part on how the message has been encoded. If the message is in the form of a written report, it can be transmitted by mail, messenger, fax machine, or increasingly, by electronic means (e-communication). If it has been entered into computer storage, it can be sent directly to another computer over phone lines or satellite. If it is expressed orally, it can be presented directly in a face-to-face meeting or over the phone. The overriding consideration in choosing a channel is to ensure that the receiver can comprehend the message.

The **channel** is the carrier of the message or the means by which the message is sent. Organizations provide information to members through a variety of channels, including face-to-face communication, websites, telephone conversations, group meetings, fax messages, memos, policy statements, reward systems, managerial behaviors, bulletin boards, and electronic means. One critical impact is the improvement in technology that has made it possible to send and receive messages thousands of times faster than was possible a few years ago. Research has shown that the communication channels must be chosen carefully to deliver the appropriate message in the right way to the right people. That is, appropriate channels for the message and the receivers can have a major impact on communication effectiveness and even managerial performance. Sometimes managers fail to understand or consider how the choice of a channel can affect a communication's impact.[10]

Jonathan Katz, CEO of Cinnabar Inc., a special-effects developer, is an example of how channels influence the effect of the message. As e-communication became more widely available, Katz and client managers began to substitute e-mail and heavy use of the company's website in place of face-to-face and direct meetings. When business dropped off as a result, Katz realized that there was not a good fit between the client, the channel, and the message. He was able to stop the decline and return to the personalized direct contacts that had been a mark of his business success.[11]

KEY TERMS

Encoding
The process that translates the sender's ideas into a systematic set of symbols or a language expressing the communicator's purpose.

Message
The tangible forms of coded symbols that are intended to give a particular meaning to the information or data.

Channel
The carrier of the message or the means by which the message is sent.

RECEIVER

The receiving person or group must make sense of the information. **Decoding** involves the translation of received messages into interpreted meanings. Once again, our abilities to accomplish this task are limited. As the workforce becomes more diverse, managers are challenged to decode messages accurately. Because receivers interpret the message based on previous experience, frames of reference, vocabulary, and culture, this process is not always successful.

FEEDBACK

In our model, **communication feedback** refers to the process of verifying messages and the receiver's attempts to ensure that the message that was decoded is what the sender really meant to convey. Feedback is a way to troubleshoot and avoid communication failure because it provides preliminary information to the sender. Through feedback, communication becomes a dynamic, two-way process. As a sender of information, it is a good idea to see if the receiver understood the meaning that you intended. It is possible to convey information to someone without being aware that the receiver interpreted the message differently than intended. Unfortunately, if you don't check for shared meaning, you are likely to become aware of this problem after a major problem or issue arises because of the confusion.[12]

LEARNING OBJECTIVE 4

Identify the primary categories of interpersonal communication.

Many organizations are beginning to realize the value of feedback from their employees and customers. For example, many give toll-free phone numbers as well as website addresses to solicit input. Offering these opportunities provides organizations with valuable feedback that they can use to improve products, strengthen the quality of customer service, and ensure employee involvement.

NOISE

Any internal or external interference with or distraction from the intended message is considered to be **noise.** Noise can cause distortion in the sending and receiving of messages due to physical conditions and emotional states that make communication more difficult. For example, a radio playing loud music while someone is trying to talk, a fading signal when using a mobile phone, construction during a class lecture, and stressful working conditions are examples of noise. Noise can occur during any stage of the communication process, and it reduces the probability of achieving common meaning between sender and receiver. Messages that are encoded poorly (for example, are written in an unclear way), decoded improperly (for example, are not comprehended), or transmitted through inappropriate channels may result in reduced communication quality and effectiveness.

Interpersonal Communication

4 Managers communicate in a variety of ways. We examine oral, written, nonverbal, and technological communication in this section.

ORAL COMMUNICATION

Oral communication consists of all forms of spoken information; it is the type of communication preferred by most managers. Research indicates that managers prefer face-to-face and telephone communication to written communication because it permits immediate feedback. For example, individuals can comment or ask questions, and points can be clarified. Managers spend most of their time sharing information orally. Just because it is used so much does not necessarily mean that it is used well. It takes practice and time to develop effective oral communication skills.

Every professional will eventually be called on to use oral communication, such as in making a formal oral presentation to a large audience, small committee or team, client or customer. As we discussed in Chapter 10, professionals are change agents. Changes have to be presented effectively and sold to achieve acceptance and implementation.[13] As a manager, your oral communication skills are vital to your work and your career success. Table 11.1 provides a checklist of key items to keep in mind when you are asked to make

KEY TERMS

Decoding
The translation of received messages into interpreted meanings.

Communication feedback
The process of verifying messages and the receiver's attempts to ensure that the message he or she decoded is what the sender really meant to convey.

Noise
Any interference with or distraction from the intended message.

Oral communication
All forms of spoken information—the type of communication preferred by most managers.

Table 11.1 Checklist for Planning More Effective Oral Presentations

1. *Establish your goals* Have a clear image of your goals or purpose. Ask yourself, "What is it that I want to accomplish?"
2. *Analyze the audience* Know your audience so you can effectively select the appropriate content, vocabulary, and visual aids. When the members of your audience are from diverse backgrounds or occupations, it is especially important to find a common bond.
3. *Diagnose the environmental conditions* Be aware of how much time you will have, and use your time effectively. Determine in advance, if possible, the audience size, physical layout of the room and speaking area, and technical equipment.
4. *Organize your material* Remember that your message can be followed easily if your material is organized. A logical flow of thoughts will help your listeners follow the message. Start with a brief introduction that provides a preview, follow with a message that develops the content, and finish with a conclusion that reviews.
5. *Design and use visual aids* Keep in mind that visual aids not only help to clarify material and heighten its impact but also keep an audience alert. Keep the visual aids simple and use them to emphasize, clarify, or pull together important information. Remember, the purpose of visual aids is to support your presentation rather than be the presentation.

Source: Adapted from *Management Skills: Practice and Experience* by P. Fandt. Copyright 1993. By permission of South-Western, a division of Thomson Learning Inc., Mason, Ohio 45040.

an oral presentation, whether to a small group or a large audience.

WRITTEN COMMUNICATION

Written communication includes letters, memos, policy manuals, reports, forms, e-mail, and other documents used to share information in an organization. Managers use written communication less often than oral communication, but there are many occasions when written documentation is important. Writing down a message and sending it as a letter or memo enables a precise statement to be made, provides a reference for later use, aids in systematic thinking, and provides an official document for the organization. Written messages can also be distributed to many members of the organization at the same time in the form of newsletters or memos.

NONVERBAL COMMUNICATION

Nonverbal communication involves all messages that are nonlanguage responses. It can be anything that sends a message. Although managers recognize that communication has a nonverbal component, they often underestimate its importance. Nonverbal cues play a large role in the messages that you send because this form of communication may contain hidden messages and can influence the process and outcomes of face-to-face communication.[14] Even a person who is silent or inactive in the presence of others may be sending a message that may or may not be what is intended.

Consider how nonverbal communication affects the impressions we make on others. For example, interviewers respond more favorably to job candidates whose nonverbal cues are positive (such as eye contact, appearance, and facial expressions) than to those displaying negative nonverbal cues (such as looking down and slouching).[15]

The physical arrangement of space, such as that found in various office and work layouts, can also send nonverbal messages. For example, some visitors tend to be uncomfortable in offices where a desk is placed between them and the person to whom they are speaking. This desk might be seen as a separation or a wall that interferes with close communication. Others might see the desk as a symbol of power of the person whose office it is and may be influenced more positively or negatively by it. A desk or table between two people might also be seen as a setting for confrontational rather than cooperative communication. Still other things that communicate nonverbal messages about an individual are the artwork and decorations found in an office, as well as its orderliness and neatness.[16] What is your view of someone who has a very clean desk? Do you see that person as having nothing important to do—so he or she has time to clean the desk—or do you see that person as very productive and efficient?

KEY TERMS

Written communication Letters, memos, policy manuals, reports, forms, and other written documents.

Nonverbal communication All messages that are nonlanguage responses.

The following are six basic types of nonverbal communication:

1. *Kinesic behavior, or body motion:* Gestures, facial expressions, eye behavior, touching, and any other movement of the body.
2. *Physical characteristics:* Body shape, physique, posture, height, weight, hair, and skin color.
3. *Paralanguage:* Voice quality, volume, speech rate, pitch, and laughing.
4. *Proxemics:* The way people use and perceive space, seating arrangements, and conversational distance.
5. *Environment:* Building and room design, furniture and interior decorating, light, noise, and cleanliness.
6. *Time:* Being late or early, keeping others waiting, and other relationships between time and status.

Keep in mind that each category of nonverbal communication becomes additionally complex when we consider diversity and multiple cultural issues in the workplace.[17]

© PETER CHRISTOPHER/MASTERFILE

These people talking around a water cooler provide a variety of possible nonverbal information.

TECHNOLOGICAL COMMUNICATION

LEARNING OBJECTIVE 5

Discuss the role of technological communication and information use in the workplace.

5 Faxes, e-mails, teleconferences, the Internet, and other types of technological communication provide opportunities to communicate with virtually anyone, anywhere, any time of the day or night. **Technological communication** is a broad category of communication that is continuously changing and rapidly influencing how, when, and where managers communicate. For example, cell phones, instant messaging, DVDs, telephone-answering devices and services, closed-circuit television systems, fax machines, the Internet, computers, and e-mail all provide communication flexibility and opportunities. Networked computers create an easy means to store and communicate vast amounts of information. Networking ties computers together, permitting individuals to share information, communicate, and access tremendous amounts of information.

KEY TERMS

Technological communication
Any communication that uses an electronic device as the channel.

Telecommuting
The practice of working at a remote site by using a computer linked to a central office or other employment location.

Telework
Another word for telecommuting.

Information technology has led many organizations to change the way in which they operate and interface with employees, customers, and stakeholders. It has enabled other organizations to streamline interactions with other businesses. Of course, information technology has made it possible for organizations to communicate and interact with customers almost exclusively electronically. Consider Amazon.com and the many e-businesses that continue to grow, as managers have learned how to manage those businesses well and meet the organization's goals.[18]

Telecommuting, or now increasingly called "**telework,**" refers to the practice of working at a remote site by using a computer linked to a central office or other employment location. It may also include those who work out of a customer's office or communicate with the office or plant via a laptop computer or mobile phone. The number of Americans employed by a company who work from home at least 1 day per month rose to 23.5 million in 2003.[19] According to a recent study, the number of people telecommuting full time accelerated 41% between 2002 and 2003, to 12.4 million from 8.8 million.[20]

Telecommuting, once primarily the domain of lower-level and technical employees, increasingly is moving into the senior-management ranks. The reasons driving the trend are diverse: faster broadband Internet connections between home and office; the September 11, 2001, terrorist attacks, which made companies recognize the value of placing executives apart geographically

Now Apply It

E Is for E-Mail Etiquette

E-mail has changed the face of business communication more than any other. It makes it much easier to communicate across time zones and across borders, so it removes some of the artificial barriers; it's also inexpensive and enables you to do things very quickly. Although e-mail is one of modern life's great conveniences, it can sometimes be a barrier to good communication. E-mail restricts us to using only part of the way that we can communicate as human beings. We pick up meaning from body language in face-to-face encounters or through tone of voice when talking on the phone. In e-mail we only have the words, and without body language or tone of voice, the recipient may interpret words differently than intended.

Before sending your next e-mail, consider the following etiquette:

- Identify your goal and be specific. What do you want to achieve with the e-mail? Is it the best way to communicate the message?
- Consider a recipient's reaction to the subject. Congratulations and commiserations are better delivered personally. If the matter is a private or sensitive one, a telephone call or a meeting will be more effective.
- Avoid replying without checking the whole e-mail. Sometimes confidential e-mails are inadvertently tagged on to the bottom of e-mail chains.
- Ensure maximum impact. Use clear subject headings, spacing, add "for information" or "action required" in the heading, and include a proper "signature."
- State the type of response you need and your deadline. Be specific and avoid terms like "ASAP."
- Use attachments effectively. Avoid sending large or unwanted documents.
- Use "reply all" and "forward" with care.
- DON'T SHOUT! Uppercase is electronic shouting.
- Check your message for spelling and punctuation errors. Text language is not appropriate on e-mail.
- Never send an e-mail when you feel annoyed.

Sources: G. Blake, "E-Mail with Feeling," *Research-Technology Management* 42 (1999): 12–14; A. Overholt, "Intel's Got Too Much Mail," *Fast Company* 44 (March 2001): 56; "The Art of Multitasking," *Fast Company* 64 (October 2002): 118; L. K. Johnson, "Does E-Mail Escalate Conflict? The Idiosyncratic Aspects of Electronic Mail Can Obviate Resolution," *MIT Sloan Management Review* 44, no. 1 (Fall 2002): 14–15. T. Theobald, "Effective Communication," *Birmingham Post*, 21 April 2004, 14; D. Booher, *E-Writing: 21st-Century Tools for Effective Communication* (New York: Pocket Books, 2001).

to help reduce disruptions; and managers' increasing comfort with the idea of working remotely.[21]

Teleworkers can essentially create a 24-hour, 7-days a week, or to use the popular phrase, a 24/7 organization. The electronic information and communication links between these workers and the organization creates a virtual organization that can reduce the need for a normal office or work space. Recall from Chapter 9, JetBlue's reservation agents work from home rather than in an expensive call center. This approach is cost efficient for the organization and has helped keep the turnover rate of reservation agents to less than 1%.[22]

Many organizations on *Fortune*'s annual list of the "100 Best Companies to Work For" provide the flexibility of telecommuting, or teleworking. Many creative freelance workers, contract and temporary workers, and small companies are using this form of communication technology, as are many well-known organizations including IBM, Xerox, American Express, Du Pont, Apple Computer, and the Environmental Protection Agency.[23]

Electronic mail (e-mail), sending messages through computerized text-processing and communication networks, provides a fast, inexpensive, and efficient means of communication. Text-based messages can be sent and received by anyone who has access to a computer terminal and has a computer mailbox on the network. Messages can be transmitted almost instantaneously to and from employees in the same building or around the world.

The use of e-mail can enhance vertical and horizontal communication because it can lead to greater information exchanges as well as encourage individuals to learn to manage the information. On the negative side, it is very easy to overload everyone with e-mails that they do not need to do their jobs. In addition, the use of e-mails could result in loss of personal interactions that may be needed for better communication in some situations.[24] Before continuing, go to the "Now Apply It" box and read about e-mail etiquette. How well do you follow these guidelines?

Video conferencing is an umbrella term referring to technologies that use live video

KEY TERMS

Electronic mail (e-mail)
A message sent with an electronic device, usually a computer.

Video conferencing
An umbrella term referring to technologies that use live video to unite widely dispersed company operations or people.

At the Forefront

FedEx Captures the Best of Communication Activities

Ten years ago, when FedEx introduced online package tracking, the web was primarily static corporate brochures and messages from CEOs displayed on gray pages. The notion that capturing web technology as a communication tool was unheard of. As FedEx's business has grown, the web has greatly increased the number of contacts that customers have with FedEx. But it's also cut FedEx's costs by $45 million a month because an online tracking request costs 2 cents versus $2.40 for a phone call.

The company has been held up as an example of how to keep employees engaged and central to its strategies. The emphasis placed on communications at FedEx is reflected in the amount of time that executives devote to it. According to T. Michael Glenn, president and CEO of FedEx Services, "Communication is at the center of everything. You can't execute strategy if you can't communicate about it."

Sources: P.A. Argenti, R. Howell, and K. Beck, "The Strategic Communication Imperative," *MIT Sloan Management Review* 46 (Spring, 2005): 83–89; O. Thomas, "What the Web Taught FedEx," from http://www.business2.com, 18 November 2004; P.A. Argenti, *Corporate Communication* (New York: McGraw-Hill/Irwin, 2002).

to unite widely dispersed organizational operations or people. This technology offers tremendous savings of time, energy, and money. Business television networks enable organizations to communicate to thousands of employees simultaneously. For example, televised instructions can provide training as well as technical assistance for employees. Video conferencing enables organizations to hold interactive meetings in which groups communicate live with each other via camera and cable transmission of the picture and sound, even though they are hundreds or even thousands of miles apart.

The meteoric growth of the **Internet** and sophisticated websites also impacts the communication in the organization. Essentially everything can be done on the Internet. To understand how thoroughly the web has permeated everyday business life, think back to the last time you tracked a package. Maybe you typed http://www.fedex.com into your browser. Or maybe you just pulled up the shipment information from a retailer's website. FedEx has had a role in changing the web and finds it can't run its business without the Internet.[26] T. Michael Glenn, president and CEO of FedEx Services says, "Communication is at the center everything."[26] (Read more about FedEx in the feature "At the Forefront.")

Websites give information potentially to all the company's stakeholders. Customers can get product and service information and can make purchases in many instances. Employees can get a variety of information. Job seekers can get information and can actually apply for a job with many companies. Stockholders can get information about the company, not only from its website but also from many investment-related sites. By using a web search, anyone can get information about almost any organization.

Organizations too can gather a variety of information with their or others' websites. Information about an applicant or a customer is recorded on the website. The number of "hits" on the site can be counted, in addition to other information about the person who accessed the site. Opinion surveys, comments, and feedback can be gathered anonymously. Perhaps the greatest impact of the new technology on communication lies in the amount of information that it makes available.

Although good communication is valuable and an essential part of the manager's job, he or she may drown in an overabundance of information. More information is not necessarily better information or even relevant information. It may encourage managers to make decisions too quickly. Rapid access to data can preclude thoughtful deliberation and make everyone a sender of messages worldwide at low cost. Managers often fail to build face-to-face relationships, so the personal touch in managing is lost. More, faster, and easier communication opens up the possibility for managers to waste a lot of time on "junk" communication.

Used correctly, technology can exert a positive influence on nearly every aspect of productivity and quality. For example, it can be the lifeline of the increasing

KEY TERMS

Internet
The vast interconnected electronic equipment that stores massive amounts of data that can be accessed with computers and related electronic equipment.

number of global economic networks and an essential tool for people who want to stay in touch with the rest of the world.[26] At UPS, technology plays a key role in disseminating information to employees. The company created upsers.com, an employee portal, that keeps people up to speed and "in the know" on everything from benefits, to health and safety, legacy, culture, business, and more.[27] Keep in mind that although technology provides more choices, it does magnify the need to make careful, informed decisions about the appropriateness of the medium.[28]

Why Managers Communicate

6 Managers communicate for many reasons: to motivate, inform, control, and satisfy social needs. Motivational communication serves the function of influencing the behavior of organizational members. Communication that is intended to motivate must be designed to influence employees to work toward the accomplishment of organizational goals. Communication has an informational purpose when it provides facts and data to be used for decision making. In addition, managers give employees information that they need to perform tasks, and employees inform managers of their progress toward meeting their objectives.

Communication also serves a control function. We discuss control more thoroughly later in the text, but it is through communication that work is coordinated and integrated, tasks and responsibilities are clarified, and records are kept to create order. Communication that controls serves the purpose of guiding and coordinating so that multiple goals and tasks can be pursued.

Finally, managers communicate to satisfy social needs. Communication fulfills social needs relating to the emotional and non-task-oriented interactions that occur in every organization.[29] For example, employees need to talk about football games, the weather, politics, the boss's personality, and so forth. This communication may not directly affect the performance of organizational tasks, but it serves important needs and can influence how employees feel about their work conditions and how connected they are with others at work.

Recall that earlier in the chapter we said that successful and effective communication results when the message is received and conveys the exact meaning that the sender intended. You have probably experienced situations in which this did not happen, and the message that you sent was not what was intended. Why does this happen? In the next section, we discuss the main barriers that prevent high-quality communication and actions that managers must take to improve communication.

Barriers to Effective Communication

7 Despite its apparent simplicity, the communication process rarely operates flawlessly. The information transmitted from one party to another may be distorted, and communication problems may result. Communication barriers interfere with organizational excellence. We turn now to common communication barriers that are summarized in Table 11.2.

LEARNING OBJECTIVE 6

Address the primary reasons why managers communicate.

CROSS-CULTURAL DIVERSITY

Communication as an exchange of meaning is bounded by culture. Individuals from different cultures may encode and decode their messages differently; they have different behaviors, styles, and ways of looking at things. All of these can lead to barriers to effective communication. Difficulties may arise between people from different geographic or ethnic groups in the same country, as well as between people from different national cultures.[30]

LEARNING OBJECTIVE 7

Explain the barriers that interfere with effective communication.

A common problem in cross-cultural communication is **ethnocentrism,** or the tendency to consider one's own culture and its values as being superior to others. Very often such tendencies are accompanied by an unwillingness to try to understand alternative points of view and take seriously the values they represent. This attitude can be highly disadvantageous when trying to conduct business and maintain effective working relationships with people from different cultures.[31]

Studies show that the greater the differences between the sender's and receiver's

KEY TERMS

Ethnocentrism
The tendency to consider one's own culture and its values as being superior to others.

Table 11.2 Sources of Communication Barriers

1. *Cross-cultural diversity:* Cultural differences may arise between people from different geographic or ethnic groups within one country as well as between people from different national cultures.
2. *Trust and credibility:* Without trust, the communicating parties concentrate their energies on defensive tactics, rather than on conveying and understanding meaning.
3. *Information overload:* Individuals can experience information overload when they are asked to handle too much information at one time.
4. *Language characteristics:* Many words or phrases are imprecise. Individuals often use different meanings or interpretations of the same word and do not realize it.
5. *Gender differences:* Since males and females are often treated differently from childhood, they tend to develop different perspectives, attitudes about life, and communication styles.
6. *Other factors:* Time pressures, physical distractions, differing perceptions, and noise can all interfere with good communication.

cultures, the greater is the chance for miscommunication. A common criticism of some U.S. business managers is that, although they have the technology and know the business, they are not prepared to deal with cultural differences.[32] Among the cultural elements that affect cross-cultural communication are level of formality, level of directness and explicitness, and perception of time.

TRUST AND CREDIBILITY

A very important barrier to effective communication is a lack of trust between the sender and the receiver. This lack of trust can cause the receiver to look for hidden meanings in the sender's message, or it can cause the sender to try to manipulate the message. A trusting relationship is almost a prerequisite for good communication. In the absence of trust and honesty, the communicating parties divert their energies to defensive tactics rather than trying to convey and understand meaning.[33] Recall our discussion earlier about TDI and the culture of trust it created.

A work environment characterized by trust does not just happen. It takes time and effort to develop. It must be nurtured and reinforced by honesty and accuracy in communication and mutual respect between communicating parties. Managers can develop trust in their working relationships with subordinates by being "trustworthy," as Steven Covey calls it. That is, managers and everyone can be trustworthy by making promises and keeping them—by doing what you say you are going to do and by not telling lies.[34]

It simply means that managers get out of their offices and communicate regularly with employees as they do their jobs. Managers who spend time walking around can greatly reduce the perceived distance between themselves and their subordinates. They can also create an atmosphere of open and free-flowing communication, which makes more and better information available for decision making and makes decisions more relevant to the needs of lower-level personnel.[35] It is no coincidence that trust continues to be an important factor in *Fortune* magazine's annual selection of "The 100 Best Companies to Work For in America."[36]

Challenges to effective communication among people from different cultural groups can be resolved by a willingness both to understand alternative points of view and to accept the values they represent.

INFORMATION OVERLOAD

Although information is the lifeblood of the organization, it is possible for managers and organizations to have too much information. The increasing use of technology in organizations often leads to **information overload,** which occurs when the amount of information that one can process is exceeded. Perhaps it would be more appropriate to talk about "data" overload. Essentially, everything is just data until and unless it has some meaning or is useful.[37] People in organizations must find ways to manage the data so that they do not become overwhelmed. Instead, they need to know how to sort and analyze the data to turn it into useful information.[38]

Information overload can be detrimental to performance unless managers develop systems for dealing with it and learn how to implement them. Knowing everything is not as important as knowing how to find the correct answers in a systematic way. Without a system, information overload can lead to:

- Failing to process or ignoring some of the information.
- Processing the information incorrectly.
- Delaying the processing of information until the information overload abates.
- Searching for people to help process some of the information.
- Lowering the quality of information processing.
- Withdrawing from the information flow.

LANGUAGE CHARACTERISTICS

The very nature of our language constitutes a source of communication barriers. Many words are imprecise. For example, suppose a manager tells a subordinate to do this task "right away." Does the manager mean for the subordinate to drop what he or she is doing and work on the new task immediately or to finish what he or she is currently working on and then do the new task?

When two individuals are using different meanings or interpretations of the same word and do not realize it, a communication barrier exists. For example, some words sound the same but have multiple meanings. *Write* (communicate), *rite* (ceremony), *right* (not left), and *right* (privilege) all sound alike, *right* (correct)? Don't assume that the meaning you give a word will be the one the receiver uses in decoding the message. Language characteristics can lead to encoding and decoding errors and mixed messages that create semantic barriers to communication. For example, a word may be interpreted differently depending on the facial expressions, hand gestures, and voice inflection that accompany it.

The imprecision and multiple meanings of words are one reason why jargon develops. **Jargon** is terminology, or language, specific to a particular profession or group. One of the best-known uses of jargon is that used at Disney. There, customers are called "guests" and employees are called "cast members." If a cast member does a job correctly, it is called a "good Mickey"; if he/she does a bad job, it is called a "bad Mickey."[39]

With more and more organizations becoming involved in e-commerce, *Fortune* magazine describes some of the Internet jargon created daily. For example, even the U.S. Postal Service is one of the ten biggest businesses that have become successful e-players or e-tailers. Or, consider "clicks-and-mortar retailers," meaning the organization has physical outlets and a sophisticated website to sell products directly to the public. Although jargon is designed to avoid communication breakdowns, in some cases, it may lead to inefficiency because not everyone will understand what is being communicated, especially new members of the organization or group.[40]

Language characteristics, including imprecision and multiple meanings, are posing an even greater threat to communication as society becomes more interconnected and mobile. The probability of contact with someone from a different background or culture who uses words differently is increasing.[41]

GENDER DIFFERENCES

Gender differences can result in barriers and lead to distorted communication and misunderstandings between men and women. Because males and females are often treated differently from childhood, they tend to develop different perspectives, attitudes about life, and communication styles. Historically, stereotypical assumptions about the differing communication styles of males and females have stimulated discrimination against female managers. In recent years, however, more realistic images of how professional men and women behave and communicate have replaced the old stereotypes.[42]

Communication barriers can be explained in part by differences in conversation styles. Research shows that women and men listen differently. Women tend to speak and hear a language of connection and intimacy, whereas men tend to speak and hear a language of status and

KEY TERMS

Information overload
A state that occurs when the amount of information that a person can process is exceeded.

Jargon
Terminology or language specific to a particular profession or group.

independence. Women are more likely to hear emotions and to communicate empathy.[43]

Women's oral communication also differs from men's in significant ways. Women are more likely to use qualifiers, phrases such as "I think" or "It seems to me." Generally, women tend to end statements with an upward inflection that makes statements sound like questions. Female voices are generally higher and softer than male voices. This makes it easy for men to overpower women's voices, and men commonly interrupt women or overlap their speech.

Although a wide range of gender differences can exist in verbal communication, nonverbal differences are even more striking. Men lean back and sit in an open-leg position that takes up considerable space, thereby communicating higher status and a greater sense of control over their environment. Women use much more eye contact than men, yet avert their gaze more often, especially when communicating with a man or someone of higher status. Women smile more frequently and are generally better at conveying and interpreting emotions.[44]

OTHER FACTORS

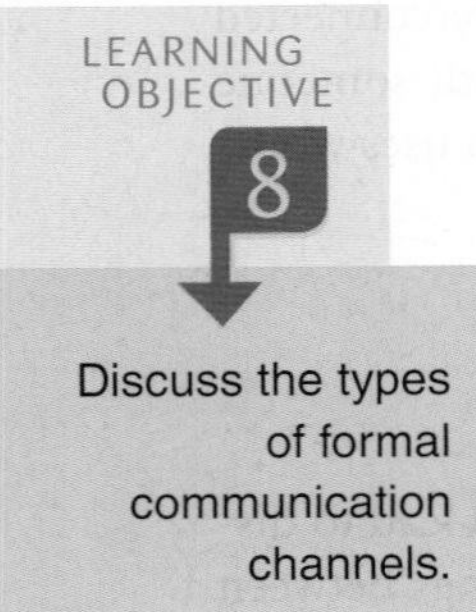

Several other factors are considered barriers to effective communication. Time pressures may cause us to focus on information that helps us make decisions quickly, although the information may not be of high quality. Feedback may be impaired or absent. In one-way communication, such as a written memo, the sender does not receive any direct and immediate feedback from the receiver. Studies show that two-way communication is more accurate and effective than one-way communication, but it is also more costly and time-consuming.

There can be many physical distractions included in nonverbal communications. A manager might not seem open or approachable if he or she sits behind a desk. Someone might be distracted by sounds in the next room or by sounds made by someone "clicking" a pen. Each person's perception influences what he or she hears and sees. This is closely related to differences in culture and gender discussed previously. Also look at the discussion of perception in Chapter 13.

Of course, noise usually is a large barrier to communication. Noise can include a wide variety of things. It might be actual noise from the surroundings—for example, birds, others speaking, the phone ringing, or the sound of equipment. Noise also includes psychological noise—that is, thinking about the death of a loved one, thinking about how hungry you are, or thinking about how silly or how good the speaker's hair looks while someone is speaking could all be noise. All of these can be barriers to good communication.

KEY TERMS

Vertical communication The flow of information both up and down the chain of command.

Downward communication Messages sent from individuals at higher levels of the organization to those at lower levels.

Communication Channels

The channel that carries information and the direction of the information can influence effectiveness. The next section focuses on these topics.

FORMAL COMMUNICATION CHANNELS

8 Formal communication follows the chain of command and is recognized as official. One way to view formal communication within organizations, as shown in Figure 11.2, is to examine how it flows—vertically and horizontally. Specific types of communication are often associated with directional flow. Briefly examining each type of directional flow will help us appreciate the problems inherent in organizational communication and identify ways to overcome these problems.

Vertical Communication

Vertical communication is the flow of information both up and down the chain of command. It involves an exchange of messages between two or more levels in the organization. When top-level managers make decisions, create strategic plans, convey directions, and so forth, they are often communicating downward. **Downward communication** flows from individuals in higher levels of the organization to those in lower levels. The most common forms of downward communication are meetings, official memos, policy statements, procedure manuals, information needed to conduct work, and company publications. Information sent downward may include new company goals, job instructions, procedures, and feedback on performance. Studies show that only 20% of an intended message sent by top-level management is intact by the time it reaches the entry-

Figure 11.2 Formal Communication Flows

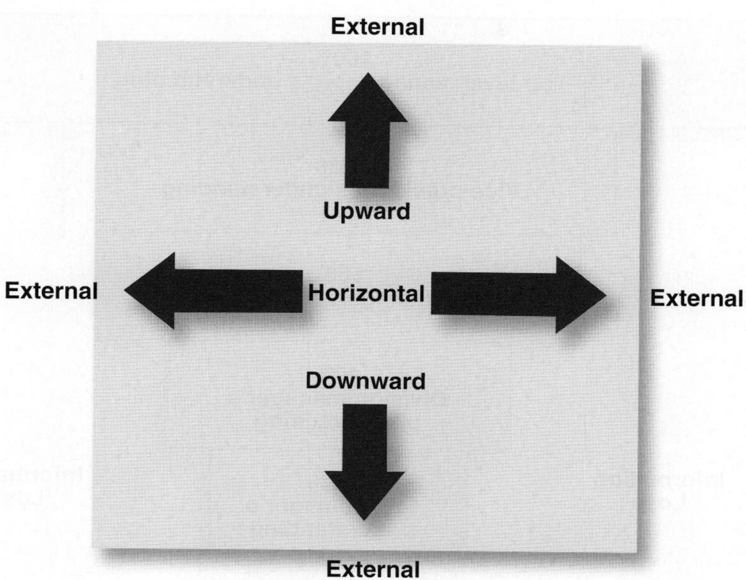

level employee[45] (Figure 11.3). This information loss occurs for several reasons. First, managers tend to rely too heavily on written channels; an avalanche of written material may cause the overloaded subordinate to ignore some messages. This is especially true with the glut of information stemming from e-communications.

Second, the oral face-to-face message, which commands more attention and can provide immediate feedback, is often underutilized. Managers may e-mail the colleague or subordinate down the hall instead of walking over for a chat. They may e-mail a business client across town instead of picking up the phone. Experts agree that managers often forget that the best way to communicate—the richest channel—is face to face, with its potential for abundant feedback.[46]

Upward communication consists of messages sent up the line from subordinates to managers. Openness to ideas and input from people in the lower levels of the organization is often the hallmark of a healthy and enjoyable organization. Effective organizations need upward communication as much as downward communication. People at all levels can and will have ideas for organizational improvement. Plus, managers need to have accurate feedback to properly guide the entire organization. Upward communication from subordinates to managers usually falls into one of the following categories:

- Personal reports of performance, problems, or concerns.
- Reports about others and their performance, problems, or concerns.
- Reactions to organizational policies and practices.
- Suggestions about what tasks need to be done and how they can be accomplished.

This type of communication is frequently sent up only one level in the organization to the person's immediate supervisor. The supervisor may send some of the information to the next higher level but usually in a modified form.

Upward communication is beneficial to both the manager and the subordinate. For the manager, it is often necessary for sound decision making. Upward communication helps managers know employees' accomplishments, problems, and attitudes and allows employees to make suggestions and feel that they are part of the decision-making process. In addition, it provides feedback, encourages ongoing two-way communication, and indicates the subordinates' receptiveness to messages. For the subordinate, upward communication may provide a release of tensions and a sense of personal worth that may lead to a feeling of commitment to the organization.[47]

For example, David Neeleman, founder and CEO of JetBlue, conducts monthly "pocket sessions," which are informal question-and-answer sessions with crew members (JetBlue's name for employees). He considers these sessions an important part of "visible leadership" and a way in which he can stay in touch with employees.[48] At JetBlue, all employees are given access to corporate information.

KEY TERMS

Upward communication Messages sent up the line from subordinates to supervisors.

Figure 11.3 Information Understanding and Loss

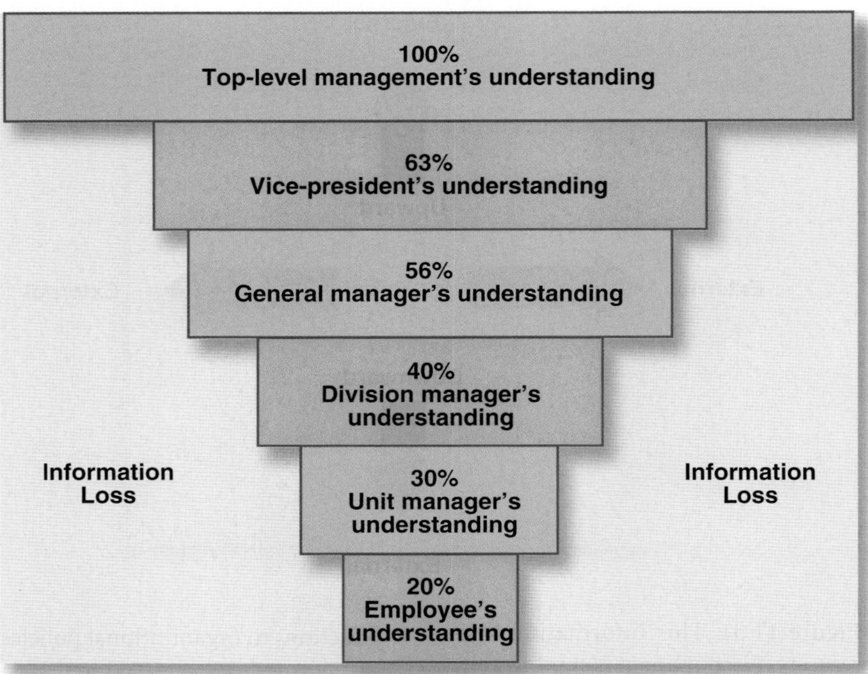

They are taught to understand it and are encouraged to ask any questions.[49]

Similar upward communication processes take place at TDI and Safeway. TDI created "Partner Roundtables" in which employees (TDI refers to them as partners) are encouraged to discuss anything that is on their mind.[50] Safeway runs "Colleague Councils" in which managers consult with groups of employees. The purpose of these is twofold: It's to inform staff and allow the business to understand how staff are feeling. Comments from Safeway staff are very positive. They claim to be impressed by the timely and appropriate communication.[51]

Achieving effective upward communication—getting open and honest messages from employees to management—is an especially difficult task. Although suggestion boxes, employee surveys, and open-door policies are often used to encourage upward communication, upper-level managers are responsible for responding to messages from lower-level employees. If they do not take advantage of this information, the chance to tap into a critical resource is lost. Managers need to act on feedback from subordinates and get back to the individuals who sent it—if only to indicate that the suggestion cannot be carried out or that progress is being made about the problem or suggestion.[52]

The track record on effectively communicating upward is not especially positive. Even for managers, on average, less than 15% of their communications is to their supervisors. Also, when managers communicate upward, their conversations tend to be shorter than discussions with peers, and they often highlight their accomplishments and downplay their mistakes if the mistakes will be looked upon unfavorably. In addition, junior managers are not trained in nor do they see good role models for how to seek needed information and pass it upward.[53]

As we discussed previously, a trusting relationship is almost a prerequisite for effective communication. Trust cannot be mandated by policy or directives. It must be earned by the manager through credible behavior and communication. Read how Julie Rodriguez created a positive communication culture in the "Leaders in Action" box. Communicating regularly, showing concern for others, and having a willingness to acknowledge mistakes helps build trust with colleagues. Here is yet another place where managers can take a crucial leadership role in setting the example of positive behavior.[54] If managers encourage all types of feedback from others in the organization and set good examples of how to do this, then effective upward communication can be developed. More will be said about this later when we discuss developing feedback skills and listening.

Leaders in Action

Listening and Learning Builds Success

Julie Rodriguez, CEO of Epic Divers and Marine, attributes the success of the company to listening and learning. When she started working in her father's small company, Rodriguez knew nothing about the Louisiana oil-field services business. Without the training and experience of a diver, she didn't know the scope of the company's qualifications for repairing offshore pipelines and platforms. Nor did Rodriguez understand accounting, contracting, or marine safety regulations.

Fifteen years ago, she took over the company and started by listening to her experienced employees, using her divers as consultants to learn about where to expand and which new customers to pursue. Her listening skills proved vital in 1994 when an Epic diver was struck and killed by a loose underwater pipeline. The fatality stunned the CEO. She also knew the accident would make it difficult to land new contracts.

Determined to recover, Rodriguez set out to reform Epic's culture around safety. She started by meeting with each employee and discussing each job with the divers in order to anticipate what tools and procedures they needed to stay safe. As a result of her communication efforts, an extensive new safety program was developed. It is still in place today, emphasizing constant communication so that employees can continually learn from one another. When an incident does happen on a job, Rodriguez uses the error to teach other divers. "It's important to share your mistakes with everybody," she says. "They go in our manual and become training tools." Today, Epic Marine has the top safety rating with all of its clients.

Sources: A. Overholt, J. McGregor, R. Underwood, and A. Sarma, "25 Top Women Business Builders," *Fast Company*, 94 (May 2005): 67–74.

Horizontal Communication

Horizontal communication is the flow of information that occurs both within and between departments. Effective organizations encourage horizontal communication because it increases coordination, collaboration, and cooperation. As you will recall from the discussion of the coordination function in Chapter 8, communication provides a means for members on the same level of an organization to share information without directly involving their supervisors. Examples include the communication that may occur between members of different departments of an organization and between coworkers in the same department. Self-managed teams create situations in which horizontal communication can flourish. In addition, more formal liaison roles may be created to support information flows. These are important to coordinate activities that support the organizational objectives.[55]

SPONTANEOUS COMMUNICATION CHANNELS

The flows of communication described so far have been part of the formal system used to accomplish the work of the organization. In addition to these formal channels, organizations have spontaneous channels of communication. **Spontaneous channels of communication** are casual, opportunistic, and informal communication paths arising from the social relationships that evolve in the organization. They are neither required nor controlled by management.[56]

A term often associated with spontaneous communication channels is the grapevine. The **grapevine** is an informal method of transmitting information, depicted as the wandering of messages throughout the organization. It typically involves small clusters of people who exchange information in all directions through unsanctioned organizational channels and networks. We refer to this as peer-to-peer conversations. This communication is a useful and important source of information for managers and employees at all levels and is used as much as the company newsletter or employee meetings. Peer-to-peer conversations may be personal, task focused, or organization focused. When people offer thoughts and guidance on personal issues or situations, it is considered personal. These discussions may not relate to

KEY TERMS

Horizontal communication
The flow of information that occurs both within and between departments.

Spontaneous channels of communication
Casual, opportunistic, and informal communication paths that arise from the social relationships that evolve in the organization.

Grapevine
An informal method of transmitting information depicted as the wandering of messages throughout the organization.

strategic objectives, but they do build relationships among coworkers, which ultimately affect culture and communication effectiveness. Conversations may relate to the task. For example, coworkers discuss the day's assignment or team projects. Or the organization may be the focus with the "inside" story on changes and company news. These spontaneous communication processes can potentially compete with or complement the formal communication system in the organization.[57]

The grapevine can be beneficial. Managers need to at least be aware of the grapevine because it is probably one of the most prevalent and reliable forms of communication. In fact, one well-known study found that approximately 80% of the information transmitted through the grapevine was correct.[58] The remaining 20%, though, can often lead to serious trouble. As you probably know from your own experience, a story can be mainly true but still be quite misleading because essential facts are omitted or distorted.

Information in the spontaneous channels is usually unverified and often includes rumors that are exaggerated and frequently wrong. To help prevent incorrect rumors, managers must keep the information that flows through informal channels accurate and rumor free. To do so, managers should share as much information as possible with employees, tell them of changes far in advance, and encourage employees to ask questions about rumors they hear.

To some extent, the spontaneous channels are always present in any organization and are more than just a means of conveying corporate gossip. The information may be less official, but it is no less important for understanding the organization. Despite being pervasive, the grapevine has escaped being directly managed in most companies. Research by Crampton, Dodge, and Jitrendra found that 92% of companies had no policy to deal with the grapevine.[59]

Communication Competency Challenges

To improve communication in the organization each person should take responsibility to assert when he or she doesn't understand a message or to suggest when and how someone could communicate more effectively. Taking this type of action requires that organizational members develop communication competency. The final section of the chapter provides material about listening and feedback competency.

It is much easier to define what effective communication is than it is to achieve communication competence. Communication is both complicated and difficult, but there is overwhelming agreement that it is very important for personal and organizational success. Les Landes, a well-known consultant, even calls it "the central nervous system of your organization."[60] Managers agree that the ability to communicate effectively is crucial to enhancing career success. More than ever before, your ability to communicate well affects your capability to thrive in today's organizations and professions. If you could strive for expertise in but one competence, communication would be the wise choice.

Even a fairly simple and straightforward exchange of factual information is subject to distortion and miscommunication. The three most important points to remember in meeting the challenge of communication competency are to (1) expect to be misunderstood by at least some listeners and readers, (2) expect to misunderstand others, and (3) strive to reduce the degree of such misunderstandings, but you should never expect total elimination of them or the ability to anticipate all possible outcomes. In this section, we focus on ways to prevent misunderstandings and improve critical aspects of communication with feedback and listening.

DEVELOPING FEEDBACK SKILLS

As we discussed earlier, communication feedback refers to the process of verifying messages from the sender. Through feedback, communication becomes a dynamic, two-way process rather than just an event. Feedback can include very personal feelings or more abstract thoughts such as reactions to others' ideas or proposals. The emotional impact of feedback varies according to how personally it is focused.

The first requirement of high-quality feedback is to recognize when it is truly intended to benefit the receiver and when it is purely an attempt to satisfy a personal need. A manager who berates an employee for a software error may actually be angry about personally failing to give clear instructions in the first place. The ability to take an active part in the feedback session can make a person more receptive to what he or she hears.[61]

In addition to giving feedback, being able to receive feedback is also important for effective communication. Learning cannot occur without feedback. Unfortunately, many people and organizations do little to encourage or cultivate useful feedback. Rather, people tend to protect themselves from getting their feelings hurt. Many tune out anything that might undermine their self-confidence. In doing so, they also forfeit an enormous opportunity for growth. You do not have to agree with all feedback. An attitude of feedback receptiveness is vital to the development of your communication skills.

Follow these five principles for giving effective feedback:

1. Give feedback that is specific rather than general. Include clear and preferably recent examples. Saying "You are a poor listener" is not as useful as saying "I watched you interact with the customer, and I believe that you did not listen to what she was saying."
2. Give feedback when the receiver appears ready to accept it. When a person is angry, upset, or defensive, it is probably not the time to bring up new issues.
3. Focus feedback on behavior rather than the person, and focus it on behavior that can be changed.
4. Provide feedback using descriptive information about what the person said or did.
5. Avoid feedback using evaluative inferences about motives, intent, or feelings.

ADVANCING LISTENING SKILLS

Of the basic communication skills—reading, writing, speaking, and listening—only one is not taught formally in schools. Most of our learning is directed toward reading, speaking, and writing, with little attention given to training in listening.[62]

The most effective leaders know when to stop talking and start listening. This is especially important in three particular situations: when emotions are high, in team situations, and when employees are sharing ideas.[63] First, listening is crucial when emotions are high. Extreme emotions, such as anger, resentment, and excitement, warrant attention from a personal and a business standpoint. On a personal level, people feel acknowledged when others validate their feelings. Managers who ignore feelings can create distance between themselves and their employees, eroding the relationship and ultimately affecting the working environment.

The second most important time to listen is in team situations. Team environments can involve multiple personalities, complex dynamics, and competing agendas. By listening carefully, managers can ensure that everyone is working toward the same goal. Listening also helps managers identify and address conflicts early, as well as facilitate healthy working relationships among team members. (Chapter 13 covers more about teams.)

Third, listening is vital when employees are sharing ideas. When managers stop listening to ideas, employees stop offering them. That means managers are essentially cut off from the creativity and expertise of the people on their team, and leadership becomes an illusion. In these and almost any situation, the advantages of listening make it worth doing well.

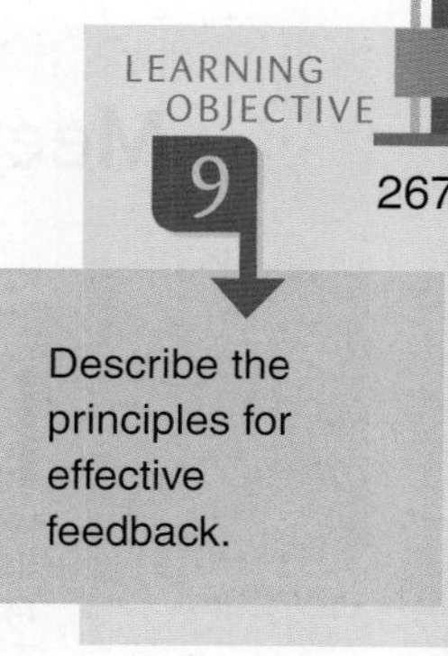

In his best-selling book, *The 7 Habits of Highly Effective People,* Stephen Covey suggests that the key to effective listening is to seek first to understand and then to be understood.[64] Communication breakdowns are the result of misleading assumptions, particularly when the listener is in the process of evaluating, approving, or disproving what another person is saying.

How good a listener are you? Before you can begin to improve your listening skills, you need to understand the demands placed on your listening capacities. Most important, listening is an active behavior; it involves careful attention and response to messages. Instead of evaluating the message or preparing a response, an effective listener tries to understand both direct and subtle meanings contained in messages. In other words, be attentive to the feelings of the sender and what he or she is not saying as well as to the verbal content of the message. Observe people while they are speaking. Watch facial expressions, gestures, body movements, and eye contact.

LEARNING OBJECTIVE 10

Specify the guidelines for becoming a good listener.

10 The following guidelines will help you be an effective listener:[65]

- Listen for message content. Try to hear exactly what is being said in the message.
- Listen for feelings. Try to identify how the sender feels about the message content. Is it pleasing or displeasing to the sender?
- Respond to feelings. Let the sender know that you recognize his or her feelings as well as the message content.
- Be sensitive to both the nonverbal and the verbal content of messages; identify mixed messages that need to be clarified.
- Reflect back to the sender, in your own words, what you think you are hearing. Paraphrase and restate the verbal and nonverbal messages as feedback to which the sender can respond with further information.
- Be attentive and listen to understand, not to reply. Most people are thinking about what they are going to say next or what is going on in the next office. Don't squirm or fidget while someone else is talking. Find a comfortable position and give 100% of your attention to the speaker.
- Be patient. Don't interrupt the speaker. Take time to digest what has been said before responding. Don't be afraid to ask questions to clarify and understand every word of what has been said. There is no shame in not knowing, only in not knowing and pretending to know.

Meeting The Challenge

TDIndustries

In the ensuing years, TDI grew to more than 1400 employees. The once informal employee conversations that were held at founder Jack Lowe, Sr.'s, home were re-created to be "Partner Roundtables." During these meetings, partners (employees) are encouraged to discuss anything that is on their mind. For example, TDI's culture and the vision and values philosophy is thoroughly debated. Discussions may include auxiliary management ideas and methods of conducting business. In addition, at least once a month every partner meets with others in his or her department and or in company-wide sessions to discuss how they can work together to make the company better.

By means of meetings, surveys, newsletters, memos, and many different communication techniques, TDI communicates and tests its business theory and other basic elements of its values and vision as it affects all partners. For example, annually all partners are required to rate their supervisors anonymously in the areas of communication, leadership, productivity, people building, motivation, and quality. The results of the survey and others are fed back to relevant parties and summaries are discussed during the frequent corporate meetings.

TDI reflects the level of trust, pride, and camaraderie that employees share with management and their peers, as well as the effect of communication practices that TDI has in place to support those things. The senior leadership of TDI believes that, to build morale, communication has to be two way. It is critical to all partners, the senior leaders, and Jack Lowe, Jr., the CEO and president.

Sources: http://www.greenleaf.org; http://www.tdindustries.com; R. Levering and M. Moskowitz, "How We Pick the Best 100," *Fortune,* 24 January 2005, 97; R. Levering and M. Moskowitz, "The 100 Best Companies to Work For," *Fortune,* 4 February 2002, 72–74; R. Levering and M. Moskowitz, "The 100 Best Companies to Work For," *Fortune,* 10 January 2000, 82–93; S. Branch, "The 100 Best Companies to Work For in America," *Fortune,* 11 January 1999, 118–131; J. Gavin and R. Mason, "The Virtuous Organization: The Value of Happiness in the Workplace," *Organizational Dynamics* 33 (December 2004): 379–392.

Listening is an active process where you make a connection with another person.[66] Effective listening behaviors include maintaining eye contact, rephrasing what has been said, listening for the message beyond the obvious and overt meaning of the words that have been spoken, and observing nonverbal messages. The key to more effective listening is the willingness to listen and respond appropriately to the feelings being expressed as well as to the content.[67]

Implications for Leaders

Organizational leaders are first and foremost in the communication business. Communication is the most important thing to be good at doing. This is clearly supported by research and beliefs of essentially all managers. That is, communication is a foundation for success of people in organizations and for success of the organization itself. Whether you are a financial planner, small-business owner, accountant, sales representative, minister, teacher, or any other type of professional, the following issues are key points to consider for managerial effectiveness:[68]

- You spend most of your time at work communicating.
- Your success is based on strong communication skills.
- Communication is becoming increasingly important in view of the changing environment including increased globalization, diversity, and technology.
- Technological communication offers new opportunities to communicate more often and more efficiently than ever before. It is an essential tool for people who want to stay in touch with the rest of world.

Whatever you do in the future, communication will probably take up a large portion of your time, and the more competent you are at communicating, the more successful you are likely to be.

One of the biggest challenges managers face is communication. And yet, communication is also one of the most critical aspects of management and leadership. Without good communication, managers can fail to gain commitment from employees, fail to achieve business goals, and fail to develop rapport with the people on their team. In short, they can fail as leaders no matter how good their intentions may be.

Effective communication takes effort. But it is effort well spent given the benefits—a more positive and more productive work setting in which everyone feels valued, ideas are shared openly, and relationships are characterized by trust. When you practice good communication, notice the effect. The results that come from communicating wisely will be the proof that communication really is the key to meeting organizational goals.[69]

SUMMARY

1. The role of communication is a critical process through which managers coordinate, lead, and influence others in the organization. The ability to be effective involves a broad array of activities including reading, listening, managing and interpreting information, writing, speech making, and using symbolic gestures. All types of communication involve a complex process that requires constant attention so that intended messages are sent and received in ways that help them be understood.

   Communication complexity results from the interaction of individuals and multiple variables including the setting, the experiences each person has had, the nature of the task, the symbolic aspects, and the changing environment—in particular, technology, global issues, and diversity in the workforce.

2. Communication is defined as a process in which one person or group evokes a meaning that is shared with or common to another person or group. Successful communication results when the message is received and conveys the exact meaning the sender intended.

3. The components of the communication process include the social context, or the setting in which the communication takes place; the sender who initiates and encodes the message; the channel, or the carrier of the message; the message itself; the receiver who decodes or translates the message; feedback, the process of verifying messages and the receiver's attempts to ensure that the message is what the sender really meant to convey; and noise, the interference with or distraction from the intended message that can cause distortion or miscommunication.

4. The categories of interpersonal communication include (a) oral communication, which includes all forms of spoken information and is the most preferred type; (b) written, which includes letters, memos, policy manuals, reports, forms, and other documents used to share information in an organization; (c) nonverbal, which includes all nonlanguage messages; and (d) technological communication, such as computer networks, e-mail, video conferencing, fax machines, and telecommuting.

5. Technological communication is a broad category of communication that is continuously changing and rapidly influencing how, when, and where managers communicate. Examples include videotape recorders, telephone-answering devices and services, closed-circuit television systems, fax machines, the Internet, computers, e-mail, mobile phones, and networked computers.

6. Managers communicate to motivate, inform, control, and satisfy social needs. Motivational communication serves the function of influencing the behavior of organizational members; informational communication provides facts and data to be used for decision making; communication that controls is intended to guide and coordinate so that multiple goals and tasks can be pursued; communication that fulfills social needs relates to the emotional and non-task-oriented interactions that occur in every organization.

7. The barriers that interfere with effective communication include cross-cultural diversity, the differences that can exist based on an individual's background and culture; lack of trust between the sender and the receiver such that the individuals involved may look for hidden meanings and misinterpret information; information overload that can lead to failing to process or ignoring information, incorrect use and delay of information, lowering the quality of information processing, or withdrawing from the information flow; language characteristics resulting from the impreciseness of words and meanings and the use of jargon; and gender differences.

8. The organization has two primary formal communication channels, vertical and horizontal. Vertical communication is the flow of information both upward and downward through the chain of command. Horizontal communication is the flow of information that occurs both within and between departments. The primary purpose of horizontal communication is coordination.

9. The principles for effective feedback include being specific rather than general, giving feedback when the receiver appears ready to accept it, focusing feedback on behavior rather than on the person and on behavior that can be changed, providing descriptive information about what the person said or did, and avoiding evaluative inferences about motives, intent, or feelings.

10. Listening is an active process. It requires that you listen for message content; listen for and respond to feelings; be sensitive to both the nonverbal and verbal content of messages; reflect back to the sender, in your own words, what you think you are hearing; be attentive and listen to understand, not to reply; and be patient and don't interrupt the speaker.

REVIEW QUESTIONS

1. (LEARNING OBJECTIVE 1) What is the role of communication in the organization, and why is it so complex for managers to understand?
2. (LEARNING OBJECTIVE 2) Define communication and discuss ways in which managers can work to achieve quality communication.
3. (LEARNING OBJECTIVE 3) Identify the components of the communication process. Explain why each is important.
4. (LEARNING OBJECTIVE 4) What are the four primary categories of interpersonal communication? Explain each of the categories and give an example.
5. (LEARNING OBJECTIVE 5) How are technological communication and information used in the workplace?
6. (LEARNING OBJECTIVE 6) Explain the essential reasons why managers communicate.
7. (LEARNING OBJECTIVE 7) Numerous barriers can interfere with effective communication. Select three and provide examples.
8. (LEARNING OBJECTIVE 8) Identify the different types of formal communication channels in the organization, and give examples.
9. (LEARNING OBJECTIVE 9) Why is feedback important? Identify the principles for effective feedback and explain why each is important.
10. (LEARNING OBJECTIVE 10) Specify the guidelines for becoming a good listener. How does each improve listening and communication?

DISCUSSION QUESTIONS

Improving Critical Thinking

1. Select one type of technological communication used in an organization and discuss how it can help to improve the communication process. Explain how it can interfere with the communication process.
2. Under what circumstances would telecommuting, or telework, be successful? When and why would it not work well?

Enhancing Communication Skills

3. With another person in your class, practice listening skills. Select a topic on which you disagree. First, ask the other person to explain his or her beliefs on the topic to you. Your role is to practice the guidelines to effective listening. Do not state your beliefs until the other person feels that you understand his or her side. Once that is accomplished, switch roles.
4. Prepare a brief oral presentation explaining how spontaneous communication channels can be both beneficial and harmful. Give examples from your own experience.

Building Teamwork

5. In a small group, brainstorm the positive sides of using e-mail. Next, brainstorm the negative aspects. Which list is longer? Why? Be prepared to summarize your ideas and report back to the class.
6. In a small group, go around the circle and have each person tell something about himself or herself that is unique. Don't write anything down, just listen. When everyone has spoken, test your listening skills by writing down each person's name and as much as you can remember about that individual's uniqueness. Compare your version and what the individual actually said. Who was the best listener in the group? What techniques were used?

Chapter

12

Leading in a Dynamic Environment

CHAPTER OVERVIEW

Societies, the broad environments of organizations, keep changing. Of course, this means that the people in the societies and the organizations change as well. The workforce is increasingly diverse in nature, has less loyalty to its employer, and has been slashed because of downsizing or other attempts to cut costs. Often these attempts are misguided because they focus on the short run. Further, organizations are becoming more borderless because of the necessary interactions between organizations (suppliers with manufacturers with retailers) and the continuing globalization of essentially all industries. To manage this successfully requires leaders who are capable of motivating and bringing together people and organizations that comprise a different kind of workforce. Further, what is needed are people who can unite a workforce at a time when confidence in leaders and institutions is at an all-time low.

Leaders face an abundance of challenging opportunities but have no clear blueprint for being a successful leader. The demand for good leaders has fascinated people throughout the ages. In fact, thousands of articles and books have been published on the subject, with many different approaches to looking at leadership. What is a leader? How do we judge a good leader? Are the methods we used to measure effectiveness a few years ago still appropriate in a changing world? Are leaders even necessary? These are the issues that we examine in this chapter.

We begin by examining the significance of leadership. Next, we explore the three broad approaches to understanding leadership: leader centered, follower centered, and interactive. The chapter continues with a discussion of current trends in leadership and concludes by examining leadership development.

LEARNING OBJECTIVES

When you have finished studying this chapter, you should be able to

1. Define leadership and explain its significance to an organization.
2. Differentiate the leader-centered approaches to leadership.
3. Describe the various types of power leaders use.
4. Explain what is meant by self-leadership and why it is important to organizations.
5. Characterize how leadership substitutes work.
6. Identify and define the variables in the situational leadership model.
7. Clarify how empowerment can increase the power and autonomy of organizational members.
8. Explain transformational leadership.
9. Describe the concept of emotional intelligence.
10. Discuss the changing role of women as leaders.

Facing The Challenge

Meg Whitman: Leading eBay

Meg Whitman, CEO of eBay, has proven herself over the last 7 years as one of the most capable leader in the high-tech history. Named by *Fortune* magazine as the most powerful woman in American business for 2004, she considers the attention as the last thing she wants. In fact, no CEO in Silicon Valley has ever been so successful at hiding herself in plain sight.

Prior to her position as CEO of eBay, Whitman was overseeing global marketing for the Mr. Potato Head and Playskool brands at Hasbro. She has a decidedly impressive corporate résumé, including degrees from Princeton and an MBA from Harvard. She worked as a marketing manager at Procter and Gamble, a consultant at Bain and Company, and held management positions with Disney, FTD, and Stride Rite. In fact, she was on track to be the typical CEO of a Fortune 500 company.

Uprooting her career and her family—a neurosurgeon husband and two sons in Boston schools—was the furthest thing from her mind. Then came a call from a Silicon Valley "headhunter." He had the perfect job for Whitman, he said. He told her all about this new website where consumers could trade their own goods for prices that they determine themselves. The recruiter wanted her to talk to the company's founder. He was prepared to offer Whitman the CEO spot. She politely said, "No way." The recruiter was persistent, though, and called Whitman a few more times over the next couple of weeks. Finally, she relented, agreeing to get on a plane and meet with eBay founder, Pierre Omidyar. While there, she saw the makings of a great brand and a profitable business.

In February 1998, Whitman signed on as eBay's CEO. Today, she is responsible for the largest operating margin of all publicly traded dot.coms—an impressive 30%. Whitman's leadership is considered to be unconventional. Her power has not come from control and size. Rather, Whitman has had to amass complex, subtle personal power. She serves as a role model for employees and the millions of people who buy and sell on the eBay site. Her image comes across positively to the public and especially to her employees. When referring to her leadership style, employees say she doesn't direct, she enables. She prides herself as being a nurturer and mentor of eBay managers. People are not threatened by her. She even wears the same outfit, navy polo shirt and khaki pants, as other eBay employees because she considers it to be egalitarian.

Whitman uses her influence carefully to establish credibility. She is known for doing what she said she was going to do, including meeting aggressive growth and profit goals for eBay. She has never missed a performance target. Today, as eBay passes the $3 billion mark a year ahead of schedule, her credibility has attracted lots of powerful admirers.

Running eBay has proved a lot more complicated than Whitman ever considered, and she has taken on a wide assortment of leadership roles. For example, a typical day might include handling the role of fielding complaints, listening in on conference calls and online chats with customers, juggling the conflicting demands of constituents, developing new strategic plans, and negotiating with international corporate presidents.

Whitman is no proponent of complacency. By expanding internationally and making bold acquisitions, such as the $1.5 billion purchase of payment processor PayPal Inc., eBay continues to expand internationally. Under her leadership, the auction company has avidly pursued relations with its overseas counterparts. In 2004, eBay acquired NeoCom Technology, Taiwan's leading operator of auction-style websites. In March 2004, eBay invested $30 million in cash to acquire a 33% interest in EachNet, an online trading community in China, and the two companies have agreed to share best practices to expand online trade there.

What's next for Whitman and eBay?

Sources: K. Bannan, "Sole Survivor," *Sales and Marketing Management* 153, no. 7 (2001): 36–41; A. Dragoon, "These Visionary CIOs and Business Leaders Have Skillfully Deployed IT to Accomplish Great Things for Their Organization CIO," 16 no. 1 (2002): 1; A. Cohen, Adam (2002). *The Perfect Store: Inside eBay.* (New York: Little, Brown, 2002); M. Copeland, E. Esfahani, S. Hamner, M. Leder, M. Maier, D. Mcdonald, T. Mucha, E. Schonfeld, P. Sloan, M. Warner, and G. P. Zachary (December 2004). "How to Succeed in 2005," *Business 2.0* 5, no. 11 (2004): 97–111; M. S. Malone (March 16, 2005). "Meet Meg Whitman," *Wall Street Journal,* 16 March 2005, A24; M. Pepe, "2002 Top 25 Executives," *CRN* 1021 (November 2002): 66–69; P. Sellers (October, 18, 2004). "eBay's Secret," *Fortune,* 18 October 2004, 160–167.

Introduction

This chapter is devoted to exploring what leadership is and how managers can develop leadership skills. Our examination of leadership provides a knowledge foundation for developing leader effectiveness in a global and diverse organizational environment. Our emphasis is on leadership in formal organizations such as business corporations, government agencies, hospitals, and universities. We examine leadership principles that can be practiced and applied and conclude with some guiding principles to get you started toward leadership effectiveness.

Throughout the chapter, we focus on individuals who demonstrate successful leadership in various ways. We also offer opportunities for you to apply leadership ideas to practice and enhance your leadership competency.

Leadership Significance

LEARNING OBJECTIVE 1

Define leadership and explain its significance to an organization.

1 We broadly define **leadership** as a social influence process. Leadership is not a position, title, or privilege; it is a responsibility and a process—an observable, understandable, learnable set of skills and practices available to everyone, anywhere in the organization.[1] Leadership is the indirect ability to influence people by setting an inspiring example—not just any sort of example but one that inspires people to pursue goals that benefit the organization. It is indirect because true leaders don't have to try to influence intentionally. Typically, leadership involves creating a vision of the future, devising a strategy for achieving that vision, and communicating the vision so that everyone understands and believes in it. Leadership also entails building a culture that will inspire and motivate people to overcome obstacles. In this way, leadership gets results and brings about change.[2]

A debate in the popular management literature concerns whether leading and managing are different behaviors. One view is that managers carry out responsibilities, exercise authority, and worry about how to get things done, whereas leaders are concerned with understanding people's beliefs and gaining their commitment. In other words, managers and leaders differ in what they attend to and in how they think, work, and interact. A related argument contends that leadership is about coping with change, whereas management is about coping with complexity.[3]

Although the leader–manager debate has generated tremendous controversy in the literature, little research exists to support the notion that certain people can be classified as leaders rather than managers or that managers cannot adopt visionary behaviors when they are required for success. We maintain that it is important for all managers to think of themselves as leaders, and consequently, we use the term *leadership* to encompass both leadership and management functions.[4]

For the purposes of our discussion of leadership, we have grouped leadership approaches into the three broad categories. Figure 12.1 shows leader-centered approaches, follower-centered approaches, and interactive approaches. We will start with leader-centered approaches.

Leadership involves creating a vision of the future, devising a strategy for achieving that vision, and communicating the vision so that everyone understands and believes in it.

© TOM McCARTHY/PHOTOEDIT

Leader-Centered Approaches

LEARNING OBJECTIVE 2

Differentiate the leader-centered approaches to leadership.

2 Leader-centered approaches focus on traits and skills, leader behavior, and power. One of the earliest approaches to studying leadership was the trait focus.

LEADER TRAITS AND SKILLS FOCUS

Underlying the **traits and skills focus** is the assumption that some people are endowed with certain physical characteristics (such as height and appearance), aspects of personality (such as self-esteem, dominance, conscientiousness, and emotional stability), and aptitudes (such as general

KEY TERMS

Leadership
A social influence process to influence people to achieve a common goal.

Traits and skill focus
The assumption that some people are born with certain physical characteristics, aspects of personality, and aptitudes that make them successful leaders.

Figure 12.1 Three Categories of Leader Approaches

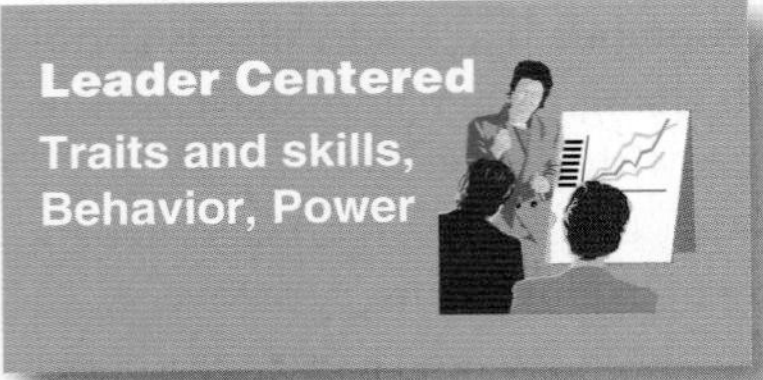

Follower Centered
Self-leadership
Leadership substitutes

Interactive
Situational leadership
Empowerment
Transformational leadership

intelligence, verbal fluency, and creativity). This research compared successful and unsuccessful leaders to see how they differed in physical characteristics, personality, ability, and certain skills.[5] The common outcome was that successful leaders possess greater (1) drive—that is, achievement, sense of responsibility, ambition, energy, tenacity, and initiative; (2) motivation, especially power; (3) honesty and integrity; (4) extraversion and self-confidence—that is, they are persuasive, diplomatic, and socially skilled; (5) conceptual ability; and (6) business knowledge. This does not mean, however, that just because a person has these characteristics that he or she will be a successful leader or even be a leader.

The evidence shows that leaders tend to differ from nonleaders with respect to the traits listed. Also, the evidence does not show that leaders are born. They are much more than a combination of traits. To succeed, leaders do not have to be intellectual geniuses or all-wise prophets, but they do have to have certain capabilities and the capacity to use their skills.[6] For example, in Chapter 1, we identified three types of skills that are relevant to managerial effectiveness. Technical skills, including knowledge about methods, processes, procedures, and techniques, are learned through formal education in specialized subjects such as accounting and computer engineering. Human skills are related to interpersonal relationships and include managing individual performance, motivating and disciplining subordinates, monitoring performance, providing feedback, and improving communications. These skills require the ability to understand the feelings, attitudes, and motives of others and the ability to communicate clearly and persuasively. Skills such as analytical ability, logical thinking, and inductive and deductive reasoning are considered conceptual skills.

A certain set of traits and skills, however, does not guarantee successful leadership. Each situation may have particular requirements that make one trait or skill more important in one situation than in another. A different trait or skill, or set of them, may be more important in another situation.[7] For example, many people are influenced by the physical height of a person; normally, the taller the person is, especially for a man, the more influential the person seems to have. A study of CEOs of Fortune 500 companies showed that over half were 6 feet or taller. Only 3% were shorter than 5 feet, 7 inches. In the past 25 elections for president of the United States, the taller man won in 21 of them.[8]

Possession of the qualities listed above does not guarantee that you will become a leader, nor does the absence of any one of them rule out the possibility of becoming an excellent leader. Because it takes more than certain traits to be successful, researchers began examining the behavior of leaders as an influence on leadership.

LEADERSHIP BEHAVIOR FOCUS

A second major leader-centered approach is the **behavior focus,** which examines what effective leaders do rather than what effective leaders are. We first examine two primary behaviors leaders use and then consider a leader's power.

Researchers examined two independent patterns of behaviors or styles that are used by effective leaders. The behavior focus assumed that what the leader does is the primary variable that determines effectiveness. Behavioral models defined a leader's effectiveness based on two orientations. The first is **task orientation** such as setting performance goals, planning and scheduling the work, coordinating activities, giving directions, setting standards, providing resources, and supervising worker performance. James Hackett, president and CEO of Steelcase, is known for his task orientation when dealing with analysts, employees, dealers, and the community.[9] The second is **relations orientation** such as showing empathy for concerns and feelings, being supportive of needs, showing trust, demonstrating appreciation, establishing trusting relationships, and allowing subordinates to participate in decision making. Elizabeth Robert, president and CEO of the Vermont Teddy Bear Company, is an example of a leader who demonstrates a strong relations orientation. When she was CFO and the company was on the verge of insolvency, employees came to her and asked for her help. When she became CEO, she kept that demeanor. For example, she listens when people come to her with an idea, she involves employees in the decision process, and she asks for input on the future direction for the company.[10]

Jack Welch, the retired CEO of General Electric, is still hailed today as one of America's most successful and influential CEOs (Table 12.1). In his earlier years, he was nicknamed "Neutron Jack," and in 1984, he was labeled as "the undisputed premier" among America's toughest bosses. He demonstrated all the task-oriented behaviors—demanding high performance standards, establishing rigid rules and procedures, autocratic decision making, and high levels of control and use of power. He is not particularly known for his use of relations-oriented behaviors.[11] However, one relations-oriented behavior does stand out. He knew how to pick people with leadership potential and provided mentoring. This includes recognizing someone for good performance.[12]

Numerous studies have examined task and relations behaviors, often with differing terms attached to the concepts of task orientation and relations orientation.[13] The general consensus is that one behavior does not occur at the expense of others. Taken together, we can conclude from the research on behaviors that (1) effective leaders use a range of behaviors, (2) these behaviors can be learned, and (3) an important characteristic of effective leaders is their ability to change and adapt to the organizational settings in which they manage.[14] However, it is still not obvious which behaviors are most effective because numerous other factors can influence performance and success. One of the most important results of the behavioral focus studies was that they directed our attention to the value of leadership training.[15] Before continuing read the "Now Apply It" box and learn some valuable tips on approaching a new promotion.

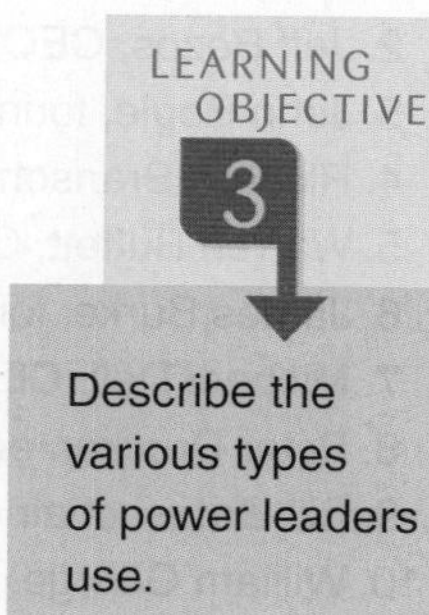

We tend to associate leaders with power. In fact, power is central to successful leadership. In the next section, we examine the power focus and how a leader can use power.

LEADERSHIP POWER FOCUS

3 **Power** is defined as the ability to use human, informational, or material resources to get something done. Let's distinguish power from authority. *Authority* is the right to get something done and is officially sanctioned; power is the ability to get results.

Power is important for leaders for influencing not only subordinates but also peers, supervisors, and people outside the organization such as clients and suppliers. Recall the power of Meg Whitman, CEO of eBay, who influences millions of eBay buyers and sellers as well as employees and stockholders. To understand the power process better, let's look at the various types of power. In addition, we consider whether the power is

KEY TERMS

Behavior focus
The study of what the effective leader does to be successful.

Task orientation
Leadership behavior that includes setting performance goals, planning and scheduling work, coordinating activities, giving directions, setting standards, providing resources, and supervising worker performance.

Relations orientation
Leadership behavior that shows empathy for concerns and feelings, being supportive of needs, showing trust, demonstrating appreciation, establishing trusting relationships, and allowing subordinates to participate in decision making.

Power
The ability to use human, informational, or material resources to get something done.

Table 12.1 The 25 Most Influential Leaders of Our Times

To celebrate the 25th anniversary of the *Nightly Business Report (NBR)*, Wharton and NBR worked to identify the 25 most influential business leaders of the past 25 years. Their goal was to find business leaders who created new and profitable ideas; affected political, civic, or social change through achievement in the business/economic world; created new business opportunities or more fully exploited existing ones; caused or influenced dramatic change in a company or industry; and/or inspired and transformed others.

1. Mary Kay Ash, founder of Mary Kay Cosmetics
2. Jeff Bezos, CEO of Amazon.com
3. John Bogle, founder of The Vanguard Group
4. Richard Branson, CEO of Virgin Group
5. Warren Buffett, CEO of Berkshire Hathaway
6. James Burke, former CEO of Johnson & Johnson
7. Michael Dell, CEO of Dell Computers
8. Peter Drucker, educator and author
9. Bill Gates, chair of Microsoft
10. William George, former CEO of Medtronics
11. Louis Gerstner, former CEO of IBM
12. Alan Greenspan, chair, U.S. Federal Reserve
13. Andy Grove, former chair of Intel
14. Lee Iacocca, former CEO of Chrysler
15. Steven Jobs, CEO of Apple Computers
16. Herb Kelleher, CEO of Southwest Airlines
17. Peter Lynch, former manager of Fidelity's Magellan Fund
18. Charles Schwab, founder of Charles Schwab Inc.
19. Frederick Smith, CEO of Federal Express
20. George Soros, founder and chair of Open Society Institute
21. Ted Turner, founder of CNN
22. Sam Walton, founder of Wal-Mart
23. Jack Welch, former CEO of General Electric
24. Oprah Winfrey, chair of the Harpo group of companies
25. Mohammed Yunus, founder of Grameen Bank

Source: "Becoming the Best: What You Can Learn from the 25 Most Influential Leaders of Our Times," from http://www.knowledge.wharton.upenn.edu, 11 February 2004.

KEY TERMS

Position power
The power attributed to one's position in an organization.

Legitimate power
The power based on formal authority.

Coercive power
The power to discipline, punish, or withhold rewards.

prescribed by the leader's position or is a result of personal attributes and to what degree the leader has a need for power.

Position Power

Power is derived in part from the opportunities inherent in a position in an organization. **Position power** includes legitimate power, coercive power, reward power, and information power.

Legitimate power stems from formal authority.[16] This authority is based on perceptions about the obligations and responsibilities associated with particular positions in an organization or social system. For example, Anne Mulcahy uses legitimate power as CEO of Xerox simply because of the formal position that she holds and because others believe that she has the legitimate right to influence them. Other people accept this power, as long as it is not abused, because they attribute legitimacy to the formal position and to the person who holds that position.

Coercive power is the power to discipline, punish, and withhold rewards. Coercive power is important largely as a potential rather than an actual type of influence. For

Now Apply It

Newly Promoted: Where Do You Start?

Congratulations, you've just been promoted to your first management job, and you have little or no training or preparation for it. However, you're not alone. Many employers provide very little training on how to manage and believe that simply having watched your own boss in action is enough to teach you how to be one. This can be a costly mistake.

According to Ben Dattner, head of Dattner Consulting in New York City (www.dattnerconsulting.com), few companies do a very good job of supporting and developing new managers. Dattner offers a few tips for new managers:

- Approach your new position as a learning process. Start with the assumption that you don't understand all that's required of you in this new role. Management positions are often complex, and the best way to take on a new responsibility is to be open to new ideas and don't be shy about asking for help.
- Avoid the trap of assuming that other people are motivated by the same things as you are. The best approach is to adapt to your new team's style and work together to develop an acceptable style.
- Expect high-quality performance but not perfection. New managers are often so intent on proving themselves that they push people to work late and come in on weekends to get everything perfect. This type of behavior may damage the work–life balance of the whole team. Be willing to back off a little.
- Encourage both individual and collective accountability. Keep reiterating the consequences: "Here's what will happen if we meet our goals, and here's what the negative results will be if we don't." This helps cultivate a sense of a shared fate. All leaders have to find ways to do it, so you may as well start now.
- Ask for suggestions or opinions if you are seriously prepared to consider them. Clarify areas that are open to discussion and negotiation and what things are not. Be explicit about the basis on which people will be rewarded. Discourage "in" and "out" groups. Employees need to see rewards based on performance, not on who likes you and supports you and who doesn't.

Source: A. Fisher, "How to Manage as a First-Time Boss," *Fortune*, 4 October 2004, 58.

example, the threat of being disciplined for not arriving at work on time is effective in influencing many employees to be punctual. Similarly, the possibility that we might get a speeding ticket is enough to cause many of us to drive within acceptable speed limits.

Another source of power that stems from a leader's position in the organization is influence over resources and rewards. **Reward power** is derived from control over tangible benefits such as a promotion, a better job, a better work schedule, a larger operating budget, an increased expense account, and formal recognition of accomplishments. Reward power is also derived from status symbols such as a larger office, an invitation to sit at the head table for visibility, or a reserved parking space. In addition to tangible benefits, leaders can also use rewards such the ones Riz Chand, senior vice president of human resources at Mary Kay, uses. He publically recognizes individuals during employee meetings for good work and deeds. In addition, he uses handwritten notes of praise to inspire employees to keep up the good work and to influence behavior. He is known as being courteous and considerate; he learns and uses employees' names and strives to be in touch with them; he knows how to use "thank you." All of these are simple yet powerful tools.[17]

Information power is control of information. It involves the leader's power to access and distribute information that is either desired by or vital to others. Managerial positions often provide opportunities to obtain information that is not directly available to subordinates or peers. However, some people acquire information power through their unique skill of always knowing all the latest news that others want and often need to know.

Consider, for example, renowned explorer Robert Swan, who was the first person to lead a team to both the North and South Poles. His belief about information was crucial in those endeavors. Swan believes that leaders are responsible for seeing that all team members have all the information needed to make wise decisions. He reasons, for example, that if only one person knows how to navigate and he or she gets sick, the whole team is going to get

KEY TERMS

Reward power
Power based on control of resources and rewards.

Information power
Power based on control of information.

lost.[18] After his successful exploration trips, he has taught businesspeople about leadership and sharing information as widely as possible at such companies as Merrill Lynch, Frito-Lay, and IBM.

With access to information only a keystroke away, power has shifted from those with titles to those with technology and the skills to use it. Considering the vast changes in the use of information technology in most organizations, you can see how information power has become a centralized focal point.[19]

Consider a very practical aspect of information power. In the past, when buying a car, the customer usually knew little about how much the dealer really paid for the car and how much markup there was. Now with information readily available on many websites, a customer can know almost exactly all the costs and markups associated with a certain car. That frequently puts the buyer in a better position to bargain when buying a new car if he or she wants to use the power and is otherwise skilled in negotiating.[20]

Personal Power

Leaders cannot rely solely on power that is derived from their position in the organization. Other sources of power must be cultivated. **Personal power** is derived from the interpersonal relationship between leaders and followers. It includes both expert and referent power.

A major source of personal power in organizations stems from expertise in solving problems and performing important tasks. **Expert power** is the power to influence another person because of expert knowledge and competence. Computer specialists often have substantial expert power in organizations because they have technical knowledge that others need. As we mentioned previously, not only is information technology influential in organizations, but also the computer systems and the individuals with the knowledge to operate them provide expertise to everyone in the organization. A technician who knows how to operate and repair office computer equipment may lack position power within the organization but has expert power.

Referent power is the ability to influence others based on personal liking, charisma, and reputation. It is manifested through imitation or emulation. Numerous reasons explain why we might attribute referent power to others. We may like their personalities, admire their accomplishments, believe in their causes, or see them as role models. Much of the power wielded by strong political leaders and professional athletes, musicians, and artists is referent power. People who feel a deep friendship or loyalty toward someone usually are willing to do special favors for that person. Mentors are usually individuals who are selected because of their referent power. Meg Whitman, president and CEO of eBay, is an example of a high-profile leader who uses her referent power. She exceeds goals by being a role model and helping others learn. In addition, she has built a culture that engages her customers, employees, and the community in the company mission.[21]

Generally, people tend to imitate the behavior of someone whom they greatly admire, and they tend to develop attitudes similar to those expressed by a person with whom they identify. Paris Hilton, Jon Stewart, Oprah Winfrey, and Tom Cruise are just a few of the many individuals who influence behavior with their referent power.

Have you ever considered whether power is good or bad, positive or negative? How do you make a judgment? To answer those questions, you need to understand how and why power is being used.

Most leadership-role requirements involve the use of power and influence. In large organizations, leaders must exercise power to influence others. For example, consider Warren Buffett, an extraordinary investor who has delivered enormous returns to investors in Berkshire Hathaway and was also highly successful as the hands-on CEO of Salomon Brothers, helping restore confidence in the Wall Street firm when it faced a severe management crisis. Buffett's power and influence derives from his moral stature and integrity. In the aftermath of scandals that have rocked U.S. companies in the past few years, it is difficult to overemphasize the importance of ethics as a factor in leadership.[22]

Leaders need to understand and use power. However, their effectiveness depends on how this need finds expression and whether it is a personalized or socialized power orientation.

A **personalized power orientation** is associated with a strong need for esteem and status; power is often used impulsively. For example, this orientation is found with centralized and controlled decision making. Information is likely to be restricted, and rewards and punishments are used to manipulate and control subordinates.

KEY TERMS

Personal power
Power derived from interpersonal relationships between leaders and followers.

Expert power
The power to influence another person because of expert knowledge and competence.

Referent power
The ability to influence others based on personal liking, charisma, and reputation.

Personalized power orientation
Associated with a strong need for esteem and status; power is often used impulsively.

Figure 12.2 Essential Strategies for Self-Leadership

- **Come to a realization about self-leadership and dispel the myths about leaders.**
- **Understand that leadership is not an external event.**
- **Take a personal inventory.**
- **Write a personal vision statement.**
- **Find a purpose or cause.**
- **Develop a plan.**
- **Establish a personal monitor, feedback, and correction system.**
- **Celebrate short-term wins.**
- **Initiate a personal reward and incentive system.**
- **Practice continuous learning and improvement.**

The opposite is true of leaders with a socialized power orientation. A **socialized power orientation** is represented by leaders who are mature, exercise power more for the benefit of others than for themselves, are less egoistic and defensive, and are willing to take advice from others in the organization. Such leaders help make subordinates feel strong and responsible.

Follower-Centered Approaches

The theme in the section on leader-centered approaches was to identify traits or behaviors leaders use to be effective. The leader-centered approaches focus on a narrow perspective: the leader in isolation. In reality, we know that leadership is affected by many factors. The second leadership category is follower-centered approaches. Let's turn our attention to self-leadership and leadership substitutes.

SELF-LEADERSHIP FOCUS

4 Although organizations spend millions annually to train potential leaders, not everyone will be a formal leader in all situations. Therefore, a high value has been placed on training potential self-leaders. Self-leadership, sometimes referred to as **followership,** is a paradigm founded on creating an organization of leaders who are ready to lead themselves.[23]

Teaching employees how to be effective self-leaders may be a wise decision. In many respects, an effective self-leader resembles an effective leader, with many of the skills that every leader must master.[24] Large organizations, discovering that an abundance of baby-boomer managers in their 40s and 50s are concerned about career plateauing, have begun to adopt leader partnerships and self-leadership training programs to assure employees that they are contributing even when they are not moving up the corporate ladder. Consider the nine leadership principles that Goldman Sachs created as a guiding model of all its employees.[25] (See the "At the Forefront" box.) Figure 12.2 offers a personalized strategy plan that lists the essential elements for self-leadership.[26]

Lincoln Electric, a Cleveland-based manufacturer of welding machines and electric motors, provides an example of the value of fostering organizational fol-

LEARNING OBJECTIVE 4

Explain what is meant by self-leadership and why it is important to organizations.

KEY TERMS

Socialized power orientation
The use of power for the benefit of others to make subordinates feel strong and responsible.

Followership
The paradigm know as self-leadership founded on creating an organization of leaders who are ready to lead themselves.

At the Forefront

What Goldman Sachs Looks For in Leaders

It took the senior leadership team at Goldman Sachs more than a year of work to create its nine leadership principles. The principles are based on the belief that good leadership is built on teamwork and change and grounded in integrity and fairness. According to Goldman Sachs, a leader must have a clear vision and the communication skills needed to execute. The nine leadership principles are as follows.

1. *Act with a profound sense of integrity and fairness* The daily stewardship and embodiment of these values is the primary responsibility of all leaders at Goldman Sachs. Integrity and fairness lie at the core of our heritage, our services to our clients, and our cultural strength. Leaders at all levels of the firm must uphold these values in their daily decisions and actions and instill them in their people as well.
2. *Deliver business results through commercial excellence and people development* The lifeblood of the organization is excellence as well as a key source of leadership credibility. Outstanding leaders create profitability not only through business development and client service but also through recruiting, coaching, developing, and retaining the best people. Leaders develop leaders and leadership demands consistent and purposeful investment of time with our people.
3. *Build strong client and other external relationships* The success of the organization depends on the quality of our relationships with a broad group of influential clients and leaders around the world. Our best leaders successfully develop long-term relationships across multiple cultures. They succeed through outstanding client service as well as playing leadership roles in external business and community groups.
4. *Drive teamwork within and between businesses* Teamwork and dedication to the organization's greatest good are competitive advantages. Leaders maintain a strong network of relationships. They cross-market products and services and actively share ideas and talent across divisional, departmental, regional, and hierarchical boundaries.
5. *Foster learning, innovation, and change* Leaders welcome and drive change. They constantly extract the learning from their own failures and successes as well as those of others who are both internal and external to Goldman Sachs. They build on our past success but also take the entrepreneurial risks necessary to innovate and grow our business.
6. *Debate freely, decide swiftly, and commit* Leaders challenge the status quo and have the courage to express and allow disagreement. However, they drive issues toward decisions and embrace decisions once they have been made.
7. *Promote meritocracy by welcoming and leveraging differences* Our clients and employees comprise a heterogeneous group of successful, influential men and women from all cultures, races, and ethnicities. Leaders create meritocracies that recognize and reward the diverse people and talents the firm requires to succeed around the world. They ensure that all employees have opportunities, free from artificial barriers, to rapidly advance to the utmost of their abilities.
8. *Develop strategy and execute* Leaders develop and articulate a clear vision and strategy for their business and set concrete goals toward realizing their strategy. They move quickly, make tough decisions, and show excellent judgment. Finally, they are relentless in prioritizing actions and executing to the highest standards.
9. *Create trust and credibility through honest communication* Our best leaders communicate fully, directly, and candidly, and they follow with action. They are also good listeners. Above all, they recognize that the power of their personal example is greater than the power of their words.

Source: Adapted from M. Goldsmith, H. Morgan, and A. J. Ogg (eds.), *Leading Organizational Learning: Harnessing the Power of Knowledge* (San Francisco: Jossey-Bass, 2004).

© SUSAN VAN ETTEN

FedEx is one company that encourages employee self-leadership.

lowership. The structure of the organization requires each employee to be accountable for his or her own behavior. Even in recessionary times, employees are loyal to the company and show their cooperation by performing duties not required by their contracts. Employees are asked to serve on an advisory board that meets weekly to assess how the company is doing in a variety of areas. The employees understand the organization and their contributions to it. They are adaptable and take responsibility for their own actions. In essence, the employees of Lincoln Electric are good followers.[27] There are numerous other successful companies that have cultures that encourage self-leadership, including ServiceMaster Clean, a national franchise of cleaning service; Microsoft; Goldman Sachs; Trader Joe's; Whole Foods Market; W. L. Gore, the inventor of Gore-Tex; FedEx; and Wegman's Food Markets.[28] Excellent examples have been discussed in previous chapters, such as Avon, JetBlue, Southwest Airlines, Aveda, Nokia, The Container Store, and General Electric.

Studies show that effective self-leaders have most of the following characteristics:[29]

1. The capacity to motivate themselves and stay focused on tasks.
2. Integrity that demands both loyalty to the organization and the willingness to act according to beliefs.
3. Understanding of the organization and their contributions to it.
4. Willingness to take the initiative to deal with problems.
5. Versatility, skillfulness, and flexibility to adapt to a changing environment.
6. Responsibility for their own careers, actions, and development.

LEADERSHIP SUBSTITUTES

Some argue that the importance of leadership is overrated and that leaders make little or no difference. In contrast to traditional models that assume that hierarchical leadership is always important, the premise of the leadership-substitutes focus is that the leader is less important, redundant, or even irrelevant.

5 **Leadership substitutes** are variables, such as individual, task, and organizational characteristics (Figure 12.3), that tend to outweigh the leader's ability to affect subordinate satisfaction and performance. These are known as neutralizers. A **neutralizer** is a condition that counteracts leader behavior or prevents the leader from having an effect on a follower or a specific situation.[30]

Follower characteristics that can serve as leadership substitutes include a high level of experience, training, ability, professional orientation, or indifference toward organizational rewards. For example, if employees have the skills and abilities to perform the job and a high need for independence, leadership is less important, and employees may resent a leader who provides structure and direction. For example, a professor in a graduate-level seminar may need to provide students with just a set of readings and materials to be studied rather than a structured course outline.

LEARNING OBJECTIVE 5

Characterize how leadership substitutes work.

Various task attributes can serve as leadership substitutes. For example, if the task is simple and repetitive, subordinates can learn the appropriate skills without extensive training. Tasks that are characterized by structure or frequent feedback can also neutralize leader behavior, as can tasks that are intrinsically satisfying.

Characteristics of the organization can also substitute for leadership. When the organization possesses high levels of formality, inflexibility, cohesive work groups, staff support, managerially independent reward structures, and spatial distance between followers and managers, the need for formal leadership decreases.[31]

KEY TERMS

Leadership substitutes
Things that guide or influence people in place of a leader, including individual, task, and organizational characteristics.

Neutralizer
A condition that counteracts leader behavior or prevents a leader's influence.

Figure 12.3 Leadership Substitutes

Individual Characteristics

Experience
Training
Ability
Professional orientation
Indifference to organizational rewards

Task Characteristics

Degree of intrinsic satisfaction
Degree of repetitiveness
Degree of structure or feedback

Organizational Characteristics

Degree of formality
Degree of flexibility
Amount of cohesiveness
Independence of reward structure
Degree of spatial distance from manager

Interactive Approaches

LEARNING OBJECTIVE 6

Identify and define the variables in the situational leadership model.

Another method of examining leadership effectiveness is to look at how leaders interact with their followers either directly, in a specific situation, or indirectly, such as how followers interpret the leader's behavior. The three approaches we have chosen to discuss are the situational leadership model, empowerment, and transformational leadership.

KEY TERMS

Situational leadership model An approach that examines the interaction between leadership style and employee readiness.

SITUATIONAL LEADERSHIP MODEL

6 The **situational leadership model** is based on the interaction of certain employee characteristics, referred to as readiness, and leadership style, based on the concern for the task and the concern for the employee (recall our earlier discussion of two primary leader behaviors—task orientation and relations orientation). To maximize employee performance, leaders must use a leadership style that is appropriate to their development or readiness.

Readiness is the extent to which a subordinate possesses the ability, knowledge, and skills, job experience, and willingness to complete a specific task. Subordinates have various degrees of readiness depending on their confidence and competence to perform a task independently, the tendency to assume additional responsibility, and the desire to achieve success.

According to the situational leadership model, a leader can adopt one of four leadership styles: telling, selling, participating, or delegating. We briefly discuss these styles and when they are most appropriate to use.

A leader using the **telling style** provides specific instructions and closely supervises performance. This is the most directive of the four styles, and the leader is primarily focused on giving explicit guidelines, setting goals, and providing structure. This style works best when employee readiness is low. The direction provided by this leadership style defines roles for employees who are unable or unwilling to take responsibility because it eliminates any insecurity about the task that must be done.

Using the **selling style,** the leader explains decisions and provides opportunities for clarification. This style offers both direction and support for employees who are not yet competent but are willing to take on responsibility. It combines a directive approach with positive support, interaction, involvement and reinforcement for maintaining enthusiasm.

The **participating style** involves sharing ideas and maintaining two-way communication to encourage and support the skills the employees have developed. It is used most appropriately for moderate to high employee readiness. The leader focuses on sharing ideas and responsibility with an emphasis more on the relationship and employee involvement than on the specifics of the task. Competent employees require supportive behavior to increase their motivation. This style helps enhance a subordinate's desire to perform a task because it shares the decision making.

Leaders use a **delegating style** to provide subordinates with minimal directions and support for the relationship. When employees have reached a high level of readiness (highly competent and confident), the leader allows them to decide how and when to do things. Because employees are able and willing to take responsibility for what needs to be done, it is appropriate for the leader to use a delegating style.

As employees gain confidence and competence, they move through different stages of readiness. Therefore, the leader's behavior changes to reflect this increased readiness. For example, as the employee increases readiness (gains confidence and competence), the leader focuses on supportive behavior and less on task behavior until the employee reaches the highest level of development, a stage referred to as high readiness. At this stage, the employee has become skilled, confident, and self-sufficient. When employees reach this stage, the leader focuses on delegating and thus provides minimal task and relations behavior.

To be successful, a leader adopting this model of behavior needs the ability to identify employee readiness for specific tasks, diagnose the demands of the situation, and choose the appropriate behavior to match the task and employee requirements. The situational leadership model shows that leaders must be flexible in choosing a leadership style. Using the appropriate leadership style maximizes productivity, increases morale, and produces long-term results.[32]

The situational leadership model has been received well by leadership practitioners, perhaps in part because it is intuitive, focuses on employees' feeling of competence, and emphasizes leadership training and development programs that are widely available.[33]

Employee picnics provide a leisure opportunity for leaders to communicate with and increase the morale of their workers.

© MICHAEL NEWMAN/PHOTOEDIT

EMPOWERMENT

One of the major forces for cultural and structural changes in organizations has been the empowerment movement. **Empowerment** is designed to increase the power and autonomy of all employees in an organization. It has its roots in the perceptions of Japanese management—the quality-circle efforts of the 1970s and the quality-of-work-life (QWL) approach—and the psychological concept of self-efficacy.[34]

7 The underlying theme of empowerment is the interaction of the leader who is giving up or sharing power with those who use it to become involved and committed to independent, high-quality performance. Such power sharing provides people with a belief in their ability and their sense of effectiveness.[35]

Empowerment is often described as delegation or devolution of power, authority, or

LEARNING OBJECTIVE 7

Clarify how empowerment can increase the power and autonomy of organizational members.

KEY TERMS

Readiness
The extent to which a subordinate possesses the ability, knowledge, and skills, job experience, and willingness to complete a specific task.

Telling style
The leader provides specific instructions and closely supervises performance.

Selling style
The leader explains decisions and provides opportunities for clarification.

Participating style
The leader shares ideas and maintains two-way communication to encourage and support the skills subordinates have developed.

Delegating style
The leader provides the subordinates with few task or relations behaviors. Authority and responsibility rest with the follower.

Empowerment
Delegating authority to the follower and holding him or her accountable. It includes making sure that the follower understands the task, has proper information, training, motivation, guidance, and skills to be successful.

Table 12.2 Primary Dimensions of Transformational Leadership

Dimension	Leader's Specific Behavior	Follower's Behavior
Individualized consideration	Acts as mentor; is attentive to achievement and growth needs.	Is motivated; feels valued.
Intellectual stimulation	Promotes innovation and creativity; reframes problems.	Is encouraged to be novel and try new approaches.
Inspirational motivation	Provides meaning and challenge through prosocial, collective action.	Is motivated by team spirit; is enthusiastic and optimistic.
Idealized influence	Shares risks; is considerate of others over own needs; is ethical and moral.	Shows admiration, respect, and trust.

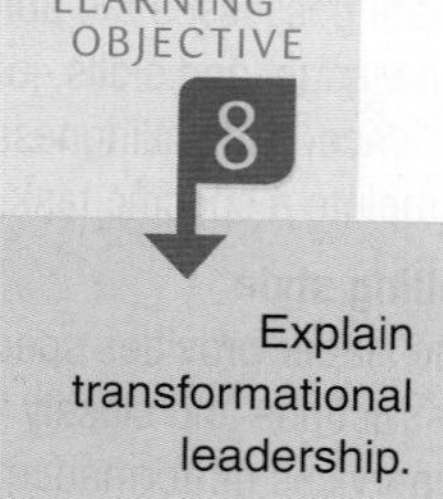

Explain transformational leadership.

responsibility by those higher in the organizational structure to those at lower levels of the organization.[36] Successful empowerment means that everyone truly understands his or her role in achieving the mission of the organization; has the skills, information, and motivation to make good decisions; is held accountable; and receives appropriate rewards for successful performance. Empowered individuals feel that what they do has meaning and significance, that they have discretion as well as obligations, and that they live in a culture of respect in which they are encouraged to act on their own. Empowered organizations generate and sustain trust as well as communicate constantly. The president of Pay Plus Benefits, John Heaton, is an example of a leader who has brought empowerment to his organization. He believes in empowering and augmenting the lives of employees, engaging them in work, and encouraging freedom, self-discipline, and the right to fail. For example, employees at Pay Plus Benefits are free to set their own hours. Heaton's goal is to create a work environment in which employees' performance can be outstanding; he believes that is more important than establishing rigid operational rules.[37]

Research and observations of many leaders strongly suggest that power sharing contributes to an organization's effectiveness if empowerment is developed effectively. Empowerment of employees can also be a powerful motivational tool, as we discuss in Chapter 14, by providing them with both control and a sense of accomplishment.[38]

KEY TERMS

Transformational leadership
Leadership in which the leader has the ability to influence subordinates to achieve more than was originally expected.

TRANSFORMATIONAL LEADERSHIP

8 **Transformational leadership** refers to the leader's ability to influence employees to achieve more than was originally expected or thought possible. This is most successful when the leader understands the vision of the organization and can articulate it to the employees. In addition, transformational leaders are able to generate feelings of trust, admiration, and loyalty, and to tap deep values and respect from followers.[39] Consequently, followers are motivated to achieve more than was originally expected and view their work as more important and as more self-congruent.[40] This motivation is created when the leader makes subordinates more aware of the importance and values of task outcomes, helps them think beyond their own self-interest to the needs of the work teams and the organization, and activates higher-order needs such as creative expression and self-actualization.[41]

Transformational leaders do not accept the status quo. They recognize the need to revitalize their organizations and challenge standard operating procedures; they institutionalize change by replacing old technical and political networks with new ones. In other words, transformational leaders transform things from what could be to what is by generating excitement.[42]

Four primary dimensions of transformational leadership include idealized influence, inspirational motivation, intellectual stimulation, and individualized consideration.[43] As shown in Table 12.2, each dimension involves specific behaviors by the leader that in turn inspire follower behavior.

Though the literature on transformational leadership focuses on CEOs and top-level managers, transformational leadership involves the actions of individuals at all levels, not just those at the top. Transformational leaders influence followers through value internalization and self-engagement with work. They motivate by activating the higher needs of followers, appealing to their moral ideas, and empowering them.

Current Perspectives on Leadership

Numerous issues and themes are related to leadership and leader development that provide insight for managers. In this next part, we discuss emotional intelligence and the relationship between gender and leadership.

EMOTIONAL INTELLIGENCE

9 An area of leadership development focused on the human and interpersonal skills of a manager is **emotional intelligence** (EI). Based on the research of Daniel Goleman and associates, EI is the capacity to effectively manage ourselves and our relationships.[44]

There are two major components of EI, personal competence and social competence. The competencies associated with each component are shown in Table 12.3. Personal competence refers to the ability to understand your own feelings, emotions, and their impact and to understand your strengths and weaknesses (based on the concept of self-awareness). The ability to manage those feelings effectively is the concept of self-management. For example, being able to contain your anger and anxiety and thereby think clearly in upsetting situations is crucial to making good decisions and influencing others.

The second component of EI is social competence. This refers to the ability to understand what others are feeling (the concept of social awareness) and having the skills to work effectively with others (based on social skill). This ability—understanding what people think and feel, knowing how to persuade and motivate them, and resolving conflicts and forging cooperation—is among the most important skill of successful leaders and managers.[45]

Goleman's research at nearly 200 large, global companies revealed that emotional intelligence, especially at the highest levels of a company, was a critical skill for leaders. EI was twice as important as cognitive (IQ) or technical skills in differentiating high performance. Without it, a person can have first-class training, an incisive mind, and an endless supply of good ideas, but he or she still won't make a great leader.[46]

Demonstrating EI at the workplace does not mean simply controlling your anger or getting along with people. Rather, it focuses on learning to be self-aware, empathetic, adept, and flexible in relationships. In addition, the underlying concept is that leadership competencies can be developed through the provision of training, ongoing assessment, and individual development strategies. Kenneth Chenault, chair and CEO of American Express, describes six distinguishing features that he believes are the foundation for becoming a skilled and exceptional leader. How many of these reflect the qualities of EI leadership? (See the "Leaders in Action" box.)

EI is now being used as a central competency in management-development programs at some of the leading global businesses. As a result, they are realizing improvements in both individual and organizational performance. For example, studies of sales teams highlight the impact of EI on the bottom line. A recent study of Fortune 500 companies—including AT&T, IBM, and PepsiCo—found salespeople with high EQ (emotional quotients, which are the measure of EI) produced twice the revenue of salespeople with average EQ scores. At American Express, financial advisers increased sales by 20% after undertaking EI training. In the service arena where the customer interface is the primary means of achieving customer loyalty, the ability to empathize, understand, and deliver exactly what the customer wants directly improves customer-retention rates.[47]

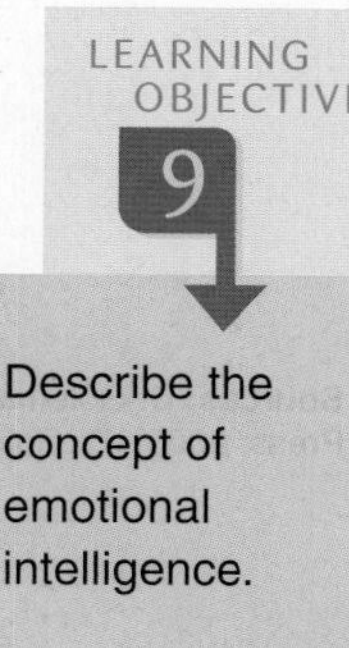

Describe the concept of emotional intelligence.

GENDER AND LEADERSHIP

Does gender affect leadership success? Do men and women differ in terms of leadership ability? Research shows that both men and women can be effective leaders, but they approach their leader positions differently. According to a new study by Caliper, a Princeton, New Jersey–based management consulting firm,

KEY TERMS

Emotional Intelligence
The capacity to effectively manage ourselves and our relationships.

Table 12.3 The Emotional Intelligence Competency Framework

Dimensions	Competencies
Personal Competence	
Self-management	*Self-control:* Keeping disruptive emotions and impulses under control
	Trustworthiness: Honesty and integrity
	Conscientiousness: Demonstrating responsibility in managing ourselves
	Adaptability: Flexibility with challenges
	Achievement orientation: Drive to improve
	Initiative: Readiness to act
Self-awareness	*Emotional self-awareness:* Recognizing emotions and their effects
	Accurate self-assessment: Knowing strengths and limits
	Self-confidence: A strong sense of self-worth and capabilities
Social Competence	
Social awareness	*Empathy and insight:* Understanding others and taking an active interest in their concerns
	Political awareness: Empathizing at the organizational level
	Service orientation: Understanding others' perspectives and feelings
Social skill	*Developing others:* Sensing others' developmental needs and bolstering their abilities
	Visionary leadership: Inspiring and guiding groups and people
	Influence: Wielding interpersonal influence tactics
	Communication: Sending clear and convincing messages and using a sense of humor
	Change catalyst: Initiating or managing change
	Conflict management: Resolving disagreements
	Building bonds: Nurturing instrumental relationships
	Teamwork and collaboration: Creating a shared vision and leveraging diversity
	Synergy in teamwork: Working with others toward shared goals

Sources: D. Goleman, R. Boyatzis, and A. McKee, *Primal Leadership: Realizing the Power of Emotional Intelligence* (Boston: Harvard Business School Press, 2003); D. Goleman "Leadership That Gets Results," *Harvard Business Review* (March/April 2000): 78–90.

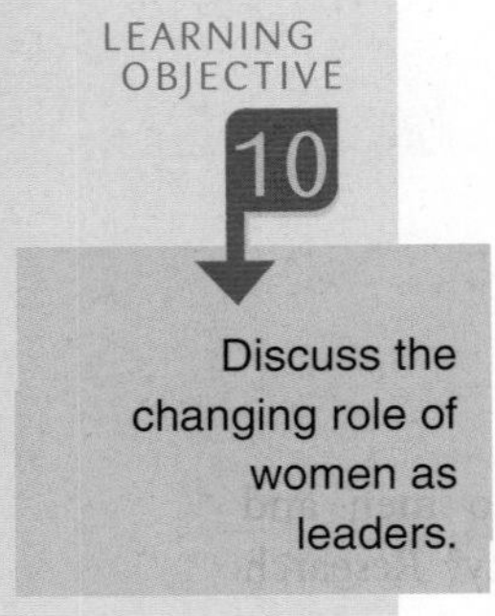

female leaders are more empathic, persuasive, better listeners, and more willing to consider others' points of view.[48] Women are better at expressing feelings and accessing their emotions, and women have an easier time switching from the verbal left brain to the emotional right brain than men do. Men show pain and distress differently than women—they tend to externalize them, whereas women tend to internalize them. In addition, male leaders showed higher levels of resilience and thoroughness than women leaders.

How well do men accept women as leaders? Research indicates that men's attitudes toward women in the workplace are gradually changing as more women enter the workforce and assume leadership positions. Studies show that both men and women executives believe that women have to be exceptional to succeed in the business world. Women leaders still face disadvantages in business and feel they must struggle harder than men to succeed.[49] In an effort to support junior female managers, Procter and Gamble pairs female employees with a senior manager for reverse mentoring to help the mostly male executives understand the issues that women face.[50]

In the past, successful leaders have been associated with stereotypical masculine attributes such as competitiveness, task orientation, and willingness to take risks.[51] Recent studies, however, show that female middle- and top-level executives no longer equate successful leadership with these masculine attributes. Both male

Leaders in Action

Kenneth Chenault on Distinguishing Features of Exceptional Leaders

According to Kenneth Chenault, chair and CEO of American Express, there are six distinguishing features or attributes that he believes are the foundation for becoming a skilled and exceptional leader. The first attribute is *integrity.* Chenault believes it is this core principle on which true leadership is built. Integrity is about being consistent in words and actions. When you are trying to lead others, they look for consistency.

The second feature is *courage.* It requires courage to offer a different perspective and challenge current or popular views. It requires courage to speak out, especially when one doesn't personally benefit from it. To build followership, one has to be courageous and come from the core value of integrity.

The third attribute is being a *team player.* Strong team players engage in confrontation when that's what is really needed. They provide constructive feedback and help the team improve.

The fourth attribute is *execution skills.* This means a personal commitment to take decisive action that benefits the organization.

The fifth distinguishing feature is *development of people.* This refers to facilitating the achievement of others and helping them to succeed. Chenault judges the success of a leader by the success of the people who are the followership.

The sixth leadership attribute is being *proactive.* A leader has to take action and make things happen.

Chenault believes that it's a lot easier to be a good leader in good times than in bad, but a reputation for leadership over the long term is established during times of change. Today, the stakes are incredibly high. The need for leaders to stand for something and act from principle is more important than ever.

Chenault confirms that personal integrity is a very big thing with him and believes that you shouldn't sell yourself to the highest bidder. If you don't believe in the product or ideals of a company or organization, he contends, don't accept the job. Dedicate yourself to a core set of values. Without them, you will never be able to find personal fulfillment, and you will never be able to lead effectively.

Sources: J. Creswell, "Ken Chenault Reshuffles His Cards," *Fortune,* 18 April 2005, 180–183; C. Clarke, "Memos from the CEOs," *Black Enterprise* 35, no. 7 (2005): 154–155; J. Roberts, "The Race to the Top," *Newsweek,* 28 January 2002, 44–49; M. Whitman-Desir, "Leadership Has Its Rewards," *Black Enterprise* 30, no. 2 (1999): 72–78.

and female leaders possess a high need for achievement and power and demonstrate assertiveness, self-reliance, risk taking, and other traits and behaviors associated with effective leadership.[52] However, a trend exists of more women making their way to the top who are not only adopting styles and habits that have proved successful for men but also drawing on the skills and attitudes they have developed from their experiences as women. Generally, women are more likely to use behaviors that are associated with transformational leadership, such as reliance on expertise, charisma, and interpersonal skills. Men are more likely to be directive.[53]

More and more organizations are being led by women. For example, some well-known women leaders include Carly Fiorina, former CEO of Hewlett-Packard; Andrea Jung, CEO of Avon (featured in Chapter 1); Meg Whitman, CEO of eBay; Anne Mulcahy, CEO of Xerox; Elisabeth Robert, CEO of Vermont Teddy Bear Company; Oprah Winfrey, chair of the Harpo group of companies; Mary Kay, the founder of Mary Kay Cosmetics; Louise Wilmot, until her retirement, the highest ranking woman (rear admiral) in the U.S. Navy; and many others.[54] Notice in Table 12.1 that only two women out of 25 people listed were considered to be the most influential business leaders of the past 25 years.

LEADERS OF THE FUTURE

With ever-increasing globalization and change, leaders will be challenged to manage relationships more than in the past. This will include the ability to interact effectively with a diversity of partners and other businesses and within the larger context of differing cultures. Predictions are that the total trade between countries will exceed the total value of trade within countries by the year 2015. This will require truly "global" leaders.

As we have been discussing throughout the book, the changing global environment is likely to continue to stimulate the transformation and revitalization of public and private institutions. Small as well as large U.S. companies such as IBM, Xerox, American Express, Hewlett-Packard, Amazon.com, and Microsoft recognize that they will have to change in order to survive.

They have embarked on programs of extensive change that must be accomplished in short periods of time. Such transformations require a new set of leadership guidelines.

It is a new era for business leaders. Emerging economic, social, and cultural pressures demand that they find better ways to align their leadership vision, core values, and everyday actions to produce desired results in all aspects of their lives, not just work.[55] It is clear that the successful leader of the 21st century will be one who promotes leadership development and encourages workers to assume his or her role as leader.[56] Individuals working in 21st-century organizations must be innovative and creative, practice continuous learning, have values (especially integrity), have a personal vision, be in charge of their own careers, motivate from within, plan, communicate, and seek harmonious relationships with stakeholders.

Implications for Leaders

We conclude this chapter on leadership with a list of guiding principles to start you toward leadership effectiveness. The topics in this book and course, plus all other topics and courses in your educational career, can help you build a competency base that will help you understand and develop your leadership. Supplemented by experience and mistakes (but you must truly learn from mistakes and not just repeat them), you can build a foundation that is necessary to establish a healthy organizational community.[57] The following ten items get to the core of what leadership is all about.[58] Following these principles will help you develop effective leadership skills.

1. *Know yourself.* You cannot be an effective leader without knowing your own strengths and weaknesses. Knowing your capabilities will allow you to improve on your weaknesses and trade on your strengths.
2. *Be a role model.* Expect no more than what you yourself are willing to give.
3. *Learn to communicate with your ears open and your mouth shut.* Most problems that leaders are asked to solve are "people" problems created because of a failure in communication. Communication failures are the result of people's hearing but not listening to and understanding one another.
4. *Know your team and be a team player.* As a leader, make the effort to know what other team members are doing, not necessarily to monitor their progress but to seek ways and means of providing assistance.
5. *Be honest with yourself as well as with others.* All good leaders make mistakes. Rarely do they make the same mistake more than once. Openly admit a mistake, learn from it, and forget it. Generally, others will forget it too.
6. *Do not avoid risks.* If you are to become an effective leader, you will need to become an effective risk taker. Take "calculated" risks and, if you make a mistake, learn from it. See problems as challenges, challenges as catalysts for change, and changes as opportunities.
7. *Believe in yourself.* All effective leaders share the characteristic of confidence in their own ability to get the job done. This personal confidence is often contagious and quick to permeate an entire organization, boosting confidence levels of all team members.
8. *Take the offense rather than the defense.* The most effective leaders are quicker to act than they are to react. Their best solution to any problem is to solve it before it becomes a problem. If they see something that needs fixing, they will do what they can to repair it before being told to do so by someone else.
9. *Know the ways of disagreement and the means of compromise.* People will disagree with one another, but remember that who wins or loses is not important. The real winner is the leader who can facilitate the opposing side's goals while achieving his or her own.
10. *Be a good follower.* Effective leaders lead as they would like to be led.

This chapter has explored many facets of leadership effectiveness for the dynamic environment in which you are or soon will be working. As we noted earlier, a considerable amount of research has been done on leadership, and many books and articles have been published on the topic. Although leadership means different things to different people, it is critical to understand that leadership is not equivalent to a rank or title, nor are leaders born. Leadership is a process, and it can be learned.

Meeting The Challenge

Meg Whitman: Leading eBay

Leadership development has been an ongoing concern of eBay's board. Meg Whitman admits that the company needs a greater emphasis on day-to-day coaching and mentoring. eBay's growth has been extremely fast from 5700 employees in 2003 to an estimated 8000 by 2006. Top executives need to develop strong leadership skills because managing 8000 people in 29 countries is a challenge difficult for any leader to comprehend.

The subject of Whitman's retirement comes up often. She has said in the past that no CEO should ever serve more than a decade; and she has already begun grooming individuals to succeed her. She can also look ahead and see that eBay's future is probably going to be grimmer than its past: The domestic online auction business is flattening (eBay having bounced the rubble in most of America's attics and garages) and the international market—especially China—does not look promising by eBay standards.

Sources: K. Bannan, "Sole Survivor," *Sales and Marketing Management* 153, no. 7 (2001): 36–41; A. Dragoon, "These Visionary CIOs and Business Leaders Have Skillfully Deployed IT to Accomplish Great Things for Their Organization CIO," 16, no. 1 (2002): 1; A. Cohen, *The Perfect Store: Inside eBay* (New York: Little, Brown, 2002); M. Copeland, E. Esfahani, S. Hamner, S. M. Leder, M. Maier, D. Mcdonald, T. Mucha, E. Schonfeld, P. Sloan, M. Warner, and G. P. Zachary, "How to Succeed in 2005" *Business 2.0* 5, no. 11 (2004): 97–111; M. S. Malone, "Meet Meg Whitman," *Wall Street Journal*, 16 March 2005, A24; M. Pepe, "2002 Top 25 Executives," *CRN* 1021 (November 2002): 66–69; P. Sellers, "eBay's Secret," *Fortune*, 18 October 2004, 160–167.

SUMMARY

1. Leadership is broadly defined as a social influence process that inspires people to pursue goals that benefit the organization.
2. There are three primary leader-centered approaches to leadership. The earliest approach was the trait focus, which is based on the assumption that some people are born with certain physical characteristics, aspects of personality, and attitudes. The second approach is the behavior focus, which examines what effective leaders do rather than what effective leaders are. The power focus is the ability to marshal human, informational, or material resources to get something done.
3. Leaders have two primary types of power—position and personal. From their position in an organization, they have legitimate, coercive, reward, and information power. Personal power is derived from the interpersonal relationship between leaders and their followers, including expert and referent power.
4. Self-leadership is a paradigm founded on creating an organization of leaders who are ready to lead themselves.
5. Leadership substitutes are variables such as individual, task, and organizational characteristics that tend to outweigh the leader's ability to influence subordinates.
6. According to the situational leadership model, effective leader behavior depends on the match between leader style and subordinate readiness. The four leader styles are telling, selling, participating, and delegating.
7. Empowerment is the delegation of power or authority by those higher in the organizational structure to those at lower levels of the organization or the sharing of power with them. It includes holding people accountable for their decisions. Successful empowerment means that everyone understands his or her role in the organization and has the proper training, motivation, and guidance to make good decisions.
8. Transformational leadership refers to leadership that influences employees to achieve more than was originally expected or thought possible.
9. Emotional intelligence (EI) focuses on human and interpersonal skills of a manager. The two components are personal competence and social competence. Personal competence refers to the ability to understand your own feelings and emotions and their impact, to understand your strengths and weaknesses,

and the ability to manage those feelings effectively. Social competence is the ability to understand what others are feeling, to work effectively with others, to understand what people think and feel and to know how to persuade and motivate them, and to resolve conflicts and forge cooperation.

10. Research shows that both men and women can be effective leaders but they approach their leadership positions differently.

REVIEW QUESTIONS

1. (LEARNING OBJECTIVE 1) Define leadership. How important is good leadership to an organization?
2. (LEARNING OBJECTIVE 2) Explain the trait and skills focus of leadership. How successful is this focus in identifying people who will be effective leaders?
3. (LEARNING OBJECTIVE 3) Explain the basis of legitimate power of a leader.
4. (LEARNING OBJECTIVE 4) Explain what is meant by self-leadership and why it is important to organizations.
5. (LEARNING OBJECTIVE 5) Identify four substitutes for leadership and give a specific example as to how each might substitute for a leader.
6. (LEARNING OBJECTIVE 6) Explain what readiness is in the situational leadership model.
7. (LEARNING OBJECTIVE 7) Explain how empowerment can help improve the effectiveness of an organization.
8. (LEARNING OBJECTIVE 8) What does a leader do to be considered transformational?
9. (LEARNING OBJECTIVE 9) Describe the concept of emotional intelligence.
10. (LEARNING OBJECTIVE 10) Explain how women and men might differ as leaders.

DISCUSSION QUESTIONS

Improving Critical Thinking

1. Under what conditions would an organization want to promote self-leadership?

2. Select a popular television show and examine how power is used by the main characters. What types of power do they use most often? Least often? Provide examples. How does the use of certain types of power affect the interactions between the main character and others?

3. Select two successful and well-known leaders. Compare the traits and characteristics of these two individuals and discuss how similar or different they are. To what degree to you think their traits led to success?

Enhancing Communication Skills

4. Read the discussion on reinforcement theory in Chapter 14. After you have done that, write a short report in which you explain the similarities between reinforcement theory and the situational leadership model.

5. Interview two women leaders and examine the types of experiences and opportunities that they have had as they have progressed to higher ranks in their organizations. Are any of their experiences common? Does either leader think that the issues women face in organizations today have changed in the past 10 years? Write your interviews as a short report.

6. Give examples of situations in which you used your power to influence your peers, your family members, and your professor. Provide specific examples either as an oral presentation or in writing, as directed by your instructor.

Building Teamwork

7. Have each team member complete the survey in the Experiential Exercise 12.1. If you are working as part of a permanent team, complete a survey

about one other team member. Follow the scoring instructions. Team members should each discuss the two behaviors with the lowest scores and then brainstorm about how practice and experience can be gained. This is a way in which each member is using relations behavior.

8. Select any leadership approach discussed in the chapter and analyze your own leadership style. When are you most effective? Ineffective? In a small group, exchange your ideas with others with whom you have worked. Discuss how your leadership style might work well with the style of another person or might conflict.

Chapter

13

Exploring Individual Differences and Team Dynamics

CHAPTER OVERVIEW

The leading organizations in the 21st century will be those whose culture allows them to move faster and react better to diverse customers, markets, and employees. They will be challenged to produce higher-quality products and services, be globally oriented, and involve everyone in a focused effort to serve ever more demanding customers. To eliminate the barriers that separate functions within them, organizations must move toward a culture that helps people understand how to work together at both the individual and the group level.

This chapter provides the foundations to understand individual behaviors. First, we examine some of the ways individuals differ in personalities, attitudes, perceptions, and abilities. We look at these factors with regard to how they affect performance. Because management effectiveness depends on the ability of different individuals to pull together and focus on a common goal, we turn our attention to understanding the impact of groups of individuals and relevant team issues. We explore the different types of groups, the inputs for designing effective groups, how groups develop, and the processes that influence groups to be effective. Finally, we take a look at how managers can work to create and support successful teams.

LEARNING OBJECTIVES

When you have finished studying this chapter, you should be able to

1. Discuss why it is important for managers to understand individual differences.
2. Define personality and briefly explain personality characteristics considered significant in the workplace.
3. Explain what is measured by both the Myers–Briggs Type Indicator and the "Big Five."
4. Explain the importance of matching personality characteristics to jobs and careers.
5. Outline the importance of perception and perceptual errors.
6. Discuss the relationship between job satisfaction and performance.
7. Comment on the various types of team member roles.
8. Identify the development phases of groups.
9. Explain how cohesiveness can impact a team.
10. Clarify the primary elements of successful teams.

Facing The Challenge

Nokia: Creating an Innovative Culture

Nokia Corporation's history stretches back more than 140 years. Until the early 1990s, it was a conglomerate with businesses as diverse as rubber products, paper, consumer electronics, and computers. During the 1990s, the company transformed itself into a focused telecommunications business supplying telecommunications network equipment and systems and mobile phones. The Nokia brand, practically unknown a decade earlier, has been ranked as one of the ten most valuable brands in the world by Interbrand Corporation, a global branding consultancy based in New York. That's why Nokia, a Scandinavian company with nearly $40 billion in annual sales in over 130 countries and 55,000 employees has been out in front for most of the mobile phone industry's short history. Nokia sells five phones every second. Its global market share, 30%, is greater than that of its nearest three rivals combined, and it boasts a 50% share of Western Europe.

Nokia isn't just the world's biggest mobile phone company. In an industry that's all about innovation, Nokia has tackled the ultimate challenge: Create a culture where innovation and flexibility are built into the way the company operates.

At Nokia, innovation was considered more than a one-time event, an exceptional idea, or an accident. CEO Jorma Ollila believed that the innovative capacity of the company would come from cooperative multifunctional teams working together to bring new insights into products and services. Restructuring of the company established more autonomous units, and reward systems were developed to encourage cooperation within teams and across the internal and external boundaries of the company.

For example, the Nokia Mobile Phone division (NMP) splintered itself into nine small, autonomous business units. This gave NMP the ability to redeploy people into completely new areas such as entertainment and imaging. Each unit taps into Nokia's central research lab for basic technology and product design and hands over end products to a shared operations/logistics team. Independent teams are profit-and-loss centers with the autonomy to create their own business model, conduct their own advanced research and development and marketing, and draft their own product road maps. According to Ollila, the team structure gives people the power to make their ideas happen. "We've created a small company soul inside a big-company body."

The strategic planning process also capitalizes on the innovative capacity of teams. Every 6 months, up to 400 people are handpicked across the company, divided into teams, and challenged to explore 5 to 15 themes that senior executives believe are most crucial to the company future. Team members interview a wide range of internal and external experts, identify markets and promising technology, and report to the executive board. Team reports are incorporated into what Nokia calls its "strategy road maps."

Selling the same goods to the same customers simply doesn't work in the fiercely competitive phone business. Products that are hot today will be cold in 6 months. The market demands a steady stream of new products. This means that Nokia's real business isn't phones but innovation. Will the innovative capacity of the company continue to come from cooperative multifunctional teams?

Sources: L. Gratton, "Managing Integration through Cooperation," *Human Resource Management* 44, no. 2 (2005): 151–158; L. Gratton and S. Ghoshal, "Beyond Best Practice," *MIT Sloan Management Review* (Spring 2005): 49–60; N. Schwartz, "Has Nokia Lost It?" *Fortune*, 24 January 2005, 98–103; I. Wylie, "Calling for a Renewable Future," *Fast Company* (May 2003): 46–47; S. Finkelstein, "Why Smart Executives Fail," *Executive Excellence* 21, no. 9 (2004): 9; J. Santos, Y. Doz, and P. Williamson, "Is Your Innovation Process Global?" *MIT Sloan Management Review* 45, no. 4 (2004): 31–37; C. Canabou, "Fast Talk," *Fast Company* (June 2004): 51–55.

Introduction

"We're all in this together." That probably should be the overall attitude of everyone in the same organization. After all, the organization would be much more successful if everyone in that organization was focused on the same mission and strategy. And no matter what the organizational goal, teams are integral to success. For example, teams have been at the core of organizational efforts to[1]:

- Reduce the time it takes to bring a new product to market.
- Provide quality customer service and speedy turnaround time on customer requests.
- Collaborate with business partners around the world.
- Reengineer the design of work processes.

- Improve the quality of products and services.
- Reduce costs and eliminate waste.
- Increase sales and improve after-sales support.
- Reduce cross-functional competition and "turf" conflicts.

Procter and Gamble (P&G) is generally considered an important U.S. pioneer in applying teams to its operations. It began work with teams in the early 1960s, although these efforts were not publicized and virtually escaped media attention. P&G envisioned the team approach as a significant competitive advantage, and through the 1980s, it attempted to deflect attention away from its efforts. The company thought of its knowledge about the team organization as a trade secret and required consultants and employees to sign nondisclosure agreements.[2]

Other prominent companies have been active with teams as well: Pfizer, U.S. Postal Service, Cummins Engine, Dell Computers, Ford, Motorola, Tektronix, Boeing, AT&T, Texas Instruments, and Xerox—to name just a few. In manufacturing, they have had extensive experience with self-managed teams, which started in the 1960s. Today they are a proven system, needing only a fine-tuning in specific sites.[3]

The use of teams in the service sector has been an exciting area of application. Service teams are well past the experimentation phase although we still have much to learn about them. Teams in government are a rapidly changing area of application. Until recently, government agencies have shown little interest in empowered teams. Now, however, driven by downsizing, teams have become a normal organizational structure.

Teams are made up of individuals. Therefore, before we direct our attention to teams, we examine individual differences and key aspects of personalities, attitudes, and abilities.

© JIM CRAIGMYLE/CORBIS

Teams are made of individuals who may have different personalities, attitudes, and abilities.

Appreciating Individual Differences

LEARNING OBJECTIVE 1

Discuss why it is important for managers to understand individual differences.

1 Individual behavior is determined to a great extent by internal elements such as attitudes, personality, perceptions, and abilities. People respond differently to the same situation because of their unique combination of these elements, called individual differences. It is a continual challenge for managers to recognize, understand, and learn to appreciate the importance of individual differences in their employees because individual differences affect the work environment and the performance of the organization overall. In the following sections, we examine some of the elements influencing individual behavior.

PERSONALITY CHARACTERISTICS

LEARNING OBJECTIVE 2

Define personality and briefly explain personality characteristics considered significant in the workplace.

2 **Personality** is an enduring, organized, and distinctive pattern of behavior that describes an individual's adaptation to a situation.[4] It is used here to represent the overall profile or combination of traits that characterize the unique nature of a person. In short, personality characteristics help us tell people apart and anticipate their behaviors.

Personality characteristics suggest tendencies to behave in certain ways and account for consistency in various situations. They can partly explain why learning certain new behaviors may be harder for some people than for others. A number of personality characteristics or traits have been convincingly

KEY TERMS

Personality
An enduring pattern of an individual's behavior.

linked to work behavior and performance. Organizational researchers have tended to focus on personality traits that are considered important in the workplace.

Self-Esteem

Self-esteem indicates the extent to which people believe they are capable, significant, and worthwhile.[5] In short, a person's self-esteem is a judgment of worthiness that is expressed in the attitudes that the individual holds toward him- or herself. A person's assessment of worthiness is affected somewhat by situations, successes or failures, the opinions of others, and thus the roles that one assumes.[6] Nevertheless, the assessments that a person makes are stable enough to be widely regarded as a basic characteristic or dimension of personality that, if positive, can enhance performance, increase the likelihood of success, and fuel motivation.

Self-esteem affects behavior in organizations and other social settings in several important ways. For example, self-esteem is related to initial vocational choice. Individuals with high self-esteem exhibit confidence, value themselves, take more risks in job selection, may be more attracted to high-status occupations, opt for occupations that match their abilities and self-perceived traits, and are more likely to choose nontraditional jobs than individuals with low self-esteem.[7] Leaders with high self-esteem are more likely to be successful in inspiring, motivating, and providing a supportive work environment for the new knowledge workers to be creative and productive.[8]

Individuals with low self-esteem set lower goals for themselves than individuals with high self-esteem and tend to be more easily influenced by the opinions of others in organizational settings. Leaders with low self-esteem who are consumed with their own insecurities are more likely to be adversarial than inspirational in their relationships with others.[9]

From a managerial perspective, it is important to understand that self-esteem is positively related to job satisfaction, motivation, and job performance. For example, employees with high self-esteem tend to have a desire for achievement and are highly competitive. They are strong performers and have a desire for growth, achievement, and success. The level of self-esteem dramatically impacts every facet of a person's life, from work performance to interactions with others. Most aspects of business activity—from leading to managing to participating in teams and from dealing with customers to engaging in research and development to responding to new challenges and new ideas—are significantly affected by the level of one's self-esteem.[10]

Locus of Control

Locus of control is a personality characteristic that reflects a person's belief in personal control in life (internality) rather than in control by outside forces or individuals (externality). It describes the extent to which individuals perceive the link between their own actions and the outcomes of those actions.[11] Before reading further, go to the Experiential Exercise 13.1 and assess your locus of control.

Individuals who have an **internal locus of control,** or internals, believe that many of the events in their lives are primarily the result of their own behavior and actions. They feel a sense of control over their lives and tend to attribute both their successes and their failures to their own efforts. As a result of such an approach, individuals with an internal locus of control tend to be more proactive and take more risks.

In contrast, individuals with an **external locus of control,** or externals, believe that much of what happens to them is controlled and determined by outside external forces such as other people, fate, or luck. Such individuals do not generally perceive that they have control over their lives. As a result, they have been found to be more reactive to events and less able to rebound from stressful situations. They tend to rely on others' judgments and conform to authority more readily than internals.

Locus of control in the workplace in particular (that is, belief that one has *control* at work) has likewise been linked to employee well-being, an important component of emotional adjustment and ability to handle stress in general life.[12] In sum, research supports the notion that internality is associated with positive well-being both on and off the job.

The many differences between an internal and an external locus of control can help explain some aspects of individual behavior in organizational settings. For example, because internals believe they control their own behavior, they are more politically and socially active, and they more actively seek information about their situations than externals. Internals are more likely to try to influence or persuade others, are less likely to be influenced by others, and may be more achievement oriented than externals. For all these reasons, internals may be more highly motivated and set higher goals than externals.

KEY TERMS

Self-esteem
The extent to which a person believes that he or she is capable, significant, successful, and worthwhile.

Locus of control
A personality characteristic that reflects a person's belief in personal control in life rather than in control by outside forces.

Internal locus of control
A belief that many of the events in one's life are primarily the result of their own behavior and actions.

External locus of control
A belief that what happens is determined by outside forces such as other people, fate, or luck.

Table 13.1 Internal versus External Locus of Control

	Internal Locus of Control	External Locus of Control
Independence	More independent and proactive; less susceptible to the influence of others.	More dependent and reactive; susceptible to influence of others.
Use of information	Good at utilizing information; active politically and socially.	Fewer attempts to acquire information; more satisfied than internals with amount of information they have.
Performance	Perform better than externals on learning and problem-solving tasks when performance leads to valued rewards; assumes personal responsibility for good and poor performance.	Perform better than internals on structured tasks when rewards are clearly proved; less likely than internals to assume responsibility for good or poor performance.
Satisfaction	Stronger job satisfaction-to-performance relationship than externals.	Less satisfied than internals; more alienated.
Motivation	Exhibit greater work motivation; expect that working hard will lead to good performance; feel more control over performance and time commitment than externals; establish difficult goals.	Feel that forces outside of their control influence performance efforts.
Risk	Engage in more risk than externals.	Show less self-control and more caution.

Table 13.1 lists further details and differences between internals and externals. Remember, the table shows the extreme behavior. Most individuals have characteristics of both internal and external locus of control.[13]

Self-Monitoring

Self-monitoring (SM) identifies the degree to which individuals are capable of reading and using cues from their environment to determine their behavior. Individuals who score high on the SM scale can read environmental and social cues about what is considered appropriate behavior and adjust accordingly. For people high on the SM scale, behavior is likely to be the result of perception of the environment and is therefore likely to adapt to the situation. People who score low on the SM scale tend to base their behaviors on internal things and are likely to appear consistent across different situations.[14]

People high on the SM scale tend to emerge as leaders more frequently and learn managerial skills more easily than do people who are low on the SM scale. High-SM managers can cope better with cross-cultural situations because they adapt their behavior more to the situation. As with almost everything, being high or low on the SM scale has advantages and disadvantages. Although someone who is a high SM is flexible, he or she might be seen as not stable in some situations. In contrast, someone who is low on the SM scale is quite consistent. That may be proper in some situations but not in others.

Studies indicates that high self-monitors are more likely to manage impressions, seek out more information, are more accurate in diagnosing social situations, take social cues more into consideration in their behavior, and are more highly skilled at presenting impressions than low self-monitors. It is important for managers to keep in mind that in an organizational setting conformity is a form of appearing socially acceptable. Therefore, high self-monitors are likely to create facades of conformity to a greater extent than low self-monitors.[15]

KEY TERMS

Self-monitoring
The degree to which individuals are capable of reading and using cues to determine behavior.

Type A and Type B Personality

The concept of Type A or Type B personality has received considerable attention as a factor having significant implications for work and nonwork behaviors and reactions to stress.[16] **Type A personality** is characterized by a sense of commitment, high standards and goals, a devotion to work, and a sense of time urgency. Type A people tend to be competitive in work and social situations and measure results against others. They often do several things at once and tend to show diffused anger, intolerance for delays, and aggressiveness.

In contrast, the **Type B personality** is characteristically easygoing and less competitive in daily events. Type B individuals appear to be more relaxed and patient and work at a more constant pace without the sense of time urgency. They are more likely to have a balanced, relaxed approach to life, listen more carefully, and communicate more precisely. Type B people may not be taken seriously because of their relaxed demeanor; their lack of concern for detail may lead to errors generally not perceived as critical. Without being driven by time constraints, the Type B personality may put off tasks or procrastinate. Type B individuals are not necessarily more or less successful than Type A people, but they are less likely to experience stress.

LEARNING OBJECTIVE 3

Explain what is measured by both the Myers–Briggs Type Indicator and the "Big Five."

Keep in mind that many of the behaviors can be positive or negative depending on the situation. For example, Xerox had some difficulties with some of its self-managed work teams. The teams were dysfunctional. Nothing was happening and members seemed to be relaxed and comfortable in their roles. An advisor to Xerox found that teams that were just forming needed a few Type A personalities who would take the leadership role, set high performance standards, push for details, and feel a sense of commitment. Once the team was launched and into its work process, the need for Type A personalities was likely to be replaced by the need for Type B personalities.[17]

KEY TERMS

Type A personality
A personality characterized by such things as a sense of urgency, impatience, and high drive.

Type B personality
A personality characterized as easygoing and less competitive in daily events.

Resiliency
The ability to absorb high levels of disruptive change.

Resilience

Resiliency is the ability to absorb high levels of disruptive change while displaying minimal dysfunctional behavior.[18] Because it is no longer sufficient to merely cope with the stress of uncertainty, employees must have the ability to move beyond mere survival and actually prosper in environments that are becoming increasingly more complex and unpredictable.[19]

A 12-year study at Illinois Bell Telephone, where employees experienced immense organizational change, found that individuals with high levels of resiliency reported high levels of coworker cohesion, supervisor support, job involvement, and responsibility. In addition, the high-resiliency individuals reported greater social support and lower levels of perceived stress and engaged in more problem-focused coping than the individuals with low resiliency.[20]

Another study conducted by Motorola found that not all individuals have high resiliency; however, resiliency can be increased through training. One of the important outcomes of the study was that the company transformed the research findings into a training program, "Transforming Stress into Resilience." At Questar, an integrated energy resource company in Salt Lake City, personal resiliency training has been linked to lower turnover and higher productivity when employees face disruption in their lives.[21]

How resilent are you? To better understand your level of resiliency, go to the "Now Apply It" box to find out.

Myers-Briggs Type Indicator

3 In the human resources area, research on personality types has reemerged as one of the most important research areas in applied organizational science as managers and researchers seek to understand why people of similar abilities differ in performance.[22] One of the most widely used instruments to assess personality is the Myers-Briggs Type Indicator, or MBTI. It examines and measures our preferred style of dealing with the world and the people in it. It can be used as a developmental tool to help us understand other people and ourselves. The MBTI examines factors that are core to individuals and can give us an indicator of typical managerial strengths and developmental needs.[23]

The *New York Times* reported that more than 3 million people take the MBTI each year, most of whom are administered the instrument by their companies.[24]

The MBTI is a series of questions that asks people to indicate their preferred way of acting, thinking, or feeling in different situations on four dimensions.[25] Responses to the questions assess where one tends to be on a continuum. Therefore, one could score toward one end or the other or somewhere in-between.

Now Apply it

How Resilient Are You?

Use a scale from 1 (very little) to 5 (very much) to rate how much each of the following applies to you. Circle the number that is most accurate. Be honest in your responses; this is not a test!

1 2 3 4 5	Curious, ask questions, want to know how things work, experiment.
1 2 3 4 5	Constantly learn from experience and the experiences of others.
1 2 3 4 5	Need and expect to have things work well for myself and others; take good care of myself.
1 2 3 4 5	Play with new developments, find the humor, laugh at self, chuckle.
1 2 3 4 5	Adapt quickly to change, highly flexible.
1 2 3 4 5	Feel comfortable with paradoxical qualities.
1 2 3 4 5	Anticipate problems and avoid difficulties.
1 2 3 4 5	Develop better self-esteem and self-confidence every year; develop a conscious self-concept of professional.
1 2 3 4 5	Listen well. Read others, including difficult people, with empathy.
1 2 3 4 5	Think up creative solutions to challenges; invent ways to solve problems; trust intuition and hunches.
1 2 3 4 5	Manage the emotional side of recovery. Grieve, honor, and let go of the past.
1 2 3 4 5	Expect tough situations to work out well and keep on going; help others and bring stability to times of uncertainty and turmoil.
1 2 3 4 5	Find the gift in accidents and bad experiences.
1 2 3 4 5	Convert misfortune into good fortune.

Add your numbers to get your total. If you scored 60–70, you're highly resilient; 50–60, you're better than most; 40–50, adequate; 30–40, struggling; under 30, seek help! *Note:* To improve your resilience, practice more of the traits above.

Source: Adapted from A. Siebert, *The Resiliency Advantage* (San Francisco: Berrett-Koehler, 2005).

A score in the center of the continuum would mean that the person has some characteristics for each.

1. Introversion/Extroversion (**I or E**). This dimension represents the source of one's energy. Introverts draw energy from inside, from themselves. They tend to enjoy being alone and prefer ideas, thoughts, and concepts. Extroverts draw energy from interacting with other people, are highly social, talkative, energetic, enthusiastic, and assertive.[26] Consequently, they tend to have a wide social network. In the United States, extroverts outnumber introverts—70% to 30%. The U.S. culture tends to encourage extroversion.
2. Sensing/Intuitive (**S or N**). The S/N dimension describes how people prefer to gather data. Sensing (S) people prefer concrete, real, factual, and structured data. They think in a careful manner, rely on facts, and are not comfortable with abstract data and theory. On the other hand, intuitive (N) people prefer the overall view, theories, new things, and become bored with details and facts. Intuitive people solve problems easily and are spontaneous in doing so although they may make errors because they neglect details and facts.
3. Feeling/Thinking (**F or T**). F/T represents how people prefer to make judgments. People who are described as feeling tend to be interested in people and feelings rather than in analysis and logic. They tend to make judgments about people and things based on empathy and harmony rather than on achieving goals that are impersonal. Thinking people rely on analysis, evidence, and logic rather than on feelings and personal values. They may seem unemotional and uninterested in people.
4. Perceiving/Judging (**P or J**). This dimension represents decision-making styles. Perceiving

KEY TERMS

I or E
A personality dimension measuring the degree to which a person is introverted or extroverted.

S or N
A personality dimension measuring whether one is sensing or intuitive in gathering data.

F or T
A personality dimension referring to whether one is feeling or thinking in making judgments.

P or J
A personality dimension representing the degree to which one is perceiving or judging in making decisions.

people tend to see all sides of a situation and welcome new perspectives and new information before deciding. Consequently, they might be indecisive and put off decisions to a point of becoming frustrated. Perceivers tend to be flexible and "roll with life." Even after deciding, they might look back at decisions and wonder if another decision might have been better. People who are considered judging are decisive and sure of themselves. They set goals and stay with them. Judging people want to get things done and move on to the next thing. Sometimes, a judging person might leave an unfinished task if it takes too long and move on to the next one.

With these four dimensions, each with two extremes, 16 possible combinations of personality types exist—ISFP, INTJ, ENTJ, to name a few. Table 13.2 summarizes possible strengths and weaknesses of the two extremes of each of the four dimensions.

The MBTI is used to help understand one's personality type and thereby to predict behavior.[27] It can be used to help select and place people in situations that are more suited to their style of behavior. For example, someone who is highly introverted probably would not be a good salesperson who must interact with large numbers of people. If a manager is a judger and the subordinate is a perceiver, at the minimum, each would have to learn to work with the other. Other options include assigning only judging types to work with judging managers. That might help the people interact well. However, it might also cause a situation in which decisions are made too quickly, without proper analysis. Overall, the MBTI should be used to help understand where a person is "coming from" so that interactions between people can be based on a better understanding. As John Bearden, chief executive of GMAC Home Services, a subsidiary of General Motors, said, "My whole decision-making and leadership process has been tremendously refined as a result of the Myers-Briggs, which helped me understand the tendencies I had to make hasty decisions;" that is, the MBTI helped him take into account hard data.[28]

LEARNING OBJECTIVE 4

Explain the importance of matching personality characteristics to jobs and careers.

KEY TERMS

Big Five
A model measuring personality traits that include extroversion, agreeableness, conscientiousness, emotional stability, and openness to experience.

The "Big Five" Personality Traits

A recent model of personality characteristics suggests that all personality characteristics can be reduced to five basic factors. It is called the Five-Factor Model, or, more commonly, the **Big Five.** These five factors are extroversion, agreeableness, conscientiousness, emotional stability, and openness to experience.[29]

1. *Extroversion:* the degree to which one is assertive, gregarious, and sociable rather than quiet, reserved, and timid.
2. *Agreeableness:* the degree to which one is agreeable, warm, and cooperative as compared to disagreeable, cold, and uncooperative.
3. *Conscientiousness:* the degree that a person is organized, dependable, and responsible. The contrast is unorganized, unreliable, and irresponsible.
4. *Emotional stability:* the degree to which a person is calm, self-confident, and secure as compared to anxious, tense, insecure, and depressed.
5. *Openness to experience:* the degree to which a person is creative, curious, and intellectual rather than very practical with narrow interests.

Overall, the Big Five is a fairly valid predictor of performance on the job. Extroversion predicts success in occupations that involve social contact, such as salespeople and managers.[30] Other research has found that people who are extroverted tend to have more promotions and higher salaries and are more satisfied with their careers than people who are less extroverted.[31] Conscientiousness is a valid predictor of high performance across essentially all occupations.[32] For more specific occupations, certain combinations of factors predict performance. People with high emotional stability, agreeableness, and openness to experience tend to perform better in customer-service jobs. As mentioned above, managers tend to do well if they are high on extroversion. Emotional stability is also associated with performance of a manager.[33] People who are more introverted and conscientious have lower absence rates.[34] Finally, people with high conscientiousness are methodical, tend to exhibit high performance, be satisfied with their jobs, and rate peers on a tougher scale than do people with high agreeableness.[35]

MATCHING PERSONALITIES WITH JOBS

4 Many "interest inventories" attempt to help a person identify careers and jobs that he or she might be interested in.[36] The most promising seems to be what is now called the RIASEC Vocational Interest Typology. This typology identifies six personality types in

Table 13.2 Possible Strengths and Weaknesses of MBTI Personality Types

Possible Strengths	Possible Weaknesses
Introvert (I)	
Independent, works alone	Avoids others, secretive
Diligent, reflective	Misunderstood by others
Careful	Dislikes being interrupted
Works with ideas	Loses opportunities to act
Extrovert (E)	
Open, interacts with others	Less independence
Is well understood	Needs change, variety
Understands the external	Impulsive, impatient
Acts decisively	Doesn't work without people
Senser (S)	
Good with detail	Loses sight of the overall
Practical	Frustrated with the complicated
Patient	Mistrusts intuition
Systematic	Doesn't see the new, caught in detail
Intuitor (N)	
Sees overall possibilities	Inattentive to detail
Imagines	Impatient with tedious
Works with complicated	Jumps to conclusions, leaps of logic
Solves novel problems	Not practical
Feeler (F)	
Considers needs of others	Not objective, is uncritical
Demonstrates feelings	Not guided by logic
Conciliatory	Less organized
Persuades, arouses	Justice based on feelings
Thinker (T)	
Logical, analytical	Feelings not important
Objective, organized	Not interested in conciliation
Is just	Shows less mercy
Stands firm	Misunderstands values of others
Perceiver (P)	
Sees all sides of issues	Indecisive, does not plan
Compromises, flexible	Does not control circumstances
Open to change	Easily distracted
Nonjudgmental, based on data	Does not finish things
Judger (J)	
Decides, plans	Unyielding, inflexible
Makes quick decisions	Judgmental
Finishes things	Controlled by task or plan
Has order, control	Decides with insufficient data

Sources: R. McCrae and T. Costa, Jr., "Reinterpreting the Myers-Briggs Type Indicator from the Perspective of the Five Factor Model of Personality," *Journal of Personality* (March 1989): 17–40; N. Quenk, *Essentials of Myers-Briggs Type Indicator Assessment* (New York: Wiley, 2000).

Figure 13.1 RIASEC Vocational Interest Typology

Realistic | Investigative | Artistic | Social | Enterprising | Conventional

Source: Based on J. Holland, *Making Vocational Choices: A Theory of Vocational Personalities and Work Environments* (Englewood Cliffs, NJ: Prentice Hall, 1985).

terms of the kind of activities and therefore jobs and careers that one would prefer.[37] They are

1. *Realistic:* Preference for physical activities that require strength, skill, and coordination.
2. *Investigative:* Preference for activities that require thinking, understanding, and organizing.
3. *Artistic:* Preference for activities that call for creative expression and are ambiguous and nonsystematic.
4. *Social:* Preference for activities that involve other people.
5. *Enterprising:* Preference for activities that allow verbal skills that can be used to influence others and gain power.
6. *Conventional:* Preference for activities that are nonambiguous and include rules and order.

This typology is based on the reasoning that if an individual's personality matches his or her job or career, then he or she will be less likely to leave. The typology has been found to be useful in that it helps individuals select a job in which they will be more satisfied. Related, it helps career counselors better suggest personality–job matches.[38]

The RIASEC Typology also uses "hexagonal calculus" (Figure 13.1). That means that the two personality types that are directly across from each other are the most opposite. For example, a realistic personality is most opposite from a social, and an investigative is most opposite from an enterprising. It also means that a personality has some overlap with the two on either side. Realistic has some overlap with investigative and with conventional.

KEY TERMS

Attitudes
The beliefs, feelings, and behavioral tendencies held by a person.

What does this hexagonal calculus mean? A realistic type of personality would be most dissatisfied in a job or career that included activities that a social personality would like, and vice versa. However, a realistic personality, although not totally satisfied, would be "OK" in an investigative setting or in a conventional setting. Of course, the same application applies to all other relationships among personality types and job settings.[39]

Attitudes

Attitudes are relatively lasting beliefs, feelings, and behavioral tendencies held by a person about specific objects, events, groups, issues, or people. Attitudes result from a person's background, personality, and life experi-

Individuals' job performance is affected by their attitudes, which are relatively lasting beliefs, feelings, and behavioral tendencies about specific objects, events, groups, issues, or people.

ences. Although these attitudes may not necessarily be factual or completely consistent with objective reality, managers still must be aware of those that have an impact on the organization, such as how satisfied individuals are with their jobs, how committed they are to the organization's values and goals, and how willing they are to expend considerable effort for the organization.[40]

People tend to want consistency among their attitudes and between their attitudes and behaviors. If differences exist, people tend to want to reconcile those differences. This is known as the theory of **cognitive dissonance,** an inconsistency among attitudes or between an attitude and a behavior.[41] For example, if a person just purchased a product that might not clearly fit his or her attitude, the person probably feels some stress or tension and would try to justify the product to fit the attitude. That is one reason why so much advertising is actually aimed at the person who just purchased a product—to help him or her feel comfortable with the product. Possibly, in this situation, attitude may have changed a bit. On the other hand, if the person continues to feel very stressed about the new product, chances are the product will be discarded.

Marketers might actually try to create cognitive dissonance as a way to get attention for a product. Consider the example of milk. It tends to not have a glamorous image. That is why a long-running campaign featured celebrities with a "milk-moustache"—to place unglamorous milk in a setting that is very glamorous. The campaign was successful in selling more milk.

What is the significance of cognitive dissonance for a manager? Leon Festinger, the originator of the theory, suggested that three things affect what a person did if he or she experienced cognitive dissonance—the importance of the factors creating the dissonance, the influence that the person has over these factors, and the rewards associated with the dissonance.[42] If the factors that create the dissonance are low in importance, then the stress related to the dissonance will be low, and the person probably will not do anything. If the factors are important, then the person will experience high stress and will want to correct the dissonance. Here is where the degree of influence that the person has comes into play. If the stress is high and the person cannot change the factors, he or she may leave the situation in order to get rid of the dissonance. Finally, rewards come into play. One example: An employee believes that doing something in the job is not ethical. However, the manager insists that the employee do it because the manager sees nothing wrong with it. If the stress is very high, the employee might, as a last resort, leave the job or rationalize doing the unethical act by saying "Well, I need a job, so I'll do it." The manager could directly influence this situation also by offering a reward. If the reward is important to the employee, then the employee can justify doing the task—"Well, I really need the promotion, so I guess this isn't so bad. Besides, doing it will make the company more successful and provide jobs for more people."

The most commonly studied work attitude is job satisfaction. **Job satisfaction** is the degree to which individuals feel positively or negatively about their jobs. It is an emotional response to tasks, leadership, peer relationships, and organizational politics, as well as other physical and social conditions of the workplace. Job satisfaction can lead to a variety of positive and negative outcomes, from both an individual and an organizational perspective.[43] It influences how employees feel about themselves, their work, and their organizations and can affect how they contribute to achieving their own goals and the organization's goals.[44]

The best-known scale that measures job satisfaction is the Job Descriptive Index (JDI). The JDI evaluates five specific characteristics of a person's job:[45]

1. The work itself: responsibility, interest, and growth.
2. Pay: adequacy of pay and perceived equity.
3. Relations with coworkers: social harmony and respect.
4. Quality of supervision: technical help and social support.
5. Promotional opportunities: chances for further advancement.

Certainly, an employee can be satisfied with some aspects of a job and at the same time be dissatisfied with others. A scale such as the JDI helps managers pinpoint sources of dissatisfaction so that they can take appropriate action.

LEARNING OBJECTIVE 6

Discuss the relationship between job satisfaction and performance.

Job Satisfaction and Performance Relationship

6 Of particular interest to managers is the relationship between job satisfaction and performance at work. Over the years, some research has shown that job satisfaction causes job performance, and other studies have indicated that job performance causes job satisfaction. Other research, however, shows no relationship between job satisfaction and performance. Contingency variables help slightly in finding relationships. The relationship

KEY TERMS

Cognitive dissonance
An inconsistency among a person's attitudes or between an attitude and a behavior.

Job satisfaction
The degree to which an individual feels positively or negatively about his or her job.

might be stronger when the employee is not controlled or constrained by other things. For example, when a job is machine paced, that influences performance more than does job satisfaction. Also, the relationship is a bit stronger for higher-level jobs.[46] The current viewpoint is that managers should not assume a simple cause-and-effect relationship between job satisfaction and job performance because the relationship between the two in any particular situation depends on a complex set of personal and situational variables. An employee's job performance depends on a large number of factors such as ability, the quality of equipment and materials used, the competence of supervision, the working environment, peer relationships, and so on.[47]

Perception

5 **Perception** refers to the way people experience, process, define, and interpret the world around them. It can be considered an information screen or filter that influences the way in which individuals communicate and become aware of sensations and stimuli that exist around them. Acting as a filter, perception means that individuals might see only certain elements in a particular situation and not the entire situation.

Perceptions are influenced by a variety of factors including an individual's experiences, needs, personality, and education. As a result, a person's perceptions are not necessarily accurate. However, they are unique and help explain why two individuals may look at the same situation or message and perceive it differently. For example, managers in the same organization but different departments, such as operations, marketing, and finance, will perceive the weekly sales data differently. An individual's cultural background also may influence his or her perception and interpretation of certain company messages or symbols.

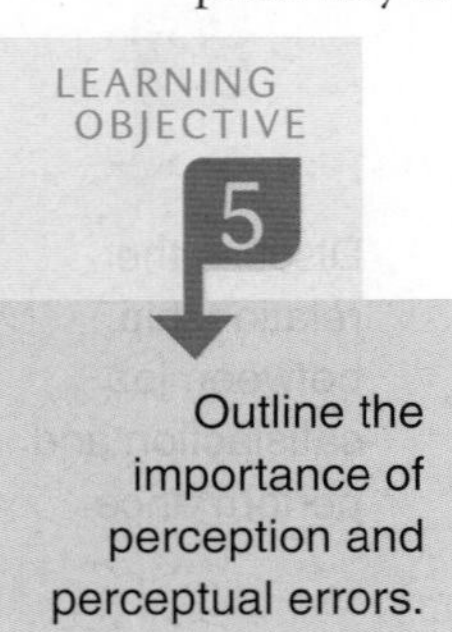

Outline the importance of perception and perceptual errors.

Perceptual Process

The perceptual process is complex and involves selection, organization, and interpretation of environmental stimuli. First, we select or pay attention to some information and ignore other information, often without consciously realizing that we are doing so. For example, a hungry person is likely to focus on the food pictured in an advertisement for fine china, whereas a person who is not hungry may focus on the color and design of the china.

After selecting, we organize the information into a pattern and interpret it. How we interpret what we perceive also varies considerably. Depending on the circumstances and our state of mind, we may interpret a wave of the hand as a friendly gesture or a threat.

The perceptual process is filled with possibilities for errors in judgment or misunderstandings. Although these perceptual errors or biases allow us to make quick judgments and provide data for making predictions, they can also result in significant mistakes that can be costly to individuals and organizations. Let's explore the following common errors or distortions in perception that have particular applications in managerial situations: (1) stereotyping, (2) the halo-and-horn effect, and (3) selective perception.

Stereotyping **Stereotyping** is generalization, or the tendency to assign attributes to a person solely on the basis of a category or group to which that person belongs rather than on individual characteristics. In many ways, stereotypes lead to misunderstandings because they are inaccurate or biased. We readily expect someone identified as a professor, carpenter, police officer, poet, or surgeon to have certain attributes, even if we have not met the individual. Even identifying an employee by such broad categories as older, female, or Native American can lead to errors and misperceptions. Stereotyping may lead the perceiver to dwell on certain characteristics expected of all persons in the assigned category and to fail to recognize the characteristics that distinguish the person as an individual.

When we face new situations, stereotypes provide guidelines to help classify people. Unfortunately, stereotyping based on false premises may lead to a distorted view of reality because it assumes that all people of one gender, race, or age, for example, have similar characteristics, which simply isn't true. Stereotypes based on such factors as gender, age, ethnicity, religion, or sexual preference, can and unfortunately still do, bias perceptions of employees in some organizations. A recent study even found gender bias in the college classroom and demonstrated that male professors were perceived to be more effective than females even though their performance ratings were identical.[48]

Some organizations have been forced by court orders and multimillion-dollar discrimination case settlements to institute training to demonstrate how stereotyping can lead to discrimination against both employees and customers and to teach employees to manage a diverse workforce. However, for the majority of organizations, training and mentoring programs have been used voluntarily to reduce stereotyping and help employees adjust to increasing workplace diversity. For example, Kodak's

KEY TERMS

Perception
The way a person experiences, processes, defines, and interprets the world.

Stereotyping
Tendency to assign attributes to someone based on the group to which that person belongs.

CEO declared diversity as a business imperative and implemented a workplace strategy called its "Winning and Inclusive Culture." The program outlines the basis of teamwork, comprehensive dimensions of diversity, and serves as the social foundation of the Kodak Operating System, the company's manufacturing framework.[49]

Halo-and-Horn Effect The **halo-and-horn effect** refers to a process in which we evaluate and form an overall impression of an individual based solely on a specific trait or dimension such as enthusiasm, gender, appearance, or intelligence. If we view the observed trait as positive, we tend to apply a halo (positive) effect to other traits and to the entire person. If we think of the observed trait as negative, we apply a horn (negative) effect. Consider, for example, the student who scores a near-perfect grade on the first exam in a course and creates a favorable impression on the professor. The professor may then assume that the student is tops in all of his or her classes, efficient, bright, and loyal. Keep in mind that when evaluations are made on the basis of traits that aren't linked, halo-and-horn effects result. Of course, many traits are in fact related; therefore, not all judgments based on the halo-and-horn effect are necessarily perceptual errors.

Selective Perception **Selective perception** is the tendency to screen out information with which we aren't comfortable or don't want to be bothered. We have all been accused of listening only to what we want to hear or "tuning out" what we don't wish to hear. Both are examples of selective perception.

A classic study of how selective perception influences managers involved executives in a manufacturing company.[50] When asked to identify the key problem in a comprehensive business strategy case, all executives in the study selected a problem consistent with their own functional area work assignments. For example, most marketing executives viewed the key problem area as sales; production people tended to see it as a production problem; and human resource people perceived it as a personnel issue. These differing viewpoints demonstrate how errors can occur and affect the way executives approach problems.

In organizations, employees often make this perceptual error. Marketing employees pay close attention to marketing problems and issues, research and development (R&D) engineers pay close attention to product technology or R&D funding, and accountants focus on issues specifically related to accounting. These employees selectively eliminate information that deals with other areas of the organization and focus only on information that is directly relevant to their own needs.

Reducing Perceptual Errors

Because perception is such an important process and plays a major role in determining our behavior, managers must recognize the common perceptual errors. Managers who fall prey to perceptual errors, such as stereotyping, lose sight of individual differences among people. The quality of their decisions can suffer, and the performance of capable people can also suffer. Simple knowledge of perceptual errors, such as stereotyping, halo-and-horn errors, and selective perception, is the first step in avoiding such mistakes.

Ability

Ability is defined as an existing capacity to perform various tasks needed in a given situation. Abilities are classified as mental, mechanical, and psychomotor. *Mental,* or *intellectual, ability* is important for problem solving because it involves the capacity to transform information, generate alternatives, memorize, and consider implications. *Mechanical ability* refers to the capacity to comprehend relationships between objects and to perceive how parts fit together. *Psychomotor ability* includes such things as manual dexterity, eye–hand coordination, and manipulative ability. In the organizational setting, ability and effort are key determinants of employee behavior and performance.

The key point is that not only do employee abilities vary substantially, but different tasks require different abilities and call for different personality characteristics. Such recognition is crucial to understanding and predicting work behaviors. This becomes even more evident when we begin to think about putting individuals together in teams. Up to this point in the chapter, we have focused on individual behavior. We now turn our attention to examining the power of individuals when they work together.

As the business environment has become more complex and uncertain, organizations have responded by increasingly using groups as their fundamental unit of organizational structure in an effort to decentralize decision making and respond more flexibly to their environments. Groups have been granted greater autonomy within organizational structures, which has brought with it the need for groups to more actively manage their cooperation and coordination with other organizational units and with management.[51]

Before we can understand how managers can create and maintain successful, high-performance teams, we need

KEY TERMS

Halo-and-horn effect
Judging a person all positive (halo) or all negative (horn) based on one trait or dimension.

Selective perception
Tendency to see or hear only what we want to see or hear.

Ability
Capacity to perform various tasks needed; may be classified as mental, mechanical, or psychomotor.

Figure 13.2 Critical Requirements of Effective Teams

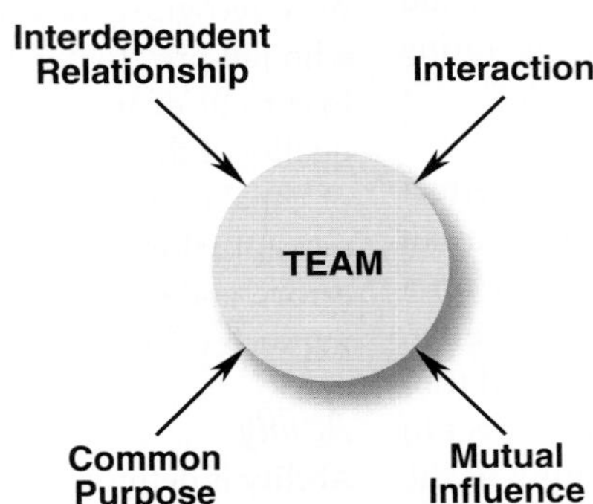

to know more about the very basic aspects of their functioning. This includes the definition of a team, the inputs for designing effective work teams, and the processes that lead to team success.

Critical Elements for Designing Effective Teams

The question of what a group or team is represents a good starting point toward a greater understanding of team and group dynamics. Organizations use numerous labels for the many types of teams. Perhaps the most basic distinction in labels surrounds the difference between a group and a team. A *group* is normally defined as two or more individuals who interact with one another.[52] A *team* is a group of interdependent individuals with shared commitments to accomplish a common purpose or goal. This suggests that a team is more than a group.[53] Our definition recognizes that success depends on the interdependent relationship and collective efforts of various team members and that members are likely to have mutual influence and significant impact on one another as they work together.[54] Although this distinction between a team and a group makes sense, determining the point at which a group becomes a team is impossible. In recent years, the word *team* has become popular in the business community, often replacing the word *group*. For our purposes in this chapter, we use the terms *group* and *team* somewhat interchangeably.

KEY TERMS

Formal group
A group that is deliberately created by managers.

Simply placing individuals together and telling them to work together does not in and of itself promote productivity or success. Team effectiveness does not magically appear when a group is formed. Members must consciously work to build and maintain the effectiveness of their team in order to first achieve success and then maintain it.

The critical requirements of an effective team are shown in Figure 13.2. First, the team members must have an interdependent relationship; they depend on each other to accomplish the tasks. Second, interdependence dictates that members must interact through conversation or work activities. Third, a team is characterized by mutual influence among members rather than having all the power held by a minority. Fourth, the team must have a clearly understood goal or common purpose that evokes high levels of commitment from all members. For a team to exist, both members and observers must be able to distinguish clearly those people who are included in the team from those who are part of the larger social system but are not included in the team.[55] Read the viewpoint of former head coach of the U.S. Women's World Cup Champion Soccer Team, Tony DiCicco, on creating successful teams in "Leaders in Action."

CHARACTERISTICS OF GROUPS

Groups come in many forms, shapes, and sizes. Most managers belong to many different groups at the same time—some at work and some in the community. In the performance of organizational work, two basic categories of teams exist—formal and informal. Both categories can influence the work performed either positively or negatively.[56]

Formal Groups

Formal groups are deliberately created by the organization's managers to accomplish goals and serve the needs

Leaders in Action

Successful Teams Share a Culture

According to Tony DiCicco, to have a successful team, you must have a shared culture. As the former head coach of the U.S. Women's World Cup Champion Soccer Team, which won Olympic gold in 1996, he should know. He built the team's culture on fitness, intensity in training, individual respect, and respect for the group, both on and off the field.

A good team member is one that arrives at training camp fit and ready to play. That kind of preparation shows respect for herself and for her team members. DiCicco also credits team success that emphasizes leadership. Each member of a team has to take responsibility, stay focused, and be accountable for meeting the team's goals. A long-term team must have a way for new people to join in successfully. To survive, new players have to buy into the team's culture. However, this means that current team members can't be afraid of new talent or new ideas. In many cases, there is a natural inclination to protect what the team has created and not to allow a new star to rise to the top. Team members have to fight against that. The bottom line is that new talent can force everyone to play at a higher level.

A successful team culture consists of four things. First, the team members must be galvanized by a common goal. That's what spurs people on and drives them to excel. Second, the members need to be driven by the team's results, not by individual results. Team members must be able to subordinate their own goals in favor of team goals. Third, the team has to be diverse and represent different skills and abilities. Fourth, on the best teams, no one hesitates to take on something that isn't in their area of responsibility. Good team players take action when it is needed.

Sources: J. Katzenbach, *Peak Performance: Aligning the Hearts and Minds of Your Employees* (Boston: Harvard Business School Press, 2000); J. Katzenbach and D. Smith, *Wisdom of Teams: Creating the High-Performance Organization* (HarperCollins, 2003); C. D. Cramton, "Finding Common Ground in Dispersed Collaboration," *Organizational Dynamics* 30, no. 4 (2002): 356–367.

---

of the organization. The major purpose of formal groups is to perform specific tasks and achieve specific objectives defined by the organization. The most common type of formal work group consists of individuals cooperating under the direction of a leader. Examples of formal groups are departments, divisions, task forces, project groups, quality circles, committees, and boards of directors. Boeing formed special quality-improvement teams when it was first testing the new 777 airplane. These are considered to be formal groups and will be maintained throughout production of the plane.

Informal Groups

Informal groups are not formed or planned by the organization's managers. Rather, they are self-created and evolve out of the formal organization for a variety of reasons such as proximity, common interests, or needs of individuals. It would be difficult to design an organization that prohibits informal working relationships from developing.

Because human beings receive reassurance from interacting with others and being part of a group, informal groups can meet a range of individual needs. Perhaps the major reason informal groups evolve is to fulfill individuals' needs for affiliation and friendship, social interaction, communication, power, safety, and status. For example, individuals who regularly eat lunch, carpool, or go to a football game together are members of an informal group that fulfills some of these needs. Although some informal groups may complement the organization's formal groups, at times they can also work against the organization's goals. A number of factors affect the ways groups operate.

In the next section, we examine the inputs for designing teams that lead to effectiveness. These include membership composition, size, and goals. Figure 13.3 illustrates the inputs.

LEARNING OBJECTIVE 7

Comment on the various types of team member roles.

MEMBERSHIP COMPOSITION

7 A critical design feature of teams concerns the individuals who comprise the teams. Team composition is the mixture of individual factors and skills included in a team. One way to understand team member input is to examine the roles of the team members.

Roles

A *role* is a set of behaviors that is characteristic of a person in a

KEY TERMS

Informal group
A group that is not formed or planned by the organization's managers.

Figure 13.3 Inputs to Designing Effective Teams

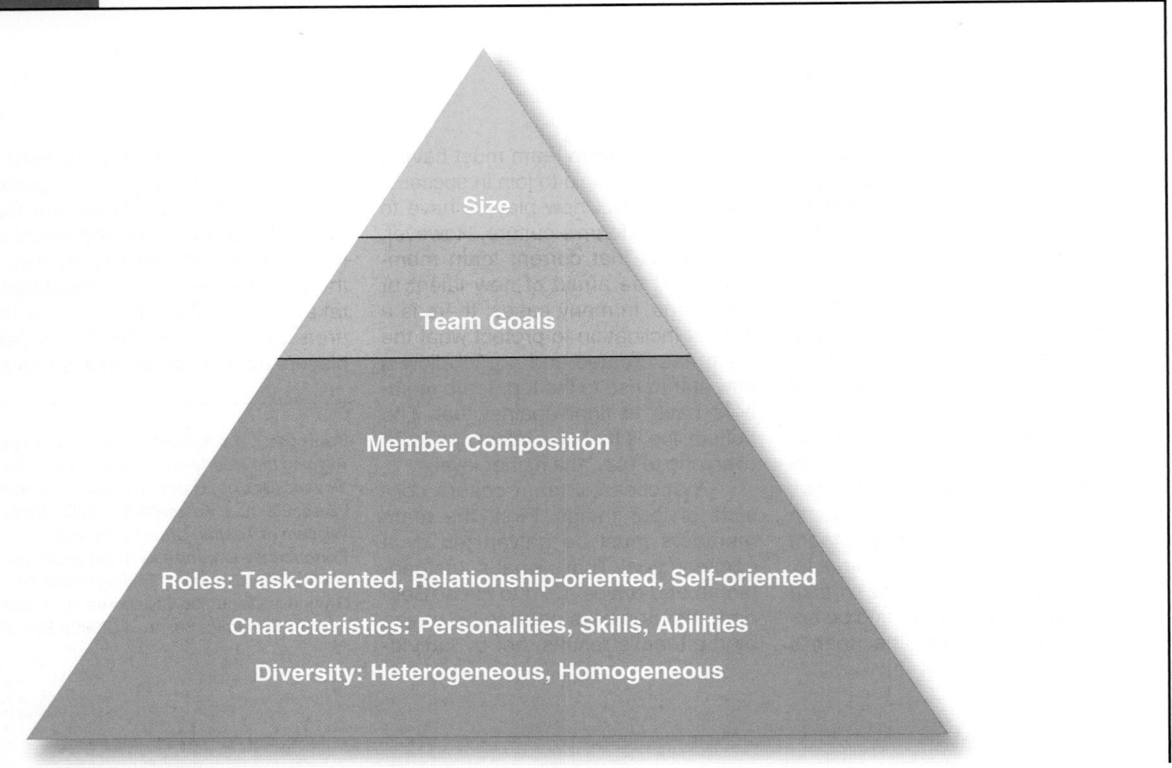

specific situation. People develop their roles and behaviors based on their own expectations, the team's expectations, and the organization's expectations—related to job description, goals that were set, and so on.[57] As employees internalize the expectations of these three sources, they develop their roles.

People often have multiple roles within the same group.[58] For example, a professor may have the roles of teacher, researcher, writer, consultant, advisor, and committee member. Our roles also extend outside the workplace. The professor may also be a family member, belong to professional and civic organizations, and have social friends, all of whom may have very different expectations about the behaviors that are appropriate.

When operating in a work group, individuals typically fulfill several roles. Member roles fit into three categories, and each has associated behaviors: (1) task-oriented roles, (2) relationship-oriented roles, and (3) self-oriented roles.[59] As Figure 13.4 shows, each of these categories includes a variety of role behaviors.

Behaviors directly related to establishing and accomplishing the goals of the group or achieving the desired outcomes are **task-oriented roles.** They include seeking and providing information, initiating actions and procedures, building on ideas, giving and seeking information, testing consensus, giving opinions, summarizing progress, and energizing the quantity and quality of output.

Relationship-oriented roles include behaviors that cultivate the well-being, continuity, and development of the group. They focus on the operation of the group and the maintenance of good relationships and help the group survive, regulate, grow, and strengthen itself. They help foster group unity, positive interpersonal relationships among group members, and the development of the members' ability to work together effectively. These behaviors include encouraging, harmonizing, checking performance, setting standards, and relieving tension.

When some personal need or goal of an individual occurs without regard for the group's problems, the

KEY TERMS

Task-oriented role
A behavior that is directly related to establishing and accomplishing the goals of the group or achieving the desired outcomes.

Relationship-oriented role
A behavior that cultivates the well-being, continuity, and development of the group.

Figure 13.4 Group Roles and Associated Behaviors

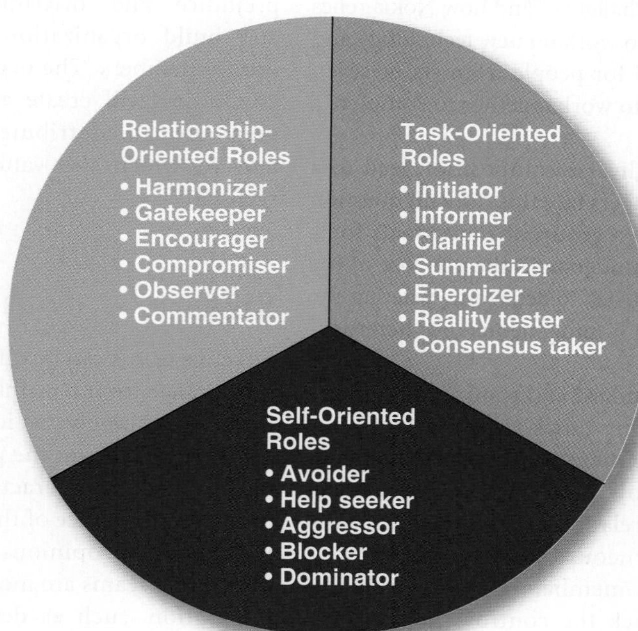

behavior is referred to as a **self-oriented role.** Such roles often have a negative influence on a group's effectiveness.[60] Examples of such behaviors include dominating the discussions, emphasizing personal issues, interrupting others, distracting the group from its work, and wasting the group's time.

Effective teams discover how to integrate relationship- and task-oriented roles. For example, the Brand Integration Group (BIG) at Ogilvy & Mather in New York has been consistently recognized for being exceptionally effective. The talented mix of artists, designers, film makers, and strategists focus on shared decision making without sacrificing personal voice.[61]

Member Characteristics

Certain member characteristics are needed to support effective working relationships, including the right combination of abilities, job-related knowledge and skills, and specific personality traits. Diversity in terms of age, race, gender, ethnicity, and functional areas certainly can help a team by providing rich input. Take, for example, the skill of handling conflict. Because some degree of conflict is beneficial for a team, members do not avoid or totally eliminate it. Instead, they encourage conflict that is constructive and discourage conflict that is destructive. With a growing emphasis on ethical business operations, the Adolph Coors Company created a highly diverse, cross-functional team to develop a code of ethics. At first, the team experienced conflict and resistance from union and employee groups. However, the team learned to function well together and the end product was a comprehensive ethics program that helps employees face situations proactively and positively.[62] Effective communication skills are required for team members to engage in informal conversation and active and objective listening. Also, team members must develop appropriate communication networks. (Refer to Chapter 11.)

Diversity

Team composition can be homogeneous (similar) or heterogeneous (diverse). A team is considered similar or **homogeneous** when it is composed of individuals having group-related characteristics, backgrounds, interests, values, and attitudes that are alike. When the individuals are dissimilar with respect to these characteristics, the group is diverse and is referred to as **heterogeneous.**

KEY TERMS

Self-oriented role
A behavior—a personal need or goal—of an individual that occurs without regard for the group's problems.

Homogeneous group
A group having many similarities.

Heterogeneous group
A group with many differences among its members.

Rapidly growing global interdependence and the increasing emphasis on teamwork result in groups with quite diverse composition. This is no longer the exception; it is the rule. Refer to "Facing the Challenge" and how Nokia relies on multifunctional teams to work on new technology and markets. It is not unusual for people from six or seven different functional areas to work together to complete a project.

Does a similar or a diverse composition lead to a more effective team? Managers face this difficult question every time they assemble a group of individuals for a task. A manager needs to understand the purpose of the team and the nature of the task to determine whether the team is better served by a homogeneous or a heterogeneous composition.

For tasks that are standard and routine, a homogeneous team functions more quickly. Membership homogeneity contributes to member satisfaction, creates less conflict and less turnover, and increases the chances for harmonious working relationships among members. If a team is too homogeneous, however, it may exert excessive pressure on its members to conform to the team's rules and may lack the controversy and perspectives essential to high-quality decision making and creativity.

For tasks that are nonroutine and require diverse skills, opinions, and behaviors, a heterogeneous group yields better results. In "Facing the Challenge," we read how Nokia's innovative culture has successfully evolved based on this concept. A diverse membership can bring a variety of skills and viewpoints to bear on problems and thus facilitate task accomplishment.[63] However, diversity may also impair collaboration, information sharing, and joint decision making. The more diverse the membership, however, the more skilled the manager or team leader will have to be in facilitating a successful experience.[64]

As organizations become increasingly diverse in terms of gender, race, ethnicity, and age, this diversity brings potential benefits such as better decision making, greater creativity and innovation, and more successful marketing to different types of customers. However, increased cultural differences within a workforce can also make it harder to develop cohesive work teams and may result in higher turnover, interpersonal conflict, and communication breakdowns.[65]

Managers must be aware of these issues as they work to create high-performance teams. They need to be trained to capitalize on the benefits of diversity while minimizing the potential costs. Additionally, managers will need to work to integrate minority-group members both formally and informally, strive to eliminate prejudice and discrimination, reduce alienation, and build organizational identity among minority group members. The organization that achieves these conditions will create an environment in which all members can contribute to their maximum potential and in which the value of diversity can be fully realized.[66]

SIZE

Effective teams can be different sizes. Many people suggest a range from 2 members to about 16. However, it is difficult to pinpoint an ideal size because the appropriate size depends on the group's purpose.[67] Size affects how individuals interact with each other as well as the overall performance of the group. As size grows, so does its diversity of opinions, values, and interests. Therefore, larger teams are more prone to problems of social integration, such as depersonalization and conflict, making it more difficult for the members of large teams to collaborate. In groups of fewer than 5 members, more personal discussion and more complete participation will occur. As a team grows beyond several members, it becomes more difficult for all members to participate effectively. Communication and coordination among members become more difficult, and the team tends to split into subgroups. As a result, the interactions become more centralized, with a few individuals taking more active roles relative to the rest; disagreements may occur more easily; and satisfaction may decline unless team members put a good deal of effort into relationship-oriented roles.[68]

As group size increases, more potential human resources are available to perform the work and accomplish needed tasks. This can boost performance, but the expanded size tends to increase turnover and absenteeism, as well as provide opportunities for free riding. **Free riding** describes a tendency of one or more team members to expend decreasing amounts of effort because their contributions are less visible.[69] They are willing to let others carry the workload.

Free riding directly challenges the logic that the productivity of the group as a whole should at least equal the sum of the productivity of each individual in the group. In other words, group size and individual performance may be inversely related. Most students are acquainted with the concept of free riding, largely as a result of negative experiences that they have encountered in working on group projects.[70] Before reading the

KEY TERMS

Free riding
A tendency for a group member to not contribute to the group's efforts but to share in the rewards.

At the Forefront

Merck Pharmaceutical: Capitalizing on the Power of Team Rewards

At the North Carolina-based Merck pharmaceutical plant, management has capitalized on the power in recognizing the small daily acts of teamwork that have ultimately lead to effective performance. Merck uses noncash team-recognition tactics, along with financial incentives, for project teams or organizational units.

The pharmaceutical plant is part of giant Merck, charged with packaging many of its well-known prescription drugs such as cholesterol-lowering Zocor, the asthma drug Singulair, medications for AIDS patients, and others for those suffering from high blood pressure or ulcers. The North Carolina plant is also the only non-union manufacturing site in Merck domestically, and all 425 of its full-time employees are salaried.

Merck Pharmaceuticals boasts three reward plans with a strong team orientation: "Reasons to Celebrate," a flexible, peer-nominated recognition plan; "Pay for Performance," a plantwide plan tied to hitting annual goals in four of the plant's operation areas; and a "Team Stock Option" reward plan for project and organizational unit teams that rewards extraordinary acts of teamwork as well as team performance against predetermined goals with Merck stock options.

The "Reasons to Celebrate" plan is a way for members of the team to recognize teammates for extraordinary effort and accomplishment and to broadcast to the plant as a whole the achievements of those teammates. They emerged from the work of a cross-functional team of employees and managers charged with rethinking reward and recognition efforts at the plant. The goal was to find new ways to support and encourage Merck's burgeoning team-based culture. Rather than having only top-down recognition, the team suggested to management a peer-nomination process: Any Merck team or employee can nominate any other Merck team employee throughout the plant under "Reasons to Celebrate." The recognition oversight committee created this list of actions that might warrant recognition, although nominators aren't limited to the list:

- Extra effort above and beyond ordinary and expected performance
- Improvements in the quality of teamwork
- Suggestions that result in product quality, worker safety, or process improvements
- Excellent customer service; cost or time savings; acquisition and use of new skills
- Perfect job attendance

"Reasons to Celebrate" is a noncash plan, following the thinking that cash awards provide a quick jolt of satisfaction but little feel-good staying power. Instead, the menu of noncash reward items in "Reasons to Celebrate" offers a choice of gift certificates for one video rental a week for a year, courtesy time off, a new set of tires, membership fees at a health club, and more. The reward is accompanied by a letter of appreciation written by nominators and copied to two levels of a nominated employee's or team's managers or coaches, in addition to public bulletin board recognition.

Cash awards are limited to a $300 equivalent for individuals and $500 for teams. When a work team is given a "Reasons" award, it decides through a vote which of the gifts it wants or whether each team member wants an individual reward item.

What actions typically are recognized? A "Reasons" award went to a team of employees who volunteered to help design and deliver a new training class to enhance plantwide knowledge of Merck's measurement of operational excellence. Six workers stepped forward and found time in their busy schedules to help deliver the course to everyone on the plant site. With the help of these part-time trainers—who delivered the content in time above-and-beyond normal work schedules—some 30 4-hour classes were delivered over a 2-month span. Other project or organizational unit teams received "Reasons" nominations for quality or process improvement suggestions that helped Merck improve its bottom line.

Sources: G. Parker, J. McAdams, and D. Zielinski, *Rewarding Teams: Lessons from the Trenches* (San Francisco: Jossey-Bass, 2000); G. Parker, J. McAdams, and D. Zielinski, "Reasons to Celebrate," *Incentive* (September 2000): 96–97.

next section on team goals, learn how Merck Pharmaceuticals capitalizes on the power of team rewards in the "At the Forefront" box.

TEAM GOALS

Another critical element for designing effective teams is team goals. *Goals* provide a clear, engaging sense of direction and specify what is going to be accomplished. For example, United Technologies Corporation (UTC) had an overall goal of reducing the costs of transportation while maintaining a certain level of service from its transportation companies. These goals united the team members in finding common transportation companies that would serve their purposes while achieving the overall corporation's goals. When members share goals, they work harder and longer on the tasks required for high performance.[71]

Figure 13.5 Stages of Team Development

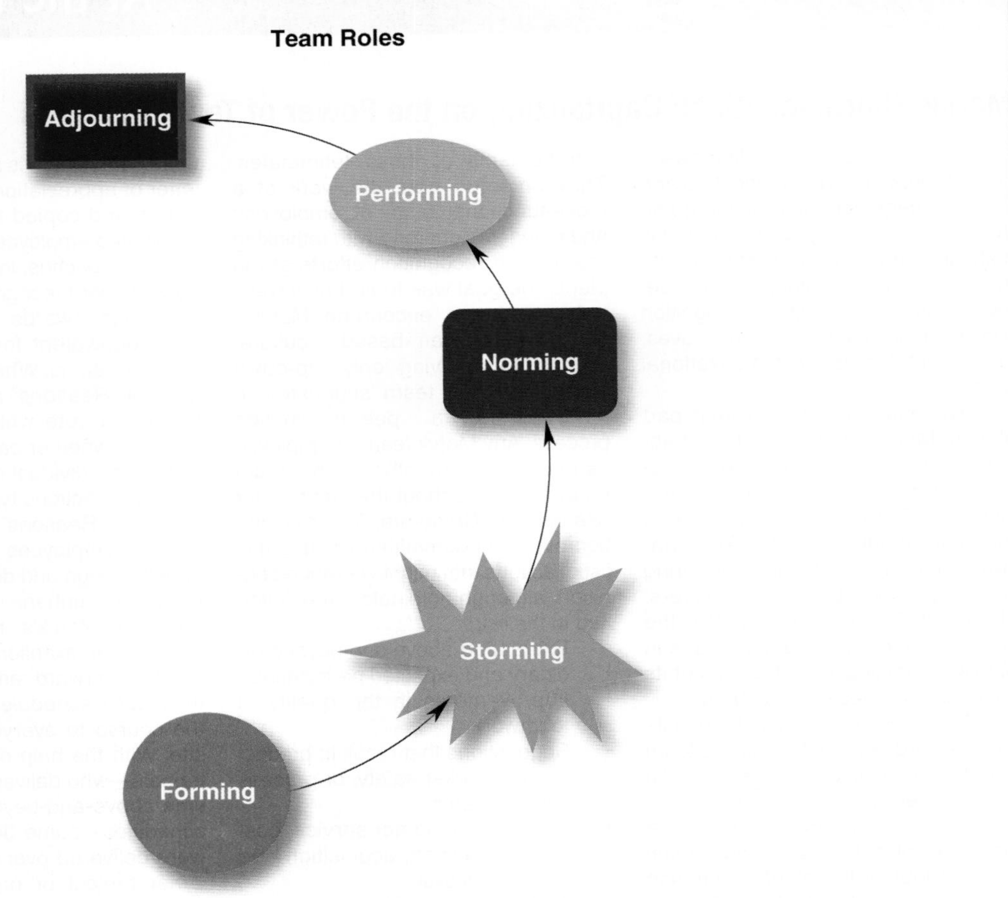

Processes for Team Effectiveness

Numerous intragroup processes can affect how a team functions. In this section, we look at the developmental stages through which most teams pass. An understanding of the developmental stages provides insight into how interactions and intrateam processes change over time and influence the team. Refer to Figure 13.5 as you examine the different stages of team progress.[72] Although no two teams develop in exactly the same way, Figure 13.5 illustrates the evolution processes.

LEARNING OBJECTIVE 8

Identify the development phases of groups.

HOW TEAMS DEVELOP AND PERFORM

8 The team development process is dynamic. Although most groups are in a continuous state of change and rarely reach complete stability, team development does follow a general pattern. Teams appear to go through a five-stage developmental sequence: forming, storming, norming, performing, and adjourning.[73]

The types of behaviors observed in groups differ from stage to stage. The length of time spent in each stage can also vary greatly, with each stage lasting until its paramount issues are resolved. The group then moves on. The stages are not clearly delineated, and some overlap exists between them. In other words, the process of development is ongoing and complex. New groups may progress through these stages, but if the group's membership changes, the group may regress to an earlier stage, at least temporarily.

Forming

In the **forming** stage, individuals come together and begin to think of themselves as members of a team. This forming stage is marked by apprehension, seeking basic information, defining goals, developing procedures for performing the task, and making a preliminary evaluation of how the team might interact to accomplish goals. A great deal of uncertainty often emerges at this point as team members begin to test the extent to which their input will be valued.

Teams in the forming stage often require some time for members to get acquainted with each other before attempting to proceed with their task responsibilities. It is a time for members to become acquainted, understand leadership and member roles, and learn what is expected of them.[74] The behaviors most common for individuals in the forming stage of team development include dependency, keeping feelings to themselves, acting more secure than they actually feel, experiencing confusion and uncertainty about what is expected, being polite, showing hesitancy about how to proceed, and sizing up the personal benefits and personal costs of being involved in the team. Jeff Zucker, president of NBC Universal Television Group, says his biggest challenge is getting a new team to maximize potential and combine together into one culture.[75]

Storming

Usually the emergence of conflict between members indicates the end of the forming stage and the beginning of the storming stage. The **storming** stage occurs as team members begin to experience conflict with one another. Being part of a team means that individuals may need to sacrifice many of their personal desires.

Arguments about roles and procedures surface, and the pleasant social interactions of the forming stage cease. Team members often experience negative emotions and become uncomfortable interacting with one another. Attempts to resolve differences of opinion about key issues, who is to be responsible for what, and the task-related direction of the leader are areas of conflict. Competition for the leadership role and conflict over goals are dominant themes at this stage. Some members may withdraw or try to isolate themselves from the emotional tension that is generated. Teams with members from diverse backgrounds or cultures may experience greater conflict than more homogenous teams.

At this stage, it is important not to suppress or withdraw from the conflict. Suppressing conflict will likely create bitterness and resentment, which will last long after members attempt to express their differences and emotions. Withdrawal can cause the team to fail more quickly.

Norming

Most teams make it through the storming stage, but the **norming** stage is a junction point.[76] If issues have not been resolved, the team will erupt into serious conflict and run the risk of failure. If mechanisms develop for handling conflict, the team will progress smoothly into the norming stage. The norming stage of development is a stage in which the team members come together and a real sense of cohesion and belonging begins to emerge. Team members feel good about each other and identify with the team. They share feelings, give and receive feedback, and begin to share a sense of success. The most important outcome of this stage of development is an increase in cohesiveness.

9 Have you ever been a member of a team whose members seemed to get along and work well with one another, were highly motivated, and worked in a coordinated way? When a team behaves in this way, it is considered to be cohesive. **Cohesiveness** is a strong sense of connectedness between team members that causes them to work together to attain an objective.[77] Think of cohesiveness as the strength of the members' desire to remain in the group, their commitment to it, and their ability to function as a unit. A team whose members have a strong desire to remain in the group and personally accept its goals would be considered highly cohesive.

LEARNING OBJECTIVE 9

Explain how cohesiveness can impact a team.

The degree of cohesiveness is an important dimension influencing group effectiveness. Cohesiveness can influence communication and the job satisfaction of group members. For example, members of cohesive groups tend to communicate more frequently, are likely to feel more satisfied with their jobs, are more committed to working through issues, think more favorably of team members, and experience less conflict than members of groups that are not cohesive.[78]

Cohesiveness among members may be a positive organizational force when it helps unite a team behind organizational goals. For example, when team members are committed, they know each other's strengths and weaknesses, they bring problems to the surface, and they work hard at being a team.[79] Unfortunately, a highly cohesive team can be a problem to an organization if the team's

KEY TERMS

Forming
First stage of group development.

Storming
Group development stage that occurs as team members begin to experience conflict with one another.

Norming
The stage of group development where norms are established.

Cohesiveness
The degree to which group members want to stay together.

goals are in conflict with the organization's goals. For example, if a team is not committed to the organization, its goals might include how much work the team can avoid or how many problems the team can cause for the manager. A highly cohesive team could cause considerable trouble in these situations.

Also, highly cohesive teams may become dysfunctional if they lead team members to groupthink. As we learned in Chapter 6, **groupthink** is an agreement-at-any-cost mentality that results in ineffective group decision making. Groupthink leads to ineffective group decisions when high cohesiveness coexists with significant conformity with the group and overrides the realistic appraisal of alternative courses of action.[80] But groupthink does not have to occur.

The other option for the cohesive team in the norming stage is the development of strong bonds between team members, thereby influencing them to work harder to achieve the collective goals. Effectiveness can be particularly high if teams vigilantly check the quality of their decisions and strive to help team members retain their individuality and to develop the potential for exchanging all kinds of information relevant to a task.[81]

The norming stage is also important because it is during this phase that team norms develop. **Norms** are unwritten, informal rules and shared beliefs that regulate the appropriate behavior expectations of team members. Norms differ from organizational rules in that they are unwritten and members must accept them and behave in ways consistent with them before they can be said to exist.[82]

Norms cannot be imposed on a group but rather develop out of the interaction among members.[83] For example, a typical work group may have norms that define how people dress, the upper and lower limits on acceptable productivity, the information that can be told to the boss, and the matters that need to remain secret. If a group member does not follow the norms, the other members will try to enforce compliance through acceptance and friendship or through such means as ridicule, ostracism, sabotage, and verbal abuse.

Work groups establish a variety of norms that may not always align with the formal standards set by the organization. Group norms can be positive, helping the group meet its objective(s), or they can be negative, hindering the group's effectiveness. Once norms are established, they are very difficult to change. Thus, the early stages of development are critical to set high standards and reward positive norms.

Although we know that disagreement among group members is beneficial for productive and critical thinking, it is often discouraged by group norms. Once a group reaches the norming stage of development, dissenters from group norm behavior are often pressured into conforming to new standards. Managers need to understand the norms of the groups that they manage and then work toward maintaining and developing positive norms while eliminating negative norms.[84]

© FIRST LIGHT/GETTY IMAGES

Cohesiveness among team members is a positive force that helps unite a team behind organizational goals.

KEY TERMS

Groupthink
An agreement-at-any-cost mentality that results in ineffective group decision making.

Norms
Unwritten, informal rules and shared beliefs that regulate the appropriate behavior expectations of team members.

Performing
Group development stage that occurs when the team is fully functional; marked by interpersonal relations and high levels of interdependence.

Performing

The **performing** stage, when the team is fully functional, is marked by interpersonal relationships and high levels of interdependence. It is also the most difficult stage to achieve. The team is oriented to maintaining good relations and to getting its task accomplished. Team members can now work well with everyone on the team, communication is constant, decisions are made with full agreement, and members understand the roles that they need to perform for the team to be highly effective.[85]

At the performing stage, the team has learned to solve complex problems and implement the solutions. Members are committed to the task and willing to experiment to solve problems. Cohesiveness has progressed to the point of collaboration. Confidence reaches a high

Meeting The Challenge

Nokia: Creating an Innovative Culture

In an effort to find fresh thinking from sources outside the company, Nokia created teams to seek out disruptive technologies, new business models, and promising entrepreneurs beyond Nokia's walls. Its U.S.-based team, called "Innovent," identifies early-stage entrepreneurs, buys options in their work, and introduces them to people at Nokia headquarters. Promoting this type of venturing behavior prevents ideas from ending up on the scrap heap or in the hands of competitors. It also keeps Nokia employees involved with creative thinkers.

In a fragmented market that is driven by style and fashion tastes rather than being primarily focused on functionality, Nokia believes it will continue to stay ahead of the fiercely competitive market. Nokia is a company that refuses to grow big, grow old, or grow slow. It's all part of an innovative culture and an ongoing emphasis on cooperative multifunctional teams.

Sources: L. Gratton, "Managing Integration through Cooperation," *Human Resource Management* 44, no. 2 (Summer 2005): 151–158; L. Gratton and S. Ghoshal, "Beyond Best Practice," *MIT Sloan Management Review* (Spring 2005): 49–60; N. Schwartz, "Has Nokia Lost It?" *Fortune*, 24 January 2005, 98–103; I. Wylie, "Calling for a Renewable Future," *Fast Company* (May 2003): 46–47; S. Finkelstein, "Why Smart Executives Fail," *Executive Excellence* 21, no. 9 (2004): 9; J. Santos, Y. Doz, and P. Williamson, "Is Your Innovation Process Global?" *MIT Sloan Management Review* 45, no. 4 (2004): 31–37; C. Canabou, "Fast Talk," *Fast Company* (June 2004): 51–55.

level for the few teams that achieve this stage. Unfortunately, even if a team reaches this stage, it still faces the difficult job of maintaining this level of success.

How effective is the team that you are currently working with? Turn to Experiential Exercise 13.2 and complete the short exercise to use as a team-building assessment.

Adjourning

The **adjourning** stage involves the termination of task behaviors and disengagement from relationship-oriented behaviors. Some groups, such as a project team created to investigate and report on a specific program within a limited time frame, have a well-defined point of adjournment. Other groups, such as an executive committee, may go on indefinitely. Adjourning for this type of group is more subtle and takes place when one or more key members leave the organization.

Implications for Leaders

10 Research indicates that the primary elements of successful teams are that they have specific, well-defined goals, develop interdependent and collaborative relationships, share leadership, provide feedback, recognize and reward performance, and celebrate victories.[86] Is there a secret to creating this type of team? No. As a manager you must create the environment for the development and nurturing of successful teams. Start by focusing on the following:

- *Trust* Team members must learn to trust. Trust leads to flexibility and information flow.
- *Involvement* Every team member's participation counts; individuals are dependent and interdependent on a team regardless of where they fit into the hierarchy.
- *Emphasis on strengths* Team members must look for ways that their strengths and weaknesses complement each other.
- *Instillment of accountability* Team members must take personal responsibility for completing tasks and supporting each other.
- *Creation of precise goals* Members need clearly defined, precise goals and specific deadlines.

The more a manager understands about his or her personality and the personalities of coworkers, the more successful the manager can be in guiding a team and in supervising individuals. It does begin with oneself.

LEARNING OBJECTIVE 10

Clarify the primary elements of successful teams.

KEY TERMS

Adjourning
Group development stage that involves the termination of task behaviors and disengagement from relationship-oriented behaviors.

SUMMARY

1. Individual differences are determined to a great extent by several internal elements such as personality, perceptions, attitudes, and abilities. People respond differently to the same situation because of the unique combination of these elements.

2. Personality is an enduring, organized, and distinctive pattern of behavior that describes an individual's adaptation to a situation. It is a combination of traits that characterizes the unique nature of a person. Many personality traits influence work behavior and performance, including self-esteem, locus of control, Type A or Type B personality, resiliency, self-monitoring, and personality traits measured by the Myers-Briggs Type Indicator and the "Big Five."

3. The Myers-Briggs Type Indicator, or MBTI examines and measures our preferred style of dealing with the world and the people in it. The dimensions are Introversion/Extroversion (I or E), Sensing/-Intuitive (S or N), Feeling/Thinking (F or T), and Perceiving/Judging (P or J). The Big Five factors are extroversion, agreeableness, conscientious, emotional stability, and openness to experience.

4. When an individual's personality matches his or her job or career, then he or she will be less likely to leave and be more satisfied. The RIASEC Vocational Interest Typology is a successful tool to assist with matching an individual's personality with jobs and careers.

5. Perception is the way people experience, process, define, and interpret the world around them and influences the way in which they communicate and become aware of sensations and stimuli. Perceptions are influenced by a variety of factors, including an individual's experiences, needs, personality, and education. Perceptual biases, such as stereotyping, halo-and-horn effects, and selective perception, cause managers to make errors that can be costly to the organization and to individuals.

6. The relationship between job satisfaction and job performance is complex because a number of personal and situational variables affect the two variables. An employee's job performance depends on a large number of factors such as ability, the quality of equipment and materials used, the competence of supervision, the working environment, and peer relationships.

7. A role is a set of behaviors that is a characteristic of a person in a specific situation. When operating in a work group, individuals typically fulfill several roles including task-oriented, relationship-oriented, and self-oriented roles. Behaviors related to establishing and accomplishing the goals of the group or achieving the desired outcomes are task-orientated roles; behaviors that cultivate the well-being, continuity, and development of the group are relationship-oriented roles; behaviors that fulfill personal needs or goals of an individual without regard for the group are self-oriented roles.

8. The team development process is dynamic, and teams pass through stages that follow a general pattern. Teams appear to go through a five-stage developmental sequence: forming, storming, norming, performing, and adjourning.

9. Cohesiveness is a strong sense of connectedness between team members that causes them to work together to attain an objective. It can influence communication and the job satisfaction of group members and help unite a team behind organizational goals. Highly cohesive teams may become dysfunctional if they lead team members to groupthink or if the team's goals are in conflict with those of the organization.

10. The primary elements of successful teams are specific, well-defined goals, development of interdependent and collaborative relationships, shared leadership, feedback, recognition and reward of performance, and celebration of victories.

REVIEW QUESTIONS

1. (LEARNING OBJECTIVE 1) Explain why managers need to learn to recognize and understand individual differences. What are the key factors that underlie individual differences?
2. (LEARNING OBJECTIVE 2) Define personality.
3. (LEARNING OBJECTIVE 2) Discuss the personality characteristics of resilience.
4. (LEARNING OBJECTIVE 2) What are some of the positive and negative aspects of Type A and Type B personality characteristics?
5. (LEARNING OBJECTIVE 3) What are the four personality dimensions measured by the MBTI?
6. (LEARNING OBJECTIVE 4) Why is it important for an individual's personality to match his or her job requirements?
7. (LEARNING OBJECTIVE 5) What is stereotyping? How is it both helpful and harmful?
8. (LEARNING OBJECTIVE 6) Why is it important for managers to understand the relationship between job satisfaction and performance?
9. (LEARNING OBJECTIVE 7) Describe the different roles team members can have on a team.
10. (LEARNING OBJECTIVE 8) What are the five primary development stages of teams?
11. (LEARNING OBJECTIVE 9) Explain how cohesiveness can impact a team.
12. (LEARNING OBJECTIVE 9) What role do norms play in a team's performance?
13. (LEARNING OBJECTIVE 10) What are the primary elements that make successful teams?

DISCUSSION QUESTIONS

Improving Critical Thinking

1. What types of careers are most appropriate for individuals with internal locus of control? High self-esteem? Low extroversion?
2. Describe an effective and an ineffective team of which you have been a member. What role(s) did you play? How cohesive was the team? What could you have done to make the team more effective?
3. Consider the development process of a team of which you have been a member. How long did the team take to pass through the different stages of development? Did the team seem to proceed through all of the stages of development? Why or why not?
4. Discuss a stereotypical group to which you belong. What people or things belong to the group? Give an example of a member of the group who does not fit the stereotype.

Enhancing Communication Skills

1. Interview several managers about ways in which they handle the job satisfaction of their employees. Write up your interview results or present them to the class as directed by your professor.
2. Explain the ways that managers can learn to reduce the perceptual errors that occur in the workplace. Prepare a presentation for a small group or the class that includes specific examples.

Building Teamwork

1. Write a brief description of a junior in college majoring in business. How would this description compare to students who attend a university different from yours? Compare your perceptions with others in a small group.
2. List different types of norms that you have experienced working in formal work teams while engaged in class projects. Form a small group and develop a combined list. Do you find any norms common to most members? Highlight these. Discuss the norms that lead to positive work performance.
3. Find an article in a current business magazine that describes how an organization is using teams. Form a small group and share your findings. Select the article that best represents an unusual use of a team and share it with the class.

Chapter

14

Motivating Organizational Members

CHAPTER OVERVIEW

An organization's energy comes from the motivation of its employees. Although ability plays a crucial role in determining employee work performance, so does motivation. Managers must ensure that employees are motivated to perform their tasks to the best of their abilities. Through motivation, managers are better able to create a working environment that is conducive to good effort and where employees are inspired to work to accomplish the organization's goals.[1]

In this chapter, we discuss motivation as the force that energizes and gives direction to behavior. The topic of motivation has been studied by industrial/organizational (I/O) psychologists at least since the 1930s.[2] It has been the subject of numerous studies and debates, and many approaches have emerged that are applicable for the contemporary manager. We examine the main approaches to motivating employees, including motivation through need satisfaction, motivation through complex processes, and the reinforcement approach to motivation. We consider several motivational challenges for today's managers, including participative management, recognition programs, money as a motivator, and motivating team performance. Finally, we discuss international perspectives to better appreciate how the diversity of the workforce influences employee motivation.

LEARNING OBJECTIVES

When you have finished studying this chapter, you should be able to

1. Explain the basic motivation process.
2. Describe the different approaches to motivation.
3. Discuss needs-based approaches to employee motivation.
4. Explain the process approaches to employee motivation.
5. Outline how goal setting is used as a tool for motivating individuals.
6. Describe how the reinforcement approach is used to increase and decrease behavior in an organizational setting.
7. Address the application of participative management.
8. Clarify the use of money as a motivator.
9. Explain how to reward team performance
10. Account for the importance of motivation from an international perspective.

Facing The Challenge

You Understand Me: Yum! Brands

In 1997 PepsiCo spun off its restaurant division under the name Tricon Global Restaurants, Inc., now Yum! Brands with David Novak selected to lead the new organization. While Novak was excited by the challenge, being spun off from PepsiCo made associates from the primary divisions—KFC, Taco Bell, Pizza Hut, Long John Silvers', and A&W—both anxious and uncertain about the future.

Novak's vision was to create a customer-focused company the right way—consistently treat those who serve customers as if they are the most important people in the company. If a company's people are treated as winners and see themselves as winners, customer satisfaction and profitability come naturally. With its emphasis on understanding people, one of the things Yum! stands for is **Y**ou **U**nderstand **M**e.

The new company was built with a strategic recognition program. Yum!'s "How We Work Together Principles" are value statements that emphasize customer focus, belief in people, recognition, coaching and support, accountability, excellence, positive energy, and teamwork. Titles were changed to reflect these values. For example, Corporate Headquarters was renamed the Restaurant Support Center, and the management team had their titles changed from managers to coaches. Yum! began investing heavily in employee training. Over 850,000 employees around the globe are trained four times a year in its Customer Mania program, which was designed to empower frontline employee to resolve customer disputes. The program recognizes employees who go the extra mile in the name of customer service.

Yum! Brands is the world's largest restaurant company with more than 33,000 restaurants in over 100 countries. That means that the company must pay special attention to the connection between employee retention and company performance. Given the high turnover in the fast-food industry, the challenge for Yum! is to keep employees engaged and motivated while achieving a remarkable record of growth.

Sources: D. Shuit, "Former PepsiCo Executives Do a 360 in Managing Yum Brands' Workforce," *Workforce Management* 84 (April 2005): 59–61; M. Barry and J. Slocum, "Slice of Reality: Changing Culture at Pizza Hut and Yum! Brands, Inc.," *Organizational Dynamics* 32 (November 2003): 319–329; R. King, "Great Things Are Starting at Yum," *Workforce Management* (November 2003); S. Hume "An Interview with Ken Blanchard," *Restaurants and Institutions* 115 (April 2005): 25; K. Blanchard, J. Ballard, and F. Finch, *Customer Mania! It's Never Too Late to Build a Customer Focused Company* (New York: Free Press, 2004); K. Blanchard, "Action: Be on Time and on Target: Leadership and the Bottom Line," *Executive Excellence* 21 (September 2004): 18.

Introduction

Steven Kerr published a classic article some time ago entitled "On the Folly of Rewarding A while Hoping for B." In the article, he argued that many organizations and managers want one thing but reward other things instead. Why do they do this? Reasons mentioned include the following:

- Managers have not clearly identified what is necessary for good performance—the behaviors, tasks, goals, and strategy that are needed.
- Managers have not determined how to measure successful performance.
- Employees do not see clear links between their performance and achievement of the goals.
- Employees may not have the right abilities to carry out the job.
- Employees want rewards different from what their supervisors think they want.
- Employees have different levels of motivation to do the job.[3]

In previous chapters, many of these issues have been addressed. These include establishing strategy, plans, and goals, selecting the right employees, determining the tasks necessary in each job, helping people to understand what is expected in their jobs, effective communication, and the relationship between leadership and employee performance.

In this chapter, our goal is to examine the motivation of people in their jobs so that we, as managers, can understand how to motivate and reward the behaviors that we really want—the behaviors that will lead to the fulfillment of goals and make individuals and the organization successful.

© SUSAN VAN ETTEN

It is important for managers to understand both what motivates employees to perform successful behaviors that achieve the goals of the corporation and what rewards employees want for their successful behaviors.

Basic Motivation Process

1 **Motivation** refers to forces, either internal or external to a person, that act as inducements or that influence action to do something. The action may be the individual's choice, effort, or persistence.[4]

How does motivation occur? How is it related to performance? Since the early work of the scientific management and human relations theorists, management scholars have developed a number of different models that help us understand what motivates people at work.[5] Although the process of motivation is complex, managers see motivation as an integral part of the performance equation at all levels in the organization.[6] This is shown in Figure 14.1 and expressed in the formula $M \times A = P$, where P refers to performance, M refers to motivation, and A refers to ability. Recall from Chapter 13 that ability is an existing capacity to perform various tasks needed in a given situation and that abilities may include mental, mechanical, and psychomotor skills.

LEARNING OBJECTIVE 1

Explain the basic motivation process.

Consider, for example, that you are motivated and have a goal to become an accountant. Motivation alone is not enough. You also must have the ability to perform the job. You are in school to gain the required knowledge, skills, and training through education. Let's look again at our formula:

Motivation	×	Ability	=	Performance
(Goal and desire)	×	(Education, knowledge)	=	Accountant

The approaches to motivation in this chapter are general approaches to the *what* and *how* of behavior. We focus on motivation as the result of the interaction between the individual and the situation. As such, the level of motivation varies both between individuals and within individuals at different times.[7] But we should remember that motivation is only one of many explanations of human behavior. For example, personality influences how individuals differ in their motivational drive.[8] Keep in mind that no single, accepted theory currently exists that can fully and accurately explain motivation.

LEARNING OBJECTIVE 2

Describe the different approaches to motivation.

Motivational Approaches

2 We discuss motivation by using three broad perspectives—need, process, and reinforcement approaches. **Needs-based approaches** emphasize specific human needs, or the factors within a person that energize, direct, and stop behavior. **Process approaches** take a complex and dynamic view of motivation. They focus on understanding the thought or cognitive

KEY TERMS

Motivation
Forces either internal or external to a person that act as inducements or that influence action to do something.

Figure 14.1 The Relationship between Motivation and Performance

Motivation × Ability → Performance

Education Knowledge

Mental Skills

Mechanical Skills

Psychomotor Skills

processes that take place within the individual's mind that influence behavior. **Reinforcement approaches** are based on learning and examine how consequences mold behavior. We begin our discussion with needs-based approaches.

NEEDS-BASED APPROACHES OF EMPLOYEE MOTIVATION

3 Many factors are believed to influence a person's desire to perform work or behave in a certain way. Approaches based on needs explain motivation primarily as a phenomenon that occurs intrinsically, or within an individual. Here we look at three widely recognized models: the hierarchy of needs (Maslow), the two-factor model (Herzberg), and the acquired-needs model.

KEY TERMS

Needs-based approach
A model of motivation that focuses on a person's needs as motivators.

Process approach
A model of motivation that focuses on understanding the thought process in influencing motivation.

Reinforcement approach
Based on learning and examine how consequences mold behavior.

Hierarchy of needs
A motivation model stating that a person has five fundamental needs.

Maslow's Hierarchy of Needs

According to the **hierarchy of needs,** a person has five fundamental needs: physiological, security, affiliation, esteem, and self-actualization.[9] Figure 14.2 shows these five needs arranged in a hierarchy, separated into higher and lower levels. Physiological and security needs are lower-order needs, which are generally satisfied externally, and affiliation, esteem, and self-actualization are higher-order needs, which are satisfied internally.

Physiological Needs At the lowest level of the hierarchy are physiological needs. Food, water, air, and shelter are all **physiological needs.** People concentrate on satisfying these needs before turning to higher-order needs. Managers must understand that to the extent employees are motivated by physiological needs, their concerns do not center on the work they are doing. They will accept any jobs that serve to meet their needs. Managers who focus on physiological needs in trying to motivate subordinates assume that people work mainly for money and are primarily concerned with comfort, avoidance of fatigue, and their rate of pay.

Security Needs Next in the hierarchy are **security needs,** which reflect the desire to have a safe physical and emotional environment. Job security, grievance procedures, health insurance, and retirement plans are used to satisfy employees' security needs. Like physiological needs, unsatisfied security needs cause people to be preoccupied with satisfying them. People who are motivated primarily by security needs value their jobs mainly as a defense against the loss of basic needs. Managers who feel that security needs are most important will often emphasize rules, job security, and fringe benefits.

Affiliation Needs **Affiliation needs** include the desire for friendship, love, and a feeling of belonging. After physiological and security needs have been satisfied, affiliation needs become more important as a motivator. When affiliation needs are primary sources of motivation,

Figure 14.2 Maslow's Hierarchy of Needs

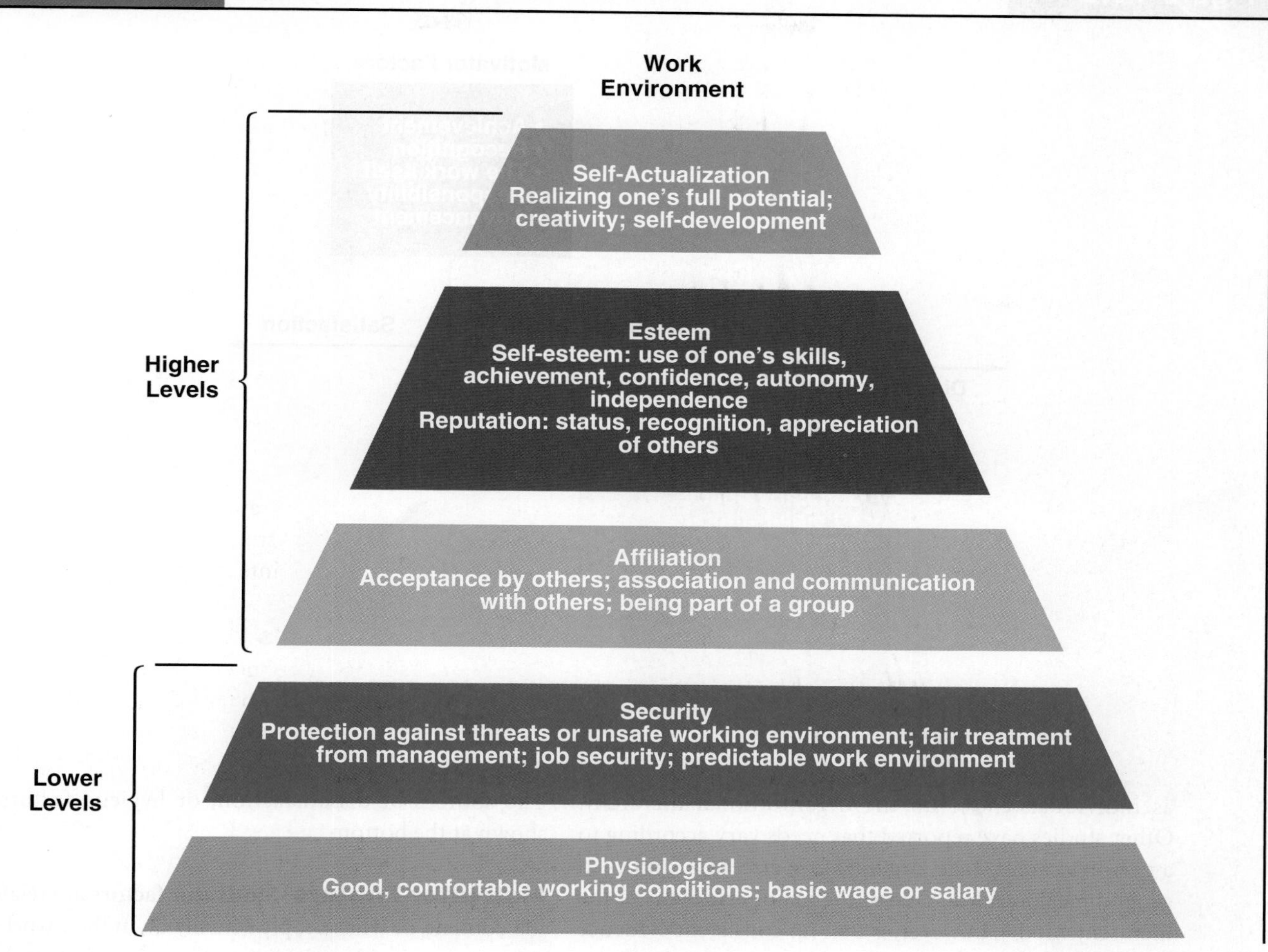

individuals value their work as an opportunity for finding and establishing friendly interpersonal relationships.

Esteem Needs Esteem needs are met by personal feelings of achievement and self-worth and by recognition, respect, and prestige from others. People with esteem needs want others to accept them and to perceive them as competent and able. Managers who focus on esteem needs try to foster employees' pride in their work and use public rewards and recognition for services to motivate them.

Self-Actualization Needs Finally, at the top of the hierarchy are self-actualization needs. Self-fulfillment and the opportunity to achieve one's potential are considered **self-actualization needs.** People who strive for self-actualization accept themselves and use their abilities to the fullest and most creative extent. Managers who emphasize self-actualization may involve employees in designing jobs or make special assignments that capitalize on employees' unique skills. Many entrepreneurs who break away from jobs in large corporations to start their own business may be looking for a way to satisfy their self-actualization needs.

In summary, the hierarchy provides a convenient framework for managers. It suggests that as individuals develop they work their way up a hierarchy based on the fulfillment of prioritized needs. Some studies show that the higher-order needs increase in importance over lower-order needs

KEY TERMS

Physiological needs
Needs such as food, water, air, and shelter; at the bottom of the hierarchy of needs.

Security needs
The desire to have a safe physical and emotional environment.

Affiliation needs
The desire for friendship, love, and a feeling of belonging.

Esteem needs
Needs for personal feelings of achievement and self-worth.

Figure 14.3 Herzberg's Two-Factor Theory

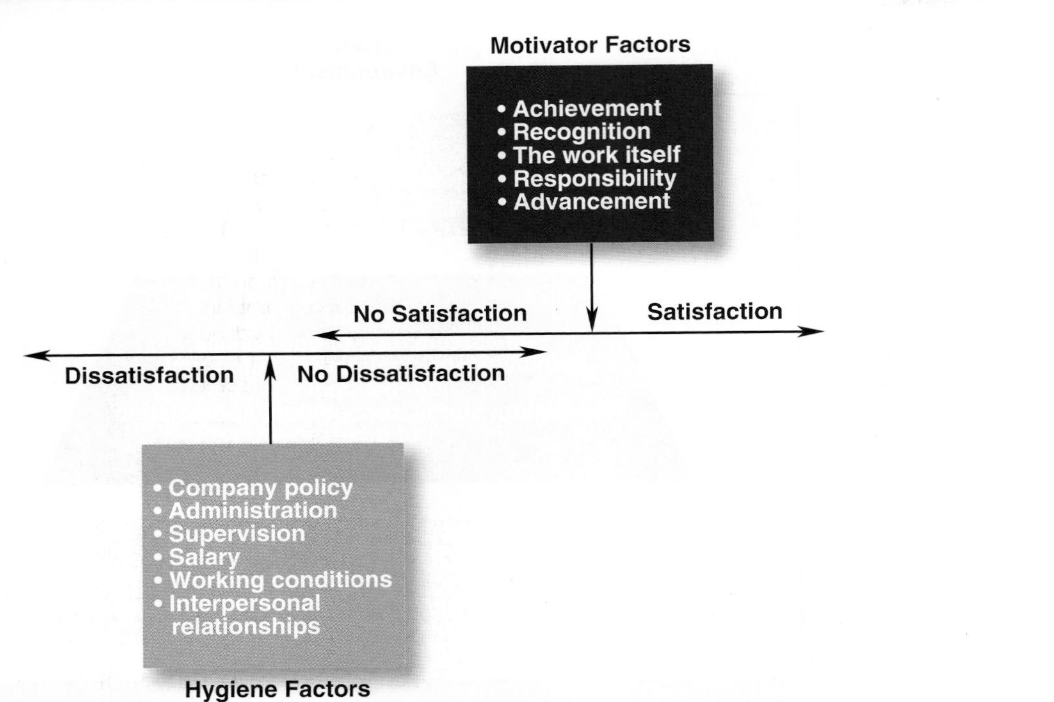

as individuals move up the organizational hierarchy. Other studies have reported that needs vary according to a person's career stage, organization size, task, and even geographical location. One of the major criticisms of the hierarchy model, however, is that no consistent evidence exists that the satisfaction of a need at one level will decrease its importance and increase the importance of the next-higher needs.

KEY TERMS

Self-actualization needs
Needs for self-fulfillment and the opportunity to achieve one's potential; at the top of the hierarchy.

Two-factor model
The model of motivation that includes motivator factors and hygiene factors.

Motivator factor
A factor related to job content.

Hygiene factor
A factor associated with the job context or environment in which the job is performed.

Two-Factor Model

The two-factor model provides another way to examine employee needs. In the **two-factor model,** Herzberg sought to understand how work activities and the nature of one's job influence motivation and performance. There are two separate and distinct influences—hence, the term *two-factor* model.[10]

The two-factor model is shown in Figure 14.3. At the top are the sources of work satisfaction, motivator factors. The sources of dissatisfaction, or hygiene factors, are shown at the bottom.

Motivator Factors **Motivator factors** are related to job content, or what people actually do in their work, and are associated with an individual's positive feelings about the job. Based on the two-factor model, motivator factors include the job itself, opportunities for achievement and advancement, responsibility, and job challenge.

Hygiene Factors **Hygiene factors** are associated with the job context or the environment in which the job is performed. Company policy and administration, technical supervision, salary, working conditions, and interpersonal relationships are examples of hygiene factors. These factors are associated with an individual's negative feelings about the job, but they do not contribute to motivation.

Studies on what managers value support the two-factor model conclusion. Achievement, recognition, and challenging work are valued more than factors such as pay or security.[11] For example, at Yum! Brands, feedback from employees showed they wanted to be part of an organization that valued and recognized their work. They helped create value statements and reward programs that were based on the company's "Founding Truth" and "How We Work Together Principles." Annual surveys

At the Forefront

Strategically Planning Recognition

As the CEO of CalPERS, the nation's largest public pension fund, James Burton created a different type of strategic plan. His strategic plan was fashioned to support the corporate goals and objectives by focusing primarily on employee recognition.

The plan was guided by two factors: (1) the company's vision for a caring community and (2) feedback from employees that was gathered through an employee-satisfaction survey. Based on this information, the company made a commitment to build a recognition-based culture.

CalPERS focused on providing recognition and reinforcement of behaviors that supported the organization's goals. Accountability measures were developed to promote quality communication. Information was shared at company-wide events. Managers were given additional training and provided opportunities to be more accessible to employees. Efforts were directed at retaining top performers. Funds were allocated for managers to host recognition-based events.

The result of the employee recognition plan was increased morale, more open communication, and more problem solutions. The program is credited for helping CalPERS achieve very aggressive business goals and objectives.

Source: *Workforce Management* online at http://www.workforce.com.

indicate that recognition for their accomplishments is one of the most important aspects of working with the organization.[12] CalPERS, the nation's largest public pension fund, is another example highlighted in the "At the Forefront" box.

However, just because many people rate motivators above hygiene factors is no guarantee that the motivators will actually increase work motivation for all employees. These findings may not be applicable to the entire population, especially as the workforce becomes more diverse.[13] Nevertheless, the two-factor model carries some clear messages for managers. The first step in motivation is to examine issues involving pay, working conditions, company policies, and so forth to be certain that they are appropriate and reasonable. Then they can address motivation itself. According to the two-factor model, managers should strive to provide opportunities for growth and advancement, achievement, and job challenge.[14]

Acquired-Needs Model

A third needs-based approach to motivation is the **acquired-needs model.** The basis of the model is that needs are acquired or learned from the life experiences in the culture or country in which we live. The acquired-needs model focuses on three particularly important needs in the work environment: achievement, power, and affiliation.[15] The model proposes that when a need is strong, it will motivate the person to engage in behaviors to satisfy that need.

Need for Achievement The **need for achievement** is represented by the drive to excel, accomplish challenging tasks, and achieve a standard of excellence. The intensity of the achievement motivation that people have depends on their childhood, their personal and occupational experiences, and the type of organization for which they work.[16] Managers who want to motivate high achievers need to ensure that such individuals have challenging but obtainable goals that allow relatively immediate feedback about their progress.

High achievers often pursue a professional career in sales and are successful in entrepreneurial activities such as running their own business, managing a self-contained unit within a large organization, or holding positions in which success depends largely on individual achievement.[17]

Need for Power Research has also focused on the desire and need for power to influence and control one's environment as a particularly important motivator in organizations. This **need for power** may involve either personal power or institutional power. Individuals with a high need for personal power want to dominate others for the

KEY TERMS

Acquired-needs model
A need that is acquired or learned from the life experiences in the culture or country in which we live and can influence behavior.

Need for achievement
The drive to excel, to accomplish, and to achieve a standard of excellence.

Need for power
The need to influence and control one's environment; may involve either personal power or institutional power.

sake of demonstrating their ability to influence and control. In contrast, individuals with a high need for institutional power want to solve problems and further organizational goals.[18]

Need for Affiliation Finally, the **need for affiliation** is the desire for friendly and close interpersonal relationships. Individuals with a high need for affiliation enjoy working in teams and are likely to gravitate toward professions that involve high levels of interaction with others, such as teaching, coaching, counseling, and sales.

Although not all individuals have the appropriate needs profile to be successful managers, the acquired-needs model of motivation argues that employees can be trained to stimulate their achievement needs.[19] If an organizational position requires a high achiever, management can select a person with a high need for achievement or develop its own candidate through training.[20]

In summary, needs-based approaches to motivation provide managers with an understanding of the underlying needs that motivate people to behave in certain ways. However, these models do not explain why people choose a particular behavior to accomplish task-related goals. As useful as they are, needs-based models still emphasize the *what* aspect of motivation by describing what motivates individuals but do not provide information on thought processes or the *how* aspect of motivation. We examine a more complex view of motivation in the next section.

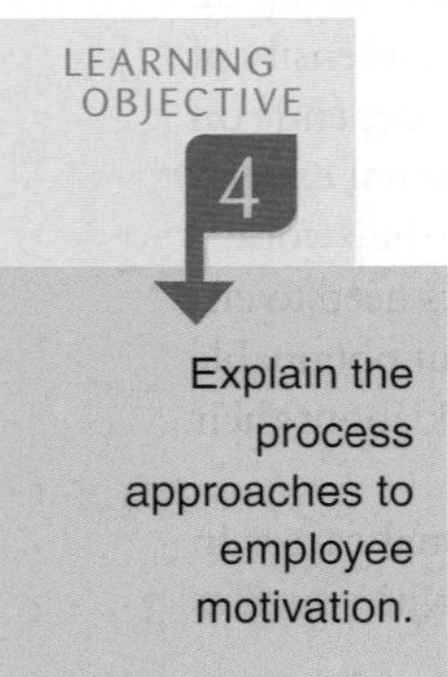

Explain the process approaches to employee motivation.

PROCESS APPROACHES TO EMPLOYEE MOTIVATION

4 Managers must have a more complete perspective on the complexities of employee motivation. It is useful to understand why different people have different needs and goals, why individuals' needs change, and how employees change to try to satisfy needs in different ways. Not all employees want the same things from their jobs. Understanding these aspects of motivation has become especially relevant as organizations deal with the diverse managerial issues associated with an increasingly global environment.[21] Some models for understanding these complex processes are the expectancy model, the equity model, and goal setting.

© SUSAN VAN ETTEN

According to the expectancy model of motivation, individuals choose the option that promises to give them the greatest reward.

Expectancy Model

The **expectancy model** suggests that behavior is purposeful, goal directed, and largely based on intentions. Behavior is determined by three basic individual perceptions: (1) Effort will lead to performance, (2) rewards are attached to performance, and (3) the outcomes or rewards are valuable to the individual.[22] Simply put, given choices, individuals choose the option that promises to give them the greatest reward. When you have three choices, you'll choose the one that provides you with the result that you value the most and has the highest probability of getting the result. The model applies to the career you select, the car you buy, the task you start the day with, the vacation site you choose, and so on. However, when individuals make choices, they must be reasonably sure that the reward they are looking for is attainable without undue risk or effort.

To help you understand the expectancy model, the next paragraphs briefly define the key terms of the model and discuss how they operate. Figure 14.4 shows how these terms are related.

Expectancy **Expectancy** is the belief that a particular level of effort will be followed by a particular level of

KEY TERMS

Need for affiliation
The desire for friendly and close interpersonal relationships.

Expectancy model
Behavior is purposeful, goal directed, and largely based on intentions.

Expectancy
The belief that a particular level of effort will be followed by a particular level of performance.

Figure 14.4 Expectancy Theory

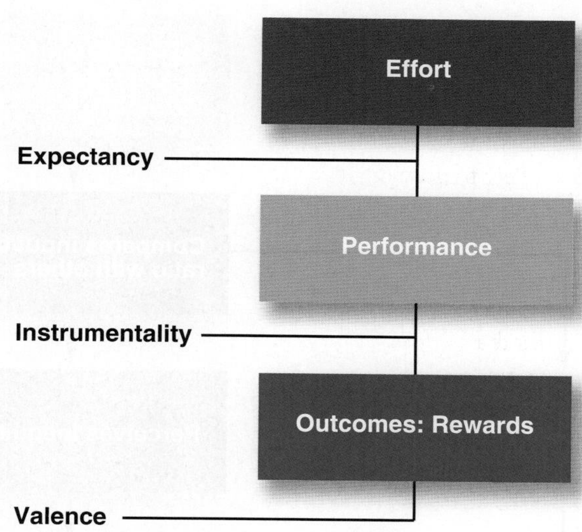

performance. This is best understood in terms of the effort–performance linkage, or the individual's perception of the probability that a given level of effort will lead to a certain level of performance.

Instrumentality **Instrumentality** is the individual's perception that a specific level of achieved task performance will lead to various work outcomes. This is the performance–reward linkage, or the degree to which the individual believes that performing at a particular level will lead to the attainment of a desired outcome.

Valence **Valence** represents the value, or importance, of the outcomes to the individual. Overall, the model says that a person will be motivated to expend effort based on his or her perceptions of the degree to which the effort will lead to performance, the degree to which rewards are tied to performance, and the value of the rewards. For motivation to be high, employees must value the outcomes that are available from high effort and good performance. Conversely, if employees do not place a high value on the outcomes and believe that there is not a strong link between effort and performance, and performance and rewards, motivation will be low.

Managers can influence expectancies by selecting individuals with the proper abilities, training them to use these abilities, supporting them by providing the needed resources, and identifying desired task goals. Instrumentalities can be influenced by making sure that rewards are tied to good performance and by helping employees see that they are. In addition, managers must try to determine the outcomes that each employee values.[23]

One of the problems with the expectancy model is that it is complex. Still, the logic of the model is clear, and the steps are useful for clarifying how managers can motivate people. Managers should first find out which rewards under their control have the highest valences for their employees. The best reward for one productive employee may be an office with large windows overlooking a scenic view of mountains or water. Other employees may value challenging work, advancement opportunities, or a flexible work schedule. Managers should then link these rewards to the performance that they desire. If any expectancies are low, managers might provide coaching, leadership, and training to raise them.[24]

Equity Model

Equity, or fairness in the workplace, has been found to be a major factor in determining employee motivation.[25] The **equity model** focuses on an individual's feelings about how fairly he or she is treated in comparison with others.[26] The model suggests that people evaluate their own performance and their attitudes by comparing them to others. They consider two primary factors in evaluating equity: (1) the ratio of their outcomes to their inputs and (2) the ratio of another's outcomes to

KEY TERMS

Instrumentality
The individual's perception that a specific level of achieved task performance will lead to outcomes or rewards.

Valence
The value of the reward to the individual.

Equity model
A motivation model focusing on an individual's feelings about how fairly he or she is treated in comparison with others.

Figure 14.5 Equity Theory

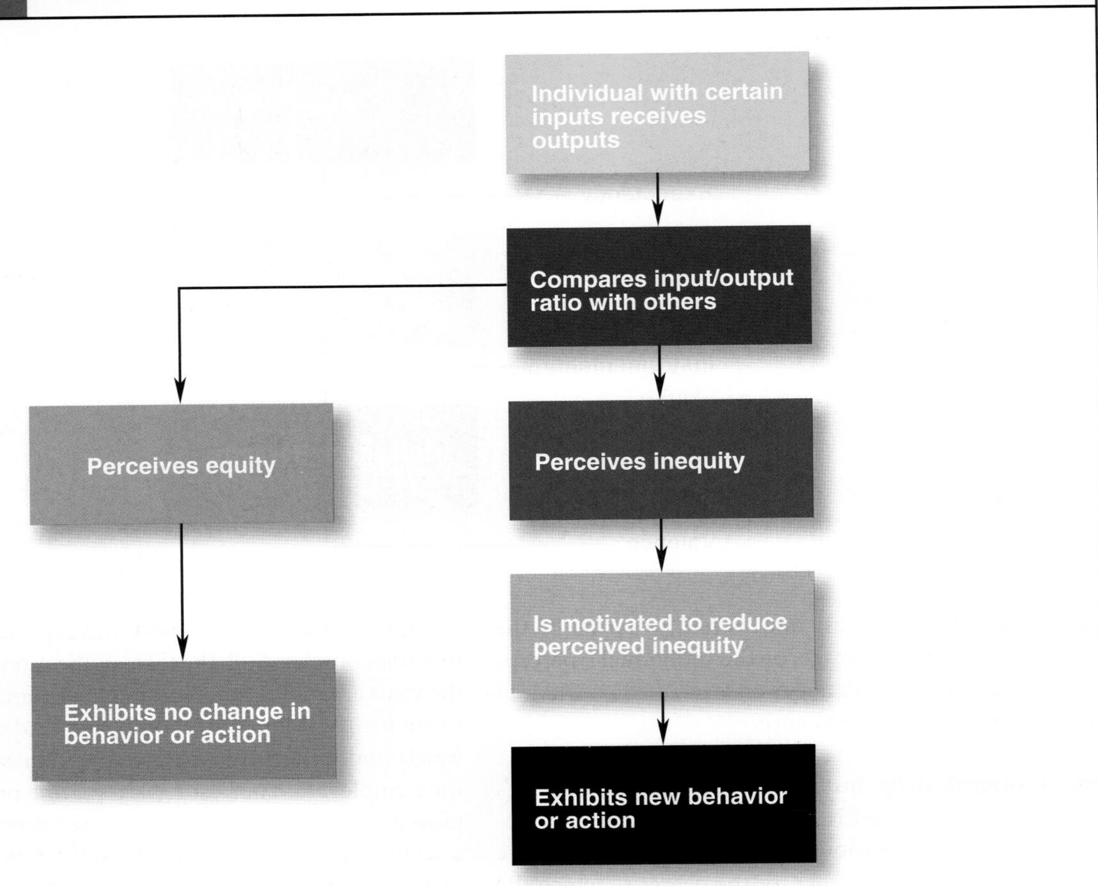

inputs. In the workplace, employees contribute their education, experience, expertise, time, and effort (inputs), and in return they get pay, security, and recognition (outputs). Figure 14.5 illustrates how the equity dynamic works in the form of input-to-outcome comparisons.

According to the equity model, we prefer a situation of balance or equity that exists when we perceive that the ratio of our inputs and outcomes is equal to the ratio of inputs and outcomes of one or more comparison persons. Given the social nature of human beings, it should come as no surprise that we compare our contributions and rewards to those of others. The comparisons may be coworkers in the group, workers elsewhere in the organization, or even persons employed by other organizations. Maintaining our self-esteem is an important priority. Therefore, if people experience inequity, they are generally motivated to change something and may respond by taking one of the following actions:

1. Change the work inputs by putting in less effort. For example, people who believe that they are underrewarded might reduce the quality of their performance, work shorter hours, or be absent frequently (output).
2. Change the outcomes received. For example, an individual may ask for improved working conditions, more favorable work assignments, or a pay increase.
3. Psychologically distort comparisons. For example, a person might rationalize or distort how hard she or he works or attempt to increase the importance of the job to the organization.
4. Change the comparison person who she or he is using to another person.
5. Change the situation. For example, quit the job or request a transfer to another department or location.

People often respond differently to the same situations, and therefore their reactions to inequity will vary. If the perceived inequity results in a change in motivation, it may alter effort and performance. You can probably think of instances in school when you believed you worked harder than others on a paper yet received a lower grade. Although working hard doesn't necessarily imply that you wrote a high-quality paper, your sense of equity was probably violated.

An important aspect in the equity model is perception. People make judgments based on perception rather than objective data. Feelings of inequity are determined solely by the individual's interpretation of the situation. Equity comparisons are common whenever managers allocate rewards that are valued. These might include vacation schedules, bonuses, raises, benefits, or preferred work assignments. Thus, it would be inaccurate to assume that all employees in a work unit will view rewards as fair. Rewards that are received with feelings of equity can foster job satisfaction and performance; rewards received with feelings of inequity can damage key work results. This conveys several clear messages to managers. First, people should be rewarded according to their contributions. Second, managers should make every effort possible to ensure that employees feel equitably treated. Finally, it is imperative for a manager to be aware that feelings of inequity are almost bound to arise. When they do, the manager should be patient and correct either the problem, if it is real, or help people recognize that things are not as inequitable as they seem.[27]

Goal-Setting

5 **Goal setting** is a process of increasing efficiency and effectiveness by specifying the desired outcomes or goals. The concept applies at all levels in the organization—individuals, groups, departments, or organization-wide.[28] Goals serve three purposes: (1) to guide and direct behavior toward overall organizational goals and strategies, (2) to provide challenges and standards against which the individual or unit can be assessed, and (3) to define what is important and provide a framework for planning.

Goal setting can be a powerful tool to motivate employees for several reasons. Goals provide a clear, engaging sense of direction and specify what is going to be accomplished. They represent the future outcomes, or the results, to achieve.[29]

For goal setting to be successful and lead to higher performance levels, goals must meet five requirements. An easy way to remember this is to use the acronym SMART: *S* stands for specific, *M* represents measurable, *A* means achievable or realistic, *R* stands for results oriented, and *T* means time related. Let's look at two different goals. One department manager establishes a goal to increase profitability. This is probably a goal that can never be met because it lacks detail. A second department manager establishes a goal to increase profitability by 10% by the end of December 2007, as compared to profitability in 2006. Do you see how important it is to provide details? The goal is now specific (10%), measurable (profitability can be measured), achievable (the manager knows how profits have been in the past), and results oriented (indicates what the outcome will be), and a time element has been given (at the end of December 2007).

Although it is not always necessary to have employees participate in the goal-setting process, participation is probably preferable to managers assigning goals especially if they anticipate that employees will resist accepting more difficult challenges. When subordinates accept the goal-setting process, they are more likely to be committed and work hard to accomplish goals. Studies suggest that employees achieve high levels of job satisfaction when they perceive that the probability of attaining goals is high and they are more satisfied when they perceive more positive than negative goals in their work environment.[30] People are more committed to their organizations when they are rewarded for achieving their job goals and when they perceive that the organization helps them achieve their personal goals.[31]

Goal setting is an increasingly important part of the motivational process for managers to understand. To use the process effectively, managers need to (1) meet regularly with subordinates, (2) work with subordinates to set goals jointly, (3) set goals that are specific and "appropriately" challenging, and (4) provide feedback about performance.

LEARNING OBJECTIVE 5

Outline how goal setting is used as a tool for motivating individuals.

REINFORCEMENT APPROACHES TO EMPLOYEE MOTIVATION

6 The reinforcement approach to motivation is based on the notion that behavior results from consequences. It is based on the role of positive and negative reinforcers, not at people's needs or reasons for choices. For example, people will repeat behaviors that are positively rewarded (reinforced positively) and avoid behaviors that are punished (not reinforced, or reinforced to avoid). From an organizational perspective, a manager can influence employee performance

LEARNING OBJECTIVE 6

Describe how the reinforcement approach is used to increase and decrease behavior in an organizational setting.

KEY TERMS

Goal setting
The process of increasing efficiency and effectiveness by specifying the desired outcomes toward which individuals, groups, departments, and organizations should work.

Figure 14.6 Four Types of Reinforcers

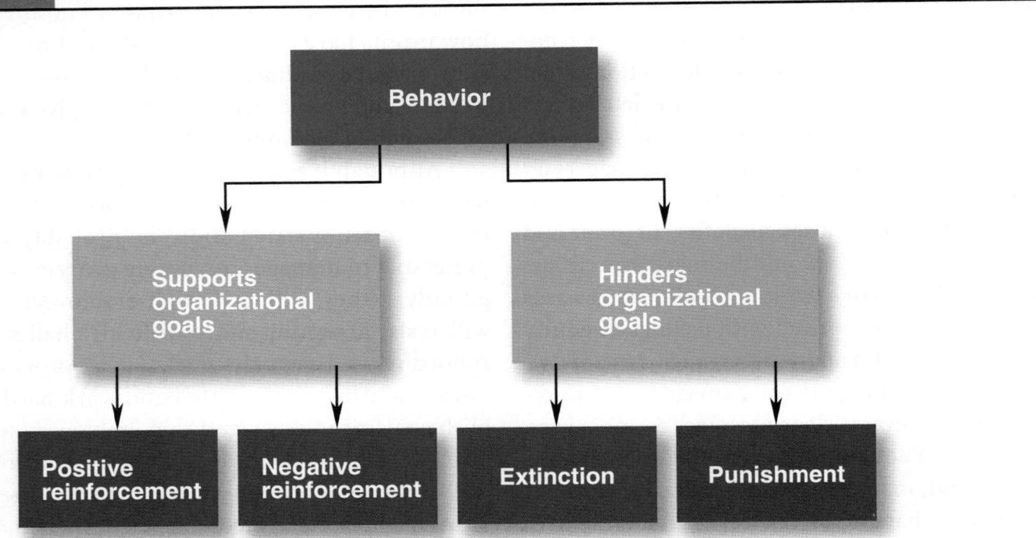

by reinforcing behavior that supports organizational goals.

The application of reinforcement theory is called **behavior modification** because it involves changing one's own behavior or the behavior of someone else. The tools of behavior modification are four basic reinforcement strategies in which either a pleasant or an unpleasant event is applied or withdrawn following a person's behavior. These four reinforcers are illustrated in Figure 14.6. To increase desired behavior, positive reinforcement or avoidance is used; to decrease undesirable behavior, extinction or punishment is used.

KEY TERMS

Behavior modification
The application of reinforcement concepts.

Positive reinforcement
The administration of positive and rewarding consequences or events following a desired behavior.

Negative reinforcement (avoidance learning)
Strengthening desired behavior by allowing escape from an undesirable consequence.

Extinction
The withdrawal of the positive reward or reinforcing consequences for an undesirable behavior.

Punishment
Administering negative consequences following undesirable behavior.

Positive Reinforcement

Positive reinforcement is the administration of positive and rewarding consequences or events following desired behavior. This tends to increase the likelihood that the person will repeat the behavior in similar settings. For example, a manager praises the marketing representative's high monthly sales performance; a student gets a good grade; a professor receives high teaching evaluations.

Negative Reinforcement

Negative reinforcement, also called **avoidance learning,** strengthens desired behavior by allowing escape from an undesirable consequence. For example, you avoid the penalties if you file your taxes by April 15.

Extinction **Extinction** is the withdrawal of the positive reward, or reinforcing consequences, for undesirable behavior. It weakens behavior because behavior that is no longer reinforced is less likely to occur in the future. For example, if an employee who is not meeting sales quotas fails to receive bonus checks, he or she will begin to realize that the behavior is not producing desired outcomes. The undesirable behavior will gradually disappear.

Punishment Administering a negative consequence following undesirable behavior is called **punishment.** This tends to reduce the likelihood that the behavior will be repeated in similar settings. For example, a manager docks an employee's pay for being rude to a customer, being late, or loafing on the job.

Which type of reinforcer is most appropriate to use? As suggested by considerable research and some popular books such as *The Enthusiastic Employee,*[32] when an employee's behavior is supportive of the organizational goals, positive reinforcement is the best action because it increases this desirable behavior. When employee behaviors do not support organizational objectives, the use of extinction is best; punishment should be used only as a last resort.

Studies have shown that consistent rewards for organizationally desirable behavior results in positive performance in the long term. In contrast, punishment as a primary motivational tool contributes little to high motivation because employees learn to avoid the punisher rather than learning appropriate behaviors.

Managers need to observe and manage the consequences of work-related behaviors carefully because individuals have different perceptions of what is a reward and what is punishment, depending on their values and needs. As the workforce becomes increasingly diverse, this issue will present greater challenges to managers.[33] The manager who positively reinforces desirable behaviors among employees achieves performance improvements without generating the fear, suspicion, and revenge that may be associated with using punishment.

Schedules of Reinforcement

To use behavior modification effectively, managers need to apply reinforcers properly. **Schedules of reinforcement** specify the basis for and timing of reinforcement. The basis for reinforcement includes interval and ratio. *Interval reinforcement* means that reinforcement is based on time. *Ratio reinforcement* means that reinforcement is based on exhibiting the desired behavior. The timing of reinforcement includes fixed or variable. *Fixed reinforcement* means that reinforcement is administered at each interval or for each desired behavior. *Variable reinforcement* means that the reinforcer is given at essentially a random time or random occurrence of the desired behavior.

A **fixed-interval schedule** rewards employees at specified time intervals, assuming that the desired behavior has continued at an appropriate level. An example is the Friday paycheck, which many employees receive.

When a reinforcer is provided after a fixed number of occurrences of the desired behavior, it is called a **fixed-ratio schedule.** For example, The Container Store offers staff members bonuses to increase their effort to hire the "right" type of employee. Workers receive $500 for every full timer hired and $200 for every part timer hired. As a result, the company often goes 8 months without placing a single classified ad.[34] Most piece-rate pay systems are considered fixed-ratio schedules.

With a **variable-interval schedule,** reinforcement is administered at random or varying times that cannot be predicted by the employee. For example, a division manager might visit a territory five times a month to comment on employee performance, varying the days and times each month.

A **variable-ratio schedule** provides a reinforcer after a varying or random number of occurrences of the desired behavior rather than after variable time periods. For example, slot machine payoff patterns, which provide rewards after a varying number of pulls on the lever, use a variable-ratio schedule. Although people anticipate that the machine will pay a jackpot after a certain number of plays, the exact number of plays is variable.

Reinforcers based on time are not very powerful in getting people to engage in and learn behaviors that are desired overall. Instead, they tend to influence people to engage in a certain behavior at a certain time. Behavior-based reinforcers are intended to teach a person to engage in behaviors that are desirable—for example, behaviors that contribute to achieving a goal of good performance.

Let's look a bit deeper at reinforcers based on desired behavior. Fixed ratio is effective during the initial learning process, but it becomes tedious and loses its value on an ongoing basis. For example, a manager might praise an employee every time he or she performs a task correctly. That would help the person learn faster. However, once the person begins to learn the task or behavior, the constant reward seems silly. Furthermore, the desired behavior tends to stop almost immediately unless the reinforcement is continued.

As an alternative, a variable-ratio reinforcement can be used. In this case, the desired behavior is rewarded intermittently rather than each time it occurs. With a variable-ratio schedule, desired behavior can be rewarded more often as encouragement during the initial learning process and less often when the behavior has been learned. The variable-ratio schedule of reinforcement tends to be the most powerful in terms of getting a person to continue desired behavior.

KEY TERMS

Schedules of reinforcement The basis for and timing of reinforcement.

Fixed-interval schedule Giving reinforcers at specified time intervals.

Fixed-ratio schedule Giving reinforcers after a fixed number of occurrences of the desired behavior.

Variable-interval schedule Giving reinforcement at varying times that cannot be predicted by the employee.

Variable-ratio schedule Giving reinforcers after varying or random number of occurrences of the desired behavior.

Table 14.1 Comparing Schedules of Reinforcement

Schedule	Form of Reinforcement	Influences on Behavior When Applied	Effects on Behavior When Withdrawn	Example
Fixed interval	Reward given on fixed time basis	Leads to average and irregular performance	Rapid extinction of behavior	Weekly or monthly paycheck
Fixed ratio	Reward tied to specific number of responses	Quickly leads to high and stable performance	Moderately fast extinction of behavior	Piece-rate system
Variable interval	Reward given at varying times	Leads to moderately high and stable performance	Slower extinction of behavior	Performance appraisals and rewards given at random times each month
Variable ratio	Reward given at variable amounts of output, or desired behavior	Leads to very high performance	Very slow extinction of behavior	Bonus given for the dollar value of sales made, with random levels of sales needed in order to get the bonus

Consider how difficult it is to walk away from a slot machine. "If it has paid out, I'll keep playing because it's likely to again. If it hasn't paid out, then it will any minute now because it's due and it might be big!" The four major types of reinforcement schedules are compared in Table 14.1.

USING BEHAVIOR MODIFICATION

Essentially, we all use the concepts in behavior modification and the reinforcement approach constantly. We perceive a response from other people for every behavior that we demonstrate. Based on our perception of the response, we tend to learn to repeat a behavior, avoid it, or stop doing it. Even if we are not aware of it, we may be influencing someone else's behavior by whether or not another person perceives a reward or punishment for certain behavior. This is especially important for managers to keep in mind because their behavior tends to set examples for the behavior of others in the organization. Hopefully, managers reward behavior of employees that is desirable for the organization—high performance—and ignore (extinction) behavior that is not or even punish it, if appropriate.

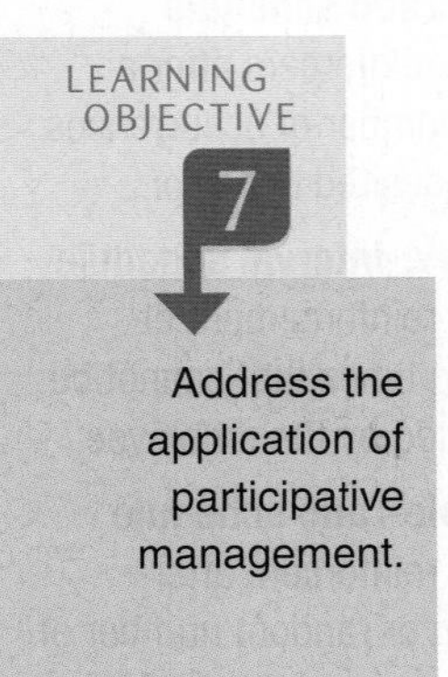

Address the application of participative management.

Do you think that managers are aware that their leadership example may reward behaviors that are not good for the organization? Recall our discussion from Chapter 12 and the role leaders play in influencing organization members.

Motivational Challenges for Today's Managers

In the past decade, the world of work has changed dramatically. The workforce is characterized by increased diversity with highly divergent needs and demands.[35] Today's managers face many challenges. Several issues related to motivation are discussed next.

PARTICIPATIVE MANAGEMENT

7 As a result of social and political developments over the past couple of decades, people today expect greater involvement in choosing directions for their lives in general and their lives at work more specifically. In addition, the changing workforce is less accepting of top-down control and expect growth, fulfillment, and dignity from their work.[36] Participative management is one way that an organization can establish a supportive environment.

Participative management is an umbrella term for programs in which employees have an opportunity for involvement in the workplace beyond the scope of their jobs. Participation management programs may include factors such as the culture and purpose of the company, leadership (especially top leadership's values and how leadership communicates), immediate supervision, job design, social relationships, codes of conduct, total rewards, opportunities for growth, community involvement, work–life benefits, and the quality of life in the workplace.[37] Sargento Foods is an example of an organization that utilizes participative management. It actively involves large numbers of people in strategy development and day-to-day operational improvement initiatives. Its commitment includes involving more than 40 senior and middle managers directly in the strategy development process, as well as "process improvement" teams focused on driving operational excellence.[38]

Participative management has emerged as an important concept underlying workforce motivation and productivity because these programs heighten the personal connection to the organization.[39] The idea draws on and is linked to a number of motivational approaches. For example, employee involvement can motivate workers by providing more opportunities for growth, responsibility, and commitment in the work itself. Similarly, the process of making and implementing a decision and then seeing the results can help satisfy an employee's need for responsibility, recognition, self-esteem, and achievement.

Participative management programs represent a shift away from traditional management styles and ways of doing business.[40] For participative management to work, however, an organization must change.[41] As we discussed in Chapter 10, the culture of an organization has to be in harmony with and accept this new way of conducting business. It is often extremely difficult for managers to give up authority and for employees to translate that surrender of power by higher-ups into lasting improvements in quality and productivity.

When organizations increase the amount of control and discretion workers have over their jobs, they are **empowering employees** and may improve the motivation of both employees and management.[42] Empowerment gives employees the tools, information, and authority they need to do their jobs with greater autonomy.[43] From a motivational perspective, it satisfies employees' higher-order needs for achievement, recognition, and self-actualization. Many companies in a variety of industries have successfully created cultures of empowerment. The list includes such well-known companies as General Electric, Texas Instruments, 3M, Pacific Gas & Electric, Marriott Corporation, and a variety of lesser-known companies like AES Corporation in Springfield, Virginia.

Do employee participation and involvement really work to motivate individuals? U.S. executives have indicated optimism toward participative management programs. These programs have been viewed as having positive influences on corporate quality, productivity, and customer service. An engaged workforce is more likely to retain its members, recommend the employer to others, be more productive, and show up at work.[44] To be successfully implemented, three core requirements are essential. Employees must (1) feel competent in what they do (have the necessary training, skills, and knowledge), (2) know what is expected and how to succeed at their jobs, and (3) have confidence in the leadership and in its ability to put together a strategy for the future.

RECOGNITION PROGRAMS

Employee recognition is a powerful element to be considered in motivating employees.[45] Top managers learned from Southwest Airlines the power of recognition to motivate employees and to elicit positive discretionary behavior among employees. Southwest separates reward from recognition and celebrates behaviors that reinforce the culture, creating an elaborate yet spontaneous process of positive behavioral feedback. Recognition is done by everyone, not just senior managers. This means that all levels of supervisors can recognize behavior, empowering those supervisors, but also ensuring that the recognition is timely, specific, and meaningful to the person who receives it.[46]

Recall our discussion earlier of Yum! Brands. The company considered employees so valuable that a strategic recognition plan was designed. For the plan to work, Yum! Brands started at the top to ensure that programs were continuous and ongoing. It built the recognition program into the communication processes and reinforced the values publically.[47] The reward and recognition programs proved to be a great way to instill company values, meet goals, and improve financial performance. A second example is how CalPERS provides recognition and reinforcement of behaviors that support the organization's goals ("At the Forefront").

MONEY AS A MOTIVATOR

LEARNING OBJECTIVE 8

Clarify the use of money as a motivator.

8 The issue of whether money motivates behavior is particularly relevant to managers. Conventional wisdom and the practice at most organizations often centers on money as the primary motivating force. As a medium of exchange, money should motivate to the degree that people perceive it as a means to acquire other things they want. Money may also have symbolic meaning, be a measure of achievement, bring recognition, or satisfy some other need.[48]

Research does show that money is a motivator when a "significant amount of

KEY TERMS

Empowering employees Increasing the amount of control and discretion workers have over their jobs.

money" is clearly tied to desired behavior. Also, money has to be desired by the person engaging in the behavior, the employee. However, overall, money tends to not be associated with productive behavior and may even motivate unwanted behavior. In situations where money does not motivate productive behavior, the reasons usually are (1) proper (productive) behavior has not been defined, (2) there are poor measures or no measures of productive behavior, and (3) the amount of money is too small to make a difference.[49] These same reasons explain why profit-sharing or gain-sharing programs frequently do not motivate individual performance.

Money may not be motivational when employees believe that a certain amount is an entitlement. Even a raise based on productive behavior, when added to the base salary for the next period of time, may be seen as an entitlement and therefore ceases to be motivational.[50] Money may motivate behavior that is not productive for an organization when people perceive that it is tied to the unwanted behavior. This of course may be due to differing perceptions and to poorly defined desired behavior.[51]

LEARNING OBJECTIVE 9

Explain how to reward team performances.

Managers need to consider the numerous ways to motivate employees that don't require money. Often these call for being creative. Complete the exercise in the "Now Apply It" box. It provides many suggestions for rewarding employees. See Table 14.2 for creative and "almost no-cost" ways to motivate employees.

© ASSOCIATED PRESS/AP

A significant part of a reward given to team members must be based on total team performance.

REWARDING TEAM PERFORMANCE

9 Recall from Chapter 13 our discussion on the use of teams in organizations and how managers can create and support successful teams. It is common for managers to experience problems getting the team members to work as a true team. Often the reason is that the reward system is established to reward an individual's performance rather than the team's

Table 14.2 Creative and "Almost No-Cost" Ways to Reward Employees

- Post a thank you note on the employee's office door.
- Call an employee into your office just to thank him or her; don't discuss any other issue.
- Volunteer to do another person's least desirable work task for a day.
- When paychecks go out, write a note on the envelope recognizing the employee's accomplishment.
- Begin a staff meeting by asking "What was the best thing that you did this week?"
- Schedule an Ugly Tie (or Crazy Sweater or Silly Socks) Day with a joke prize for the winner.
- Take a daily humor break. Designate someone to share a joke or funny story with the rest of the staff.
- Bring a Polaroid camera to work. Take candid shots of employees and post the results throughout the office.
- Give everyone an opportunity to arrive an hour late or leave an hour early 1 day a week.
- Recognize employee birthdays with a card or note.
- Create a Hall of Fame wall with photos of outstanding employees.
- Take a photo of the person being congratulated by his or her boss's boss. Frame the photo. Place photos of top performers in the lobby.
- Have lunch or coffee with an employee who you normally don't see.
- Write a thank you card by hand.
- Designate a bulletin board as a place for employees to post favorite jokes, cartoons, and the like.
- Make a bowl of popcorn and stop by staff members' offices to share.

Now Apply It

Refer to Table 14.2 and the suggestions for rewarding employees. For each of the following 16 items, select the ones that would motivate you as an employee. Next, select the ones that as a manager you would feel comfortable initiating. What suggestions do you have to add to the list?

SUGGESTION	WOULD MOTIVATE ME AS AN EMPLOYEE	I WOULD INITIATE AS A MANAGER
Post a thank you note on the employee's office door.		
Call an employee into your office just to thank him or her; don't discuss any other issue.		
Volunteer to do another person's least desirable work task for a day.		
When paychecks go out, write a note on the envelope recognizing the employee's accomplishment.		
Begin a staff meeting by asking "What was the best thing that you did this week?"		
Schedule an Ugly Tie (or Crazy Sweater or Silly Socks) Day with a joke prize for the winner.		
Take a daily humor break. Designate someone to share a joke or funny story with the rest of the staff.		
Bring a Polaroid camera to work. Take candid shots of employees and post the results throughout the office.		
Give everyone an opportunity to arrive an hour late or leave an hour early 1 day a week.		
Recognize employee birthdays with a card or note.		
Create a Hall of Fame wall with photos of outstanding employees.		
Take a photo of the person being congratulated by his or her boss's boss. Frame the photo. Place photos of top performers in the lobby.		
Have lunch or coffee with an employee who you normally don't see.		
Write a thank you card by hand.		
Designate a bulletin board as a place for employees to post favorite jokes, cartoons, and the like.		
Make a bowl of popcorn and stop by staff members' offices to share.		

performance.[52] So how do you reward team performance? First, a significant part of the reward given to team members must be based on total team performance. That will motivate the team to work together for the same goal. Second, individual rewards need to be based on how the employee contributed to the team's success, effort, and functioning and not for individual performance itself.[53] Toyota has been successful using team-based reward systems. Each team takes complete responsibility for the quality and management of its products. It conducts member performance reviews and establishes rewards. The system provides a challenging yet positive experience for workers and it reduces the need for bureaucracy because the people essentially manage themselves.[54]

International Perspectives

10 Just as no single approach to motivation fits everyone in the United States, the differences in what motivates individuals become greater as we go to other countries.[55] Here are just a few examples.

LEARNING OBJECTIVE 10

Account for the importance of motivation from an international perspective.

The United States is an achievement-oriented society that has historically encouraged and honored individual accomplishment and the attainment of material prosperity. Individualism, independence, self-confidence, and speaking out against injustice and threats are important elements of the U.S. character. Japanese motivations and values are very different, with obvious implications for management practices.[56] The Japanese place greater emphasis on socially oriented qualities. Their society is arranged in a rigid hierarchy, and all members are expected to maintain loyalty and obedience to authority. Dependency and security are part of the Japanese upbringing, whereas autonomy and early independence are typically American. In their corporate life, the Japanese show great dependency and are highly conforming and obedient. Japanese managers recognize that these characteristics can inhibit creativity and innovation and are consequently encouraging programs in their schools that will develop the creativity and ingenuity that they envy in Americans.[57]

The cross-cultural research on achievement has been relatively consistent across cultures, stimulated by the realization that managers in multinational corporations must be sensitive to the underlying values and needs of their diverse employees.[58] For example, managers in New Zealand appear to follow an achievement pattern developed in the United States. In general, managers in Anglo countries, such as the United States, Canada, and Great Britain, tend to have a high need for achievement as well as a high need to produce and a strong willingness to accept risk. In contrast, managers in countries such as Chile and Portugal tend to have a lower need for achievement. Keep in mind, however, that the word *achievement* itself is difficult to translate into other languages, and this influences any cross-cultural research findings.

The implications for managerial style, practices, and motivational planning for a U.S.-based company that is operating branches in other countries are apparent.[59] Consider the challenge facing Yum! Brands as the company continues its strong international expansion.[60] Managers must take the social character, values, and cultural practices of each country into consideration. A well-managed, diverse workforce is instrumental for a firm's competitive advantage. Read how Paul Mak, president of Mary Kay China, has successfully translated the traditional Mary Kay culture to fit his sales force in China (see the "Leaders in Action" box).[61] To develop or maintain such an advantage, managers need to consider a broad definition of motivation when determining compensation packages, responsibilities, rules and procedures, organizational structure, control systems, job design, and management techniques.[62]

Implications for Leaders

Here are important conclusions that we can draw from the study of motivation:

- *Individuals have different needs and wants.* Find out what motivates each person because the same thing will not motivate everyone.
- *Treat people fairly.* This includes fair pay, benefits, and job security. These days, employees especially need medical benefits.
- *Recognition is important.* In a classic study first conducted in the 1940s and repeated in the 1980s and the 1990s, Lawrence Lindahl asked managers to list, in order of importance, what they thought were

Leaders in Action

Mary Kay in China

In 1963 when Texan Mary Kay Ash founded Mary Kay Cosmetics, she probably did not consider that her products might be popular in China. Her business model was founded on personal initiative combined with a strong message of female empowerment, not necessarily advocated by the Chinese culture.

Despite the cultural differences, Paul Mak, president of Mary Kay China, says that Mary Kay products are very much in demand and his company has experienced rapid annual growth rates. The company has over 370 full-time employees and 25,000 registered "beauty consultants," independent contractors who sell directly to consumers.

Mak has had to make some adjustments to adapt the traditional Mary Kay values to the Chinese culture. For example, the Mary Kay corporate motto "God first, family second, career third," was modified by substituting *Principle* for the word *God.* Mak also has to help employees understand the Mary Kay notion that family is more important than career.

As the company leader, Mak strives to encourage the sales force by creating a holistic experience. His goal is "to motivate the heart." For example, he teaches the sales force not to sell to people but to care for people. In America, the company mission is to "enrich each woman's life." In China, the focus is "well-being and harmony" with special attention that these values are more important than money.

What about the traditional Mary Kay incentive—the legendary pink Cadillac? In China, Mak uses pink cell phones as rewards but says that the pink Cadillac will be available to top sellers in a few months.

Source: M. Booe, "Sales Force at Mary Kay China Embraces the American Way," *Workforce Management* (April 2005): 24–25.; A. Lo, "Selling Dreams: The American Way," AsiaWeek.com, 16 July 2005.

most important to their employees. These lists were compared to those in which employees ranked what was important to them. Managers said that their employees wanted good wages, job security, and promotion opportunities more than anything else. The employees ranked recognition for a good job as number 1; their managers ranked it number 8. Number 2 in importance to employees was "feeling in on things." Managers ranked it number 10, or last, in the 1–10 scale. Number 3 in importance to employees was "empathic managers!" This seems to be a cruel irony because empathic managers would tune into what their subordinates wanted for rewards.

- *Link rewards to the behavior that you want repeated.* Managers have to clearly link rewards that people value to the performance/behavior that is productive for the organization. That of course requires a clear mission, strategy, and goals so that what is "good" behavior or performance can be clearly seen and measured.
- *Help people see what the right behavior and performance are.* Select, train, teach, guide, encourage, and coach people so they can achieve the goals.[63] Hold them accountable for results. Here is one place where the manager can set a positive example by his or her own behavior.

As a manager, you probably can't make your employees be motivated. You can, however, create an environment that lends itself to greater motivation. We conclude this chapter with a prescription for greater motivation that involves building value into people's work and increasing their expectation that they can be successful in attaining the rewards that they want:[64]

1. *Tell people what you expect them to do.* On a regular, periodic basis, tell employees what your goals are as well as your standards of performance. People need goals. No human activity exists without them. Don't assume that they know what you want. Tell them as specifically as possible.
2. *Make the work valuable.* When you can, assign people to the kinds of work they like and can do well—work that they regard as valuable to them. Give them work that enables them to achieve their personal goals such as growth, advancement, self-esteem, professional recognition, and status.
3. *Make the work doable.* Increase employees' confidence that they can do what you expect by training, coaching, mentoring, listening, scheduling, providing resources, and so on.

4. *Give feedback.* Provide employees feedback on how well they are doing. Positive feedback tells them what they need to continue doing; give criticism in ways that help them correct mistakes and truly learn from the mistakes.
5. *Reward successful performance.* When employees have done what you asked them to do, reward them with both monetary and nonmonetary recognition.

In this chapter, we have examined motivation as a key management tool that organizations can use to energize employees. An organization can help create a motivating atmosphere by making the work environment positive and conducive to productive output. The organization that achieves these conditions will create a culture in which all members can contribute to their maximum potential and in which the value of diversity can be fully realized. Many companies are attempting to improve working conditions for employees based on the premise that a motivated workforce can reduce absenteeism and turnover, increase efficiency and effectiveness, encourage labor–management harmony, lead to a better product or service, and ultimately achieve organizational goals.

Meeting The Challenge

You Understand Me: Yum! Brands

The retention of employees is reflected in Yum! Brands' bottom line. Managers know that a lower turnover rate among hourly employees will lead to better service to customers and better profitability. This means that the company must not only attract quality people but retain excellent employees.

In an effort to reduce turnover, reward systems, training programs, and performance measures were aligned with the "How We Work Together Principles." To measure how well the company was adhering the principles, an annual company-wide survey was created. Restaurant support centers established programs to recognize employees. In many of the offices, employees can fill out "walk the talk" cards that give recognition to a coworker who has done something great. The company also rewards performance by providing upward mobility to many people. Some employees start as team members and work their way up to managing restaurants. Others work their way through school using the tuition-reimbursement program. Open communication sessions are held with employees quarterly and annually along with recognition ceremonies. In addition, a 360-degree-performance review program was implemented.

With 33,000 restaurants, over 22 million customers daily around the world, and employees in 100 countries, Yum! Brands' workforce is diverse with highly divergent needs and demands. According to David Novak, the phrase "you understand me" means that you understand not only my unique needs but also universal needs such as recognition that apply across cultures. Regardless of where employees live, he believes that recognition drives performance.

Top managers at Yum! Brands had the capacity to envision and enact a culture that inspired intense locality, strong commitment, increased productivity, and even greater profitability. Management practices have resulted in a motivated workforce and a financially successful organization.

Sources: D. Shuit, "Former PepsiCo Executives Do a 360 in Managing Yum Brands' Workforce," *Workforce Management* 84 (April 2005): 59–61; M. Barry and J. Slocum, "Slice of Reality: Changing Culture at Pizza Hut and Yum! Brands, Inc.," *Organizational Dynamics* 32 (November 2003): 319–329; R. King, "Great Things Are Starting at Yum," *Workforce Management* (November 2003); S. Hume, "An Interview with Ken Blanchard," *Restaurants and Institutions* 115 (April 2005): 25; K. Blanchard, J. Ballard, and F. Finch, *Customer Mania! It's Never Too Late to Build a Customer Focused Company* (New York: Free Press, 2004); K. Blanchard, "Action: Be on Time and on Target: Leadership and the Bottom Line," *Executive Excellence* 21(September 2004): 18; E. Lambert, "Sell the Sizzle," *Forbes*, 1 November 2004, 164.

SUMMARY

1. Motivation is generally defined as the forces either internal or external to a person that act as inducements or that influence action to do something.

2. Managers can draw on several different approaches to motivation. Needs-based approaches emphasize specific human needs or the factors within a person that energize, direct, and stop behavior. They explain motivation as a phenomenon primarily occurring intrinsically, or within an individual. Process approaches take a more dynamic view of motivation. These models focus on understanding how the individual's thought or cognitive processes act to affect behavior. The reinforcement approach is based on learning and examines how consequences mold behavior.

3. Three needs-based models were examined. The hierarchy of needs explains that a person has five fundamental needs: physiological, security, affiliation, esteem, and self-actualization. Physiological and security needs are lower-order needs, which are generally satisfied externally, and affiliation, esteem, and self-actualization are higher-order needs, which are satisfied internally. The two-factor model examines the relationship between job satisfaction and productivity. The sources of work satisfaction are motivator factors. The sources of dissatisfaction are hygiene factors. The acquired-needs model focuses on three particularly important or relevant needs in the work environment: achievement, affiliation, and power. The model proposes that when a need is strong, it will motivate the person to engage in behaviors to satisfy that need.

4. Three process approaches were examined. The expectancy model suggests that work motivation is determined by an individual's perceptions about the relationship between effort and performance, the relationship between performance and outcomes, and the desirability of the outcomes or rewards. Individuals choose the option that promises to give them the greatest reward and that is most valued. The equity model focuses on individuals' feelings about how fairly they are treated in comparison with others. It assumes that individuals evaluate their interpersonal relationships just as they evaluate any exchange process and compare their situations with those of others to determine the equity of their own situation. Goal setting is a process of increasing efficiency and effectiveness by specifying the desired outcomes.

5. As a motivational tool, goal setting helps employees by serving three purposes: to guide and direct behavior toward supportive organizational goals, to provide challenges and standards against which the individual can be assessed, and to define what is important and provide a framework for planning. Goals must be specific, measurable, achievable, realistic, and timely.

6. The reinforcement approach explains how a person learns to repeat certain behavior or to stop the behavior based on the consequences of that behavior. If the behavior is positively reinforced, the person will learn to repeat it. If the behavior is ignored or punished, the person will learn to stop. The tools of reinforcement theory are four basic reinforcement strategies. To increase desired behavior, positive reinforcement or negative reinforcement, also known as avoidance, can be used. Positive reinforcement is the administration of positive and rewarding consequences or events following desired behavior. Negative reinforcement, or avoidance, strengthens desired behavior by allowing escape from undesirable consequences. To decrease undesirable behavior, extinction or punishment is used. Extinction is the withdrawal of the positive reward or reinforcing consequences for undesirable behavior. It weakens behavior because behavior that is no longer reinforced is less likely to occur in the future. Administering negative consequences following undesirable behavior is called punishment. This tends to reduce the likelihood that the behavior will be repeated in similar settings.

7. Participative management encompasses various activities in which subordinates share a significant degree of decision-making power with their immediate superiors. It involves any process in which power, knowledge, information, and rewards are moved downward in the organization. Participative management motivates workers by providing more opportunities for growth, responsibility, and commitment in the work itself. In addition, the process of making and implementing a decision and then seeing the results can help satisfy an employee's need for responsibility, pride, recognition, growth, self-esteem, and achievement.

8. Money is a motivator to the degree that people perceive it as a means to acquire other things that they want. It may have symbolic meaning, be a measure of achievement, bring recognition, or satisfy a need. To motivate with money, it must be important to the employee and must be perceived as a reward for performance. The same ideas apply to employee ownership because the ownership is related to monetary outcomes.

9. To get true teamwork, a significant part of the reward to individual team members must be based on overall team results. The rest of an individual's reward should be based on his or her contribution to the team's success or functioning.

10. In the international arena, managers must take the social character, values, and cultural practices of each country into consideration when applying motivation concepts. People of other cultures perceive work differently. Reward systems need to be designed carefully to ensure that the rewards are truly motivational in the local cultural framework.

REVIEW QUESTIONS

1. (LEARNING OBJECTIVE 1) Define motivation.
2. (LEARNING OBJECTIVE 1) Explain how motivation is related to performance by describing the model $M \times A = P$.
3. (LEARNING OBJECTIVE 2) How do needs-based models differ from process models of motivation?
4. (LEARNING OBJECTIVE 3) Clarify hygiene and motivator factors in the two-factor model of motivation. How is satisfaction involved in the model?
5. (LEARNING OBJECTIVE 3) Discuss the acquired-needs model of motivation and the three needs that are the basis for understanding the model.
6. (LEARNING OBJECTIVE 4) If people experience inequity, what are they generally motivated to change?
7. (LEARNING OBJECTIVE 5) Describe how goal setting can help employees become motivated.
8. (LEARNING OBJECTIVE 5) For goal setting to be successful, what are the requirements that goals must have?
9. (LEARNING OBJECTIVE 6) As a manager, you decide that you need to decrease a behavior of an employee. What type of reinforcer will be appropriate to use and why?
10. (LEARNING OBJECTIVE 7) Select and discuss some of the reasons why participative management is successful in organizations.
11. (LEARNING OBJECTIVE 8) Explain when and why money might not be a good motivator of work performance.
12. (LEARNING OBJECTIVE 9) Explain how to reward individual team members so that they will contribute to a successful team.
13. (LEARNING OBJECTIVE 10) Discuss why managers need to be aware of international perspectives when trying to motivate employees from different cultures.

DISCUSSION QUESTIONS

Improving Critical Thinking

1. Explain what a manager could do if one of his or her subordinates does not perceive a relationship between effort and performance in a job.
2. Think about the best job you have ever had. What motivational approach was used in the organization or by your manager?
3. Explain why the variable-ratio schedule of reinforcement is more effective than the other schedules in motivating behavior.
4. What occupations or professions are people with a high need for affiliation likely to choose? A high need for achievement? A high need for power?

Enhancing Communication Skills

5. Think about the worst job you have ever had. What motivational approach was used in the organization? Prepare a short presentation that describes this job, citing specific examples of motivational approaches. Make suggestions for possible changes.

6. Research the acquired-needs model in more depth. Write a short paper in which you explain how one acquires the various needs.

Building Teamwork

7. In a team of four, discuss how to reward individual team members in order to achieve a successful team.

8. In a small group, identify a local health club or diet center that uses reinforcement theory or behavior modification as one of its tools. Ask for an interview with the manager and discuss the use of the reinforcers and the schedules of reinforcement. Be prepared to present your findings.

part 5

Control Challenges in the 21st Century

Chapter

15

Organizational Control in a Complex Business Environment

CHAPTER OVERVIEW

Control is the last of the four major management functions to be covered in this text. It is a critically important managerial function because it helps ensure that all of our planning, organizing, and leading have gone as we intended. In today's rapidly changing and highly competitive global business environment, organizations can experience a rapid reversal of fortunes if they fail to control all aspects of their operations adequately. Individual and group behaviors and all organizational performance must be in line with the strategic focus of the organization. When economic, technological, political, societal, global, or competitive forces change, control systems must be capable of adjusting behaviors and performance to make them compatible with these shifts. The essence of the control process requires that business leaders determine performance standards, measure actual performance, compare actual performance with standards, and take corrective action when necessary.

In this chapter, we begin by examining the steps in the control process. After this, we discuss several control system–design considerations, criteria for effective control, and keys to selecting the proper amount of control. Because the control process can be implemented at almost any stage in an organization's operations, we examine the three basic organizational control focal points. In addition, we explore two opposing philosophies of control and raise some thought-provoking ethical issues in the control of employee behavior. After examining these two philosophies, we examine several commonly used and important techniques and methods for establishing financial control in an organization. We conclude the chapter by examining some controversial mechanisms to control the behavior of individuals and groups within organizations. Thought provoking questions are raised regarding the ethical implications of drug testing, undercover surveillance, and computer monitoring.

LEARNING OBJECTIVES

When you have finished studying this chapter, you should be able to

1. Define and discuss the importance of organizational control.
2. Identify the sequence of steps to be undertaken in a thorough control system.
3. Identify the factors that are important considerations in the design of a control system.
4. Describe the various criteria of effective control.
5. Identify the factors that help determine the proper amount of control.
6. Define feedforward control, concurrent control, and feedback control.
7. Describe the difference between the philosophies of bureaucratic control and organic control.
8. Describe some of the more important techniques and methods for establishing financial control.
9. Discuss some of the ethical issues related to the control of employee behavior.

Facing The Challenge

Berner Foods: The Biggest Cheese Maker You Never Heard Of

When a group of dairy farmers banded together in 1943 to form a co-op that provided milk for the cheeses they were to produce, the Berner Cheese Company was formed. Berner was one of many "corner cheese factories" sprinkled around Wisconsin and northern Illinois. This is the heart of America's dairy land, so the location was a natural. For the first 45 years of its existence, Berner was best known as a contract manufacturer producing Swiss cheese for companies like Alpine Lace. In 1988, after noticing a void in the processed-cheese arena, Berner management decided to build the company's first processed-cheese plant, which began mass producing a private-label cheddar cheese sauce. Berner's product line quickly expanded. Today the company offers a variety of natural cheeses (Lacey Swiss, Baby Swiss, Muenster, and Havarti), as well as reduced fat versions of these items, revolutionary cholesterol-free cheeses (made from milk that has had the butter fat replaced with natural vegetable oils), an assortment of processed cheese and snack dips, and a variety of dairy-based toppings. Berner products are packaged in assorted sizes in glass jars, portion-control cups, aerosol cans, and plastic bowls, bottles, cups, and tubs. The company has also ventured into soy products and now operates the nation's largest food-grade soy production platform. With the beginning of this diversity in operations and products, the company changed its name to Berner Foods.

When it started out as a simple cheese-making company, Berner processed less than 100,000 pounds of milk per year. The company now processes almost 1.5 million pounds of milk per day! Berner's 100+ workforce generates annual sales of about $110 million, with markets in North, Central, and South America; Europe; and Asia. As impressive as these numbers are, most of us would probably never recognize a Berner product on a grocery store shelf. That is because Berner is a private-label manufacturer, making the previously listed products and then putting some national or store brand label on them. Approximately 70% of all private-label cheese sauces and spreads, 85% of all private-label salsa con queso products, and 90% of all private-label aerosol canned cheese products in North America are manufactured by Berner Foods.

This way of doing business presents some unique challenges because private-label manufacturers often have a fairly small number of fairly large customers. With increasing consolidation of retailers, Berner has all its "eggs" in fewer and fewer baskets. Loss of one customer can have a devastating impact on a company like Berner. Furthermore, private-label manufacturers typically contend with tight margins, necessitating maximum efficiency, visibility, and productivity in their manufacturing operations to ensure profitability. This is due in part to the size of consolidated retailers, who can leverage that size to put price pressure on companies that supply them. Berner is also challenged to meet increasing regulatory scrutiny from the Food and Drug Administration (FDA) and the U.S. Department of Agriculture (USDA). Furthermore, the company must meet the record-keeping and traceability requirements of the Bioterrorism Act (BTA) of 2002, which requires that Berner have the ability to trace quickly products and supplies all the way from the raw-material sources to the destinations where products are shipped. In addition to quality control mandates from regulatory bodies, Berner must meet the quality expectations of its customers. Berner had to respond to these challenges to continue providing a consistent quality product. Every day Berner takes in an inconsistent product (raw material with considerable variablilty) and must turn out a consistent one. To make matters more difficult, in 2004 international concerns over mad cow disease, coupled with a national herd-size reduction, put an additional strain on Berner's already paper-thin margins.

Sources: E. Rennie, "Brand New World: What's in Store for Food and Beverage Manufacturers?" *APICS Magazine* (May 2005): 31–34; "Private Label Manufacturer Achieves Results with ERP System," *Food Manufacturing* (September 2004): 24; P. A. Smith, "Midwestern Stronghold, America's Agricultural Heartland Is Home to Some of the Industry's Most Successful Independent Players," *Dairyfield Magazine* (July 2004); "Berner Foods Enables Quality Assurance and Regulatory Compliance with Ross Systems," *Business Wire,* 25 May 2004, 5476; "Industry-Specific Functionality, Compliance, Collaboration among Hot Topics at Ross Systems User Conference," *Business Wire,* 17 November 2003, 5020; "Berner Celebrates its 60th," *Private Label Buyer* (April 2003): 14; "Berner Launches Naturally Cultured, Cholesterol-Free Cheese Product Line," "Ross Systems Joins Top Private Label Industry Association," "Berner Cheese Receives Governor's Export Award," "Recent Trade Journal Interview with Stephen A. Kneubuehl, President—Berner Foods, Inc." (last four are Berner Foods press releases) from http://www.bernerfoods.com.

Introduction

Berner Foods faced some significant challenges as it strived to maintain profitability and increase its product base in the private-label manufacturing segment of the cheese-product industry. Some of these challenges came from its customers, some from government regulatory agencies, and some were self-imposed. But, regardless of the source, these challenges would require that Berner have proper control mechanisms in place so that the company could keep its customers happy and remain profitable while doing so.

Control is the last of the four major management functions that we have been discussing. By its very nature, control is concerned with making sure that all of our planning, organizing, and leading have gone as we anticipated. Control is a critical function within any organization because negative or even disastrous consequences can be associated with not meeting the established standards of performance. For example, poor inventory control can result in lost business because of a product shortage. Poor quality control may result in angry customers, lost business, and the necessity to provide customers with replacement products. Poor cost control can lead to negative profitability and perhaps even bankruptcy. The list of potential control problems is almost limitless. These problems all point to the fact that improving operational effectiveness and quality is virtually impossible without stringent control mechanisms.

Furthermore, in a world where quality often means the difference between success and failure, organizations simply cannot tolerate substandard product or service outputs. Organizations must develop and maintain control mechanisms capable of identifying and responding to deviations in organizational performance.

While the need for control is evident in all organizations, multinational organizations have particularly challenging and unique control needs. Maintaining internal control of units located in markets and regions around the globe can be far more problematic than maintaining control over a set of domestic operating units. Thus, control mechanisms must often be specifically designed to meet the challenges of global management.

In this chapter, we examine several aspects of the control process. We begin by describing the basic steps in the control process and then build on these basics.

Control Process for Diverse and Multinational Organizations

1 **Organizational control** is defined as the systematic process through which managers regulate organizational activities to make them consistent with the expectations established in plans and to help them achieve all predetermined standards of performance.[1] This definition implies that managers must establish performance standards and develop mechanisms for gathering performance information in order to assess the degree to which standards are being met. Control, then, is a systematic set of four steps that must be undertaken: (1) setting standards of performance, (2) measuring actual performance, (3) comparing actual performance with standards, and (4) responding to deviations.[2] Figure 15.1 illustrates this sequence of steps. Let's examine each step in greater detail.

LEARNING OBJECTIVE 1

Define and discuss the importance of organizational control.

SETTING STANDARDS OF PERFORMANCE

LEARNING OBJECTIVE 2

Identify the sequence of steps to be undertaken in a thorough control system.

2 The control process should begin with the establishment of standards of performance against which organizational activities can be compared. Standards of performance begin to evolve only after the organization has developed its overall strategic plan and managers have defined goals for organizational departments. In some instances, performance standards are generated from within an organization. Sometimes, however, the impetus for specific performance standards may originate with some outside source. For example, the FDA sets standards on allowable levels of certain chemicals or contaminants in food and beverage products, and food-processing organizations must adhere to these standards. Failure to comply can

KEY TERMS

Organizational control
A process through which leaders regulate organizational activities to make them consistent with the expectations established in plans and to help them achieve all predetermined standards of performance.

Figure 15.1 Steps in the Control Process

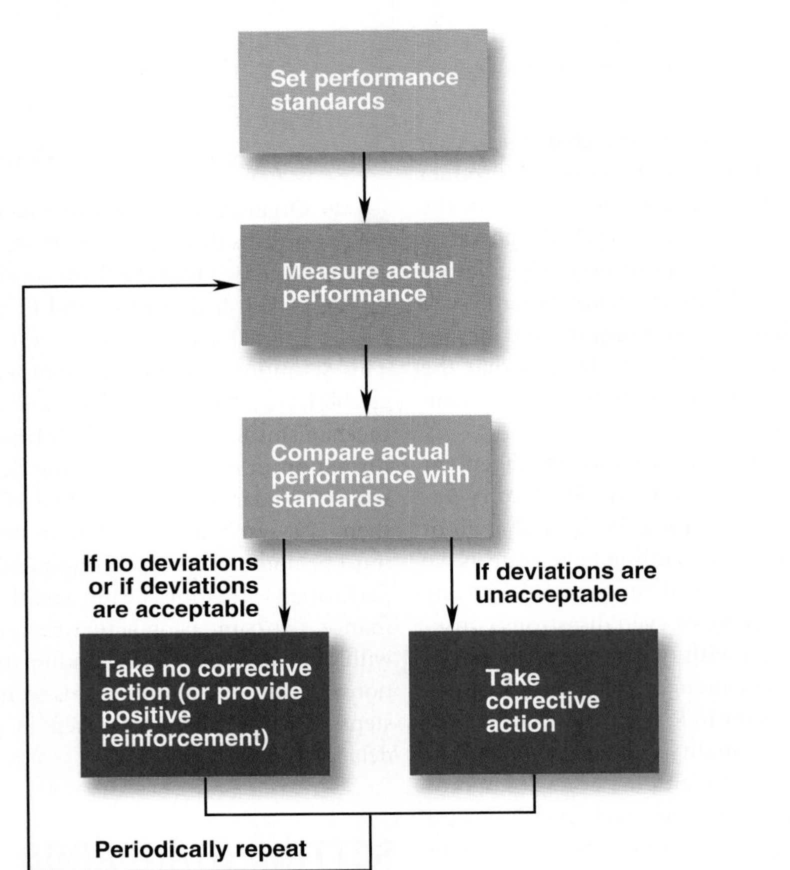

have costly consequences, as evidenced by the mid-2002 nationwide recall of ConAgra processed ground beef.[3] Examples like this are too numerous to list. To see for yourself, just check out the website www.fda.gov/oc/po/firmrecalls/archive, and you will find a day-by-day archive listing of recalls, market withdrawals, and safety alerts from the FDA over the past several years. In the opening "Facing the Challenge," Berner Foods was faced with these types of constraints from the FDA, the USDA, and the requirements of the BTA.

In other cases, the desires and needs of the customer may dictate the standards set by both manufacturers and the providers of services. In fact, in today's environment, the emphasis on quality and customer satisfaction is increasing the influence that customers have on organizational standards of performance.

The organizational activities to be controlled may involve individual behavior, group behavior, production output, service delivery, and so forth. Whenever possible, the standards should be set in a manner that allows them to be compared with actual performance. Consider the professor who wishes to communicate to students the standards of classroom performance for his management class. Simply stating that "students should be prepared for class" is vague and provides little guidance to the students. However, if the syllabus says that "students should have read the assigned material prior to each class and should be prepared to discuss the issues when called upon in class," much more clarity is provided.

These brief examples hardly illustrate the wide diversity of performance standards that might be established. Standards of performance can be set for virtually any activity or behavior within an organization. For example, it is not unusual to find organizations that set standards for employee dress or grooming. For many years, IBM required the men in its male-dominated supervisory positions to wear white dress shirts. The Walt Disney Company maintains strict standards for employee dress, grooming, jewelry, cosmetics, and even artificial hair coloring. As today's workforce becomes more diverse, setting and enforcing standards of individual behavior and performance can sometimes be more difficult. We have seen

© PHOTODISC/GETTY IMAGES

Organizational control involves establishing a variety of performance standards that may be set for virtually any employee activity or behavior. It is not unusual to find organizations that set standards for employee dress or grooming.

repeatedly throughout this book that the workplace is no longer composed of homogeneous individuals. Ethnic, racial, and gender differences often lead to different sets of individual values and expectations.

Furthermore, multinational organizations with operations in several countries often find it difficult if not impossible to maintain the same standards in all countries. It is difficult to establish organization-wide standards for subsidiaries that function within diverse sociocultural, technological, political–legal, and economic environments. For example, a multinational organization's facilities may have very different productivity targets in light of the different work attitudes in various countries. Similarly, plants in different nations may employ technologies with various levels of sophistication suitable to the education and skill levels of the local workforce; consequently, the plants may experience significant variation in productivity rates. Clearly, such circumstances can impede the development of organizationwide performance standards.

MEASURING ACTUAL PERFORMANCE

In some cases, measuring actual performance can be relatively simple, but in others it can be quite complex. We have to decide such things as (1) what to measure (that is, a single item or multiple items such as sales, costs, profits, rejects, or orders), (2) when to measure, and (3) how frequently to measure. As we noted earlier, standards should be stated as clearly as possible so that they can be compared with performance. Doing this is simple when the performance criteria are quantitative in nature and can be measured objectively. Sometimes, however, performance criteria are more qualitative in nature and do not easily lend themselves to absolute units of measure. Instead, they require a subjective assessment to determine whether the standard is being met. For example, even though a management student has read the assigned material and discussed the issues when called upon in class, the professor's assessment of the student's performance can be subjective when the issues do not have a single correct interpretation.

Suppose the Chicago Cutlery Company states that its knives "must be honed to a high degree of sharpness, and the wooden handles must be polished to a bright luster." This is also a qualitative performance measure because determining whether a particular knife was sharp enough or bright enough would not be easy. But regardless of whether the stated performance measure is quantitative or qualitative in nature, actual performance must be recorded for subsequent comparison with the performance standard.

COMPARING ACTUAL PERFORMANCE WITH STANDARDS

The first two steps of the control process provide managers with the information that allows them to make comparisons between actual performance and standards. When viewing any control situation, if the actual performance is identical to the standard, then no deviation has occurred. Rarely, however, is there absolutely no deviation between actual and planned performance. Fortunately, in most real-world situations, actual performance does not always have to be identical to the standard.

Typically, the performance standard has a stated acceptable deviation. For example, suppose leaders at Berner Foods set an average productivity standard in the Baby Swiss Cheese manufacturing area of 500 pounds of cheese per worker per day, with an acceptable deviation of plus or minus 50 pounds. The acceptable deviations would define the control limits for this process. If productivity is between 450 and 550 pounds of Baby Swiss per worker per day, then the process is said to be in control, meaning that no corrective action is necessary. Measurements outside this range indicate an out-of-control situation that requires corrective action.

Continuing with the Berner example, an actual productivity of 470 pounds per worker per day suggests that no corrective action is required. Suppose, on the other hand, that productivity is 580 pounds per worker per day. Now the deviation from the standard is outside of the in-control range, and the subsequent steps in the control process should attempt to correct it. One might initially think that this deviation (with its extra output) would be considered desirable and that no attempts would be made to correct it. But this deviation could lead to problems if the company has no market for the excess output or no room to store it. It is also possible that the extra production is using a resource (raw milk) that was to be used in some other product. This Berner example provides an illustration in which unacceptable deviations occur on either side of the standard. This need not always be the case. When the Federal Aviation Administration (FAA) determined that aircraft must maintain a minimum clearance standard of 500 feet above an obstacle to reduce an aircraft phenomenon known as "controlled flight into terrain," Minimum Safe-Altitude Warning Systems were installed in commercial aircraft. These systems alert pilots when the 500-foot clearance standard is not being observed. In this case, actual clearances of more than 500 feet would be acceptable. However, any deviation in the other direction has the potential to be catastrophic and will immediately trigger an alarm.[4]

For a more personal example, suppose you have established a performance standard of at least 85 for your scores on the midterm and final exams to help you achieve your goal of receiving a grade of B in your management course. If your midterm exam score is only 75, you would have an undesirable deviation. However, any score above 85 would prove to have an acceptable deviation from your established standard.

RESPONDING TO DEVIATIONS

After comparing actual performance with standards, we can choose to either (1) take no corrective action or (2) take corrective action. If the deviation was acceptable or if there was no deviation, then the response should be to take no corrective action because the performance or behavior is acceptable in light of the standards. If, however, the deviation was unacceptable, then the response should be to take corrective action. Corrective action usually requires making a change in some behavior, activity, or aspect of the organization to bring performance into line with the standards. Even when no corrective action is necessary, it is often useful to provide positive feedback (and in some cases even rewards) to the responsible individuals so that they are motivated to continue performing to the standards.

Return to the earlier example in which you set a standard of 85 for your midterm and final exam scores. If your midterm exam score is only 75, the undesirable deviation requires a response on your part. You might attempt to compensate by preparing more thoroughly for the final exam. (Or you might decide to drop the course and try again another semester!) If your score on the midterm exam is 90, you do not need to take corrective action in preparing for the final exam (unless, of course, you decide to raise your goal to a course grade of A and reestablish your performance standard for the final exam to achieve this goal).

When exercising control in business organizations, a variety of types of changes are possible, depending on the particular situation. Changes in materials, equipment, process, or staffing might be made. In some cases, the corrective action might even involve changing the original performance standards. For example, an organization whose standards are rarely met might determine that the standards were set unrealistically high, making them too difficult to achieve consistently. Regardless of whether corrective action is taken, the control process does not end here. Even if performance standards are currently being achieved, there is no guarantee that this will be true in the future. Consequently, the measurement and comparison steps must be repeated periodically.

Developing and implementing creative and constructive responses to undesirable deviations can be exceptionally difficult for multinational organizations. Because the organization's managers might have less understanding of each individual unit when units are scattered around the globe, developing solutions requires a substantial amount of information gathering. Furthermore, the development of solutions that are acceptable to both subsidiary and headquarters managers may require active participation by key personnel at each level. Consequently, it may take longer to determine and implement the necessary corrective action, and that action may come at the expense of significant managerial time and energy.

Up to this point, we have seen that the basic process of control involves a few very fundamental steps: (1) establishing standards of performance, (2) measuring actual performance, (3) comparing actual performance with standards, and (4) responding to deviations when necessary. However, knowing the four steps in the control process is not enough to ensure that an effective control system will be developed. As we see in the next sections, several other issues must be considered.

Designing Quality and Effectiveness into the Control System

Designing an effective control system can be far more complex than simply performing the four steps in the control process. Several other important factors must be con-

Figure 15.2 Control System–Design Issues

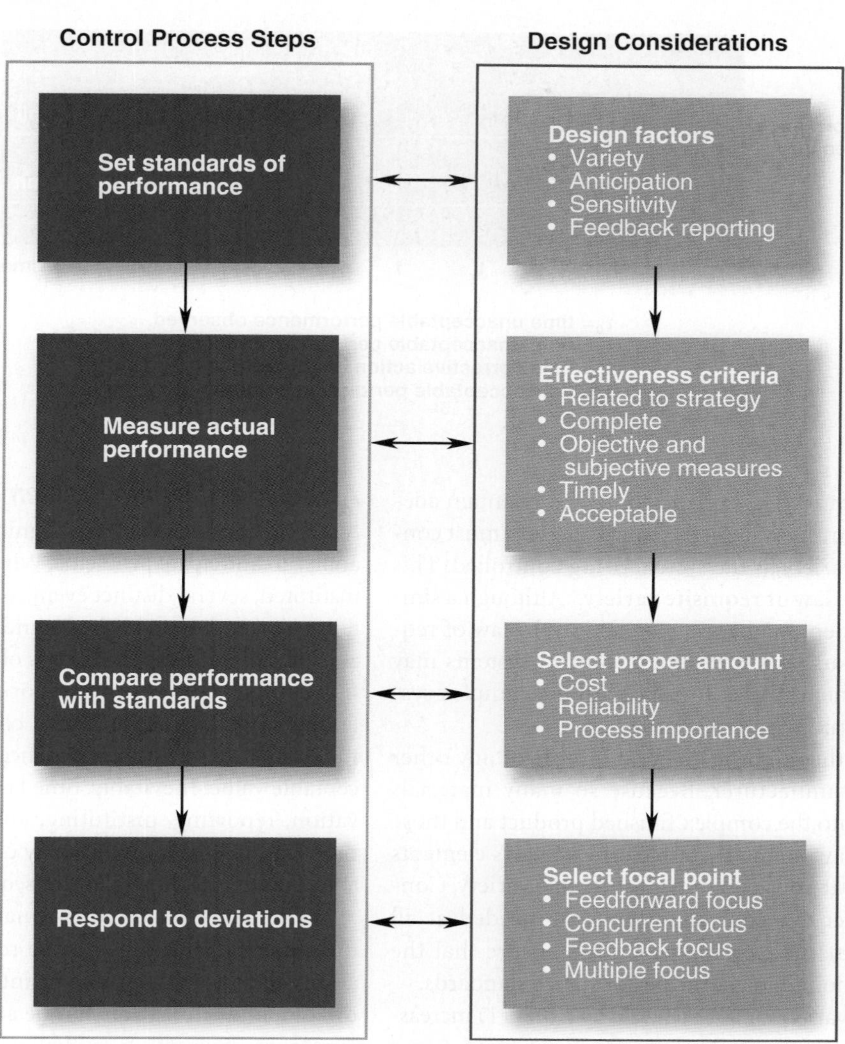

sidered as well. Once the control system has been designed and implemented, several criteria are available to help determine how effective it will be. Additionally, it is necessary to select the amount of control to be used and the point in the organization where the control effort will be focused. These issues must be considered as each step in the control process unfolds, as Figure 15.2 illustrates. We begin our treatment of control system–design issues by examining several important design factors.

DESIGN FACTORS AFFECTING CONTROL SYSTEM QUALITY

3 When designing a control system, four important factors must be considered: (1) the amount of variety in the control system, (2) the ability to anticipate problems, (3) the sensitivity of the measuring device, and (4) the composition of the feedback reports. Let's examine each of these factors more thoroughly.

LEARNING OBJECTIVE 3

Identify the factors that are important considerations in the design of a control system.

Amount of Variety in the Control System

One important design consideration is the amount of variety in the control system. Variety refers to the number of activities, processes, or items that are measured and controlled. Systems become more complex as the number of system elements and number of possible interactions among them increase. More uncertainty exists in complex systems because more things can go wrong with them. In other words,

Figure 15.3 Time Lags in Control

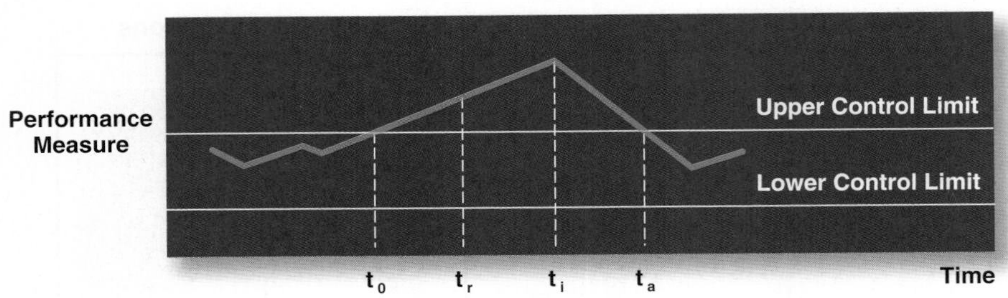

t_0= time unacceptable performance observed
t_r= time unacceptable performance reported
t_i= time corrective action instituted
t_a= time acceptable performance returns

more variety leads to less predictability. To maintain adequate control in any system, the control system must contain as much variety as the system being controlled. This is known as the **law of requisite variety.**[5] Although a simple control system might seem attractive, the law of requisite variety suggests that simple control systems may not have sufficient variety to cope with the complex systems that they are trying to control.[6]

Consider the plight of General Motors or any other automobile manufacturer. Because so many materials and parts go into the complex finished product and those components have so many sources, the system's elements and their interactions contain considerable variety. Consequently, extensive control systems are needed at all stages in the manufacturing process to ensure that the finished automobiles meet the performance standards.

Requisite variety can be achieved by either (1) increasing the amount of variety in the control system or (2) reducing the amount of variety in the system being controlled. Increased variety in the control system can be achieved by increasing the number of performance standards and the number of items controlled. In the case of General Motors, top-level leaders will set a performance standard for finished product quality. To ensure that this standard is achieved, lower-level managers and supervisors will employ additional performance standards to provide raw material input control, production scrap control, labor control, quality control, and similar other control systems. If the lower-level managers and supervisors are successful in achieving these standards, it is likely that the top-level standard for product quality will also be achieved.

KEY TERMS

Law of requisite variety
Control systems must have enough variety to cope with the variety in the systems they are trying to control.

Ability to Anticipate Problems

A second consideration in designing a control system is its ability to anticipate problems. When the control process is instituted, several distinct events occur when performance fails to meet the established standards. First, the undesirable deviation from standards is observed. Then, the situation is reported to the person or persons responsible for taking corrective action. Next, corrective action is instituted, and eventually, performance should return to an acceptable value. Inevitably, time lags occur between observation, reporting, instituting, and return. During these time lags, the performance may continue to be unacceptable. Figure 15.3 illustrates this sequence of events.

The damage caused by unacceptable performance during these time lags can be reduced by building the ability to anticipate problems into the control system. If unacceptable deviation can be anticipated before it occurs, corrective action can be instituted in a more timely fashion, and the negative consequences of the deviation can be reduced. This is precisely the situation with the FAA Minimum Safe-Altitude Warning Systems described earlier. Not only are they designed to sound an alarm when the 500-foot clearance standard is not being observed, but they also can project a plane's descent path and alert the pilot and control tower when it appears that the plane is on course to violate the 500-foot rule.

To further illustrate the ability to anticipate problems, consider how the Georgia-Pacific Lumber Company manages its timber reserves. It is a fact of nature that forest fires sometimes occur. If standard performance is defined as a fire-free forest, then a forest fire represents an undesirable deviation that needs corrective action. Georgia-Pacific can anticipate that fires are more likely to occur during prolonged dry periods. By staffing watch towers, using spotter aircraft and reconnaissance

Air-traffic controllers rely on a control system design that anticipates problems and corrects them quickly.

satellites, and keeping fire-fighting equipment in a state of readiness during these periods, the company increases its anticipatory capability, enabling it to respond more quickly to the undesirable situation.

Sensitivity of the Measuring Device

A third consideration in control system design is the sensitivity of the measuring device. Sensitivity refers to the precision with which the measurement can be made. Care must be taken to use the appropriate measuring device for the system under consideration. For example, Seagate Technology, which manufactures computer components and other electronic equipment, might need a high-precision micrometer to measure the diameter of the spindles used in its computer disk drive. However, it would be highly unnecessary for the Georgia-Pacific Lumber Company to use such a measuring device to check the thickness of two-by-four wall studs. A simple tape measure will suffice in this situation because tolerances need to be expressed only in fractions of inches, not microns. It is critical that consistent units of measurement be used if proper control is to be attained in any process. Failure to do this resulted in the destruction of NASA's $125 million Mars *Climate Orbiter.* While flight computers on the ground performed calculations based on pounds of thrust per second, the spacecraft's computer used metric system units called newtons. A check to make sure the units were compatible was never performed, which resulted in the orbiter burning up in the Mars atmosphere.[7]

Composition of Feedback Reports

A final consideration in control system design involves the composition of feedback reports. As the control process measures performance and compares it with standards, much information and data are generated. Reports to leaders and managers will be based on these data. But what data should be included in the reports? A simple answer and one that users of such reports will view favorably is "Don't tell me what is right with the system; tell me what is wrong." **Variance reporting** fulfills this desire by highlighting only those items that fail to meet the established standards. Focusing on the elements that are not meeting the standards provides the capability for **management by exception.** In this approach, management targets the trouble areas. If the system is operating acceptably, no information needs to come to the manager's attention. In the cheese-making processes used at Berner Foods, temperature is an important variable as milk is converted into cheese products. As long as temperature readings are acceptable, no one needs to be alerted. However, if the temperature of a vat of milk being processed is out of the acceptable range, someone needs to be alerted.

Now that we have examined the factors that are important in the design of a control system, let's look at several criteria that measure the system's effectiveness.

CRITERIA FOR EFFECTIVE CONTROL

4 To be effective in detecting and correcting unacceptable performance, a control system must satisfy several criteria. The system must (1) be related to organizational strategy, (2) use all steps in the control process, (3) be composed of objective and subjective measures, (4) be timely in feedback reporting, and (5) be acceptable to a diverse workforce.[8] The next sections examine these criteria more closely.

LEARNING OBJECTIVE 4

Describe the various criteria of effective control.

Related to Organizational Strategy

In designing a control system, one must make sure that it measures what is important now and what will be important in the future, not what was important in the past. As an organization's strategic focus shifts over time, the measures and standards of performance that are important to the organization must also shift. When

KEY TERMS

Variance reporting
Highlighting only those things that fail to meet the established standards.

Management by exception
Focusing on the elements that are not meeting the standards.

the control system is linked to organizational strategy, it recognizes strategic shifts and is flexible enough to measure what is important as indicated by the firm's strategy.

This issue also has implications for the standards of behavior and performance that are set for individuals and groups within the organization. As the workforce becomes more racially, ethnically, and gender diverse, organizations will often have to adjust their expectations of workers and performance standards in response to the differing attitudes, abilities, and cultural biases of their employees.

Multinational corporations often find it useful to maintain a centralized, integrated system of controls consistent with the strategic orientation of the organization. If the network of organizational units is to benefit from the organization's global orientation, there must be sufficient coordination and control of the units to ensure that such benefits are achieved. General Motors maintains a number of units that are interdependent through each of the sequential steps in the manufacturing process (for example, GM's Brazilian subsidiary supplies its U.S. subsidiary with engines); therefore, GM must have control systems that ensure that production processes are not disrupted.[9]

Uses All Steps in the Control Process

To be effective, a control system must employ all steps in the control process. Standards of performance must be set, measurements of actual performance taken, comparisons of standards with actual performance made, and when necessary, corrective action taken. Omitting any of these steps will detract from the system's effectiveness.

To return to our more personal example of your quest for a grade of B in your management course, suppose you never bothered to check your posted grade on the midterm exam. In that case, your control system would be incomplete. Without knowing your midterm exam score, you could not compare your actual performance with your standard. Consequently, you would not know whether there was an undesirable deviation and whether you should study harder for the final exam.

Composed of Objective and Subjective Measures

It is unlikely that a control system will lend itself to the use of a single performance measure. More often than not, a number of performance measures are needed. As we discussed earlier, some of these performance measures may be objective and easily quantified, whereas others may be qualitative and more subjective. For example, management may have set specific targets for productivity. This performance goal has a precise formula for measurement, as we will see in the next chapter. Suppose, in that same situation, management has also expressed a desire to achieve high levels of worker satisfaction. Such a qualitative criterion is more difficult if not impossible to measure accurately. Situations like this often require managers to blend quantitative (objective) and qualitative (subjective) performance measures in their control systems.

Incorporates Timeliness In Feedback Reporting

Timeliness is the degree to which the control system provides information when it is needed. The key issue here is not how fast the feedback information is provided but whether it is provided quickly enough to permit a response to an unacceptable deviation. For example, consider the air traffic controller at Chicago's O'Hare Airport who observes on the radar screen that an aircraft is descending too close to an obstacle. Feedback information on the position of the aircraft is needed very quickly if a tragedy is to be averted. Here timeliness would be measured in seconds. Now consider the manager of a Christmas tree farm who monitors the annual growth rate of the trees. If the amount of growth falls below standards in a particular year, an application of fertilizer might be called for as a corrective action. In this case, timeliness might be measured in weeks or even months.

A graphic example of the importance of timeliness presents itself in a U.S. naval accident that occurred in early 2005. The crew of the nuclear submarine USS *San Francisco* violated the feedback timeliness requirement with near-catastrophic consequences. In short, the submarine smashed into an undersea mountain. A subsequent naval investigation revealed that the crew should have checked the water depth more frequently, should not have been traveling at high speed, and failed to take into account a variety of danger signs, all of which contributed to the underwater accident.[10] In the "Leaders in Action" box, we see how LINPAC Plastics struggled when feedback information for control was not provided in a timely manner. We further see how the organization benefited when company leaders selected and implemented a more appropriate feedback-reporting system.

Let's return to the personal example of your grade. Suppose the midterm exam was administered in the eighth week of the semester and the results were not posted until the tenth week. This feedback would not be timely if the deadline for dropping the course was in the ninth week of the semester.

Acceptable to a Diverse Workforce

To be effective, organizational controls must be accepted by employees. The control system should motivate workers to recognize standards and act to achieve them. If the control system discourages employees, they are likely to ignore the standards, and undesirable deviations are likely to follow. The more committed that employees are

Leaders in Action

LINPAC Plastics

LINPAC Plastics is a global manufacturer of plastic-packaging products for packers and retailers in the contemporary food, catering, and fast-food retailing industry. The company has 26 manufacturing sites around the world, including facilities in England, Germany, France, Spain, Italy, Poland, South Africa, Chile, Uruguay, and the United States, employing nearly 3500 people. Among the items they manufacture are packages for meat, fish, poultry, fresh fruit, and produce; ready meals; bakery items; and egg cartons. Until recently, company leadership struggled to effectively coordinate inventory and production. One of the main causes of those struggles was inadequate feedback information. The report-writing tools in use could deliver only monthly or quarterly data. This simply wasn't adequate because there was a need to analyze and manage sales on a daily basis. Furthermore, management recognized that users needed to be able to interact with the feedback information and analyze it in depth. Unfortunately, these reports were static in nature and did not offer users such interactive capability.

Leaders at LINPAC recognized that a solution would be had only if the feedback-reporting system was totally overhauled. To accomplish this, a new system that could integrate LINPAC's major business functions was needed. A commercially available, modularized software system was selected. LINPAC initially implemented the sales and inventory modules, followed soon after by the finance module. LINPAC has realized several benefits since the implementation. The more frequent and highly interactive feedback reports have enabled the company to reduce inventory costs, more effectively forecast and plan production, eliminate bottlenecks and overproduction, and significantly reduce costs. At one site alone, the company has been able to reduce inventory levels by about $900,000 without negatively affecting customer service.

Sources: "The Power of Information: Business Intelligence Solution Delivers Heightened Inventory Efficiency," *APICS: The Performance Advantage* (January 2005): 20; "LINPAC Plastics Case Study," *Information Week* (April 2005); LINPAC Plastics website at www.linpac-plastics.co.uk.

to the control system, the more successful the system will be.[11] In the increasingly diverse workplaces of today's organizations, one of the challenges to managers is to develop control systems and establish standards that are acceptable and understandable to all workers.

To illustrate acceptability, consider your situation as a student in a management course. Suppose your professor has no problem assigning course grades of B or lower but says that a grade of A can be achieved only by students who read a new chapter and five related journal articles every day and submit a 20-page, typewritten synopsis of these readings each day. Would you be discouraged from attempting to earn a grade of A? Most if not all students probably would be discouraged and would resign themselves to a grade of no higher than a B for the course.

Up to this point, we have seen several factors that are essential to the design of an effective control system. To assist managers in developing effective control systems, the "Now Apply It" box presents a checklist that can be used to make sure that all important factors and characteristics have been included in the design of any control system.

Now that the control system has been established, it is necessary to determine how much control should be used. The amount of control needed depends on several factors, as we see in the next section.

SELECTING THE PROPER AMOUNT OF CONTROL

LEARNING OBJECTIVE 5

Identify the factors that help determine the proper amount of control.

5 In almost any task, reasonable limits exist on the amount of energy that should be expended. This is also true in the area of control. In theory, the amount of control that a manager exercises over some aspect of the organization can vary from a minimum of zero control to a maximum of infinite control. It is possible for management to go too far and overcontrol some aspect of the organization or not go far enough and thereby undercontrol. The result in either case is a suboptimal control system and suboptimal performance, which will decrease the overall effectiveness and efficiency of the organization.

Choosing the proper amount of control is critical to organizations that strive for quality in everything they do. Deciding how much control is enough is not a simple matter, however. Several factors can be used to help determine the proper amount of control. These factors, which vary in their degree of objectivity, include the costs and benefits of a control system, the reliability of the item or process being controlled, and the importance of the thing or process being controlled.[12]

Now Apply It

Checklist for Designing Effective Control Systems

Frequently, systems for management control of some process in an organization are inadequately designed or ill thought out. After designing your system for control, answer the following questions to ensure that all important aspects of the control system have been included.

- Have performance standards been explicitly stated with a degree of clarity that allows them to be compared with actual performance?
- Have standards been defined in a manner that permits measurement of actual performance?
- Are guidelines in place for responding with corrective actions to undesirable deviations?
- Is there sufficient variety in the control system to deal with the variety in the process being controlled?
- Does the control system have the capability to anticipate problems before they get out of hand?
- Is the precision of the measuring devices appropriate for the performance being measured?
- Is the feedback system designed to report what is wrong with the process rather than what is right with the process?
- Is the control system measuring what is important as indicated by the organization's strategy?
- Is feedback information provided in a timely fashion?
- Is the control system acceptable to your employees?

Costs in Control Systems

Two basic categories of costs need to be considered in control systems: (1) the costs associated with the information needed to perform the control process and (2) the costs associated with undesirable deviations from standards. These costs behave differently as the amount of control effort varies.[13]

Control systems rely on information. As the amount of control effort increases, information feedback is needed in greater amounts and with greater frequency. This information does not come without a cost. Time, effort, resources, and money must be expended to gather and assimilate information. Consequently, as the level of control effort increases, the information costs of the control system also increase.

As the level of control effort increases, undesirable deviations from performance standards will decrease. As a consequence, the costs associated with undesirable performance will also decrease. Reductions in the costs due to undesirable performance represent the benefits of control systems. Examples of these costs include costs to correct the problem that is causing the undesirable deviations; material-scrap costs and rework costs when defective parts are detected in the manufacturing process; product warranty, repair, and replacement costs when defective output reaches the consumer; worker compensation costs when workers are injured due to behaviors or actions that do not conform to standards; and liability costs when consumers are harmed by nonconforming products. When these relationships are displayed in a graphical format, as in Figure 15.4, they reveal that from an economic standpoint there is an ideal amount of control to be exercised. This optimal amount of control corresponds to the minimum total cost.

From a practical standpoint, this optimal value is not always easy to identify. When performance improvements are many and varied, quantifying the precise costs and benefits of the control system may be difficult. This is particularly true in situations like the FAA's Minimum Safe-Altitude Warning Systems or in the monitoring of parts being manufactured for space shuttles. Undesirable deviations can result in catastrophic failures and corresponding loss of human life in both of these situations. In such cases, the value of the control system might be assessed by simply examining the number of areas of improvement and the level of improvement in each area.

Reliability of the System

Reliability refers to the probability that the object or process being controlled will consistently behave in an acceptable manner. The basic premise is that the more reliable the process, the less control is needed. Here is a situation that is familiar to most of us. It seems that physicians are notorious for having poor handwriting, resulting in prescriptions that are difficult to decipher. This often leads to extra work on the part of the pharmacist (checkup calls to physicians) and sometimes incorrect medications being dispensed. These problems can be eliminated thanks to the Allscript Corporation, which developed a wireless, handheld electronic prescription pad. When a physician

Figure 15.4 Cost Trade-Offs in a Control System

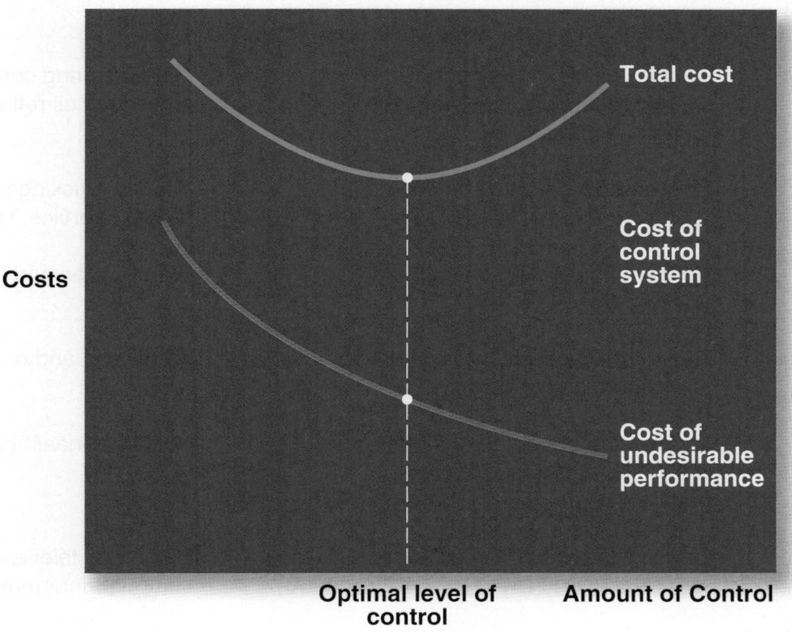

enters a prescription, the system can check for interactions with any other drugs the patient may be taking and also check for patient drug allergies. With a few clicks, the prescription can be e-mailed to the patient's drug store. This new technology improves the process, reduces the controls necessary, and virtually eliminates the problems associated with unintelligibly written prescriptions.[14]

© AMY ETRA/PHOTOEDIT

Equipment reliability can often be measured objectively, but human operators present some uncertainty for a variety of reasons ranging from amount of work experience to use of illegal substances on the job.

Process reliability is often difficult to assess because it is affected by the operating characteristics of the physical equipment and by the experience and attitudes of the workers. Equipment reliability can often be measured objectively; human operators present a bit more uncertainty. Although reliability can be expected to increase with worker experience, there is no way to accurately predict when a worker will have a "bad day." And of course, at times extraneous conditions (such as bad weather in the case of airline pilots) might impact the reliability of the workers. Business leaders must often make subjective judgments on the human aspect of reliability to aid in determining the proper amount of control.

Importance of the Process Being Controlled

Common sense suggests that the more important the object or process being controlled, the greater the amount of control that should be exercised. The difficulty here lies in selecting a measure for importance. Frequently, cost or value is used as a substitute for importance. The more valuable the item, the more important it is and therefore the more control it deserves. In the area of inventory control, a relatively small percentage of a company's inventory items (perhaps 20%) often account for a large percentage of the total inventory value (perhaps 80%). Although the percentages may vary, this "20/80 rule," as it has become known, would suggest that an "important few" items deserve close inventory control.

Table 15.1 Descriptions and Examples of Operations Transformation Processes

Transformation	Description	Examples
Physical or chemical	Cutting, bending, joining, or chemically altering raw materials to make a product	Manufacturing company, chemical processor, oil refinery
Locational	Provide transportation function	Airlines, trucking companies, package delivery service, U.S. Postal Service
Storage	Hold and then release a commodity or item	Warehouses and banks
Exchange	Transfer possession and ownership of a commodity or item	Wholesale and retail organizations
Physiological	Improve the physical or mental well-being of sick and injured people	Hospitals, healthcare clinics
Informational	Transmit information to customers	Radio and television news departments, computer information services
Entertainment	Impart an attitudinal change to their customers	Motion picture industry, programming departments of television networks
Educational	Impart knowledge to customers	Schools, universities

The others (the "trivial many") require considerably less control.[15]

You should not automatically assume that importance can always be measured by cost or value. At first glance, it might seem that extensive control systems are not needed to monitor quality in the manufacture of an inexpensive bolt. However, if that bolt is used to secure a window washer to the outside of a high-rise building, it has assumed a high level of importance despite its low cost. In a similar vein, Berner Foods must closely control the quality of each "relatively inexpensive" package of cheese because a contaminated product has the potential to sicken or even kill an unsuspecting consumer.

Now that the question of how much control is needed has been addressed, let's examine where in the transformation process control should be used. The place where control is applied is called the focal point for control.

SELECTING THE FOCAL POINT FOR CONTROL

Before managers design and implement a control system, they must decide where the control effort will be focused. Virtually all organizations maintain a structure in which inputs are subjected to a transformation process that converts them into usable and marketable outputs. Despite this similarity, inputs, transformations, and outputs can vary considerably among organizations.

Although Chapter 16 provides a much more extensive examination of the operations aspects of the input transformation process, we do need to note here that inputs can include such items as raw materials, supplies, people, capital, land, buildings, equipment, utilities, and information. Outputs of the transformation process will be either physical products or services. The list of transformation processes is lengthy and varied. Table 15.1 provides descriptions and examples of these processes.

In Chapter 5, we were introduced to the concept of feedforward and feedback controls in the context of the overall strategic mission of the organization. At an operational level, controls are necessary at various points in the process of transforming inputs into outputs. Control can focus on the inputs, the transformation process, or the outputs of the operating system. These three different focal points yield three different types of control: (1) feedforward control, (2) concurrent control, and (3) feedback control.[16] These control focal points are il-

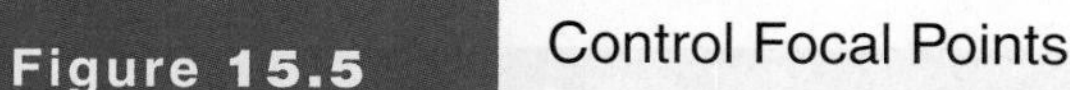

Control Focal Points

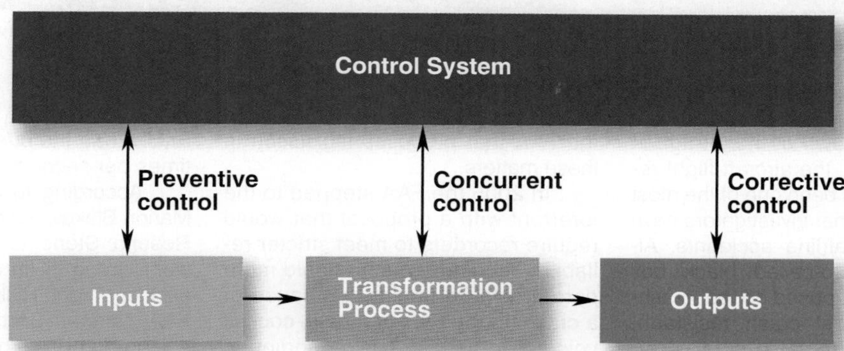

lustrated in Figure 15.5. The next sections examine them in greater detail.

Feedforward Control

6 When control focuses on the material, financial, or human resources that serve as inputs to the transformation process, it is referred to as **feedforward control.** This type of control is sometimes called **preventive control** because it is designed to ensure that the quality of inputs is high enough to prevent problems in the transformation process. For example, think about the preventive controls that might take place prior to the manufacture of blue jeans. A primary input for manufacturers such as Levi Strauss is denim fabric. Long bolts of this material will have patterns overlaid and cut prior to the sewing operations. Before the patterns are laid out on the fabric, a system of preventive control could be used to inspect the denim fabric for knots, runs, tears, color variations, and other imperfections. If the fabric contains many imperfections, there could well be excessive levels of imperfections in the finished blue jeans. In such a case, the corrective action suggested by the preventive control system might be to reject the entire bolt of fabric rather than trying to cut around the imperfections. Berner Foods exercises feedforward control as it tests the raw milk input that will eventually be converted into cheese products.

Concurrent Control

When control focuses on the transformation phase, it is referred to as **concurrent control.** This form of control is designed to monitor ongoing activities to ensure that the transformation process is functioning properly and achieving the desired results. To illustrate, consider again the manufacture of blue jeans by Levi Strauss. Sewing-machine operators must continuously monitor their process to ensure that seams are being sewn straight and threads are interlocking appropriately. If these standards are not being met, corrective actions such as changing needles, adjusting thread tension, lubricating machines, and so forth may need to be taken. In the case of Berner Foods, concurrent controls are actively used as temperature, time, and other variables are continuously monitored in the cheese-making process.

Feedback Control

When control focuses on the output phase of Figure 15.5, it is referred to as **feedback control.** This type of control is sometimes referred to as **corrective control** because it is intended to discover undesirable output and implement corrective action. We can illustrate this focal point by again considering the manufacture of blue jeans. After the jeans have been assembled, a final inspection is normally performed. Individuals responsible for assessing the quality of the jeans compare the finished product with established standards of performance. If an undesirable amount of deviation from the standards is identified, then corrective action must be prescribed. For example, if the design stitching on the back pockets is misaligned, corrective action would be needed at the pocket-stitching operation to correct this problem. With

LEARNING OBJECTIVE 6

Define feedforward control, concurrent control, and feedback control.

KEY TERMS

Feedforward (preventive) control
Focuses on detecting undesirable material, financial, or human resources that serve as inputs to the transformation process.

Concurrent control
Focuses on the transformation process to ensure that it is functioning properly.

Feedback (corrective) control
Focuses on discovering undesirable output and implementing corrective action.

At the Forefront

FAA Proposes New "Black Box" Rules

Since the dawn of the jet age in the 1950s, the aircraft-flight recorder has been one of the most important tools that investigators have to understand airline accidents. Although these so-called black box devices are supposed to be crash-proof (or at least crash resistant), several times in recent years poorly functioning, inadequate, or damaged recorders have hindered major accident investigations. Some might think that this doesn't much matter because the damage has already been done. However, successful determination of the cause of an airline crash is crucial to ensuring that this cause does not result in another similar incident. The National Transportation Safety Board (NTSB) has recommended upgrades in recorders for years. Although the NTSB investigates accidents, it unfortunately has no regulatory power. It is the FAA that proposes legislation in these matters.

In 2005 the FAA stepped to the forefront with a proposal that would require recorders to meet stricter reliability requirements and hold more data crucial to finding the cause of a crash. In the FAA proposal, cockpit voice recorders would be equipped with backup power supplies, rendering them impervious to power failures on the aircraft. Furthermore, recording time would be increased to 2 hours from the current upper limit of 30 minutes. Instead of storing sound and data on magnetic tape, this information would be stored on computer chips, which are much more capable of surviving a crash. The systems will also collect more details on how cockpit controls were used during a flight, storing data on flight controls 16 times per second rather than the current standard of 2 times per second.

According to FAA Administrator Marion Blakey, "Good data is often the Rosetta Stone to deciphering what went wrong in an aircraft incident or accident." John Hickey, the head of the FAA Aircraft-Certification Division, said the proposal hit the "sweet spot." It mandates the most important aspects of the NTSB wish list but doesn't burden the airlines with unreasonable costs. You can expect these improved flight recorders to appear on aircraft in 2006, which will ultimately make the skies safer to navigate.

Source: A. Levin, "FAA Proposes New Airliner 'Black Box' Rules," *USA Today,* 25 February 2005, 3A.; Leslie Miller, "FAA Proposes New Black Box Rules," New York: Associated Press, 24 February 2005.

Berner Foods, before products are shipped, feedback control is instituted with the testing of cheese products to ensure their safety for consumption.

In the "At the Forefront" box, we can see how the FAA has focused on improving the quality and amount of feedback-control data in aircraft flight recorders. A 2005 FAA proposal would require more frequent recording of data in those so called black boxes and at the same time change the data-storage medium to make the data more impervious to a crash. These changes will greatly aid in any postincident or postcrash investigations.

Multiple Focal Points

Very few organizations rely on a single point of focus for their control process. Instead, most organizations use several control systems focused on various phases of the transformation process.[17] This way, managers are better able to control resource inputs, ongoing transformation activities, and final outputs simultaneously. This approach gives the manager the capability to determine (1) whether current output is in accordance with standards and (2) whether any impending problems are looming on the horizon.

Not unlike Berner Foods, the McDonald's restaurant chain provides a familiar example of a company that uses control mechanisms that are focused on inputs, transformation processes, and outputs. In its attempts to maintain consistency in its french fried potatoes, McDonald's uses preventive control with a stringent set of standards for purchased raw potatoes. It uses concurrent control by monitoring the oil temperature and frying time used in the cooking process and the amount of salt used in seasoning the french fries. Finally, it uses corrective control when the output (cooked french fries) is examined. If examination reveals improper color or excess oiliness, the cooking oil, the temperature of the cooking oil, the cooking time, or perhaps some combination of all three may need to be changed to attain the desired results. Multiple focal points are important here because, if only the finished product were monitored, potential problems caused by a bad batch of raw potatoes or a defective fryer thermostat would not be revealed until defective french fries were produced.

Because today's business organizations incorporate many highly interrelated and overlapping functional specialties, control systems must be implemented in all functional specialty areas of the organization. Management, marketing, finance, and accounting activities all play a critical role in the success of the organization, and as such, each has many aspects that require control mechanisms. Management theorist Peter Drucker has identified eight areas in which performance objectives should be set and results measured. These areas—marketing, financial resources, productivity, physical resources, human organization, profit requirements, social responsibility, and innovation—extend through all of the interrelated functional specialties of the business.[18]

Control Philosophies for Managers

Instituting a control system requires that leaders do more than simply select the appropriate focal points. It is also necessary to make a choice between two philosophical control styles: bureaucratic control and organic control (often referred to as clan control).

BUREAUCRATIC CONTROL

7 **Bureaucratic control** involves the use of rules, procedures, policies, hierarchy of authority, written documents, reward systems, and other formal mechanisms to influence behavior, assess performance, and correct unacceptable deviations from standards.[19] This type of control is typical of the bureaucratic style of management introduced in Chapter 2. In this method of control, standard operating procedures and policies prescribe acceptable employee behavior and standards for employee performance. A rigid hierarchy of authority extends from the top down through the organization. Formal authority for the control process lies at the supervisor level, and lower-level employees are not expected to participate in the control process. Bureaucratic control relies on highly formalized mechanisms for selecting and training workers, and it emphasizes the use of monetary rewards for controlling employee performance. Formal quantitative tools such as budgets or financial reports and ratios are frequently used to monitor and evaluate performance in bureaucratic control systems.

As we discussed in Chapter 2, the bureaucratic style often has a negative connotation due to its very formal structure and perceived lack of flexibility. However, this method of control should not be viewed as a mechanism to restrain, force, coerce, or manipulate workers. Instead, it should be viewed as an effective although rigid mechanism to ensure that performance standards are met.

ORGANIC CONTROL

Organic control, often called **clan control,** is quite different from bureaucratic control. It relies on social values, traditions, shared beliefs, flexible authority, looser job descriptions, and trust to assess performance and correct unacceptable deviations. The philosophy behind organic control is that employees are to be trusted and that they are willing to perform correctly without extensive rules and supervision. With its empowered workers and team concept, Berner Foods relies heavily on this control philosophy. This type of control is particularly appropriate when there is a strong organizational culture and the values are shared by all employees. When cohesive peer groups exist, less top-down bureaucratic control is necessary because employees are likely to pressure coworkers into adhering to group norms. When employees exercise self-discipline and self-control and believe in doing a fair day's work for their pay, managers can take advantage of this self-discipline and use fewer bureaucratic control methods.

Such cohesiveness and self-discipline are characteristic of self-managed teams (SMTs), as you will recall from earlier chapters.[20] Organic control is an appropriate style to use in conjunction with SMTs. Although organic control is less rigid than bureaucratic control, it would be a mistake to assume that it is a better method. Both the bureaucratic and organic approaches can be useful for organizational control, and most organizations use some aspects of both in their control mechanisms. Table 15.2 provides a brief comparison of the bureaucratic and organic methods of control.

Before deciding which of these two control styles to use in a particular situation, managers must first evaluate several factors of their organization. The next sections describe the factors that help determine an appropriate choice of control style.

LEARNING OBJECTIVE 7

Describe the difference between the philosophies of bureaucratic control and organic control.

KEY TERMS

Bureaucratic control
Use of formal mechanisms to influence behavior, assess performance, and correct unacceptable deviations from standards.

Organic (clan) control
Reliance on social values, traditions, shared beliefs, flexible authority, and trust to assess performance and correct unacceptable deviations.

Table 15.2 Bureaucratic and Organic Methods of Control

	Bureaucratic	Organic
Purpose	Employee compliance	Employee commitment
Technique	Rigid rules and policies, strict hierarchy, formalized selection and training	Corporate culture, individual self-discipline, cohesive peer groups, selection and socialization
Performance expectation	Clearly defined standards of individual performance	Emphasizes group or system performance
Organizational structure	Tall structure, top-down controls Rules and procedures for coordination and control Authority resides in position	Flat structure, mutual influence Shared values, goals, and traditions for coordination and control Authority resides with knowledge and expertise
Rewards	Based upon individual employee achievements	Based upon group achievements and equity across employees
Participation	Formalized and narrow	Informal and broad

Source: Adapted and reprinted by permission of *Harvard Business Review.* An exhibit from "From Control to Commitment in the Workplace" by R. E. Walton, March/April 1985, 76–85.

SELECTING A CONTROL STYLE IN TODAY'S DIVERSE AND MULTINATIONAL ORGANIZATIONS

The bureaucratic and organic approaches present two distinctly opposite control philosophies. Top-level leaders are often faced with a dilemma in choosing a style for their organization. This decision can be made more easily if managers first evaluate these four factors: (1) individual management style, (2) organizational culture, (3) employee professionalism, and (4) performance measures.[21]

Individual management style refers to whether the manager has a task-oriented or a relationship-oriented leadership style. These concepts were described in Chapter 12 where we discussed behavioral approaches to understanding leadership. If a manager uses more relationship-oriented behaviors when interacting with subordinates, then an organic-control style would tend to be more compatible with his or her leadership style. Examples of relationship-oriented behaviors include extending a high degree of trust, friendship, and respect to subordinates. In contrast, if a leader displays more task-oriented behaviors when interacting with subordinates, then a bureaucratic-control style would tend to be more compatible with his or her leadership style. Task-oriented behavior occurs when the leader assumes the responsibility for planning, directing, providing job information, and maintaining standards of performance for subordinates. The key is that the control style needs to be consistent with the manager's leadership style.

The second factor that determines a control style is organizational culture. If the organizational culture encourages employees to participate in decision making and rewards them for this participation and loyalty, then an organic-control style is more appropriate. If the organizational culture favors decision making at the top and avoids employee participation, then a bureaucratic-control style will be the better choice.

Employee professionalism can also influence the control style that an organization uses. Employees who are highly educated, highly trained, and professional are more likely to want to participate in decision making and are more likely to accept the high standards of behavior displayed in the group's norms. These employees will be good candidates for an organic-control style. Employees who lack experience, training, or the desire to participate would be better candidates for a bureaucratic-control style.

Finally, performance measures influence the choice of control style. If performance can be quantified and explicitly measured, then a bureaucratic-control style will work well. However, if task performance is difficult to measure or quantify, then an organic-control style will be more appropriate.

You should recognize from the preceding discussion that achieving quality in the control process requires a good fit between the situation and the control system. Care must be taken to accurately assess management style, organizational culture, employee professionalism, and types of performance measures before selecting a philosophical approach to control. The choice of a control style is contingent on all these situational factors.

The selection of a control style for a multinational organization presents some unique challenges. Although most multinational organizations develop control systems that are a blend of bureaucratic and organic control, the high level of standardization in many multinational organizations permits a heavier use of bureaucratic control because company manuals and specific rules, procedures, and policies may be applicable across certain subgroups of operating units. For example, because General Motors maintains a number of subsidiaries around the globe that manufacture the same types of engines, it has the potential to use bureaucratic controls in these units. Nevertheless, organic-control mechanisms may also play an important part in the control process for multinational organizations because it is critical that each organizational subunit understand the role that it plays in the network of subsidiaries. Strong shared values and philosophies help ensure that behaviors and output at the subsidiary level are compatible with organization-wide initiatives.[22]

Impact of Information Technology on Organizational Control

Advances and developments in information technology have had a profound and positive effect on organizational control. The very essence of control is deeply rooted in information. Just look at how the topics have progressed in this chapter. One of the basic steps in the control process involves gathering information on actual performance and then comparing it with preestablished standards of performance. Furthermore, the final step in the control process requires that feedback be provided, which is nothing more than the dissemination of information. As the chapter has unfolded, we have seen that it is critical to gather information and to disseminate feedback information in a timely fashion. We live in an age when advances in information-processing hardware and software occur at almost dizzying speed. All these technological advances and improvements serve to get critical control information to managers in a more timely fashion, allow managers to make the proper control responses more quickly, and finally disseminate the information on those decisions more quickly so that the negative consequences associated with out-of-control situations can be minimized.

There is an important footnote to the notion that technology can have a positive impact on control. When technology does not operate as it should, the impact on the control systems can be equally strong but in the wrong direction. This was evident for Hershey Foods Corporation, the nation's largest candy maker. A few years ago, trouble with the company's new $112 million computer system for orders and deliveries fouled up distribution for the biggest candy-buying holiday of the year—Halloween. Distribution difficulties caused Hershey to lose as much as $100 million in sales during the quarter spanning that holiday.[23]

Mechanisms for Financial Control

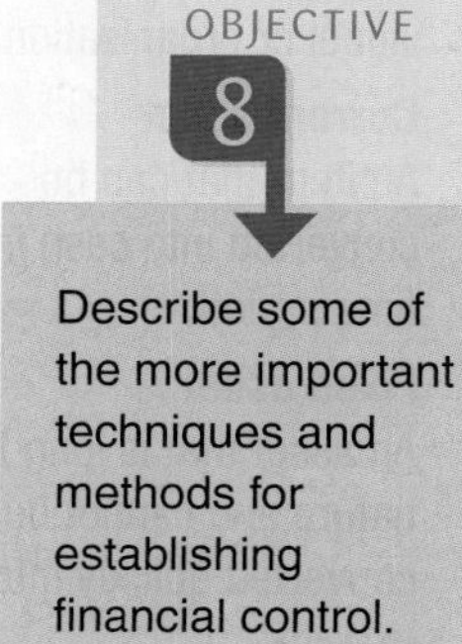

8 One of the most important areas in which control must be exercised is in the finances of an organization. At times, financial performance may not be meeting standards, or it may fall short of expectations. If such situations go undetected and corrective actions are not taken, the company's survival might be at stake. We only briefly examine some of the more important techniques and methods for establishing financial control. More thorough coverage of these topics is left to your accounting and finance classes.

FINANCIAL STATEMENTS

Two financial statements provide much of the information needed to calculate ratios that are used to assess an organization's financial health. These statements are the balance sheet and the income statement.

Table 15.3 Balance Sheet

Cestaro Manufacturing Company
Balance Sheet
December 31, 2006

ASSETS			LIABILITIES AND OWNERS' EQUITY		
Current assets:			Current liabilities:		
Cash	$ 30,000		Accounts payable	$ 20,000	
Accounts receivable	50,000		Accrued expenses	10,000	
Inventory	200,000		Income tax payable	40,000	
Total current assets		$280,000	Total current liabilities		$ 70,000
Fixed assets:			Long-term liabilities		
Land	$150,000		Mortgages	$300,000	
Buildings & equipment	400,000		Bonds	100,000	
Total fixed assets		550,000	Total long-term liabilities		400,000
			Owner's equity:		
			Common stock	$300,000	
			Retained earnings	60,000	
			Total owner's equity		360,000
Total assets		$830,000	Total liabilities and owner's equity		$830,000

Balance Sheet

The **balance sheet** provides a picture of an organization's financial position at a given point in time. It usually shows the financial status at the end of a fiscal year or a calendar year although the time interval can certainly be shorter (for example, at the end of each quarter). The balance sheet summarizes three types of information: assets, liabilities, and owner's equity.

Assets are the things of value that the company owns; they are usually divided into current assets and fixed assets. **Current assets** are those items that can be converted into cash in a short time period; they include such items as accounts receivable, inventory, and, of course, cash. **Fixed assets** are longer term in nature and include such things as buildings, land, and equipment.

Liabilities include the firm's debts and obligations. They can be divided into current liabilities and long-term liabilities. **Current liabilities** are the debts that must be paid in the near future; they include such obligations as accounts payable and not-yet-paid salaries earned by workers. **Long-term liabilities** are the debts payable over a long time span and include such obligations as payments on bonds and bank loans and mortgages for buildings and land.

Owner's equity is the difference between the assets and liabilities. It represents the company's net worth and consists of common stock and retained earnings. Table 15.3 shows an example of a balance sheet. Note that the totals on both sides of the balance sheet are equal; this must always be the case.

Income Statement

The **income statement** summarizes the organization's financial performance over a given time interval, typically 1 year. It shows the revenues that have come into the organization, the expenses that have been incurred, and the bottom-line profit or loss realized by the firm for the given time interval. For this reason, the income statement is often called a **profit-and-loss statement.** Table 15.4 shows the general structure of an income statement.

FINANCIAL RATIOS

Several financial ratios can be used to interpret company performance. Each ratio is simply a comparison of a few

KEY TERMS

Balance sheet
A summary of an organization's financial position at a given point in time, showing assets, liabilities, and owner's equity.

Asset
A thing of value that an individual or organization owns.

Current asset
An item that can be converted into cash in a short time period.

Fixed asset
An asset that is long term in nature and cannot be converted quickly into cash.

Liability
A debt or obligation of the firm.

Current liability
A debt that must be paid in the near future.

Long-term liability
A debt that is payable over a long time span.

Table 15.4 Income Statement

Cestaro Manufacturing Company
Income Statement
December 31, 2006

Gross sales	$2,400,000	
Less sales returns	100,000	
Net sales		$2,300,000
Less expenses and cost of goods sold:		
Cost of goods sold	$1,600,000	
Depreciation	50,000	
Sales expense	150,000	
Administrative expense	80,000	1,880,000
Operating profit		$ 420,000
Other income		10,000
Gross income		$ 430,000
Less interest expense		40,000
Taxable income		$ 390,000
Less taxes		160,000
Net income		$ 230,000

pieces of financial data. These ratios can be used to compare a company's current performance with its past performance, or they can be used to compare the company's performance with the performance of other companies in the same industry.

Liquidity Ratios

Liquidity ratios indicate the firm's ability to meet its short-term debts and obligations. The most commonly used liquidity ratio is the *current ratio,* which is determined by dividing current assets by current liabilities. The current ratio for the Cestaro Manufacturing Company, as illustrated in Tables 15.3 and 15.4, is 280,000/70,000, or 4. This ratio indicates that Cestaro has $4 of liquid assets for each dollar of short-term debt. Another liquidity ratio is the *quick ratio,* which is calculated by dividing current assets less inventory by the current liabilities. This ratio assesses how well a firm can expect to meet short-term obligations without having to dispose of inventories. For the Cestaro Company, the quick ratio is (280,000 − 200,000)/70,000, or 1.14.

Profitability Ratios

Profitability ratios indicate the relative effectiveness of the organization. One important profitability ratio is the profit margin on sales, which is calculated as net income divided by sales. For the Cestaro Company, this ratio is 230,000/2,300,000, or 0.1 (10%). Another profitability measure is return on total assets (ROA), which is calculated by dividing the net income by total assets. For Cestaro, this ratio is 230,000/830,000, or 0.28 (28%). ROA is a valuable yardstick for potential investors because it tells them how effective management is in using its assets to earn additional profits.

Debt Ratios

Debt ratios indicate the firm's ability to handle long-term debt. The most common debt ratio is calculated by dividing total liabilities by total assets. The debt ratio for Cestaro is 470,000/830,000, or 0.57 (57%). This indicates that the firm has 57 cents in debt for each dollar of assets. The lower the debt ratio, the better is the financial health of the organization.

Activity Ratios

Activity ratios measure performance with respect to key activities defined by management. For example, the total cost of goods sold divided by the average daily inventory

KEY TERMS

Owner's equity
The portion of a business that is owned by the shareholders; the difference between the assets of an organization and its liabilities.

Income statement (profit-and-loss statement)
A summary of an organization's financial performance over a given time interval, showing revenues, expenses, and bottom-line profit or loss.

Liquidity ratio
An indicator of the firm's ability to meet its short-term debts and obligations.

Profitability ratio
An indicator of the relative effectiveness, or profitability, of the organization.

Debt ratio
An indicator of the firm's ability to handle long-term debt.

indicates how efficiently the firm is forecasting sales and ordering merchandise. When total sales are divided by average inventory, an inventory turnover ratio is calculated. This ratio indicates the number of times inventory is turned over to meet the total sales. A low figure means that inventory sits too long and money is wasted.[24]

These and other similar ratios should be used to gain insights into a company's financial relationships and to identify areas that are out of control so that corrective action can be taken. When a ratio is out of line with either past company performance or the performance of comparable companies within the industry, managers must probe through the numbers carefully to determine the cause of the problem and devise a solution. Many of the numbers on the balance sheet and income statement are interrelated, and making a change to improve one ratio may have an undesirable impact on another. Therefore, managers must be very familiar with company operations in order to arrive at a proper remedy when using financial controls.

Ethical Issues in the Control of a Diverse Workforce

9 Organizations are increasingly employing controversial mechanisms to control the behavior of individuals and groups within the organization. Sometimes these control mechanisms are known to the individuals, and sometimes the individuals are totally oblivious to their existence. Considerable controversy exists over the ethics of using such control methods as drug testing, undercover surveillance, and computer monitoring. The next sections briefly review the debates over these practices.

LEARNING OBJECTIVE 9

Discuss some of the ethical issues related to the control of employee behavior.

DRUG TESTING

It has been estimated that the use of illegal drugs is costing U.S. organizations close to $100 billion per year.[25] Drug abuse results in increases in defective output, absenteeism, workplace accidents, healthcare costs, and insurance claims. To combat the costs associated with these drug-related problems, organizations have increasingly turned to drug testing. One type of drug testing is preemployment testing.[26] As the name suggests, organizations that use this approach require job applicants to submit to a drug detection test.

Another type of drug testing focuses on testing current employees. Organizations that test existing employees can follow any of three policies. Random testing subjects employees to unannounced and unscheduled examinations. Testing can also be based on probable cause. If an employee exhibits suspicious or erratic behavior or if drug paraphernalia are found in an employee's locker, there may be probable cause for testing. Finally, testing may be prescribed after an accident. Because it is conceivable that impaired motor skills may be the cause of the accident, this is a reasonable time for a drug test. The Motorola Corporation began screening all employees for illegal drug use in 1990. Motorola estimates that lost productivity and absenteeism costs could be reduced by $190 million annually if drug addicts were removed from the workplace.[27]

The ethical issue posed by drug testing hinges on whether it constitutes an invasion of privacy. Do individuals have the right to do as they please with regard to drugs while on their own time, or do organizations have the right to test for drugs in an effort to reduce medical costs, lost-productivity costs, absenteeism costs, and accidents in the workplace?[28] This ethical issue has even spilled out of the workplace and onto the home front. Because of the large number of drug-related crimes in and around one of its housing projects, Atlanta-based developer Trammel Crow Residential began requiring prospective residents to pass drug tests to gain entry. Furthermore, current residents were subjected to the same tests before their leases could be renewed.[29] There are no easy answers to the ethical questions raised by drug testing. The debate over drug testing continues and will undoubtedly continue for quite some time.

UNDERCOVER SURVEILLANCE

Organizations are constantly subjected to a variety of illegal activities that add to operating costs and decrease profit. Therefore, they are constantly looking for ways to control such activities. These activities include theft (such as pilferage, shoplifting, embezzlement, and burglary), fraud (such as credit card fraud, check fraud, and insurance fraud), and malicious destruction of property (such as vandalism, arson, and most recently, the threat of terrorism).[30] Organizations often resort to a variety of surveillance techniques to control these illicit activities. Surveillance may be conducted by undercover internal security staffs, external security firms, or electronic devices. For example, General Electric uses tiny cameras hidden behind

KEY TERMS

Activity ratio
An indicator of performance with respect to key activities defined by management.

walls and ceilings to watch employees suspected of crimes, Du Pont uses hidden cameras to monitor its loading docks, and Las Vegas casinos use ceiling-mounted cameras to observe activities on the gaming floors.[31]

Few would find fault when surveillance attempts to detect illegal activities being performed by individuals who are not part of the organization. However, undercover surveillance becomes a delicate issue when an organization's own employees are the subject of the scrutiny.[32] Again, the issue of invasion of privacy often surfaces in such instances, as does the concern that management has a low regard for and little trust in its own employees. Another concern is the potential abuse of such technology. Recently Caesar's Atlantic City Hotel Casino was heavily fined when it was discovered that security technicians were using the "eye in the sky" surveillance cameras to look for low-cut blouses on female employees and customers sitting at casino tables.[33]

COMPUTER MONITORING

In many businesses, employees spend much of their time working at computer terminals and other electronic devices. Among these employees are data processors, word processors, airline reservations clerks, insurance claims workers, telemarketers, communications network personnel, and workers in many other occupations. Technology has evolved to the point where the work of these employees can be monitored electronically without their knowledge through the computers with which they interface.[34]

Although it is a form of undercover surveillance, computer monitoring is concerned with measuring employee performance rather than detecting illegal activities. This form of surveillance raises serious questions as to whether it violates a worker's right to privacy.[35] Many would question the appropriateness of the organization's "electronically peeking over the workers' shoulders" to monitor their actions. They might argue that it is more appropriate to judge the net output of employees' efforts periodically (daily, weekly, or monthly) rather than to constantly monitor their every action or decision.[36] There are no easy answers to the ethical questions raised by these control methods.

Implications for Leaders

Throughout this book, we have been continually stressing that the successful organizations in the new millennium will be those that achieve quality in all aspects of their operations. Successful managers in these organizations will be those who can ensure that, once plans have been set into place, all activities will be directed toward successfully carrying out those plans. The most effective device that managers have for assessing the success of organizational activities is a basic control system. In a sense, control systems help leaders chart a course or set a direction when standards of behavior or performance are established. Control systems also help tell them whether they are on course by providing a way to monitor performance. Leaders monitor behavior or performance by measuring what has been done and comparing it to what should have been done. Finally, when organizations stray off course, control systems help guide them back onto the right path by forcing leaders to consider corrective actions to remove undesirable deviations from standards.

Successful business leaders of the future will be those who

- Develop a control system for each important product, service, process, or activity within the organization.
- Incorporate sufficient variety, sensitivity, anticipation capability, and feedback into the control system.
- Gauge the control system's effectiveness by considering its relationship to corporate strategy, its completeness, the degree to which it incorporates objective and subjective performance measures, its timeliness, and its acceptability to individuals within the organization.
- Determine the appropriate points within the organization where control systems should be focused.
- Understand the intricacies of the financial data contained in the organization's financial statements and can use various financial control techniques to assess the organization's financial health.
- Adopt a philosophy of control that is consistent with the management style, organizational culture, employee professionalism, and performance measures present within the organization.

The checklist shown earlier in "Now Apply It" can be helpful in determining whether or not a control system has been designed effectively.

In short, the concepts of control presented in this chapter provide us with a mechanism for determining whether our plans and actions have turned out as we had expected or hoped they would. If they haven't, we will be alerted to that fact, allowing us to take the appropriate corrective action to keep matters on their proper course. By remaining on course, we stand a better chance of being successful in our organizational activities.

Meeting The Challenge

Berner Foods: Controlling Its Destiny

We saw in the opening to this chapter that the challenges facing Berner Foods were many and varied. To deal with the issues originating with the FDA, USDA, and BTA, a lot of data needed to be collected, and it needed to be gathered very quickly. After all, the law dictates that companies must be able to reply to a recall request within 4 hours. This could not be accomplished manually, so Berner implemented a computer control system that would address quality-control issues, manage regulatory compliance and food safety, and produce real bottom-line improvements. Berner now responds successfully to all food-safety measures required by the government. Gary Gold, Berner vice president of Quality Systems notes that, prior to implementation, mock recalls were taking up to 8 hours. Now they are done in about 30 minutes. Gold further notes that "with full lot tracing, we can determine the disposition of any raw ingredient, throughout production and distribution of all finished products, and quickly contain the scope of a potential recall." With regard to tracing, he adds that employees are "able to go forward and backward—as well as even sideways in some cases—and do it very quickly."

Berner's system integrated manufacturing operations, quality control, supplier management, financials, and regulatory management. The company was able to achieve more accurate inventory levels, more exact forecasts and plans, lowered costs, and improved profitability. The software system has allowed Berner to be more competitive in the cutthroat grocery business and create new efficiencies. The company has reduced overall costs by 5% through increased production throughput, facility consolidation, improved product quality, and more robust inventory tracking capabilities. In addition, stock outs have been reduced by 99%, and customer complaints due to quality issues have gone down dramatically. As icing on the cake, Berner has been able to reduce system administration and maintenance overhead by 96%. All in all, Berner's implementation of a new system for controls has proved to be a very worthwhile venture.

Sources: E. Rennie, "Brand New World: What's in Store for Food and Beverage Manufacturers?" *APICS Magazine* (May 2005): 31–34; "Private Label Manufacturer Achieves Results with ERP System," *Food Manufacturing* (September 2004): 24; "Berner Foods Enables Quality Assurance and Regulatory Compliance with Ross Systems," *Business Wire,* 25 May 2004, 5476; "Berner Foods Selects Enterprise Software," "Berner to Increase Efficiency with ERP Software," "Berner Foods Enables Quality Assurance and Regulatory Compliances with Ross Systems," "Berner Foods Invests in Retort Technology" (last four are Berner Foods press releases) from http://www.bernerfoods.com.

SUMMARY

1. Organizational control is the systematic process through which business leaders regulate organizational activities to make them consistent with the expectations established in plans, targets, and standards of performance. Control is an extremely important managerial function because it ensures that all of the planning, organizing, and leading has gone as we hoped it would. If things have not gone as planned, this situation can result in a variety of negative consequences to the organization.

2. An organized system for control requires that (a) standards of performance be established, (b) actual performance be measured, (c) comparisons be made between standards and actual performance, and (d) corrective action be taken when unacceptable deviations of the actual performance from the standards occur.

3. When designing a control system, one should consider the amount of variety to include in the system, its ability to anticipate problems before they occur, the amount of sensitivity needed in the measuring instruments, and the type of data and information to be included in the feedback report.

4. To be effective, the control system should be related to the organizational strategy, incorporate all the steps in the control process, blend both objective and subjective performance measures, provide timely feedback, and be accepted by members of the organization.

5. To determine the proper amount of control that should be exercised in a given situation, several factors must be examined. The costs and benefits of the control effort must be assessed. The amount of control can also be affected by the reliability of the system being controlled or the importance of the item being controlled.

6. Feedforward (preventive) control systems focus on the inputs to the transformation process. Concurrent control systems focus on the ongoing activities of the transformation process. Feedback (corrective) control systems focus on the outputs of the transformation process.

7. Bureaucratic control is a more rigid philosophy of control that relies on prescribed rules and policies, a hierarchy of authority, written documents, and other formal mechanisms to influence behavior, assess performance, and correct unacceptable deviations from standards. Organic control is a more flexible philosophy that relies on social values, traditions, flexible authority, and trust to assess performance and correct unacceptable deviations.

8. Several financial control devices are available to assess an organization's financial health. The balance sheet and income statement are two important financial statements. In addition, several financial ratios can be used to interpret company performance.

9. It is becoming more common for organizations to test their employees for drug use, conduct undercover surveillance of their employees, and engage in computer monitoring. Such control procedures raise ethical questions of invasion of privacy and lack of confidence and trust in the employees.

REVIEW QUESTIONS

1. (LEARNING OBJECTIVE 1) Why is control such a critical managerial function?
2. (LEARNING OBJECTIVE 2) Discuss each of the four steps that should be taken in a systematic process of control.
3. (LEARNING OBJECTIVE 3) Discuss the important factors that should be considered when designing a control system.
4. (LEARNING OBJECTIVE 4) Discuss the various criteria that must be satisfied if a control system is to be effective.
5. (LEARNING OBJECTIVE 5) Describe the factors that should be considered when trying to determine the proper amount of control to be exercised.
6. (LEARNING OBJECTIVE 6) Describe the difference between feedforward control, concurrent control, and feedback control.
7. (LEARNING OBJECTIVE 7) Explain the difference between a bureaucratic-control philosophy and an organic-control philosophy.
8. (LEARNING OBJECTIVE 8) Describe the differences between a balance sheet and an income statement.
9. (LEARNING OBJECTIVE 9) Discuss some of the organizational control practices that raise ethical dilemmas.

DISCUSSION QUESTIONS

Improving Critical Thinking

1. Through your personal observations, identify a situation in which the use of technology seems to be enhancing the control effort and one in which the use of technology seems to be detracting from the control effort. Discuss the reasons why you feel each situation is either enhanced or detracted from by the use of technology.

2. Recall some situations that you have encountered in which electronic or undercover surveillance was being performed. Discuss how you felt about those practices.

Enhancing Communication Skills

3. Think about your approach to this course and your quest for a particular grade. Then design a system with which you could control this activity. Be specific in describing the activity, how you would perform each of the steps in the control process, and the potential corrective actions you could take if your performance was not up to your standards. To enhance your written communication skills, write a short essay (one to two pages) in which you describe the design of this control system.

4. The chapter cited two brief examples (air traffic controller and tree farm manager) in which the response times for control feedback were quite different. Identify several situations with varying response-time

requirements. Try to come up with examples having response times in seconds, minutes, hours, days, and months. To enhance your oral communication skills, prepare a short (10–15 minutes) presentation for the class in which you describe your examples of each of these categories of response time.

Building Teamwork

5. Identify two situations that you have observed in which you think the sensitivity of the measuring device is inappropriate. One of those situations should have a device that is too sensitive and the other a device that is not sensitive enough. Thoroughly describe what is being measured and the device that is being used to measure it. Indicate why you feel that the sensitivity of the devices is inappropriate. To refine your teamwork skills, meet with a small group of students who have been given this same assignment. Compare and discuss your selections and then reach a consensus on the two best choices (one overly sensitive device and one insufficiently sensitive device). Select a spokesperson to present your choices to the rest of the class.

6. Try to identify two situations in which the costs would suggest very different levels of control. In one situation, the cost trade-offs should suggest that high levels of control are warranted, and in the other they should suggest that low levels of control are appropriate. To refine your teamwork skills, meet with a small group of students who have been given this same assignment. Compare and discuss your selections and then reach a consensus on the two best choices (one requiring low levels of control and one requiring high levels of control). Sketch the cost trade-off graphs for each situation. Then select a spokesperson to present your team's choices and graphs to the rest of the class.

Chapter

16

Productivity and Quality in Operations

CHAPTER OVERVIEW

All business organizations engage in operations that transform inputs into outputs. Regardless of whether their organization manufactures a product or provides a service, business leaders have one fundamental concern—to provide the customers what they want, when they want it. As simple as this concept sounds, leaders must make many decisions prior to delivering the product or service. To achieve quality in operations, they must understand (1) the nature of the various decisions they will face and (2) the various tools, techniques, and approaches that can help them make these decisions. How business leaders should approach these decisions depends to a large extent on whether their organization is predominantly product or service oriented and on the structural characteristics of the operating system.

In this chapter, we first examine the differences between manufacturing and service organizations and review the basic system configurations that these organizations may exhibit. We then briefly examine some of the more important managerial decision areas for the long-term design of these systems, as well as some of the important decisions for their short-term operation and control. Because productivity and quality have a major impact upon the efficiency and effectiveness of operations decisions, ways to measure and improve them are examined. We also discuss the roles that productivity and quality play in achieving excellence in operations. The chapter concludes with an examination of some contributions of the most prominent contemporary quality philosophers.

LEARNING OBJECTIVES

When you have finished studying this chapter, you should be able to

1. Identify the major differences between manufacturing and service organizations.
2. Describe the volume/variety continuum for identifying different operating system configurations and identify the different types of manufacturing and service organizations that might exist, as well as their locations on the volume/variety continuum.
3. Identify the two broad categories of decision-making areas within operating systems and describe some of the important decisions in each category.
4. Define the concept of productivity and identify the three approaches to improving productivity.
5. Provide definitions of quality from both a consumer perspective and a producer perspective.
6. Identify factors that can be used to assess the quality of products and services.
7. Describe the four categories of quality-related costs.
8. Identify the various areas of concentration and commitment for a program of total quality management.
9. Describe the major contributions of the most prominent contemporary quality philosophers.

Facing The Challenge

Summit Industrial Products: Victimized by Its Own Success

Summit Industrial Products, located in Tyler, Texas, is an industry leader in the development and manufacture of quality synthetic lubricants and other industrial products. Although the company is not a household name and although you and I would never be directly interested in Summit's products, we would quickly feel the impact of their disappearance. You see, Summit makes the products that keep the manufacturing machines running smoothly. Food processors, consumer products manufacturers, chemical processors, and countless other industries rely on Summit's precision manufactured compressor lubricants, specialty oils, degreasing chemicals, scale removal chemicals, and oil–water separator equipment to keep the manufacturing plants humming.

Summit has built a strong reputation on delivering the highest-quality product in a timely manner to thousands of manufacturers around the world. Lubricant technology is sophisticated because equipment-operating temperature, speed, load, and environmental conditions dictate the use of unique lubricant solutions. In conjunction with its parent organization, the Klüber Group, Summit can offer more than 5000 specific formulations. Ever-changing market demands and increasingly difficult technical requirements constantly result in new formulations being developed.

Eventually, Summit came to be a victim of its own success. As a result of high demand and Summit's expanded product offerings, the company was facing numerous challenges. Delivery lead times had begun to slide. Inventory tracking and labeling had become increasingly labor intensive. Coordinating individual product and business transactions with Summit divisions in Mexico and New Hampshire had become progressively more difficult. Company leaders needed to figure out a way to manage each stage of the manufacturing process to ensure that internal and external customer expectations could be met.

Sources: "ERP Solution Keeps Texas Manufacturing Plant Running Smoothly," *APICS—The Performance Advantage* (November/December 2004): 64; "Summit Industrial Products Achieves Stellar Customer Satisfaction Levels with Ross Systems," *Business Wire,* 9 June 2004, 5055; http://www.klsummit.com.

Introduction

Summit Industrial Products was not unique in the challenges that it faced. A desire to deliver the highest-quality products in the face of increasing global competition presents challenges to most chemical manufacturers today. Summit, with its focus on delivering superior products in a timely manner, would have to make use of the latest advances in operations technology if it was going to maintain its competitive edge.

In this chapter, we focus on issues of productivity and quality in operations. Recall that in Chapter 15 we presented a simple model for operations. It described a process in which inputs are subjected to a transformation process that converts them into the product or service outputs of the organization. We see that operations management has a strong decision-making orientation and contains several design and operating decision areas. How managers should approach these decisions depends on the structural characteristics of their own operating systems and whether their organizations are predominantly engaged in manufacturing products or providing services. Let's begin by examining those structural characteristics so that we can see how manufacturing and service organizations differ.

What Is Operations Management?

Operations management is concerned with the design, planning, and control of the factors that enable us to provide the product or service outputs of the organization. Decision making is central to operations management. Operations managers must make decisions to ensure that the firm's product or service output happens (1) in the amount demanded, (2) at the right time, (3) with the chosen quality level, and (4) in a manner that is compatible with the organization's goals.

The first three aspects of the operations manager's function are fairly straightforward: Provide what the customers want, when they want it, and with a quality level that is acceptable to them. The fourth aspect can be a bit trickier. As we saw in Chapter 4, organizations often have multiple goals, and some may be in conflict with one another. When this happens, operations management decisions cannot satisfy all organizational goals simultaneously. Consider, for example, the dilemma you would face if you were in charge of operations in a steel mill. Suppose two of your organization's many goals were to (1) maximize bottom-line profits and (2) reduce the amount of pollutants that the mill discharges into the atmosphere. Installing scrubbers in the mill's smokestacks would reduce pollution, but the expense of these scrubbers would detract from your organization's bottom-line profits. Likewise, consider the dilemma faced by the home-delivery pizza industry in recent years. A reasonable goal might be to deliver pizzas to the customers in as short a time as possible. Another reasonable goal might be to promote public safety in the delivery of the pizzas. These two goals are at odds with one another. Speedier delivery of the pizzas can result in dangerous driving practices on the part of delivery personnel. In fact, it was a dilemma like this that caused the major pizza delivery companies like Pizza Hut, Domino's, Papa John's, and many others to eliminate such traditional time guarantees as "30-minute delivery or the pizza is free."

The decisions faced by operations managers can be conveniently separated into two broad categories. The first set of decisions relates to the design of the operating system. After the system has been designed and built, operations managers must then make the operating and control decisions necessary to keep the system running smoothly and efficiently. Managers can draw on many tools, techniques, and models to help them make these decisions. For many operations decisions, the proper decision-making tools depend on whether the system is a manufacturing or service system. We see later in the chapter that the manufacturing-versus-service distinction also influences how quality and productivity are measured. Decision-making tool selection also depends on the structural characteristics of the operating system. Consequently, before we explore the important operations management decision areas, we first examine the differences between manufacturing and service organizations and the structural differences among various manufacturing and service organizations.

© MICHAEL NEWMAN/PHOTOEDIT

Major pizza-delivery companies reflect the conflicts organizations face when their goals may be in conflict with one another.

MANUFACTURING VERSUS SERVICE OPERATING SYSTEMS

1 Although manufacturing and service organizations both display the same input-to-output transformation process, a fundamental output characteristic distinguishes manufacturing organizations from most service organizations. The output of manufacturing will always be a physical product—something that can be touched, measured, weighed, or otherwise examined. For example, IBM makes computers, General Motors makes automobiles, RCA makes audio and video equipment, and Nike makes athletic apparel.

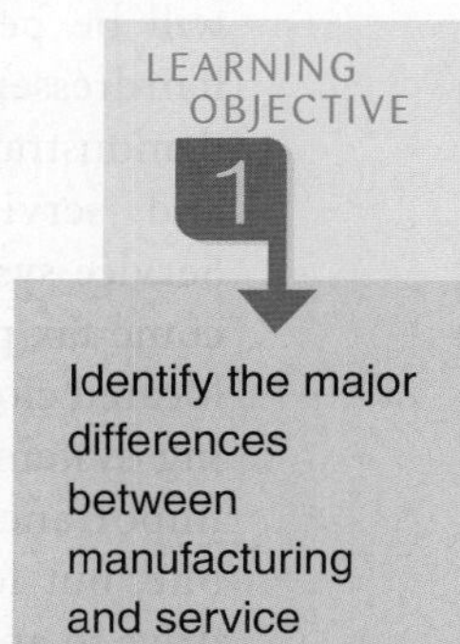

Outputs of service organizations often lack physical properties. For example, H&R Block processes income tax returns, hospitals treat sick and injured people, and your college professors deliver lectures and convey knowledge to you. Sometimes, however, the outputs of service organizations do possess physical properties.

When you order a hamburger at a fast-food restaurant, your selection certainly has physical properties associated with it. Does this make the fast-food restaurant a manufacturing organization? Not really. The physical characteristic of outputs is not the only feature that distinguishes manufacturing from service organizations. As we take a closer look at other differences, continue to think about fast-food restaurants. You should have a definite opinion as to whether they are manufacturing or service organizations by the time we get to the end of the discussion.

Several of the differences between manufacturing and service stem from the physical nature of the output. Manufacturing can stockpile inventories of finished products in advance of customer demand.[1] Service organizations usually cannot. For example, a barbershop cannot stockpile a supply of haircuts prior to the Saturday morning peak-demand period, and H&R Block cannot stockpile an inventory of completed income tax returns prior to April's peak demand. Even when a physical product is made, stockpiling in advance of demand can sometimes be impractical. This is certainly true in the case of fast-food restaurants, as discussed in more detail shortly. Service capacity is often described as being time perishable.[2] This means that if a service organization has excess capacity that goes unused, that service capability has been lost forever. On the other hand, a manufacturing organization with excess capacity can use the surplus capacity to produce additional product for later consumption.

Another difference is that production and consumption usually occur simultaneously (or within a short time of one another) in service organizations. In addition, the customer is normally a participant in the service process.[3] For example, you must show up at the barbershop or beauty salon to receive a haircut, and it will be performed while you sit in the barber's or hairdresser's chair. These two characteristics also demonstrate another difference between manufacturing and service—the system location considerations. Service systems, such as barbershops, restaurants, income tax preparation firms, and hospitals, need to be located close to their customers, whereas manufacturing systems would not consider this to be of prime importance.[4] Most adult Americans own an automobile, but few live within walking distance or an easy drive to an automobile-manufacturing plant. However, most would like to have reasonable access to an automobile repair shop because none of us would want to take our automobile back to Detroit (or Japan!) for repair service.

A final difference between manufacturing and service relates to the measurement of quality and productivity. The quality of a product is usually much easier to assess than the quality of a service.[5] Physical products are designed to meet various specifications that involve physical traits such as weight, dimensions, color, durability, and so forth. After manufacture, precise objective measurements of these characteristics can be made to determine the degree to which the product meets the quality standards. For example, once manufactured, a Dell computer or a Hewlett-Packard printer can be put through a variety of tests to ensure that they operate exactly as they were designed. Such precision is usually more difficult when assessing the quality of a service output. In many instances, only subjective assessments can be made of the quality of the service output. Precise standards usually do not exist to determine how good the haircut is, how accurately the income tax return was prepared, or how tasty the hamburger was. Productivity, which gauges the relationship between inputs and outputs, is also easier to assess in manufacturing situations in which the physical nature of the inputs and outputs allows them to be precisely measured.[6] The "Now Apply It" box presents a checklist for determining whether an organization is predominantly a manufacturing organization or a service organization. Apply the checklist to any of the U.S. Big Three automakers (General Motors, DaimlerChrysler, and Ford). Into which category—manufacturing or service—do they fall?

Now let's think again about fast-food restaurants and the checklist in "Now Apply It." The service capacity of a restaurant is usually time perishable. Excess capacity early in the day will go unused; it cannot be used to satisfy the needs of the lunch or dinner crowd. Using that early-morning excess capacity to stockpile inventory in advance of the meal-hour rush is of limited practicality. Hamburgers cannot be cooked early in the day and then stored until the rush hours. In these situations, production and consumption must occur almost simultaneously, and the customer is an active participant in the process. The vast multitude of locations also points to a service orientation. One centralized McDonald's restaurant will not suffice. There must be plenty of outlets scattered about so that they are near the customers in order to facilitate direct interaction between the customer and the service system. Thus, when all the tests are applied, a service classification proves to be more appropriate for fast-food restaurants.

Let's now turn our attention to an examination of the structural differences that can exist among manufacturing and service organizations.

Now Apply It

Checklist for Manufacturing/Service Classification

To determine whether a business firm is a manufacturing organization or a service organization, answer the following questions with a zero (0) for no and a one (1) for yes.

1. Does the firm provide a tangible, physical output?
2. Can the output be stored in inventory for future use or consumption?
3. Can the output be transported to distant locations?
4. Can excess capacity be used when there is no immediate demand?
5. Can the output be produced well in advance of its consumption?
6. Can the system operate without having the consumer of the output as an active participant?
7. Is it reasonable to have the system located a great distance from the consumer of the output?
8. Is productivity relatively easy to measure?
9. Is quality relatively easy to assess?

Total the value of your responses. The closer the total is to 9, the more inclined we would be to classify the system as a manufacturing organization. The closer the total is to 0, the more inclined we would be to classify the system as a service organization.

STRUCTURAL DIFFERENCES AMONG OPERATING SYSTEMS

LEARNING OBJECTIVE 2

Describe the volume/variety continuum for identifying different operating system configurations and identify the different types of manufacturing and service organizations that might exist, as well as their locations on the volume/variety continuum.

2 Individual operating systems can be categorized along a volume/variety continuum, as illustrated in Figure 16.1. Companies can differ in the variety of outputs produced, as well as in the volume of each item that is provided. As you move toward the left extreme of low variety and high volume, you encounter systems that provide very few different types of output but deliver a large quantity of each. Toward the right extreme of high variety and low volume, you encounter systems that provide a very wide variety of different types of output but deliver a small number of each. The endpoints of this line represent two extremes in both manufacturing and service organizations. Let's take a closer look at these configurations, first in manufacturing organizations and then in service organizations.

Types of Manufacturing Systems

The left portion of the continuum represents systems that have a specific purpose. Because such systems often focus on a limited number of specific products, they are often referred to as **product systems.**[7] The extreme left reflects companies that make only one product but produce it in large quantities. In such a system, operations can be standardized. When the product being made takes the form of discrete, individual units, the system is called a **repetitive, assembly-line,** or **mass-production system.** For example, a company that makes only yellow number 2 pencils with an eraser would be at the left end of the continuum. When a product is made in a continuous stream and not in discrete units, the system is called a **continuous-flow production system.** Examples here would include an ExxonMobil oil refinery, a Coors brewery, or perhaps a USX steel mill that produces long, continuous rolls of sheet steel. You may recall from Chapter 2 that Joan Woodward identified these two types of production systems as mass-production technology and continuous-process technology when she proposed that managerial style would be affected by the organization's technology. In that context, she also identified a third type of technology that she called small-batch technology, which is described next.

At the right end of the continuum are systems that have a flexible purpose. Such systems typically have a variety of outputs and focus on the processes that produce them. Hence, these systems are often referred to as **process systems.** The extreme right reflects companies that make many different types of items but produce only one of each. This would be a custom-manufacturing situation. In

KEY TERMS

Product system
An operating system that produces a limited variety of items, with high volumes of each.

Figure 16.1 Classification Scheme for Different Operating Systems

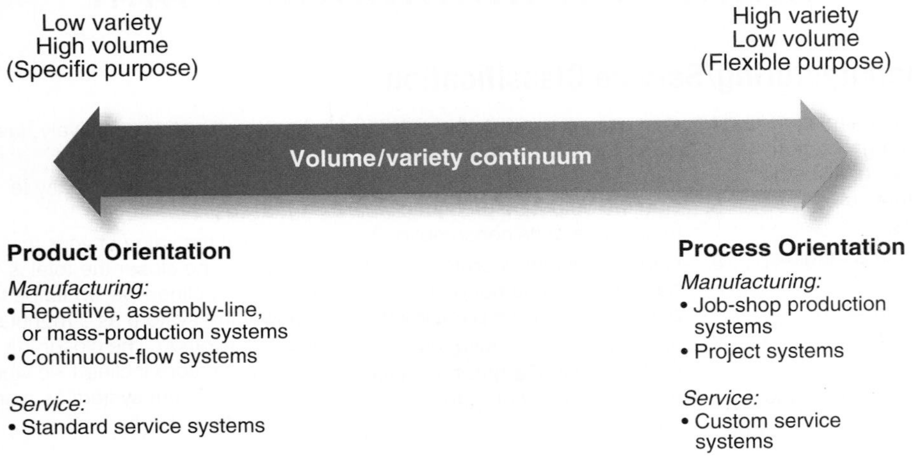

such a system, operations cannot be standardized; instead, they must be flexible enough to accommodate the wide variety of items that will be manufactured. When the items to be made require small to moderate amounts of resources and time (hours or days), the system is referred to as a **job-shop production system.** The term *unit production* is often used to signify systems that manufacture only a single unit of a particular item. A sign shop that custom-fabricates neon advertising signs for small businesses would be an example of a company near the right extreme of this continuum. Xtek, Inc., described in the "At the Forefront" box, is a manufacturer that lies at the right extreme of the continuum. Here we see that Xtek manufactures large, heat-treated steel gears, gear couplings, steel rollers, and many other components of large industrial equipment, and each item is made according to unique, custom specifications. At any one time, the company might have more than 3500 active jobs in process, with no two being identical.

KEY TERMS

Repetitive, assembly-line, or mass-production system
A product system that produces a high volume of discrete items.

Continuous-flow production system
A product system that produces a high volume of a continuous product or nondiscrete item.

Process system
An operating system that produces a high variety of items, with limited volumes of each.

Job-shop production system
A process system that produces small quantities of a wide variety of specialized items.

Project productions system
A process system that produces large-scale, unique items.

Sometimes flexible-purpose systems produce items that consume massive amounts of resources and require large amounts of time to complete (months or years). Such systems are referred to as **project production systems.** Examples here would include construction companies that develop shopping centers, build roads and bridges, and so forth.[8]

Although the endpoints have been neatly defined for the continuum of Figure 16.1, it is unusual to find an organization that lies at either extreme. Although pencil manufacturer Dixon Ticonderoga is noted for its yellow number 2 pencils with erasers, this company makes more than just that one product. It turns out pencils in a variety of colors with different types of lead. In addition, it also makes a variety of pens and marking pencils. All these different writing instruments are produced in very large quantities. Consequently, Dixon Ticonderoga exhibits mass-production characteristics because it lies close to the left extreme of the volume/variety continuum. Because of its unique product ingredients and its 5000+ compound configurations, Summit Industrial Products, described in "Facing the Challenge," can be viewed as a process system.

Types of Service Systems

The continuum of Figure 16.1 also applies to different types of service systems. The left extreme reflects organizations that provide standard services, and the right extreme reflects organizations that provide custom services. Consider, for example, a college dormitory cafeteria line. It has all the characteristics of an assembly line as each customer moving through the line is serviced in exactly the same manner at each serving station. In contrast, a walk-in emergency clinic might exhibit all the character-

At the Forefront

Xtek Employs Advanced Planning and Scheduling System

Xtek, Inc., located in Cincinnati, Ohio, is a manufacturer of custom-machined and heat-treated parts for heavy-duty power transmission and industrial component applications. Among Xtek's products are large gears, gear couplings, steel rollers for steel mills, steel wheels for cranes, and assorted other heat-treated components. Because most of the products manufactured by Xtek are one-of-a-kind items, the company is a true job-shop production system. Xtek had earned a reputation for excellence within the industries that it served. Despite this reputation, Xtek managers found that work scheduling had recently become a daily challenge. The company often had more than 3500 active jobs in the shop at one time. Xtek's legacy software systems didn't provide the capability of tracking and managing jobs effectively. Furthermore, because Xtek always tried to respond quickly to customers who had experienced an equipment breakdown, there was often chaos in the management of the resulting rush jobs. This caused concern among Xtek leaders because one of the company's key differentiators in the industry had been its ability to accommodate such urgent jobs.

Xtek management recognized that they needed an effective advanced planning-and-scheduling (APS) system if they were going to remain at the forefront in this industry. Such a system would have to be capable of providing on-time delivery for customers, quoting accurate lead times on projects, effectively managing shop capacity, tracking jobs on the floor, and accommodating rush jobs. Furthermore, Xtek management wanted a way to reduce the work in process inventory on the shop floor by scheduling parts and assemblies as needed instead of dispatching them when an order was started, as had been the case.

After a careful search, Xtek leaders selected a scheduling system called NaView. NaView helps Xtek plan, predict, and control shop operations in a fashion that allows the company to meet business goals and exceed customer expectations. The system's immediate impact was with the here and now. Xtek could better perform the daily schedule management functions such as modifying the schedule to meet shifting requirements and changing customer demands. Within 3 months of implementation, Xtek had achieved a 25% cycle-time reduction throughout the facility. At the same time, on-time delivery of high priority jobs went up 19%. This was impressive because these improvements occurred in the face of increased orders due to market growth. The roll department alone had shipped about 30% more output while these improvements were occurring. Beyond the here and now, the system also gave Xtek predictive capabilities that allowed the company to examine "what-if" scenarios. The company can now use hypothetical scenarios to determine the impact on capital and labor resource needs. When the system anticipated the need for new machines and more shop workers, these resource adjustments proved to be an easy sell to management. The needed resources were acquired, helping Xtek stay at the forefront in this industry.

Sources: "Hardcore Rewards," *APICS Magazine* (March 2005): 66; http://www.xtek.com.

istics of a custom job shop because most patients are likely to have different types of injuries and illnesses and consequently will require different services.

As in the case of manufacturing, service organizations can easily lie somewhere between the extremes. The cafeteria line might have á la carte selections in which case some customers might receive slightly different service. Likewise, the emergency clinic might have a few patients with broken arms whose service requirements are virtually identical. The wound will be cleaned and dressed, X-rays taken, and a cast applied for each of them.[9]

Whether an organization is a manufacturing or a service entity and wherever it fits on the volume/variety continuum, its operations managers will have to make decisions. In the next section, we examine the many decisions that must be made for both the design and operation of manufacturing and service organizations.

OPERATIONS MANAGEMENT DECISION AREAS

LEARNING OBJECTIVE 3

Identify the two broad categories of decision-making areas within operating systems and describe some of the important decisions in each category.

3 To operate any business organization, a number of decisions must be made. Based on the time frame involved, these decisions can be conveniently categorized as long-term system design decisions or as short-term operating and control decisions.[10] It is not our intention to present a thorough description of each of the operations management decision areas. That level of detail is best left to separate operations management courses with their specialized textbooks. Instead, we provide a brief, introductory overview

of some of the more important operations management decision areas.

Long-Term System Design Decisions

Long-term system design decisions require substantial investments of time, energy, money, and resources. As the name implies, they commit the decision maker to a particular system configuration (that is, an arrangement of buildings and equipment) that will exist for many years, if not the entire life of the organization. Once these decisions are made and implemented, changing them would be costly. Although a thorough treatment of these various decisions would require several chapters, the following brief overview will provide a basic understanding.

Choice of a Product or Service Prior to the development and start-up of any business, a fundamental decision must be made about what product or service will be provided. This decision is linked directly to the corporate strategy because it answers the question, What business are we in? The choice of product or service will ultimately dictate what inputs will be necessary and what type of transformation will be performed. To make a viable product/service selection decision, considerable interaction with the marketing function will be needed. This interaction will help the decision maker accurately assess the wants and needs of the marketplace as well as the strength of the competition so that the product or service selected has a reasonable chance of success.

© MARY KATE DENNY/PHOTOEDIT

A college cafeteria has all of the characteristics of an assembly line as each customer moving through the line is provided with the same service at each serving station.

Product or Service Design From a manufacturing standpoint, the development of a product involves a sequence of steps, as illustrated in Figure 16.2.[11] These

Figure 16.2 Steps in Product Design

Concept Development → Preliminary Design → Make versus Buy Decisions → Transformation Process Design / Seek Suppliers

steps might also be applied in certain service situations that involve physical output. The sequence of design steps requires (1) development of a concept, (2) development of a preliminary design or prototype, (3) development of make-versus-buy choices, and (4) selection of production methods, equipment, and suppliers.

Although each step in the design process is usually carried out by a different unit of the organization, design quality is facilitated when all participants from marketing, engineering, production, purchasing, and any other relevant areas work together as a design team. The instant feedback and enhanced interactions within the team help achieve more rapid product development. The design process can also be facilitated by such recent high-tech developments as computer-aided design (CAD), computer-aided engineering (CAE), and computer-aided manufacturing (CAM). By using virtual prototypes on computers to design and test cars, the U.S. Big Three automakers have made marked progress in reducing the time required to develop new vehicles, which will save them billions of dollars in costs.[12]

System Capacity Another decision to be made involves the capacity of the system.[13] This decision will determine the level of product or service output that the system will be able to provide. It is here that the firm will make its major investment decisions. The number of facilities to be built, the size of each facility, their individual capabilities, and the amount and type of equipment to be purchased must all be determined. To make high-quality decisions in this area, the decision maker must forecast the market demand for the product or service to be offered and assess the competition so that the organization's market-share potential can be estimated. Next, the amount of labor and equipment needed to meet these market-share projections must be calculated. Marketing will play a key role here because accurate projections of market demand and competition will help establish the size of the system being developed. As a company's business grows, it may become necessary to revise that capacity decision (that is, capacity expansion).

Process Selection The selection of a framework for the transformation process will depend on how the firm is likely to be categorized. Recall our classification scheme that categorized manufacturing and service organizations along a volume/variety continuum. An organization's self-assessment of the volume, variety, and type of product or service output likely to be generated will help indicate the type of process to be selected. In a manufacturing setting, answers to these questions will indicate the types of material flows that can be expected through the system. This in turn will determine the process configuration to be selected—that is, whether the organization will be configured as a continuous-flow, repetitive, job-shop, or project system. In a service setting, the self-assessment of volume, variety, and type of service will determine whether the system process will provide custom or standard services. Once the decision makers select the process configuration, the firm can obtain machinery and equipment compatible with that process.

Facility Location The facility location decision involves the selection of a geographic site on which to establish the organization's operations. This decision is extremely important because once the physical structure has been built or acquired, its high cost usually dictates that the location decision will remain in effect for a considerable amount of time. In the "Leaders in Action" box, we can see that the Target Laser & Machining Company's initial location decision carried it for the first 20 years of its existence. Eventually, market conditions dictated that capacity be expanded, but the current site was not capable of accommodating a capacity expansion. In this case, a "relocation" decision was necessary, so once again this issue had to be addressed. We can see here some of the questions that had to be answered in the course of making a sound relocation decision.

Manufacturing and service organizations emphasize very different factors in making the location decision. Consider what would be important to a hospital, a gasoline service station, a fast-food restaurant, an automobile-manufacturing plant, a cement-processing plant, and a ballpoint pen–manufacturing plant. Some factors might be common to all, whereas other factors might be important for only certain types of systems. Survey data show that manufacturing location decisions are dominated by five factors: (1) favorable labor climate, (2) proximity to markets, (3) quality of life, (4) proximity to suppliers and resources, and (5) proximity to the parent company's facilities.[14] Table 16.1 describes these factors further. Summit Industrial Products' location in Tyler, Texas, places the company's main operations close to the Texas oil fields that serve as a prime source of supply for raw materials.

In service organizations, proximity to customers is often the primary location factor to be considered. Because customers must usually interact directly with service organizations, convenient locations are crucial. Barbershops, dry cleaners, supermarkets, gasoline service stations, and restaurants would do very little business if they were situated in remote, inaccessible areas. Traffic volume, residential population density, competition, and income levels all play an important part in the location decision for service organizations.

Leaders in Action

Target Laser & Machining: Company on the Move

Whenever a company outgrows its existing space, it's a nice problem. After all, it is a sign that business has been good and the company has grown. So, what's the issue? Well, for starters, the company has to decide where it can put the new workers and machines that will be needed to accommodate the growth.

That is exactly the problem that faced Target Laser & Machining of Rockford, Illinois. Target is a supplier of laser-cut steel parts to equipment manufacturers in the agricultural, heavy industrial equipment, automotive, and aerospace industries. For its first 20 years of existence, Target managed to survive in a 20,000-square-foot factory. Eventually, though, increasing business was making it difficult for the company to keep up with demand. It was project manager Mike Kubera's job to come up with a solution.

The basic options in a case like this are limited. One can expand the existing facility, build a new facility, or find a suitable existing facility as a replacement. The first two options often require significant construction costs and a considerable wait for construction to be completed. That was apparent to Kubera when he quickly determined that the company could do much better by acquiring existing space than by engaging in a construction effort. Because the company was in business for the long haul, Kubera also decided that it made more sense to purchase than to rent.

Once these decisions were made, it became necessary to examine the available properties in the area (there were more than two dozen prospects). As luck would have it, one of those properties was a 50-year-old, 50,000-square-foot building right across the street that was being vacated by its current tenant. Seems like a no-brainer, right? Well, don't be too hasty. Kubera recognized that there was a lot to be considered before closing the deal. What about asbestos and other hidden issues that come with an existing building? Financers want to know about such things, and the company certainly needs to know whether it is buying into a potential lawsuit. The complete history of hazardous material use in the building needed to be researched. Structural soundness also needed to be checked. The building would have to be assessed to determine what, if any, modifications would be needed to make it functional, energy efficient, and aesthetically pleasing. Questions about parking spaces also needed to be addressed. In summary, this "short move" was not quite the no-brainer that our first instincts might have suggested. However, Kubera did do the homework and got favorable responses to all the questions that arose. Ultimately, the decision was made, and beginning in 2004 the move progressed in stages so that operations would not be totally disrupted. Because of the actions of Kubera, Target's move promises to be a smooth transition.

Sources: C. M Wright, "On the Move," *APICS—The Performance Advantage* (February 2005): 22–25; http://www.targetlaser.com.

Table 16.1 Major Factors in Manufacturing Location Decisions

1. *Favorable labor climate* Management's assessment of the labor climate would be based on such parameters as union activity, wage rates, available labor skill levels, required labor training, worker attitudes, and worker productivity.
2. *Proximity to markets* Consideration would be given to both the actual distance to the markets and the modes of transportation available to deliver the products.
3. *Quality of life* Attention would be paid to the quality and availability of schools, housing, shopping, recreation facilities, and other lifestyle indicators that reflect the quality of life.
4. *Proximity to suppliers and resources* When companies rely on bulky or heavy raw materials and supplies, this factor is of prime concern. Distance and transportation modes would influence this factor.
5. *Proximity to the parent company's facilities* This factor is important for companies with multiplant configurations. When parts and materials must be transferred between operating facilities, frequent interactions, communication, and coordination will be necessary. Additionally, the time and cost of material transfers must be minimized. All of this can be facilitated by geographical proximity between the facilities.

The location criteria mentioned here should not be interpreted as an exhaustive list. The Russell Stover Candy Company recently incorporated a somewhat unusual factor in its location decision. Although it had committed to building a plant in Corsicana, Texas, that decision was put on hold when plans were announced for an animal parts–processing plant in the same town. Russell Stover officials feared that odors from the animal-rendering facility would contaminate its sweets. The candy company gave the go-ahead with its construction plans only after the animal-rendering plant was paid by town officials to locate elsewhere.[15]

Facility Layout The primary objective of the facility layout decision is to arrange the work areas and equipment so that inputs progress through the transformation process in as orderly a fashion as possible. This will result in a smooth flow of materials or customers through the system. The precise configuration for a given system will depend on where the system fits into the volume/variety continuum. Systems at the flexible-purpose extreme, which must be able to handle a wide variety of product or customer-service demands, will use a **process layout.** Conversely, systems at the specific-purpose extreme, in which all products or services are essentially the same, will use a **product layout.**

Lying between these extremes are a variety of systems that need layouts combining aspects of each of the extreme cases. These systems would incorporate a **hybrid layout.** Finally, a system that produces extremely large or bulky items may use a **fixed-position layout** in which the item remains stationary while workers and equipment move to the item to provide processing. Just how important is the layout decision? Consider these examples. Recently, Toys "R" Us embarked on a massive project to revamp the layout of its stores by removing the maze of parallel aisles in an effort to rekindle customer interest.[16] Similar revolutionary changes are being tested in Albertsons and Food Lion grocery stores where aisles have been replaced with clusters of grocery departments and service centers to spark consumer interest. In addition, Subway restaurants has begun a makeover of the layout and décor of its units to add a Tuscany flair.[17]

Some of these long-term system design decisions present unique managerial challenges to multinational organizations. For example, before selecting and designing a product or service, the sociocultural and economic environments of the global markets in which the organization will operate must be assessed. In addition, it would be unwise to select international locations for operating units of the organization without first considering the political–legal climate, economic conditions, state of technological development, and cultural values of the workforce in the potential locations. Success will come more easily to multinational organizations that thoroughly research all of these parameters in their long-term system design decisions.

Short-Term Operating and Control Decisions

After the long-term system design decisions have been made and the system is operational, it is time to begin making the short-term operating and control decisions. These decisions are made frequently (daily, weekly, or perhaps monthly), can be readily changed, and in many cases are directly involved with the scheduling of work activities. In today's organizations, managers face new challenges as they schedule, lead, and control labor in the increasingly diverse workforce. Ethnic, racial, and gender differences often lead to different individual values and expectations. Hence, standards of individual behavior, performance, and productivity are sometimes more difficult to set and enforce.

Aggregate Planning Before initiating any detailed day-to-day or week-to-week scheduling activities in a manufacturing firm, management must first make a series of decisions designed to set the overall level of operations for a planning horizon that generally spans the upcoming year. At this point, management uses demand forecasts to make rough production, labor-scheduling, and inventory decisions that will set the tone for the overall level of operations during the year. The goal is to ensure that customer demand can be satisfied, the firm's resources won't be overtaxed, and the relevant costs will be held to a minimum. These decisions constitute what is known as **aggregate planning.** This set of planning decisions represents the link between the more general business-planning activities and the more specific master plans for short-range operation and control aspects of the firm.

In aggregate planning, management formulates a

KEY TERMS

Process layout
A configuration flexible enough to accommodate a wide diversity of products or customers.

Product layout
A configuration set for a specific purpose, with all product or service demands essentially identical.

Hybrid layout
A configuration containing some degree of flexibility, lying between the extremes of process and product layouts.

Fixed-position layout
A configuration used for large or bulky items that remain stationary in the manufacturing process.

Aggregate planning
A link between the more general business-planning activities and the more specific master-planning activities.

plan that involves such factors as production scheduling, workforce-level adjusting, inventory scheduling, production subcontracting, and employment scheduling so that enough product or service will be available to satisfy customer demands.[18] By their very nature, aggregate plans are rather rough. They are usually stated in terms of product families rather than individual products. Their monthly or quarterly time periods are incapable of directing the day-to-day scheduling of operations. The main purpose of aggregate plans is to provide broad production scheduling, inventory scheduling, and human resource scheduling guidelines within which more detailed scheduling decisions eventually will be made.

Master Production Scheduling Although the rough schedule provided by aggregate planning will be useful for projecting the overall levels of production and labor requirements over an intermediate planning horizon, it will not contain enough detail and information for scheduling the various production activities. Another schedule is needed that not only contains detailed information about individual product identities but also divides the planning horizon into finer increments of time. Such a schedule, which is known as the master production schedule, will be used to drive all the ensuing production scheduling activities within the system.

The **master production schedule** is a detailed statement of projected production quantities for each item in each time period.[19] Time periods are typically weekly intervals. The master production schedule is often thought of as an anticipated build schedule for finished products. A major constraint in the development of the master production schedule is that the total number of units scheduled for production must be compatible with the aggregate plan. Because the master production schedule is simply a more detailed breakdown of the aggregate plan, the sum of the parts (the master production schedule units) must equal the whole (the aggregate plan).

KEY TERMS

Master production schedule
A detailed statement of projected production quantities for each item in each time period.

Material requirements planning (MRP)
A methodology that uses the production schedule for the finished products to derive demand and production schedules for component items that make up the final products.

Inventory Management One of the most studied of the short-term decisions deals with the control of inventories. Items in inventory may exist in any of four forms: (1) raw materials, (2) work-in-process, (3) finished goods, and (4) supplies. Raw materials are the basic inputs that have not yet been subjected to any processing transactions. Work-in-process represents semifinished items that are in various stages of completion. Finished goods are items that have had all processing transactions performed and are ready for delivery to the customer. Supplies represent purchased items that facilitate the completion of some production or service activity.[20] Two fundamental decisions must be made with respect to the replenishment of any item maintained in inventory: (1) how many should be ordered and (2) when they should be ordered. These decisions are referred to as lot-sizing and lot-timing decisions. The objective of inventory management is to make those decisions in a manner that minimizes the total of inventory-related costs.

Many models have been developed to aid in making lot-sizing and lot-timing decisions under varying conditions. The earliest and perhaps best known of these models is the classic economic order quantity (EOQ) model. Table 16.2 provides a brief overview of the specifics of this model.

Material Requirements Planning Excellence in inventory control requires that lot-sizing and lot-timing decisions be made correctly for all items used to construct a product. EOQ models of the type described are capable of making the proper sizing and timing decisions for finished products. Unfortunately, they do a poor job of controlling the various raw materials, parts, and components that are assembled into those finished products. **Material requirements planning (MRP)** is a methodology that derives component demands from finished product–manufacturing schedules and then uses this information to make the timing and sizing decisions for these lower-level items.

The basic approach of MRP requires that lot-sizing and lot-timing decisions be made first for the finished product so that sufficient finished product will be available to support the master production schedule. These timing and sizing decisions for the finished product will determine the needs for the various components that combine directly into the finished product (that is, the components that are one level of production removed from the finished product). The timing and sizing decisions can then be made for these components so that sufficient amounts will be available to support the planned production of the finished product. Once this has been done, attention is focused on the next lower level of manufacture. By continually linking the successive levels of manufacture, lot-sizing and lot-timing decisions for all raw materials, parts, and components used in making the finished product will be coordinated to ensure that the master production schedule will be met.[21] Because most multistage manufacturing

Table 16.2 Economic Order Quantity Model

- Relevant costs: Annual ordering cost and annual carrying cost
- Symbols used: D = annual demand or usage
  S = cost per order (setup cost or purchase order cost)
  H = carrying cost per unit per year
  Q = order size (which is to be determined)

Model Structure

The total annual carrying cost is the average inventory level multiplied by the cost to carry a unit in inventory for a year. In symbolic form, the average inventory level is Q/2; therefore,

Total annual carrying cost $= (Q/2)(H)$

The total annual ordering cost is equal to the number of orders placed during the year times the cost per order. In symbolic form, the number of orders placed per year is D/Q; therefore,

Total annual ordering cost $= (D/Q)(S)$

Combining these two costs yields a total cost of

$$TC = (Q/2)(H) + (D/Q)(S)$$

Determination of *EOQ*

Take the derivative of TC with respect to Q and set equal to zero and then solve for Q:

$$H/2 - DS/Q^2 = 0$$

An algebraic rearrangement of terms yields the following:

$$Q^2 = 2DS/H$$

and

$$Q = \sqrt{2DS/H} \quad \text{(Also called the EOQ)}$$

This is called the EOQ because this is the most economic order quantity.

systems have products that consist of hundreds or even thousands of individual raw materials, parts, components, subassemblies, and assemblies spanning dozens of levels of manufacture, a computerized system is necessary to perform the massive data-handling and manipulation chores of the MRP process.

Just-in-Time Inventory Management A phenomenon that has strong implications in the area of inventory control is a philosophy known as just-in-time (JIT) inventory management. This concept initially received considerable attention and refinement within the Japanese industrial community, but its application quickly spread worldwide. Despite its concern with inventory, JIT is more than just a technique for dealing with inventory. **Just-in-time (JIT) inventory management** is an overall manufacturing philosophy that advocates eliminating waste, solving problems, and striving for continual improvement in operations.[22]

JIT attempts to reduce inventory because inventory can be costly and can hide problems. For example, problems such as machine breakdowns, high levels of defective output, and worker absenteeism may not cause noticeable disruptions to flow when high levels of inventory exist to "ride over" those problems. JIT attempts to reduce inven-

KEY TERMS

Just-in-time (JIT) inventory management
A philosophy that advocates eliminating waste, solving problems, and striving for continual improvement in operations.

tory by scheduling smaller but more frequent shipments from internal and external suppliers. Because the ultimate goal is the almost total elimination of inventory, JIT systems are often referred to as zero-inventory systems or stockless production systems.[23] Successful JIT requires close cooperation between the supplier and user of a commodity.

Because little inventory exists in a JIT system, there can be little tolerance for problems because these will inevitably disrupt flow and perhaps stop system output. This happened to General Motors when a 17-day labor strike occurred at two of its brake suppliers. GM was forced to close 22 of its 29 car and truck plants in North America until the labor problem was resolved.[24] This is why JIT is regarded as a broader philosophy of problem solving, waste elimination, and continual improvement. In addition to the zero-inventory ideal, JIT also seeks to attain zero defects (perfect quality), zero breakdowns, zero disruptions, and in general, zero problems. In such systems, workers play an important role in attaining these goals. Not only are workers responsible for their own manufacturing efforts, but they are also responsible for such things as quality control, equipment maintenance, housekeeping duties in the work area, and general problem solving in the workplace.[25]

Just-in-time (JIT) inventory management strives to reduce inventory by scheduling smaller but more frequent shipments from internal and external suppliers.

Supply-Chain Management One of the most important areas of focus in recent years has been in the area of supply-chain management (SCM). A **supply chain** is the entire network of activities involved in the delivery of a finished product or service to the customer. These activities include the acquisition of raw materials and parts, order entry, manufacturing and assembling the products, warehousing, distribution, order tracking, and delivery to the customer. **Supply-chain management** is the business function that coordinates and manages all these activities. This process is facilitated by an information system that allows relevant information such as sales data, sales forecasts, and promotional campaigns to be shared among all participants in the supply chain.

Sharing accurate demand information between all members of a supply chain is critical. Inaccurate or distorted information can cause erratic replenishment orders to be placed at different levels in the supply chain, and these replenishment orders may have no apparent link to the final product or service demand. There are several potential negative consequences of this, including excess inventory investment, misused production capacity, ineffective transportation use, poor customer-service levels, and lost revenues. When accurate information is shared, synchronization can be attained between all participants in a supply chain. Each of those participants can then schedule its operations in a manner that will be consistent with the ultimate customer demand.[26] As will be seen later in "Meeting the Challenge," Summit Industrial Products was attentive to SCM issues. The Summit system provides inventory management and logistics capabilities that extend across company, division, and site boundaries, enabling

KEY TERMS

Supply chain
The entire network of activities involved in the delivery of a finished product or service to the customer.

Supply-chain management (SCM)
The business function that coordinates and manages all the activities involved in the delivery of a product or service to the customer.

the company to quickly manage the distribution of each order placed.

Today most organizations face challenges and opportunities brought about by our continuously shrinking world and our global marketplace. Multinational organizations with operating units in different countries may have to set different productivity goals to accommodate differences in work attitudes across national boundaries. In addition, the level of technological development may differ among nations, resulting in significant differences in attainable productivity rates. Political factors may also affect the way the organization can operate in foreign countries.

Even organizations that view themselves as purely domestic are not untouched by aspects of the global marketplace. As we saw in our brief treatment of SCM, raw material inputs, purchased parts, and supplies needed in their transformation processes often originate in foreign countries. In these instances, purchasing agreements must cut across national boundaries. Consequently, these so-called domestic companies must be sensitive to the sociocultural, political–legal, technological, and economic environments of the supplying countries.

In addition to global challenges and opportunities, many businesses face challenges and opportunities spawned by ever-increasing sophistication in technology and information-processing capabilities. Even traditional bookstores and music stores will see changes in the way they conduct business. Maintaining inventories may not be as important as in the past if the technologies described next take off. Sprout, Inc., has an arrangement with Borders Books that would allow them to deliver books on demand to customers. The bookstores would be able to download digital versions of books from Sprout, then digitally print, assemble, and bind using a normal paperback-binding process. The entire process would be completed in 15 minutes.[27] In a similar vein, Sony Music Entertainment revealed plans to make more than 4000 albums from its catalog available on demand. Digitally recorded music can be sent directly to stores via a high-speed computer network. A compact disc, complete with liner notes and artwork, would be made while the customer waits.[28] And of course, nowadays music connoisseurs can even bypass the music store entirely and simply download the music of their choice from a variety of legitimate sources.

Thus far, we have seen that operations managers face a wide variety of decisions. To improve the quality of their operations, managers must make these decisions in a way that supports the goals of the organization. We have already noted that organizations can have a variety of goals. When this is the case, managers can move toward achieving excellence in operations by focusing on productivity and quality.

The Role of Productivity and Quality in Operations

4 Organizational goals can be many and varied. In firms operating on a for-profit basis, bottom-line profit will always have a high priority, whereas not-for-profit organizations will be more inclined to view service and customer satisfaction as the prime goals. However, any of these firms might also strive to achieve other goals such as market share, improved satisfaction and welfare of its workforce, heightened social and environmental responsibility, and so forth. Operations managers rarely find it easy to relate their decisions directly to these system goals. Fortunately, there are two measures of operations efficiency and effectiveness that indirectly relate to these system goals. In the next section, we see that productivity is a measure of operations efficiency and quality is a measure of operations effectiveness. Every decision that an operations manager makes—whether a long-term design decision or a short-term operating and control decision—has an impact on productivity and quality. Let's turn our attention to the fundamentals of productivity and examine the ways in which productivity can be improved.

LEARNING OBJECTIVE 4

Define the concept of productivity and identify the three approaches to improving productivity.

FUNDAMENTALS OF PRODUCTIVITY

In Chapter 15, we saw a diagram that showed how all operating systems engage in the transformation of inputs into outputs. **Productivity** is a measure of the efficiency with which a firm performs that transformation process. In the broadest sense, productivity can be defined as the ratio of system outputs to system inputs, or

$$\text{Productivity} = \frac{\text{Output}}{\text{Input}}$$

Measuring productivity is often easier said than done because outputs can be quite varied and inputs quite diverse. Table 16.3 shows some of the various inputs and outputs for a few manufacturing and nonmanufacturing examples.

KEY TERMS

Productivity
A measure of the efficiency with which a firm transforms inputs into goods and services.

Table 16.3 Examples of Inputs and Outputs for Productivity Measurement

Output	Input
Number of refrigerators manufactured	Direct labor hours, raw materials, machinery, supervisory hours, capital
Number of patients treated	Doctor hours, nurse hours, lab technician hours, hospital beds, medical equipment, medicine and drugs, surgical supplies
Number of income tax returns prepared	Staff accounting hours, desktop computers, printers, calculators, typewriters, supplies

Interest in productivity has increased in the United States during recent years, in large part because of the alarming decline in international competitiveness suffered by many U.S. companies. In the last four decades of the 20th century, the United States had one of the lowest annual productivity increases of any of the industrialized nations. Its average annual increase of 3% was less than half that of Japan.[29] A lower level of productivity can result because less output is being produced from a given level of input or because more input is needed to achieve a given level of output. In either case, the cost incurred to produce a unit of the good or service will be higher as will the purchase cost for the customers. This leads to a decline in sales volume, which results in decreased revenues. With less operating revenue, business and industry are likely to lower employment levels, which leads to idle capacity. This is likely to reduce productivity even further, resulting in a snowball effect. Fortunately, in recent years, most U.S. industries have recognized this phenomenon. Many firms are attempting to break this vicious cycle by instituting productivity improvement programs.

Improving Productivity

Any increase in the numerator or decrease in the denominator of the productivity equation will result in a productivity increase. Simply stated, to increase productivity, all that is needed is an increase in output, a decrease in input, or a combination of both. Such changes can be achieved in several ways. We can categorize the productivity-enhancing tactics as being related to technology, people, or design.[30]

Productivity Improvement through Technology Productivity can be improved through the use of new technology. If, for example, old office equipment and computers are replaced with newer, faster versions, the number of tax returns prepared per labor hour might be expected to increase. Likewise, in the case of manufacturing, if faster equipment replaces slower equipment, more units might be produced per labor hour.

Another technological approach to improving productivity is to substitute capital for labor. For example, certain operations that are performed manually may be done by a machine or robot. If the machine has a lower hourly operating cost, higher output rate, and greater precision than a human operator, then the substitution should be considered as a possible means to improve productivity.

Productivity Improvement through People One of the most important inputs to the productivity equation is the human resource element. We have seen repeatedly throughout this book that the workforce is becoming increasingly more racially, ethnically, and gender diverse. These groups of individuals all have unique sets of values, expectations, motivations, and skills. Their interaction often has a synergistic effect on the work team, enabling the team to achieve results that exceed previous norms.

Effective management of people can often result in significant increases in output without an appreciable increase in the labor cost. This feat can be accomplished through the use of employee compensation programs and employee teams. Many companies have found that compensation can encourage higher productivity. For example, the practice of paying employees bonuses based on productivity and company profitability has become more popular in recent years.

The most common form of the employee team in current practice is the quality circle, which is described more fully later in this chapter. Various companies have given their employee teams different names, but they all have the general objective of increasing employee satisfaction and productivity by providing them with more autonomy and a greater degree of involvement in the decision-making and problem-solving process.

Productivity Improvement through Design Several system design issues were described earlier in this chapter. These design decisions can have a direct bearing on productivity. If a product is designed in a way that makes it easier to produce, less time will be spent producing the item, fewer defective units will be produced, and less scrap will result. These improvements will ultimately lead to an increase in productivity. Ford Motor Company used design simplification to its advantage when it redesigned an instrument panel to contain 6 parts instead of the 22 parts contained in an earlier model. This simplified design led to productivity enhancements.

Process design can also have a significant impact on productivity. If the process has been designed poorly, material flow may be restricted by bottlenecks. Inappropriate placement of work areas and tools can lead to inefficient material flows through the system. These inefficiencies will ultimately lead to greater production time per unit and reduced productivity. Not only did Ford take advantage of simplified product design, as we just described, but the company also streamlined many production processes, which resulted in improved productivity.[31]

As we discussed in Chapter 7, job design is the third design area that can impact productivity. If a worker's assigned job has been defined so narrowly that there is no job fulfillment, boredom and a lack of interest are likely to result. In such a situation, the quality of work can be expected to suffer. The resulting defects, scrap, and rework will diminish the level of productivity. To avoid these problems associated with excessive job specialization, many companies adopt philosophies of job enrichment, job enlargement, and job rotation.

As we continue through this chapter, we encounter more and more evidence suggesting that productivity and quality are intertwined. Improvements in quality are likely to result in improved productivity. Later in this chapter, we see more specifically how this occurs when we examine the five-step chain reaction of the late W. Edwards Deming, one of the world's foremost authorities on quality. But first, let's examine the fundamentals of quality.

FUNDAMENTALS OF QUALITY

5 People sometimes have an inaccurate perception about quality. Too often they assume that quality implies a high degree of luxury or expense. Grandeur, luxuriousness, and expense are not the prime determinants of quality, however. The following two perspectives provide more accurate definitions of quality. From a consumer perspective, quality can be defined as the degree to which the product or service meets the expectations of the customer. From a producer perspective, quality can be defined as the degree to which the product or service conforms to design specifications. The more effective the organization is in meeting customer expectations and design specifications, the higher will be the implied quality level of its output.[32]

The Mercedes Benz and Honda Accord are two automobiles with very different prices and quite different features and accessories. However, this does not automatically mean that the more expensive and more elaborate Mercedes has a higher level of quality than the Honda. As the consumer perspective indicates, the test of quality is based on user expectations. Each automobile has as its function the conveyance of passengers in a particular style, and those styles are different by design.

A similar observation could be made for service organizations. Ritz-Carlton Hotels and Holiday Inns both provide overnight lodging for guests. Ritz-Carlton Hotels feature larger, more elaborately decorated rooms with more amenities than Holiday Inns provide. However, one fact remains common to both. Each provides overnight sleeping and bathing accommodations for travelers. Ultimately, it is the individual guest who must determine the level of quality associated with these accommodations.

Once an organization selects the product or service it will provide, design decisions are made that ultimately shape the product or service design characteristics. If the completed product or service output meets those design characteristics, the output will be viewed as high quality from the production perspective. If this output fails to meet customer expectations, however, then the initial design was probably inadequate because the customer is not likely to purchase it regardless of the quality level that production perceives. Businesses are increasingly adopting this consumer perspective on quality.

LEARNING OBJECTIVE 5

Provide definitions of quality from both a consumer perspective and a producer perspective.

Although the terms *quality control, quality assurance,* and *total quality management* (or *total quality control*) are often used interchangeably, these concepts are not identical. **Quality control (QC)** has the narrowest focus; it refers to the actual measurement and assessment of output to determine whether the specifications are being met. The responsibility for taking corrective actions when standards are not being met is also in the

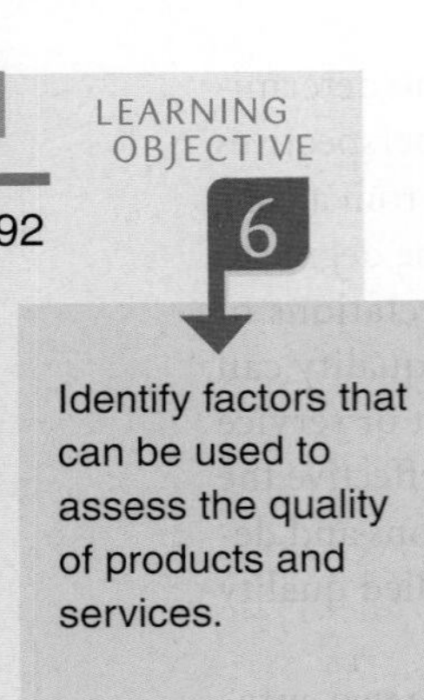

Identify factors that can be used to assess the quality of products and services.

domain of quality control. Statistical procedures are useful in quality control. **Quality assurance (QA)** concerns itself with any activity that influences the maintenance of quality at the desired level. It refers to the entire system of policies, procedures, and guidelines that the organization has established to achieve and maintain quality. Quality assurance extends from the design of products and processes to the quality assessment of the system outputs. **Total quality management (TQM)** has an even broader focus than quality assurance because its goal is to manage the entire organization in a manner that allows it to excel in the delivery of a product or service that meets customer needs. Before we look at TQM in more detail, it will be helpful to examine the factors for assessing quality.

Factors for Assessing Quality

6 A customer might evaluate many aspects of a product or service to determine whether it meets expectations. These aspects differ slightly for products and services.

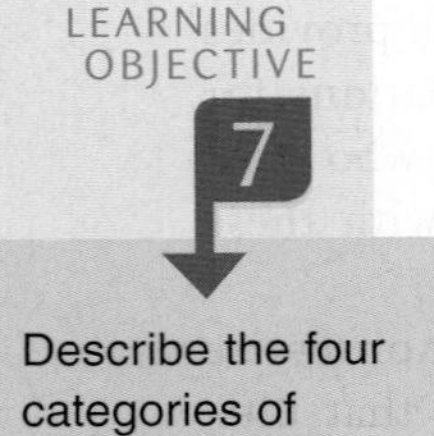

Describe the four categories of quality-related costs.

Product Factors When evaluating the quality of a product, a customer will probably first notice *aesthetic* characteristics, which are usually perceived by sensory reactions. The customer will observe how the product looks, sounds, feels, smells, or tastes. A product's *features* are also likely to be judged early. If you were about to purchase an automobile, for example, you might look for such features as a stereo system, air bags, and power seats. *Performance* is another aspect that helps determine whether the product meets the customer's needs and expectations. If you do a lot of highway driving, acceleration and passing power are probably important to you, so you would check these performance characteristics before making your purchase decision. Another important aspect of quality is *reliability*, which refers to the likelihood that the product will continue to perform satisfactorily through its guarantee period. You might ascertain this through product warranty information or by referring to a consumer magazine.

The *serviceability* aspect of a product's quality refers to the difficulty, time, and expense of getting repairs. In the case of your automobile purchase, you might assess this by considering the location and business hours of the dealer's automobile service center. The *durability* aspect refers to the length of time the product is likely to last. Both the manufacturer and independent consumer agencies might be a source of data here. *Conformance* reflects the degree to which the product meets the specifications set by the designers. For example, you will undoubtedly check to be sure that the automobile possesses all the accessories that the advertising suggests it will have. A final aspect is *perceived quality*, which has been described as an overall feeling of confidence based on observations of the potential purchase, the reputation of the company, and any past experiences with purchases of this type.[33]

Service Factors The product quality factors just described can be relevant to a service encounter if some physical commodity is delivered to the customer. For example, when you dine at a restaurant, the meal can be judged according to most of those characteristics. Unfortunately, service quality is sometimes more difficult to assess with quantitative measures. Suppose you visit a dentist for emergency treatment of a broken tooth. In this case, you would use other attributes to measure your satisfaction with service quality. *Responsiveness* reflects the willingness and speed with which the service personnel (that is, the dentist, dental technician, and receptionist) attend to you. *Reliability* is a measure of the dependability and accuracy of the service performed. *Assurance* refers to the feeling of trust and confidence you have in the service personnel. *Empathy* reflects the degree of attention and caring that the service personnel provide to you. Finally, *tangibles* are an assessment of such factors as the appearance of the service personnel, cleanliness of the equipment and physical system, and comfort of the surroundings.[34]

You should not get the mistaken impression that the list of product factors is applicable only to manufacturing situations and the list of service factors only to service encounters. Depending on the type of product or service being judged, items from either list might be applicable. These lists of product and service factors must be viewed as neither exclusive nor exhaustive.

Cost of Quality

7 Any costs that a company incurs because it has produced less-than-perfect quality output or costs that it incurs to prevent less-than-perfect quality

KEY TERMS

Quality control (QC)
Focuses on the actual measurement of output to see whether specifications have been met.

Quality assurance (QA)
Focuses on any activity that influences the maintenance of quality at the desired level.

Total quality management (TQM)
A systematic approach for enhancing products, services, processes, and operational quality control.

Figure 16.3 Quality Costs

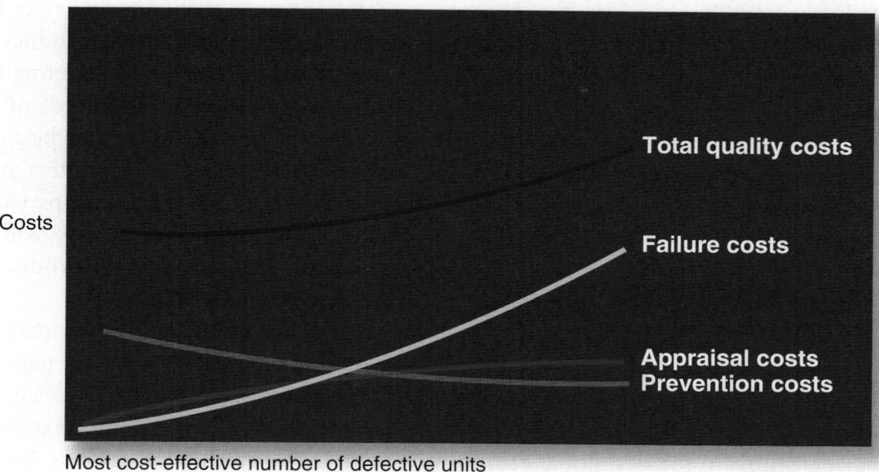

output are referred to as the cost of quality. The cost of quality can be organized into the following four major categories:[35]

- Prior to the production of the product or the delivery of the service, several activities can be performed in an attempt to prevent defective output from occurring. These activities include designing products, processes, and jobs for quality; reviewing designs; educating and training workers in quality concepts; and working with suppliers. The costs of these activities are the **prevention costs.**
- **Appraisal costs** are incurred to assess the quality of the product that has been manufactured or the service that has been provided. They include the costs of testing equipment and instruments, the costs of maintaining that equipment, and the labor costs associated with performing the inspections.
- Defective output that is detected before it leaves the system will either be scrapped (discarded) or reworked (repaired). If it is scrapped, the company incurs the cost of all materials and labor that went into the production of that output. If it is reworked, a cost is incurred for the material and labor that went into the defective portion that was replaced or repaired. In addition, more material and labor costs are incurred for the rework activities. These costs all contribute to the **internal-failure costs.**
- Defective output that is not detected before being delivered to the customer incurs **external-failure costs.** This category consists of the costs associated with customer complaints, returns, warranty claims, product recalls, and product liability suits.

The current popular view holds that prevention costs do not have to be increased substantially to reduce the number of defective units. Furthermore, this view suggests that as prevention costs increase, appraisal costs will decrease because less testing and inspection will be necessary due to inherently lower numbers of defective units. Meanwhile, failure costs will also decrease with the reduced number of defective units.[36] Figure 16.3 displays these cost relationships and suggests that the most cost-effective way of doing business is close to if not at the zero-defect level.

Although these concepts of quality-related costs may seem to apply only to the physical products of manufacturing systems, service organizations can also benefit from paying attention to quality-related costs. Providing poor-

KEY TERMS

Prevention cost
The cost associated with any activity that is performed in an attempt to prevent defective output from occurring.

Appraisal cost
The cost associated with any activity that is performed in an attempt to assess the quality of the product that has been manufactured or the service that has been provided.

Internal-failure cost
The cost associated with the repair or disposition of defective output that is detected prior to delivery to the customer.

External-failure cost
The cost resulting from defective output that is not detected prior to delivery to the customer.

quality service will lead to failure costs, just as with poor-quality products. However, in the case of service organizations, external-failure costs tend to be much greater than internal-failure costs. This is a result of the customer's direct involvement in the service transaction. There is usually little opportunity to check the quality of the service before the service encounter with the customer. Defective service is generally not detected until the service act has transpired. At that point, failure costs are by definition in the external category.

TOTAL QUALITY MANAGEMENT AS A TOOL FOR GLOBAL COMPETITIVENESS

8 Emphasis on quality is a key to achieving excellence in operations in today's global economy. This emphasis on quality is crucial for two reasons: (1) Customers are becoming increasingly conscious of quality in their choice of products and services, and (2) increased quality leads to increased productivity and its associated benefits. It is no secret that in recent years U.S. manufacturers have struggled with the loss of market share to foreign competitors in the global marketplace. These losses have been attributed to the notion (in some cases real and in some cases perceived) that the foreign competitors have been able to supply products of higher quality and at a lower price. People who are trying to get the most from their disposable income have understandably been attracted to these products. These shifts to foreign manufacturers are evidence that consumers do consider the product factors discussed earlier prior to making purchase decisions. Any manufacturer who hopes to reverse this declining market share can begin to do so by focusing on the quality aspects of the product. A TQM program is one of the most effective ways to enhance an organization's competitive position.

LEARNING OBJECTIVE 8

Identify the various areas of concentration and commitment for a program of total quality management.

KEY TERMS

External customer
User of an item who is not a part of the organization that supplies the item.

Internal customer
User of an item who is a member of or employee of the organization that supplies the item.

Customer-Driven Standards

Because one definition of quality centers on meeting customer expectations, the external customer should play a central role in establishing product or service standards. An **external customer** is a user who is not part of the organization that supplies the product or service. The external customer can be the ultimate consumer (that is, end user), or it can be some intermediary encountered as the product or service works its way toward the end user. Marketing will be instrumental in assessing the wants and needs of external customers. These wants and needs can then be conveyed to design engineers, who will make the product and service design decisions. Process design decisions will then follow. Ultimately, the product or service will be easier to sell if customers recognize that the product or service has been designed to satisfy their needs.

In some cases, a customer may be an **internal customer,** which is a user who is part of the organization that supplies the product or service. For example, the internal customer might be the next worker or next department in the production process. Internal customers also have quality requirements that must be considered in the product or service design stage. In essence, everybody in the organization is a supplier to some customer, and these supplier–customer links represent a major area of concern in total quality management. The quality focus of Summit Industrial Products was clearly consumer oriented, given the company's focus on meeting the expectations of not only regulatory agencies but also all internal and external customers.

Management and Labor Commitment

Recall from Chapter 10 the concepts of organizational culture and organizational change. If TQM is to pervade all levels of an organization successfully, management must develop an organizational culture in which all workers are committed to the philosophy. This requires a strong commitment from top-level management from which the values to be shared by the organization originate. If all parts of the organization are to coordinate toward a common goal, then this goal must be embraced at the top. Top-level management must not only communicate this goal but also demonstrate a commitment to the goal through its actions, policies, and decisions. Management must back up slogans and catchy phrases with a willingness to institute changes, a receptiveness to employee suggestions, and recognition and reward for improvements.

Organization and Coordination of Efforts

We have already seen that TQM will result in a wide variety of diverse personnel interactions. Marketing serves as an intermediary between external customers and design engineers, who in turn interact with production personnel. To improve their operations, companies will often compare their own products, services, or processes against those of industry leaders. This process, called

benchmarking, is a useful aid in understanding how outstanding companies do things so that their excellence in operations can be replicated. The internal supplier–customer links lead to many interactions among production personnel. Purchasing must interact with external suppliers. If TQM is to be successful, communication links must be established between all these internal and external entities to achieve proper coordination. As we saw in Chapter 8, such coordination efforts lead to a teamwork philosophy among all participants in the organization. A fundamental principle of TQM is that all participants should be focused on making continuous improvements, or what the Japanese refer to as ***kaizen.*** Because more and more organizations are buying and selling in international markets, many of these firms are striving to conform to a set of standards devised by the International Organization for Standardization (ISO). ISO standards govern documentation of a quality program within a company. Upon becoming certified, companies are listed in a directory so that potential customers can see who has been certified. Summit Industrial Products proudly proclaims that it is one of the first companies in its industry to achieve ISO certification.[37]

Employee Participation

A central theme of the TQM approach is that all employees should be brought into the decision-making and problem-solving processes. After all, those who are doing the work are closest to the action and will probably have valuable opinions about methods for quality improvement. This is an outgrowth of what we learned in Chapter 6 about participative decision making and the advantages it can bring to an organization. By providing the workers with an opportunity to express their opinions, worker morale and motivation are enhanced. Workers develop more of a sense of responsibility and connection to their jobs. Worker participation is further enhanced by the use of teams. Two of the more popular types of teams are quality circles and special-purpose teams.

Quality Circles A **quality circle** is a small group of supervisors and employees from the same work area.[38] Most quality circles have between 6 and 12 members, and membership is voluntary. Quality circles meet on a regular basis (usually weekly) to identify, analyze, and solve production and quality problems related to the work done in their part of the company. Many benefits accrue from quality circles. When workers are allowed to help shape their work, they usually take more pride and interest in it. Furthermore, quality circles have the potential to uncover and solve many problems or suggest ways to achieve improvements in operations. Even though some of these improvements may be minor, collectively they can result in substantial cost savings, quality improvements, and productivity increases in the organization.

Special-Purpose Teams On occasion, a **special-purpose team** may have to be formed to solve a special or nonrecurring problem.[39] Unlike quality circles, special-purpose teams are likely to draw their members from many departments or work areas and bring together people from different functional specialties. For example, if some characteristic of a product no longer conforms to customer needs, marketing personnel will be needed on the team to explain the wants and needs of the customers. Design engineers will be needed to help translate those needs into new product design specifications. Production personnel will also be needed to determine whether and how the redesigned product can be manufactured. Special-purpose teams also differ from quality circles in longevity. Quality circles are standing teams that continue in existence over time. Special-purpose teams are ad hoc groups that disband after the problem has been resolved.

LEARNING OBJECTIVE 9

Describe the major contributions of the most prominent contemporary quality philosophers.

PROMINENT QUALITY MANAGEMENT PHILOSOPHERS

9 Many of today's business organizations are placing more and more emphasis on quality because they are aware of how much it has helped their competition. It is safe to say that, in general, U.S. business organizations were a step behind many of their foreign competitors. Those competitors were able to get a head start in quality by taking the advice of some of the noted quality philosophers and consultants long before U.S. organizations did.

Perhaps the most prominent quality philosopher was W. Edwards Deming, an American who was considered the father of quality control in Japan. Deming emphasized the importance of improving quality through his five-step chain reaction, which proposes that when quality is improved (1) costs decrease because of less

KEY TERMS

Benchmarking
The process of comparing one's own products, services, or processes against those of industry leaders for the purpose of improvement.

Kaizen
A Japanese term referring to the total quality management principle of continuous improvement.

Quality circle
A work team that meets regularly to identify, analyze, and solve problems related to its work area.

Special-purpose team
A temporary team formed to solve a special or nonrecurring problem.

rework, fewer mistakes, fewer delays, and better use of time and materials, (2) productivity improves, (3) market-share increases with better quality and lower prices, (4) the company increases profitability and stays in business, and (5) the number of jobs increases.[40] Deming devised a 14-point plan (Table 16.4) to summarize his philosophy on quality improvement.

Joseph Juran is another of the pioneers in quality management. Juran's experiences revealed that over 80% of quality defects are caused by factors controllable by management. This led Juran to develop a trilogy of quality planning, control, and improvement.[41] Quality planning involves linking product and service design with process design to achieve the quality characteristics desired. Quality control involves comparing products or services to standards and then correcting undesirable deviations. (This part of the trilogy relates directly to what we learned about control in Chapter 15.) The final part of the trilogy involves getting into the habit of making significant improvements every year. An area with chronic quality problems is selected and analyzed, and an alternative is selected and implemented.

Other notable names in the area of quality are Armand Feigenbaum, Kaoru Ishikawa, and Phillip Crosby. Feigenbaum is credited with introducing the concept of total quality control and developing the quality cost categories described earlier in this chapter.[42] Ishikawa is credited with introducing quality circles, and he also developed the fishbone diagram (or cause-and-effect diagram), which helps identify the causes of quality problems.[43] Crosby introduced the philosophy that "quality is free."[44] In his opinion, the most cost-effective level of defects is zero defects. Crosby contends that with no defects, rework costs are saved, scrap is eliminated, labor and machine-time costs are reduced, and product failure costs are eliminated. Crosby believes that these cost reductions far outweigh the costs incurred in creating an environment that promotes the achievement of high quality. Crosby's philosophy is very much like the old adage "An ounce of prevention is worth a pound of cure."

NASA's experience with the *Hubble Space Telescope* dramatically illustrates this point. This $1.5 billion orbiting laboratory was launched for the purpose of viewing outer space. Not long after the launch, astronomers discovered that the telescope's view of the stars was somewhat blurred due to the incorrect grinding and polishing of its primary mirror. A relatively simple test costing a few hundred thousand dollars could have detected this flaw, but this test was omitted in an effort to reduce costs. As it turned out, repairs didn't come this easily or cheaply to NASA. To correct this defect and make a variety of other repairs, the space shuttle *Endeavour* embarked upon an 11-day mission. The repairs required five separate space walks by astronauts spaced over 5 days. The mission cost $750 million—$250 million for replacement parts and $500 million for the shuttle flight.[45]

We first learned in Chapter 1 of the increasing level of diversity in the workplace, and we continued to see the implications of such diversity throughout this book. NASA provides one of the most visible examples of increasing diversity in the workforce. Astronaut crews on shuttle missions have become more diverse in race, nationality, and gender over the years. Kathy Thornton was one of the four astronauts who spent more than 35 space-walking hours

Table 16.4 Deming's 14 Points

1. Create constancy of purpose for improvement of product and service, and communicate this aim to all employees.
2. Learn and adopt the new philosophy throughout all levels within the organization.
3. Understand that inspection only measures problems but does not correct them; quality comes from improving processes.
4. Reduce the number of suppliers, and do not award business on the basis of price tag alone.
5. Constantly improve processes, products, and services while reducing waste.
6. Institute modern aids to training on the job.
7. Improve supervision.
8. Drive out fear of expressing ideas and reporting problems.
9. Break down barriers between departments and get people working toward the goals of the organization as a team.
10. Eliminate slogans, exhortations, and targets for the workforce.
11. Eliminate numerical quotas for production; concentrate on quality, not quantity.
12. Remove barriers that rob people of pride of workmanship.
13. Institute a program of education and self-improvement for everyone.
14. Put everyone in the organization to work to accomplish the transformation.

Source: W. Edwards Deming, *Out of the Crisis* (Cambridge, MA: MIT, Center for Advanced Engineering Study, 1986).

repairing the ailing *Hubble Telescope.*[46] In late 1996, astronaut Shannon Lucid completed more than 6 months aboard space station *Mir,* eclipsing the space endurance record for women and, in the process, spending more time in space than any American astronaut before her.[47] And in mid-1999, Eileen Collins became the first woman to serve as commander of a space shuttle flight when she took the helm of *Columbia* on its 5-day mission to deliver the *Chandra X-ray Observatory* into earth orbit.[48]

Impact of Information Technology on Productivity and Quality

Advances and developments in information technology have had a profound and positive effect on productivity in operations. A quick reflection on the productivity formula (output divided by input) suggests that anything that enables one to achieve more output with the same amount of input or the same amount of output with less input will improve an organization's productivity. In the past few decades, the many advances in information-processing capabilities have positively influenced productivity. Computer-aided design and computer-aided manufacturing allow firms to link and manipulate information electronically, facilitating coordination of the design and manufacturing functions. Efficient designs and efficient manufacturing processes lead to less waste, smoother manufacturing, and a correspondingly higher level of productivity.

On an even broader basis, businesses are finding it increasingly important to integrate all internal functional areas. Decisions are constantly being made in the areas of production and materials, sales and marketing, finance and accounting, and human resources. Because a transaction in any one of these areas impacts the other functional areas, it is important that all areas are fully integrated, sharing a common database. The tool used to achieve such coordination is called an **enterprise resource planning (ERP) system.** ERP systems are characterized by software that is designed to organize and manage business processes by sharing information across all functional areas of an organization. In fact, the newer ERP systems go beyond coordinating just the internal business functions of an organization and extend that coordination to all participants in the organization's supply chain.[49] As you will see shortly, an ERP software system was critical for Summit Industrial Products to meet the challenges described at the opening of this chapter.

Advances in information-processing capabilities have also allowed companies to gravitate toward being lean production systems (LPS). These systems combine an understanding of quality with a desire to eliminate all kinds of waste. The JIT, MRP, and SCM systems described earlier in this chapter are compatible with this waste-elimination philosophy as they strive to have the right parts available in the right quantities and at the right time. The use of information technology to boost productivity is not restricted to manufacturing organizations. Ryder Systems, Inc., a seemingly low-tech trucking company, is actually on the cutting edge when it comes to using information technology to improve productivity and become more competitive. Its Fast Track Maintenance Service uses a computer chip to record information from electronic sensors on a truck's engine while the truck is being driven. When routine maintenance is due or when a problem occurs, that information can be downloaded, resulting in greatly reduced downtime for maintenance or repair.[50]

It should not go unnoticed in this discussion that the technological advances that enhance productivity will also have a positive effect on quality. With more efficient and effective design tools, products and services that satisfy customer needs should result. With more efficient and effective production and delivery systems, there is a greater likelihood that the delivered goods or services will meet their design specifications while satisfying the wants and needs of the customers.

In this chapter, we have seen that operations management has a strong decision-making orientation in both manufacturing and service organizations. We have also learned that the concepts of productivity and quality are extremely important for assessing the efficiency and effectiveness of operations decisions. Let's conclude the chapter by considering the implications of these concepts for tomorrow's leaders.

Implications for Leaders

Excellence in operations can be achieved only if business leaders strive to achieve perfection in all of the decision-making areas related to operations. Particular attention should be paid to long-term system design decisions. Because of the difficulty in reversing decisions

KEY TERMS

Enterprise resource planning (ERP) system
A software system designed to organize and manage business processes by sharing information across all functional areas of an organization.

Meeting The Challenge

Summit Industrial Products: Improvement through ERP

To address the challenges brought about by its expanding product line and increasing demand, leadership at Summit Industrial Products decided to implement a new ERP system. Summit conducted a widespread search to find a software partner with an understanding of its process manufacturing needs. Summit eventually selected a system that gave the company control over all materials and products throughout the entire manufacturing process, ensuring that products would meet the expectations of internal customers, external customers, and regulatory agencies. Summit can now custom tailor the labeling of products, which allows the company to deliver and track both standardized and customized products. Summit's new ERP solution has provided systemwide visibility, from finance to manufacturing to distribution, allowing the company to streamline production and distribution operations. The ERP system has also enabled Summit to more easily coordinate operations with its sister sites in Mexico and New Hampshire.

The results have been impressive. Within 6 months of implementation, Summit greatly improved its inventory tracking and labeling protocol and streamlined its order processing. Summit's enhanced organization-wide visibility enabled the company to greatly improve the order turnaround process—products are now shipped to customers in less than 1 day. The inventory management and visibility capabilities of the system allow Summit to store materials, process orders, and place shipments across international borders while consistently meeting customer expectations. Summit has been able to reduce its finished-goods inventory by 7% while increasing sales by 48% and production output by more than 65%. In addition, the supply-chain component of the system provides inventory management and logistics capabilities across multicompany, multidivision, and multisite environments, enabling Summit to store materials at its sister sites and quickly manage the distribution of each customer order. In the words of Kelly Starr, Summit vice president for finance, when speaking about the coordination among all Summit sites, "We are better able to work together to meet our customers' needs. In our warehouse here in Texas, we can store materials, process orders, and place shipments for our sister company in New Hampshire, knowing that each order will be shipped in a timely fashion. It's this inventory management and visibility that helps Summit be a leader in its industry."

Sources: "ERP Solution Keeps Texas Manufacturing Plant Running Smoothly," *APICS—The Performance Advantage* (November/December 2004): 64; "Summit Industrial Products Achieves Stellar Customer Satisfaction Levels with Ross Systems," *Business Wire,* 9 June 2004, 5055; http://www.klsummit.com.

in this area, leaders may get only one chance at them. If a poor decision is made, operations may have to suffer the negative consequences for quite some time. Once the design decisions are behind them, leaders must shift their attention to short-term operating and control decisions. These decisions will continue to recur throughout the life of the organization, so leaders should strive for continual improvement in this decision-making focus.

If leaders are to make high-quality design and operating decisions, they will have to become thoroughly familiar with the nature of the specific decision issues in these broad areas while equipping themselves with the tools and techniques that can aid in making those decisions. In short, tomorrow's business leaders must

- Be prepared to make the tough decisions that commit to a long-term design for the operating system.
- Strive for perfection in making recurring short-term operating and control decisions.
- Focus on achieving continual improvement because these operating and control decisions are made repeatedly throughout the life of the organization.
- Be aware of the importance of productivity to organizational success and understand the ways in which productivity can be improved.
- Recognize the links between productivity and quality.
- Focus on improving the quality of the product or service provided.

The quality–productivity link is best illustrated by Deming's five-step chain reaction, which states that improved quality leads to lower labor and material costs, which lead to an improvement in productivity, which results in higher-quality and lower-cost items (and an associated increase in market share), which lead to increased profitability and an increase in the number of jobs. Emphasis on quality will enable tomorrow's business leaders to reap the benefits of this quality–productivity chain reaction.

SUMMARY

1. Manufacturing organizations produce a physical product that can be stored in inventory and transported to different locations. Productivity and quality of this physical output are usually easy to measure. Service organizations differ in that their capacity is time perishable, customers are typically active participants in the service process, and their locations must be close to the customers.

2. Operating systems can lie anywhere along a volume/variety continuum that extends from high volume and low variety on one extreme to low volume and high variety on the other extreme. Manufacturing organizations can be classified as repetitive manufacturing systems or continuous-flow systems at the high-volume and low-variety extreme and job-shop systems or project systems at the low-volume and high-variety extreme. Service organizations can be classified as standard service systems at the high-volume and low-variety extreme and custom-service systems at the low-volume and high-variety extreme.

3. Most operations management decisions can be classified as either long-term system design decisions or short-term operating and control decisions. Important long-term system design decisions include choice of a product or service, product or service design, system capacity, process selection, facility location, and facility layout. Important short-term operating and control decisions include aggregate planning, master production scheduling, inventory management, material requirements planning, just-in-time inventory management, and supply-chain management.

4. Productivity is a measure of the efficiency with which an organization converts inputs to outputs. It is measured as a ratio of system outputs to system inputs. Productivity can be improved through technology, people, or design.

5. From a consumer perspective, quality can be defined as the degree to which the product or service meets the expectations of the customer. From a producer perspective, quality can be defined as the degree to which the product or service conforms to design specifications.

6. When evaluating the quality of a physical product, consumers often base their judgments on their sensory perceptions of the product (its look, sound, feel, smell, or taste), its features, performance, reliability, serviceability, durability, and conformance to specifications. In the case of service encounters, consumers' assessments of quality might also include consideration of their feeling of trust and confidence in the service personnel, the responsiveness and empathy provided by the service personnel, the dependability and accuracy of the service performance, and various tangible factors associated with the service environment.

7. There are four categories of quality-related costs. Prevention costs are incurred to prevent defective output from occurring. Appraisal costs are incurred to assess the quality of the output. Internal-failure costs are associated with defective units that are detected before they reach the customers. External-failure costs are associated with defective units that are not detected before they reach the customers.

8. To achieve a successful total quality management program, concentration, commitment, and improvement should be focused on meeting customer expectations, attaining commitment to the philosophy and participation from every individual within the organization, and achieving coordination among all departments and functional specialties within the organization.

9. W. Edwards Deming proposed a five-step chain reaction in which excellence in quality eventually leads to improved productivity, increased market share, increased profitability, and more jobs. Joseph Juran developed a trilogy of quality planning, control, and improvement. Armand Feigenbaum is credited with originating the concept of total quality control, Kaoru Ishikawa introduced the idea of quality circles, and Phillip Crosby developed the philosophy that quality is free.

REVIEW QUESTIONS

1. (LEARNING OBJECTIVE 1) Discuss the differences between manufacturing and service organizations.
2. (LEARNING OBJECTIVE 2) Discuss the volume/variety continuum for categorizing operating systems and provide examples of both manufacturing and service organizations for each of the major categories.
3. (LEARNING OBJECTIVE 3) Identify the two major categories for classifying the decisions faced by the operations function and list the decision that operations managers face in each of these categories.
4. (LEARNING OBJECTIVE 4) List and briefly describe the three categories of tactics that might be used to enhance productivity.
5. (LEARNING OBJECTIVE 5) Provide a definition of quality from a consumer perspective and a definition from a producer perspective.
6. (LEARNING OBJECTIVE 6) List the different aspects of a product that might be judged in an attempt to assess its quality and list the different aspects of a service that might be judged in an attempt to assess its quality.
7. (LEARNING OBJECTIVE 7) Briefly describe the four categories of quality costs and provide an example of each.
8. (LEARNING OBJECTIVE 8) Briefly describe the areas of concentration and commitment for a program of total quality management.
9. (LEARNING OBJECTIVE 9) Describe the major contributions of several prominent quality philosophers.

DISCUSSION QUESTIONS

Improving Critical Thinking

1. JIT advocates a holistic view of workers that takes advantage of all their skills, knowledge, and experiences and gives the workers added duties and responsibilities. Discuss these added duties and responsibilities and compare this view with the traditional manufacturing view of workers. How do you feel these enhanced responsibilities might affect worker motivation and dedication to the job?
2. It has often been said that poor quality and poor productivity will detract from a company's competitiveness. Discuss the chain of events that you think would lead from poor quality and poor productivity to the eventual loss of competitiveness.

Enhancing Communication Skills

3. Imagine the way material would flow through a custom machine shop that fabricates metal parts for customers. Then imagine the way patients would flow through a walk-in emergency clinic. Discuss the similarities between the flows in these two systems. To enhance your oral communication skills, prepare a short (10–15-minute) presentation for the class in which you describe the flow similarities in these two systems.
4. Consider the aggregate planning problem in which the demand for a product or service is seasonal. List as many strategies as you can that could be used to cope with the fluctuating demand pattern. Try to identify strategies that you might use from an operations standpoint and try to envision strategies that you might use from a marketing standpoint (in an attempt to induce changes in the demand pattern). Finally, indicate which of your strategies might not be viable in a service organization. To enhance your written communication skills, prepare a short (one- to two-page) essay in which you describe the strategies in each category and explain which strategies probably aren't appropriate for service organizations.

Building Teamwork

5. The Crosby "quality is free" philosophy suggests that the only acceptable level of behavior is zero defects. Try to think of examples that might contradict this philosophy; that is, identify situations where the cost of totally eliminating

defects might be higher than the failure cost incurred with a moderate level of defects. To refine your teamwork skills, meet with a small group of students who have been given the same assignment. Compare and discuss your selections and then reach a consensus on the two best choices. Select a spokesperson to present your choices to the rest of the class.

6. Meet with a small group of students as directed by your instructor. To refine your teamwork skills, this group will operate as a quality circle. Discuss with one another some of the problems you have encountered in conjunction with your college education. These problems can cover any aspect of your education and may relate to interactions with administration, faculty, or support services (for example, the library, the computer center, and the like). Reach a consensus on the most important or urgent problem and then conduct a brainstorming session to develop potential solutions to this problem. Select a spokesperson to present your problem and potential solutions to the rest of the class.

Chapter

17

Information Technology and Control

CHAPTER OVERVIEW

Although an abundance of information is available to assist organizational decision makers, it is high-quality information that is a necessity for good decision making. High-quality information provides knowledge about past and current conditions in the organization and, if used carefully, can provide insights into possible future conditions. Ultimately, high-quality information provides a means of understanding the organization and its activities and a means for making decisions on how to control the organizational system. The process of acquiring, processing, maintaining, and distributing this information increasingly involves information systems and information technology (IT).

This chapter introduces the basic concepts of information as well as the information systems and technology that can be used to collect and distribute the information. We first examine information systems from an organizational perspective by focusing on worldwide changes that have altered the environment of business and have made it more reliant on information technology. We complete this organizational perspective by examining the basic intent and purpose of the different information systems that support workers at the different levels within an organization's hierarchy. We then shift our viewpoint to a technical perspective. Here we provide an introductory overview of the various components, or building blocks, of information systems. Some important points are made here on the distinction between data and information. This discussion also outlines the characteristics of good information. The technical overview next provides a description of the process used to develop high-quality information systems and an overview of some of the new information technologies. We conclude the chapter with a look at the impact of technology on the organization and some of the limitations of computer-based information systems.

LEARNING OBJECTIVES

When you have finished studying this chapter, you should be able to

1. Discuss the recent changes that have altered the environment of business and made it more reliant on information technology.
2. Describe the four levels of decision specialties and their functions within an organization's hierarchy.
3. Describe the general types of information systems that would support decision makers at the different levels within an organization's hierarchy.
4. Describe the various components in an information system.
5. Explain the differences between data and information and discuss the characteristics of useful information.
6. Identify the steps in the development of an information system.
7. Describe the emerging technologies that are changing the way we work.
8. Discuss the impact of information technology on the organization.
9. Explain the limitations of information technology.

Facing The Challenge

Torino, Italy: Lots to Do to Stage the Olympic Games

Can you imagine spending roughly 2 billion U.S. dollars on an assortment of projects for an event that will last exactly 17 days? Well, that's a task the city of Torino (referred to as Turin in most of the English-speaking world) began to embark upon when on June 19, 1999, the International Olympic Committee awarded the 2006 Olympic Winter Games to that Italian city. From February 10 through the 26 in 2006, approximately 2500 athletes, 10,000 journalists and media personnel, 650 judges and referees, 2500 coaches and national team officials, 2300 officials from 85 National Olympic Committees, 6000 guests of sponsors, and 1.5 million spectators would descend on this town in northwest Italy for the XXth Olympic Winter Games. To accommodate 84 medal events, venues had to be distributed among eight competition sites scattered within 50 miles of Torino.

In some cases, construction of new facilities was necessary; in others it was possible to renovate existing facilities to ensure adequate competition sites and adequate housing for athletes, officials, and media personnel. The Torino Organizing Committee (TOROC) identified a total of 65 projects that would have to be completed to ensure that competition venues would be first rate, accommodations would be available for the "Olympic family" (which needed over 20,000 rooms), and an efficient transport system would be in place to take spectators to the competition venues. These are the things an average spectator sees. Enrico Frascari, director of TOROC, observed that "large scale use of information technology tools is essential in order to guarantee the success of the Games." He further noted that we have all come to expect seeing push-off times, intermediate times, partial classifications, and final results on the television screen. But, very few realize that all this requires an articulated information system network. Systems would be needed for the timing and scoring of events, diffusing information to the press and broadcasters, delivering venue results, and dealing with athlete accreditation, transportation, accommodations, arrivals and departures, medical encounters, qualifications, and protocol. A local telecommunications network would need to be put into place, as would long-distance services, PBX systems, and mobile telephone systems. Computer and audio/video equipment would have to be assembled; an Internet website would have to be developed. The list of needed systems goes on and on. And by the way, the very nature of the event dictates that all this would be put into place in an area where weather conditions would be less than ideal—the alpine locations for many of the outdoor events had upwards of 40 inches of snow and temperatures that were constantly hovering around the freezing point. The challenges this project presented were indeed formidable. If these challenges were not met, an estimated 3 billion worldwide TV viewers would be quick to notice.

Sources: B. Shewchuk, "Kiev or Kyiv? Turin or Torino?" *CBC News Online*, 26 November 2004; http://www.olympic.org/; http://www.torino2006.org/comitato; http://www.torino2006.org/evento.

Introduction

On being selected to host the 2006 Winter Olympics, the Torino Organizing Committee (TOROC) faced a huge challenge not apparent to many observers. Most of us would recognize that TOROC was faced with major projects in the construction of the venues for athletic competition, the construction of housing to accommodate athletes and visitors, and the construction of a transportation infrastructure to move people between venues (after all, the venues were scattered among eight sites within a 50-mile radius of the host city). However, what was not readily apparent to most observers was the challenge of developing information systems to make the Olympics work. TOROC recognized early that it would take a coordinated effort among many IT partners to ensure that the Olympics ran smoothly. Event results had to be recorded, tabulated, and disseminated quickly. Athletes and spectators had to be transported smoothly between venues. Communications networks needed to be established. The list goes on and on. Fortunately, TOROC was prepared for this challenge. We see throughout this chapter and in "Meeting the Challenge" that TOROC took this challenge head-on with its coordinated partner approach.

The dizzying rate at which new technologies are evolving and existing technologies are expanding is having a dramatic impact on organizations and society. The interaction between people and computers is growing rapidly. At the organizational level, an ever-increasing number of activities are relying on these human–machine interactions. On a personal level, an ever-increasing number of activities in our daily lives are also relying on such interactions. Although once relegated exclusively to such recurring activities as payroll processing and inventory monitoring, computerized information systems within organizations are now routinely applied to complex managerial decisions such as the evaluation of mergers and acquisitions. Business executives almost universally recognize that information technology is vital to their companies' success. The fundamental purpose of information technology is to monitor, process, and disseminate information to assist in managing, controlling, and making decisions for the organization. Although information technology in the world of business is barely 40 years old, it holds great promise for improving and even changing the way we manage and run our organizations.

Organizational Foundations of Information Systems

If one were asked to characterize the current time in which we live and work, the response likely would be that we live in the "Information Age." Today, more than ever, businesses are using information to gain an advantage over their competitors. The fundamental principles (which we saw in detail in Chapter 16) are simple. Businesses and organizations must service their customers. To provide high-level service to customers, businesses and organizations must provide the customers what they want, when they want it, and where they want it. The marketing discipline often refers to these requirements as the customers' form, time, and location requirements. Organizations that can satisfy these requirements efficiently and cost effectively stand to gain a coveted competitive advantage. Having knowledge of the customer form, time, and place requirements will enhance the organization's ability to meet those requirements. That knowledge comes from having information. Gaining knowledge through information is the role of information technology in today's information-based businesses. Information technology can help provide the right people with the right information so that the best decisions possible can be made regarding the servicing of customers.

As this chapter unfolds, we will see that several types of information systems are prevalent in today's organizations. Computer applications that were once confined to simple transaction processing and monitoring are moving toward more sophisticated systems for analyzing problems and implementing solutions. As we transition into the 21st century, we are seeing an increasing trend toward providing managers with information systems that can assist them directly in their most important task: making decisions.[1] Before examining some of the different types of information systems available to management, let's first look at some of the recently occurring powerful, worldwide changes that have altered the face of business and made organizations much more reliant on information systems.

THE CHANGING BUSINESS ENVIRONMENT

LEARNING OBJECTIVE 1

Discuss the recent changes that have altered the environment of business and made it more reliant on information technology.

1 The world has seen several changes in the recent years that have altered the environment of business. In the last few decades of the 20th century, we saw the emergence and strengthening of the global economy, the transformation of many industrial economies to knowledge-based and information-based service economies, profound changes in the hierarchical structure of many organizations, and the emergence of technology-driven innovations like the virtual workplace, telecommuting, and electronic commerce. In one way or another, each of these phenomena is impacted by or reliant upon information technology.

Increasing Globalization

Look around you. It would be difficult to find an item within reach that can be classified as totally domestic. The pages in the book you are reading may well be printed on paper that originated in Canada. The pencil you use to jot down notes may have been manufactured in China, using wood that was harvested in South America. A rapidly growing percentage of the businesses in the advanced industrial economies rely more and more on imports and exports. Globalization is a reality that will continue to shape tomorrow's business. Globalization is a result of such factors as improved worldwide transportation and telecommunications, deregulation, the emergence of transnational firms (firms that produce and sell products and services in countries all over the world), and the organization of trade blocs (such as the World Trade Organization, the European Union, and the North American Free Trade Agreement).

Information is crucial to firms that operate on a global basis. Organizations whose operations extend to the far reaches of the globe face the challenges of communicating with distributors and suppliers (often on a 24-hour basis due to time differences) while servicing local and international reporting needs. Information systems can provide the communication and analytic power needed to meet these challenges, enabling organizations to become effective and competitive participants in these international markets.

Shifting Economies

In recent years, we have seen the relocation of many manufacturing industries to low-wage countries. At the same time, the economies of the United States, Germany, Japan, and other major industrial powers have shifted in the direction of knowledge-based and information-based service economies. In these types of economies, knowledge and information are key ingredients in the creation of wealth.

At the beginning of the 20th century, more than 70% of the United States workforce was engaged in farming or were blue-collar workers employed in manufacturing. Less than 20% of U.S. workers were white-collar employees in offices. The number of white-collar workers did not exceed farm workers, service workers, and blue-collar workers until the mid-1970s, when it grew to about 40% of the workforce. As we entered the 21st century, most people in the United States did not work on farms or in factories. Instead, most were involved in jobs that worked with, distributed, or created new knowledge and information. These jobs are found in such areas as banking, healthcare, education, sales, computer programming, insurance firms, and law firms. As the new millennium began, the number of white-collar workers employed in knowledge and information work accounted for almost 60% of the U.S. workforce and generated nearly 60% of the gross domestic product.[2]

We have seen the emergence of new kinds of knowledge-intense and information-intense organizations whose sole purpose is to produce, process, and distribute information. Even those industries that are engaged in the manufacture of traditional products have seen an intensification of knowledge utilization. Consider for the moment the automobile industry in which design and production now rely heavily on knowledge-intensive information technology. This industry has seen an increase in the number of computer specialists, engineers, designers, and computer-controlled robots and a concurrent reduction in the number of blue-collar production workers. Information and the technology that delivers it have become strategic assets for many firms. Information systems are needed to streamline the flow of information and knowledge in these organizations. When such systems are present, management will be better equipped to properly utilize the firm's knowledge and information resources.

KEY TERMS

Virtual workplace
A workplace with no walls and no boundaries; workers can work anytime, anywhere by linking to other people and information through technology.

Telecommuting
The practice of working at a remote site by using a computer linked to a central office or other employment location.

Flattening of Organizations

We saw in Chapter 1 that the traditional business organization is often viewed as a pyramid, narrow at the top and wide at the bottom. Between these extremes lies a hierarchical arrangement of workers and supervisors, each with different skills and responsibilities. Many large, bureaucratic organizations with this structure have proven to be inefficient, slow to change, and less competitive in recent years. Consequently, a trend has emerged toward reducing the number of employees and the number of levels in many organizational hierarchies. We've all heard of the phenomenon: corporate downsizing (often euphemistically referred to as "rightsizing"). In Chapter 1, we learned that the new organizational model could be lean and flexible. Because flatter organizations have fewer levels of management, lower-level employees tend to have greater decision-making authority.

These organizational-structural changes rely heavily on information technology. Information systems have been able to put more and better information into the hands of the workers so they can make decisions that had previously been made by managers. A flexible arrangement of teams and individuals working in task groups is often used to achieve coordination among employees as they work toward satisfying customer needs. A networked information system accessible to all workers helps facilitate this coordination.

Emerging Technology-Driven Innovations

In the restructured organization described above, IT innovations can result in teams and work groups that are no longer bound by departmental barriers. We have seen the emergence of a concept called the **virtual workplace.** Computerized information systems allow workers to be linked to other people and the information that they need at any time and from any place. There are no walls and no boundaries.[3] Communication can also be established by voice mail, fax, e-mail, and videoconferencing. In essence, people can work together or individually on their work-related tasks without "coming in to the office." The concept is called **telecommuting** and will be discussed in more depth later in this chapter.[4] In many cases, the success of the virtual workplace and telecommuting depends on the organization's ability to do business

© SPENCER GRANT/PHOTOEDIT
Telecommuting allows an organization's employees to work at home.

electronically. **Electronic commerce** (which will be examined in more detail later in the chapter) is the process of buying and selling goods and services electronically with computerized business transactions. Manual and paper-based procedures are replaced with electronic transmissions over information networks. The need for face-to-face interactions between the participants can be eliminated.[5] These and many other technology-driven innovations are changing the face of business today. More attention will be paid to these technical innovations later in this chapter.

Types of Information Systems

2 It would simplify our understanding of this topic if there were a single information system within organizations. Unfortunately, this is not the case. Most organizations develop a wide array of computerized information systems and attempt to maintain some level of integration among them. Despite the wide array of information systems, the basic structure of all of them is quite similar. An **information system** is a set of interrelated components that collects (or retrieves), processes, stores, and distributes information to support the activities of an organization. The simple structure (which will be expanded upon later in Figure 17.4) is that inputs are subjected to a transformation process that converts them into outputs. It is this basic transformation process that produces the information that organizations need for making decisions, controlling operations, analyzing problems, and creating new products or services. At the input point, raw data are collected from within the organization or from its external environment. At the processing point, the raw input is converted into a more meaningful form. This processing may entail classifying, arranging, or performing calculations on the input. At the output point, the converted information is transferred to the people who will use it or to the organizational activities for which it is needed.

No single system can satisfy all the information needs of an organization. In its preparation for the 2006 Olympic Winter Games, the TOROC IT team recognized this as it oversaw the development of several major information systems. Different system architectures are often needed in an organization because there are different specialties and interests at the various levels within that organization. Figure 17.1 illustrates the typical pyramid structure of decision specialties within an organization.[6] In this pyramid structure, we see an operational level at the base, composed of operational managers who must monitor and control the day-to-day operations of the organization. **Operational-level information systems** support operational managers by keeping track of the basic activities and transactions of the organization, such as the flow of materials, sales, receipts, and payroll activities. Above the operational level is the knowledge level, composed of knowledge workers and data workers. Generally speaking, knowledge workers create new information and knowledge. They normally hold university degrees and are typically members of a recognized profession such as scientists, engineers, doctors, and lawyers. Data workers usually have less formal education, may lack college degrees, and generally process rather than create information. Data workers consist primarily of secretaries, filing clerks, accountants, and other workers whose job it is to manipulate and disseminate information. **Knowledge-level**

LEARNING OBJECTIVE

2

Describe the four levels of decision specialties and their functions within an organization's hierarchy.

KEY TERMS

Electronic commerce (e-commerce)
The process of buying and selling goods and services electronically with computerized business transactions.

Information system
A set of interrelated components that collects (or retrieves), processes, stores, and distributes information to support the activities of an organization.

Operational-level information system
An information system that supports operational managers by keeping track of the basic activities and transactions of the organization.

Knowledge-level information system
An information system that helps knowledge workers to discover, organize, and integrate new knowledge into the business or helps data workers to control the flow of paperwork and information.

Figure 17.1 Decision Specialties within an Organizational Hierarchy

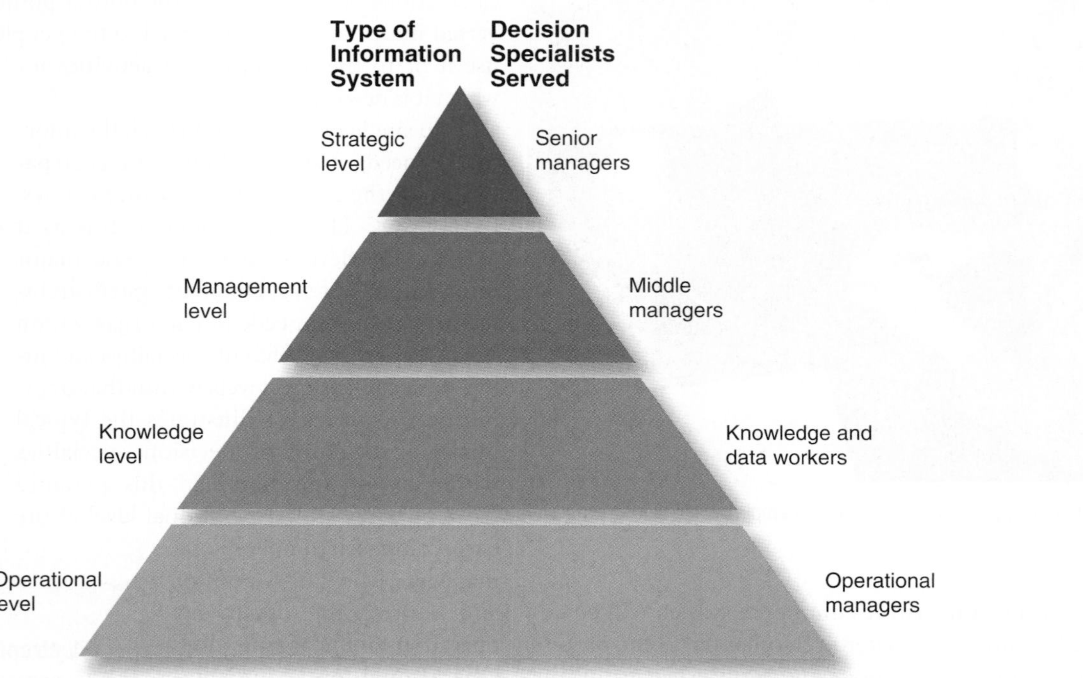

KEY TERMS

Management-level information system
An information system that assists in the administrative activities of middle managers and aids in decision making and the monitoring and controlling of operations.

Strategic-level information system
An information system that aids senior management as they address strategic issues and long-term decision making.

Transaction processing system (TPS)
An information system that supports workers at the operational level of the organization by recording daily business transactions and performing the routine, clerical record-keeping activities of the organization.

information systems help knowledge workers discover, organize, and integrate new knowledge into the business or help data workers control the flow of paperwork and information.

Directly above the knowledge level lies the management level, which is composed of middle managers who are responsible for monitoring and controlling the activities of the business and also responsible for making many routine and nonroutine decisions. **Management-level information systems** assist in the administrative activities of middle managers and aid in decision making and the monitoring and controlling of operations. Finally, at the top of the pyramid lies the strategic level, which is composed of senior-level managers. **Strategic-level information systems** aid senior management as they address strategic issues and long-term decision making.

Operational-Level Information Systems

3 **Transaction processing systems (TPSs)** are the information systems that support workers at the operational level of the organization. They record daily business transactions and generally perform the routine, clerical record-keeping activities of the organization. These activities can be varied; therefore, most organizations will have several types of TPSs. Table 17.1 displays the different categories of TPSs. We see from this table that a TPS can be classified as sales/marketing systems, manufacturing/production systems, finance/accounting systems, human resource systems, or industry-specific systems. An example in the manufacturing/production category would be an inventory TPS, which will record all additions to and withdrawals from inventory so that an accurate inventory count can be retrieved at any time. An example in the finance/accounting cate-

LEARNING OBJECTIVE 3

Describe the general types of information systems that would support decision makers at the different levels within an organization's hierarchy.

gory would be a payroll TPS, which will record time-clock information and couple that with employee pay rates to generate paychecks, withholding statements, and any other payroll reports of interest to management and government agencies. At the 2006 Winter Olympic Games, the Timing and Scoring System represented an industry-specific type of TPS. Here raw data on athletes' times and scores were recorded and assembled for further processing.

Table 17.1 Categories of Transaction Processing Systems

Types of TPSs
• Sales/Marketing Systems
• Manufacturing/Production Systems
• Finance/Accounting Systems
• Human Resource Systems
• Industry-Specific Systems

Knowledge-Level Information Systems

Knowledge management systems (KMSs) and **office automation systems (OASs)** are the information systems that support workers at the knowledge level of the organization. KMSs help knowledge workers create, organize, and make available important business knowledge wherever and whenever it is needed in an organization. This includes processes, procedures, patents, reference works, formulas, best practices, forecasts, and fixes.[7] OASs are IT applications designed to increase the productivity of data workers. Systems for office automation are typically computer-based information systems that assist the organization in the processing, storage, collection, and transmission of electronic documents and messages among individuals, work groups, and organizations. For example, OASs might handle and manage documents via word processing, desktop publishing, digital document imaging, and digital filing and communication might be handled via electronic mail, voice mail, and videoconferencing. The TOROC clerical staff used many such applications in the systems that provided updates to broadcasters and media representatives at the 2006 Olympic Winter Games. Figure 17.2 shows the full range of components in OASs. Many of these systems are important on their own merits, but when combined, they create an overall environment that supports all document and message processing.[8]

Management-Level Information Systems

Management information systems (MISs) and **decision support systems (DSSs)** are the information systems that support middle managers of the organization. MISs provide managers with periodic reports that summarize the organization's performance. MISs are designed primarily to summarize what has occurred and point people toward the existence of problems or opportunities. These systems are generally not flexible and have little analytical capability. Furthermore, MIS reports rarely tell someone why a problem exists or offer solutions. In many MISs, information is available on demand to facilitate monitoring exception conditions and to monitor moment-by-moment activities if desired. However, unanticipated reporting requirements and unusual operating conditions are not typically well supported by the systematic, structured nature of a traditional MIS.

DSSs are designed to help decision makers formulate high-quality decisions about ad hoc, semistructured problems—situations in which procedures can be only partially specified in advance. Because the situations occur infrequently, the organization does not have routine procedures for dealing with them. This lack of routine

Figure 17.2 Components of Office Automation Systems

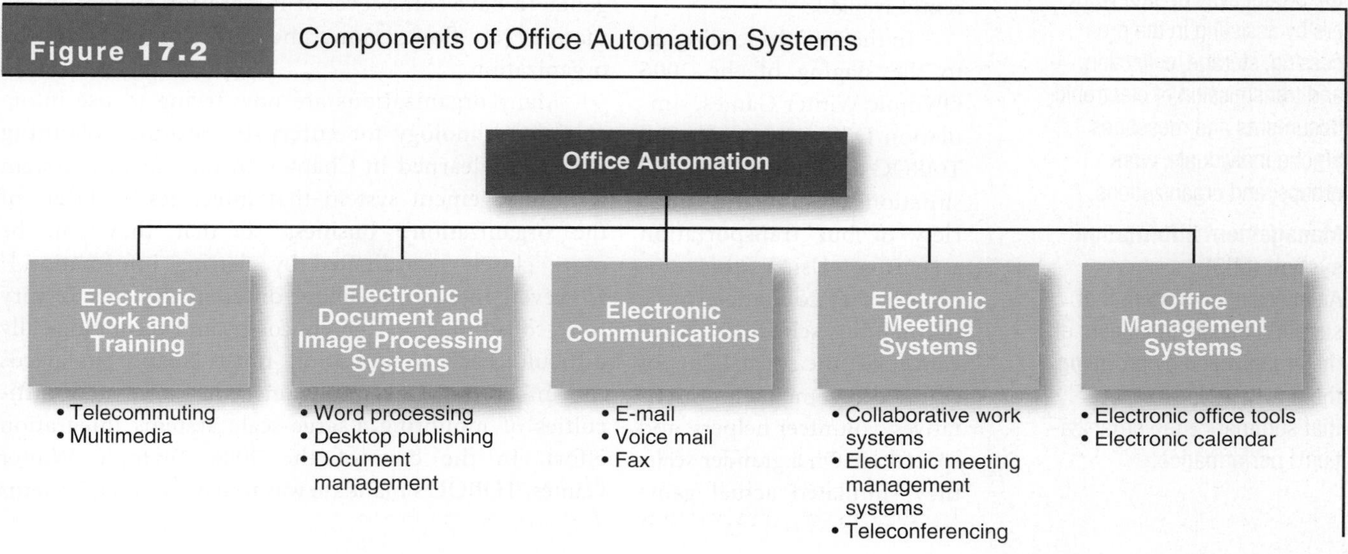

Table 17.2 Characteristics and Capabilities of Executive Support Systems

- Is tailored to individual user.
- Allows user to filter, expand, compress, and track critical information.
- Provides an up-to-date status report.
- Gives access to broad range of internal and external information and data.
- Is user-friendly and easily learned.
- Supports electronic communications.
- Provides a variety of data-analysis tools.
- Often includes tools for personal productivity.

means there are limited rules to guide decision behavior; therefore, outcomes are less predictable or obvious. DSSs have more analytical power than other systems and are built with a variety of models to analyze and condense data into a form that can be used by decision makers. A DSS allows users to combine their own insights and judgment with the analytical models and information from the database to examine alternative approaches and solutions to the situation. In particular, "what-if" analysis can be performed using the DSS. In other words, the decision maker can assess a variety of decision choices by modeling the expected outcomes of those decisions with the information that is currently available.

In the months leading up to the staging of the 2006 Olympic Winter Games, simulation DSS systems allowed TOROC to examine "what-if" situations by simulating a variety of bus transportation scenarios. Using this approach, they could determine optimal bus schedules in advance of the onslaught of competitors, media representatives, volunteer helpers, and spectators. On a grander scale, they simulated actual game time competitions and conditions in the final months of 2005 to see the entire system in action.

KEY TERMS

Knowledge management system (KMS)
An information system that supports workers at the knowledge level of the organization by helping create, organize, and make available important business knowledge wherever and whenever it is needed in an organization.

Office automation system (OAS)
An information technology application designed to increase the productivity of data workers by assisting in the processing, storage, collection, and transmission of electronic documents and messages among individuals, work groups, and organizations.

Management information system (MIS)
An information system that supports middle managers of the organization by providing them with periodic reports that summarize the organization's performance.

Strategic-Level Information Systems

Executive support systems (ESSs) are the information systems that support senior managers at the strategic level of the organization. An ESS is a highly interactive MIS combined with DSSs for helping senior managers identify and address problems and opportunities from a strategic perspective. ESSs are not designed to solve specific problems; instead, they provide a generalized computing and telecommunications capacity that can be applied to a changing array of unstructured decisions and problems. For example, ESSs can assist in answering such strategic questions as, What business should we be in? What acquisitions might help protect us from cyclical business swings? How can we raise cash for acquisitions? What are our competitors doing?[9] Table 17.2 summarizes many of the characteristics and capabilities of an ESS.[10]

INTEGRATION OF SYSTEMS

Figure 17.3 illustrates ways that different types of information systems in an organization might relate to one another. Logic would suggest value in upward transfer of information between the systems at the different levels within an organization. In addition, there are a few places where there may be some utility in having information flow to lower-level systems or horizontally between systems at the same level, as Figure 17.3 shows. A difficult question facing any organization is, How much can and should these systems be integrated? Unfortunately, the standard answer is that "there is no one right level of integration and centralization."[11] It would certainly be advantageous to have some level of integration so that information can flow among the different parts of the organization.

Many organizations are now trying to use information technology for **enterprise resource planning (ERP).** We learned in Chapter 16 that an ERP system is a management system that integrates all facets of the organization's business so that they can be more closely coordinated by sharing information.[12] However, integrating many different systems is very time-consuming, extremely costly, and technologically difficult. Each organization must balance its needs for integrating systems against the costs and difficulties of mounting a large-scale systems integration effort. In the case of the 2006 Olympic Winter Games, TOROC's mandate was to have all their systems

Figure 17.3 Interrelationships between Organizational Information Systems

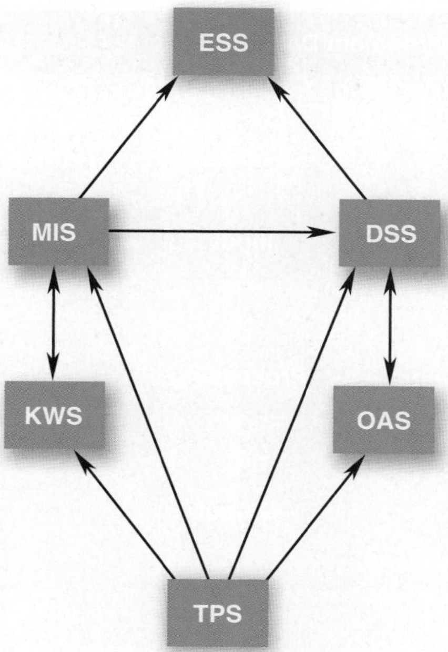

totally integrated. This was a costly venture, but the TOROC information technology budget of almost $400 million was prepared to support that level of integration.

Technical Foundations of Information Systems

4 The fundamental idea behind information systems is that they provide a systematic approach for collecting, manipulating, maintaining, and distributing information throughout an organization. Despite the common misconception, an information system does *not* require a computer. Systems of managing information existed long before computers. Even with the rapid increase in computers in recent years, many organizations still maintain systems for managing information that are not computerized. Nevertheless, computer systems and other advances in information technology are providing organizations and their workers with virtually unlimited opportunities to collect, explore, and manage information. These are opportunities that were not available a short time ago.

INFORMATION SYSTEM COMPONENTS

LEARNING OBJECTIVE 4

Describe the various components in an information system.

A general system consists of five basic components: inputs, the processing or transformation area, outputs, procedures for providing feedback to the system, and a means of controlling the system. As Figure 17.4 shows, a computer-based information system closely resembles the traditional general system model except that the former also includes hardware, software, and a database. The next few sections provide a summary glimpse of each of those components of a computer-based information system.

Input

The input portion of a computer-based information system consists of any type of computer input device that can provide data to the system. For example, the scanner cash registers, often called point-of-sale terminals, provide input to the information system. We

KEY TERMS

Decision support system (DSS)
An information system that supports middle managers of the organization by assisting them in the formulation of high-quality decisions about ad hoc, semi-structured problems.

Executive support system (ESS)
An information system that supports senior managers at the strategic level of the organization by helping them identify and address problems and opportunities from a strategic perspective.

Figure 17.4 General Information Systems

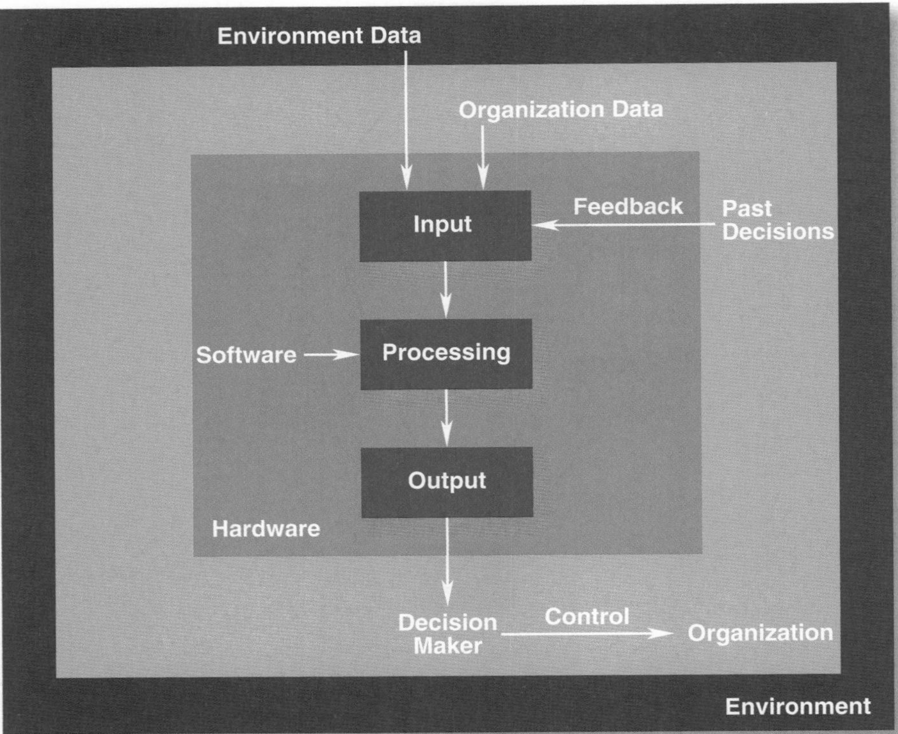

see these devices every day in grocery stores and department stores. Although not visible to most of us, similar technology is also used by the U.S. Postal Service and with good reason. One person can manually sort only about 500 pieces of mail per hour, but a scanning machine can sort 30,000 to 40,000 pieces in the same amount of time.[13] Sensors and monitoring equipment in a manufacturing or production facility can provide input as can the timing devices used at the Olympic Winter Games. Input can also come via telephone lines, satellite transmission, and archival data stored on computer disks and tapes. Input data can also be directly entered into the system by a user at a terminal or microcomputer through a bar code reader and now even through pen-based computer systems that recognize handwriting. A more recent innovation is the use of radio-frequency identification (RFID) chips, which are placed on materials moving through supply chains, to enter data into a computer information system. The "Leaders

KEY TERMS

Enterprise resource planning (ERP)
A management system that integrates all facets of the organization's business so that they can be more closely coordinated by sharing information.

It takes one postal worker an hour to sort 500 pieces of mail. A scanning machine can sort 30,000 to 40,000 pieces of mail in the same amount of time.

Leaders in Action

Beaver Street Fisheries: Poster Child for RFID

Ever heard of RFID? This is the technology that is destined to replace bar coding and bar code scanners in the delivery of products and materials through supply chains. RFID stands for radio-frequency identification. RFID chips can be encoded with assorted information about a box, carton, or pallet of items and then attached to that container. As the container moves through the various points in the supply chain, that encoded information can be interpreted by RFID readers, and transactions automatically entered into the information-processing systems of all participants in the supply chain. The type of information encoded on the RFID chip is virtually unlimited. Product identity, amount of product in the container, manufacturer, expiration date, and temperature requirements are just a few examples of the kind of information that might reside on the chip. Many large organizations are beginning to require that their suppliers adopt RFID technology. In mid-2003, Wal-Mart informed its top 100 suppliers that all boxes and pallets shipped to Wal-Mart distribution centers must be equipped with RFID chips by January 1, 2005. By January 1, 2006, all Wal-Mart suppliers were to have met this requirement.

This is where the story of Beaver Street Fisheries begins. Beaver Street is a small supplier of frozen seafood and meats. This Jacksonville, Florida, company is not one of the top 100 suppliers to Wal-Mart, and it has no illusions of ever reaching that stature of the global multinationals that make up the top tier of Wal-Mart suppliers. Although many suppliers grumbled about the Wal-Mart mandate, Howard Stockdale, chief information officer of Beaver Street Fisheries noted that "you can complain about the mandate all you want, or you can embrace it and figure out how to make it work." About 2 years ahead of schedule, Stockdale sought permission to be included in the top 100 timeline and communications network. Permission was granted, and Beaver Street was off and running.

Stockdale began by devising a three-phase implementation plan to bring RFID into company operations. In phase one, Beaver Street developed an EZ-RFID slap-and-ship station for its own use. This enabled the company to print, code, and ship RFID labels. This portable, stainless-steel station was designed to move throughout the company as needed. In phase two, the company moved on to find efficiencies in the process. One such example was the development of a corner wrap that is one long label instead of two, meeting the demand for labels on adjacent sides of a box. Another was the development of hybrid labels that meet both human readability and RFID demands. In addition, Beaver Street integrated RFID procedures into its inline production system. Phase Three involved the integration of the RFID environment into its warehouse management and ERP systems.

Stockdale aspired to have Beaver Street achieve the status as a model for small and midsized businesses integrating RFID into their relationships with Wal-Mart. In his words, "We wanted to be the poster child for small and medium-sized businesses." The company achieved that goal (more than a year ahead of schedule!) and then some. Beaver Street Fisheries has started its own integration company to help others looking to employ RFID technology.

Sources: M. Weil, "Angling to Be the Poster Child of RFID," *APICS Magazine* (March 2005): 53; M. Weil, "Life after the Deadline," *APICS Magazine* (March 2005): 51–53; J. Proctor, "The RFID Race," *APICS Magazine* (June 2005): 25–27; M. Weil, "RFID Confusion and Possibility," *APICS—The Performance Advantage* (February 2004): 51–54.

in Action" box describes how one small supplier to Wal-Mart was at the cutting edge in the use of this technology.

Processing

The processing component of an information system—what we typically think of as the "brains" of the computer—is called the central processing unit (CPU). When we think of a computer, we usually mean the CPU. This is the portion of the system where the raw data are manipulated and transformed into meaningful and useful information that can then be distributed to the relevant decision makers.

Output

The output portion of the system distributes the information that is the result of processing. Output can take a variety of forms including paper printouts; electronic data stored on computer disks, CDs, or magnetic tape; electronic transmissions through telephone systems or via satellite; displays on computer monitors; and sounds or synthetic voices made available through speakers for audio use. Output can even be made available through the control and manipulation of computer-controlled machinery. In the general systems model, the output process provides information to the decision makers, who can then manage and control the larger organizational system. Feedback occurs when the decision makers interpret the information to determine what should occur next. The decisions that result from the interpretation and use of the information are a means of controlling the system.

Hardware

The physical components of the information system—the computer, terminals, monitors, printers, and so on—are the hardware. The storage devices, such as hard drives, floppy disks, CDs, DVDs, zip disks, memory sticks, and magnetic tapes, are also hardware components. A wide variety of hardware components are available, and they can be combined as needed to meet organizational information-processing needs. A variety of hardware components were critical to the success of the TOROC information systems, and their numbers were prodigious. Among the computer hardware items needed to support the 2006 Olympic Winter Games were 5000 computers and workstations, 400 servers, and nearly 1000 printers.

LEARNING OBJECTIVE 5

Explain the differences between data and information and discuss the characteristics of useful information.

Software

The software portion of an information system consists of the various types of programs that are used to tell the hardware how to function. Software controls how the data are processed. Examples of software include word processing, spreadsheet, and accounting packages; other business applications; and even the computer games that we commonly play. Ultimately, software governs how the information is stored and distributed.

KEY TERMS

Database
The archived data and information used by an organization.

Database management system (DBMS)
Software that allows an organization to store data, manage them efficiently, and provide access to stored data.

Data
The raw facts or details that represent some type of transaction or activity within an organization.

Information
Data that have been processed or transformed into a meaningful and useful form.

Database

A **database** is the archived data and information that the organization uses. A database typically contains a vast amount of related information on company operations, financial records, employee data, customers, and so on. In the past, much of this information was maintained in separate files, which were often paper based. As a result, the data were often inconsistent and hard to locate and retrieve. Even early, computerized systems often maintained data in separate files, leading to similar problems. These problems can be overcome with modern database management systems. In the "At the Forefront" box on page 485 we can see a graphic example of a company that overcame a variety of problems in its production process by implementing a unified information system with a centralized database.

A database management system (DBMS) is the software that allows an organization to store data, manage them efficiently, and provide access to the stored data. When an application program needs a particular type of data, the DBMS acts as an interface between the program and the physical data files. The DBMS finds and retrieves the necessary item from the database and then delivers it to the application program. For example, a program that generates payroll for hourly workers would have the DBMS retrieve each worker's wage rate from the database and that information would be used to prepare paychecks. An extensive database was in place at the 2006 Olympic Winter Games to enable systems to compare competition results with results from prior Olympic and World Championship competitions, thereby generating Olympic and world-record information for broadcasters and media representatives.

INFORMATION VERSUS DATA

5 Several times we have used the terms *data* and *information* in our discussions. Often these words are used interchangeably. In the organizational context, however, a significant difference in meaning may exist. **Data** are the raw facts or details that represent some type of transaction or activity within an organization. For example, the sale of items at a grocery store or the sale of an automobile creates a great deal of data representing that event. Data are therefore the objective measurements of the characteristics of the objects or transactions that are occurring in an organization. In relation to the Olympic Winter Games described in "Facing the Challenge," you and I might view the elapsed time for a single run of a bobsled team as a piece of raw data.

Information is the result of the process of transforming data into a meaningful and useful form for a specific purpose. In other words, data go through a process whereby meaning is added, thus yielding information. In data processing, the data are aggregated and organized, manipulated through analysis, and placed in a proper context for evaluation and use by the end user. In a grocery store, the price and inventory amount for a particular product are examples of raw data. As sales occur, the inventory changes. The changes in inventory for this product, as well as the broader inventory changes that occur for all items available in the store, are examples of information. Each individual transaction is not that important in isolation; once combined, however, the transaction and sales figures provide useful information. Continuing with the Olympics example, when a bobsled team has finished all its runs, the individual times can be accumulated into a total time, which can be compared to the total times of all other teams. When these totals are sorted, we have information about medal winners.

Other aspects of the data–information relationship also add complexity to organizational decision making and control. Information for one person may be data to another. For example, as customers make their purchases at the grocery store, the store's inventory is altered. If the store has automated cash registers, it can update the inventory immediately. If the store does not have automated registers, the inventory will have to be updated and reconciled manually at the end of the day. The transaction data, generated by and representing details of customer purchases, are important to the store manager. From these raw data, the manager derives information on the store's sales, the success or failure of specific specials, and inventories that need to be restocked as well as other such operations details. The regional manager for this chain of stores, however, is not as interested in the details of specific transactions. Instead, the regional manager is concerned with broader issues of how the stores as a whole are doing. Is one store in the region performing better than another? Do different specials or different store layouts generate better sales? Because the regional manager is interested in several stores as a unit, rather than in one store or individual customers, the information needs are different. In summary, information for the store managers is data for the regional manager.

In a similar vein, as a viewer of the Olympic Winter Games, your bobsledding interest might be limited to knowing which team had the lowest cumulative time for all runs. One team's individual time on one of its runs might not hold particular interest to you—it is merely a piece of raw data that will eventually contribute to the team's total (the piece of information of interest to you). However, to members of that bobsled team, this individual run time could represent a valuable piece of information that influences their actions and preparations for a subsequent run (for example, strive for a longer, more vigorous push-off at start, crouch lower for improved aerodynamics, and achieve better team balance in sled to avoid wall touches, among others).

CHARACTERISTICS OF USEFUL INFORMATION

When data are processed into information, the information must be in a form that is useful to decision makers and management. Useful information has several fundamental characteristics. First, its quality must be very high. Second, it must be available to decision makers in a timely fashion. Finally, the information must be complete and relevant. As we examine those characteristics in more detail, refer to Figure 17.5 for an illustration of the relationship among these three primary characteristics of information.

Figure 17.5 Characteristics of Useful Information

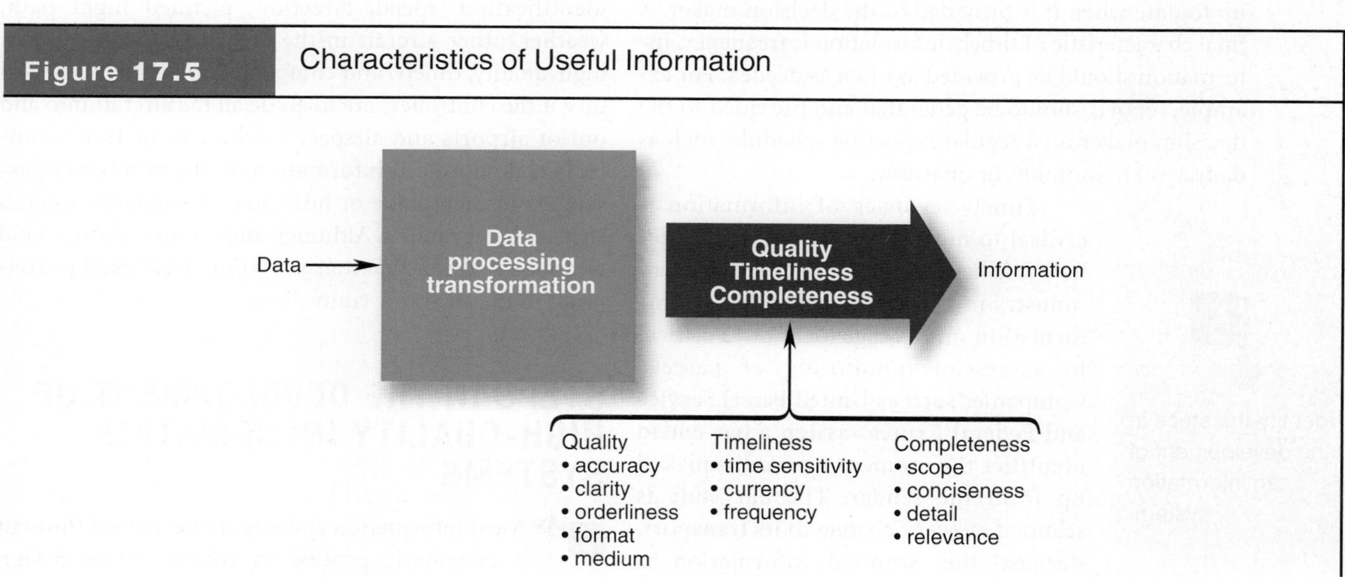

Quality

Quality is perhaps the single most important characteristic of information. Without high quality, the information is of little use. Quality consists of several attributes. One of these is accuracy. If the details do not accurately reflect current conditions, then any decision made using the information may be adversely affected. Clarity is another attribute of high-quality information. The meaning and intent of the information must be clear to the decision maker. Orderliness and format are two more attributes of high-quality information. If information is presented in an orderly arrangement and in a format that assists the decision maker, the decision-making process will be facilitated. Finally, the medium through which the information is communicated is important. For example, providing the decision maker with a massive computer printout would be an inappropriate medium if a short e-mail transmission summarizing exceptions from standards conveyed all the information needed by the decision maker. Consider the time results for the competitors in the Olympic downhill skiing competition. Judges, broadcasters, competitors, and spectators would all like to have precise time measurements, sorted from fastest to slowest, so that the winners can be quickly identified.

Timeliness

Most organizational decision making requires timely information because many of these decisions must be made on a frequent basis. Timely information has several ingredients. One of them is time sensitivity, which refers to the information being provided when it is needed—not too late and, by the same token, not too early. This way the decision maker has the information when it is needed to support making a decision. A second key ingredient of timely information is currency. Information should be up to date when it is provided to the decision maker. A final characteristic of timely information is frequency. Information should be provided as often as needed. For example, reports should be generated and provided to the decision maker on a regular reporting schedule, such as daily, weekly, monthly, or quarterly.

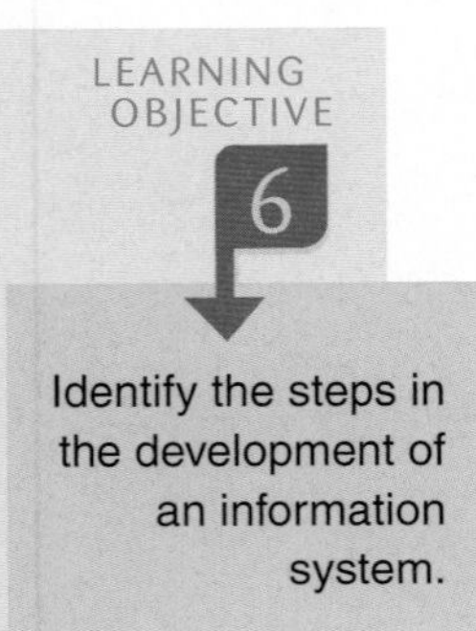

Identify the steps in the development of an information system.

Timely feedback of information is critical to most organizations. Consider how it is handled in the package-delivery industry in which timely feedback of information on package location is critical to successful monitoring of parcels. Companies such as United Parcel Service and Federal Express assign a bar-coded identifier the moment a parcel is picked up from the sender. The bar code is scanned at every change in its transport. Because this scanned information is communicated to a central computer, an up-to-date record of the status and location of each package is constantly maintained.[14] In the case of the Olympic Winter Games, information needs to be provided immediately on the completion of each performance in a particular competitive event.

Completeness

If information is to contribute to making good decisions, it must be complete. It would be impossible to determine the winner of a speed skating event if all competitors' times were not reported. Information completeness consists of several primary attributes. The scope of the information must be sufficient to allow the decision maker to make an accurate assessment of the situation and to arrive at a suitable decision. Where appropriate, decision makers should have access to not only current information but also past history and future plans for the organization. Conciseness and detail are two additional attributes of completeness. Information should be presented to the decision maker in as concise a form as possible, but there should be sufficient detail to provide the decision maker with enough depth and breadth for the current situation. Too much detail, however, can overwhelm the decision maker, causing information overload, distracting from the decision, or making it virtually impossible to focus on the important information. A final attribute of complete information is relevance. Only information that is relevant to the decision at hand needs to be provided. Once again, too much information may do more harm than good.

To illustrate these concepts, consider this example. Imagine the job of air traffic controllers who must manage a number of aircraft flying through a designated airspace. The relevant information consists of aircraft identification, speed, direction, planned flight path, weather, other aircraft in the area, and so on. Clearly, high-quality, timely, and complete information is necessary if the controllers are to guide all the aircraft into and out of airports and airspace safely. The air traffic controllers do not need information on the number of passengers in each plane or how many passengers ordered special dietary meals. Although such information is vital to others in the airline transportation network, it is irrelevant to the air traffic controllers.

STEPS IN THE DEVELOPMENT OF HIGH-QUALITY INFORMATION SYSTEMS

Most information systems are developed through a systematic process in which system design

Figure 17.6 Steps in the Design of Information Systems

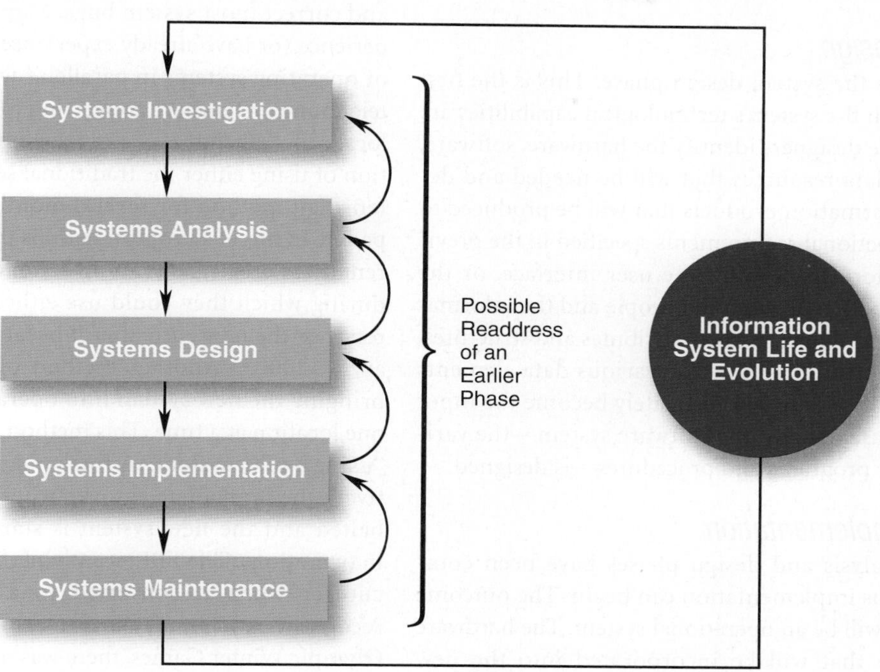

specialists and programmers collaborate with the end users. **End users** are all the people who will use and interact with the information system, particularly the decision makers in the organization. This process, depicted in Figure 17.6, is often called systems analysis and design.

Investigation

The initial phase in the development of an information system is systems investigation. During this phase, the organization determines whether a problem or opportunity exists that an information system can address. In addition, it performs a feasibility study to determine whether a new information system is attainable. Once an organization ascertains that an information system is both appropriate and feasible, it develops a plan for managing the project and obtaining management approval. Determining that an information system was appropriate was a "no-brainer" for TOROC. Without information systems, event results could not be quickly determined and disseminated to the world; events could not be smoothly scheduled and coordinated; and spectators, judges, media, event workers, and competitors could not be moved around efficiently. This list could go on and on.

Systems Analysis

Once the plan has been devised and management's approval has been obtained, the second phase, called systems analysis, begins. The purpose of this phase is to develop the functional requirements for the information system. In other words, this phase concentrates on what needs to be done to provide the desired information. This phase begins with an examination and analysis of the current systems in use, an assessment of the organizational environment, and a detailed assessment of the information needs of the end users. The organizational environment consists of both internal factors, such as the organization's structure, people, and activities, and external factors, such as industry considerations and the competition.

After studying these components, the system designers develop a set of functional requirements, or a detailed description of the necessary functional performance capabilities of the information system. These requirements focus on the type of information that decision makers need, the response times the users will need, and the format, frequency, and volume of information that should be produced and distributed. The TOROC IT team recognized in this phase of the process that there was a multitude of functional requirements, which resulted in several subprojects identified in "Meeting the

KEY TERMS

End user
The person who will use and interact with the information system, particularly the decision maker(s) in the organization.

Challenge." Each of these subprojects was responsible for bringing forward specific systems, infrastructure, and services for the 2006 Olympic Winter Games.

Systems Design

Phase three is the system design phase. This is the first phase in which the system's technological capabilities are addressed. The designers identify the hardware, software, people, and data resources that will be needed and describe the information products that will be produced to satisfy the functional requirements specified in the previous phase. More specifically, the user interface, or the point of interaction between the people and the information, is designed. The data, their attributes and structures, and the relationships among the various data elements are created. These data will ultimately become the input for the database. Finally, the software system—the various computer programs and procedures—is designed.

Systems Implementation

Once the analysis and design phases have been completed, systems implementation can begin. The outcome of this phase will be an operational system. The hardware and software that will be incorporated into the new information system are developed or acquired. As the system is put together, extensive testing is necessary to ensure that the system will meet all specified requirements. Any problems can be corrected more easily at this phase than at any later phase. The TOROC IT team performed extensive testing to ensure that the systems and venues would be ready for the 2006 Games. This testing was particularly critical to ensure that the systems were ready by February 10, 2006, the starting date of the Games. Unlike some commercial systems projects that can delay implementation when problems arise, TOROC could not push back their deployment date, and they could not "work out the bugs" during the early weeks of implementation. The systems, equipment, and applications had to work correctly on the first day of competition, and they needed to continue working correctly throughout the Games.

Documentation of the new system, or the relationships among the various pieces of hardware and software, should also be emphasized. The information system may not work perfectly, and the individuals who designed and developed it will not always be around to maintain it. Therefore, detailed and accurate descriptions of what was done, why it was done, and how it all works together are needed to assist in managing and maintaining the system.

Once the testing is completed, the system is ready for use, and the organization can switch from its old procedures to the new information system. This transition process may require operating both the new and the old system for a time in parallel. Operating the systems in parallel gives people time to learn and become comfortable with the new system and an opportunity to identify and correct most system bugs. Many of us will soon experience (or have already experienced) this phenomenon of operating systems in parallel if we live in areas whose telephone systems are converting to ten-digit dialing for local calls. When this occurs, customers are given the option of using either the traditional seven-digit or the new ten-digit method for several months. In a similar vein, people in the 11 European nations that merged their currencies to create a common currency had a few months during which they could use either their national currency or the new euro after it became available on January 1, 2002.[15] Another method of transition involves bringing the new system into operation on a trial basis, one location at a time. This method is often referred to as "using a pilot system." A final and more abrupt alternative is the immediate cutover, whereby the old system is halted and the new system is started with no overlap in operations. The FBI recently performed an immediate cutover when it converted to a digital fingerprint-recognition system.[16] Of course, in the case of the 2006 Olympic Winter Games, there was no "old" system, so the only option was to simply implement the new system for the control of the Games. All these transition methods have positive and negative aspects. The organization should carefully assess the benefits and potential costs before selecting an approach.[17]

Systems Maintenance

The final phase in the development of an information system is systems maintenance. Like an automobile, a house, or any piece of machinery, an information system will need to be maintained to keep it in top shape and to ensure that it will not encounter problems that could have been prevented. New hardware may be added to the system to address new needs or to replace older equipment. Software updates—new versions with added capabilities—often become available. Despite extensive testing, most systems will contain errors or bugs, some of them major. In addition, as the users work with the information system, they will discover additional things that need to be added, better ways of doing some things, and possibly areas that can be removed from the system. Although maintenance issues such as these are important for the information systems of most organizations, they were not particularly relevant to the TOROC systems. In less than a month after the start of the Games, the bulk of the systems would cease to be used.

One final aspect of any new information system is user training. The success of an information system depends on more than just thorough analysis, design, and implementation. Success also, and perhaps ultimately, depends on the people who will use the system on a daily basis to assist in making decisions. To facilitate their use of the system, the users need to be trained in what the system can and cannot do and in how to accomplish the needed tasks. Training may be for simple tasks such as data entry or for very complex monitoring and operations of critical machinery within the organization. In larger organizations, the training role is commonly fulfilled by an information center.[18] As cultural diversity increases in the workplace, the training process can become more difficult due to language barriers and communication problems. In addition, as with any type of change, the process can be slower and more tedious when cultural backgrounds cause resistance to change.

ATTRIBUTES OF SUCCESSFUL INFORMATION SYSTEMS

If the steps in the development of an information system have been successful, the resulting system will possess two important attributes. These attributes relate to the system's feasibility and the system's ability to meet the needs and expectations of its users.

Feasibility

An assessment of the information system's feasibility focuses on evaluating alternative systems that will best meet the needs of the organization and its workers. Feasibility has several dimensions.[19] **Organizational feasibility** examines how well the proposed system supports the strategic objectives of the organization as a whole. Systems that do not directly contribute to the short-range and long-range goals of the organization should be rejected. **Economic feasibility** focuses on whether the expected benefits will be able to cover the anticipated costs. A system whose benefits do not match or exceed the costs should not be approved unless mandated by other considerations, such as government regulations.

Technical feasibility addresses the hardware and software capabilities of the proposed system. Is the system, as proposed, capable of reliably providing the needed information to the appropriate people? Can the decision makers get the right kinds and amounts of data to support the desired decision making? And will the information be available when needed? The last type of feasibility is **operational feasibility,** which focuses on the willingness and ability of all concerned parties to operate, use, and support the information system as it is proposed and implemented. If any one of the relevant constituencies, such as management, employees, customers, or suppliers, does not support or use the system, it is doomed to failure. For example, if the system is too difficult for the employees to use successfully, they will reject it and use other approaches to do their work. Others who depend on the employees' use of the system for information will be unable to get what they need, leading to a further loss of opportunity.

Ability to Meet Needs of Diverse Users

A second attribute of successful system design is that the system should ultimately meet the needs and expectations of its users. Many reasons explain why an information system might fail to meet the needs and expectations of its users, and they can all doom the system to failure. The investigation, analysis, and design process is time-consuming and can be very costly. Time and cost often put pressure on designers to take shortcuts that may lead to an inferior or flawed system that does not meet users' needs. Failure to meet the users' needs can also occur because users have difficulty describing their information needs adequately. This problem is exacerbated when, as is often the case, the systems specialists have little or no previous experience with the types of problems currently under consideration. Therefore, if care is not taken, the resulting system may not live up to the expectations of the users. In addition, as the users become more familiar with the system, their demands and expectations may increase.[20] Fortunately, such problems did not befall the development of the information systems for the 2006 Olympic Winter Games. The TOROC IT team started early and cut no corners (its almost $400 million IT budget allowed that luxury!). Furthermore, the TOROC used Atos Origin as its major IT partner. Atos Origin is one of the world's leading IT and business services companies with extensive experience and proven skills in event management, having provided successful technology systems to prior Olympic Games, World Cup Soccer, and other major sporting events.

Another potential problem is that the users may resist the new system. This situation is especially common when workers are afraid that the new information technology may make some currently existing jobs unnecessary. Resistance is

KEY TERMS

Organizational feasibility How well the proposed information system supports the strategic objectives of the organization.

Economic feasibility Focuses on whether the expected benefits of an information system will be able to cover the anticipated costs.

Technical feasibility The capability of the hardware and software of the proposed information system to provide the decision makers in the organization with the needed information.

Operational feasibility The willingness and ability of all concerned parties to operate and support the information system as it is proposed and implemented.

Now Apply It

Checklist for Successful Information System Design

Frequently, management information systems fail to do the job they were supposed to do because they were inadequately designed or poorly thought out. Before, during, and after the design of the information system, system designers should see whether they could provide a positive response to the questions on the following checklist:

- Is the information provided to the decision maker accurate and clear?
- Is the information provided to the decision maker current?
- Is the information provided to the decision maker in a timely fashion?
- Is the information provided to the decision maker frequently enough?
- Is the information provided to the decision maker complete?
- Have all the steps in the information system development process been completely performed?
- Does the information system support the strategic objectives of the organization?
- Do the benefits of the information system outweigh the costs?
- Are the hardware and software capable of providing the needed information to the appropriate people?
- Does the information system meet the users' needs and expectations?

also more likely when the people who must work with the information systems are excluded from participating in its design and development. Not only does this lead to an incomplete analysis and design process, but it can also generate resentment toward the new system.[21] These potential pitfalls and problems underscore the importance of thoroughness in the analysis and design steps in the development of the information system. Because information systems frequently fail to do the job they were supposed to do, system designers can benefit from using the checklist in the "Now Apply It" box to improve their chances of achieving a successful information system design.

LEARNING OBJECTIVE 7

Describe the emerging technologies that are changing the way we work.

The New Technologies

7 In addition to the six organizational-level specific types of information systems described early in this chapter, organizations may take advantage of several other types of information technology. Many of these are used at all levels of the organization to assist in communication, information transmission, and decision making. An interesting phenomenon has accompanied the rapid advancements and new developments in information technology. An unprecedented number of entrepreneurial ventures by engineers, scientists, and technical experts is being spawned. We all know of the entrepreneurial success of Microsoft chairman Bill Gates, "The World's Richest Person," but there are many other success stories that aren't quite this prominent. Many engineers, scientists, and technical experts have been concocting their own schemes to grab that elusive brass ring. Consider John Pelka, a former Harris Corporation engineer, who cofounded Quali-Tool, a successful computer hardware manufacturer, or Don Schmaltz, former NASA engineer, and Peter Atwal, former Siemens engineer, who cofounded ISR Global Telecom, Inc. With a little help from a marketing consultant, they successfully launched their new telecommunications software package.[22]

Before you get the mistaken impression that such success stories are limited to the technical experts and computer "geeks" of the world, consider the story of Tricia Grady. This shrewd Tampa, Florida, homemaker realized that there is potential buyer for almost everything. She also understood that the local garage sales, flea markets, and estate sales were exposing their merchandise to a rather limited pool of potential customers. Grady started frequenting these events and began purchasing items that she thought might hold interest and appeal to someone beyond the local neighborhood. She then began placing those items on the eBay auction site, in effect putting the items up for sale to the entire world. Success was instantaneous and in some cases staggering. Percent returns on some items were in the quadruple-digit range.[23] On almost a daily basis, we learn of more success stories like these through the news media.

TELECOMMUNICATIONS AND NETWORKING

Telecommunications is the transmission of information in any form from one location to another using electronic or optical means. This definition applies to all types of telecommunications, including the ordinary telephone call. Generally, however, the term implies that computer systems and the people who use them can communicate from almost any location.

The global integration of organizations is rapidly increasing the need for international phone calls and information transmission. For example, the number of international calls made annually to or from the United States has increased almost tenfold during the past decade.[24] These numbers do not include the data and information that are transmitted through private communication systems.

The more advanced ideas in telecommunications typically concern the connection of multiple computer systems and multiple users in what is usually called a network. A **local-area network (LAN)** connects information systems and users within a small area such as a building, an office, or a manufacturing plant. The computer network on a college campus is usually a LAN or may contain several LANs.[25] The notion of a LAN is even beginning to filter down to the level of the home. Several corporations are selling or preparing to sell home networking systems. Among the early entrants into this area are Bell Atlantic, IBM, Lucent Technologies, and Motorola. Compaq was among the first computer companies to announce that it would sell computers equipped with home networking cards. The first home networking applications will connect PCs and printers, but eventually video surveillance cameras, heating and air conditioning systems, and other electrical devices within the home might be connected. Some experts even envision the day when a home network will keep an inventory of a refrigerator's contents and automatically order more items as necessary.[26]

One of the IT projects associated with the 2006 Olympic Winter Games was the establishment of a telecommunications network to carry voice, data, video, and audio traffic between all venues and offices during the Games. One of the TOROC IT partners developed a fiber optic–based LAN to accomplish this. Additional Olympic telecommunications capabilities were provided in the form of a long-distance system, a mobile telephone and pager system, and a broadband communications system. Some of the accompanying hardware for these systems included thousands of fiber miles of fiber-optic cable, 13,000 telephones, 14 telephone exchanges, and thousands of two-way radios.

A network that stretches over a wide geographic area, such as a city, a region, a country, and even the world, is typically called a **wide-area network (WAN).** For example, Wal-Mart, Sears, and CVS Pharmacy, as well as many other companies, can easily communicate with their stores through a WAN. Network arrangements are becoming

The 2006 Olympic Winter Games implemented a telecommunications network that carried voice, data, video, and audio traffic between all venues and offices during the Games. A related database system compared competition results with results from prior Olympic and World Championship competitions, which were provided to broadcasters and media representatives.

KEY TERMS

Telecommunication
The transmission of information in any form from one location to another using electronic or optical means.

Local-area network (LAN)
An information system that connects users in a small area such as a building, an office, or a manufacturing plant.

Wide-area network (WAN)
An information system that extends over a broad geographic area such as cities, regions, countries, or the world.

increasingly common in organizations that need to transmit and receive day-to-day information on business operations from their employees, customers, suppliers, and other organizations. In addition, each day more and more of us are adapting to that widest of WANs, the Internet's World Wide Web. Almost daily we seem to see new software that has been developed to facilitate the blending of desktop computing with the multimedia technology of the World Wide Web. This new technology will make it easier to find information, whether it is on the computer's hard drive or on the Internet. Furthermore, each piece of material created on a personal computer—whether an e-mail message, a memo to the boss, or any other type of document—could easily be embellished with images, audio, and video.[27]

A warning should accompany the rapid proliferation of information available on the Internet. There is no guarantee that the information to be found will always be accurate. With the explosion of electronic commerce (which will be discussed shortly), the distinction between objective information and advertising has become clouded. For example, most of us know of Dr. C. Everett Koop, who became one of America's most authoritative, recognizable, and trusted public figures during the 8 years he served as the U.S. Surgeon General. After leaving that position, Dr. Koop became the subject of intense criticism from medical ethicists who complained that his health information website (http://www.drkoop.com) had frequently blurred the line between its objective information and its advertising or promotional content.[28] The caveat here is "Let the user of the information beware!"

Some profound sociological implications should be considered as the World Wide Web gets more and more refined and as we see more and more people using the web for their own entertainment and enlightenment or to conduct business. The Internet might change the way that we live and work as a society. Because the Internet will allow some people to work almost anywhere, workers may move away from major cities and spread to rural areas. Furthermore, if these workers are parents, they will be able to monitor their children's activities and well-being at day-care centers. Many child-care facilities have already begun installing monitoring cameras whose images are accessible via the Internet to parents possessing the proper password. Even the concept of communities may change as geographically dispersed people gather and interact online.

KEY TERMS

Electronic data interchange (EDI)
Electronic transmission of transaction data using telecommunications.

Electronic funds transfer (EFT)
Electronic manipulation of financial transactions.

Many activities are now possible due to the ease of access and relatively low cost of telecommunications. **Electronic data interchange (EDI)** is the electronic transmission of transaction data using telecommunications. These data can include sales invoices, purchase orders, shipping notices, and so on. EDI provides an almost immediate transmission of the data and allows for a significant savings in printing, mailing, and labor costs as well as in time. In addition, because the orders and information are transferred electronically, fewer people have to handle the data, thereby reducing the chances for data-entry and mishandling errors. Some companies have reported decreases of 25 to 50% in the amount of time it takes to receive and fill customer orders since adopting EDI. RCA has estimated that the cost to fill an order will drop from $50 to around $4 due to labor-saving use of EDI. General Motors has required all of its suppliers to use EDI, leading to estimated savings of about $200 per automobile produced. Likewise, the U.S. Department of Defense is moving toward a similar requirement for its suppliers.[29] Boeing Aircraft Company relies on telecommunications to support its new global approach to building airplanes. The new Boeing 787 Dreamliner will have most of its structural and internal components outsourced to production plants in many countries around the world. The pieces will then be shipped to Seattle where they will be assembled within 3 days in Boeing's main assembly plant. In an endeavor like this, precise engineering specifications must be transmitted to all participants if the parts are to fit to the required tolerances of thousandths of an inch.[30] Campbell Soup Company has put EDI to good use in coordinating orders placed by its customers. Implementing some of these new advances resulted in multimillion-dollar annual savings to Campbell, and in some cases a 50% increase in profit for some of its retail customers.[31]

EDI is not just for giant manufacturers and government, however. For example, InterDesign, of Solon, Ohio, makes plastic clocks, refrigerator magnets, soap dishes, and the like. Under pressure from a large retailer, the company adopted EDI. Now over half of the orders to InterDesign arrive via modems connected to its computer system instead of by mail or through a phone call. Virtually all order-entry and shipping errors have been eliminated. Now employees who used to staff phones taking orders spend their time collecting valuable information that the company couldn't afford to collect before. Sales are tracked by product, color, customer, region, and so on.[32] According to some predictions, early in this new millennium as many as one half of all business documents will be transmitted by EDI.

The banking and retail industries are moving increasingly toward an environment of **electronic funds transfer (EFT)**, where all financial transactions are done

At the Forefront

Remy International: Centralized Database Key to Success

Through its operations in North America, South America, Europe, and Asia, Remy International (familiar to many readers by its former name, DelcoRemy) manufactures electrical, power train, and drive train components for automobiles, light trucks, heavy-duty trucks, and other heavy-duty vehicles. Remy starter motors, alternators, engines, torque converters, and fuel systems are shipped to approximately 3500 customers worldwide. Remy relies on 500 worldwide suppliers for the parts and components used in its manufacturing processes.

In recent years, Remy had experienced problems with slowdowns in work processes because of bottlenecks. Requests for quotes (RFQ) and engineering change orders (ECO) required information that was often difficult to retrieve and often inaccurate. The slowdowns were inhibiting revenue growth and customer satisfaction. RFQ and ECO projects became sidetracked when workers and managers would have to spend time searching for a multitude of supporting documents stored at different locations in different systems. Often these critical documents would reside on an individual engineer's computer. With more than 100,000 part drawings on file, searching for the right document added significant amounts of time and cost to the process.

Rick Huibregtse, vice president of Engineering at Remy, noted that "mistakes [were] made because documents with incorrect revisions were sometimes used. Workers [who were] expected to complete final assembly operations would find that the wrong parts had been ordered, or that components didn't fit because an engineering change hadn't been coordinated properly." Huibregtse realized that much of the documentation and related information were stored in separate databases. Moreover, because each database had its own format and each stored only particular types of information, there was limited communication capability among them, and no consistent means of working together collaboratively.

Remy corrected this defect by implementing a unified information system called Product Sight Lifecycle Environment (PSLE). PSLE allows each worker to access a central database and display information relevant to each particular job. Workers can exchange real-time status information, while managers can see progress and bottlenecks, enabling them to make well-informed decisions. This shared information system has sped up work flow by synchronizing data and enabling workers to get what they need, when they need it. Remy's unified information system has yielded many beneficial results. ECOs are now completed in less than half the time they formerly took. Increased efficiency has resulted from the time and cost savings with the new system. Mistakes are down, quality is up, and the company is now much more responsive to customers.

Sources: "Share and Share Alike," *APICS Magazine,* (April 2005): 43–44; "Delco Remy Takes on New Name," *Grand Rapids Press,* 27 July 2004, C2; http://www.remyinc.com.

electronically. Many of us already depend on EFT for our banking and financial transactions. The automatic teller machine is one example of EFT. Being able to pay bills over the phone is another example. Furthermore, many of the point-of-sale terminals in retail stores depend on EFT as checks are approved and debit or credit cards are swiped.

Many organizations around the world are discovering that they can benefit from telecommunications. In its quest to help small and medium-sized businesses in developing countries become involved in world trade, the United Nations has established a global electronic trading network. It is the United Nations' hope that the network will stimulate growth in international trade by helping those target businesses locate information that would help them enter global markets.[33]

Telecommuting, another facet of telecommunications described earlier in this chapter, is a relatively new way to work. When workers telecommute, they operate from a remote location, such as a branch office or their home, and communicate with the office via telecommunications. Many jobs do not require an individual to be at the main office all of the time. In fact, some people find that working from a remote site, such as their home, provides some big benefits.

American Express Travel Services has been experimenting with telecommuting for some of its employees. These jobs are oriented around providing customer service and information by telephone. Many employees located in the Houston area had a 60- to 90-minute commute to and from work each day. By telecommuting from home, the workers found they had more time to spend with their families and were not stressed by the chore of driving in heavy traffic or bad weather. American Express has also seen some significant benefits. Thus far, workers have been able to handle 26% more calls with no reduction in the quality of service. In addition, the rent that would normally have been spent for office space for these employees could be saved. In New York, American Express estimates that it can save about $4400 annually for every travel counselor who telecommutes. In addition, with advances in technology, managers can still monitor the employees' work performance in responding to customer phone calls.[34] In a similar vein, the entire reservation system for JetBlue Airlines consists of 400 reservation agents working from their homes in the Salt Lake City area. In fact, by early 2004, 23.5 million employees of U.S. companies worked from their homes. This amounted to 16% of the American labor force![35]

In an effort to help reduce pollution caused by automobiles, California became one of the first states to recognize the benefits of telecommuting when it instituted legislation that encouraged businesses to allow workers to telecommute.[36] In the last decade of the 20th century, an earthquake near Los Angeles did so much damage to the interstate highway system in the area that commuting times were significantly lengthened, sometimes by as much as 2 or 3 hours each way.[37] Telecommuting offers a way for companies to alleviate this type of difficulty. More recently, the events of the 9/11 attack on America have caused a dramatic surge in the interest in telecommuting. Concerns that the workplace could be a target of anthrax-tainted mail or another terrorist attack has many workers staying away and using technology to get the job done.[38]

Another advance that has grown out of telecommunications is **electronic mail (e-mail)** networks and bulletin board systems. E-mail systems, which are often a part of office automation systems (discussed later), are changing the way we work and communicate. You can think of e-mail as being like the postal system except that the messages and information are transmitted electronically through computer networks instead of being sent through the mail. Many Internet access companies offer e-mail services. Among the largest and most recognizable of these are America Online, Microsoft's MSN, AT&T Corporation's WorldNet, NetZero, and EarthLink. Communication speeds are very fast. Whenever the people receiving messages are ready, they can read their mail.

KEY TERMS

Electronic mail (e-mail) A computer-based system that allows individuals to exchange and store messages through computerized text-processing and communication networks.

ELECTRONIC COMMERCE

In recent years Internet technology has served as a catalyst for change in the ways organizations are conducting business. Thousands of organizations can be linked together into a single network via the Internet. Through such a linkage, prospective buyers and sellers can exchange information, products, services, and payments. In effect, they are acting as an electronic marketplace. Because the Internet knows no national boundaries and pays attention to no clock, this electronic marketplace is indeed global in scope, and it is open 24 hours per day. This linkage forms the basis for electronic commerce (e-commerce), which was described earlier as the process of buying and selling goods and services electronically by means of computerized business transactions. The Internet has emerged as the dominant technology for conducting e-commerce. On almost a daily basis, we read in the newspaper of some new organization that will sell its product or service online. Computers, books, cars, stereos, appliances, tools, airline tickets, flowers, and countless other items can be obtained in this fashion.[39] In mid-2005, U.S. Census Bureau data revealed that e-commerce is accounting for a steadily increasing percentage of U.S. retail sales. As a percent of sales, e-commerce has risen from less than 1% in 2000 to well over 2% by 2005. These percentages may not sound like much, but the total revenue generated is substantial. Since the start of the new millennium, e-commerce retail sales increased from slightly less than $27 billion in 2000 to almost $70 billion in 2004. Projections indicated that this figure would rise to over $85 billion in 2005.[40]

E-commerce has several advantages. By using electronic ordering rather than the traditional manual and paper-based procedures, ordering, delivery, and payment can be accelerated. Often companies can achieve higher profits and at the same time charge lower prices due to the removal of intermediate steps in the distribution and sales process. That is the approach used by such companies as the Dell Computer Corporation and Gateway Computers. Companies can face risks associated with offering their products online. Traditional retail outlets for their products often view such a process as taking away some of their business. This feeling caused Dell rivals IBM, Compaq, and Hewlett-Packard to initially move tentatively in this arena in fear of alienating the wholesalers and retailers who have helped make them among the world's top computer makers.[41] Such potential alienation of wholesalers and retailers is evidenced in a letter Home Depot recently sent to its suppliers warning them to consider the consequences of selling online. The letter stated that "We, too, have the right to be selective in regard to vendors we select, and we trust that you can understand that a company may be hesitant to do business with its competitors."[42] Such a feeling has caused many manufacturers to think twice before offending retailers that sell their products or quickly reverse their decision, as was the case with Gibson Musical Instruments of Nashville. When the company decided to offer its guitars through the Internet at a 10% discount, Gibson dealers were irate. Fearing that this new practice would jeopardize relations with its dealers, Gibson discontinued its web sales of guitars within a month and changed its web strategy. The company put its parts catalog on the web and now uses the web only for the sale of strings, accessories, and repair parts.[43]

Another hot area that has evolved recently in electronic commerce is the online auction forum. Using e-mail and other interactive features of the Internet, people can make online bids for any number of items that someone else wants to sell. The system receives bids for items entered on the Internet, evaluates the bids, and notifies the highest bidder. One of the most visible success stories in this area is that of eBay. The company was founded in 1995 to sell Pez dispensers, but it has quickly evolved well beyond that under the leadership of CEO Meg Whitman, who has risen to the status of the world's richest female CEO, with a net worth well over $1 billion. In 2004 eBay generated a net income of almost $800 million from revenue of $3.3 billion. eBay's website receives roughly 2 million unique visitors per day, providing the company with the status of one of the top ten businesses on the Internet. The website sees a constant daily flurry of deals for Beanie Babies, Star Wars toys, antiques, collectibles, and a wide variety of other items.[44]

As business transactions are made via the Internet, remuneration is typically made by means of an electronic payment. Such technologies as EFT, credit cards, smart cards, debit cards, and new Internet-based payment systems can be used to pay for products and services. Security of electronic communications is a major control issue for companies that engage in e-commerce. All information being transmitted between buyers and sellers must be kept confidential and secure as it is being transmitted electronically. This includes information related to the details of the order as well as information related to the mechanism for payment. Most organizations rely on sophisticated encryption procedures to protect sensitive information as it is transmitted over networks. **Encryption** refers to the coding and scrambling of information to make it unintelligible to unauthorized viewers. Encryption is especially useful to protect transmission of payment data such as credit card information. Several methods of encryption exist, each with its own proprietary methodology. These encryption methodologies will continue to change and new ones will evolve as businesses strive to keep confidential e-commerce information out of sight of those not authorized to see it.

ARTIFICIAL INTELLIGENCE

Artificial intelligence (AI) has the goal of developing computers and computer systems that can behave intelligently. Work in this area is derived from research in a variety of disciplines including computer science, psychology, linguistics, mathematics, and engineering. Probably the most widely known application of artificial intelligence is in computer programs that play chess, some at or near the level of a grand master. But AI applications go well beyond this. Two primary areas of research that have had some success in recent years are expert systems and robotics.

Expert Systems

An **expert system** is a knowledge-based information system. In other words, it is a computer-based system that contains and can use knowledge about a specific, relatively narrow, complex application. The knowledge that the expert system contains and the way it is programmed to use this knowledge allow it to behave as an expert consultant to end users.

Fundamentally, an expert system is a type of software in which expert knowledge has been programmed to assist decision makers in a complex decision environment. The knowledge in an expert system has been painstakingly acquired from one or more experts in the knowledge domain of interest. Knowledge engineers, the expert system specialists, take this knowledge and carefully construct a knowledge base and the software that can use it. Users can then tap into this knowledge through the expert system and use it to provide expertise in difficult decision situations. Texas Instruments has developed an expert system called IEFCARES (Information Engineering Facility Customer Response Expert System) to assist in providing service and support for their CASE product called IEF. Like many other credit companies, both ITT Commercial Finance Corporation and American Express have expert systems to assist in managing and monitoring credit requests and approvals. Expert systems are also commonly used for tasks such as loan portfolio analysis, diagnostic troubleshooting, design and layout configuration, and process monitoring and control.[45]

KEY TERMS

Encryption
The coding and scrambling of sensitive information transmitted over networks to make it unintelligible to unauthorized viewers.

Artificial intelligence (AI)
A process in which computers and computer systems behave intelligently.

Expert system
A computer-based system that contains and can use knowledge about a specific, relatively narrow, complex application.

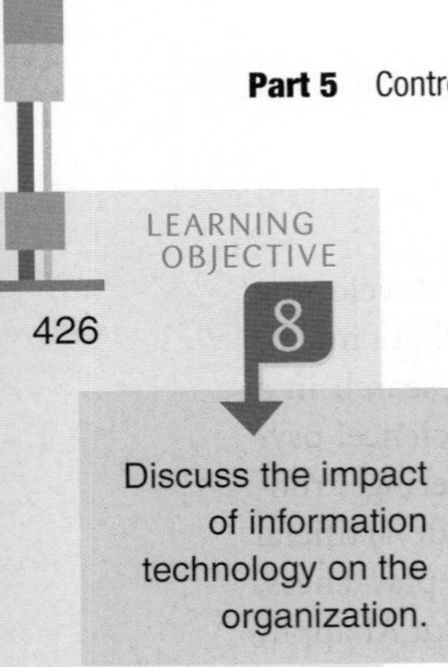

Discuss the impact of information technology on the organization.

Robotics

The technology of building and using machines with humanlike characteristics, such as dexterity, movement, vision, and strength, is called **robotics.** A robot contains computer intelligence and uses research knowledge from artificial intelligence, engineering, and physiology. Robots are often called "steel-collar" workers because they are frequently used to perform manufacturing tasks that were previously done by blue-collar workers. When used in this fashion, they are programmed to perform specific, repetitive tasks in exactly the same way with each repetition. These automated machines offer significant benefits. They can be programmed to do very complex tasks that require a variety of movements and strength over and over again with precision. Robots don't have some of the weaknesses of human workers, such as illness, fatigue, and absenteeism. In addition, robots can be valuable in hazardous work areas and with tasks that are dangerous for humans. For example, robots have been developed that can distance humans from dangerous situations such as assisting police bomb-squads in the removal of hazardous materials or aiding in the dismantling of damaged nuclear power plants. They can also be valuable in going where humans simply cannot go. Japanese electronics companies have developed micromachines smaller than a coin. They are capable of crawling into the tiniest gaps around bundles of pipes, performing inspections, and even making repairs at electric and nuclear power plants while the plants keep running.[46] And the latest from the medical field is Pillcam ESO, a pill-sized gadget that replaces the more invasive and uncomfortable endoscope for diagnosing esophageal disorders. Patients merely swallow the Pillcam and its two cameras will transmit seven photos per second wirelessly to a nearby storage device.[47] NASA continues to be a leader in the use of robotics with its unmanned space explorers that attempt to map foreign worlds. One of the latest of these ventures is the mission to perform geological surveys on the surface of Mars. Rovers *Spirit* and *Opportunity* were still going strong after a year of Martian exploration.[48] NASA has funded the Robotics Engineering Consortium, which is devoted to turning robotic ideas into practical machines. Some of its successful developments thus far include an excavator for Caterpillar, an off-road vehicle for Boeing, and a forklift system for Ford. New Holland North America provides an illustration of just how sophisticated these robots can be. Its computer-driven harvester uses the satellite-based global positioning system (GPS), wheel sensors, and a video camera to "see" a crop line so it can harvest a field without a driver or a remote operator.[49]

KEY TERMS

Robotics
The technology of building and using machines with humanlike characteristics such as dexterity, movement, vision, and strength.

Impact of Information Technology on Dynamic Organizations

8 An organization is a sociotechnical system that consists of people and their tasks, as well as the organization's culture, structure, and environment. All of these things are affected by and will affect technology. Information technology will have a profound impact on management efficiency, social relationships, and organizational structure.

Information systems must produce useful and relevant information for management. Many of the areas that have been computerized have not yet resulted in the desired or expected gains. In part, this is because many organizations have used these new systems simply to replace traditional business practices instead of reassessing and redesigning the organization and the decision-making process to take advantage of the new technology's capabilities. Viewed another way, the primary, or first-order, effect of initial investments in information technology was simply to improve efficiency. Organizations still have a lot of room for improving the design and management of their information systems. Furthermore, we are discovering that the second-order effects, which are unintended and impossible to predict, are often more interesting and provide greater opportunities than the first-order effects.[50] These unintended and unanticipated effects lead to a second area of impact.

If only isolated individuals used information systems, the systems would have minimal impact on the social relationships among people. Currently, however, the very essence of the use of information technology within organizations is to enhance communication between people. Therefore, whenever information systems are used in this manner, they have a social component and potential social effects.

For example, what are the new technologies doing to power relationships within the organization? Does the technology change the dimensions and directions of determining priorities? If the use of the technology has negative consequences, who is accountable for the results? Furthermore, the expanding use of and dependence on information technology have created an interesting paradox. Information technology, like globalization, can extend an organization, making it less personal and less social. However, the effect of the technology often rewards intimacy.[51] These social implications suggest other, broader effects of information technology.

In the early years of computer-based information systems, the technology was so limited that it was difficult to computerize even one division of the organization. As a result, data-processing services tended to be decentralized. During the 1960s and 1970s, computer systems became much more powerful, and large systems were often able to handle many of the computing needs for the whole organization. This led to greater centralization of control over computer resources. The advent of the microcomputer in the late 1970s and the 1980s led to increased demands for computing access and power, creating a great deal of confusion and conflict within organizations as they struggled to manage the rapid proliferation of varieties of hardware and software.

Neither centralization nor decentralization alone is the appropriate response. Instead, organizations should examine their specific computing needs and try to align their information technology to those needs. Some aspects of information processing in an organization may require greater centralization of computing resources, while others may lend themselves to greater decentralization.

Many note that information technology can help managers control the interdependencies of their organizations. In particular, as the competitive environment has become more complex, so have the information needs of the decision makers. Information technology can help managers respond to this competitive environment. For example, unlike the situation during the Industrial Revolution, when the goal was to separate tasks and then make them simple and routine, current trends in information technology and data communications are to flatten the organization, fuse departments, create cross-functional teams, and increase and improve communications among employees, suppliers, and customers.[52] The structure of the organization can then be adjusted to take advantage of the varying needs. Despite its great promise, information technology also has limitations. We turn to them in the next section.

Limitations of Computer-Based Information Systems

9 As we have seen, although investments in computer-based information systems have been substantial, the improvements that can be traced directly to the investment in technology have in some instances been minimal. Several factors may explain this low return on investments in technology.

First, the technology has been changing so rapidly in the last 10 years that organizations have had difficulty keeping up. In 1981 IBM produced its first microcomputer, marking for many the beginning of the rapid proliferation of computers in organizations and homes. Apple introduced its Macintosh system in 1984 as an easier-to-use alternative to the DOS (disk operating system) environment of IBM and IBM-compatible machines. In 1986 the Intel 386 microchip became the norm for microcomputer systems. Five years later, the Intel 486 was released, and a few years later the Pentium microchip began to show up in microcomputers. The Pentium II chip soon replaced the Pentium and thus became the standard for processing speed. Then, by 1999 the Pentium III had surfaced, establishing a new standard for speed.[53] The new millennium saw that speed eclipsed by the Pentium 4. When it was introduced in 2000, it boasted a speed 50% greater than the Pentium III.[54] In fact, Gordon Moore, cofounder of Intel, predicted in 1965 that the number of transistors on a computer chip would double about every 2 years. That prophecy has pretty much held true because the top chips in 2005 contained more than 600 million transistors.[55] By the time you read this, advances could be well beyond this new standard. Where will this dizzying escalation end? Looming on the distant horizon but still in the research stage are quantum computers. Instead of the traditional architecture of transistors mounted on microprocessor chips, these computers will do calculations using the spin of atoms. It is estimated that such a computer would be able to perform calculations 1 billion times faster than a Pentium 4 and search the entire Internet in the blink of an eye![56] All these advances in technology have increased computing speed at a very low cost; they have also allowed larger and more sophisticated programs to be developed and have enabled almost all users to do types of computing that could be performed only on mainframe computers just a few years ago. As computers have become more powerful, so have software programs. However, this vast array of new hardware and software systems has made it difficult for organizations to maintain consistency throughout the organization. Furthermore, many people are reluctant to change their way of working to take full advantage of the capabilities of the technology.

LEARNING OBJECTIVE 9

Explain the limitations of information technology.

Table 17.3 21st Century Issues in the Use of Information Technology

1. Information architecture—creating a high-level map of the information requirements of the organization.
2. Data resources—data are now viewed as the important factor of production.
3. Strategic planning—considered one of the most important issues, it involves the close alignment of technology with business plans.
4. Human resources—recognition of the limited number of information systems professionals available to develop and maintain increasingly technical and complex organizational computing environments.
5. Organizational learning—learning how to make appropriate use of information technology.
6. Technology infrastructure—a new issue for this survey, it involves building an infrastructure that will support current operations while remaining flexible enough to adapt to changing technology and evolving organizational needs.
7. Information system organization alignment—effectiveness of support for organizational activities and operations without constraining either the technology or the organization.
8. Competitive advantage—technology is no longer the sole arbiter of competitive advantage but is becoming the necessary, but not sufficient condition. Competitive advantage comes from the proper role of information technology in streamlining internal business processes, forging electronic links with suppliers and customers, and shaping the organization's design.
9. Software development—developing new tools and techniques to facilitate the rapid and error-free development of needed software systems.
10. Telecommunications system planning—can be used to reduce structural, time, and spatial limits on organizational relationships.

Source: Adapted from F. Niederman, J. C. Brancheau, and J. C. Wetherbe, "Information Systems Management Issues for the 1990s," *MIS Quarterly* (15:4), 1991, pp. 475–500. © 1991, Regents of the University of Minnesota. Reprinted by permission.

Implications for Leaders

Most organizations are only now coming to realize that the ways they incorporate technology into the workplace have a significant impact on their success or failure. A recent survey asked senior information system executives to name the ten issues that are most important for the management and organizational use of information technology as we move into the 21st century. Their responses are listed in Table 17.3.

We have seen in this chapter that there are several different types of computerized information systems, serving several different types of decision specialists at different levels of the organization. Despite this diversity, there is one common element to all these information systems: They support decision making within the organization. Leaders must be competent in their understanding of the information systems that can provide support to their decision-making efforts. Successful leaders of the future will be those who

- Understand the importance of quality information that is obtained in a timely fashion.
- Employ information systems capable of providing quality information that is both timely and complete.
- Are able to use that information to their advantage in the organizational decision-making process.
- Are well versed in the latest technological innovations for information gathering, processing, and disseminating.
- Are aware of the impact of information technology on management efficiency, organizational social relationships, and organizational structure.
- Are aware of the limitations of computer-based information systems.

As we have seen throughout this chapter, the ultimate success or failure of information technology is not always immediately clear. Technology is not the solution for all organizational problems, and technology will not in and of itself provide relief from poor organizational practices. The benefits that can be gained from technology are many, but the ultimate benefits from technology are the vast amounts of information that can be processed and distributed more easily. Management success—and, on a larger scale, organizational success—is still based primarily on the skills and insightful decisions of the leaders. Still, it is up to the organization and its decision makers to take advantage of and properly use the information that becomes available.

Meeting The Challenge

TOROC Pulls It Together to Stage the Winter Olympics

The Torino Organizing Committee (TOROC) was up to the challenge of assembling the hardware, software, telecommunications, and technology services for the 2006 Olympic Winter Games. TOROC began its journey into this project shortly after the conclusion of the 2002 Salt Lake City Olympic Winter Games. In April 2002, representatives from the Salt Lake Olympic Committee (SLOC) and TOROC engaged in a week-long series of meetings, presentations, and debriefings so that TOROC could get a better sense of what it would take to stage a successful Olympics. A special 3-day session was dedicated to the technological aspects of Salt Lake City, focusing on telecommunications systems, computer systems, and the Internet. Through these encounters, TOROC members gained some valuable insights, which would later serve them well.

To successfully complete an undertaking of this magnitude (the IT budget alone was close to $400 million), the International Olympic Committee (IOC) and TOROC assembled a consortium of leading companies to design, develop, and operate the technology required for the games. Atos Origin, Olympic Games IT partner since 2001, was once again chosen to integrate and manage the vast IT systems that were vital to the successful operation of the games. That technology would eventually consist of 5000 computers, 400 servers, hundreds of printers and photocopiers, 13,000 telephones, 14 telephone exchanges, thousands of fiber miles of fiber-optic cable, and countless two-way radios and mobile phones. The Torino Olympic Broadcasting Organization (TOBO) had scheduled nearly 1000 hours of live television coverage via its 400+ cameras and 900 audio and video positions. To reach the estimated worldwide viewing audience of 3 billion people, TOBO would provide material to 80 broadcasters, such as the familiar NBC, CNN, and BBC, and assorted other national broadcasting networks from around the world. Partnering in this endeavor was Eutelstat, a French telecommunications company that is one of the largest telecommunications operations in the world. Its fleet of 23 geostationary satellites provided transmission capacity for more than 1300 television channels. Eutelstat would also provide closed-circuit satellite transmissions to 5000 locations for use by athletes and companions in the three Olympic villages, members of the IOC, all national Olympic committees in their hotels, and journalists in the Main Press Centre, the International Broadcasting Centre, and the press halls at the venue sites. Another technology partner would once again be Swatch, a Swiss company that would provide timing and scoring information as well as photo-finish technology.

The TOROC IT project had very unique dynamics. While most commercial IT systems projects can delay implementation when problems or issues arise, Olympic organizing committees cannot push back their deployment dates. In addition, they don't have the luxury of working through the bugs during the first weeks that new systems are live. The equipment and applications deployed for the games must work correctly on the first day of competition. As a result, development processes and testing procedures were well planned out and thoroughly tested. Simulations of events at al venues were conducted well in advance of the start of the games. By late 2005, everything was in the ready for what TOROC hoped would be remembered as the most successful Olympic winter games ever.

Sources: "IOC to Sign Extension to Technology Partnership, IOC press release, 28 June 2005; "Swatch: Precision Timing for the Olympic Games," IOC press release, 26 August 2004; "Atos Origin: Delivering Results Faster Than Ever," IOC press release, 24 August 2004; "IOC and Atos Origin Extend Partnership to 2012," IOC press release, 1 July 2005; "Torino 2006: More Than 900 Hours of Programming Planned for Winter Games," IOC press release, 3 March 2005; http://www.torino2006.org/comitato.

SUMMARY

1. In recent years, the world has seen the strengthening of the global economy, the transformation of many industrial economies to knowledge-based and information-based service economies, changes in the hierarchical structure of many organizations, and the emergence of many technology-driven innovations. These forces have altered the environment of business and made it more reliant on information technology.

2. Many organizations possess a hierarchical structure with a strategic level at the top, composed of senior-level managers who address strategic issues and long-term decision making. Directly below this lies a management level, composed of middle managers who monitor and control the organization's operations. Immediately below this lies a knowledge level, composed of knowledge workers and data workers who create new information and knowledge or process the organization's information. Finally, at the bottom of the structure lies an operational level, which is composed of operational managers who keep track of the basic activities and transactions of the organization.

3. Strategic-level information systems consist of executive support systems (ESSs) and enterprise resource planning (ERP) systems. Management-level information systems consist of management information systems (MISs) and decision support systems (DSSs). Knowledge-level information systems consist of knowledge management systems (KMSs) and office automation systems (OASs). Operational-level information systems consist of transaction processing systems (TPSs).

4. In general, the components of an information system consist of hardware, software, and data. The hardware consists of the input, processing, output, storage, and data-transmission devices. The software consists of the various programs, which are the instructions that tell the hardware components what to do and how to do it. Data, which are often stored and maintained in a database, are the objective measures of an organization's activities.

5. Data are the raw facts, details, or objective measures that represent some type of transaction or activity within an organization. Data processing is the process in which the data are aggregated and organized, manipulated through analysis, and placed in a proper context for evaluation and use by the end user. Information is the result of the process of transforming data into a meaningful form for a specific purpose. To facilitate good decision making, the people making decisions must have useful information. Useful information has three primary characteristics: (a) The quality of the information produced and distributed to decision makers must be very high, (b) the information must be available in a timely fashion, and (c) the information must be complete in its scope.

6. The development of an information system is a systematic process of examining and analyzing the current activities needed to maintain organizational operations. The systems design process involves several steps: (a) investigation, (b) systems analysis, (c) systems design, (d) systems implementation, and (e) systems maintenance. The systems development life cycle (SDLC) is a common model for how information systems evolve over time within an organization.

7. Various types of information technology are changing the way we work. Telecommunications and networking are especially important. Electronic data interchange (EDI) and electronic funds transfer (EFT) are allowing organizations to establish and maintain business relationships without direct person-to-person contact. Among the most rapidly growing technology-based processes emerging is electronic commerce (e-commerce), which is the process of buying and selling goods and services electronically with computerized business transactions. Telecommuting is allowing more workers to conduct business activities at home or on the road with the customer. Applications of artificial intelligence, such as expert systems and robotics, are enabling technology to do tasks that were previously done by workers. Office automation is creating a technology-supported office environment to assist in the management and processing of office work and information.

8. Information technology will have an impact on management efficiency, social relationships, and the structure within an organization. Efficiency will improve only when the organization and the decision-making process are reassessed and redesigned to take advantage of the capabilities of the technology. When information systems are used to enhance communication between people in the organization, there is a social impact. Finally, as more aspects of an organization become integrated into the information system, more centralization of control over computer resources may occur.

9. Among the limitations of information technology are (a) the difficulty in keeping up with technological advances, (b) the potentially high cost and time involved in changing technologies, and (c) the failure of many people to take advantage of the technology because of their reluctance to change the way they work.

REVIEW QUESTIONS

1. (LEARNING OBJECTIVE 1) Briefly describe the recent changes that have altered the environment of business and made it more reliant on information technology.
2. (LEARNING OBJECTIVE 2) List the four levels of decision specialists within an organization's hierarchy and identify the major function of each.
3. (LEARNING OBJECTIVE 3) Describe the types of information systems available to support decision makers at the different levels of an organization's hierarchy.
4. (LEARNING OBJECTIVE 4) Briefly describe the various components in an information system.
5. (LEARNING OBJECTIVE 5) Describe how data and information differ and identify the characteristics of useful information.
6. (LEARNING OBJECTIVE 6) List and describe the steps in the development of an information system.
7. (LEARNING OBJECTIVE 7) Describe some of the IT-related advances that are changing the way that we work.
8. (LEARNING OBJECTIVE 8) Identify and discuss the various effects information technology can have on an organization.
9. (LEARNING OBJECTIVE 9) What are some of the limitations of information technology? Briefly discuss the causes and outcomes of each type of limitation.

DISCUSSION QUESTIONS

Improving Critical Thinking

1. Assume that the health center at your school wishes to install an information system. Identify the major tasks necessary for each phase of a systems design process for the health center. What difficulties in design and development might you expect to encounter in each phase?

2. Explain the concept of expert systems. If it is possible to capture the knowledge of an expert and place it in an expert system, one can argue that there is no longer a need for an expert. Furthermore, if the data are in a database, the knowledge of the expert becomes permanent. It can be transferred to different settings and even reproduced through copying processes. Can an expert system produce more consistent, reproducible results than the human expert on whom it is based? Why or why not? Is it desirable to seek this result? Explain.

3. What can you do to ensure that you will have the technical knowledge and skills related to information technology necessary to compete effectively in the job market?

Enhancing Communication Skills

4. Examine the library at your school. What major types of activities must the library support as part of its mission? Which of these activities could be computerized? Can these various activities be integrated into one larger information system? Explain. Identify additional library functions that could be computerized. To enhance your oral communication skills, prepare a short (10- to 15-minute) presentation of your answer for the class.

5. What news stories dealing with e-commerce have appeared in the news lately? What impact do you think this technology will have on organizations and management? To enhance your written communication skills, write a short (one- to two-page) essay in which you discuss these impacts.

Building Teamwork

6. What do you think the office or organization of the future will be like? What technology do you think the office of the future will use? To refine your team-

work skills, meet with a small group of students who have been given this same assignment. Compare your visions of the office of the future and then reach a consensus about how this office will look. Select a spokesperson to present your team's vision to the rest of the class.

7. Identify several types of data that might be collected in a full-service bank. Think about how the information that can be derived from the data would differ for each hierarchical level in the bank. In other words, how might the various levels in the organization make different uses of the same basic data? To refine your teamwork skills, meet with a small group of students who have been given this same assignment. Compare your lists and then, by consensus, consolidate your lists into a single list of the best four types of data. Select a spokesperson to present your team's findings to the rest of the class.

Glossary

A

Ability
Capacity to perform various tasks needed; may be classified as mental, mechanical, or psychomotor.

Accommodation
An approach to corporate social responsibility that adapts to public policy in doing more than the minimum required.

Accountability
Responsibility to the supervisor for results of decisions made and actions taken with delegated authority.

Acquired-needs model
A need that is acquired or learned from the life experiences in the culture or country in which we live and they can influence behavior.

Activity ratio
An indicator of performance with respect to key activities defined by management.

Adjourning
Group development stage that involves the termination of task behaviors and disengagement from relationship-oriented behaviors.

Administrative management
Perspective on management that focuses on managers and the functions they perform.

Affiliation needs
The desire for friendship, love, and a feeling of belonging.

Affirmative action
Emphasizing the recruiting, hiring, and promoting of members of minority groups and other protected classes if such individuals are underrepresented in the organization.

Aggregate planning
A link between the more general business-planning activities and the more specific master-planning activities.

Alternative
A strategy that might be implemented in a decision-making situation.

Application form
A form used to gather information about a job applicant.

Appraisal cost
The cost associated with any activity that is performed in an attempt to assess the quality of the product that has been manufactured or the service that has been provided.

Artificial intelligence (AI)
A process in which computers and computer systems behave intelligently.

Asset
A thing of value that an individual or organization owns.

Assessment center
A type of simulation of a more complex or higher-level managerial job used to predict a job applicant's performance.

Attitudes
The beliefs, feelings, and behavioral tendencies held by a person.

Authority
The formal right inherent in an organizational position to make decisions.

Autonomy
The degree to which a job includes freedom, independence, and decision-making authority.

B

Balanced Scorecard
A planning system that aligns the goals of individual employees with the strategic goals of the organization.

Balance sheet
A summary of an organization's financial position at a given point in time, showing assets, liabilities, and owner's equity.

BCG matrix
A business portfolio matrix that uses market growth rate and relative market share as the indicators of the firm's strategic position.

Behavioral decision model
A descriptive framework for understanding that a person's cognitive ability to process information is limited.

Behavior focus
The study of what the effective leader does to be successful.

Behavior modification
The application of reinforcement concepts.

Benchmarking
The process of comparing one's own products, services, or processes against those of industry leaders for the purpose of improvement.

Benefits
Indirect compensation given to employees as a reward for organizational membership.

Best-cost provider strategy
A strategy based on achieving the benefits of both low-cost and differentiation strategies.

Big Five
A model measuring personality traits that include extroversion, agreeableness, conscientiousness, emotional stability, and openness to experience.

Bona fide occupational qualification
A qualification of a job that is legal to use even if it tends to rule out members of employee classes protected by Title VII.

Boundary-spanning role
A lateral relationship that helps to integrate and coordinate the activities of the organization (liaisons, committees, task forces, integrating positions, and cross-functional work teams).

Bounded rationality
Recognizes that people are limited by such organizational constraints as time, information, resources, and their own mental capacities.

Brainstorming
A technique used to enhance creativity that encourages group members to generate as many novel ideas as possible on a given topic without evaluating them.

Budgets
Plans that specify how financial resources should be allocated.

Bureaucratic management
Perspective on management that focuses on the overall organizational system.

Business ethics
The application of general ethics to business behavior.

Business level strategy
Focused plans that define how each business unit in an organization's corporate portfolio will operate in its market arena.

Business portfolio matrix
A two-dimensional grid that compares the strategic positions of each of the organization's businesses.

B2B
An initialism representing business-to-business transactions.

B2C
An initialism representing business-to-consumer interactions.

Bottom-up
Planning that starts at the lower levels in the organization.

Bureaucratic control
Use of formal mechanisms to influence behavior, assess performance, and correct unacceptable deviations from standards.

C

Cash cow
A business that falls into the low market-growth/low market-share cell of a BCG matrix.

Central tendency
Judging all employees as average, even though their performance varies.

Centralized
Authority decision making is at the top of the organization.

Channel
The carrier of the message or the means by which the message is sent.

Chain of command
The line of authority and responsibility that flows throughout the organization.

Charismatic authority
Subordinates voluntarily comply with a leader because of his or her special personal qualities or abilities.

Closed systems
Systems that do not interact with the environment.

Code of ethics
The general value system, principles, and specific rules that a company follows.

Coercive power
The power to discipline, punish, or withhold rewards.

Cognitive dissonance
An inconsistency among a person's attitudes or between an attitude and a behavior.

Cohesiveness
The degree to which group members want to stay together.

Communication
A process in which one person or group evokes an identical or common meaning in another person or group.

Communication feedback
The process of verifying messages and the receiver's attempts to ensure that the message he or she decoded is what the sender really meant to convey.

Compensation
Direct and indirect payments to employees.

Competencies
The things that an organization can do well; the skills and abilities.

Competitive advantage
An advantage over competitors.

Competitive analysis
Analysis conducted to understand the strengths and weaknesses of competitors.

Competitive structure
The nature and type of competition between competitors in an industry.

Conceptual skill
The ability to analyze complex situations.

Concurrent control
Focuses on the transformation process to ensure that it is functioning properly.

Contingency perspective
Perspective on management which proposed that the best managerial approach is contingent on key variables in a given organizational situation.

Contingency planning
Development of two or more plans each based on different conditions.

Continuous-flow production system
A product system that produces a high volume of a continuous product or non-discrete item.

Contrast error
The tendency to rate employees relative to each other rather than to performance standards.

Coordinating
Keeping organization units that interact with or influence each other in contact with each to share information and other things in a way that enhances accomplishment of tasks.

Corporate level strategy
Decisions and actions at the top level of the organization that define the portfolio of business units that an organization maintains.

Corporate social responsibility
The interaction between business and the social environment in which it exists. More specifically, the obligation that an organization has to society.

Cost leadership strategy
A strategy for competing on the basis of low per unit cost.

Cross-training
Teaching a variety of skills to a jobholder, usually skills that can be used in other, similar jobs.

Current asset
An item that can be converted into cash in a short time period.

Current liability
A debt that must be paid in the near future.

Customer capital
The value of established relationships with customers and suppliers.

Customer divisional structure
An organizational structure focused on customer groups.

Customer profile
A description of customers that will help managers understand what products and services customers wish to purchase.

D

Data
The raw facts or details that represent some type of transaction or activity within an organization.

Database
The archived data and information used by an organization.

Database management system (DBMS)
Software that allows an organization to store data, manage them efficiently, and provide access to stored data.

Debt ratio
An indicator of the firm's ability to handle long-term debt.

Decentralized
Authority decision making is at the lower levels of the organization.

Decision making
The process through which managers and leaders identify and resolve problems and capitalize on opportunities.

Decision support system (DSS)
An information system that supports middle managers of the organization by assisting them in the formulation of high-quality decisions about ad hoc, semi-structured problems.

Decisional role
The role in which a manager processes information and reaches conclusions.

Decoding
The translation of received messages into interpreted meanings.

Defense
An approach to corporate social responsibility that an organization takes only when it is necessary to defend its current position.

Delegating style
The leader provides the subordinates with few task or relations behaviors. Authority and responsibility rest with the follower.

Delegation
The process of transferring the authority for a specific activity or task to another member of the organization and empowering that individual to accomplish the task effectively.

Delphi technique
An approach that uses experts to make predictions and forecasts about future events without meeting face to face.

Demand forecasting
Determining the number of employees that the organization will need in the future as well as the knowledge, skills, and abilities these employees must possess.

Devil's advocacy
An approach in which an individual or subgroup is appointed to critique a proposed course of action and identify problems to consider before the decision is final.

Dialectical inquiry
A method that approaches a decision from two opposite points and structures a debate between conflicting views.

Differentiation strategy
A strategy for competing by offering products or services that are different from those of competitors.

Distinctive competency
A unique organizational skill or knowledge that will help an organization accomplish something better than its competitors.

Diversification
Adding new products, services, or businesses to an organization.

Diversity
The heterogeneity of the workforce, mostly in terms of gender and race.

Divisional structure
A structure in which members of the organization are grouped on the basis of common products, geographic markets, or customers served.

Dog
A business that falls into the low market-growth/low market-share cell of a BCG matrix.

Downward communication
Messages sent from individuals at higher levels of the organization to those at lower levels.

Driving forces
The forces that push for change.

Dynamic network
A network structure that makes extensive use of outsourcing through alliances with outside organizations.

E

Economic environment
The economic components of the general environment.

Economic feasibility
Focuses on whether the expected benefits of an information system will be able to cover the anticipated costs.

Economic responsibility
The perspective that says the social responsibility of an organization is to make profits and provide attractive returns on investment.

Effectiveness
The degree to which goals are achieved; doing the right things.

Efficiency
Using the fewest inputs to generate a given output; doing things right.

Electronic commerce (e-commerce)
The process of buying and selling goods and services electronically with computerized business transactions.

Electronic data interchange (EDI)
Electronic transmission of transaction data using telecommunications.

Electronic funds transfer (EFT)
Electronic manipulation of financial transactions.

Electronic mail (e-mail)
A message sent with an electronic device, usually a computer.

Electronic mail (e-mail)
A computer-based system that allows individuals to exchange and store messages through computerized text-processing and communication networks.

Emotional intelligence
The capacity to effectively manage ourselves and our relationships.

Employee-centered work redesign
An approach whereby employees design their work roles to benefit the organization and satisfy their individual goals.

Employee fairness
Expectations that individuals on a given job are paid fairly relative to coworkers on the same job.

Employment test
Any instrument or device used to assess the qualifications of a job applicant.

Empowering employees
Increasing the amount of control and discretion workers have over their jobs.

Empowerment
Delegating authority to the follower and holding him or her accountable. It includes making sure the follower understands the task, has proper information, training, motivation, guidance, and skills to be successful.

Encoding
The process that translates the sender's ideas into a systematic set of symbols or a language expressing the communicator's purpose.

Encryption
The coding and scrambling of sensitive information transmitted over networks to make it unintelligible to unauthorized viewers.

End user
The person who will use and interact with the information system, particularly the decision maker(s) in the organization.

Enterprise resource planning (ERP)
A management system that integrates all facets of the organization's business so that they can be more closely coordinated by sharing information.

Enterprise resource planning (ERP) system
A software system designed to organize and manage business processes by sharing information across all functional areas of an organization.

Entropy
The tendency for systems to decay over time.

Equity model
A motivation model focusing on an individual's feelings about how fairly he or she is treated in comparison with others.

Escalation of commitment
The tendency to increase commitment to a previously selected course of action beyond the level that would be expected if the manager followed an effective decision-making process.

Esteem needs
Needs for personal feelings of achievement and self-worth.

Ethical behavior
Behavior that is morally accepted as good or right as opposed to bad or wrong.

Ethical behavior
Behavior that is considered by most to be acceptable.

Ethical dilemma
A situation in which a person must decide whether or not to do something that, although benefiting oneself or the organization, may be considered unethical and perhaps illegal.

Ethical responsibility
The perspective that an organization should respond to the spirit as well as the letter of the law.

Ethics
Reflects established customs and morals.

Ethnocentrism
The tendency to consider one's own culture and its values as being superior to others.

Evaluation and control
The methods by which the performance of the organization is monitored.

Executive support system (ESS)
An information system that supports senior managers at the strategic level of the organization by helping them identify and address problems and opportunities from a strategic perspective.

Expectancy
The belief that a particular level of effort will be followed by a particular level of performance.

Expectancy model
Behavior is purposeful, goal directed, and largely based on intentions.

Expert power
The power to influence another person because of expert knowledge and competence.

Expert system
A computer-based system that contains and can use knowledge about a specific, relatively narrow, complex application.

External customer
User of an item who is not a part of the organization that supplies the item.

External environment
The setting in which an organization operates; the markets and industry.

External-failure cost
The cost resulting from defective output that is not detected prior to delivery to the customer.

External fairness
Pay in one organization is fair relative to the pay for the same job in other organizations.

External forces
Forces that are fundamentally beyond the control of management.

External locus of control
A belief that what happens is determined by outside forces such as other people, fate, or luck.

Extinction
The withdrawal of the positive reward or reinforcing consequences for an undesirable behavior.

F

F or T
A personality dimension referring to whether one is feeling or thinking in making judgments.

Feedback
Information about the status and performance of a given effort or system.

Feedback control
A control that compares the actual performance of the organization to its planned performance.

Feedback (corrective) control
Focuses on discovering undesirable output and implementing corrective action.

Feedforward control
A control designed to predict changes in the external environment or the internal operations of the organization that may affect an organization's ability to fulfill its mission.

Feedforward (preventive) control
Focuses on detecting undesirable material, financial, or human resources that serve as inputs to the transformation process.

First-line manager
The manager who supervises the operational employees.

Five forces model
A model developed by Michael Porter that uses five forces to assess the competitive structure of an industry.

Fixed assets
An asset that is long term in nature and cannot be converted quickly into cash.

Fixed-interval schedule
Giving reinforcers at specified time intervals.

Fixed-ratio schedule
Giving reinforcers after a fixed number of occurrences of the desired behavior.

Focus strategy
A strategy for competing by targeting a specific and narrow segment of the market.

Followership
The paradigm known as self-leadership founded on creating an organization of leaders who are ready to lead themselves.

Force-field analysis
A systematic process for examining pressures that support or resist a proposed change.

Formal authority
Authority inherent in an organizational position.

Formal groups
A group that is deliberately created by managers.

Forming
First stage of group development.

Free riding
A tendency for a group member to not contribute to the group's efforts but to share in the rewards.

Functional-level strategy
Strategy at the department level that specifies such things as the production, research and development, financial, human resource management, and/or marketing activities necessary to implement the organization's corporate and business strategies.

Functional manager
A manager who is responsible for managing a work unit that is grouped based on the function served.

Functional structure
A structure in which tasks and jobs are grouped according to the function they perform within the organization.

G

GE matrix
A business portfolio matrix that uses industry attractiveness and business strength as the indicators of the firm's strategic position.

General environment
Those environmental forces outside of the organization over which the organization may have no control.

General manager
A manager who is responsible for managing several different departments that are responsible for different tasks.

Generic strategy
The fundamental way in which an organization competes in the marketplace.

Geographic divisional structure
A structure in which the activities of the organization are grouped according to the geographic markets served.

Globalization
Various companies moving to multiple countries and doing business in multiple countries.

Goal setting
The process of increasing efficiency and effectiveness by specifying the desired outcomes toward which individuals, groups, departments, and organizations should work.

Grand strategy
A comprehensive, general approach for achieving the strategic goals of an organization.

Grapevine
An informal method of transmitting information depicted as the wandering of messages throughout the organization.

Groupthink
An agreement-at-any-cost mentality that results in ineffective group decisions.

H

Halo-and-horn effect
Judging a person all positive (halo) or all negative (horn) based on one trait or dimension.

Halo effect
Rating an employee high or low on all items because of one characteristic.

Hawthorne effect
Phenomenon whereby individual or group performance is influenced by human behavior factors.

Heterogeneous group
A group with many differences among its members.

Hierarchy of needs
A motivation model stating that a person has five fundamental needs.

Homogeneous group
A group having many similarities.

Horizontal communication
The flow of information that occurs both within and between departments.

Hostile environment harassment
Harassment produced by workplace conduct and/or setting that is considered to make an abusive working environment.

Human capital
The cumulative skills and knowledge of the organization.

Human rights approach
A situation in which decisions are made in light of the moral entitlements of human beings.

Human skill
The ability to work effectively with others.

Hybrid layout
A configuration containing some degree of flexibility, lying between the extremes of process and product layouts.

Hygiene factor
A factor associated with the job context or environment in which the job is performed.

I

I or E
A personality dimension measuring the degree to which a person is introverted or extroverted.

Income statement (profit-and-loss statement)
A summary of an organization's financial performance over a given time interval, showing revenues, expenses, and bottom-line profit or loss.

Informal authority
Ability to influence others that is based on personal characteristics or skills.

Informal groups
A group that is not formed or planned by the organization's managers.

Information
Data that have been processed or transformed into a meaningful and useful form.

Informational role
The manager's responsibility for gathering and disseminating information to the stakeholders of the organization.

Information overload
A state that occurs when the amount of information that a person can process is exceeded.

Information power
Power based on control of information.

Information system
A set of interrelated components that collects (or retrieves), processes, stores, and distributes information to support the activities of an organization.

Inputs
Such diverse items as materials, workers, capital, land, equipment, customers, and information used in creating products and services.

Instrumentality
The individual's perception that a specific level of achieved task performance will lead to outcomes or rewards.

Instrumental value
A standard of conduct or method for attaining an end.

Integrating mechanisms
A method for managing the flow of information, resources, and tasks within the organization.

Interdependence
The degree to which work groups are interrelated.

Internal analysis
Assessment of the strengths and weaknesses of an organization.

Internal customer
User of an item who is a member of or employee of the organization that supplies the item.

Internal-failure cost
The cost associated with the repair or disposition of defective output that is detected prior to delivery to the customer.

Internal fairness
Pay for the job within the organization is fair relative to the pay of higher- and lower-level jobs in the same organization.

Internal forces
Forces that are generally within the control of management.

Internal locus of control
A belief that many of the events in one's life are primarily the result of their own behavior and actions.

Internal network
A network structure that relies on internally developed units to provide services to a core organizational unit.

Internet
The vast interconnected electronic equipment that stores massive amounts of data that can be accessed with computers and related electronic equipment.

Interpersonal role
The role of a manager that involves relationships with organizational members and other constituents.

Interview
Relatively formal, in-depth conversations used to assess a candidate's readiness for a job, and to provide information to the candidate.

Intuition
An unconscious analysis based on past experience.

J

Jargon
Terminology or language specific to a particular profession or group.

Job analysis
Studying a job to understand what knowledge, skills, abilities, and attitudes are required for successful performance.

Job description
Details of the responsibilities and tasks required by a job.

Job description
Details of the responsibilities and tasks associated with a given position.

Job design
The set of tasks and activities that are grouped together to define a particular job.

Job enlargement
Adding more if similar tasks to a job.

Job enrichment
Adding tasks to a job that require a wider range of skills.

Job depth
Adding tasks to a job that require a wider range of skills, usually including autonomy.

Job rotation
Assigning individuals to a variety of job positions, usually positions at a similar level.

Job satisfaction
The degree to which a individual feels positively or negatively about his or her job.

Job scope
The number of different activities required in a job and the frequency with which each activity is performed.

Job-shop production system
A process system that produces small quantities of a wide variety of specialized items.

Job specification
A list of the knowledge, skills, abilities, and other employee characteristics needed to perform the job.

Just-in-time (JIT) inventory management
A philosophy that advocates eliminating waste, solving problems, and striving for continual improvement in operations.

Justice approach
A situation in which decisions are based on an equitable, fair, and impartial distribution of benefits and costs among individuals and groups.

K

Kaizen
A Japanese term referring to the total quality management principle of continuous improvement.

Knowledge-level information system
An information system that helps knowledge workers to discover, organize, and integrate new knowledge into the business or helps data workers to control the flow of paperwork and information.

Knowledge management system (KMS)
An information system that supports workers at the knowledge level of the organization by helping create, organize, and make available important business knowledge wherever and whenever it is needed in an organization.

L

Labor-management relations
The formal process through which labor unions represent employees in negotiating with management.

Language, metaphors, and symbols
The way that organizational members typically express themselves and communicate with each other.

Law of requisite variety
Control systems must have enough variety to cope with the variety in the systems they are trying to control.

Leadership
A social influence process to influence people to achieve a common goal.

Leadership substitutes
Things that guide or influence people in place of a leader, including individual, task and organizational characteristics.

Leading
Motivating and directing the members of the organization so that they contribute to the achievement of the goals of the organization.

Legal responsibility
The perspective that the social responsibility of an organization is to obey laws and public policy.

Legitimate power
The power based on formal authority.

Leniency error
Evaluating someone in a group higher than the person should be rated or when the rater in unjustifiably easy in evaluating performance.

Liability
A debt or obligation of the firm.

Line department
An organizational unit that is not directly involved in delivering the products and services of the organization but provides support for line personnel.

Liquidity ratio
An indicator of the firm's ability to meet its short-term debts and obligations.

Local-area network (LAN)
An information system that connects users in a small area such as a building, an office, or a manufacturing plant.

Locus of control
A personality characteristic that reflects a person's belief in personal control in life (internality) rather than in control by outside forces or individual (externality).

Locus of decision making
The level of the organization at which decision are made.

Long-term liability
A debt that is payable over a long time span.

M

Management
The process of administering and coordinating resources effectively and efficiently in an effort to achieve the goals of the organization.

Management by exception
Focusing on the elements that are not meeting the standards.

Management by objectives
A method for developing individualized plans that guide the activities of individual members of an organization.

Management information system (MIS)
An information system that supports middle managers of the organization by providing them with periodic reports that summarize the organization's performance.

Management-level information system
An information system that assists in the administrative activities of middle managers and aids in decision making and the monitoring and controlling of operations.

Manager
An organizational member who is responsible for planning, organizing, leading, and controlling the activities of the organization so that its goals are achieved.

Master production schedule
A detailed statement of projected production quantities for each item in each time period.

Material requirements planning (MRP)
A methodology that uses the production schedule for the finished products to derive demand and production schedules for component items that make up the final products.

Matrix structure
A technique that arranges work groups on two dimensions simultaneously.

MBO
Management by objectives.

Message
The tangible forms of coded symbols that are intended to give a particular meaning to the information or data.

Middle manager
A manager who supervises the first-line managers or staff departments.

Mission
The reasons for which the organization exists.

Moral agent
A business's obligation to act honorably and to reflect and enforce values that are consistent with those of society.

Motivation
Forces either internal or external to a person that act as inducements or that influence action to do something.

Motivator factors
Factors related to job content.

N

Need for achievement
The drive to excel, to accomplish, and to achieve a standard of excellence.

Need for affiliation
The desire for friendly and close interpersonal relationships.

Need for power
The need to influence and control one's environment; may involve either personal power or institutional power.

Needs-based approach
A model of motivation that focuses on a person's needs as motivators.

Negative reinforcement (avoidance learning)
Strengthening desired behavior by allowing escape from an undesirable consequence.

Network structure
An organization that has a core coordinating with other organizations or organizational units.

Neutralizer
A condition that counteracts leader behavior or prevents a leader's influence.

Noise
Any interference with or distraction from the intended message.

Nominal group technique (NGT)
A structured process designed to stimulate creative group decision making where agreement is lacking or where the members have incomplete knowledge concerning the nature of the problem.

Nonprogrammed decision
Decision made in response to a situation that is unique, unstructured, or poorly defined.

Nonverbal communication
All messages that are nonlanguage responses.

Norming
The stage of group development where norms are established.

Norms
Unwritten, informal rules and shared beliefs that regulate the appropriate behavior expectations of team members.

O

Objective
The desired result to be attained when making decisions.

Office automation system (OAS)
An information technology application designed to increase the productivity of data workers by assisting in the processing, storage, collection, and transmission of electronic documents and messages among individuals, work groups, and organizations.

Open systems
Systems that must interact with the external environment to survive.

Operational feasibility
The willingness and ability of all concerned parties to operate and support the information system as it is proposed and implemented.

Operational-level information systems
An information system that supports operational managers by keeping track of the basic activities and transactions of the organization.

Operational planning
The process of determining the day-to-day activities that are necessary to achieve the long-term goals of the organization.

Operational plans
An outline of the tactical activities necessary to support and implement the strategic plans of the organization.

Opportunities
Environmental trends on which the organization can capitalize.

Opportunity
A situation that has the potential to provide additional beneficial outcomes.

Oral communication
All forms of spoken information—the type of communication preferred by most managers.

Organic (clan) control
Reliances upon social values, traditions, shared beliefs, flexible authority, and trust to assess performance and correct unacceptable deviations.

Organization
A group of individuals who work together toward common goals.

Organizational chart
The chart, or "picture" of the organizational structure.

Organizational change
Any alteration of activities in an organization.

Organizational control
A process through which leaders regulate organizational activities to make them consistent with the expectations established in plans and to help them achieve all predetermined standards of performance.

Organizational culture
The shared beliefs, values, and norms in an organization.

Organizational design
The way in which the activities of an organization are arranged and coordinated so that its mission can be achieved.

Organizational feasibility
How well the proposed information system supports the strategic objectives of the organizations.

Organizational structure
A phrase referring to the primary reporting relationships that exist within an organization.

Organizing
The process of determining the tasks to be done, who will do them, and how those tasks will be managed and coordinated.

Orientation
The process of familiarizing new employees with the organization, their job, and their work unit.

Outputs
The physical commodity, or intangible service or information, that is desired by the customers or users of the system.

Outsourcing
Using other companies to provide operations that were previously done inside the company.

Owner's equity
The portion of a business that is owned by the shareholders, the difference between the assets of an organization and its liabilities.

P

P or J
A personality dimension representing the degree to which one is perceiving or judging in making decisions.

Paralysis by analysis
While planning, spending so much time on analysis that nothing is accomplished.

Participating style
The leader shares ideas and maintains two-way communication to encourage and support the skills subordinates have developed.

Perception
The way a person experiences, processes, defines, and interprets the world.

Performance appraisal
Any method used to assess a person's performance on the job.

Performing
Group development stage that occurs when the team is fully functional; marked by interpersonal relations and high levels of interdependence.

Personalized power orientation
Associated with a strong need for esteem and status; power is often used impulsively.

Personality
An enduring pattern of an individual's behavior.

Personality test
Assessment of personality characteristics of a job applicant.

Personal power
Power derived from interpersonal relationships between leaders and followers.

Philanthropic responsibility
The perspective that organizations should be good corporate citizens; organizations should seek to improve the welfare of society.

Physiological needs
Needs such as food, water, air, and shelter; at the bottom of the hierarchy of needs.

Plan
A blueprint for action that prescribes the activities necessary for the organization to realize its goals.

Plan B
Referring to a second, contingency plan.

Planning
Setting goals and defining the actions necessary to achieve those goals.

Policies
Guidelines for decision making within the organization.

Political-legal environment
The part of the external environment that includes political and legal issues that affect organizations.

Pooled interdependence
When organizational units have a common resource but no interrelationship with one another.

Position power
The power attributed to one's position in an organization.

Positive reinforcement
The administration of positive and rewarding consequences or events following a desired behavior.

Power
The ability to use human, informational or material resources to get something done.

Prevention cost
The cost associated with any activity that is performed in an attempt to prevent defective output from occurring.

Proaction
An approach to corporate social responsibility that includes behaviors that improve society.

Problem
A situation in which some aspect of organizational performance is less than desirable.

Procedures
Instructions on how to complete recurring tasks.

Process layout
A configuration flexible enough to accommodate a wide diversity of products or customers.

Process approach
A model of motivation that focuses on understanding the thought process in influencing motivation.

Process system
An operating system that produces a high variety of items, with limited volumes of each.

Product divisional structure
A structure in which the activities of the organization are grouped according to specific products or product lines.

Product layout
A configuration set for a specific purpose, with all product or service demands essentially identical.

Product system
An operating system that produces a limited variety of items, with high volumes of each.

Productivity
A measure of the efficiency with which a firm transforms inputs into goods and services.

Profitability ratio
An indicator of the relative effectiveness, or profitability, of the organization.

Programmed decision
A decision made in response to a situation that is routine or recurring.

Programs
Single-use plans that govern a comprehensive set of activities designed to accomplish a particular set of goals.

Project productions system
A process system that produces large-scale, unique items.

Projects
Directs the efforts of individuals or work groups toward the achievements of a specific goal.

Punishment
Administering negative consequences following undesirable behavior.

Q

Quality assurance (QA)
Focuses on any activity that influences the maintenance of quality at the desires level.

Quality circle
A work team that meets regularly to identify, analyze, and solve problems related to its work area.

Quality control (QC)
Focuses on the actual measurement of output to see whether specifications have been met.

Question mark
A business that falls into the high market-growth/low market-share cell of a BCG matrix.

"Quid pro quo" harassment
Sexual harassment requiring sexual favors in exchange for positive job treatment.

R

Rational-economic decision model
A model that focuses on how decisions should be made.

Rational-legal authority
Subordinates comply with a leader because of a set of impersonal rules and regulations that apply to all employees.

Reaction
An approach to corporate social responsibility that includes an organization denying responsibility for its actions.

Readiness
The extent to which a subordinate possesses the ability, knowledge, and skills, job experience, and willingness to complete a specific task.

Reciprocal interdependence
Occurs when information, resources, and tasks must be passed back and forth between work groups.

Recruitment
Finding and attracting qualified job candidates.

Referent power
The ability to influence others based on personal liking, charisma, and reputation.

Refreezing
The act of applying the new approaches and behaviors.

Related diversification
Adding products, services, or businesses that have some relationship to the ones an organization currently has—or share a core competency.

Relationship-oriented role
A behavior that cultivates the well-being, continuity, and development of the group.

Relations orientation
Leadership behavior that shows empathy for concerns and feelings, being supportive of needs, showing trust, demonstrating appreciation, establishing trusting relationships, and allowing subordinates to participate in decision making.

Reinforcement approach
Based on learning and examines how consequences mold behavior.

Repetitive, assembly-line, or mass-production system
A product system that produces a high volume of discrete items.

Resiliency
The ability to absorb high levels of disruptive change.

Resource
An input that an organization can use to achieve its strategy.

Responsibility
The obligation to perform the duties assigned.

Restraining forces
The forces to keep the status quo.

Résumé
Information prepared by a job applicant usually stating career goal, qualifications, and some related information.

Reward power
Power based on control of resources and rewards.

Rites, rituals, and ceremonies
Relatively dramatic events that have special meaning for organizational members.

Robotics
The technology of building and using machines with humanlike characteristics such as dexterity, movement, vision, and strength.

Role
The behavior that is expected in a particular situation.

Rules
Detailed and specific regulations for action.

S

S or N
A personality dimension measuring whether one is sensing or intuitive in gathering data.

Satisficing
The search for and acceptance of something that is satisfactory rather than perfect or optimal.

SBU
Strategic business unit.

Schedules of reinforcement
The basis for and timing of reinforcement.

Scientific management
Perspective on management that focuses on the productivity of the individual worker.

Security needs
The desire to have a safe physical and emotional environment.

Selection
The process of evaluating and choosing the best-qualified candidate from the pool of applicants available for the position.

Selective perception
Tendency to see or hear only what we want to see or hear.

Self-actualization needs
Needs for self-fulfillment and the opportunity to achieve one's potential; at the top of the hierarchy.

Self-esteem
The extent to which a person believes that he or she is capable, significant, successful, and worthwhile.

Self-managed teams (SMT)
A group of employees who design their jobs and work responsibilities to achieve the self-determined goals and objectives of the team.

Self-monitoring
The degree to which individuals are capable of reading and using cues to determine behavior.

Self-oriented role
A behavior—or goal—of an individual that occurs without regard for the group's problems.

Selling style
The leader explains decisions and provides opportunities for clarification.

Sender
The person who initiates the communication process by encoding his or her meaning and sending the message through a channel.

Sequential interdependence
When organizational units must coordinate the flow of information, resources, and tasks from one unit to another.

Severity error
Being unjustifiably harsh in evaluating employee performance.

Sexual harassment
Actions that are sexually directed, are unwanted, and subject the worker to adverse employment conditions.

Single-use plans
Plans that address specific organizational situations that typically do not recur.

Situational leadership model
An approach that examines the interaction between leadership style, and employee readiness.

Skill variety
The degree to which a job challenges the jobholder to use various skills and abilities.

SMART
The acronym standing for the characteristics that goals should possess; specific, measurable, achievable, results-oriented, and time line.

Socialized power orientation
The use of power for the benefit of others to make subordinates feel strong and responsible.

Social context
The setting in which the communication takes place.

Social contract
An implied set of rights and obligations that are inherent in social policy and assumed by business.

Sociocultural environment
The attitudes, behavior patterns, and lifestyles of individuals who purchase products and services of organizations.

SOP
Standard operating procedure.

Span of control
The number of employees reporting to a particular manager.

Special-purpose team
A temporary team formed to solve a special or nonrecurring problem.

Spontaneous channels of communication
Casual, opportunistic, and informal communication paths that arise from the social relationships that evolve in the organization.

Stable environment
An external environment that contains little change.

Stable network
A network structure that continually uses a set of alliance partners.

Staff department
An organization unit that is not directly involved in delivering the products and services of the organization but provides support for line personnel.

Stakeholders
All those who are affected by or can affect the activities of the organization.

Standing plans
Plans that deal with organizational issues and problems that recur frequently.

Star
A business that falls into the high market-growth/high market-share cell of a BCG matrix.

Stereotyping
Tendency to assign attributes to someone based on the group to which that person belongs.

Strategic analysis
An assessment of the external and internal environments of an organization.

Strategic business unit
A part of an organization that is responsible for its outcomes.

Strategic decision-making matrix
A two-dimensional grid used to select the best strategic alternative in light of multiple organizational objectives.

Strategic direction
Direction of the organization toward success in the long-run.

Strategic goal
The result that an organization seeks to achieve in the long term.

Strategic human resource management (SHRM)
Managing in such a way as to coordinate all human resource components and focus them on achieving organizational goals and overall strategy.

Strategic-level information system
An information system that aids senior management as they address strategic issues and long-term decision making.

Strategic management
Overall, long-run management.

Strategic plan
A comprehensive plan that provides overall direction for the organization.

Strategic planning
The process of making plans and decisions that are focused on long-run performance.

Strategy formulation
Establishing strategy and tactics necessary to achieve the mission of the organization.

Strategy implementation
Doing the things necessary to ensure that the strategy of the organization is achieved effectively and efficiently.

Stretch goal
A goal that is intended to be high.

Stories and sagas
Narratives based on true events, frequently embellished.

Storming
Group development stage that occurs as team members begin to experience conflict with one another.

Supply chain
The entire network of activities involved in the delivery of a finished product or service to the customer.

Supply-chain management (SCM)
The business function that coordinates and manages all the activities involved in the delivery of a product or service to the customer.

Supply forecasting
Determining what human resources will be available both inside and outside the organization.

Synergy
A phenomenon whereby an organization can accomplish more when its subsystems work together than it can accomplish when they work independently.

Systems analysis
An approach to problem solving that attacks complex systems by breaking them down into their constituent elements.

T

Task environment
Those environmental forces that are within the firm's operating environment and over which the organization may have some degree of control.

Task identity
The degree to which a job includes the completion of an identifiable piece of work.

Task orientation
Leadership behavior that includes setting performance goals, planning and scheduling work, coordinating activities, giving directions, setting standards, providing resources, and supervising worker performance.

Task-oriented role
A behavior that is directly related to establishing and accomplishing the goals of the group or achieving the desired outcomes.

Task significance
The degree to which a job contributes to the overall efforts of the organization.

Technical feasibility
The capability of the hardware and software of the proposed information system to provide the decision makers in the organization with the needed information.

Technical skill
The ability to utilize tools, techniques, and procedures that are specific to a particular field.

Technological communication
Any communication that uses an electronic device as the channel.

Technological environment
Changes in technology in the external environment.

Telecommunication
The transmission of information in any form from one location to another using electronic or optical means.

Telecommuting
The practice of working at a remote site by using a computer linked to a central office or other employment location.

Telework
Another word for telecommuting.

Telling style
The leader provides specific instructions and closely supervises performance.

Terminal value
A goal an individual will ultimately strive to achieve.

Theory X
Managers perceive that subordinates have an inherent dislike of work and will avoid it if possible.

Theory Y
Managers perceive that subordinates enjoy work and will gain satisfactions from their jobs.

Theory Z
Advocates that managers place trust in the employees and make them feel like an integral part of the organization.

Threat
A condition in the environment that may cause trouble for the organization.

360-degree feedback
Feedback from the supervisor, subordinates, coworkers, and self-appraisal.

Top-down
Planning that starts at the top-level of the organization.

Top-level manager
A manager who provides the strategic direction for the organization.

Total quality management (TQM)
A systematic approach for enhancing products, services, processes, and operational quality control.

Traditional authority
Subordinates comply with a leader because of custom or tradition.

Training
A planned effort to assist employees in learning job-related behaviors that will improve their performance.

Traits and skill focus
The assumption that some people are born with certain physical characteristics, aspects of personality, and aptitudes that make them successful leaders.

Transaction processing system (TPS)
An information system that supports workers at the operational level of the organization by recording daily business transactions and performing the routine, clerical record-keeping activities of the organization.

Transformational leadership
Leadership in which the leader has the ability to influence subordinates to achieve more than was originally expected.

Transformation process
The mechanism by which inputs are converted to outputs.

Turbulent environments
An external environment that includes rapid and significant change.

Two-factor model
The model of motivation that includes motivator factors and hygiene factors.

Type A personality
A personality characteristic characterized by such things as a sense of urgency, impatience, and high drive.

Type B personality
A personality characterized as easygoing and less competitive in daily events.

U

Unfreezing
Developing an awareness of the need for change and the forces supporting and resisting change.

Unity of command
An employee in the organization is accountable to one and only one supervisor.

Universal
Something that applies in all situations. The basic management principles apply in all situations.

Unrelated diversification
Adding products, services, or businesses that are different from the ones an organization currently has.

Upward communication
Messages sent up the line from subordinates to supervisors.

Utility approach
A situation in which decisions are based on an evaluation of the overall amount of good that will result.

V

Valence
The value of the reward to the individual.

Validity
An employment tool must show that it predicts actual job performance.

Values
Relatively permanent and deeply held preferences upon which individuals form attitudes and personal choices.

Variable-interval schedule
Giving reinforcement at varying times that cannot be predicted by the employee.

Variable-ratio schedule
Giving reinforcers after varying or random number of occurrences of the desired behavior.

Variance reporting
Highlighting only those things that fail to meet the established standards.

Vertical communication
The flow of information both up and down the chain of command.

Video conferencing
An umbrella term referring to technologies that use live video to unite widely dispersed company operations or people.

Vigilance
The concern for and attention to the process of making a decision that occurs when the decision maker considers seven critical procedures.

Virtual workplace
A workplace with no walls and no boundaries; workers can work anytime, anywhere by linking to other people and information through technology.

Vision
The ability to predict opportunities and threats in the future.

Vision statement
A statement representing what the organization wants to become and where it wants to be in the future.

W

Whistle-blowing
Reporting alleged organizational misconduct or wrongdoing to the public.

Wide-area network (WAN)
An information system that extends over a broad geographic area, such as cities, regions, countries, or the world.

Work sample
A small part of an actual job completed by an applicant to predict performance on the job.

Written communication
Letters, memos, policy manuals, reports, forms, and other written documents.

Endnotes

CHAPTER 1

1. "The Best & Worst Managers of the Year," *BusinessWeek,* 10 January 2005, 55–68.
2. Ibid., 62.
3. D. Foust, "Gone Flat," *BusinessWeek,* 20 December 2004, 76–82.
4. "The Best & Worst Managers," 55–68.
5. "eBay's Secret," *Fortune,* 18 October 2004, 161–178.
6. "Who's Up? Who's Down?" *Fortune,* 18 October 2004, 181–198.
7. A. Bernasek, "Okay, Now What?" *Fortune,* 11 July 2001, 98–106; S. Finkelstein, "The Myth of Managerial Superiority in Internet Startups: An Autopsy," *Organizational Dynamics,* Fall 2001, 172–185; T. Mulaney, "Break Out the Black Ink," *BusinessWeek,* 13 May 2002; R. Hof, "The Wizard of Web Retailing," *BusinessWeek,* 20 December 2004, 18.
8. D. Ketchen, C. Snow, and V. Street, "Improving Firm Performance by Matching Strategic Decision-Making to Competitive Dynamics," *Academy of Management Executive* 18, no. 4 (2004): 29–43.
9. M. Follett, "Dynamic Administration," in *Dynamic Administration: The Collected Papers of Mary Parker Follett,* ed. H. Metcalf and L. Urwick (New York: Harper & Row, 1942).
10. P. Drucker, *The Effective Executive* (New York: Harper & Row, 1967); P. Drucker, "What Makes an Effective Executive," *Harvard Business Review* 82 (June 2004): 58.
11. Foust, 76–82.
12. H. Willmott, "Images and Ideals of Managerial Work: A Critical Examination of Conceptual and Empirical Accounts," *Journal of Management Studies* 21 (1984): 349–368; C. Hales, "What Do Managers Do? A Critical Review of the Evidence," *Journal of Management Studies* 23 (1986): 88–113; H. Willmott, "Studying Managerial Work: A Critique and a Proposal," *Journal of Management Studies* 24 (1987): 249–270; R. Webber, "General Management Past and Future," *Financial Times Mastering Management,* 1997; J. Collins, "Don't Rewrite the Rules of the Road," *BusinessWeek,* 28 August 2000, 206–208; J. Cortada, *21st Century Business* (London: Financial Times/Prentice Hall, 2001).
13. "Human Capital Index: 2001/2002 Survey Report," Watson Wyatt Worldwide, Washington, D.C.
14. H. Mintzberg, "The Manager's Job: Folklore and Fact," *Harvard Business Review* (September–October 1974): 91; H. Mintzberg, "The Manager's Job: Folklore and Fact," *Harvard Business Review* (March–April 1990): 49–61; H. Mintzberg and J. Gosling, "Educating Managers Beyond Borders," *Academy of Management Learning and Education* (September 2002): 64–76.
15. A. Kraut, P. Pedigo, D. McKenna, and M. Dunnette, "The Role of the Manager: What's Really Important in Different Management Jobs," *Academy of Management Executive* (November 1989): 286–293; M. Martinko and W. Gardner, "Structured Observation of Managerial Work: A Replication and Synthesis," *Journal of Management Studies* (May 1990): 330–357.
16. C. Pavett and A. Lau, "Managerial Work: The Influence of Hierarchical Level and Functional Specialty," *Academy of Management Journal* (1983): 170–177; C. Bartlett and S. Goshal, "The Myth of the Generic Manager: New Personal Competencies for New Management Roles," *California Management Review* 40, no. 1 (1997): 92–116.
17. Q. Huy, "In Praise of Middle Managers," *Harvard Business Review* (September 2001): 72–79.
18. R. Katz, "Skills of an Effective Administrator," *Harvard Business Review* (September–October 1974): 92.
19. A. Lustgarten, "A Hot, Steaming Cup of Customer Awareness: Howard Schultz," *Fortune,* 15 November 2004, 192.
20. R. Edmondson, "What Ghosn Will Do With Renault," *BusinessWeek,* 25 April 2005, 54.
21. H. Collingwood and D. Coutu, "Jack on Jack: The HBR Interview," *Harvard Business Review* (February 2002): 88–94.
22. J. Garten, "Andy Grove Made the Elephant Dance," *BusinessWeek,* 11 April 2005, 26.
23. See, for example, J. Doherty, "Same Old Story," *Barron's,* 10 December 2001, 13–16; J. Cooper and K. Madigan, "The Second Half Should be Healthier," *BusinessWeek,* 13 August 2001, 25–27; J. Byrne, "A Highflier's Legacy: Low Comedy," *BusinessWeek,* 14 January 2002, 16–19.
24. R. Hof and H. Green, "How Amazon Cleared That Hurdle," *BusinessWeek,* 4 Februrary 2002, 60–61.
25. H. Hof, "The Wizard of Web Retailing," *BusinessWeek,* 20 December 2004, 18.
26. J. Useem, "Dot-coms: What Have We Learned?" *Fortune,* 30 October 2000, 82–104; R. Hof and S. Hamm, "How E-Biz Rose, Fell, and Will Rise Anew," *BusinessWeek,* 13 May 2002, 64–72; T. Mulaney, "Break Out the Black Ink," *BusinessWeek,* 13 May 2002, 74–76.
27. Hof and Green, 60.
28. T. Mullaney and R. Hof, "E-Tailing Finally Hits Its Stride," *BusinessWeek,* 20 December 2004, 36–37.
29. D. Rynecki, "Make Their Pain Your Gain," *Fortune,* 9 July 2001, 158–159.
30. J. Weber and A. Therese, "How the Net Is Remaking the Mall," *BusinessWeek,* 9 May 2005, 60–61.
31. S. Baker and H. Green, "Blogs Will Change Your Business," *BusinessWeek,* 2 May 2005, 57–67.
32. See M. Porter, "Strategy and the Internet," *Harvard Business Review* (March 2001): 63–78 for a very good discussion on how the Internet has changed certain aspects of business.
33. A. Fisher, "Offshoring Could Boost Your Career," *Fortune,* 24 January 2005, 36. Also see askannie@fortunemail.com.
34. J. Garten, "The High-Tech Threat from China," *BusinessWeek,* 31 January 2005, 22.
35. P. Engardio and B. Einhorn, "Outsourcing Innovation: Special Report," *BusinessWeek,* 21 March 2005, 84–94;

D. Roberts, F. Balfour, P. Engardio, and J. Weber, "China Goes Shopping," *BusinessWeek,* 20 December 2004, 32–34. Also see Y. Luo, "Selling China: Foreign Direct Investment during the Reform Era," *Academy of Management Review* 30, no. 1 (January 2005): 200–203.

36. S. Hamm, P. Engardio, and F. Balfour, "Big Blue's Bold Step into China," *BusinessWeek,* 20 December 2004, 35–36.
37. See, for example, the entire edition of the *Academy of Management Executive* 19 (May 2005): 2.
38. A. Morrison and M. Von Glinow, "Women and Minorities in Management," *American Psychologist* 45 (1990): 200–208; "The Best Managers," *BusinessWeek,* 10 January 2005, 57.
39. G. Hickman and A. Creighton-Zollar, "Diverse Self-Directed Work Teams: Developing Strategic Initiatives for 21st Century Organizations," *Personnel Management* 27, no. 2 (Summer 1998): 187–200.
40. J. Crockett, "Diversity: Winning Competitive Advantage through a Diverse Workforce," *HR Focus* 76, no. 5 (May 1999): 9–10; J. Crockett, "Diversity as a Business Strategy," *Management Review* 88, no. 5 (May 1999): 62–63; "The Best Managers," *BusinessWeek,* 10 January 2005, 57.
41. P. Coy, "The Creative Economy," *BusinessWeek,* 21 August 2000, 76–82.
42. W. Miller, "Building the Ultimate Resource," *Management Review* 88, no. 1 (January 1999): 42–45; H. Oh, M. Chung, and G. Labianca, "Group Social Capital and Group Effectiveness: The Role of Informal Socializing Ties," *Academy of Management Journal* 47, no. 6 (December 2004): 875; A. Inkpen and E. Tsang, "Social Capital, Networks, and Knowledge Transfer," *Academy of Management Review* 30, no. 1 (January 2005): 146–165.
43. T. Stewart, *Intellectual Capital: The New Wealth of Organizations* (New York: Doubleday, 1998).
44. "They Fought the Law: A Parade of Alleged Corporate Wrongdoers Faced Their Accusers," *BusinessWeek,* 10 January 2005, 82–83.
45. "P. Shinkle, "Former Charter Executive Pleads Guilty," *St. Louis Post-Dispatch,* 27 January 2005, C1–C2.
46. D. Nicklaus, "Businesses Are Pushing against Requirements of Sarbanes–Oxley Act," *St. Louis Post-Dispatch,* 26 January 2005, C1; also see F. Clarke, G. Dean, and K. Oliver, "Corporate Collapse: Accounting, Regulatory and Ethical Failure," *Academy of Management Review* 30, no. 1 (January 2005): 192–196.
47. G. Colvin, "Ebbers, Lay & Scrushy: A Trifecta for the Feds," *Fortune,* 24 January 2005, 54.
48. "Jury Is Selected in Tyco Execs' Retrial," *St. Louis Post-Dispatch,* 26 January 2005, C2.
49. *Academy of Management Executive* 18, no. 2 (May 2004).

CHAPTER 2

1. "Sony Names Stringer First Foreign CEO," *PC Magazine,* March 2005 and "Sony Timeline," *Online Reporter,* 22 February 2003 (both from Thomson Higher Education computer database); "Sony Corporate Fact Sheet," http://www.sony.com; "Transformation 60—Confirming Sony's Position as a Leading Consumer Brand in the 21st Century," Sony Corporation press release, http://www.sony.com.
2. J. Smeltzer, "Java Fans Get a Jolt," *Orlando Sentinel,* 19 March 2005, C1ff.; D. Mercado, "Coffee Lovers Swallow Brew's Higher Cost," *Orlando Sentinel,* 19 March 2005, C1ff.
3. J. Snyder, "Storms Hammer Home the Competition for Customers," *Central Florida Business,* 18 October 2004, 18–19; J. Snyder, "Ace Hardware Stores Build Loyal, Post-Hurricanes Following," *Central Florida Business,* 18 October 2004, 18–19.
4. K. Griffith, "Signs Litter Landscape Long after Hurricanes, *Orlando Sentinel,* 27 December 2004, B1ff.
5. "Katrina Slams Gulf," *Orlando Sentinel,* 30 August 2005, A1ff.
6. J. Ball and J. White, "GM Offers to Enhance Job Security," *Wall Street Journal,* 7 September 1999, A3ff.
7. J. A. Conger, "Leadership: The Art of Empowering Others," *Academy of Management Executive* 3 (1989): 17–24.
8. F. Norris, "Krispy Kreme's Sticky Situation," *Orlando Sentinel,* 5 January 2005, C1ff.; P. Nowell, "Doughy Downturn," *Orlando Sentinel,* 23 November 2004, C1; M. Schneider, "State Agency Challenges OJ Labeling," *Orlando Sentinel,* 16 December 2004, C1ff.
9. "Nike, Inc. Increases Pay for Workers in Indonesia," *Orlando Sentinel,* 24 March 1999, B5.
10. E. Thompson, "Growers Leaving Tobacco Farming," *Orlando Sentinel,* 23 April 2005, A23.
11. L. J. Krajewski and L. P. Ritzman, *Operations Management: Strategy and Analysis,* 5th ed. (Reading, MA: Addison-Wesley, 1999).
12. "Neglect Internet? Compaq Brass Did," *Orlando Sentinel,* 20 April 1999, B5.
13. J. R. Evans, D. R. Anderson, D. J. Sweeney, and T. A. Williams, *Applied Production and Operations Management,* 3rd ed. (St. Paul: West, 1990), 423–428.
14. J. Evans and W. Lindsay, *Production/Operations Management: A Focus on Quality* (St. Paul: West, 1993).
15. B. Brocka and M. S. Brocka, *Quality Management* (Homewood, Ill.: Business One Irwin, 1992), 18.
16. D. Wren, *Evolution of Management Thought,* 2nd ed. (New York: Wiley, 1979).
17. F. W. Taylor, *Scientific Management* (New York: Harper & Row, 1911).
18. C. Wrege and A. G. Peroni, "Taylor's Pig-Tale: A Historical Analysis of Frederick W. Taylor's Pig-Iron Experiments," *Academy of Management Journal* 17 (March 1974): 6–27.
19. C. Wrege and A. M. Stotka, "Cooke Creates a Classic: The Story behind F.W. Taylor's Principles of Scientific Management," *Academy of Management Review* 3 (October 1978): 736–749.
20. M. Himmelberg, "Perks Other Than Money Keep Workers Happy," *Orlando Sentinel,* 9 May 1999, H1ff.
21. Wren, *Evolution of Management Thought.*
22. F. B. Gilbreth, *Principles of Scientific Management* (New York: Van Nostrand, 1911).
23. M. K. Starr, *Operations Management: A Systems Approach* (Danvers, MA: Boyd & Fraser, 1996), 375.
24. H. Fayol, *Industrial and General Administration* (New York: Pitman, 1930).
25. C. George, Jr., *The History of Management Thought* (Englewood Cliffs, NJ: Prentice-Hall, 1968).

26. J. F. Mee, "Pioneers of Management," *Advanced Management–Office Executive,* October 1962, 26–29.
27. M. Weber, *General Economic History,* trans. F. H. Knight (London: Allen & Unwin, 1927).
28. Wren, *Evolution of Management Thought.*
29. M. Weber, *The Theory of Social and Economic Organizations,* ed. and trans. A. M. Henderson and T. Parsons (New York: Free Press, 1947).
30. Ibid.
31. "Shareholders of Compaq Fume at Meeting," *Orlando Sentinel,* 23 April 1999, B6.
32. D. Ignatius, "The Egyptian Bureaucracy Galls Both the Public and Foreign Investors," *Wall Street Journal,* 24 March 1983.
33. M. P. Follett, *Creative Experience* (London: Longmans, Green, 1934).
34. M. P. Follett, "Dynamic Administration," in *Dynamic Administration: The Collected Papers of Mary Parker Follett,* ed. H. Metcalf and L. F. Urwick (New York: Harper & Row, 1942).
35. H. M. Parson, "What Happened at Hawthorne?" *Science* 183 (1974): 922–932.
36. J. A. Sonnenfeld, "Shedding Light on the Hawthorne Studies," *Journal of Occupational Behavior* 6 (1985): 111–130.
37. F. Kast and J. Rosenzweig, *Organization and Management: A Systems and Contingency Approach* (New York: McGraw-Hill, 1979).
38. D. McGregor, *The Human Side of Enterprise* (New York: McGraw-Hill, 1960), 33–58.
39. Ibid.
40. R. A. Baron and P. B. Paulus, *Understanding Human Relations: A Practical Guide to People at Work* (Needham Heights, MA: Allyn & Bacon, 1991), 312–313.
41. C. Barnard, *The Functions of the Executive* (Cambridge, MA: Harvard University Press, 1938).
42. B. Render and R. M. Stair, Jr., *Introduction to Quantitative Models for Management* (Englewood Cliffs, NJ: Prentice-Hall, 1996).
43. L. Austin and J. Burns, *Management Science* (New York: Macmillan, 1985).
44. T. Cook and R. Russell, *Introduction to Management Science* (Englewood Cliffs, NJ: Prentice-Hall, 1985), 6–20.
45. K. Boulding, "General Systems Theory—The Skeleton of Science," *Management Science* 2 (April 1956): 197–208.
46. Krajewski and Ritzman, *Operations Management,* 3–4.
47. Kast and Rosenzweig, *Organization and Management,* 102.
48. F. Luthans, "The Contingency Theory of Management: A Path Out of the Jungle," *Business Horizons* 16 (June 1973): 62–72.
49. J. Woodward, *Industrial Organizations: Theory and Practice,* 2nd ed. (London: Oxford University Press, 1980).
50. Ibid.
51. F. Kast and J. Rosenzweig, *Contingency Views of Organizations and Management* (Chicago: Science Research Associates, 1973).
52. F. Robert, "As UPS Tries to Deliver More to Its Customers, Labor Problem Grows," *Wall Street Journal,* 23 May 1994.
53. "More Businesses Hispanic-Owned, Government Says," *Orlando Sentinel,* 12 July 1996, B1.
54. M. A. Vonderembse and G. P. White, *Operations Management: Concepts, Methods and Strategies,* 3rd ed. (Minneapolis: West, 1996), 638–651.
55. Starr, *Operations Management,* 144.
56. J. Healey, "Global Competition Fells Japan Tradition," *USA Today,* 27 October 1999, 1B; J. Schmit, "Placard: Will Work for Pride," *USA Today,* 12 November 1999, 1B; J. Schmit and P. Hadfield, "Japan's Students Uneasy about Jobs," *USA Today,* 1 April 1999, 5B.
57. W. Ouchi, *Theory Z: How American Business Can Meet the Japanese Challenge* (Reading, MA: Addison-Wesley, 1981), 60.
58. All from Thomson Higher Education computer database: "Business Week Sends Advice to Sony's Stringer," *Online Reporter,* 25 March 2005, 18; "Westerner to Run Sony," *Client Server News,* 14 March 2005, 6; "Stringer: A Shared Vision and a Will to Manage," *Online Reporter,* 12 March 2005, 16; "Behind the Smiles at Sony," *Economist.com,* 10 March 2005; "Sony Names Stringer First Foreign CEO," *eWeek,* 7 March 2005; "Sony Corporation Announces New Management Structure," *JCNNewswire,* 7 March 2005; "Hitachi, Sony to Adopt US-Style Incentive Pay," *Online Reporter,* 8 November 2003; "Sony to Cut 20,000 Jobs over Three Years," *Information Week,* 28 October 2003.

CHAPTER 3

1. J. Lubin, P. Davies and A.M. Squeo, "Bristol-Myers to Settle U.S. Probe," *Wall Street Journal,* 6 June 2005, A3, A12; D. Brady and M. Vickers, "AIG: What Went Wrong," *BusinessWeek,* 11 April 2005, 32–35; G. Colvin, "Ebbers, Lay & Scrushy: A Trifecta for the Feds," *Fortune,* 24 January 2005, 54.
2. A. Lawrence, J. Weber, and J. Post, *Business and Society: Stakeholders, Ethics, Public Policy,* 11th ed. (New York: McGraw-Hill Irwin, 2005), 7; J. Post, L. Preston, and S. Sachs, *Redefining the Corporation: Stakeholder Management and Organizational Wealth* (Palo Alto, CA: Stanford University Press, 2002); T. Donaldson and L. Preston, "The Stakeholder Theory of the Corporation: Concepts, Evidence, Implications," *Academy of Management Review* (January 1995): 71–83.
3. M. Javidan, G. Stahl, F. Brodbeck, and C. Wilderom, "Cross-Border Transfer of Knowledge: Culture Lessons from Project GLOBE," *Academy of Management Executive* 19 (May 2005):59–76; G. McDonald and P. Pak, "It's All Fair in Love, War, and Business: Cognitive Philosophies in Ethical Decision Making," *Journal of Business Ethics* 15 (1996): 973–996.
4. E. White, "PR Firms Advise Corporations on Social Responsibility Issues," *Wall Street Journal,* 13 November 2002, B10; M. Pava, "The Talmudic Concept of 'Beyond the Letter of the Law': Relevance to Business Social Responsibilities," *Journal of Business Ethics* 15 (1996): 941–950.
5. H. R. Bowen, *Social Responsibilities of the Businessman* (New York: Harper & Row, 1953), 6.
6. Most of this discussion comes from S. Wartick and P. Cochran, "The Evolution of the Corporate Social Performance Model," *Academy of Management Review* 10 (1985): 758–769.

7. A. Carroll and A. Buchholtz, *Business & Society: Ethics and Stakeholder Management,* 6th ed. (Mason, OH: Thomson South-Western, 2006), 38.
8. J. Useem, "Should We Admire Wal-Mart?" *Fortune,* 8 March 2004, 118–120.
9. J. Snider, R. P. Hill, D. Martin, "Corporate Social Responsibility in the 21st Century: A View from the World's Most Successful Firms," *Journal of Business Ethics* 48, no. 2 (December 2003): 175–188; "A CEO Forum: What Corporate Social Responsibility Means to Me," *Business and Society Review* (Spring 1992).
10. L. Preston and J. Post, "Private Management and Public Policy," *California Management Review* 23 (1991): 57.
11. A. Carroll, "The Four Faces of Corporate Citizenship," *Business and Society Review* 100 (1998): 1–7; A. Carroll, "The Pyramid of Corporate Social Responsibility: Toward the Moral Management of Organizational Stakeholders," *Business Horizons* (July/August 1991): 39–48.
12. L. Armstrong, "Are You Ready for a Hybrid?" *BusinessWeek,* 25 April 2005, 118–126.
13. "It's Time To Turn Up the Heat on Global Warming," *Fortune,* 3 October 2005: 21.
14. A. Carroll and A. Buchholtz—see endnote #15, pages 54–60; *and* B. Grow, "The Debate over Doing Good," *BusinessWeek,* 15 August 2005, 76–78.
15. K. Grit, "Corporate Citizenship: How to Strengthen the Social Responsibility of Managers," *Journal of Business Ethics* (August 2004): 97–107; E. Schrage, "Supply and the Brand;" G. Zwetsloot, "From Management to Systems to Corporate Social Responsibility," *Journal of Business Ethics* 44, no. 2/3 (May 2003): 201–208; B. Daviss, "Profits from Principle," *Futurist* (March 1999): 28–33.
16. D. Dalton and R. Cosier, "The Four Faces of Social Responsibility," *Business Horizons* (May/June 1982): 19–27. Also see Carroll and Buchholtz, *Business & Society,* 179–180, for a related discussion.
17. Carroll and Buchholtz, *Business & Society,* 48.
18. J. Dubashi, "Insulated from Reality," *Financial World* 158 (June 1989): 64–66; S. Gellerman, "Why 'Good' Managers Make Bad Ethical Choices," *Harvard Business Review* (July/August 1986): 85–90.
19. Hampel, "Why They Keep on Lying."
20. B. Blackstone, "U.S. Antismoking Plan Is Criticized," *Wall Street Journal,* 9 June 2005, B2.
21. Ibid; Hampel, "Why They Keep on Lying."
22. N. Byrnes,"The Tobacco Suit That's Going Up in Smoke," *BusinessWeek,* 27 June 2005, 70–71.
23. J. Harrison and R. Freeman, "Stakeholders, Social Responsibility, and Performance: Empirical Evidence and Theoretical Perspectives," *Academy of Management Journal* 42 (1999): 479–485.
24. Target advertisement, *St. Louis Post-Dispatch,* 15 May 2005, A7; L. Armstrong, "Are You Ready for a Hybrid?" *BusinessWeek,* 25 April 2005, 118–136; L. Alberthal, "Corporate Policy on Community Outreach and Philanthropy," *Executive Speeches* (April/May 1999): 1–5.
25. J. Useem, "America's Most Admired Companies," *Fortune,* 7 March 2005, 66–70; "The Best & Worst Managers of the Year," *BusinessWeek,* 10 January 2005, 55–68; C. Neal, "A Conscious Change in the Workplace," *Journal of Quality and Participation* (March/April 1999): 27–30.
26. L. Grossmanx, "Rating Corporate Social Responsibility," *Business Date* 12, no. 4 (August 2004): 5–8; "Royal Standard for Enterprising Business," *Energy & Environmental Management* (September/October 2002): 12.
27. Zwetsloot, "From Management to Systems."
28. L. Alexander and W. Mathews, "The Ten Commandments of Corporate Social Responsibility," *Business and Society Review* 50 (1984): 62–66.
29. Colvin, "Ebbers, Lay, & Scrushy"; J. Veiga, "Bringing Ethics into the Mainstream: An Introduction to the Special Topic," *Academy of Management Executive* 18, no. 2 (2004): 37–38.
30. T. Thomas, J. Schermerhorn, J. Dienhart, "Strategic Leadership of Ethical Behavior in Business," *Academy of Management Executive* 18, no. 2 (2004): 56–66.
31. L. Trevino and M. Brown, "Managing to Be Ethical: Debunking Five Business Ethics Myths," *Academy of Management Executive* 18, no. 2 (2004): 69–81.
32. R. Berenbeim, "One Company, One Market, One Code, One World," *Vital Speeches of the Day* 65, no. 22 (September 1999): 696–698.
33. J. Beyer and D. Nino, "Ethics and Cultures in International Business," *Journal of Management Inquiry* 8, no. 3 (September 1999): 287–297; R. Berenbeim, "Global Corporate Ethics Practices," *Conference Board Research Report,* 121243–00-RR, 1999.
34. M. Rokeach, *The Nature of Human Values* (New York: Free Press, 1973).
35. G. Cavanaugh, *American Business Values in Transition* (Upper Saddle River, NJ: Prentice-Hall, 1980).
36. See, for example, "Leadership and Business Ethics: Does It Matter? Implications for Management," *Journal of Business Ethics* 20, no. 4 (July 1999): 327–335.
37. "The Chairman of the Board Looks Back," *Fortune,* 28 May 2001, 63–76.
38. A. Serwer, "The Waltons: Inside America's Richest Family," *Fortune,* 15 November 2004, 86–116.
39. For a discussion on value-based culture, see P. Pruzan, "From Control to Value-Based Management and Accountability," *Journal of Business Ethics* 17, no. 13 (October 1998): 1379–1394.
40. "Exposure in Cyberspace," *Wall Street Journal,* 21 March 2001, B1; S. Henderson and C. Snyder, "Personal Information Privacy: Implications for MIS Managers," *Information and Management* 36, no. 4 (October 1999): 213–220.
41. "New Technology Strains Ethics," *USA Today,* June 1999, 4.
42. J. Anders, "Congress Is Wasting No Time in Effort to Address Major Issues Raised by Web," *Wall Street Journal,* 27 February 2001, B13; "Putting the Ethics in E-Business," *Computerworld,* 6 November 2000, 34, 45, 81.
43. J. Veiga, "Bringing Ethics into the Mainstream: An Introduction to the Special Topic," *Academy of Management Executive* 18, no. 2 (May 2004): 37–38.
44. R. Perloff, "Self-Interest and Personal Responsibility Redux," *American Psychologist* 42 (1987): 3–11; V. Barry, *Moral Issues in Business* (Belmont, CA: Wadsworth, 1979), 43.

45. M. Valasquez, D. Moberg, and G. Cavanagh, "Organizational Statesmanship and Dirty Politics: Ethical Guidelines for the Organizational Politician," *Organizational Dynamics* (Autumn 1993): 65–80.
46. D. Luban, "Judicial Activism and the Concept of Rights," Report from the Institute for Philosophy and Public Policy (College Park, MD: University of Maryland, Winter/Spring 1994), 12–17.
47. For a discussion on this approach, see M. Weinstein, "Bringing Logic to Bear on the Liberal Dogman," *New York Times,* 1 December 2002, 5; J. Rawls, *A Theory of Justice* (Cambridge, MA: Harvard University Press, 1971).
48. T. Thomas, J. Schermerhorn, and J. Dienhart, "Strategic Leadership of Ethical Behavior in Business," *Academy of Management Executive* 18, no. 2 (May 2004): 56–66; D. Morf, M. Schumacer, and S. Vitel, "A Survey of Ethics Officers in Large Organizations," *Journal of Business Ethics* 20, no. 3 (July 1999): 265–271.
49. S. Wall, "Executive Commentary," *Academy of Management Executive* 28, no. 2 (May 2004): 82.
50. B. Gaumnitz and J. Lere, "A Classification Scheme for Codes of Business Ethics," *Journal of Business Ethics* (February 2004): 329; C. Wiley, "The ABC's of Business Ethics: Definitions, Philosophies and Implementation," *Industrial Management* 37, no. 1 (January/February 1995): 22–27.
51. S. Modic, "Corporate Ethics: From Commandments to Commitment," *Industry Week* (December 1987): 33–36.
52. R. Gilmartin, "Innovation, Ethics and Core Values: Keys to Global Success," *Vital Speeches of the Day* 65, no. 7 (January 1999): 209–213; R. Berenbeim, "Global Corporate Ethics Practices," *Conference Board Research Report,* 121243–99-RR, 1999.
53. A. Murray, "Citigroup CEO Pursues Culture of Ethics," *Wall Street Journal* 2 March 2005, A2.
54. Thomas et al., "Strategic Leadership."
55. Bernbeim, "Global Corporate."
56. G. Weaver, L. Trevino, and P. Cochran, "Corporate Ethics Programs as Control Systems: Influences of Executive Commitment and Environmental Factors," *Academy of Management Journal* 42 (1999): 41–57.
57. G. Steiner and J. Steiner, *Business, Government, and Society: A Managerial Perspective,* 11th ed. (New York: McGraw-Hill Irwin, 2006), 201–203.
58. J. Byrne, "After Enron: The Ideal Corporation," *BusinessWeek,* 19 August 2002, 68–71; D. Rice and C. Dreilinger, "Rights and Wrongs of Ethics Training," *Training & Development Journal* (May 1990): 103–109.
59. M. Miceli and J. Near, "Whistleblowing: Reaping the Benefits," *Academy of Management Executive* 8, no. 3 (1994): 65–72.
60. L. Driscoll, "A Better Way to Handle Whistle-Blowers: Let Them Speak," *BusinessWeek,* 27 July 1999, 36.
61. J. Near, M. Rehg, J. Van Scotter, and M. Miceli, "Does Type of Wrongdoing Affect the Whistle-Blowing Processs?" *Business Ethics Quarterly* 14, no. 2 (April 2004): 219.
62. T. Mohr and D. Slovin, "Making Tough Calls Easy," *Security Management* 49, no. 3 (March 2005): 51–56.
63. N. Swartz, "Whistleblower Complaints Growing," *Information Management Journal* 39, no. 3 (May/June 2005): 8.
64. Driscoll, "A Better Way to Handle Whistle-Blowers."
65. Ibid.
66. W. Zellner, S. Anderson, and L. Cohn, "A Hero and a Smoking-Gun Letter," *BusinessWeek,* 28 January 2002, 34–35.
67. S. Amer, "Do the Right Thing," *Successful Meetings* 54, no. 3 (March 2005): 72.
68. R. Lacayo and A. Ripley, "Persons of the Year," *Time,* 30 December 2002, 30–33.
69. For a discussion on this topic, see Carroll and Buchholtz, *Business & Society,* 55–56.
70. R. Parloff, "Is the $200 Billion Tobacco Deal Going Up in Smoke?" *Fortune,* 7 March 2005, 126–140.
71. J. Bruno, "Citigroup Agrees to $2 Billion Enron Case Settlement," *St. Louis Post-Dispatch,* 11 June 2005, B1.
72. G. Morgenson, "Companies Behaving Badly," *New York Times,* 6 March 2005, Section 3, 1.
73. Thomas et al., "Strategic Leadership."

CHAPTER 4

1. D. Hambrick and J. Fredrickson, "Are You Sure You Have a Strategy?" *Academy of Management Executive* 15, no. 4 (2001): 48–59; H. Mintzberg, "Crafting Strategy," *Harvard Business Review* (July/August 1987): 66–75; R. Evered, "So What Is Strategy?" *Long Range Planning* 16 (1983): 57–72.
2. M. Goold and J. Quinn, "The Paradox of Strategic Control," *Strategic Management Journal* 11 (1990): 43–57.
3. Mintzberg, "Crafting Strategy."
4. D. Ketchen, C. Snow, and V. Hoover, "Improving Firm Performance by Matching Strategic Decision-Making Processes to Competitive Dynamics," *Academy of Management Executive* 18, no. 4 (2004): 29–43; P. J. H. Schoemaker, "How to Link Strategic Vision to Core Capabilities," *Sloan Management Review* (Fall 1992): 67–81.
5. S. Stershirc, "Mission Statements Can Be a Field of Dreams," *Marketing News,* 1 February 1993, 7ff.
6. D. Calfee, "Get Your Mission Statement Working," *Management Review* (January 1993): 54–57.
7. B. Bartkus, M. Glassman, and R. Bruce McAffe, "Mission Statements: Are They Smoke and Mirrors?" *Business Horizons* (November 2000): 23–36.
8. See, for example, A. H. Van de Ven, "Medtronic's Chairman William George on How Mission-Driven Companies Create Long-Term Shareholder Value," *Academy of Management Executive* (November 2001): 39–48.
9. "Mission Possible," *BusinessWeek,* 16 August 1999, 12.
10. "On a Mission," *Gallup Management Journal* (Winter 2001): 6–7.
11. R. Tedlow, "What the Titans Can Teach Us," *Harvard Business Review* (December 2001): 70–78.
12. J. Cosco, "Down to the Sea in Ships," *Journal of Business Strategy* (November/December 1995): 48.
13. S. Kaplan and E. Beinhocker, "The Real Value of Strategic Planning," *MIT Sloan Management Review* 44, no. 2 (Winter 2003): 71–76.
14. T. Wheelen and D. J. Hunger, *Strategic Management and Business Policy,* 8th ed. (Upper Saddle River, NJ: Prentice

Hall, 2002), 57; T. Wheelen and D. J. Hunger, *Strategic Management* (Reading, MA: Addison-Wesley, 1990), 100.
15. P. Bray, "Dentsply Extracts Market Share," *NASDAQ* (June 2002): 50–54.
16. P. Engardio and B. Einhorn, "Outsourcing Innovation," *BusinessWeek,* 21 March 2005, 84–94.
17. "Why Moonves Didn't Lose Letterman," *BusinessWeek,* 25 March 2002, 62; "Home Center Industry Tailors Itself to Consumers," *Chain Store Age* (August 1999): A26–A28; E. Fisher, "Levi's Panting for Youth Sales," *Insight on the News,* 28 December 1998, 40; J. Wyatt, "Playing the Woofie Card," *Fortune,* 6 February 1995, 130–132.
18. S. Shinn, "Beauty King," *BizEd* (July/August 2005): 20–23.
19. M. Jortberg, "Markets of One: Creating Customer-Unique Value through Mass Customization," *Journal of Product Innovation Management* 18, no. 2 (March 2001): 129–131.
20. "Alone in America," *Futurist* (September/October 1995): 56–57.
21. "Population Growth Slowing as Nation Ages," *Daily Tribune* (Ames, IA), 14 March 1996, A7.
22. L. Armstrong, "Are You Ready for a Hybrid?" *BusinessWeek,* 25 April 2005, 118–126; "Royal Standard for Enterprising Business," *Energy & Environmental Management* (September/October 2002): 12.
23. "Ground Wars," *BusinessWeek,* 21 May 2001, 64; "Out of the Box at UPS," *BusinessWeek,* 10 January 2000, 76.
24. "Electronic Capabilities Prompting Changing Trends in Cardiovascular Monitoring," *Health Industry Today* (February 2000): 8.
25. "The Man Who Built Pixar's Incredible Innovation Machine," *Fortune,* 15 November 2004, 207–212.
26. G. Anders, "AOL's True Believers," *Fast Company* (July 2002): 96–105.
27. F. Vogelstein, "10 Tech Trends to Watch in 2005," *Fortune,* 10 January 2005, 43–60.
28. T. Bisoux, "The Sarbanes–Oxley Effect," *BizEd* (July/August 2005): 24–29.
29. "The Good News in All That Bad News: The Painful Cleansing Taking Place Could Usher in a Stronger, Healthier Market," *BusinessWeek,* 29 July 2002, 201.
30. "Best Practices Are Hard to Copy," *Harvard Business Review* 83, no. 5 (May 2005): 79.
31. L. Grant, "Why Warren Buffet's Betting Big on American Express," *Fortune,* 30 October 1995, 70–84.
32. M. McNamee, "Don't Leave Home without a Freebie," *BusinessWeek,* 8 November 1999, 150–152; R. Buckman, "American Express Plans to Overhaul, Relaunch Online-Brokerage Operation," *Wall Street Journal,* 6 October 1999, C7; "AmEx Gets the Blues, but Smiles," *Credit Card Management* 12, no. 7 (October 1999): 10–12.
33. G. Anders, "The View from the Top: The Past, Present, and Future of the Internet Economy, as Seen by Amazon.com's Jeff Bezos," *Wall Street Journal,* 12 July 1999, R52.
34. B. Gimbel, "Southwest's New Flight Plan," *Fortune,* 16 May 2005, 93–98; S. Shinn, "Luv, Colleen," *BizEd* (March/April 2003): 18–23.
35. R. Nakashima, "On Road to Hog Heaven," *St. Louis Post-Dispatch,* 28 June 2005, C3.
36. M. Porter, "How Competitive Forces Shape Strategy," *Harvard Business Review* 57, no. 2 (March/April 1979): 137–145.
37. S. Zahra and S. Chaples, "Blind Spots in Competitive Analysis," *Academy of Management Executive* 7, no. 2 (1993): 7–28.
38. "Labor Shortage Unlikely to Cause Soaring Wages in First Half of 2000," *HR Focus* (March 2000): 8.
39. M. Conlin, "The Big Squeeze on Workers," *BusinessWeek,* 13 May 2002, 96.
40. See, for example, N. Wingfield, "E-Commerce (A Special Report)—the Industries—Reading the Riot Act: Amazon.com Isn't Bad, Says an Independent Bookseller; It's Just Dangerous," *Wall Street Journal,* 12 July 1999, R46.
41. C. Snow and L. Hrebiniak, "Strategy, Distinctive Competence, and Organizational Performance," *Administrative Science Quarterly* 25 (June 1980): 317–337.
42. M. Hitt, R. D. Ireland, and R. Hoskisson, *Strategic Management: Competitiveness and Globalization,* (Mason, OH: Thomson South-Western, 2003), 72–105.
43. J. Barney, "Looking Inside for Competitive Advantage," *Academy of Management Executive* 9, 4 (1995): 49–61.
44. J. Heskett, *Southwest Airlines 2002: An Industry under Siege* (Boston: Harvard Business School Publishing, 2003).
45. S. Holmes, "First the Music, Then the Coffee," *BusinessWeek,* 22 November 2004, 64; A. Brown, "What's Brewing at Starbucks?" *Black Enterprise* 35, no. 1 (August 2004): 25; C. Daniels, "Mr. Coffee," *Fortune,* 14 April 2003, 139.
46. B. Gimbel, "Southwest's New Flight Plan," *Fortune,* 16 May 2005, 93–98.
47. G. Hamel and C. K. Prahalad, "Strategic Intent," *Harvard Business Review* 83, no. 7 (July/August 2005): 148; G. Hamel and C. K. Prahalad, "Strategic Intent," *Harvard Business Review* 67, no. 3 (May/June 1989): 63–77.
48. M. Mankins and R. Steele, "Turning Great Strategy into Great Performance," *Harvard Business Review* 83, no. 7 (July/August 2005): 64; Barney, "Looking Inside."
49. J. Pfeffer, "Dare to Be Different Great Companies," *Business 2.0* 5, 8 (September 2004): 58.
50. J. Garten, "Andy Grove Made the Elephant Dance," *BusinessWeek,* 11 April 2005, 26.
51. R. Robinson, "Planned Patterns of Strategic Behavior and Their Relationship to Business-Unit Performance," *Strategic Management Journal* 9 (1988): 43–60.
52. S. Kerr, "Establishing Organizational Goals and Rewards," *Academy of Management Executive* 18, no. 4 (November 2004): 122–123; G. Latham, "The Motivational Benefits of Goal-Setting," *Academy of Management Executive* 18, no. 4 (November 2004): 126–129; E. Locke, "Linking Goals to Monetary Incentives," *Academy of Management Executive* 18, no. 4 (November 2004): 130–133; S. Kerr and S. Landauer, "Using Stretch Goals to Promote Organizational Effectiveness and Personal Growth: General Electric and Goldman Sachs," *Academy of Management Executive* 18, no. 4 (November 2004): 134–138; K. Shaw, "Changing the Goal-Setting Process at Microsoft," *Academy of Management Executive* 18, no. 4 (November 2004): 139–142; R. Renn, "Moderation by Goal Commitment of the Feedback-Performance Relationship: Theoretical Explanation and Preliminary

Study," *Human Resource Management Review* 13, no. 4 (Winter 2003): 561–581; J. Lebediker, "The Supervisor as a Coach: 4 Essential Models for Setting Performance Expectations," *Supervision* 56, no. 12 (December 1995): 14–18; J. Collins, "Turning Goals into Results: The Power of Catalytic Mechanisms," *Harvard Business Review* (July/August 1999): 71–82.

53. Kerr and Landauer, "Using Stretch Goals."
54. Collins, "Turning Goals into Results."
55. Robinson, "Planned Patterns of Strategic Behavior."
56. "The Clouds Keep Getting Thicker," *BusinessWeek,* 26 November 2001, 46.
57. "The Fortunes—and Misfortunes—of War," *BusinessWeek,* 14 January 2002, 90.
58. M. Porter, *Competitive Advantage: Creating and Sustaining Superior Performance* (New York: Free Press, 1985),
59. J. Bachmann, "Competitive Strategy: It's OK to Be Different," *Academy of Management Executive* 16, no. 2 (2002): 61–65.
60. A. Thompson and A. J. Strickland, *Strategic Management: Concepts and Cases* (New York: McGraw-Hill Irwin, 2003), 151, 167–168; C. Hill, "Differentiation versus Low Cost of Differentiation and Low Cost: A Contingency Framework," *Academy of Management Review* 13, no. 3 (1988): 401–412.
61. Ibid.
62. M. Corboy and D. O'Corrbui, "The Seven Deadly Sins of Strategy," *Management Accounting* 77, no. 10 (November 1999): 29–30.
63. K. Shimizu and M. Hitt, "Strategic Flexibility: Organizational Preparedness to Reverse Ineffective Strategic Decisions," *Academy of Management Executive* 18, no. 4 (November 2004): 44–59; L. Huston, "Using Total Quality to Put Strategic Intent into Motion," *Conference Executive Summary* (September/October 1992): 21–23.
64. Mankins and Steele, "Turning Great Strategy."
65. C. Rhoads, "Motorola's Modernizer," *Wall Street Journal,* 23 June 2005: B1, B5.
66. Bisoux, "The Sarbanes–Oxley Effect."
67. P. Lorange and D. Murphy, "Considerations in Implementing Strategic Control," *Journal of Business Strategy* 4 (Spring 1984): 27–35.
68. J. Eckhouse, "In Search of the Customer-Centric Enterprise," *Informationweek,* 6 December 1999, 209–210.
69. N. Tay and R. Lusch, "A Preliminary Test of Hunt's General Theory of Competition: Using Artificial Adaptive Agents to Study Complex and Ill-Defined Environments," *Journal of Business Research* 58, no. 9 (September 2005): 1155–1168.

CHAPTER 5

1. A. DeGeus, "Planning as Learning," *Harvard Business Review* (March/April 1988): 70–74.
2. S. Kaplan and E. Beinhocker, "The Real Value of Strategic Planning," *MIT Sloan Management Review* 44, no. 2 (Winter 2003): 71–76; P. Drucker, *Managing for Results* (New York: Harber & Row, 1964); P. Drucker, *The Effective Executive* (New York: Harper & Row, 1967).
3. B. Matherne, "If You Fail to Plan, Do You Plan to Fail?" *Academy of Management Executive* 18, no. 4 (November 2004): 156–157.
4. J. Foster, "General Malaise at General Mills," *BusinessWeek,* 1 July 2002, 96–104.
5. W. Shea, "Strategic Planning Clears Up Alice in Wonderland Thinking," *Wichita Business Journal* at http://www.bizjournals.com/wichita/stories/1999/07/12/editorial3.html, 26 July 2005.
6. C. Miller and L. Cardinal, "Strategic Planning and Firm Performance: A Synthesis of More Than Two Decades of Research," *Academy of Management Journal* (March 1994) 1649–1685; N. Capon, J. Farley, and J. Hulbert, "Strategic Planning and Financial Performance: More Evidence," *Journal of Management Studies* (January 1994): 22–38.
7. Kaplan and Beinhocker, "The Real Value of Strategic Planning"; P. Brews and M. Hunt, "Learning to Plan and Planning to Learn: Resolving the Planning School/Learning School Debate," *Strategic Management Journal* (December 1999): 889–913.
8. B. Gimbel, "Southwest's New Flight Plan," *Fortune,* 16 May 2005, 93–98; S. Shinn, "Luv, Colleen," *BizEd* (March/April 2003): 18–23; "The Chairman of the Board Looks Back," *Fortune,* 28 May 2001, 63–74.
9. D. Aaker and E. Joachimsthaler, "The Lure of Global Branding," *Harvard Business Review* 77, no. 6 (November/December 1999): 137–144.
10. R. Michaels, "Planning: An Effective Management Tool or Corporate Pastime?" *Journal of Marketing Management* (Spring 1986): 259.
11. H. Mintzberg, "Rethinking Strategic Planning. Part I: Pitfalls and Falacies," *Long Range Planning* 27 (1994): 12–21.
12. "How Planning Can Destroy Value," *Harvard Business Review* 77, no. 2 (March/April 1999): 42–43.
13. F. Delmar and S. Shane, "Does Business Planning Facilitate the Development of New Businesses?" *Strategic Management Journal* 24, no. 12 (2003): 1165–1185.
14. W. Chan Kim and R. Mauborgne, "Charting Your Company's Future," *Harvard Business Review* (June 2002): 77–84.
15. Delmar and Shane, "Does Business Planning."
16. "How Planning Can Destroy Value."
17. W. Brickner and D. Cope, *The Planning Process* (Boston: Winthrop, 1977), 52–56.
18. D. Hambrick and J. Fredrickson, "Are You Sure You Have a Strategy?" *Academy of Management Executive* 15, no. 4 (2001): 48–59.
19. D. Ketchen, C. Snow, and V. Hoover, "Improving Firm Performance by Matching Strategic Decision-Making Processes to Competitive Dynamics," *Academy of Management Executive* 18, no. 4 (2004): 29–43.
20. S. Wheelwright, "Strategy, Management, and Strategic Planning Approaches," *Interfaces* 14 (1984): 19–33.
21. M. Porter, "From Competitive Advantage to Corporate Strategy," *Harvard Business Review* (May/June 1987): 43–59.
22. H. Ansoff, "Critique of Henry Mintzberg's 'The Design School: Reconsidering the Basic Premises of Strategic

Management,'" *Strategic Management Journal* (February 1991): 449–461.

23. N. Byrnes, "Restocking Pepsi," *BusinessWeek,* 11 April 2005, 46; "The Best Managers: Steven Reinemund," *BusinessWeek,* 10 January 2005, 57; "PepsiCo and Quaker Complete Their Merger, Forming the Fifth Largest Food and Beverage Company," *PR Newswire,* 2 August 2001.
24. R. Burgelman and A. Grove, "Strategic Dissonance," *California Management Review,* 1996, 38, no. 2 (1996): 8–28.
25. D. Mills and G. Friesen, "Emerging Business Realities," *Journal of Management Consulting* 10, no. 4 (November 1999): 39–45.
26. Byrnes, "Restocking Pepsi."
27. S. Zahra, "An Interview with Peter Drucker," *Academy of Management Executive* 17, no. 3 (2003): 9–12.
28. M. Crossan, "Altering Theories of Learning and Action: An Interview with Chris Argyris," *Academy of Management Executive* 17, no. 2 (2003): 40–46.
29. A. Grandey, "When 'The Show Must Go On': Surface Acting and Deep Acting as Determinants of Emotional Exhaustion and Peer-Rated Service Delivery," *Academy of Management Journal* 46, no. 1 (2003): 86–96.
30. K. Eddleston, D. Kidder, and B. Litzky, "Who's the Boss? Contending with Competing Expectations from Customers and Management," *Academy of Management Executive* 16, no. 4 (2002): 85–95.
31. J. Crockett, "Diversity: Winning Competitive Advantage through a Diverse Workforce," *HR Focus* 76, no. 5 (May 1999): 9–10.
32. P. Drucker, *The Practice of Management* (New York: Harper, 1954).
33. E. Marlow and R. Schilhavy, "Expectation Issues in Management by Objectives Programs," *Industrial Management* 33, no. 4 (1991): 29; K. Davis and J. Newstrom, *Human Behavior at Work in Organizational Behavior* (New York: McGraw-Hill, 1989), 209.
34. J. Gordon, *Management and Organizational Behavior* (Boston: Allyn & Bacon, 1990), 129–132.
35. J. Muczyk and B. Reimann, "MBO as a Complement to Effective Leadership," *Academy of Management Executive* 3 (1989): 131–138.
36. J. Kondrasuk, "Studies in MBO Effectiveness," *Academy of Management Review* 6 (1981): 419–430.
37. J. Ewing, "Siemens Climbs Back," *BusinessWeek,* 5 June 2000, 79–82.
38. J. Kaplan and D. Norton, *The Strategy-Focused Organization: How Balanced Scorecard Companies Thrive in the New Business Environment* (Boston: Harvard Business School Press, 2000).
39. D. Ketchen, Jr., "An Interview with Raymond E. Miles and Charles C. Snow," *Academy of Management Executive* 17, no. 4 (2003): 97–103.
40. A. Zardkoohi, "Do Real Options Lead to Escalation of Commitment?" *Academy of Management Review* 29, no. 1 (2004): 111–119.
41. D. McConkey, "Planning for Uncertainty," *Business Horizons* (January/February 1987): 40–43.
42. Kaplan and Beinhocker, "The Real Value of Strategic Planning."
43. I. Wylie, "There Is No Alternative Too . . . ," *Fast Company* (July 2002): 106–111.
44. L. Gerstner, "Can Strategic Planning Pay Off?" in *Perspectives on Strategic Marketing Management* (Boston: Allyn & Bacon, 1980).
45. S. Covey, *The 7 Habits of Highly Effective People* (New York: Simon & Schuster, 1989).
46. "Strategic Planning Is Back," *BusinessWeek,* 25 August 1996, 25–30; J. Rosenzweig, F. Kast, and T. Mitchell, *The Frank and Ernest Manager* (Los Altos, CA: Crisp Publications, 1992).
47. See, for example, J. Fernandez and M. Barr, *The Diversity Advantage: How American Business Can Outperform Japanese and European Companies in the Global Marketplace* (New York: Lexington Books, 1993); M. Gentile, ed., *Differences That Work: Organizational Excellence through Diversity* (Boston: Harvard Business School Press, 1994).
48. L. Martel, "The Principles of High Performance—and How to Apply Them," *Journal of Organizational Excellence* (Autumn 2002): 45–59.
49. See, for example, E. DeBono, *Six Thinking Hats* (Boston: Little, Brown, 1985); K. Albrecht, *Brain Power: Learn to Improve Your Thinking Skills* (Upper Saddle River, NJ: Prentice-Hall, 1990).
50. Kaplan and Beinhocker, "The Real Value of Strategic Planning."

CHAPTER 6

1. S. Hale, "Cypress Gardens to Close Its Gates, *Orlando Sentinel,* 11 April 2003, A1ff.; L. Roberts, "Cypress Gardens Drew Tourists Long Before Disney," *Orlando Sentinel,* 11 April 2003, A10.
2. M. J. Hicks, *Problem Solving in Business and Management* (London: Chapman & Hall, 1991).
3. "Ford Recalling Pickups, SUVs," *Orlando Sentinel,* 28 January 2005, A11.
4. S. Jacobson and S. Powers, "Deadly Crash on Turnpike Stresses Need for Guardrails," *Orlando Sentinel,* 30 November 2004, A1ff.; S. Powers, "Barriers Will Be Installed on Turnpike, Other Roads," *Orlando Sentinel,* 3 March 2005, B5ff.
5. C. Sherman, "Teen Dies Day after Gas Exposure," *Orlando Sentinel,* 10 January 2005, B1ff.; G. Taylor, "Restaurants Change Their CO_2 Systems Following Fatal Accident," *Orlando Sentinel,* 12 February 2005, C1ff.
6. M. Kaufman, "Canada Finds 3rd Case of Mad-Cow Disease," *Orlando Sentinel,* 12 January 2005, A3; J. Neuman, "Possible Case of Mad-Cow Reported," *Orlando Sentinel,* 19 November 2004, A3; J. Jackson, "Rockin' Back to Its Roots," *Orlando Sentinel,* 21 February 2002, C1ff.
7. J. Gecker, "Asian Diners Force Menu Makeover," *Orlando Sentinel,* 21 January 2005, A4.
8. "Pepsi Puts Freshness Dates on Diet Soda Bottles, Cans," *Orlando Sentinel,* 31 March 1994, B5.
9. J. Fineman, "Coca Cola to Add Lime-Flavored Coke," *Orlando Sentinel,* 8 January 2005, C3; D. Tommelleo, "Town Turns Out for 'Vanilla Day,'" *Orlando Sentinel,* 9 May 2002, C3.
10. "Coke Will Introduce New Zero-Calorie Cola," *Orlando Sentinel,* 22 March 2005, C3.
11. A. Pham, "iPod Craze Sprouts New Gadgets," *Orlando Sentinel,* 6 January 2005, C1ff.

12. C. Sheehan. "Bayer Cranks Up Cipro Output," *Orlando Sentinel,* 17 October 2001, B1ff.
13. J. Schmeltzer, "Airport Security Draws Giants," *Orlando Sentinel,* 17 October 2002, C2; "Lockheed Martin Team Awarded Homeland Security Contract to Plan, Coordinate Heightened Airport Security Measures," Lockheed Martin press release, 25 April 2002.
14. I. Rodriguez, "Danger Drives Up Demand: South Florida Armored Car Suppliers Grow to Meet Increased Need for Security," *South Florida Sun-Sentinel,* 13 March 2005, 1B; I. Rodriguez, "Danger Drives Demand for Armored-Car Makers," *Orlando Sentinel,* 26 March 2005, C1ff.
15. D. Haugh, "Product Placement: Nike Execs Hope to Get Plenty of Mileage Out of Tiger Woods' Amazing Shot at the Masters," *Orlando Sentinel,* 13 April 2005, A1ff.; "Nike to Launch Ad Campaign on Woods' Shot," Forbes.com, 13 April 2005; T. Spousta, "Woods' Chip Lodged in Masters Lore, k181K5n3 USAToday.com, 12 April 2005.
16. C. Deutsch, "The Handwriting on the Post-It Note," *New York Times,* 6 July 1999, C1ff.; S. Tully, "Why Go for Stretch Targets," *Fortune,* 14 November 1994, 148–150; "The Mass Production of Ideas, and Other Impossibilities," *Economist,* 18 March 1995, 72.
17. P. Fandt, *Management Skills: Practice and Experiences* (St. Paul: West, 1994).
18. C. O'Reilly, "Variations in Decision Makers' Use of Information Sources," *Academy of Management Journal* 25 (1982): 756–771; C. O'Reilly, "The Use of Information in Organizational Decision Making: A Model and Some Propositions," in *Research in Organizational Behavior,* vol. 5, ed. B. Staw and L. Cummings (Greenwich, CT: JAI Press, 1983), 103–139.
19. A. Goldman, "Mattel Updates Aging Barbie," *Orlando Sentinel,* 10 February 2002, H1ff.
20. "Coke's Brand-Loyalty Lesson," *Fortune,* 5 August 1985, 44–46.
21. D. Vaughan, "Autonomy, Interdependence, and Social Control: NASA and the Space Shuttle *Challenger,*" *Administrative Science Quarterly* 35 (1990): 225–257.
22. D. Jones and E. Neuborne, "Fate, Fortune Ride on Flow of Critical Data," *USA Today,* 2 July 1996, B1–B2.
23. D. Tracy, "Fallen Foam Likely Cause; Missing Tiles from Re-Entry Crucial to Investigation," *Orlando Sentinel,* 4 February 2003, A1ff.
24. D. Snachez, "Burger King Sees How New Menu Stacks Up," *Orlando Sentinel,* 8 December 2001, B1ff.
25. S. H. Meitner, "Breakfast Bulks Up," *Orlando Sentinel,* 29 March 2005, C1ff.
26. J. Slater, "Big-Burger Lovers Rejoice," *Orlando Sentinel,* 16 November 2004, C3.
27. K. Eisenhardt, "Making Fast Strategic Decisions in High-Velocity Environments," *Academy of Management Journal* 32 (1989): 543–576.
28. M. A. Verespej, "Gutsy Decisions of 1994: Gerstner Looked before Leaping," *Industry Week,* 23 January 1995, 36.
29. "Long Distance: Innovative MCI Unit Finds Culture Shock in Colorado Springs," *Wall Street Journal,* 25 June 1996.
30. S. W. Floyd and B. Wooldridge, "Managing the Strategic Consensus: The Foundation of Effective Implementation," *Academy of Management Executive* 6 (1992): 27–39.
31. A. Adler, "Saturn Recalls All Cars Made before April '93 for Fire Risk," *Columbia SC State,* 11 August 1993, A1; B. Meier, "Engine Fires Prompt G.M. to Issue Recall of 80% of Saturns," *New York Times,* 11 August 1993, A1; O. Suris, "Recall by Saturn Could Tarnish Its Reputation," *Wall Street Journal,* 11 August 1993, A3; R. Truett, "Calls Swamp Saturn Dealers since Recall," *Orlando Sentinel,* 11 August 1993, A1.
32. H. Mintzberg, "The Manager's Job: Folklore and Fact," *Harvard Business Review* (March/April 1990): 163–176.
33. J. G. March, "Decision Making Perspective," in *Perspectives on Organization Design and Behavior,* ed. A. H. Van de Ven and W. S. Joyce (New York: Wiley, 1981).
34. N. J. Adler, *International Dimensions of Organizational Behavior,* 2nd ed. (Boston: PWS-Kent, 1991); P. Sethi, N. Maniki, and C. Swanson, *The False Promise of the Japanese Miracle* (Marshfield, MA: Pitman, 1984).
35. F. N. Brady, *Ethical Managing: Rules and Results* (New York: Macmillan, 1990).
36. Adapted from S.W. Gellerman, "Why 'Good' Managers Make Bad Ethical Choices," *Harvard Business Review* (July/August 1986) 85–90; and K. H. Blanchard and N. V. Peale, *The Power of Ethical Management* (Homewood, IL: Irwin, 1987).
37. H. A. Simon, *Model of Man* (New York: Wiley, 1957).
38. O. Behling and N. L. Eckel, "Making Sense Out of Intuition," *Academy of Management Executive* 5 (1991): 46–54.
39. R. Rowen, *The Intuitive Manager* (Boston: Little, Brown, 1986).
40. Robert Johnson, "Universal Orlando's New Thrill Seeker," *Central Florida Business,* 15 April 2002, 14–15; Robert Johnson, "Universal Orlando Thinks Big," *Orlando Sentinel,* 16 March 2002, A1ff.
41. Behling and Eckel, "Making Sense."
42. J. Schmit, "PC Maker Realizes a Dream," *USA Today,* 17 July 1996, B4.
43. C. R. Schwenk, "Information, Cognitive Biases, and Commitment to a Course of Action," *Academy of Management Review* 11 (1986): 298–310.
44. M. H. Bazerman, *Judgment in Managerial Decision Making* (New York: Wiley, 1986).
45. T. R. Weiss, "United Axes Troubled Baggage System at Denver International Airport," *Computerworld Online,* 10 June 2005.
46. I. Janis and L. Mann, *Decision Making: A Psychological Analysis of Conflict, Choice, and Commitment* (New York: Free Press, 1977).
47. D. Ciampa, *Total Quality* (Reading, MA: Addison-Wesley, 1992).
48. V. H. Vroom and P. W. Yetton, *Leadership and Decision Making* (Pittsburgh, PA: University of Pittsburgh, 1973).
49. V. H. Vroom and A. G. Jago, *The New Leadership: Managing Participation in Organizations* (Upper Saddle River, NJ: Prentice Hall, 1988).
50. V. H. Vroom, "Leadership and the Decision-Making Process," *Organizational Dynamics* (Spring 2000): 82–94.
51. Vroom and Jago, *The New Leadership.*
52. R. A. Cooke and J. A. Kernagan, "Estimating the Difference between Group versus Individual Performance on Problem-Solving Tasks," *Group and Organization Studies* 12 (1987): 319–342.

53. W. L. Ury, J. M. Brett, and S. B. Goldberg, *Getting Disputes Resolved* (San Francisco: Jossey-Bass, 1989).
54. I. L. Janis, *Victims of Groupthink* (Boston: Houghton Mifflin, 1972).
55. L. R. Beach, *Making the Right Decision: Organizational Culture, Vision, and Planning* (Upper Saddle River, NJ: Prentice Hall, 1993).
56. R. Whyte, "Groupthink Reconsidered," *Academy of Management Journal* 14 (1989): 40–55.
57. Adapted from C. R. Schwenk and R. A. Cosier, "Effect of the Expert, Devil's Advocate, and Dialectic Inquiry Methods on Prediction Performance," *Organizational Behavior and Human Performance* 1 (1980): 409–424.
58. Beach, *Making the Right Decision.*
59. D. M. Schweiger, W. R. Sandberg, and J. W. Ragan, "Group Approaches for Improving Strategic Decision Making: Analysis of Dialectical Inquiry, Devil's Advocacy, and Consensus," *Academy of Management Journal* 29 (1986): 51–71.
60. A. F. Osborn, *Applied Imagination*, rev. ed. (New York: Scribner, 1957).
61. Ibid.
62. B. Schlender, "How Bill Gates Keeps the Magic Going," *Fortune,* 18 June 1990, 82–89.
63. A. Delbecq, A. Van de Ven, and D. Gustafson, "Guidelines for Conducting NGT Meetings," in *Group Techniques for Program Planning* (Glenview, IL: Scott Foresman, 1975).
64. R. DeStephen and R. Hirokawa, "Small Group Consensus: Stability of Group Support of the Decision, Task Process, and Group Relationships," *Small Group Behavior* 19 (1988): 227–239.
65. D. M. Hegedus and R. V. Rasmussen, "Task Effectiveness and Interaction Process of a Modified Nominal Group Technique in Solving an Evaluation Problem," *Journal of Management* 12 (1986): 545–560.
66. R. Cosier and C. Schwenk, "Agreement and Thinking Alike: Ingredients for Poor Decisions," *Academy of Management Executive* 4 (1990): 69–74.
67. Schwenk and Cosier, "Effect of the Expert."
68. Ibid.
69. H. A. Simon, *The New Science of Management* (Upper Saddle River, NJ: Prentice Hall, 1977), 47.
70. Z. Espinosa, "The Comeback Rig—Schwinn Bounces Back with a Hot New Suspension Bike," *Mountain Bike* (February 1995): 50–52.
71. J. M. Kopf, J. G. Krevze, and H. H. Beam, "Using a Strategic Planning Matrix to Improve a Firm's Competitive Position," *Journal of Accountancy* 175 (July 1993): 97–101.
72. F. R. David, "The Strategic Planning Matrix—A Quantitative Approach," *Long Range Planning,* 19 October 1986, 102.
73. F. R. David, *Strategic Management*, 4th ed. (New York: Macmillan, 1993), 234.
74. A. A. Thompson, Jr., and A. J. Strickland III, *Strategic Management: Concepts and Cases* (Homewood, IL: Irwin, 1992), 193.
75. J. A. Pearce III and R. B. Robinson, Jr., *Strategic Management: Formulation, Implementation, and Control*, 4th ed. (Homewood, IL: Irwin, 1991), 263.
76. David, *Strategic Management*, 225–227.
77. R. Burnett, "Olive Gardens Get Rush Order," *Orlando Sentinel,* 25 March 2005, C1ff.
78. "Smokey Bones Celebration," *Central Florida Business,* 14 March 2005, 3; S. H. Meitner, "Hungry for Diners: Smokey Bones Ready to Grow," *Orlando Sentinel,* 6 February 2005, H1ff.
79. S. H. Meitner, "Darden's Not Rushing 'Casual Elegance' Chain," *Orlando Sentinel,* 15 February 2005, C1ff.
80. P. Haspeslagh, "Portfolio Planning: Uses and Limitations," *Harvard Business Review* 60 (January/February 1982): 58–173.
81. D. F. Abell and J. S. Hammond, *Strategic Market Planning: Problems & Analytical Approaches* (Upper Saddle River, NJ: Prentice Hall, 1979).
82. Thompson and Strickland, *Strategic Management.*
83. S. C. Certo and J. P. Peter, *Strategic Management: Concepts and Applications*, 2nd ed. (New York: McGraw-Hill, 1991), 107–110.
84. Pearce and Robinson, *Strategic Management,* 267–272.
85. C. W. Hofer and D. Schendel, *Strategy Formulation: Analytical Concepts* (St. Paul: West, 1978), 33.
86. R. Johnson, "Disney Zeros in on Resort Pools," *Central Florida Business,* 24 December 2001, 8.
87. "Burger King to Hire More Former Welfare Recipients," *Orlando Sentinel,* 27 February 1999, C10.
88. "GM to Equip Cars with Sensors to Open Trunks," *Orlando Sentinel,* 8 June 1999, A3.
89. "Colt Exiting Handgun Business," *Orlando Sentinel,* 11 October 1999, A3.
90. R. Roy, "Expressway Not a Dead End for Homeless—Program Will Give Them Jobs," *Orlando Sentinel,* 21 April 1993, B1ff.
91. "Boss Divides $128 Million among 550 Loyal Workers," *Jacksonville Times-Union,* 12 September 1999, A14.
92. "Mattel Leads Hunt for Safer Plastics," *Orlando Sentinel,* 9 December 1999, B5.

CHAPTER 7

1. K. Rogg, D. Schmidt, C. Shull, and N. Schmitt, "Human Resource Practices, Organizational Climate, and Customer Satisfaction," *Journal of Management* 27 (2001): 431–439; P. Wright, B. Dunford, and S. Snell, "Human Resources and the Resource-Based View of the Firm," *Journal of Management* 27, (2001): 701–721.
2. J. Hackman, G. Oldham, R. Janson, and K. Purdy, "A New Strategy for Job Enrichment," *California Management Review* 17 (Summer 1975): 57–71.
3. Ibid., 58.
4. N. Dodd and D. Ganster, "The Interactive Effects of Variety, Autonomy, and Feedback on Attitudes and Performance," *Journal of Organizational Behavior* 17 (1996): 329–347.
5. "Learning without Limits," *Fast Company* (July/August 1999) 461. See also C. Sittenfeld, "Letter Perfect," *Fast Company* (April 2002): 50.
6. See, for example, T. Galpin, *The Human Side of Change* (San Francisco: Joseey-Bass, 1996).
7. A. Markels, "The Wisdom of Chairman Ko," *Fast Company* (November 1999): 258–276.

8. G. Johns, J. Xie, and F. Yongqing, "Mediating and Moderating Effects in Job Design," *Journal of Management* 18 (1992): 657–676; J. Dean, Jr., and S. Snell, "Integrated Manufacturing and Job Design: Moderating Effects of Organizational Inertia," *Academy of Management Journal* 34 (1991): 776–804.
9. S. Papmarcos and L. Sama, "Managing Diversity: Individual Differences in Work-Related Values, Gender, and the Job Characteristics–Job Involvement Linkage," *International Journal of Management* 15, no. 4 (December 1998): 431–441.
10. H. Sondak, "Review of 'Employing Bureaucracy: Managers, Unions, and the Transformation of Work in the 20th Century,'" *Academy of Management Review* 30, no. 3 (July 2005): 637–639.
11. A. Smith, *The Wealth of Nations* (New York: Modern Library, 1937).
12. P. Cappelli, "A Market Driven Approach to Retaining Talent," *Harvard Business Review* (January 2000): 103.
13. J. Cunningham and T. Eberle, "A Guide to Job Enrichment and Redesign," 67 *Personnel* (February 1990): 56–61.
14. R. Zemke, C. Raines, and B. Filipczak, *Generations at Work: Managing the Clash of Veterans, Boomers, Xers, and Nexters in Your Workplace* (New York: American Management Association, March 2000).
15. "Flexibility Is No Key to Stability," *BusinessWeek*, 5 March 2001, 30.
16. M. Campion, L. Cheraskin, and M. Stevens, "Career-Related Antecedents and Outcomes of Job Rotation," *Academy of Management Journal* 37, no. 6 (1994): 1518–1542.
17. W. Byham, "Grooming Leaders," *Executive Excellence* 16, no. 6 (June 1999): 181; L. Thach, "14 Ways to Groom Executives," *Training* 35, no. 8 (August 1998): 52–55.
18. S. Harryson, "How Cannon and Sony Drive Product Innovation through Networking and Application-Focused R&D," *Journal of Product Innovation Management* 14, no. 4 (July 1997): 288–295.
19. L. Burke, "Developing High-Potential Employees in the New Business Reality," *Business Horizons* 40, no. 2 (March/April 1997): 18–24.
20. I. Mitroff, R. Mason, and C. Pearson, "Radical Surgery: What Will Tomorrow's Organizations Look Like?" *Academy of Management Executive* 8 (1994): 11–21.
21. S. Perlman, "Employees Redesign Their Jobs," *Personnel Journal* 67 (November 1990): 37–40.
22. J. Neal and C. Tromley, "From Incremental Change to Retrofit: Creating High-Performance Work Systems," *Academy of Management Executive* 9 (1995): 42–54.
23. S. Shellenbarger, "Three Myths That Make Managers Push Staff to the Edge of Burnout," *Wall Street Journal* 17 March 1999, B1.
24. S. Shellenbarger, "Are Saner Workloads the Unexpected Key to More Productivity?" *Wall Street Journal* (Eastern Edition), 10 March 1999, B1.
25. C. Farren, "A Smart Team Makes the Difference," *Human Resource Professional* 12, no. 1 (January/February 1999): 12–16; A. Gregory, "Solving the Teambuilding Jigsaw," *Works Management* 52, no. 1 (January 1999): 56–59.
26. S. Bishop, "Cross-Functional Project Teams in Functionally Aligned Organizations," *Project Management Journal* 30, no. 3 (September 1999): 61.
27. M. Campion and A. Higgs, "Design Work Teams to Increase Productivity and Satisfaction," *HR Magazine* (October 1995): 101–107.
28. M. Belbin, *Management Teams—Why They Succeed or Fail* (Boston: Butterworth-Heinemann, 1996).
29. L. Gilson, J. Mathieu, C. Shalley, and T. Ruddy, "Creativity and Standardization: Complementary or Conflicting Drivers of Team Effectiveness?" *Academy of Management Journal* 48, no. 3 (2005): 521–531; M. Campion, E. Papper, and G. Medsker, "Relations between Work Team Characteristics and Effectiveness: A Replication and Extension," *Personnel Psychology* 49 (1996): 429–452.
30. M. Moravec, O. Johannessen, and T. Hjelmas, "The Well-Managed SMT," *Management Review* 87, no. 6 (June 1998): 56–58.
31. C. Christensen and M. Overdorf, "Meeting the Challenge of Disruptive Change," *Harvard Business Review* (March 2000): 66.
32. C. Solomon, "Building Teams across Borders," *Workforce* 3, no. 6 (November 1998): 12–17.
33. J. Lipnack and J. Stamps, "Virtual Teams," *Executive Excellence* 16, no. 5 (May 1999): 14–15; "See Your Online," *Fortune* (Winter 1999): 190.
34. D. Van Fleet and A. Bedeian, "A History of the Span of Management," *Academy of Management Review* 2 (1997): 356–372.
35. "Managers Oversee," *Wall Street Journal* 9 January 2001, A1.
36. For a general background, see P. Collins and F. Hull, "Technology and Span of Control: Woodward Revisited," *Journal of Management Studies* 23 (March 1986): 143–164.
37. B. Dive, "When Is An Organization Too Flat?" *Across the Board* (July/August 2003): 20–23.
38. P. Jehiel, "Information Aggregation and Communication in Organizations," *Management Science* 45, no. 5 (May 1999): 659–669.
39. B. Davison, "Management Span of Control: How Wide Is Too Wide?" *Journal of Business Strategy* 24, no. 4 (2003): 22–29.
40. L. Thompson, "Improving the Creativity of Organizational Work Groups," *Academy of Management Executive* 17, no. 1 (2003): 96–109.
41. W. Cascio, "Strategies for Responsible Restructuring," *Academy of Management Executive* 16, no. 3 (2002): 80–81.
42. S. Wetlaufer, "Organizing for Empowerment: An Interview with AES's Roger Sant and Dennis Bakke," *Harvard Business Review* (January/February 1999): 110–123.
43. N. Van Yperen and M. Hagedoorn, "Do High Job Demands Increase Intrinsic Motivation or Fatigue or Both? The Role of Job Control and Job Social Support," *Academy of Management Journal* 46, no. 3 (2003): 339–348; N. Biggart and R. Delbridge, "Systems of Exchange," *Academy of Management Review* 29, no. 1 (2004): 28–49.

44. S. Zahra, "The Practice of Management: Reflections on Peter F. Drucker's Landmark Book," *Academy of Management Executive* 17, no. 3 (2003): 16–23.
45. R. Maruca, "Fighting the Urge to Fight Fires," *Harvard Business Review* (November/December 1999): 30–32.
46. P. Mills and G. Ungson, "Reassessing the Limits of Structural Empowerment: Organizational Constitution and Trust as Controls," *Academy of Management Review* 28, no. 1 (2003): 143–153; L. Bossidy, "The Job No CEO Should Delegate," *Harvard Business Review* 79, no. 3 (2001): 47.
47. S. Bistayi, "Delegate—or Not?" *Forbes* 21 (April 1997): 20–21.
48. S. Bushardt, D. Duhon, and A. Fowler, Jr., "Management Delegation Myths and the Paradox of Task Assignment," *Business Horizons* 34 (March/April 1991): 37–43.
49. M. Douglas, "How to Delegate Safely," *Training and Development Journal* (February 1987): 8.
50. "Top 10 Leadership Tips from Jeff Immelt," *Fast Company* 81 (April 2001): 96.
51. M. Schrage, "I Know What You Mean and I Can't Do Anything about It," *Fortune,* 2 April 2001, 186.
52. F. Reichheld, "Manager's Journal: September 11's Loyalty Dividend," *Wall Street Journal* 10 September 2002, B4.
53. "Chris Galvin on the Record," *BusinessWeek* 16 July 2001, 76.
54. "The Best Managers: Steven Reinemund," *BusinessWeek,* 10 January 2005, 57.
55. P. Senge, "Learning Leaders," *Executive Excellence* 16, no. 11 (November 1999): 12–13.
56. D. Vinton, "Delegation for Employee Development," *Training and Development Journal* (January 1987): 65–67.
57. P. Adler, "Building Better Bureaucracies," *Academy of Management Executive* 13, no. 4 (November 1999): 36–49.
58. J. Rau, "Two Stages of Decision Making," *Management Review* 88, no. 11 (December 1999): 101.
59. Ibid.
60. M. Yate, "Delegation: The Key to Empowerment," *Training and Development Journal* (April 1991): 23–24.
61. A. Balsamo, "The Power of Empowerment," *Management Review* 88, no. 10 (November 1999): 111.
62. J. Carter, "Minimizing the Risks from Delegation," *Supervisory Management* (February 1992): 1–2.
63. S. Gracie, "Delegate Don't Abdicate," *Management Today* (March 1999): 92–94.
64. R. Rohrer, "Does the Buck Ever Really Stop?" *Supervision* 60, no. 4 (April 1999): 11–12.
65. M. Douglas, "How to Delegate Safely."
66. Yate, "Delegation: The Key."
67. Vinton, "Delegation for Employee Development."
68. R. Wilkinson, "Think before You Open Your Mouth!" *Supervision* 52 (May 1991): 17–19.
69. M. Townsend, "Let the Employees Carry the Ball," *Personnel Journal* 69 (October 1990): 30–31.
70. M. Haynes, "Delegation: There's More to It Than Letting Someone Else Do It," *Supervisory Management* 25 (January 1980): 9–15.
71. T. Horton, "Delegation and Team Building: No Solo Acts Please," *Management Review* (September 1992): 58–61.

CHAPTER 8

1. L. Kikulis, T. Slack, and C. Hinings, "Sector-Specific Patterns of Organizational Design Change," *Journal of Management Studies* 32 (January 1995): 67–100; M. Burke and K. Tulett, "Impact of Information Needs on Organizational Design," *Journal of the American Society for Information Science* 50, no. 4 (April 1999): 380–381.
2. C. Claycomb, C. Droge, and R. Germain, "The Effects of Just-in-Time with Customers on Organizational Design and Performance," *International Journal of Logistics Management* 10, no. 1 (1999): 37–58.
3. U. Tsolmon, "Review of *Strategic Restructuring for Nonprofit Organizations: Mergers, Integrations, and Alliances* by A. Kohm and D. La Piana," *Academy of Management Review* 30, no. 3 (July 2005): 643–645; A. Kohm and D. La Piana, *Strategic Restructuring for Nonprofit Organizations: Mergers, Integrations, and Alliances* (Westport, CT: Praeger, 2003).
4. J. Clancy and P. Cappelli, "Is Loyalty Dead?" *Across the Board* 36, no. 6 (June 1999): 14–19; B. Carroll, "Self-Managed Knowledge Teams Simplify High-Tech Manufacturing," *National Productivity Review* 18, no. 2 (Spring 1999): 35–39.
5. S. Hamm, "Beyond Blue," *BusinessWeek,* 18 April 2005, 68–76; W. Schaff, "Restructuring Pays Off for Motorola," *Information Week,* 26 July 2004, 72; P. Sellers, "P&G: Teaching an Old Dog New Tricks," *Fortune,* 31 May 2004, 166–180; S. Shinn, "The Maverick CEO," *BizEd* (January/February 2004): 16–21; M. Good and A. Campbell, "Do You Have a Well-Designed Organization?" *Harvard Business Review* (March 2002): 117–124.
6. D. Jennings and S. Seaman, "High and Low Levels of Organizational Adaptation: An Empirical Analysis of Strategy, Structure, and Performance," *Strategic Management Journal* (July 1994): 459–475; H. Boschken, "Strategy and Structure: Reconceiving the Relationship," *Journal of Management* (March 1990): 135–150; D. Miller, "Relating Porter's Business Strategies to Environment and Structure: Analysis and Performance Implications," *Academy of Management Journal* 31 (1988): 280–308; D. Miller, C. Droge, and J. Toulouse, "Strategic Process and Content as Mediator between Organizational Context and Structure," *Academy of Management Journal* 31 (1988): 544–569; R. Miles and C. Snow, *Organizational Strategy, Structure, and Process* (New York: McGraw-Hill, 1978).
7. Hamm, "Beyond Blue."
8. Sellers, "P&G."
9. J. Gamble, "PepsiCo's Acquisition of Quaker Oats," in *Strategic Management: Concepts and Cases,* eds. A. Thompson, Jr., and A. Strickland III (New York: McGraw-Hill Irwin, 2003), 502–535.
10. "Illinois Central Deal Spurs Reorganization by Canadian National," *Wall Street Journal,* 15 April 1999, A4.
11. R. Sookdeo, "The New Global Consumer," *Fortune* (Autumn/Winter 1993): 68–77.
12. P. Lewis and P. Fandt, "The Strategy-Structure Fit in Multinational Corporations: A Revised Model," *International Journal of Management* (June 1990): 137–146.

13. Kellogg Company, 2001 Annual Report.
14. "HM Creates International Division," *Publishers Weekly* 246, no. 2 (January 1999): 12.
15. "GE Reorganizes into Six Units," *St. Louis Post-Dispatch,* 24 June 2005, C2.
16. L. Heller, "Amazon Sees Retail Service Reshaping Company Future," *DSN Retailing Today,* 23 June 2003, 12.
17. S. Johnston, "Microsoft Reorganizes," *InformationWeek*, 5 April 1999, 30.
18. D. Cackowski, M. Najdawi, and Q. Chung, "Object Analysis in Organizational Design: A Solution for Matrix Organizations," *Project Management Journal* 31, no. 3 (September 2000): 44–51.
19. L. Thompson, "Improving the Creativity of Organizational Work Groups," *Academy of Management Executive* 17, no. 1 (2003): 96–109; W. Casico, "Strategies for Responsible Restructuring," *Academy of Management Executive* 16, no. 3 (2002): 80–81.
20. W. Bernasco, P. Weerd-Nederhof, H. Tillema, and H. Boer, "Balanced Matrix Structure and New Product Development Process at Texas Instruments' Material and Controls Division," *R&D Management* 29, no. 2 (April 1999): 121–131.
21. B. Dyer, A. Gupa, and D. Wilemon, "What First-to-Market Companies Do Differently," *Research Technology Management* 42, no. 2 (March/April 1999): 15–21.
22. Hamm, "Beyond Blue"; D. Nadler and M. Tushman, *Competing by Design* (New York: Oxford Press, 1997).
23. Ibid.; S. Tully, "The Modular Corporation," *Fortune,* 8 February 1993, 106–114.
24. A. Serwer, "The Education of Michael Dell," *Fortune,* 7 March 2005, 72–82; J. Byrne, "The Virtual Corporation," *BusinessWeek,* February 1993, 98–103.
25. S. Cohen and D. Mankin, "Complex Collaborations for the New Global Economy," *Organizational Dynamics* 31, no. 2 (2002): 117–133; D. Tapscott, "Rethinking Strategy in a Networked World," *Strategy & Business* 24 (2001): 34–41.
26. D. Hambrick and J. Fredrickson, "Are You Sure You Have a Strategy?" *Academy of Management Executive* 15, no. 4 (2001): 48–59.
27. Serwer, "The Education."
28. B. Nussbaum, "The Power of Design," *BusinessWeek,* 17 May 2004, 86–94.
29. A. Goerzen, "Managing Alliance Networks: Emerging Practices of Multinational Corporations," *Academy of Management Executive,* 19, no. 2 (May 2005): 94–107.
30. C. Snow, R. Miles, and H. Coleman, Jr., "Managing 21st Century Network Organizations," *Organizational Dynamics* 10 (February 1992): 5–20.
31. Ibid.
32. Ibid.
33. S. Pritchard, "Inside Dell's Lean Machine," *Works Management* 55, no. 12 (December 2002): 14–16.
34. Hambrick and Fredrickson, "Are You Sure."
35. Snow et al., "Managing 21st Century."
36. Hamm, "Beyond Blue."
37. P. Siekman, "The Snap-Together Business Jet," *Fortune,* 21 January 2002, 104A–104H.
38. J. Bush and A. Frohman, "Communication in a 'Network' Organization," *Organizational Dynamics,* 20, no. 2 (1991): 23–36.
39. J. Sampler and J. Short, "Strategy in Dynamic Information-Intensive Environments," *Journal of Management Studies* 35, no. 4 (July 1998): 429–436.
40. See, for example, J. Ito and R. Peterson, "Effects of Task Difficulty and Interunit Interdependence on Information Processing Systems," *Academy of Management Journal* 4 (1986): 139–149; J. Chency, "Interdependence and Coordination in Organizations: A Role-System Analysis," *Academy of Management Journal* 26 (1983): 156–162; J. McCann and D. Ferry, "An Approach for Assessing and Managing Inter-Unit Interdependence," *Academy of Management Review* 4 (1979): 113–120.
41. J. Thompson, *Organizations in Action* (New York: McGraw-Hill, 1967).
42. J. Galbraith, "Organizational Design: An Information Processing View," *Interfaces* 4 (May 1974): 3.
43. Sellers, "P&G"; Gamble, "PepsiCo's Acquisition of Quaker Oats."
44. B. Flynn and F. Flynn, "Information-Processing Alternatives for Coping with Manufacturing Environment Complexity," *Decision Sciences* 30, no. 4 (Fall 1999): 1021–1052.
45. A. Serwer, "The Waltons: Inside America's Richest Family," *Fortune,* 15 November 2004, 86–116.
46. S. Cliffe, "Knowledge Management: The Well-Connected Business," *Harvard Business Review* (July/August 1998): 17–21.
47. P. Adler, "Building Better Bureaucracies," *Academy of Management Executive* 13, no. 4 (November 1999): 36–49; S. Mohrman, "Integrating Roles and Structure in the Lateral Organization," in *Organizing for the Future,* ed. J. Galbraith, E. Lawler III, and Associates (San Francisco: Jossey-Bass, 1993).
48. D. Sobek II, J. Liker, and A. Ward, "Another Look at How Toyota Integrates Product Development," *Harvard Business Review* (July/August 1998): 36–49.
49. A. Townsend, S. DeMarie, and A. Hendrickson, "Virtual Teams: Technology and the Workplace of the Future," *Academy of Management Executive* 12, no. 3 (August 1998): 17–29.
50. "Sharing Knowledge through BP's Virtual Team Network," *Harvard Business Review* (September/October 1997): 152–153. See also Flynn and Flynn, "Information-Processing."
51. See, for example, B. Milligan, "Despite Attempts to Break Them, Functional Silos Live On," *Purchasing* 127, no. 7 (November 1999): 24–46.
52. G. Garnier, "Context and Decision Making Autonomy in Foreign Affiliates of U.S. Multinational Corporations," *Academy of Management Journal* 25 (1982): 893–908.
53. A. Ferner, "Being Local World-wide: ABB and the Challenge of Global Management Relations," *Industrielles* 55, no. 3 (Summer 2000): 527–529.
54. See, for example, E. Moltzen, "The 1999 Top 25 Executives: The Comeback Kids," *Computer Reseller News,* 15 November 1999, 165; S. Berglas, "What You Can Learn

From Steve Jobs," Inc. 21, no. 14 (October 1999): 29–32; J. Sculley, *Odyssey: Pepsi to Apple—A Journey of Adventures Ideas for the Future* (New York: Harper & Row, 1987).

55. "Best Managers: Edward Breen," *BusinessWeek*, 10 January 2005, 63; S. Tully, "Mr. Cleanup," *Fortune*, 15 November 2004, 151–163.
56. P. Kafta, "Diversify and Conquer," *Forbes*, 12 May 2002, 102.
57. C. Bendersky, "Organizational Dispute Resolution Systems: A Complementarities Model," *Academy of Management Review* 29, no. 4 (2003): 643–656.
58. C. Claycomb, C. Droge, and R. Germain, "The Effect of Just-in-Time with Customers on Organizational Design and Performance," *International Journal of Logistics Management* 10, no. 1 (1999): 37–58.
59. S. Kalagnanam and M. Lindsay, "The Use of Organic Models of Control in JIT Firms: Generalizing Woodward's Findings to Modern Manufacturing Practices," *Accounting, Organizations and Society* 24, no. 1 (January 1999): 1–30.
60. C. Rhoads, "Handset Sales Help Motorola Return to Profit," *Wall Street Journal*, 20 July 2005, A1; "The Best Advice I Ever Got," *Fortune*, 21 March 2005, 104; Serwer, "The Education"; "Hello Moto," *Economist* 370, no. 8357 (January 2004): 58.
61. P. Lawrence and J. Lorsch, *Organization and Environment* (Burr Ridge, IL: Irwin, 1967.)

CHAPTER 9

1. J. Collins, *Good to Great: Why Some Companies Make the Leap and Others Don't* (New York: HarperCollins, 2001).
2. J. Pfeffer, "How Companies Get Smart," *Business 2.0* (January 2005): x; J. Collins, *Good to Great*; S. Daniels, "Employee Training: A Strategic Approach to Better Return on Investment, *Journal of Business Strategy* 24 (2003): 39–42.
3. K. Rogg, D. Schmidt, C. Shull, and N. Schmitt, "Human Resource Practices, Organizational Climate, and Customer Satisfaction," *Journal of Management* 27 (2001): 431–449.
4. L. Berry, *Discovering the Soul of Service: The Nine Drivers of Sustainable Business Success* (New York: Free Press, 1999).
5. S. Musselman, "Linking Culture, Strategy Builds Business Success," *Hotel and Motel Management*, 2 May 2005, 14–15.
6. L. Soupata, "Prepare for the Future," *Executive Excellence* 21 (November 2004): 15–17.
7. C. Salter, "And Now the Hard Part," *Fast Company* (May 2004): 66–73.
8. D. Creelman, "Six Easy Pieces," *Workforce Management*, 24 May 2005.
9. L. Bassi, S. Cheney, and E. Lewis, "Trends in Workplace Learning: Supply and Demand in Interesting Times," *Training and Development* (November 1998): 51–69.
10. D. Shuit, "Where Paying Dues Delivers," *Workforce Management* 84 (May 2005): 38; Soupata, "Prepare for the Future."
11. C. Kong-Pin, "External Recruitment as an Incentive Device," *Journal of Labor Economics* 23 (2005): 259–277.
12. J. Post, (May 2005). "Online, In-house," *Workforce Management* 84 (May 2005): 49.
13. V. Powers, "Finding Workers Who Fit," *Business 2.0* (November 2004): 74.
14. Post, "Online, In-house."
15. M. Clausing, "Bills Reopen Debate over Visa Limit," *New York Times*, 31 August 1999, A6; P. Van Slambrouck, "Controversy Surrounds Demand for Imported High-Tech Labor," *Christian Science Monitor*, 30 August 1999, 21; C. Lockheed, "Tech Firms' Plea for Work Visas Draws Criticism," *San Francisco Chronicle*, 8 August 1999, A3.
16. D. Wentland, (2003). "The Strategic Training of Employees Model: Balancing Organizational Constraints and Training Content," *SAM Advanced Management Journal* 68 (2003): 56–63.
17. J. Mintz, (March 1, 2005). "Large Firms Increasingly Rely on Employees for Job Referrals," *Wall Street Journal*, March 2005, B4.
18. R. Barnes, "More Employers Are Using Assessment Tests to Hire the Right Workers," *Knight Ridder Tribune Business News*, 7 May 2005, 1; A. Eunjung Cha, "Employers Relying on Personality Tests to Screen Applicants," *Washington Post*, 27 March 2005, A1
19. I. Robertson and R. Kandola, "Work Sample Tests: Validity, Adverse Impact, and Applicant Reaction," *Journal of Occupational Psychology* 55 (1982): 171–183.
20. Barnes, "More Employers Are Using Assessment Tests."
21. P. Carbonara, "Hire for Attitude, Train for Skill," *Fast Company* (August 1996).
22. Berry, *Discovering the Soul of Service.*
23. Wentland, "The Strategic Training of Employees Model"; R. Noe, *Employee Training and Development* (New York: McGraw-Hill, 2004).
24. Daniels, "Employee Training."
25. R. Mathis and J. Jackson, *Human Resource Management*, 10th ed. (Mason, OH: South-Western, 2004).
26. Daniels, "Employee Training."
27. Salter, "And Now the Hard Part."
28. T. Stewart, "Mystified by Training? Here Are Some Clues," *Fortune*, 2 April 2001, 184.
29. An overview of rewarding performance can be found in E. Lawler, *Rewarding Excellence* (San Francisco: Jossey-Bass, 2000); E. Lawler, "Reward Practices and Performance Management: System Effectiveness," *Organizational Dynamics* 32 (November 2003): 396–404.
30. Refer to a detailed discussion in Mathis and Jackson, *Human Resource Management.*
31. Noe, *Employee Training and Development.*
32. F. Luthans and S. Peterson, "360-Degree Feedback with Systematic Coaching: Empirical Analysis Suggests a Winning Combination," *Human Resource Management* 42 (Fall 2003): 243–256; D. Waldman, I. Atwater, and D. Antonioni, "Has 360-Degree Feedback Gone Amok?" *Academy of Management Executive* (May 1998): 86–94; C. Wick, "The Course Isn't the Finish Line: Keep Them Learning Long after the Training Ends," *Training and Development* 57 (November 2003): 17–19.
33. Lawler, "Reward Practices and Performance Management."
34. Wentland, "The Strategic Training of Employees Model."
35. Anonymous, "Will Employees Perform Better if You Reward Them?" *HR Focus*, 81 (December 2004): 10.
36. A. Fisher, "Companies Serve Up New Pay Option," *Fortune*, 19 April 2004, 54.

37. K. Taylor, "Life in the Balance: Work–Life Programs Used to Be Viewed as a Nice Perk," *Incentive* 179 (January 2005): 16–19; B. Nelson, *1001 Ways to Reward Employees* (New York: Workman, 2005).
38. For a more detailed discussion of benefits, see Mathis and Jackson, *Human Resource Management.*
39. S. Curry, "Retention Getters," *Incentives*, 179 (April 2005): 15–19.
40. G. Milkovich and J. Newman, *Compensation* (Homewood, IL: BPI/Irwin, 1990).
41. J. T. Childs, "Managing Workforce Diversity at IBM: A Global HR Topic That Has Arrived," *Human Resources Management,* 44 (2004): 73–77.
42. L. Joel III, *Every Employee's Guide to the Law* (New York: Pantheon Books, 1994).
43. H. O'Neill, "California Undoing Affirmative Action," *Los Angeles Times,* 17 November 1996.
44. P. Babcock, "Down to the Letter," *HR Magazine* 49 (June 2004): 90–94.
45. A. Wellner, "Welcoming Back MOM," *HR Magazine* 49 (June 2004): 76–80.
46. Childs, "Managing Workforce Diversity at IBM."
47. Soupata, "Prepare for the Future."
48. S. Webber and L. Donahue, "Impact of Highly and Less Job-Related Diversity on Work Group Cohesion and Performance: A Meta-Analysis," *Journal of Management* 27 (2001): 141–162.
49. G. Powell, "Sexual Harassment: Confronting the Issue of Definition," *Business Horizons* (July/August 1983): 24–28.
50. Mathis and Jackson, *Human Resource Management.*
51. T. Bland and S. Stalcup, "Managing Harassment," *Human Resource Management* 40, no. 1 (Spring 2001): 51–61.
52. T. Hennerman, "Acceptance of Gays, Lesbians Is a Big Part of Kodak's Diversity Picture," *Workforce Management* 83 (December 2004): 68–70.
53. Editorial, "Labor of Politics," *Wall Street Journal*, 4 March 2005, A14.
54. R. Walton and R. McKersie, *A Behavioral Theory of Labor Negotiations: An Analysis of a Social Interaction System* (New York: McGraw-Hill, 1965).
55. Editorial, "Labor of Politics."
56. J. Marquez, "Wal-Mart Gives an Assist to Its Store Managers," *Workforce Management*, 84 (May 2005): 18; D. Soderquist, *The Wal-Mart Way: The Inside Story of the Success of the World's Largest Company*. (New York: Thomas Nelson, 2005).
57. J. Wyndbrandt, *Flying High: How JetBlue Founder and CEO David Neeleman Beats the Competition . . . Even in the World's Most Turbulent Industry* (New York: Wiley, 2004).

CHAPTER 10

1. F. Stone, "Making Change," *Leadership Excellence* 22 (March 2005): 19–20.
2. L. Gerstner, *Who Says Elephants Can't Dance?: Inside IBM's Historic Turnaround* (New York: HarperCollins, 2002); A. Deutschman, "Change or Die," *Fast Company* 94 (May 2005): 53–60.
3. D. Collins and K. Rainwater, "Managing Change at Sears: A Sideways Look at a Tale of Corporate Transformation," *Journal of Organizational Change Management* 18 (January 2005): 16–30.
4. J. Kouzes and B. Posner, *Leadership Challenges*, 3rd ed. (San Francisco: Jossey-Bass, 2002).
5. H. Trice and J. Beyer, *The Cultures of Work Organizations* (Upper Saddle River, NJ: Prentice Hall, 1993).
6. Aveda website (http://www.aveda.com); H. Rechelbacher, *Rejuvenation* (Rochester, VT: Healing Arts Press, 1987); H. Rechelbacher, *Aveda Rituals* (New York: Holt, 1999); New York, NY.; GreenMoneyJournal.com 13, no. 53 (Winter 2004–2005).
7. L. Berry, *Discovering the Soul of Service: The Nine Drivers of Sustainable Business Success* (New York: Free Press, 1999); J. Gavin, and R. Mason, "The Virtuous Organization: The Value of Happiness in the Workplace," *Organizational Dynamics* 33 (December 2004): 379–392.
8. Gavin and Mason, "The Virtuous Organization."
9. C. Flash, "Amazon Maintaining Its Tight-Lipped Style as It Moves to Town," *News Tribune* (Tacoma, WA), 19 October 1999, D7; "Personalization Features Set Amazon.com Apart," *Computerworld,* 18 October, 1999, 40–42.
10. D. Soderquist, *The Wal-Mart Way: The Inside Story of the Success of the World's Largest Company* (New York: Nelson, 2005).
11. E. Cabrera and J. Bonache, "An Expert Human Resource System for Aligning Organizational Culture and Strategy," *Human Resource Planning* (March 1999): 51–63.
12. Gerstner, *Who Says Elephants Can't Dance?*
13. L. Beach, *Making the Right Decision: Organizational Culture, Vision, and Planning* (Upper Saddle River, NJ: Prentice Hall, 1993).
14. S. Musselman, "Linking Culture, Strategy Builds Business Success," *Hotel and Motel Management*, 2 May 2005, 14–15.
15. D. Rosseau, "Assessing Organizational Culture: The Case for Multiple Methods" in *Organization Climate and Culture,* ed. B. Schneider (San Francisco: Jossey-Bass, 1990).
16. H. Trice and J. Beyer, "Studying Organizational Cultures through Rites and Rituals," *Academy of Management Review* 9 (1984): 653–669.
17. A. Perlit, "The Ten-Minute Manager's Guide to Conserving Culture," *Restaurants and Institutions* 115 (February 2005): 18–20.
18. J. Saranow, "Leadership (A Special Report): Anybody Want to Take a Nap?" *Wall Street Journal*, 24 January 2005, R5.
19. C. Bernick, "When Your Culture Needs a Makeover," *Harvard Business Review* (June 2001): 53–60; M. Ash, *Mary Kay on People Management* (New York: Warner Books, 1984).
20. See examples in A. Harrington, "Hall of Fame," *Fortune,* 24 January 2005, 94.
21. K. Friedberg, "Changing and Creating Organizational Cultures" in *The Cultures of Work Organizations* ed. H. Trice and J. Beyer (Upper Saddle River, NJ: Prentice Hall, 1993), 418.
22. S. Morgan and R. Dennehy, "The Power of Organizational Storytelling: A Management Development Perspective," *Journal of Management Development* 16 (1997):

494–501; K. Rogg, D. Schmidt, C. Shull, and N. Schmitt, "Human Resource Practices, Organizational Climate, and Customer Satisfaction," *Journal of Management* 27 (2001): 431–449.

23. N. Tichy, "No Ordinary Boot Camp," *Harvard Business Review* (April 2001): 63–70.
24. P. C. Neuhauser, *Corporate Legends & Lore* (New York: McGraw-Hill, 1993).
25. D. Welch and G. Khermouch, "Can GM Save an Icon?" *BusinessWeek,* 8 April 2002, 60–67.
26. Fairburn, "HR as a Strategic Partner."
27. J. Amore, "Best Practices," *Potentials* 37 (September 2004): 69; see examples in Harrington, "Hall of Fame."
28. Childs, "Managing Workforce Diversity at IBM."
29. P. Drucker and J. Maciariello, (2004). *The Daily Drucker* (New York: Harper Business, 2004).
30. Aveda website (http://www.aveda.com).
31. Rechelbacher, *Aveda Rituals*; GreenMoneyJournal.com.
32. Katzenbach, *Real Change Leaders.*
33. J. Folaron, "The Human Side of Change Leadership," *Quality Progress* 38 (2005): 30–43.
34. V. Powers, "Finding Workers Who Fit," *Business 2.0* (November 2004): 74.
35. Harrington "Hall of Fame."
36. J. Kotter, "Leading Change: Why Transformation Efforts Fail," *Harvard Business Review* (March/April 1995): 59–67.
37 J. Kotter, and D. Cohen, *Heart of Change: Real Life Stories of How People Change Their Organizations* (Boston: Harvard Business School, 2002); J. Kotter and L. Schlesinger, "Choosing Strategies for Change," *Harvard Business Review* (March/April 1979): 109–112; F. Stone, "Making Change," *Leadership Excellence* 22 (2005): 19–20.
38. K. Lewis, *Field Theory in Social Science* (New York: Harper & Row, 1951).
39. R. Jones, N. Jimmieson, and A. Griffiths, "The Impact of Organizational Culture and Reshaping Capabilities on Change Implementation Success: The Mediating Role of Readiness for Change," *Journal of Management Studies* 42 (2005): 361–366.
40. Summarized from *Work USA Survey* (Washington, DC: Wyatt Company, 2003).
41. Deutschman, "Change or Die."
42. W. Bridges, *Managing Transitions: Making the Most of Change*. (Boulder, Colorado, Perseus, 2003).
43. K. Blanchard, *Executive Excellence* (Provo, UT: Excellence, 1999).
44. K. Murrell and M. Meredith, *Empowering Employees* (New York: McGraw-Hill, 2002).
45. M. Joffe and S. Glynn, "Facilitating Change and Empowering Employees," *Journal of Change Management* 2, no. 4 (2002): 369–379; E. Lawler, "Reward Practices and Performance Management: System Effectiveness," *Organizational Dynamics* 32 (November 2003): 396–404.
46. Stone, "Making Change."
47. M. Denham, N. Blackwell, and R. Dickhout, "Designing the Right Change Program for You and Your Organization," *Ivey Business Journal* 64 (2000): 26–39; Kotter and Schlesinger, "Choosing Strategies for Change."

CHAPTER 11

1. J. Goodman and C. Truss, Catherine. "The Medium and the Message: Communicating Effectively during a Major Change Initiative," *Journal of Change Management* 33 (2004): 318–328; J. Lloyd, "Employees Aren't Mind Readers: Communicate to Avoid Turnover," *Business Journal* 21 (June 2004): 23; London. P. J. Kitchen and F. Daly, "Internal Communication during Change Management," *Corporate Communications: An International Journal* 15, no. 2 (2002): 169–83.
2. T. Petzinger, *The New Pioneers: The Men and Women Who Are Transforming the Workplace and Marketplace* (New York: Random House, 1999).
3. M. Joffe and S. Glynn, "Facilitating Change and Empowering Employees, *Journal of Change Management*, 2, no. 4 (2002): 369–79; L. Croft, and N. Cochrane, "Communicating Change Effectively," *Management Services* 49 (Spring 2005): 18–33.
4. L. Landes, "Real-Life, Real-Time Communication," *Communication World*, 19 (December 2001/January 2002): 20–23; L. Penley, E. Alexander, I. Jernigan, and C. Henwood, "Communication Abilities of Managers: The Relationship of Performance," *Journal of Management* 17 (1991): 57–76.
5. J. Conger, "Inspiring Others: The Language of Leadership," *Academy of Management Executive* 5 no. 1 (1991): 310–345.
6. For a thorough discussion, see Munter, *Guide to Managerial Communication.*
7. K. Roberts, *Communication in Organizations* (Chicago: Science Research Associates, 1984).
8. M. Messmer, "Communicating Effectively with Employees," *Strategic Finance* 86 (February 2005): 15–16.
9. Goodman and Truss. "The Medium and the Message"; R. Lengel and R. Daft, "The Selection of Communication Media as an Executive Skill," *Academy of Management Executive* 2 (1988): 225–232.
10. Goodman and Truss, "The Medium and the Message"; Croft and Cochrane, "Communicating Change Effectively."
11. "The Technocrats," *Inc.* (February 1999): 55.
12. F. Hesselbein, "The Art of Listening," *Leader to Leader* 29 (Summer 2003): 4–6.
13. D. Garvin and M. Roberto, "Change through Persuasion," *Harvard Business Review* 83 (February 2005): 104ff.
14. J. Collins, "Aligning Action and Values" in *Leader to Leader,* ed. F. Hesselbein and P. Cohen (San Francisco: Jossey-Bass, 1999); K. Blanchard, "Translating Body Talk," *Success*, (April 1986): 10.
15. H. Sims and C. Manz, *Company of Heroes* (New York: Wiley, 1996).
16. E. Schein, *The Corporate Culture Survival Guide: Sense and Nonsense about Culture Change* (San Francisco: Jossey-Bass, 1999); P. Morrow and J. McElroy, "Interior Office Design and Visitor Response: A Constructive Replication," *Journal of Applied Psychology* 66, (1981): 646–650.
17. J. Lloyd, (December 14, 2001). "Managers Need to Shine a Light on Their Expectations," *San Antonio Business Journal*, 14 December 2001, 15.

18. R. Hof and S. Hamm, "How E-Biz Rose, Fell, and Will Rise Anew," *Business Week,* 13 May 2002, 64–72; S. Levy, "How the Bust Saved Silicon Valley," *Newsweek,* 25 March 2002, 42–50.
19. K. Maher, "Corner Office Shift: Telecommuting Rises in Executive Ranks," *Wall Street Journal*, 21 September 2004, B1; M. Strum, "Telework, Telecommuting, Virtual Officing . . . : Redefining the 9–5 Routine," *Afp Exchange*, (May/June 2001): 36–41.
20. Research conducted by the Dieringer Research Group, Milwaukee, Wisconsin, on behalf of The International Telework Association and Council (ITAC).
21. Maher, "Corner Office Shift."
22. A. Rottier, "The Skies Are JetBlue," *Workforce* 80 (September 2001): 22.
23. For example, see R. Levering and M. Moskowitz, "The 100 Best Companies to Work For," *Fortune*, 24 January 2005, 72–84.
24. D. Booher, *E-Writing: 21st-Century Tools for Effective Communication* (Pocket Books, 2001); G. Blake, (1999). "E-Mail with Feeling, *Research-Technology Management* 42 (1999): 12–14.
25. O. Thomas, "What the Web Taught FedEx," from http://www.business2.com, 18 November 2004.
26. P.A. Argenti, R. Howell, and K. Beck, "The Strategic Communication Imperative," *MIT Sloan Management Review* 46 (Spring, 2005): 83–89.
27. L. Soupata, "Prepare for the Future," *Executive Excellence* 21 (November 2004): 15–17.
28. Goodman and Truss, "The Medium and the Message"; J. Lloyd, "Employees Aren't Mind Readers: Communicate to Avoid Turnover," *Business Journal* 21 (June 2004): 23.
29. D. Sirota, L. Mischkind, and M. Meltzer, *The Enthusiastic Employee: How Companies Profit by Giving Workers What They Want* (Wharton School Publishing/Pearson, 2005).
30. M. Kets de Vries and E. Florent-Treacy, *The New Global Leaders: Richard Branson, Percy Barnevik, David Simon and the Remaking of International Business* (San Francisco: Jossey-Bass, 1999); N. Zaidman, "Cultural Codes and Language Strategies in Business Communication," *Management Communication Quarterly* (February 2001): 408–441.
31. S. Cady, P. Fandt, and D. Fernandez, "Investigating Cultural Differences in Personal Success: Implications for Designing Effective Reward Systems," *Journal of Value-Based Management* 6 (1993): 65–80.
32. D. Raths, "Communication Is Key to Cross-Cultural Success," *InfoWorld* 21 (November 1999): 83–85.
33. S. Currall and M. J. Epstein, "The Fragility of Organization Level Trust: Lessons from the Rise and Fall of Enron," *Organizational Dynamics* 32 (May 2003): 193–206.
34. S. Covey, *The 7 Habits of Highly Effective People* (New York: Simon & Schuster, 1989).
35. M. Joffe and S. Glynn, "Facilitating Change"; M. Sinetar, "Building Trust into Corporate Relationships," *Organizational Dynamics* 16 (Winter 1988): 73–79.
36. A. Harrington, "Hall of Fame," *Fortune,* 24 January 2005, 94.
37. I. Jay, "On Communicating Well," *HRMagazine* 50, (January 2005): 87–90.
38. Booher, *E-Writing.*
39. M. Cooper, D. Friedman, and J. Koenig, "Empire of the Sun," *U.S. News & World Report*, 28 May 1990, 44–51.
40. F. Griffin, "Idioms and Back Translation," *Business Communication Quarterly* 67 (December 2004): 455–464.
41. P. Marren, Patrick. (2004). "'Impact' as a Verb and the Decline of Western Civilization," *Journal of Business Strategy* 25 (2004): 5–7.
42. K. Ashcraft, "Empowering 'Professional' Relationships," *Management Communication Quarterly* 13 (2000): 347–393.
43. D. Borisoff, "Gender Issues and Listening" in *Listening in Everyday Life: A Personal and Professional Approach,* eds. D. Borisoff and M. Purdy (Lanham, MD: University Press of America, 1992).
44. A thorough discussion can be found in D. Kolb, J. Williams, and C. Frohlinger, *Her Place at the Table: A Woman's Guide to Negotiating Five Key Challenges to Leadership Success* (New York: Wiley, 2004).
45. S. Kirmeyer and T. Lin, "Social Support: Its Relationship to Observed Communication with Peers and Superiors," *Academy of Management Journal* 30 (1987): 138–151.
46. Jay, "On Communicating Well"; W. Cascio, Managing a Virtual Workplace," *Academy of Management Executive* 14 no. 3 (2000): 81–90.
47. Argenti, Howell, and Beck, "The Strategic Communication Imperative"; J. Lloyd, "Employees Aren't Mind Readers"; Messmer, "Communicating Effectively with Employees."
48. J. Wyndbrandt, *Flying High: How JetBlue Founder and CEO David Neeleman Beats the Competition . . . Even in the World's Most Turbulent Industry* (New York: Wiley, 2004).
49. G. Cancelada, "New Strategy Puts Workers Operating like Owners," *St. Louis Post-Dispatch,* 2 May 2002, C1.
50. "The Virtuous Organization: The Value of Happiness in the Workplace," *Organizational Dynamics* 33, (2004): 379–392.
51. S. Bashford "Every Incentive," *Human Resources* (January 2004): 44.
52. M. Montoya-Weiss, A. Massey, and M. Song, "Getting It Together: Temporal Coordination and Conflict Management in Global Virtual Teams," *Academy of Management Journal* 44, no. 6 (2001): 1251–1262.
53. V. Baker, "Traps in Diagnosing Organization Failure," *Journal of Business Strategy* 26 (2005): 44–53; J. Glauser, "Upward Information Flows in Organizations: Review and Conceptual Analysis," *Human Relations* 37 (1984): 113–143.
54. Sinetar, "Building Trust."
55. Cascio, "Managing a Virtual Workplace"; C. D. Cramton, "Finding Common Ground in Dispersed Collaboration," *Organizational Dynamics* 30 no. 4 (2002): 356–367. Messmer, "Communicating Effectively with Employees."
56. R. Cross, N. Nohria, and A. Parker, "Six Myths about Informal Networks—and How to Overcome Them," *MIT Sloan Management Review* 43 no. 3 (2002): 67–75.
57. S. Rosen, "Carry On the Conversation," *Communication World* 22 (March/April 2004): 24–26.
58. E. Walton, "How Efficient Is the Grapevine?" *Personnel* 28 (1961): 45–48.
59. Rosen, "Carry on the Conversation."

60. Landes, "Real-life, Real-time Communication."
61. M. Buckingham, "What Great Managers Do," *Harvard Business Review* 83 (March 2005): 70–79.
62. Covey, *The 7 Habits.*
63. Jay, "On Communicating Well."
64. Covey, *The 7 Habits.*
65. Rosen, "Carry on the Conversation"; J. McKay, "Want to Improve Communication Skills? Practice, Practice, Practice," *Pittsburgh Post-Gazette,* 6 February 2005, P1.
66. Hesselbein, "The Art of Listening."
67. E. Rautalinko, and H. O. Lisper, "Effects of Training Reflective Listening in a Corporate Setting," *Journal of Business and Psychology* 18 (Spring 2004): 281–299.
68. Adapted from M. Munter, *Guide to Managerial Communication,* xii.
69. Jay, "On Communicating Well"; Joffe Glynn, "Facilitating Change and Empowering Employees"; K. Murray, "Create a Listening Organization," *Strategic Communication Management* 8 (August/September 2004): 5–12.

CHAPTER 12

1. G. Yukl, *Leadership in Organizations,* 5th ed. (Upper Saddle River, NJ: Prentice Hall, 2002).
2. J. Kouzes and B. Posner, *The Leadership Challenge,* 3rd ed. (San Francisco: Jossey-Bass, 2003); D. Goleman, "Leadership That Gets Results," *Harvard Business Review,* 78, no. 2 (2000): 78–90; G. Hernez-Broome and R. L. Hughes, "Leadership Development: Past, Present, and Future," *Human Resource Planning* 27, no. 1 (2004): 24–32.
3. J. Kotter, *The Leadership Factor* (New York: Simon & Schuster, 1987).
4. C. Hickman, *Mind of a Manager, Soul of a Leader* (New York: Wiley, 1990).
5. Summarized in Yukl, *Leadership in Organizations,* and T. A. Judge, J. Bono, R. Ilies, and M. Gerhardt, "Personality and Leadership: A Qualitative and Quantitative Review," *Journal of Applied Psychology* 87, no. 4 (2002): 766–780.
6. D. Rooke and W. Torbert, "Seven Transformations of Leadership: Leaders Are Made, Not Born, and How They Develop Is Critical for Organizational Change," *Harvard Business Review* 83 (April 2005): 66–78.
7. Kouzes and Posner, *The Leadership Challenge.*
8. M. Leibovich, "Reich Rises above Height Issue in Run for Governor," *St. Louis Post-Dispatch,* 17 March 2002, A19.
9. P. B. Brown, (June 2005). "The Case for Design." *Fast Company* 95 (June 2005): 100.
10. J. Marquez, "Leading Indicators," *Workforce Management* (July 2005): 49–52.
11. N. Tichy and S. Sherman, *Control Your Destiny or Someone Else Will* (New York: HarperCollins, 2005); S. Flax, "The Toughest Bosses in America," *Fortune,* 6 August 1984, 90–107.
12. D. Brady, "The Education of Jeff Immelt: The Jack Welch Era Is History," *BusinessWeek,* 29 April 2002, 80–87.
13. Task orientation may also be referred to as initiating structure, concern for production, job centered, or authoritarian. Relationship orientation may also be referred to as democratic, people centered, employee centered, and consideration. For a review of earlier research findings, see S. Kirkpatrick and E. Locke, "Leadership: Do Traits Matter?" *Academy of Management Executive* 5 (1991): 48–59; R. Stogdill, *Handbook of Leadership* (New York: Free Press, 1974); R. Stogdill and A. Coons, *Leader Behavior: Its Description and Measurement* (Columbus: Ohio State University Bureau of Business Research, 1957); R. Tannenbaum and W. Schmidt, "How to Choose a Leadership Pattern," *Harvard Business Review* (March/April 1958): 95–101; R. Blake and J. Mouton, "How to Choose a Leadership Style," *Training and Development Journal* (February 1986): 39–46.
14. An excellent discussion is found in P. Drucker, *Managing for the Future: The 1990s and Beyond* (New York: Plume Books, 1993); P. Drucker, *The Essential Drucker: The Best of Sixty Years of Peter Drucker's Essential Writings on Management* (New York: Harper Business, 2001); T. Petzinger, *The New Pioneers: The Men and Women Who Are Transforming the Workplace and Marketplace* (New York: Simon & Schuster, 2000).
15. Hernez-Broome and Hughes, "Leadership Development."
16. J. French and B. Raven, "The Bases of Social Power" in *Studies of Social Power,* ed. D. Cartwright (Ann Arbor, MI: Institute for Social Research, 1959).
17. A. Perele, "What Makes Companies Well Loved?" *Workforce Management* 77 (April 1998): 125–126.
18. C. Sittenfeld, "Leader on the Edge," *Fast Company* (October 1999): 212–226.
19. W. G. Bennis and R. J. Thomas, *Geeks & Geezers* (Boston: Harvard Business School Press, 2002); S. Hays, "Our Future Requires Collaborative Leadership," *Workforce* (December 1999): 30–34; B. Avolio and S. Kahai, Adding the "E" to Leadership: How It May Impact Your Leadership," *Organizational Dynamics* 31, no. 4 (2003): 325–338.
20. T. Diamante and M. London, "Expansive Leadership in the Age of Digital Technology," *Journal of Management Development* 21, no. 5–6 (2002): 404–416.
21. Marquez, "Leading Indicators."
22. "Becoming the Best: What You Can Learn from the 25 Most Influential Leaders of Our Times," http://knowledge.wharton.upenn.edu, published 11 February 2004.
23. This term is used by H. Sims and C. Manz, *Company of Heroes* (New York: Wiley, 1999). There are other perspectives that are developed around self-leadership. See, for example, H. Sims and P. Lorenzi, *The New Leadership Paradigm: Social Learning and Cognition in Organizations* (Newbury Park, CA: Sage, 1992); Kouzes and Posner, *The Leadership Challenge.*
24. I. Chaleff, *The Courageous Follower: Standing Up to and for Our Leaders* (San Francisco: Berrett-Koehler, 1995).
25. Adapted from M. Goldsmith, H. Morgan, A. J. Ogg (eds.), *Leading Organizational Learning: Harnessing the Power of Knowledge* (San Francisco, Jossey-Bass, 2004).
26. I. Chaleff, *The Courageous Follower.*
27. D. Roth, "How to Cut Pay, Lay Off 8,000 People, and Still Have Workers Who Love You," *Fortune,* 4 February 2002, 64–68; D. Eisenberg, (June 18, 2001). "Where People Are Never Let Go," *Time,* 18 July 2001, 40.

28. A. Harrington, "Hall of Fame," *Fortune,* 24 January 2005, 94; R. Levering, M. Moskowitz, J. Boorstin, and C. Tkaczyk, "The 100 Best Companies to Work For," *Fortune,* 12 January 2004, 56.
29. C. Lee, "Followership: The Essence of Leadership," *Training* (January 1991): 27–35; M. Abramson and J. Scanlon, "The Five Dimensions of Leadership," *Government Executive* (July 1991): 20–25; J. M. Howell and B. Shamir, "The Role of Followers in the Charismatic Leadership Process: Relationships and Their Consequences," *Academy of Management Review* 30, no. 1 (2005): 96–114.
30. S. Kerr and J. Jermier, "Substitutes for Leadership: Their Meaning and Measurement," *Organizational Behavior and Human Performance* (1978): 375–403; P. Podsakoff, B. Niehoff, S. MacKenzie, and M. Williams, "Do Substitutes for Leadership Really Substitute for Leadership? An Empirical Examination of Kerr and Jermier's Situational Leadership Model," *Organizational Behavior and Human Decision Processes* (February 1993): 1–44.
31. P. Podsakoff et al., "Do Substitutes for Leadership."
32. P. Hersey and K. Blanchard, *Management of Organizational Behavior: Utilizing Human Resources*, 5th. ed. (Upper Saddle River, NJ: Prentice Hall, 1988).
33. A proliferation of books and articles have been published by Ken Blanchard and his colleagues regarding this topic. See K. Blanchard, S. Fowler, and L. Hawkins, *Self Leadership and the One Minute Manager: Increasing Effectiveness Through Situational Self Leadership* (New York: HarperCollins, 2005) or at http://www.kenblanchard.com.
34. R. Ford and M. Fottler, "Empowerment: A Matter of Degree," *Academy of Management Executive* 9 (1995): 21–30; G. Chen and R. Klimoski, "The Impact of Expectations on Newcomer Performance in Teams as Mediated by Work Characteristics, Social Exchanges, and Empowerment," *Academy of Management Journal* 46, no. 5 (2003): 591–607.
35. W. A. Randolph, "Re-thinking Empowerment: Why Is It So Hard to Achieve?" *Organizational Dynamics* 29 (2000): 94–107.
36. S. Wall, *The New Strategists: Creating Leaders at All Levels* (New York: Free Press 1995); M. Joffe and S. Glynn, "Facilitating Change and Empowering Employees," *Journal of Change Management* 2 no. 4 (2002): 369–379; S. Seibert, G. Johns, and F. Ntalianis, "Taking Empowerment to the Next Level: A Multiple-Level Model of Empowerment, Performance, and Satisfaction," *Academy of Management Journal* 47, no. 3 (2004): 332–349.
37. R. Cummins, "John Heaton: Leading an Organization to Prevent Disruptions in Your Team," *Journal for Quality and Participation* 28, no. 1 (2005): 16–19.
38. S. Kerr, "GE's Collective Genius" in *Leader to Leader,* ed. F. Hesselbein and P. Cohen (San Francisco: Jossey-Bass, 1999), 227–236.
39. P. Northhouse, *Leadership Theory and Practice* (London: Sage, 2004).
40. J. Bono and T. Judge, "Self-Concordance at Work: Toward Understanding the Motivational Effects of Transformational Leaders," *Academy of Management Journal* 46, no. 5 (2003): 554–570; Hernez-Broome and Hughes, "Leadership Development."
41. R. Pillai, "Crisis and the Emergence of Charismatic Leadership in Groups: An Experimental Investigation," *Journal of Applied Social Psychology* 26 (1996): 543–562; Kouzes and Posner, *The Leadership Challenge;* J. Sparks and J. Schenk, "Explaining the Effects of Transformational Leadership: An Investigation of the Effects of Higher-Order Motives in Multilevel Marketing Organizations," *Journal of Organizational Behavior* 22 (2001): 849–869.
42. B. Breen, "The Clear Leader," *Fast Company* 92 (March 2005): 65; Bono and Judge, "Self-Concordance at Work."
43. J. Sosik and L. Megerian, "Understanding Leader Emotional Intelligence and Performance: The Role of Self–Other Agreement on Transformational Leadership Perceptions," *Group & Organization Management* 24 (1999): 367–390; See also J. Seltzer and B. Bass, "Transformational Leadership: Beyond Initiation and Consideration," *Journal of Management* (December 1990): 693–703.
44. D. Goleman, *Emotional Intelligence* (New York: Bantam Books, 1995).
45. Goleman, "Leadership That Gets Results"; Goleman, *Emotional Intelligence.*
46. K. Bunker and M. Wakefield, "In Search of Authenticity: Now More Than Ever, Soft Skills Are Needed," *Leadership in Action* 24, no. 1 (2004): 17–21.
47. L. Herkenhoff, "Culturally Tuned Emotional Intelligence: An Effective Change Management Tool?" *Strategic Change* 13, no. 2 (2004): 73–81; R. E. Boyatzis, "Self-Directed Learning," *Executive Excellence* 21, no. 2 (2004): 11–12; P. Cairo, D. L. Dotlich, and S. H. Rhinesmith, "The Unnatural Leader," *Training and Development* 59, no. 3 (2005): 26–30.
48. Summarized in S. Taylor, "Breaking All the Rules," *Chicago Tribune,* 8 June 2005, 2; the complete study results are available at http://www.caliperonline.com.
49. J. Rosener, "Ways Women Lead," *Harvard Business Review* (November/December 1990): 119–125.
50. Diamante and London, "Expansive Leadership."
51. On how gender may affect management style, see reviews in G. Powell, *Women and Men in Management,* 2nd ed. (Newbury Park, CA: Sage, 1993).
52. G. Powell, "One More Time: Do Female and Male Managers Differ?" *Academy of Management Executive* 3 (August 1990): 68–75; http://www.caliperonline.com.
53. J. Tingley, *Genderflex: Men and Women Speaking Each Other's Language at Work* (New York: American Management Association, 1994); R. Sharpe, "As Leaders, Women Rule," *BusinessWeek,* 20 November 2000, 75–84.
54. P. Drucker *Managing the Next Society* (New York: St. Martin's Press, 2002); S. Kirsner, "4 Leaders You Need to Know," *Fast Company* (February 2005): 68–72.
55. F. Hesselbein, "A Star to Steer By," *Leader to Leader* 1 (Summer 1996): 4–5.
56. A. Karaevli, and D. T. Hall, "Growing Leaders for Turbulent Times: Is Succession Planning Up to the Challenge?" *Organizational Dynamics* 32, no. 1 (2003): 62–79.
57. K. Groves, "Linking Leader Skills, Follower Attitudes, and Contextual Variables via an Integrated Model of Charismatic Leadership," *Journal of Management* 31 (2005): 255–278.

58. Adapted from J. Schiro, 1999; and L. Ludewig, "The Ten Commandments of Leadership," *NASPA Journal* (Spring 1988): 297.

CHAPTER 13

1. G. Parker, J. McAdams, and D. Zielinski (2000). *Rewarding Teams: Lessons from the Trenches* (San Francisco: Jossey-Bass, 2000).
2. H. Sims and C. Manz, *Company of Heroes: Unleashing the Power of Self-Leadership* (New York: Wiley, 1996); H. Sims and P. Lorenzi, *The New Leadership Paradigm* (Newbury Park, CA: Sage Press, 1992).
3. Sims and Manz, *Company of Heroes.*
4. For a thorough summary and critique of 25 years of research and theory on the role of personality in organizational contexts, see B. Schneider and B. Smith, *Personality and Organizations* (Mahwah, NJ: Lawrence Erlbaum, 2004).
5. E. Robinson, *Why Aren't You More Like Me?* 2nd ed. (Human Resource Development Press, 1995); M. Rosenberg, C. Schooler, C. Schoenbach, and F. Rosenberg, "Global Self-Esteem and Specific Self-Esteem: Different Concepts, Different Outcome," *American Sociological Review* 60 (1995): 141–156.
6. M. Mitchell and P. Fandt, "Examining the Relationship between Role-Defining Characteristics and Self-Esteem of College Students," *College Student Journal* 33 (1995) 99–120; D. J. McAllister and G. A. Bigley, "Work Context and the Definition of Self: How Organizational Care Influences Organization-Based Self-Esteem," *Academy of Management Journal* 45, no. 5, (2002): 894–905; J. Brockner, *Self-Esteem at Work* (Lexington, MA: Lexington Books, 1988).
7. T. A. Judge and J. E. Bono, "Relationship of Core Self-Evaluations Traits—Self-Esteem, Generalized Self-Efficacy, Locus of Control, and Emotional Stability—with Job Satisfaction and Job Performance: A Meta-Analysis," *Journal of Applied Psychology* 86 (2001): 80–92; T. A. Judge, J. E. Bono, and E. A. Locke, "Personality and Job Satisfaction: The Mediating Role of Job Characteristics," *Journal of Applied Psychology* 85 (2000): 237–249; A. Korman, "Self-Esteem Variable in Vocational Choice," *Journal of Applied Psychology* 50 (1966): 479–486; A. Korman, "Relevance of Personal Need Satisfaction for Overall Satisfaction as a Function of Self-Esteem," *Journal of Applied Psychology* 51 (1967): 533–538.
8. N. Branden, *Self-Esteem at Work: How Confident People Make Powerful Companies* (San Francisco: Jossey-Bass, 1998).
9. G. Mitchell and P. Fandt, "Confident Role Models for Tomorrow's Classrooms: The Self-Esteem of Education Majors," *Education* 113 (1993): 556–562.
10. Judge and Bono, (2001). "Relationship of Core Self-Evaluations Traits"; J. Brockner, *Self-Esteem at Work: Research, Theory, and Practice* (Lexington, MA: Heath, 1988); Branden, *Self-Esteem at Work;* U. Raja, G. Johns, and F. Ntalianis, "The Impact of Personality on Psychological Contracts," *Academy of Management Journal* 47, no. 3 (2004): 350–367.
11. J. Rotter, "Generalized Expectancies for Internal versus External Control of Reinforcement," *Psychological Monographs* 80 (1966): 1–28; P. Spector, "Locus of Control and Well-Being at Work: How Generalizable Are Western Findings?" *Academy of Management Journal* 45, no. 2 (2002): 453–466.
12. P. Spector, "Development of the Work Locus of Control Scale," *Journal of Occupational Psychology* 61 (1988): 335–340.
13. Spector, "Locus of Control and Well-Being at Work"; Spector, P. "Behavior in Organizations as a Function of Employees' Locus of Control," *Psychological Bulletin* 91 (1982): 482–497; Spector, "Development of the Work Locus of Control Scale."
14. M. Snyder and S. Gangestad, "On the Nature of Self-Monitoring: Matters of Assessment, Matters of Validity," *Journal of Personality and Social Psychology* 51 (1986): 123–139.
15. P. F. Hewlin, "And the Award for Best Actor Goes to . . . : Facades of Conformity in Organizational Settings," *Academy of Management Review* 28, no. 4 (2003): 633–642.
16. Based on M. Jamal, "Type A Behavior and Job Performance: Some Suggestive Findings," *Journal of Human Stress* (Summer 1985): 60–68.
17. M. Fischetti, "Team Doctors, Report to ER," *Fast Company* (February 1998): 170–172.
18. A. Siebert, *The Resiliency Advantage* (Williston VT: Berrett-Koehler, 2005); A. Seibert, *The Survivor Personality: Why Some People Are Stronger, Smarter, and More Skillful at Handling Life's Difficulties* (New York: Perigee Trade, 1996).
19. S. Maddi, and D. Khoshaba, *Resilience at Work: How to Succeed No Matter What Life Throws at You* (New York: AMACOM, 2005).
20. Ibid.
21. M. Guttman, "Resilience," *USA Weekend,* 7 March 1999, 4–5.
22. S. A. Berr, A. H. Church, and J. Waclawski, "The Right Relationship Is Everything: Linking Personality Preferences to Managerial Behaviors," *Human Resource Development Quarterly* 11, no. 2 (2000): 133–157.
23. J. Curd, F. Dent, and M. Carr, "Development Challenges: Looking at the Future," *Training Journal* (January 2005): 36–39.
24. C. Carr, "Redesigning the Management Psyche," *New York Times,* 26 May 2002, 3.14.
25. I. Briggs-Myers, *Introduction to Type* (Palo Alto, CA: Consulting Psychologists Press, 1980).
26. Siebert, *The Resiliency Advantage;* Maddi and Khoshaba, *Resilience at Work.*
27. Berr et al., "The Right Relationship Is Everything."
28. Carr, "Redesigning the Management Psyche."
29. J. Digman, "Personality Structure: Emergence of a Five-Factor Model," *Annual Review of Psychology* 41 (1990): 417–440; Seibert, *The Survivor Personality.*
30. M. Barrick and M. Mount, "The Big Five Personality Dimensions and Job Performance: A Meta-Analysis," *Personnel Psychology* 44 (1991): 1–26; Seibert, *The Survivor Personality.*
31. S. Seibert and M. Kraimer, "The Five-Factor Model of Personality and Career Success," *Journal of Vocational Behavior* 58 (2001): 1–21.

32. L. Hough, N. Eaton, M. Dunnette, J. Kamp, and R. McCloy, "Criterion-Related Validities of Personality Constructs and the Effect of Response Distortion on Those Validities," *Journal of Applied Psychology* 75 (1990) 581–595; Barrick and Mount, "The Big Five"; J. Salgado, "The Five-Factor Model of Personality and Job Performance in the European Community," *Journal of Applied Psychology* 82 (1997): 30–43; F. De Fruyt, Filip, I. Mervielde, and Ivan, "Riasec Types and Big Five Traits as Predictors of Employment Status and Nature of Employment," *Personnel Psychology* 52 (Autumn 1999): 701–728.
33. G. Hurtz and J. Donovan, "Personality and Job Performance: The Big Five Revisited," *Journal of Applied Psychology* 85 (2000): 869–879.
34. Seibert and Kraimer, "The Five-Factor Model of Personality."
35. Ibid.
36. T. A. Wright, "What Every Manager Should Know: Does Personality Help Drive Employee Motivation?" *Academy of Management Executive* 17, no. 2 (2003): 131–133.
37. J. Holland, *Making Vocational Choices: A Theory of Vocational Personalities and Work Environments* (Englewood Cliffs, NJ: Prentice Hall, 1985); J. Holland, *Making Vocational Choices: A Theory of Vocational Personalities and Environments* (Odessa, FL: Psychological Assessment Resources, 1997).
38. M. J. Miller, and T. A. Miller, "Theoretical Application of Holland's Theory to Individual Decision-Making Styles: Implications for Career Counselors," *Journal of Employment Counseling* 42, no. 1 (2005): 20–28; M. J. Miller, and C. Bass, Application of Holland's Theory to a Nonprofessional Occupation," *Journal of Employment Counseling* 40, no. 1 (2003): 17–23.
39. J. Holland, *Making Vocational Choices,* 3rd ed.
40. L. Porter, R. Steers, R. Mowday, and P. Boulian, "Organizational Commitment, Job Satisfaction, and Turnover among Psychiatric Technicians," *Journal of Applied Psychology* 5 (1974): 603.
41. L. Festinger, *A Theory of Cognitive Dissonance* (Stanford, CA: Stanford University Press, 1957).
42. Ibid.
43. B. L. Kirkman, and D. L. Shapiro, "The Impact of Cultural Values on Job Satisfaction and Organizational Commitment in Self-Managing Work Teams: The Mediating Role of Employee Resistance," *Academy of Management Journal* 44 (2001): 557–569, Judge et al., "Personality and Job Satisfaction"; J. P. Meyer, D. J. Stanley, L. Herscovitch, and L. Topolnytsky, "Affective, Continuance, and Normative Commitment to the Organization: A Meta-Analysis of Antecedents, Correlates, and Consequences," *Journal of Vocational Behavior* 61 (2002): 20–52; P. Smith, L. Kendall, and C. Hulin, *The Measurement of Satisfaction in Work and Retirement* (Chicago: Rand McNally, 1969).
44. L. Hill, "New Manager Development for the 21st Century," *Academy of Management Executive* 18, no. 3 (2004): 121–126.
45. Smith et al., *The Measurement of Satisfaction.*
46. M. Petty, G. McGee, and J. Cavender, "A Meta-Analysis of the Relationship between Individual Job Satisfaction and Individual Performance," *Academy of Management Review* (October 1984): 712–721; A. Cooper-Hakim and C. Visvesvaran, "The Construct of Work Commitment: Testing an Integrative Framework," *Psychological Bulletin* 131, no. 2 (2005): 241–259; Judge et al., "Personality and Job Satisfaction."
47. C. Pearson and C. Porath, "On the Nature, Consequences and Remedies of Workplace Civility: No Time for Nice? Think Again," *Academy of Management Executive* 19, no. 1 (2005): 7–18; S. Jo and S. W. Shim, "Paradigm Shift of Employee Communication: The Effect of Management Communication on Trusting Relationships," *Public Relations Review* 31, no. 2 (2005): 277–280; J. Collins, *Good to Great: Why Some Companies Make the Leap and Others Don't* (New York: HarperCollins, 2001).
48. P. Fandt and G. Stevens, "Evaluation Bias in the Business Classroom: Evidence Related to the Effects of Previous Experiences," *Journal of Psychology* 125 (1991): 469–477.
49. T. Hennerman, "Acceptance of Gays, Lesbians Is a Big Part of Kodak's Diversity Picture," *Workforce Management* 83 (December 2004): 68–70.
50. D. Dearborn and H. Simon, "Selection Perception: A Note on the Departmental Identification of Executives," *Sociometry* 21 (1958) 140–144.
51. O. Hongseok, C. Myung-Ho, and G. Labianca, "Group Social Capital and Group Effectiveness: The Role of Informal Socializing Ties," *Academy of Management Journal* 47, no. 6 (2004): 860–876.
52. D. Johnson and P. Johnson, *Joining Together: Group Theory and Skills,* 8th ed. (New York: Allyn & Bacon, 2002).
53. Further differences are discussed in J. Katzenbach and D. Smith, *Wisdom of Teams: Creating the High-Performance Organization* (New York: HarperCollins, 2003).
54. G. Steward, C. Manz, and H. Sims, *Team Work and Group Dynamics* (New York: Wiley, 1999); D. Johnson and R. Johnson, *Cooperation and Competition: Theory and Research* (Edina, MN: Interaction Book, 1989); G. Parker, J. McAdams, and D. Zielinski, *Rewarding Teams: Lessons from the Trenches* (Jossey-Bass, 2000).
55. B. Beersma, J. R. Hollenbeck, S. E. Humphrey, H. Moon, D. E. Conlon, and D. R. Ilgen, "Cooperation, Competition, and Team Performance: Toward a Contingency Approach," *Academy of Management Journal* 46, no. 5 (2003): 572–590.
56. L. Thompson, *Making the Team* (New York: Prentice Hall, 2003).
57. M. Shaw, R. Robbin, and J. Belser, *Group Dynamics,* 3rd ed. (New York: McGraw-Hill, 1990).
58. Johnson and Johnson, *Joining Together.*
59. P. Scholtes, B. Joiner, and B. Streibel, *The Team Handbook,* 3rd ed. (Madison, WI: Oriel, 2003).
60. Based on K. Benne and P. Sheats, "Functional Roles of Group Members," *Journal of Social Issues* 4 (1948): 42–47.
61. L. Tischler, "Blowing Out Advertising's Walls," *Fast Company* 95 (June 2005): 63–65.
62. S. Greengard, "Golden Values at Coors," *Workforce Management* (March 2005): 52–53.
63. S. Jackson, "Team Composition in Organizational Settings: Issues in Managing and Increasingly Diverse Work Force" in *Group Process and Productivity,* ed. S. Worchell, W. Wood, and J. Simpson (Newbury Park, CA: Sage, 1992), 138–173; D. Hambrick, T. Cho, and M. Jen, "The Influence of Top Management Team Heterogeneity on Firms' Competitive

Moves," *Administrative Science Quarterly* 41 (1996): 650–684; R. L. Moreland and J. M. Levine, "The Composition of Small Groups" in *Advances in Group Processes,* vol. 9, ed. E. J. Lawler, B. Markovsky, C. Ridgeway, and H. Walker (Greenwich, CT: JAI Press, 1992), 237–280.

64. R. Hackman and R. Wageman, "A Theory of Team Coaching," *Academy of Management Review* 30, no. 2 (2005): 269–288; J. R. Hackman, R. Wageman, T. M. Ruddy, and C. R. Ray, "Team Effectiveness in Theory and Practice" in *Industrial and Organizational Psychology: Theory and Practice,* ed. C. Cooper and E. A. Locke (Oxford: Blackwell, 2000), 109–129.
65. H. Park, P. Lewis, and P. Fandt, "Ethnocentrism and Group Cohesiveness in International Joint Ventures" in *Multinational Strategic Alliances,* ed. R. Culpan (Binghamton, NY: International Business Press, 1993).
66. Hackman and Wageman, "A Theory of Team Coaching."
67. K. G. Smith, K. A. Smith, J. D. Olian, H. P. Sims, D. P. O'Bannon, and J. A. Scully, "Top Management Team Demography and Process: The Role of Social Integration and Communication," *Administrative Sciences Quarterly* 39 (1994): 412–438; B. Berelson and G. Steiner, *Human Behaviors: An Inventory of Scientific Findings* (New York: Harcourt, Brace & World, 1964), 356–360; A. B. Henley and K. Price, "Want a Better Team? Foster a Climate of Fairness," *Academy of Management Executive* 16, no. 3 (2002): 153–155.
68. Z. Simsek, J. F. Veiga, M. H. Lubatkin, and R. N. Dino, "Modeling the Multilevel Determinants of Top Management Team Behavioral Integration," *Academy of Management Journal* 48, no. 1 (2005): 69–82; K. Y. Williams, and C. A. O'Reilly, "Demography and Diversity in Organizations: A review of 40 Years of Research" in *Research in Organizational Behavior,* ed., L. L. Cummings and B. M. Staw (Greenwich, CT: JAI Press, 1998), 77–140.
69. N. Kerr and S. Bruun, "The Dispensability of Member Effort and Group Motivation Losses: Free-Rider Effects," *Journal of Personality and Social Psychology* 44 (1983): 78–94.
70. For more information, see Johnson and Johnson, *Joining Together.*
71. A. O'Leary-Kelly, J. Martocchio, and D. Frink, "A Review of the Influence of Group Goals on Group Performance," *Academy of Management Review* 37 (1994): 128–301.
72. D. J. Beal, R. R. Cohen, M. J. Burke, and C. L. McLendon, "Cohesion and Performance in Groups: A Meta-Analytic Clarification of Construct Relations," *Journal of Applied Psychology* 88 (2003): 989–1004.
73. B. Tuckman and M. Jensen, "Stages of Small Group Development Revisited," *Group and Organization Studies* 2 (1977): 419–427.
74. G. Chen and R. Klimoski, "The Impact of Expectations on Newcomer Performance in Teams as Mediated by Work Characteristics, Social Exchanges, and Empowerment," *Academy of Management Journal* 46, no. 5 (2003): 591–607.
75. P. Brown, "What I Know Now," *Fast Company* 90 (January 2005): 96.
76. S. Wheelan, *Creating Effective Teams: A Guide for Members and Leaders* (Thousand Oaks, CA: Sage, 1999).
77. R. T. Keller, "Cross-Functional Project Groups in Research and New Product Development: Diversity, Communications, Job Stress, and Outcomes," *Academy of Management Journal* 44, no. 3 (2001): 547–556.
78. N. Evans and P. Jarvis, "Group Cohesion: A Review and Reevaluation," *Small Group Behavior* 11 (1980): 359–370.
79. B. S. Kuipers and M. C. de Witte, "Teamwork: A Case Study on Development and Performance," *International Journal of Human Resource Management* 16, no. 2 (2005): 185–201; T. Kayser, *Building Team Power: How to Unleash the Collaborative Genius of Work Teams* (Burr Ridge, IL: Irwin, 1994); J. Katzenbach and D. Smith, *Wisdom of Teams: Creating the High-Performance Organization* (New York: Harper Collins, 2003).
80. Beal et al., "Cohesion and Performance in Groups"; I. L. Janis, *Victims of Groupthink,* 2nd ed. (Boston: Houghton Mifflin, 1982); I. L. Janis, *Groupthink: Psychological Studies of Policy Decisions and Fiascoes* (Boston: Houghton Mifflin, 1986).
81. G. Whyte, "Groupthink Reconsidered," *Academy of Management Review* 14 (1989): 40–55.
82. Hongseok et al., "Group Social Capital and Group Effectiveness."
83. Hackman and Wageman, "A Theory of Team Coaching."
84. Hackman et al., "Team Effectiveness."
85. Scholtes et al., *The Team Handbook;* Wheelan, *Creating Effective Teams;* Parker et al., *Rewarding Teams.*
86. M. McIntyre, *The Management Team Handbook: Five Key Strategies for Maximizing Group Performance* (San Francisco: Jossey-Bass, 1998); Curd et al., "Development Challenges"; Hackman and Wageman, "A Theory of Team Coaching."

CHAPTER 14

1. J. Gavin and R. Mason, "The Virtuous Organization: The Value of Happiness in the Workplace," *Organizational Dynamics* 33 (December 2004): 379–392; N. Nicholsonn, "How to Motivate Your Problem People," *Harvard Business Review* 81 (January 2003): 56–72.
2. E. A. Locke and G. Latham, "What Should We Do about Motivation Theory? Six Recommendations for the Twenty-First Century," *Academy of Management Review* 29 (2004): 388–403; N. Qubein, "Ten Principles of Motivation," *Executive Excellence* 20 (October 2003): 12–13.
3. S. Kerr, "On the Folly of Rewarding A while Hoping for B," *Academy of Management Executive* 9, no. 1 (1995): 7–14.
4. Locke and Latham, "What Should We Do about Motivation Theory?"
5. An overview is provided in R. Steers, R. Mowday, and D. Shaprio, "The Future of Work Motivation Theory," *Academy of Management Review* 29, no. 3 (2004): 379–387.
6. "Will Employees Perform Better if You Reward Them? *HR Focus* 81 (December, 2004): 10.
7. H. Kehr, "Integrating Implicit Motives, Explicit Motives, and Perceived Abilities: The Compensatory Model of Work Motivation and Volition," *Academy of Management Review* 29 (2004): 479–499.
8. For example, see T. A. Wright, "What Every Manager Should Know: Does Personality Help Drive Employee Motivation?" *Academy of Management Executive* 17, no. 2 (2003): 131ff.; M. Barrick and M. Mount, "Select on Con-

scientiousness and Emotional Stablity," in *Handbook of Principles of Organizational Behavior,* ed. E. Locke Malden, MA: Blackwell, 2000), 15–28; R. Ilies and T. Judge, "On the Heritability of Job Satisfaction: The Mediating Role of Personality," *Journal of Applied Psychology* 88, no. 4 (2003): 750–759.

9. A. Maslow, "A Theory of Human Motivation," *Psychological Review* 50 (1943): 270–396; M. Wahba and L. Bridwell, "Maslow Reconsidered: A Review of Research and the Need Hierarchy," *Organizational Behavior and Human Performance* 16 (1976): 212–240.
10. F. Herzberg, "One More Time: How Do You Motivate Employees?" *Harvard Business Review* (January/February 1968): 53–68.
11. K. Blanchard, J. Ballard, and F. Finch, *Customer Mania! It's Never Too Late to Build a Customer Focused Company* (New York: Free Press, 2004); D. Sirota, L. Mischkind, and M. I. Meltzer, *The Enthusiastic Employee: How Companies Profit by Giving Workers What They Want* (New York: Wharton School Publishing/Pearson, 2005).
12. D. Shuit, "Former Pepsico Executives Do a 360 in Managing Yum Brands' Workforce," *Workforce Management* 84 (April 2005): 59–61; R. King, "Great Things are Starting at Yum," Workforce Management Online, November 2003.
13. R. Kanfer and P. Ackerman, "Aging, Adult Development, and Work Motivation," *Academy of Management Review* 29, no. 3 (2004): 440–458.
14. J. Lloyd, "Managers Need to Shine a Light on Their Expectations," *San Antonio Business Journal* 15 (December 2001): 29.
15. D. McClelland, *The Achieving Society* (New York: Van Nostrand Reinhold, 1961).
16. D. McClelland, *Human Motivation* (Glenview, IL: Scott, Foresman, 1985); for an overview see Steers et al., "The Future of Work Motivation Theory."
17. D. Miron and D. McClelland, "The Impact of Achievement Motivation Training on Small Businesses," *California Management Review* (Summer 1979): 13–28.
18. D. McClelland and H. Burnham, "Power Is the Great Motivator," *Harvard Business Review* 54 (March/April 1976): 100–110.
19. A. Durik and J. Harackiewic, "Achievement Goals and Intrinsic Motivation: Coherence, Concordance, and Achievement Orientation," *Journal of Experimental Social Psychology* 39 (2003): 378–385.
20. E. Apospori, N. Papalexandris, and E. Galanaki, "Entrepreneurial and Professional CEOs: Differences in Motive and Responsibility Profile," *Leadership and Organization Development Journal* 26 (2005): 141–162.
21. J. T. Childs, "Managing Workforce Diversity at IBM: A Global HR Topic That Has Arrived," *Human Resources Management* 44 (2004): 73–77.
22. V. Vroom, *Work and Motivation* (New York: Jossey-Bass, 1994).
23. Sirota et al., *The Enthusiastic Employee.*
24. R. Mowday and K. Colwell, "Employee Reactions to Unfair Outcomes in the Workplace: The Contributions of Adams' Equity Theory to Understanding Work Motivation" in *Motivation and Work Behavior,* 7th ed., eds. L. W. Porter, G. A. Bigley, and R. M. Steers (Burr Ridge, IL: Irwin/McGraw-Hill, 2003), 65–82.
25. S. Adams, "Toward an Understanding of Inequity," *Journal of Abnormal and Social Psychology* 67 (1963): 422–436.
26. Ibid.; S. Adams, "Inequity in Social Exchange" in *Advances in Experimental Social Psychology,* vol. 2, ed. L. Berkowitz (New York: Academic Press, 1965), 267–300.
27. M. Gagné and E. Deci, "Self-Determination Theory and Work Motivation," *Journal of Organizational Behavior* 26 (2005): 331–362; A. Bowey, "Motivation: The Art of Putting Theory into Practice," *European Business Forum* 20 (Winter 2005): 17–21.
28. Goal-setting theory is well documented in E. Locke and G. Latham, *A Theory of Goal Setting and Task Performance* (Englewood Cliffs, NJ: Prentice Hall, 1990).
29. For a detailed review, see E. Locke and G. Latham, "Building a Practically Useful Theory of Goal Setting and Task Motivation: A 35-Year Odysesy," *American Psychologist* 57 (2002): 705–717.
30. S. Kerr and S. Landauer, "Using Stretch Goals to Promote Organizational Effectiveness and Personal Growth: General Electric and Goldman Sachs," *Academy of Management Executive* 18 no. 4 (2004): 134–138.
31. G. Chen and R. Klimoski, "The Impact of Expectations on Newcomer Performance in Teams as Mediated by Work Characteristics, Social Exchanges, and Empowerment," *Academy of Management Journal* 46, no. 5 (2003): 591–607; Y. Fried and L. Slowik, "Enriching Goal-Setting Theory with Time: An Integrated Approach," *Academy of Management Review* 29 (2004): 404–422.
32. Sirota et al., *The Enthusiastic Employee.*
33. R. Kanfer and P. Ackerman, "Aging, Adult Development, and Work Motivation," *Academy of Management Review* 29, no. 3 (2004): 440–458; K. Ayers, "Creating a Responsible Workplace: Stop Holding People Accountable. Use These Tools to Let Them Choose to Be Accountable," *HRM Magazine* 50 (February 2005): 111–115.
34. V. Powers, "Finding Workers Who Fit," *Business 2.0* (November 2004): 74.
35. Steers et al., "The Future of Work Motivation Theory."
36. Kanfer "Aging, Adult Development, and Work Motivation"; B. Nelson, "The Ironies of Motivation," *Strategy & Leadership* (January/February 1999): 26–31.
37. E. Gubman, *The Engaging Leader* (Chicago: Dearborn, 2003).
38. B. Gannon and J. Sterling, "Company Culture Provides Competitive Edge for Sargento Foods. *Strategy & Leadership* 32 (2004): 31–38.
39. E. Gubman, "From Engagement to Passion for Work: The Search for the Missing Person," *Human Resource Planning* 27 (2004): 42–46.
40. J. Harter, F. Schmidt, and T. L. Hayes, "Business-Unit-Level Relationship between Employee Satisfaction, Employee Engagement, and Business Outcomes: A Meta-Analysis," *Journal of Applied Psychology* 87 (2002): 268–279.
41. J. Harter, "Managerial Talent, Employee Engagement, and Business-Unit Performance," *Psychologist-Manager Journal* 4 (2000): 215–224; Harter et al., "Business-Unit-Level Relationship"; S. Stern, "Forever Changing," *Management Today*, 7 February 2005, 40–42.

42. W. A. Randolph, "Re-thinking Empowerment: Why Is It So Hard to Achieve?" *Organizational Dynamics* 29 (2000): 94–107; J. Vogt and K. Murrell, *Empowerment in Organizations: How to Spark Exceptional Performance* (San Diego: University Associates, 1990).
43. S. Seibert, G. Johns, and F. Ntalianis, "Taking Empowerment to the Next Level: A Multiple-Level Model of Empowerment, Performance, and Satisfaction," *Academy of Management Journal* 47, no. 3 (2004): 332–349.
44. M. Buckingham, "What Great Managers Do," *Harvard Business Review* 83 (March 2005): 70–79; M. Buckingham and C. Coffman, *First, Break All The Rules: What the World's Greatest Managers Do Differently* (Simon & Schuster, 1999).
45. J. Katzenbach, *Peak Performance: Aligning the Hearts and Minds of Your Employees* (Boston: Harvard Business School Press, 2000).
46. M. Barry and J. Slocum, "Slice of Reality: Changing Culture at Pizza Hut and Yum! Brands, Inc.," *Organizational Dynamics* 32 (November 2003): 319–329.
47. Ibid.; Blanchard et al., *Customer Mania!*
48. J. Katzenbach, *Why Pride Matters More Than Money: The Power of the World's Greatest Motivational Force* (Crown Business, 2003).
49. Katzenbach, *Peak Performance;* E. Locke, "Linking Goals to Monetary Incentives," *Academy of Management Executive* 18, no. 4 (2004): 130–133.
50. W. Murphy, "In Pursuit of Short-Term Goals: Anticipating the Unintended Consequences of Using Special Incentives to Motivate the Sales Force," *Journal of Business Research* 57 (2004): 1265–1275.
51. L. Hughes, "Motivating Your Employees," *Women in Business* 55 (March/April 2003): 17.
52. N. Ellemers, D. de Gilder, and Haslam, S. A. "Motivating Individuals and Groups at Work: A Social Identity Perspective on Leadership and Group Performance," *Academy of Management Review* 29, no. 3 (2004): 459–478; R. Oxoby, "Status Characteristics, Cognitive Bias, and Incentives in Team," *Journal of Socio-Economics* 31 (2002): 301–316.
53. D. Knight, C. Durham, and E. Locke, "The Relationship of Team Goals, Incentives, and Efficacy to Strategic Risk, Tactical Implementation, and Performance," *Academy of Management Journal* 44 (2001): 326–338.
54. Sirota et al., *The Enthusiastic Employee.*
55. Bowey, "Motivation."
56. M. Erez, "Make Management Practice Fit National Culture," *Handbook of Principles of Organizational Behavior,* ed. E. Locke (Malden, MA: Blackwell, 2000), 418–434.
57. J. Spence, "Achievement American Style: The Rewards and Costs of Individualism," *American Psychologist* 40 (1985): 1285–1294; N. Zaidman, "Cultural Codes and Language Strategies in Business Communication," *Management Communication Quarterly* (February 2001): 408–441.
58. S. Cady, P. Fandt, and D. Fernandez, "Investigating Cultural Differences in Personal Success: Implications for Designing Effective Reward Systems," *Journal of Value Based Management* 6 (1993): 65–80; N. Adler, *International Dimensions of Organizational Behavior* (Boston: PWS Kent, 1991).
59. V. Chirkov, R. M. Ryan, Y. Kim, and U. Kaplan, "Differentiating Autonomy from Individualism and Independence: A Self-Determination Theory Perspective on Internalization of Cultural Orientations and Well-Being," *Journal of Personality and Social Psychology* 84 (2003): 97–109.
60. Shuit, "Former Pepsico Executives"; E. Lambert, "Sell the Sizzle," *Forbes*, 1 November 2004, 164.
61. M. Booe, "Sales Force at Mary Kay China Embraces the American Way," *Workforce Management* (April 2005): 24–25.
62. P. Early, *Face, Harmony, and Social Structure: An Analysis of Organizational Behavior across Cultures* (New York: Oxford University Press, 1997); R. Steers, and C. Sanchez-Runde, "Culture, Motivation, and Work Behavior" in *Handbook of Cross-Cultural Management,* ed. M. Gannon and K. Newman (London: Blackwell, 2001), 190–215.
63. F. Luthans and S. Peterson, "360-Degree Feedback with Systematic Coaching: Empirical Analysis Suggests a Winning Combination," *Human Resource Management* 42 (Fall 2003): 243–256.
64. Sirota et al., *The Enthusiastic Employee.*

CHAPTER 15

1. K. A. Merchant, *Control in Business Organizations* (Marshfield, MA: Pitman, 1985).
2. T. Lowe and J. L. Machin, *New Perspectives on Management Control* (New York: Macmillan, 1987).
3. D. Paletta, "*E. Coli* Outbreak Has Stores Asking Consumers to Return Beef," *Orlando Sentinel,* 26 July 2002, B1ff.
4. A. Levin, "Without Warning," *USA Today,* 18 October 1999, 1Aff.
5. W. R. Ashby, *Introduction to Cybernetics* (New York: Wiley, 1963).
6. S. Beer, *Cybernetics and Management* (New York: Wiley, 1959), 44.
7. M. Cabbage, "Faulty Math Botched Mars Probe," *Orlando Sentinel,* 11 November 1999, A4.
8. M. Goold and J. Quinn, "The Paradox of Strategic Controls," *Strategic Management Journal* (January 1990): 43–57.
9. D. Cray, "Control and Coordination in Multinational Corporations," *Journal of International Business Studies* (Fall 1984): 85–98.
10. C. Drew, "Deadly Undersea Crash Nearly Doomed U.S. Sub," *Orlando Sentinel,* 19 May 2005, A1ff.; "Sub Missed Warning Signs Before It Crashed, Navy Says," *Orlando Sentinel,* 13 March 2005, A10; "Old Charts Might Have Played Part in Sub Crash," *Orlando Sentinel,* 16 January 2005, A10.
11. P. Lorange and D. Murphy, "Considerations in Implementing Strategic Control," *Journal of Business Strategy* 4 (Spring 1984): 27–35.
12. P. P. Schoderbek, R. A. Cosier, and J. C. Aplin, *Management* (San Diego: Harcourt Brace Jovanovich, 1991).
13. J. R. Evans and W. M. Lindsay, *The Management and Control of Quality* (St. Paul: West, 1993).
14. "Doctors Get an Rx for Messy Handwriting-Digital Prescriptions," *Orlando Sentinel,* 13 November 1999, A8.

15. L. Krajewski and L. Ritzman, *Operations Management: Strategy and Analysis*, 5th ed. (Reading, MA: Addison-Wesley, 1999), 552.
16. W. H. Newman, *Construction Control* (Upper Saddle River, NJ: Prentice Hall, 1975).
17. P. Lorange, M. F. S. Morton, and G. Sumantra, *Strategic Control* (St. Paul: West, 1986).
18. P. F. Drucker, *Management: Tasks, Responsibilities, Practices* (New York: Harper & Row, 1973), 100.
19. W. G. Ouchi, "Markets, Bureaucracies, and Clans," *Administrative Science Quarterly* 25 (1980): 128–141.
20. H. P. Sims, Jr., and C. C. Manz, *SuperLeadership: Leading Others to Lead Themselves* (New York: Simon & Schuster, 1989).
21. C. Cortland and D. A. Nadler, "Fit Control Systems to Your Managerial Style," *Harvard Business Review* (January/February 1976): 65–72.
22. B. R. Baliga and A. M. Jaeger, "Multinational Corporations: Control Systems and Delegation Issues," *Journal of International Business Studies* (Fall 1984): 25–40.
23. "Computer Troubles Cast Wicked Spell on Hershey," *Orlando Sentinel*, 30 October 1999, C1ff.
24. E. Brigham, *Financial Management: Theory and Practice*, 4th ed. (Chicago: Dryden Press, 1985).
25. F. J. Tasco and A. J. Gajda, "Substance Abuse in the Workplace," *Compensation and Benefits Management* (Winter 1990): 140–144.
26. T. Shoulberg, "Drug-Free Workplace Can Save on Premiums," *Central Florida Business Report*, 29 November 1999, 25; M. A. McDaniel, "Does Pre-Employment Drug Use Predict On-the-Job Suitability?" *Personnel Psychology* (Winter 1988): 717–730.
27. T. W. Ferguson, "Motorola Aims High, So Motorolans Won't Be Getting High," *Wall Street Journal*, 26 June 1990, A19.
28. R. L. Campbell and R. E. Langford, *Substance Abuse in the Workplace* (Boca Raton, FL: Lewis, 1995).
29. "Housing Complex Requires Drug Tests for Tenants," *Orlando Sentinel*, 28 July 1996, B3.
30. "Preventing Crime on the Job," *Nation's Business* (July 1990): 36–37.
31. J. Rothfeder, M. Galen, and L. Driscoll, "Is Your Boss Spying on You?" *BusinessWeek*, 15 January 1990, 74–75.
32. N. H. Snyder and K. E. Blair, "Dealing with Employee Theft," *Business Horizons* (May/June 1989): 27–34.
33. "Casino Hit with $80,000 Fine for Improper Use of Cameras," *Orlando Sentinel*, 16 December 2004, A21.
34. B. Dumaine, "Corporate Spies Snoop to Conquer," *Fortune*, 7 November 1988, 68–76.
35. M. McDonald, "They've Got Your Number," *Dallas Morning News*, 7 April 1991, F1.
36. H. J. Chalykoff and T. A. Kochan, "Computer-Aided Monitoring: Its Influence on Employee Job Satisfaction and Turnover," *Personnel Psychology* (Winter 1989): 807–834.

CHAPTER 16

1. L. J. Krajewski and L.P. Ritzman, *Operations Management: Strategy and Analysis*, 5th ed. (Reading, MA: Addison-Wesley, 1999).
2. J. R. Evans, *Applied Production and Operations Management*, 5th ed. (St. Paul: West, 1997).
3. R. B. Chase and N. J. Acquilano, *Production and Operations Management: A Life Cycle Approach*, 8th ed. (Homewood, IL: Irwin, 1997).
4. Krajewski and Ritzman, *Operations Management: Strategy and Analysis.*
5. M. A. Vonderembse and G. P. White, *Operations Management: Concepts, Methods, and Strategies*, 3rd ed. (St. Paul: West, 1996).
6. Krajewski and Ritzman, *Operations Management: Strategy and Analysis.*
7. Vonderembse and White, *Operations Management: Concepts, Methods, and Strategies.*
8. R. J. Schonberger and E. M. Knod, Jr., *Operations Management: Improving Customer Service*, 6th ed. (Homewood, IL: Irwin, 1996).
9. Chase and Acquilano, *Production and Operations Management: A Life Cycle Approach.*
10. Krajewski and Ritzman, *Operations Management: Strategy and Analysis.*
11. Vonderembse and White, *Operations and Management: Concepts, Methods, and Strategies.*
12. R. Blumenstein, "Big Three Pare Design Time for New Autos," *Wall Street Journal*, 9 August 1996, A3; M. Maynard, "GM Heads Down Road to Quick Development Time," *USA Today*, 9 August 1996, B2.
13. Vonderembse and White, *Operations and Management: Concepts, Methods, and Strategies.*
14. R. W. Schmenner, *Making Business Decisions* (Upper Saddle River, NJ: Prentice Hall, 1982).
15. "Plant's Plan Causes a Stink in Small Town," *Orlando Sentinel*, 27 June 1996, B5; "Candy Plant to Be Built in Corsicana," *Dallas Morning News*, 14 August 1996, D12.
16. B. Kuhn, "Toys R Us Plays Around with Image," *Orlando Sentinel*, 13 July 1996, C1ff.
17. J. Jackson, "Subway to Redecorate with a Tuscany Flair," *Central Florida Business*, 27 May 2002, 4; C. Boyd, "Pretty Stores May Bag More Profits," *Orlando Sentinel*, 28 July 1999, B1ff.; C. Boyd, "Grocery Stores Are Reinventing Themselves," *Orlando Sentinel*, 13 June 1999, H1ff.
18. Krajewski and Ritzman, *Operations Management: Strategy and Analysis.*
19. J. Heizer and B. Render, *Operations Management*, 5th ed. (Upper Saddle River, NJ: Prentice Hall, 1999).
20. Evans, *Applied Production and Operations Management.*
21. Krajewski and Ritzman, *Operations Management: Strategy and Analysis.*
22. N. Gaither, *Production and Operations Management*, 7th ed. (Belmont, CA: Wadsworth, 1996).
23. Vonderembse and White, *Operations Management: Concepts, Methods, and Strategies.*
24. T. Minaham, "Did GM Strike Prove That JIT Doesn't Work?" *Purchasing* 120 no. 7 (1996).
25. Evans, *Applied Production and Operations Management.*
26. R. D. Reid and N. R. Sanders, *Operations Management: An Integrated Approach* (New York: Wiley, 2005), 101–112.
27. "Borders, Partner Will Provide Paperbacks Printed on Demand," *Orlando Sentinel*, 2 June 1999, B5.

28. "You Know That Album You Can Never Find? Sony Has a Solution," *Orlando Sentinel,* 11 June 1999, B5
29. Vonderembse and White, *Operations Management: Concepts, Methods, and Strategies.*
30. Evans, *Applied Production and Operations Management.*
31. N. Templin, "Team Spirit: A Decisive Response to Crisis Brought Ford Enhanced Productivity," *Wall Street Journal,* 15 December 1992, A1; A. Taylor III, "Ford's $6 Billion Baby," *Fortune,* 28 June 1993, 76–81
32. Krajewski and Ritzman, *Operations Management: Strategy and Analysis.*
33. J. R. Evans and W. M. Lindsay, *The Management and Control of Quality,* 4th ed. (Cincinnati: South-Western, 1999).
34. Ibid.
35. Evans, *Applied Production and Operations Management.*
36. Vonderembse and White, *Operations Management: Concepts, Methods, and Strategies.*
37. http://www.klsummit.com.
38. Evans, *Applied Production and Operations Management.*
39. Krajewski and Ritzman, *Operations Management: Strategy and Analysis.*
40. W. E. Deming, "Improvement of Quality and Productivity through Action by Management," *National Productivity Review* (Winter 1981–1982): 12–22.
41. J. M. Juran and F. Gryna, Jr., *Quality Planning and Analysis,* 2nd ed. (New York: McGraw-Hill, 1980).
42. A. V. Feigenbaum, *Total Quality Control,* 3rd ed. (New York: McGraw-Hill, 1983).
43. K. Ishikawa, *Guide to Quality Control* (Tokyo: Asian Productivity Organization, 1972).
44. P. B. Crosby, *Quality Is Free* (New York: McGraw-Hill, 1979).
45. S. Date, "No Gazing Off into Space on This Trip," *Orlando Sentinel,* 4 December 1993, A1ff.
46. S. Date, "Endeavour Opens Some Eyes as Hubble Mission Ends at KSC," *Orlando Sentinel,* 13 December 1993, A1ff.
47. "Shannon Lucid Leaves *Mir,* Boards Atlantis for Trip Back," *Orlando Sentinel,* 20 September 1996, A14.
48. M. Cabbage, "Shuttle Finally Roars to Life," *Orlando Sentinel,* 23 July 1999, A1ff.
49. Reid and Sanders, *Operations Management: An Integrated Approach,* 522–527.
50. R. Henkoff, "Delivering the Goods," *Fortune,* 28 November 1994, 64–78; I. Sager, "The Great Equalizer," *BusinessWeek,* Special Issue on the Information Revolution (1994): 100–107.

CHAPTER 17

1. E. Turban and J. E. Aronson, *Decision Support Systems and Intelligent Systems* (Upper Saddle River, NJ: Prentice Hall, 2001), 8.
2. K. D. Laudon and J. P. Laudon, *Management Information Systems: Organization and Technology in the Networked Enterprise,* 6th ed. (Upper Saddle River, NJ: Prentice Hall, 2000), 5–6.
3. S. Haag, M. Cummings, and J. Dawkins, *Management Information Systems for the Information Age,* 2nd ed. (Boston: Irwin McGraw-Hill, 2000), 13–14.
4. Ibid., 14.
5. Ibid., 14–17.
6. Laudon and Laudon, *Management Information Systems,* 37–38.
7. J. A. O'Brien, *Introduction to Information Systems,* 9th ed. (Boston: Irwin McGraw-Hill, 2000), 360–361.
8. Ibid., 279–280.
9. J. F. Rockart and M. E. Treacy, "The CEO Goes On-line," *Harvard Business Review* (January/February 1982).
10. J. Rockart and D. DeLong, *Executive Support Systems: The Emergence of Top Management Computer Use* (Homewood, IL: Dow Jones-Irwin, 1988).
11. Laudon and Laudon, *Management Information Systems,* 48.
12. T. Davenport, "Living with ERP," *CIO,* 19 December 1998; D. Slater, "The Hidden Costs of Enterprise Software," *CIO,* 15 January 1998.
13. "Dynacorp Takes High-Tech to Mail-Carrying Business," *Central Penn Business Journal,* 4 April 1994.
14. "When Is Package Tracking Really Tracking?" *UPS Public Relations,* 9 February 1999; J. Moad, "Can High Performance Be Cloned? Should It Be?" *Datamation,* 1 March 1995; L. M. Grossman, "Federal Express, UPS Face Off on Computers," *Wall Street Journal,* 17 September 1993, B1ff.
15. E. Hale, "The Euro Becomes Legal Tender," *USA Today On-line,* 31 December 2001; E. Hale, "Euro Queries and Answers," *USA Today On-line,* 16 December 2001; E. Hale, "Europeans Make Change to Euro," *USA Today On-line,* 16 December 2001; T. Kamm, "Emergence of Euro Embodies Challenge and Hope for Europe," *Wall Street Journal,* 4 January 1999.
16. G. Fields, "FBI Digitizes Fingerprint System Today," *USA Today,* 10 August 1999, 1Aff.
17. E. W. Martin, D. DeHayes, J. Hoffer, and W. Perkins, *Managing Information Technology: What Managers Need to Know* (New York: Wiley-Interscience, 1971).
18. D. Amoroso and P. Cheney, "Testing a Causal Model for End User Applications Effectiveness," *Journal of Management Information Systems* (Summer 1991); K. Christoff, *Managing the Information Center* (Glenview, IL: Scott Foresman/Little, Brown, 1990).
19. J. A. O'Brien, *Management Information Systems: A Managerial End User Perspective,* 2nd ed. (Homewood, IL: Irwin, 1993).
20. R. R. Panko, *End User Computing: Management, Applications, and Technology* (New York: Wiley, 1988).
21. L. Fried, "A Blueprint for Change," *Computerworld,* 2 December 1991, 91–93.
22. R. Burnett, "More 'Geeks' Braving Business World," *Orlando Sentinel,* 1 September 1996, H1ff.; "Gates Gets 26% Raise," *Orlando Sentinel,* 28 September 1996, C1.
23. Personal interview with Tricia Grady.
24. "Welcome to the Revolution," *Fortune,* 13 December 1993, 66–78.
25. W. Stallings and R. Van Slyke, *Business Data Communications,* 2nd ed. (New York: Macmillan, 1994).
26. C. Cobbs, "Electronics Get Home Makeover," *Orlando Sentinel,* 25 February 2005, C1ff.; "Get Set to Network with Your Refrigerator," *USA Today,* 3 February 1999, 3B.

27. "Microsoft to Blend Desktop Computing, Global Networking," *Orlando Sentinel,* 22 July 1996, B5.
28. "Koop Slammed for Corporate Link in Latex-Glove Flap," *Orlando Sentinel,* 30 October 1999, C10; "Former Surgeon General Attacked for Web Site," *Orlando Sentinel,* 5 September 1999, A7.
29. "The Strategic Value of EDI," *I/S Analyzer* (August 1989).
30. D. Greising and M. O'Neal, "Blueprint for the Future," *Orlando Sentinel,* 26 February 2005, C1ff.
31. "Invoice? What's an Invoice?" *BusinessWeek,* 10 June 1996, 110–112.
32. "Welcome to the Revolution."
33. L. Radosevich, "United Nations Launches Worldwide Network," *Computerworld,* 24 October 1994, 64.
34. "Information Technology Special Report," *Fortune* (Autumn 1993) 15.
35. T. L. Friedman, *The World Is Flat* (New York: Farrar, Straus and Giroux, 2005), 36–37.
36. "The Race to Rewire," *Fortune*, 19 April 1993, 42–61.
37. "Quake Tosses L.A. Around: Buildings, Roads Fall in Tremblers Onslaught," *Orlando Sentinel,* 18 January 1994, A1ff.
38. S. Armour, "Worried Workers Turn to Telecommuting," *USA Today On-line,* 17 October 2001.
39. J. Jackson, "Flower, Fruit Companies Smell Success on Web," *Central Florida Business Report,* 7 June 1999, 18–19; E. Eldrige, "GM Pursues .Com Goals," *USA Today,* 11 August 1999, 6B; D. Levy, "Superstores Seek Online Customers," *USA Today,* 16 March 1999, 3B; "Sears Puts Appliances Online," *Orlando Sentinel,* 13 May 1999, B1; "Home Depot Targets Internet," *Orlando Sentinel,* 2 March 1999, B1.
40. "Quarterly Retail E-Commerce Sales," *U.S. Census Bureau News,* 29 May 2005.
41. "Dell Clicks with Buyers by Deleting Middlemen," *Orlando Sentinel,* 22 June 1999, B1ff.
42. S. Nathan, "Defining the Seller in On-Line Market," *USA Today,* 26 August 1999, 3B.
43. C. Wilder, "E-Commerce—Old Line Moves On-line," *Information Week,* 11 January 1999; S. Kalin, "Conflict Resolution," *CIO,* 1 February 1998.
44. J. Niccolai, "eBay Buys Shopping.com for $620M," *Computerworld Online,* 2 June 2005; "ebay CEO Ventures a Bid—Wins Big," *Orlando Sentinel*, 6 June 1999, H8.
45. Turban and Aronson, *Decision Support Systems and Intelligent Systems.*
46. "Ant-Sized Robots Designed to Fix, Inspect Plants," *Orlando Sentinel,* 22 June 1999, B1.
47. D. Kohn, "Camera Films on Location—in Patient's Esophagus," *Orlando Sentinel,* 3 May 2005, C1ff.
48. G. K. Shaw, "Mars Rover Goes Strong on 1st Birthday," *Orlando Sentinel,* 4 January 2005, A6.
49. "Center Devoted to Robotic Revolution," *Orlando Sentinel,* 21 August 1996, B1ff.
50. "Welcome to the Revolution."
51. D. Schuler, "Social Computing," *Communications of the ACM,* Special Issue (January 1994): 28–29.
52. "Welcome to the Revolution."
53. "Fast Processor," *USA Today,* 24 February 1999, 1B; "Pentium III Breaks Speed Record," *Orlando Sentinel,* 24 February 1999, B7; "Faster Than a Speeding Pentium: Latest Is Here," *Orlando Sentinel,* 18 May 1999, B5.
54. "Intel Rolls Out Pentium 4," *USA Today On-line,* 20 November 2000; "Intel Unveils Pentium 4 Chip," *USA Today On-line,* 28 June 2000.
55. C. Cobbs, "Speeding Up: Moore's Law Has Ruled Computers for 40 Years," *Orlando Sentinel,* 19 April 2005, C1ff.
56. K. Maney, "Beyond the PC: Atomic QC," *USA Today,* 14 July 1999, 1Bff.
57. "Another State Opts to Sell Income Data," *Orlando Sentinel,* 4 June 1999, B5.
58. "Privacy Rules Are Set by Bank of America," *Orlando Sentinel,* 12 June 1999, C10.
59. "Another State Opts to Sell Income Data."

Name Index

Company Index

Subject Index

D

E

J

K

L

M

T

U

V

W